CIM
STUDY TEXT

Diploma

Strategic Marketing Management: Planning and Control

New in this July 2001 edition

- Comprehensively updated 'Marketing at Work' examples with website references

- Greater reference to the Internet and e-commerce

- Updated Exam Tips

- More coverage of globalisation and the reaction to it, and innovation

- Links to other papers at Diploma level identified throughout the text

First edition July 1999
Third edition July 2001

ISBN 0 7517 4122 1 (previous edition 0 7517 4110 8)

British Library Cataloguing-in-Publication Data
A catalogue record for this book
is available from the British Library

Published by

BPP Publishing Limited
Aldine House, Aldine Place
London W12 8AW

www.bpp.com

Printed in England by
DACOSTA PRINT
1A Mildmay Avenue
London N1 4RS
Tel: 0207 354 6200

We are grateful to the Chartered Institute of Marketing for permission to reproduce in this text the syllabus, tutor's guidance notes, and past examination questions.

Contents

Page

BPP
PUBLISHING

Contents

HOW TO USE THIS STUDY TEXT

Aims of this Study Text

To provide you with the knowledge and understanding, skills and applied techniques required for passing the exam

The Study Text has been written around the CIM syllabus (reproduced below, and cross-referenced to where in the text each topic is covered) and the CIM's Tutor's Manual.

- It is **comprehensive**. We do not omit sections of the syllabus as the examiner is liable to examine any angle of any part of the syllabus - and you do not want to be left high and dry.

- It is **on-target** - we do not include any material which is not examinable. You can therefore rely on the BPP Study Text as the stand-alone source of all your information for the exam.

To allow you to study in the way that best suits your learning style and the time you have available, by following your personal Study Plan (see below)

You may be studying at home on your own until the date of the exam, or you may be attending a full-time course. You may like to (and have time to) read every word, or you may prefer to (or only have time to) skim-read and devote the remainder of your time to question practice. Wherever you fall in the spectrum, you will find the BPP Study Text meets your needs in designing and following your personal Study Plan.

To tie in with the other components of the BPP Effective Study Package to ensure you have the best possible chance of passing the exam

Recommended period of use	Elements of BPP Effective Study Package
3 – 12 months before exam	**Study Text** Acquisition of knowledge, understanding, skills and applied techniques
1 – 6 months before exam	**Practice and Revision Kit (9/2001)** Tutorial questions and helpful checklists of the key points lead you into each area. There are then numerous examination questions to try, graded by topic area along with realistic suggested solutions prepared by marketing professionals in the light of the Examiner's Reports. The September 2001 edition will include the December 2000 and June 2001 papers.
1 – 6 months before exam	**Success Tapes** Audio cassettes covering the vital elements of your syllabus in less than 90 minutes per subject. Each tape also contains exam hints to help you fine tune your strategy.

BPP PUBLISHING

Settling down to study

By this stage in your career you may be a very experienced learner and taker of exams. But have you ever thought about *how* you learn? Let's have a quick look at the key elements required for effective learning. You can then identify your learning style and go on to design your own approach to how you are going to study this text - your personal Study Plan.

Key element of learning	Using the BPP Study Text
Motivation	You can rely on the comprehensiveness and technical quality of BPP. You've chosen the right Study Text - so you're in pole position to pass your exam!
Clear objectives and standards	Do you want to be a prizewinner or simply achieve a moderate pass? Decide.
Feedback	Follow through the examples in this text and do the Action Programme and the Quick Quizzes. Evaluate your efforts critically - how are you doing?
Study Plan	You need to be honest about your progress to yourself - do not be over-confident, but don't be negative either. Make your Study Plan (see below) and try to stick to it. Focus on the short-term objectives – completing two chapters a night, say - but beware of losing sight of your study objectives.
Practice	Use the Quick Quizzes and Chapter Roundups to refresh your memory regularly after you have completed your initial study of each chapter.

These introductory pages let you see exactly what you are up against. However you study, you should:

- **Read through the syllabus and teaching guide** - this will help you to identify areas you have already covered, perhaps at a lower level of detail, and areas that are totally new to you

- **Study the examination paper section**, where we show you the format of the exam (how many and what kind of questions etc)

Key study steps

The following steps are, in our experience, the ideal way to study for professional exams. You can of course adapt it for your particular learning style (see below).

Tackle the chapters in the order you find them in the Study Text. Taking into account your individual learning style, follow these key study steps for each chapter.

Key study steps	Activity
Step 1 *Chapter Topic List*	Study the list. Each numbered topic denotes a **numbered section** in the chapter.
Step 2 *Setting the Scene*	Read it through. It is designed to show you **why the topics in the chapter need to be studied** - how they lead on from previous topics, and how they lead into subsequent ones.
Step 3 *Explanations*	Proceed **methodically** through the chapter, reading each section thoroughly and making sure you understand.
Step 4 *Key Concepts*	**Key Concepts** can often earn you **easy marks** if you state them clearly and correctly in an appropriate exam.
Step 5 *Exam Tips*	These give you a good idea of how the examiner tends to examine certain topics – pinpointing **easy marks** and highlighting **pitfalls**.
Step 6 *Note taking*	Take **brief notes** if you wish, avoiding the temptation to copy out too much.
Step 7 *Marketing at Work*	Study each one, and try if you can to add flesh to them from your **own experience** - they are designed to show how the topics you are studying come alive (and often come unstuck) in the **real world**. You can also update yourself on these companies by going on to the World Wide Web.
Step 8 *Action Programme*	Make a very good attempt at each one in each chapter. These are designed to put your **knowledge into practice** in much the same way as you will be required to do in the exam. Check the answer at the end of the chapter in the **Action Programme Review**, and make sure you understand the reasons why yours may be different.
Step 9 *Chapter Roundup*	Check through it very carefully, to make sure you have grasped the **major points** it is highlighting.
Step 10 *Quick Quiz*	When you are happy that you have covered the chapter, use the **Quick Quiz** to check your recall of the topics covered. The answers are in the paragraphs in the chapter that we refer you to.
Step 11 *Illustrative questions*	Either at this point, or later when you are thinking about revising, make a full attempt at the **illustrative questions**. You can find these at the end of the Study Text, along with the **answers** so you can see how you did.

BPP PUBLISHING

Developing your personal Study Plan

Preparing a Study Plan (and sticking closely to it) is one of the key elements in learning success.

First you need to be aware of your style of learning. There are four typical learning styles. Consider yourself in the light of the following descriptions and work out which you fit most closely. You can then plan to follow the key study steps in the sequence suggested.

Learning styles	Characteristics	Sequence of key study steps in the BPP Study Text
Theorist	Seeks to understand principles before applying them in practice	1, 2, 3, 7, 4, 5, 8, 9, 10, 11 (6 continuous)
Reflector	Seeks to observe phenomena, thinks about them and then chooses to act	
Activist	Prefers to deal with practical, active problems; does not have much patience with theory	1, 2, 8 (read through), 7, 4, 5, 9, 3, 8 (full attempt), 10, 11 (6 continuous)
Pragmatist	Prefers to study only if a direct link to practical problems can be seen; not interested in theory for its own sake	8 (read through), 2, 4, 5, 7, 9, 1, 3, 8 (full attempt), 10, 11 (6 continuous)

Next you should complete the following checklist.

Am I motivated?   (a) ☐

Do I have an objective and a standard that I want to achieve?   (b) ☐

Am I a theorist, a reflector, an activist or a pragmatist?   (c) ☐

How much time do I have available per week, given: (d) ☐

- the standard I have set myself

- the time I need to set aside later for work on the Practice and Revision Kit.

- the other exam(s) I am sitting, and (of course)

- practical matters such as work, travel, exercise, sleep and social life?

Now:

- take the time you have available per week for this Study Text (d), and multiply it by the number of weeks available to give (e).   (e) ☐

- divide (e) by the number of chapters to give (f).   (f) ☐

- set about studying each chapter in the time represented by (f), following the key study steps in the order suggested by your particular learning style.

This is your personal **Study Plan**.

Short of time?

Whatever your objectives, standards or style, you may find you simply do not have the time available to follow all the key study steps for each chapter, however you adapt them for your particular learning style. If this is the case, follow the Skim Study technique below (the icons in the Study Text will help you to do this).

Skim Study technique

Study the chapters in the order you find them in the Study Text. For each chapter, follow the key study steps 1-2, and then skim-read through step 3. Jump to step 9, and then go back to steps 4-5. Follow through step 7, and prepare outline Answers to the Action Programme (step 8). Try the Quick Quiz (step 10), following up any items you can't answer, then do a plan for the illustrative question (step 11), comparing it against our answers. You should probably still follow step 6 (note taking).

Moving on...

However you study, when you are ready to embark on the practice and revision phase of the BPP Effective Study Package, you should still refer back to this Study Text:

- As a source of **reference** (you should find the list of Key Concepts and the index particularly helpful for this)

- As a **refresher** (the Chapter Roundups and Quick Quizzes help you here)

A note on pronouns

On occasions in this Study Text, 'he' is used for 'he or she', 'him' for 'him or her' and so forth. Whilst we try to avoid this practice it is sometimes necessary for reasons of style. No prejudice or stereotyping according to sex is intended or assumed.

BPP PUBLISHING

SYLLABUS

Aims and objectives

- To enable students to develop a sound theoretical and practical understanding of marketing planning and control

- To enable students to understand the theoretical concepts, techniques and models that underpin the marketing planning process

- To build practical skills associated with the management of the planning process

- To enable students to justify their strategic decisions and recommendations

- To develop an understanding of the barriers that exist to effective implementation of strategy

- To appreciate the need to tailor marketing plans and process to allow for the specific sector and situational factors that apply to any given organisation

- To develop an awareness of the techniques that underpin innovation and creativity in organisations

Learning outcomes

Students will be able to:

- Understand and critically appraise a wide variety of marketing techniques, concepts and models

- Conduct and evaluate a detailed marketing audit, both internally and externally

- Identify the elements that can be used to create competitive advantage

- Compare and contrast strategic options

- Specify a clear rationale when choosing between strategic alternatives

- Prepare effective and realistic marketing plans

- Initiate control systems for marketing planning

- Understand and evaluate the processes that can be used to overcome barriers to effective implementation of marketing strategies and plans

- Evaluate a range of techniques that facilitate innovation in organisations

Indicative content and weighting

Covered in Chapter

1 Market-led approach to planning (10%)

1.1 Adopting a market-led orientation — 1

- Marketing orientation
- Role of marketing in market-led strategic management
- Drivers of change in the business environment

1.2 The strategic marketing process — 2, 3

- Corporate strategy/marketing interface
- The basis of planning and control: the structure of planning and the cycle of control
- The nature of strategic, tactical and contingency planning

2 Analysis (25%)

2.1 External analysis   4, 5

- Environmental analysis, industry analysis
- Market analysis
- Competitor analysis, customer analysis

2.2 Internal analysis   6, 8

- Resource-based approach:
  Organisational assets, capabilities and competencies
  Technical resources
  Financial standing
  Managerial skills
  Organisation
  Information systems
- Asset-based approach:
  Customer-based assets
  Distribution-based assets
  Alliance-based asset
  Internal assets
- Marketing activities audit:
  Marketing strategy audit
  Marketing structures audit
  Marketing systems audit
  Productivity audit
  Marketing functions audit
- Innovation audit:
  The organisational climate
  Rate of new product development
  Customer satisfaction ratings
  The innovation/value matrix
  The balance of cognitive styles of the senior management team

3 Techniques for analysis and strategy development (20%)

3.1 Techniques for developing a future orientation   10

- Trend extrapolation
- Modelling
- Intuitive forecasting:
  Individual or genius forecasting
- Consensus forecasting:
  Jury forecasting
  Delphi forecasts
- Scenario planning
- Market sensing - examines the way in which managers develop new ways
  of looking at the outside world, in order to improve the way they develop
  market strategies and deliver marketing programmes

BPP
PUBLISHING

TUTOR'S GUIDANCE NOTES

Extracted from the CIM's online Tutor Manual, these websites are specific to this paper.

Websources

Syllabus Section	Web Address	Description
Market-led approach to planning	www.marketing.haynet.com/keynote/index/html	Useful notes on the preparation of marketing plans, and access to research data
	www.amazon.co.uk	Classic example of ground-breaking online customer service and the marketing orientation in practice.
Analysis	www.financewise.com	Specialist index of websites providing links to information on all aspects of finance (registration required)
	http://web.utk.edu/~jwachowi/wacho_world.html	Exhaustive listing of web financial resources presented with a student perspective
	www.gbn.org	The Global Business Network which encourages collaborative exploration of the future using forecasting tools such as scenario planning
Strategy Formulation and Selection	www.mckinseyquarterly.com	Free full text articles on strategy issues from one of the world's premier business journals
	(see 'strategy' section) www.bprc.warwick.ac.uk	Business Processes Resource Centre at the University of Warwick. Has links to research on BPR, knowledge management and strategy development
	www.strategy-business.com	Online journal on the topic of business strategy, with good search facilities
Implementation and Control	www.change-management.org	The Change Management Resource Library containing useful articles and links
	www.bpmg.org	The Business Process Management Group, an interest group developed to understand and support the implementation of change. Site contains a number of useful case studies. Free Associate membership, fee charged for additional services
	www.dti.gov.uk/mbp	A wide range of information and services designed to help firms improve their performance through benchmarking against best practice

THE EXAM PAPER

Assessment methods and format of the paper

Number of marks

Part A: one compulsory mini case study (maybe in the form of an article extract) with two questions of 20 marks each — 40

Part B: three questions from six (20 marks each) — 60

100

Time allowed: 3 hours

Analysis of past papers

The analysis below shows the topics which have been examined in recent sittings of the syllabus.

June 2001

Part A

1   Major UK retailers falling on hard times

 (a)   Strategic position analysis
 (b)   Recommendations

Part B

2   Overcoming resistance to a market-led culture
3   Innovation: quantity and price
4   Market share and profitability
5   Defining mission and objectives
6   Segmentation in new markets
7   Product life cycle: pros and cons

December 2000

Part A

1   Profile of a company making battery-less portable radios and electronic equipment

 (a)   Developing mission, goals and objectives
 (b)   Successful segmentation, targeting and positioning

Part B

2   Repositioning a brand for a charity
3   Competitor analysis
4   BCG matrix and Shell Directional Policy Matrix
5   Focus strategy
6   Internet and marketing
7   Alliances in retailing

(xv)

The exam paper

June 2000

Part A

1   Profile of a cereal manufacturer

    (a)   Strategic options in a price war
    (b)   Auditing process necessary to review innovation activities

Part B

2   Value chain
3   Evaluation of target markets
4   Balanced score card approach
5   Branding issues
6   Motivation for strategic partnership and critical success issues
7   Scenario planning

December 2000

Part A

1   Profile of a low cost UK based airline

    (a)   Identification of core capabilities, using the value chain
    (b)   Branding strategy for future developments

Part B

2   Problems in effective marketing planning
3   Geodemographic segmentation and direct marketing
4   Formulation of and influences on strategic objectives
5   Forming a view of the future: market sensing and market research
6   New product development
7   Dangers and causes of strategic wear out

June 1999

Part A

1   The wet shave market

    (a)   Briefing paper on new product development and promotion
    (b)   Evaluate the strategic options

Part B

2   Pan-European branding
3   PIMS
4   Internal cultural barriers
5   Market-led strategic change
6   Potential market segments
7   Relationship marketing strategy

December 1998/New syllabus specimen paper

Part A

1   A UK retailer specialises in selling photographic equipment

    (a)   Competitive position and competitive advantage
    (b)   Internal marketing

Part B

2   Weakness of BCG
3   Defending position
4   Franchising
5   Lifestyle segmentation and international markets
6   Innovation in a domestic appliance business
7   Product life cycle

BPP PUBLISHING

STUDY CHECKLIST

This page is designed to help you chart your progress through the Study Text, including the Action Programme and illustrative questions. You can tick off each topic as you study and try questions on it. Insert the dates you complete the chapters, Action Programme and questions in the relevant boxes. You will thus ensure that you are on track to complete your study before the exam.

	Text chapters	Action Programme		Illustrative questions	
	Date completed	Number	Date completed	Number	Date completed

PART A: THE MARKET-LED APPROACH TO PLANNING

1 Adopting a market-led orientation
2 The basis of planning and control
3 The corporate strategy/marketing interface

PART B: ANALYSIS

4 External environmental analysis
5 External situation analysis
6 Internal situation analysis

PART C: TECHNIQUES FOR ANALYSIS AND STRATEGY DEVELOPMENT

7 Auditing tools
8 Marketing audits and SWOT
9 Financial analysis
10 Techniques for developing a future orientation

PART D: STRATEGY FORMULATION AND SELECTION

11 Strategic intent
12 Approaches to creating strategic advantage
13 Developing a specific competitive position
14 The marketing mix
15 Strategic choice evaluation

PART E: IMPLEMENTATION AND CONTROL

16 Implementation
17 Control

PART F: THE EXAMINATION

18 Mini-cases in the examination

Part A
The Market-led Approach to Planning

1 Adopting a Market-led Orientation

Chapter Topic List	Syllabus reference
1 Setting the scene	
2 Market orientation	1.1
3 Role of marketing in market-led strategic management	1.1
4 Drivers of change	1.1

Learning Outcomes

- Understand and critically appraise a wide variety of marketing techniques, concepts and models.

Key Concepts Introduced

- Marketing
- Market orientation

Examples of Marketing at Work

- Wedgwood
- Halifax
- Royal Doulton

1 SETTING THE SCENE

1.1 This chapter introduces you to some of the dynamic changes in the environment and some of the issues that underline this paper.

1.2 Section 2 aims to help you break out of the 'functional' box to ensure that the market is **everybody's** concern in the company.

1.3 Section 3 shows how the 'market-orientation' will affect the role and activities of marketing personnel.

1.4 Although the environment is covered in Chapters 5 and 6, we indicate here some of the drivers of strategic changes.

Impact on other papers

1.5 The content of each chapter does represent the 'Western' industrial world. In some societies, you will find in the International Marketing Strategy paper, even basic 'marketing' is difficult owing to lack of resources or an insufficiently acculturated workforce or customer base.

2 MARKET ORIENTATION

2.1 A 'market' is a group of customers. 'Marketing' is a process or activity. Here are some definitions of marketing.

Key Concept

(a) **Marketing** is 'the management process responsible for identifying and satisfying customers' needs profitably.' (CIM)

(b) The American Marketing Association's definition is: 'The process of planning and executing the conception, pricing, promotion, and distribution of ideas, goods and services to create exchanges that satisfy individual and organisational goals.'

2.2 Note in passing that both (b) and (c) include 'ideas'. This has some important implications.

(a) 'Ideas' can be intellectual property, such as software and so forth, which can be sold as products. Marketing is not limited to FMCG products.

(b) Many industries are 'knowledge'-based industries. The ability to tap knowledge and create ideas might be instrumental in corporate success, as might be the ability to communicate these ideas.

(c) Ideas can include information that will help customers determine whether the product will, in fact, be able to satisfy their needs. Marketing therefore encompasses many of the qualities that businesses need to have in order to survive.

2.3 'Marketing' can also refer to a department within an organisation, with its own professional staff with specialist expertise, and 'potential' interests in terms of other business functions. We cover this briefly in Chapter 3.

Marketing-led and market-led orientation

2.4 Given that marketing is a process, an organisational function, and an academic discipline, it is worth going back to first principles. A **market** is customer or group of customers.

Key Concept

Market orientation is 'an organisational culture where beating the competition through the creation of superior customer value is the paramount objective throughout the business'. (Piercy)

2.5 **A marketing-led organisation is led by the marketing department.** Marketing orientation might just refer to increased power for marketing personnel. The customer, however, is not necessarily at the heart of **everyone's** thinking.

2.6 In a company with a market orientation, the aim of providing superior customer value dominates **all** thinking.

- What the business is
- Which markets to service
- Investments and acquisitions
- Which people to employ and how to promote them

2.7   In **market-led** organisations, the marketing department is **not** in a world of its own. Customer value is designed and created by **multi-function** product teams supporting **all the business functions.**

2.8   Focusing on customers and their needs is something which should be your meat and drink. Hooley, Saunders and Piercy identify the following components of a market orientation.

- **Customers:** know them well enough to give superior value.

- **Competition:** what are their short- and long-term capabilities?

- **Inter-functional:** mobilise the entire company to create superior customer value.

- **Culture:** employee behaviour should be managed to ensure customer satisfaction.

- **Long term profit focus:** have a strategic but realistic vision.

2.9   Those issues will be discussed in later chapters.

3   ROLE OF MARKETING IN MARKET-LED STRATEGIC MANAGEMENT   6/01

3.1   Marketing expertise and personnel are important drivers in taking a firm to the customer, as the example below suggests.

Marketing at Work

Waterford Wedgwood/Royal Doulton

From *Financial Times 1 May 2001*

Royal Doulton, one of the great names in British ceramics, is shrinking to survive. A philosophy of winning sales at all cost triggered a series of loses and a management shake-up under Hamish Grossart, the company director appointed in 1998. The contraction of Royal Doulton, which is based in Stoke-on-Trent, mirrors a decline in the whole Staffordshire ceramics industry.

Wedgwood, Royal Doulton's main rival, seems curiously insulated from the pain. At its pretty campus-style site just outside Stoke-on-Trent, robot delivery trucks glide quietly between the workbenches where craftspeople assemble items for its classic Jasperware range.

The business, a division of Waterford Wedgwood, the Irish luxury goods group chaired by Sir Anthony O'Reilly, made operating profits last year of €18.7m (£11.6m). This compared with a loss of £9.6m at Royal Doulton. Wedgwood's sales were a third higher than its rival, while its workforce was two-thirds smaller.

At Royal Doulton, Mr Nutbeen (CEO) is resigned to indifference from the City.

Redmond O'Donoghue, Waterford Wedgwood's genial president, frets that its shares trade on a prospective p/e of about 12 compared to multiples of some more than 20 for luxury goods business such as Bulgari, Tiffany and LVMH. That Mr O'Donoghue can afford such aspirational worries is partly the result of Waterford Wedgwood's revamp its ceramics division in the late 1990s. At the time, it was sharply criticised by some analysts for investing about £30m in automating what may saw as a dying business.

But the move was justified by revival in sales, triggered by the reinvention of the previously fusty Wedgwood brand using experience and knowledge gained in the Waterford glassware business. Independent designers, such as Paul Costellow, brought their own followings to the brand, as well as fresh design thinking.

Marketing, not production, now drives the business. The Duchess of York, retained expensively for a few day's work a year, has proved an improbably potent ambassador for the brand in the US.

BPP PUBLISHING

Waterford Wedgwood's glossy magazine includes interviews with Washington socialites and features on vacations in the Hamptons.

The next fundamental shift, says Mr O'Donoghue, is for Wedgwood to crank up its sales in giftware, as Waterford has already done.

Royal Doulton also likes to think of itself as a luxury giftware group. If Mr Nutbeen is serious about this, lines such as resin *Mr Men* figurines, at £8 each, seem unlikely to survive a cull this summer. Royal Doulton executives resent suggestions they are copying Wedgwood's ideas. But whatever the inspiration, the losses are falling. Mr Nutbeen says they will eventually be replaced by 'double-digit returns'.

Both businesses would be envious of the 10 percent profit margin achieved by Portmeirion, a much smaller Stoke-on-Trent ceramics company.

Website addresses

www.wedgwood.co.uk
www.royal-doulton.com

Market-led strategic change

3.2 Market-led strategic change rests on the following assumptions (Piercy, 1997).

Assumptions	Application in Wedgwood and Royal Doulton
All organisations must follow the dictates of the market to survive.	Risk of relying on current tableware market. Company had to find new customers.
Organisational effectiveness can be pursued by being market-led, focusing on the customer.	Winning sales at all costs. The firm needed **marketing** knowledge and implementation skills, by reinventing Wedgwood Brand.
Barriers to being market-led come, not from ignorance of customer characteristics, but from the way organisations are run.	Experience in one part of the business was applied elsewhere. There must have been good communications to ensure knowledge transfer.
Becoming market-led often needs an upheaval.	New designers, and more resources focused on the customer communications.
Deep seated strategic change, not just hiring a marketing executive.	Change from providing tableware to offering giftware.

3.3 In short the pursuit of **customer satisfaction** is at the heart of the market-led company. Piercy (1997) makes a distinction between **marketing** and **going to market**. Markets are more important than marketing, per se, and markets and customers are important for everyone in a company (not just the marketing department). 'Going to market is a process owned by everyone in the organisation ... the context for marketing should be the **process** of going to market, not the marketing department.'

3.4 The process of going to market needs to be **managed**. (Piercy, 1992)

(a) Strategies are based on customers and markets.

(b) Internal programmes and external actions are driven by such strategies.

(c) The company must 'get its act together' in order to deliver its strategy into the market. This involves more than the marketing department.

(d) Cross-functional teams cross organisational boundaries to get the job done.

(e) New types of relationships are created.

(f) New ways of doing business are supported by a new information technology infrastructure.

Challenges for the market-led organisation

3.5 Four broad issues arise for the market-led organisation (Piercy, 1997).

Issue	Comment
'New' customers	• Rising expectations: customers exposed to world class service will expect it everywhere
	• Sophistication: customers can see through marketing-speak, and want transparency
	• Increased cynicism about marketing
New competitors	• From overseas
	• Reinventing the business (eg Direct Line Insurance)
New type of organisation	• Outsourcing arrangements
	• Collaboration arrangements
	• Alliances (eg airlines)
	• Stakeholder influences
New ways of doing business	• Customer-specific marketing
	• Databases are used to develop profiles of individual customers to entice them into a **relationship**
	• Internet marketing: buyers and sellers can conduct a dialogue as the internet is interactive
	• Customer co-operatives: internet newsgroups and chatrooms enable customers to get together perhaps to negotiate discounts or to share experience of a brand

Role of 'marketing' in market-led firms

3.6 What might be the role of marketing and marketing management in this particular context? Kashani (*Financial Times*, Mastering Management) argues that the role of 'marketing' has changed significantly but has also become much more important to the activities of many firms. The changes he notes are these.

(a) **From staff to line.** Marketing thinking and action are better integrated into the day to day decisions of managers running important parts of the business. In other words, instead of a separate, 'staff' marketing department going its own sweet way and putting a promotional gloss on what the organisation does, marketing is more involved in line decisions, such as segment or product management.

(b) **From specialist to strategic.** 'Marketing in the organisation has evolved beyond its traditional specialist focus. Tasks once exclusively associated with marketing, such as market and competitive assessment or end-user communication, are now only a part of a far more integrated marketing process that may include other functions such as upstream product development or downstream management of distribution.'

(c) **From isolated to widespread.** Marketing has become more diffused within the organisation, and is no longer the concern of the few. In short, Kashani argues, the market orientation is spreading.

(i) 'Companies are inculcating their managers in various 'back office' functions with market and customer-mindedness - the very attributes that were the exclusive domain of marketing people.

BPP
PUBLISHING

(ii) A widespread appreciation of market forces and customer needs and how parts of an organisation may contribute to creating a superior customer value is a necessity if the entire organisation is to become market responsive.'

Marketing at Work

In September 1997 *Marketing Business* described change in the financial services sector. In a service business such as the *Halifax*, group marketing staff report to a main board director who is head of *personnel*. This is because service businesses are people businesses, and 'in a corporate brand, the brand is everybody and the brand strategy is the corporate strategy'. Whether this will change in the proposed merger with the Bank of Scotland is not certain.

Website address: www.halifax.co.uk

Exam Tip

It is worth emphasising that this paper is about strategy rather than the design of tactical marketing programmes. The list below, Piercy (1997), covers some of the issues.

- **Customers**: does the firm take customers seriously and work for customer satisfaction? How do you create a customer-focused organisation?

- How are markets **defined and segmented** around issues that **matter** to customers?

- How do we create a **value proposition** based on our mission and our ability to differentiate from competitors?

Action Programme 1

An IMD survey put 'knowledge of other [business] functions beyond marketing' as fairly low on the list (4th from bottom). Given that this survey covered only *marketing* managers, how significant do you think it is that they seem relatively unconcerned with understanding other business functions such as the production department and the finance department? Do they know enough already, or do you think a failure to understand how the rest of the organisation works could be a weakness, especially given that a market-led company embodies everybody?

Role of marketing in strategic management: summary

3.7   *Step 1.*   Identify customer requirements and disseminate information

       Step 2.   Determine competitive positioning (matching customer needs with organisational resources)

       Step 3.   Implement the strategy to deliver satisfaction. Internal marketing is needed here.

4   DRIVERS OF CHANGE

Marketing and the 'strategic triangle'

4.1   An IMD survey identified **competition** as a major worry for marketing managers. The reason why businesses and firms need a competitive orientation is that customers have a choice, and they can compare the firm's offering with what competitors are offering.

4.2   Given that the marketing orientation needs to be present in all the areas of the organisation, we are led to **Ohmae's** strategic triangle: company, competitors and customers.

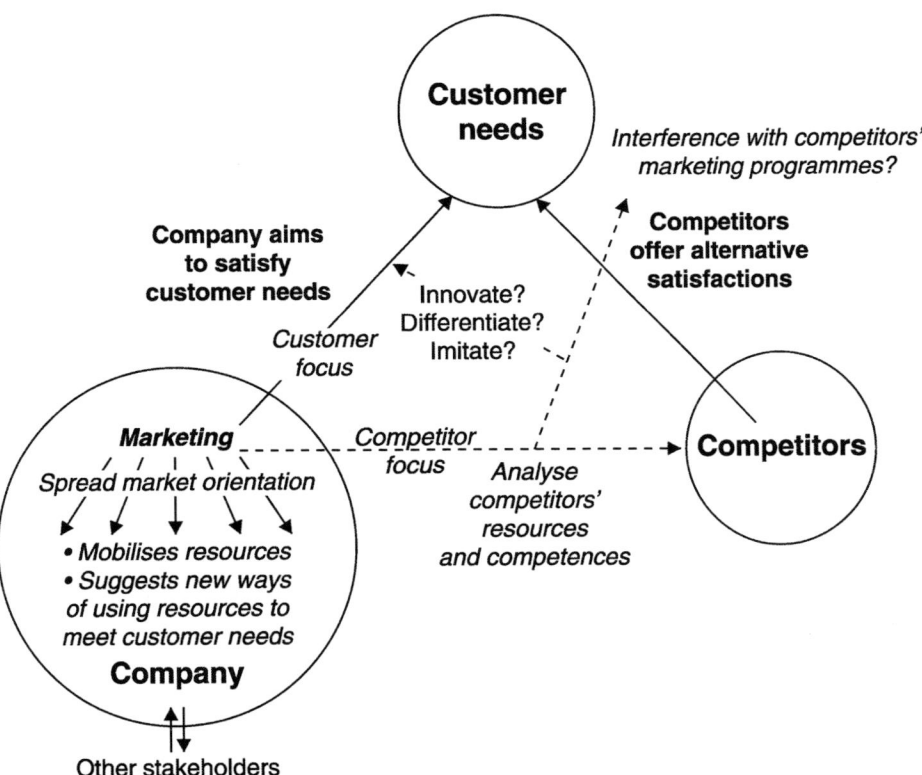

4.3   All organisations are subject to increasing change. It has been said that change is the only business certainty. It follows that the possibility of change should be incorporated in every business strategy. Drummond and Ensor (1999) pose the following questions about this.

(a)   **What drives change?** An analysis of PEST forces is useful here (political, economic, social and technological).

(b)   **How does change impact on our business environment?** Even the most mature and traditional markets may change with customer needs and expectations. Marks & Spencer has suffered from a shift in the middle market of fashion retailing, as customers become increasingly polarised between 'designer' and 'value' outlets. Intense competition and shorter product life cycles make it difficult to predict the future.

(c)   **What is the result of change on the organisation's strategy?** Change brings opportunities for those companies that are willing and able to take them, and also implies that old ways of doing business (however well they served the company in the past) must be reassessed to reflect the new needs of the marketplace.

The view from 2005

4.4   It is worth having a look at how certain trends might affect how things will appear in a few years time. Introducing the Financial Times *Mastering Marketing* series, **Kotler** made the following predictions.

Trend	Comment
Disintermediation	All products can be bought off in the internet, meaning that there is less need for intermediaries
Retailers	Simple shopping is out, as people can buy supplies over the internet. Shops become entertainment venues (eg bookshops with coffee shops)
Mass customisation	Customers can order bespoke products but these can be produced with the efficiency of mass production
Data mining	Firms get more information about customers and use it for cross selling
Management information	Real information about customer profitability can be obtained
Long-term supplies	Customers will be offered 'life-time' supplies
Outsourcing	This will be the norm
Franchising	Most field sales people will become franchisees
End of mass TV	TV advertising takes on the characteristics of magazine advertising, with a proliferation of TV and internet channels made possible with digital TV
Sustainable competitive advantages	Benchmarking, reverse engineering and technological leapfrogging

Exam Tip

New developments were covered explicitly in an essay question set in December 1997 in the old syllabus. However, such developments, especially in relation to IT, can be brought into any question. Before you get carried away, you must bear in mind that change, particularly in relation to technology, moves at different paces in different market **segments**. So, for example, despite the Internet, marketers will still have to address people who are afraid of, or not interested in, new technology.

Marketing in non-profit-making organisations

4.5 **Governments** and **non-profit-making organisations** might adopt a marketing orientation to achieve their objectives more effectively. The marketer's skills are relevant but the 'profit' aspect of marketing is absent.

(a) Governments wish to promote or discourage certain activities or attitudes.

(b) The main purpose of a non-profit-making organisation will be to satisfy the needs and wants of a group or section of a community.

Action Programme 2

What would be the effects of introducing a marketing approach to a charity?

4.6 'Non-profit marketing' differs from marketing for profit.

(a) Whereas marketers in a profit-making organisation can focus mainly on customers, many non-profit-making organisations have two major 'publics' that they must satisfy.

- Donors (who provide the funds, the 'customers')
- Beneficiaries (the 'consumers')

(b) Whereas profit-making organisations can work primarily towards a profit objective, non-profit-making organisations are likely to have **complex multiple objectives**, which are hard to measure.

(c) Non-profit-making organisations often come under more public scrutiny than profit-making organisations.

Chapter Roundup

- A **market-led firm** is a company in which everyone puts the customer at the centre of decision-making. The customer is not 'owned' by the marketing department.

- Elements of a **market-orientation** include culture, capabilities, organisation, and strategic thinking.

- **Marketing personnel are catalysts** in generating a market-orientation and promoting market-led strategic change.

- **Barriers** to being market-led mainly rest in the way the business is run.

- The role of marketing has changed from being an isolated, specialist staff department to being **integrated** with line management, **widespread** in the organisation and involved in strategic decision making.

- Marketers need to attend to the **strategic triangle**: customers, competitors and the company (and its stakeholders).

- **Challenges** are new customer expectations, new competitors and ways of doing business, and new types of organisation.

- The **internet** will break down barriers between end-consumers and producers.

- Most marketing activities for businesses have to be justified in terms of **increasing long-term shareholder wealth**. Customer satisfaction is a means to that end.

Now try illustrative question 1 at the end of the Study Text

Quick Quiz

1 What is marketing? (see para 2.1)

2 What is a market orientation? (2.4)

3 What distinguishes a market-led from a marketing-led organisation? (2.5, 2.7)

4 What are the underlying assumptions of market-led strategic change? (3.2)

5 What changes might affect the role of marketing expertise and personnel in a market-led organisation? (3.6)

6 Identify some key issues for market-led companies. (3.5)

7 What makes up Ohmae's strategic triangle? (4.2)

8 What three questions may be asked about change? (4.3)

Action Programme Review _____

1   If market-led strategy is necessary throughout the company, then understanding how other functions in the company work would seem significant – otherwise marketing will be conducted in a vacuum.

2   (a) The reasons for the organisation's existence should be expressed in terms of the consumer or client.

     (b) Marketing research should be used to find out:

(i)   Who needs help, and in what ways, and how satisfactory is the current help provided

(ii)   Where funds should be raised, and what the best approaches should be

(iii)   Which political figures are susceptible to 'lobbying' and how such lobbying should best be conducted

(c)   'Target markets' would be identified for charitable acts, fund-raising and influencing.

(d)   The charity might also wish to promote an image to the public, perhaps by means of public relations work.

(e)   The management of the charity will be aware that they are in competition for funds with other charities, and in competition with other ways of spending money in trying to obtain funds from the public. It should organise its 'sales and marketing' systems to raise funds in the most effective way.

(i)   Many charities now engage in telemarketing.

(ii)   Many charities have acquired logos - even NHS hospitals have acquired them.

2 The Basis of Planning and Control

Chapter Topic List	Syllabus reference
1 Setting the scene	
2 The management context	1.2
3 Planning and control	1.2
4 The strategic planning process	1.2
5 Other models for setting direction	1.2
6 Tactical and resource planning	1.2
7 Contingency planning	1.2

Learning Outcomes

- Appreciate theoretical concepts and techniques underpinning the marketing planning process.

- Prepare effective and realistic marketing plans.

Key Concepts Introduced

- Management
- Planning
- Corporate planning
- Control
- Goals

- Objectives
- Aims
- Strategy
- Tactics
- Corporate strategy

- Business strategy
- Critical success factors, key tasks, priorities
- Contingencies

Examples of Marketing at Work

- Body Shop
- Europe's defence industry

- Coca-Cola
- Honda

1   SETTING THE SCENE

1.1   This chapter is concerned with the processes of planning and control. These relate to the roles of management in general.

1.2 We introduce planning and control at the level of corporate **strategy**, and show how this is related. The same issues are relevant further down the a hierarchy, to marketing and other functional activities. Some of these steps are covered in detail in later chapters.

1.3 In Chapter 3, we describe the marketing plan, how it relates to other functional plans and where the marketing function fits in the organisation. Control is covered in more detail in Chapter 17.

Links to other papers

1.4 Planning and control techniques discussed here are fundamental to the other papers at Diploma.

- International Marketing Strategy: plans are likely to be more complex to execute, and the marketing process may need to be delegated.

- Integrated Marketing Communications: the 'campaign' aspect of this subject makes planning skills very important.

2 THE MANAGEMENT CONTEXT

Key Concept

Management is the 'process' of getting things done through people'. (Rosemary Stewart)

2.1 Managers are concerned with:

- **Process**: forecasting, planning, monitoring and controlling
- **People**: motivation, leadership, delegation and **relationship management** in general both within the organisation and with groups outside it

2.2 An IMD survey identified a number of managerial competences which marketing managers are supposed to have, to cope with the new challenges and the enhanced external roles of marketing. The **three most important competences for future marketing managers** were held to be the following.

- Strategic thinking
- Communication capability (listening as well as talking)
- Sensitivity to customers

Specialist marketing skills came at the bottom, the least relevant to marketing **management** performance.

Marketing at Work

Corporate culture, as a dimension of management theory, has only attracted attention since the 1970s. In companies such as *Body Shop* the culture is obvious and is used as a marketing platform. It is sustained through the selection of new franchisees with similar cultural values and ideals.

Website address: www.the-body-shop.com

Managerial 'roles'

2.3 Managers perform various 'roles' (Mintzberg). These are relevant to **marketing** management. In the *Analysis and Decision* case, you have to adopt a role and you must be sensitive to your position.

Interpersonal roles

- **Figurehead** — Performing ceremonial and social duties as the organisation's representative, for example at conferences

- **Leader** — Uniting and inspiring the team to achieve objectives (eg sales team)

- **Liaison** — Communication with people outside the manager's work group or the organisation, for example about customer needs

Informational roles

- **Monitor** — Receiving information about the organisation's performance and comparing it with objectives

- **Disseminator** — Passing on information

- **Spokesperson** — Transmitting information outside the unit or organisation, on behalf of the unit or organisation

Decisional roles

- **Entrepreneur** — Being a 'fixer' - mobilising resources to get things done and to seize opportunities

- **Disturbance-handler** — Rectifying mistakes and getting operations - and relationships - back on course - customer call?

- **Resource allocator** — Distributing resources in the way that will most efficiently achieve defined objectives: planning

- **Negotiator** — Bargaining for required resources and influence

---

Action Programme 1

Identify which 'management' tasks are currently performed by:

(a) You
(b) Your boss

---

3 PLANNING AND CONTROL

12/99

3.1 Planning and control are at the heart of this syllabus.

Key Concept

Planning involves:

- setting objectives, quantifying targets for achievement and communicating these targets to others
- selecting strategies, tactics, policies, programmes and procedures for achieving the objective

(Fayol)

BPP PUBLISHING

Action Programme 2

In business, the process of planning is formal, but you are already very skilled in a more informal version of the same activity. Take some time to analyse the steps you would take when planning a holiday, a long car journey or a dinner party. Make a note of these. As you work through the remainder of this chapter identify the business activity parallel to each of your planning steps.

Importance of planning

3.2 Planning therefore involves decisions about:

- **What** to do in the future (objectives)
- **How** to do it (strategy)
- **When** to do it (tactics)
- **Who** is to do it (tactics)

3.3 Planning is a fundamental part of the manager's role.

(a) It helps to **drive the organisation forward by co-ordinating resources** and channelling them towards the achievement of pre-determined goals.

(b) Planning gives us some **influence over an uncertain future**. By deciding what you want to achieve or what you want to happen in the future, you can take logical steps which will help you to achieve this goal.

(c) A plan **communicates** the objectives and what is needed to achieve them to other people.

Key Concept

Corporate planning is quite simply planning undertaken at a corporate level, ie involving the **whole** organisation. It has been described as follows, by Argenti.

It is 'a systematic and disciplined study designed to help identify the objective of any organisation or corporate body, determine an appropriate target, decide upon suitable constraints, and devise a practical plan by which the objective may be achieved.'   (Argenti 1968)

What is control?

3.4 The purpose of planning is to direct resources to achieve results in the future. However, managers need to monitor actual performance in the light of the plan.

Key Concept

Control is a review of actual results against planned performance and the taking of corrective action if needed.

The cycle of planning and control

3.5 Planning is part of a cycle of planning and control cycle which has six steps.

Step 1. **Make a plan.** Decide what to do and identify the desired results.

Step 2. **Record the plan.** The plan should incorporate standards of efficiency or targets of performance.

Step 3. **Carry out the plan.**

Step 4. **Compare actual results** against the plan.

Step 5. **Evaluate the comparison**, and decide whether further action is necessary to ensure the plan is achieved.

Step 6. Take **corrective action** if necessary, or adjust.

3.6 EXAMPLE

Managers often plan and control at the same time. For example, a sales manager might receive information saying that sales volumes were less than planned. After investigating the variance the sales manager might:

(a) Inform superiors that sales forecasts for the rest of the year will need to be revised (planning activity) and/or

(b) Take action in an attempt to improve the current sales effort (control activity).

Barriers to good planning

3.7 Many managers are reluctant to make formal plans, and prefer to operate without them, dealing with problems only when and if they arise.

(a) **Lack of knowledge** (or interest) about the purpose and goals of the organisation as a whole.

(b) **Reluctance to be committed to one set of targets.** Managers might want to keep their options open.

(c) **Fear of blame or criticism for failing to achieve planned targets.** The motivation to plan for inefficient performance will also be strong, since the likelihood of 'failure' will then be relatively low.

(d) **Lack of confidence in performing the job efficiently and effectively**, or a lack of confidence in the organisation's senior management to **provide the resources** needed to achieve planned targets.

(e) **Lack of information about what is going on in the 'environment'** (ie customers, markets, competition, social and economic change).

(f) **Resentment of plans made by others.**

3.8 **Overcoming barriers to planning**

(a) **Participation.** All levels of staff should be involved (to a greater or less degree) in the planning process.

(b) **Information.** Planners must be provided with the information they need to plan properly.

(c) **Motivation.**

(d) **Education.** Planning techniques can be taught.

(e) **Compulsion.**

Exam Tip

The Analysis and Decision case study often requires you to prepare a **marketing plan**, programming the decisions on the basis of your analyses. Learning planning disciplines is therefore important.

17

Elements of all plans

3.9 All good plans contain the following elements. We have analysed them as Key Concepts.

Key Concepts

Goals: what you are trying to achieve; the intention behind any action.

Objectives: a goal which can be quantified. *Example*: increase profits by 30% over the next 12 months. The achievement of an objective can be measured. Objectives should be SMART • Specific • Measurable • Attainable • Results oriented • Time-bounded.

Aims: goals which cannot be measured usefully. *Example:* customer satisfaction is an aim, but it is a continuous process and does not stop when one target has been achieved.

3.10 How you achieve the goals is indicated by strategy and tactics.

Key Concepts

Strategy: the method chosen to achieve goals or objectives. *Example:* we will achieve our objective of increasing profits by growing market share in existing markets.

Tactics: how resources are deployed in an agreed strategy. *Example:* we will set up a new telephone call centre and target new customers.

3.11 There are different ways of achieving the same objective, hence the need to choose a strategy. Similarly, there are many tactics we can exploit while executing a strategy. For example, increasing profits by 30% could be achieved in a number of ways:

- Growing revenue, by targeting new and existing customers
- Cutting costs

What if the plan goes wrong?

3.12 All plans are based on assumptions. Some managers are able to identify the type of things that could go wrong. We will cover contingency planning shortly.

4 THE STRATEGIC PLANNING PROCESS

Marketing at Work

The European *defence industry* faces lower government spending, a changed strategic environment, and greater competition as contracts are put out to open tender. There is greater competition in export markets.

Planning

A number of assumptions can be made about the environment and customer demands.

- Military needs are for mobile and flexible forces, with fewer tanks, and more flexible 'high-tech' weaponry.

- For economic reasons, reliability and maintainability are desired.

- There should be military applications of civilian technology.

- The Ministry of Defence has also tightened up on procurement, replacing cost-plus contracts with competitive tenders.

- Defence is big business. Most European firms have been hampered by their small size in comparison with US firms. Mergers are in progress.

- The strategic environment is changing with 'rogue states' and so on, the target of US concern.

Since the recent incident in which a US spy plane crash landed in China, there has been a 'war' between American and Chinese computer hackers. A sign of things to come?

Defence firms are undertaking strategic management. All firms are concerned with cash flow and productivity. **Strategic planning departments** have been set up to provide necessary inputs and analyses.

Website address: www.defence-data.com

Levels of strategy

4.1 Planning takes place at different levels. Hofer and Schendel refer to three levels of strategy.

- Corporate strategies
- Business strategies
- Operational and functional strategies, as in the diagram below

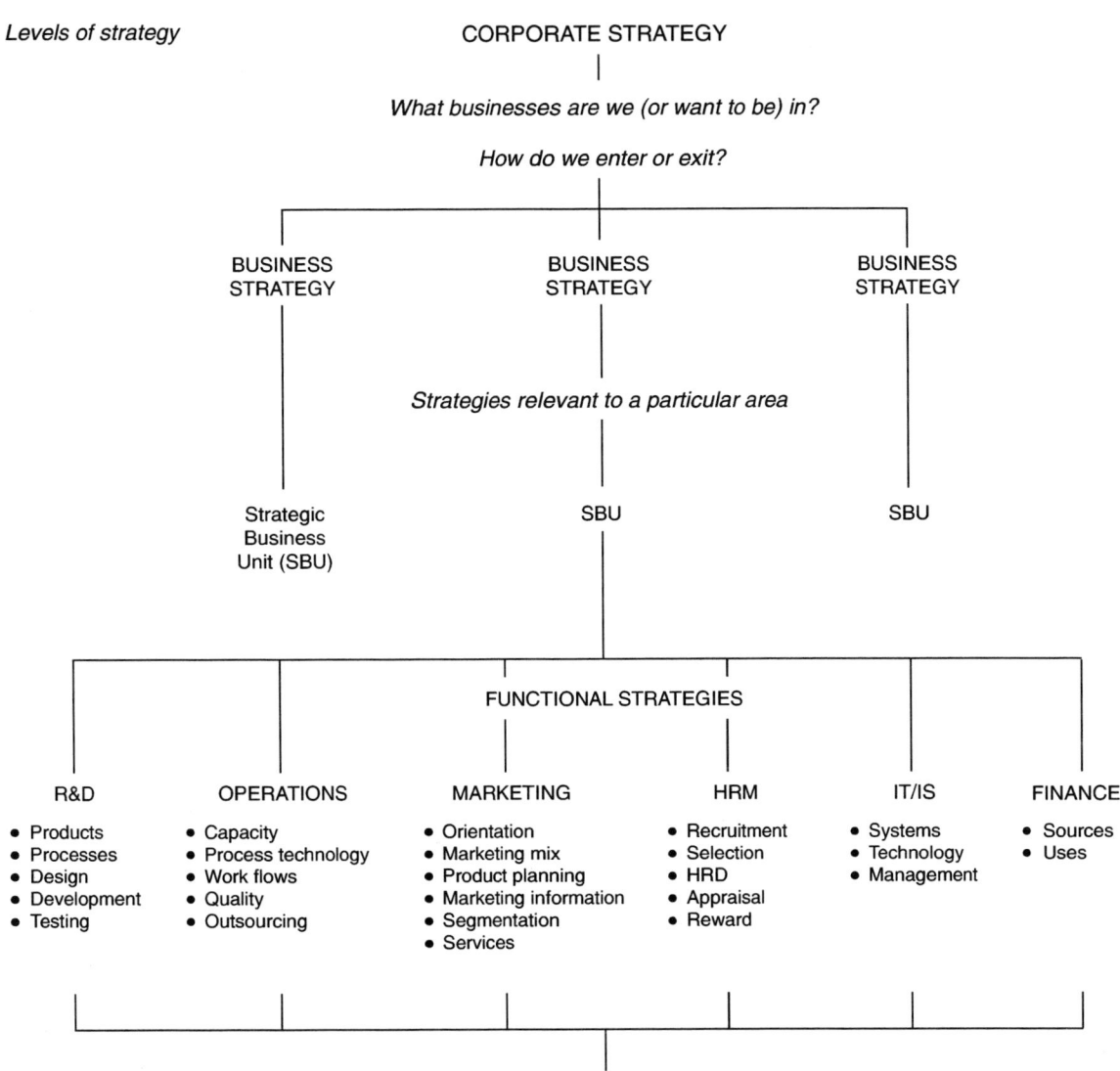

BPP PUBLISHING

Corporate strategies

> ## Key Concept
>
> **Corporate strategy** is concerned with what types of business the organisation is in. It 'denotes the most general level of strategy in an organisation' (Johnson and Scholes).

4.2   Corporate strategy might involve diversifying into a new line of business or closing a business down. It might mean global expansion or contraction.

Business strategy

> ## Key Concept
>
> **Business strategy**: how an organisation approaches a particular product market area.

4.3   This can involve decisions as to whether, in principle, a company should:

- Segment the market and specialise in particularly profitable areas
- Compete by offering a wider range of products
- Offer a differentiated product

4.4   Some large, diversified firms have separate **strategic business units** dealing with particular areas.

Functional/operational strategies

4.5   Functional/operational strategies deal with specialised areas of activity, as shown on the diagram in paragraph 4.1.

Marketing at Work

BT, Vodafone and *J-phone* (*Financial Times, 1 May 2001*).

BT had hoped to build up a mobile phone presence in Japan, but high levels of debt led it to announce the sale of its Japanese interests in J-phone to Vodafone for £3bn. Vodafone now has full control of J-phone. J-phone has been growing but apparently Vodafone wants it to compete more aggressively with *NTT DoCoMo*, Japan's largest mobile phone company, but behind Vodafone globally. J-phone has cutting edge technology, is innovative and highly profitable, but has 16% of the market compared to NTT CoCoMo's 60%.

Website addresses

www.vodafone.com
www.nttdocomo.com
www.bt.co.uk

A corporate strategic planning model

4.6   On the next page is one model of the corporate strategic planning process. We have identified **three** stages. These are described briefly in the paragraphs below.

Strategic analysis

4.7   Strategic analysis is concerned with understanding the strategic position of the organisation.

(a) **Environmental analysis** (external appraisal) is the scanning of the business's environment for factors relevant to the organisation's current and future activities.

(b) **Position or situation audit.** The current state of the business in respect of resources, brands, markets etc.

(c) **Mission**

(i)   The firm's long-term approach to business

(ii)   The organisation's value system

(d) **Goals** interpret the mission to the needs of different stakeholders (eg customers, employees, shareholders).

(e) **Objectives** should embody mission and goals. Generally, they are **quantitative** measures, against which actual performance can be assessed.

(f) **Corporate appraisal.** A critical assessment of the Strengths, Weaknesses, Opportunities and Threats in relation to the internal and environmental factors affecting an organisation.

(g) **Gap analysis.** A projection of current activities into the future to identify if there is a difference between the firm's objectives and the results from the continuation of current activities.

4.8   Note that you **might** decide the mission **after** assessing the needs of the organisation and its environmental situation.

Exam Tip

You may have to suggest a new mission, sometimes for the organisation as a whole and sometimes for the marketing function.

Strategic choice

4.9   **Strategic choice** is based on strategic analysis.

(a) **Strategic options generation.** Here are some examples.

- Increase market share
- International growth
- Concentration on core competences
- Acquisition

(b) **Strategic options evaluation.** Alternative strategies are developed and each is then examined on its merits.

- Acceptability to the organisation's stakeholders
- Suitability
- Feasibility

(c) **Strategy selection**

- **Competitive strategy** is the generic strategy determining **how you compete.**
- **Product-market strategy** determines **where you compete.**
- Institutional strategies determine the **method of growth.**

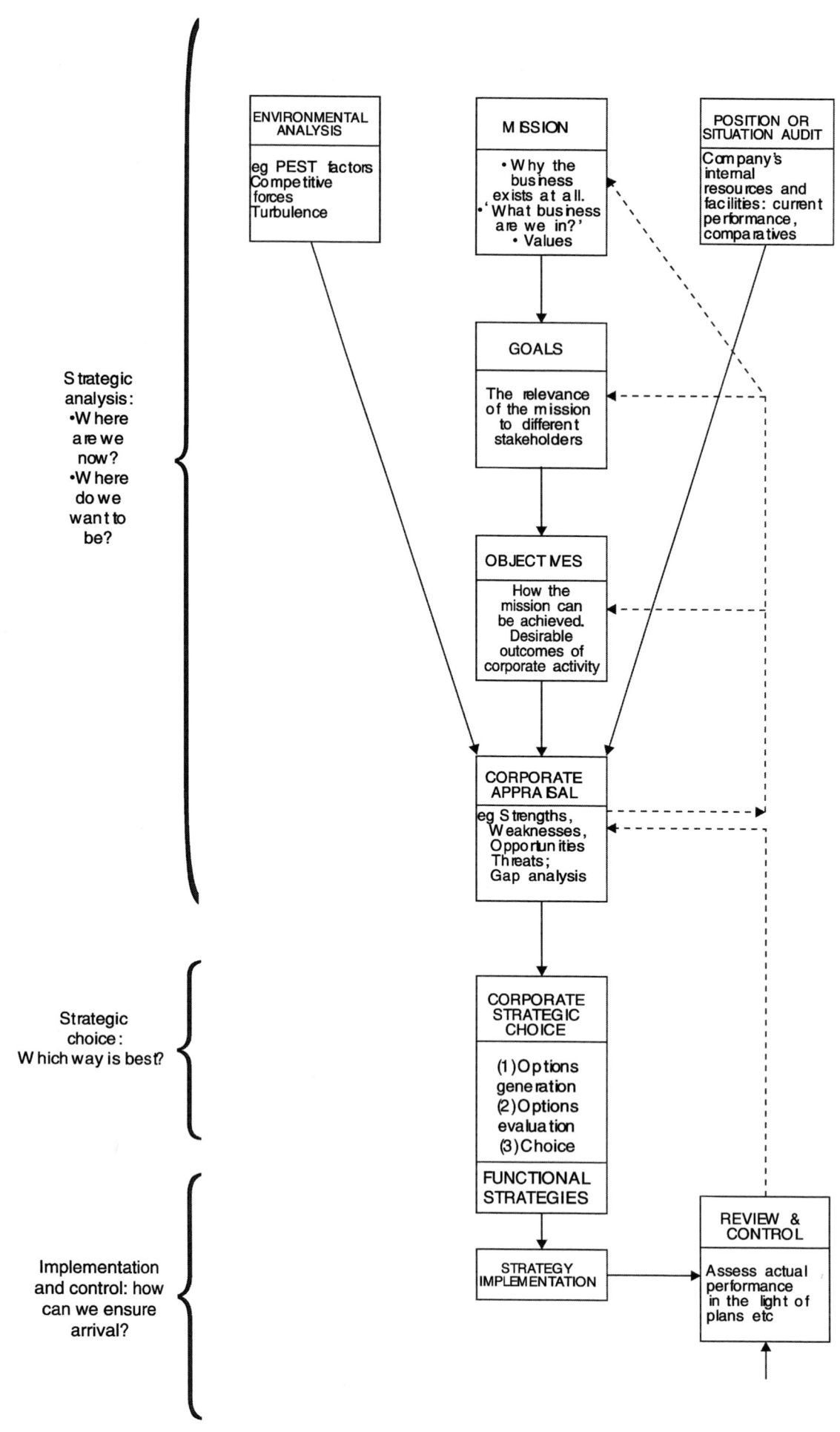

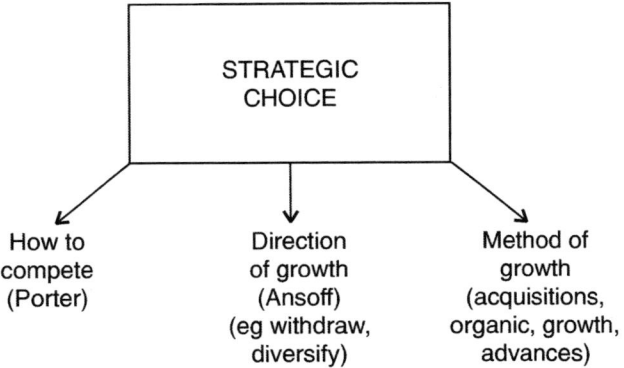

Implementation

4.10 The implementation of the strategy has to be planned. This is the conversion of the strategy into detailed **plans or objectives for operating units.**

(a) Some plans go into detailed **specifications** as to how the activities should be carried out.

(b) Others will specify **targets** which managers are expected to reach on their own initiative.

(c) The planning of implementation has several aspects.

(i) **Resource planning** (ie finance, personnel). This involves assessing the key tasks, and the resources to be allocated to them.

(ii) **Systems.** Systems are necessary to provide the necessary strategic information, as well as essential operational procedures. Control systems are used to assess performance.

(iii) Organisation structure.

Action Programme 3

Ganymede Ltd is a company selling widgets. The finance director says 'We plan to issue more shares to raise money for new plant capacity - which will enable us to enter the vital and growing widget markets of Latin America. After all, we've promised the shareholders 5% profit growth this year, and trading is tough'.

Identify the corporate, business and functional strategies in the above quotation.

Is strategic planning necessary?

4.11 **Advantages of a formal system of strategic planning**

Advantages	Comment
Identifies risks	Strategic planning helps in managing risks.
Forces managers to think	Strategic planning can encourage creativity and initiative by tapping the ideas of the management team.
Forces decision-making	Companies cannot remain static - they have to cope with changes in the environment. A strategic plan helps to chart the future possible areas where the company may be involved and draws attention to the need to keep on changing and adapting, not just to 'stand still' and survive.
Better control	Management control can be better exercised if targets are explicit.

Advantages	Comment
Enforces consistency at all levels	Long-term, medium-term and short-term objectives, plans and controls can be made consistent with one another. Otherwise, strategies can be rendered ineffective by budgeting systems with performance measures which have no strategic content.
Public knowledge	Drucker has argued that an entrepreneur who builds a long-lasting business has 'a theory of the business' which informs his or her business decisions. In large organisations that theory of the business has to become public knowledge, as decisions cannot be taken only by one person. As Drucker says 'business enterprise ... requires that entrepreneurship be systemised, spelled out as a discipline and organised as work'.
Time horizon	Some plans are needed for the long term.
Co-ordinates	Activities of different business functions need to be directed towards a common goal.
Clarifies objectives	Managers are forced to define what they want to achieve.
Allocates responsibility	A plan shows people where they fit in.

4.12 The problem is that the further ahead you look the more imprecise planning becomes.

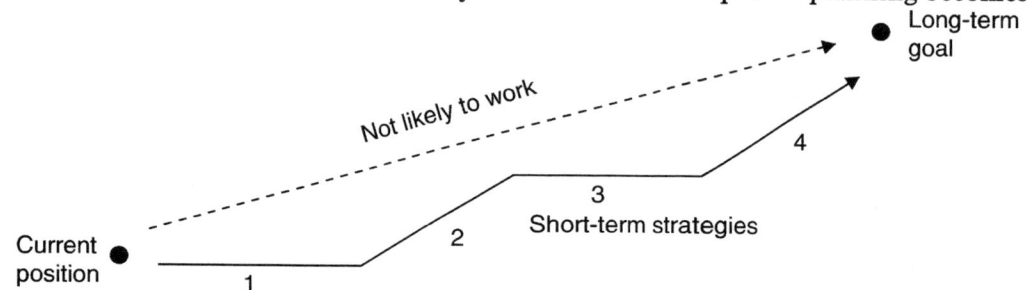

Forecasting becomes more uncertain with each key variable, such as interest rates and employment levels, becoming more and more difficult to predict. Long-term plans therefore have to be 'broad brush' pictures of the organisation's future. Modification will be necessary as more information becomes available and managers need to be clear that long-term goals are most likely to be achieved by a series of short-term strategies which may not follow a direct path.

4.13 Long-term **thinking**, even beyond the **planning horizon** (the furthest time ahead for which plans can be usefully quantified) is still a useful activity as it provides managers with a picture of how the organisation should be developing a **vision** for the future.

Exam Tip

One of the mistakes often made by CIM students is to develop plans which are unrealistic. A frequent factor in this is the failure to consider the time frame of plans. Here is an example.

(a) *Objective:* to double sales over the next twelve months.

(b) *Student's proposed strategy:* to double the sales force.

(c) *Reality.* Such a decision taken and implemented today might increase sales by perhaps 50%, but not the required 100%. This is because the plan fails to consider the time lags and practical issues involved in implementing the strategy. Recruitment, selection and training of the additional sales team is likely to take at least six months to complete. The additional sales team will therefore only be effective for about half a year.

5   OTHER MODELS FOR SETTING DIRECTION

5.1   The case example below is an example of planning and control which went horribly wrong. (*Tutorial note.* You might yawn when you see Coca-Cola, yet again, in a marketing text - however, as Coca-Cola is one of the world's most successful consumer marketing companies, it seems perverse to exclude it.)

Marketing at Work

This is a classic example of what can go wrong.

In the 1980s, *Coca-Cola* decided to change its flavour to compete with Pepsi. Market research, taste tests and so forth elicited favourable responses to the change, and so the new formulation was introduced.

A small group of consumers vociferously opposed the change. This opposition spread suddenly and rapidly like an epidemic, forcing Coca-Cola to re-introduce the old formula. It was hard to detect the reasons for this, but if some consumers perceived Coke to symbolise 'American values', then changing the formula appeared to be an assault on them.

This case exemplifies four issues.

1   The limitations of planning and research. Clearly the emotional impact of the brand change had not been considered.

2   The environment is not predictable (as it rapidly became fashionable not to drink the new formula).

3   Small causes (a few disaffected Coke-drinkers) can generate major consequences.

4   The limitations to organisational gathering of information.

Consumers, who had initially favoured the product, turned against it, for reasons that could not be predicted by market researchers.

Website address: www.coca-cola.co.uk (or local equivalent)

5.2   Criticisms of the strategic planning model concern how it has worked in **practice** and more fundamental problems of **theory**. Many of these criticisms were made by Henry Minztberg.

5.3   **Criticisms of strategic planning in practice**

Problem	Comments
Practical failure	Empirical studies have not proved that formal **planning** processes ('the delineation of steps, the application of checklists and techniques') contribute to success.
Routine and regular	Strategic planning occurs often in an **annual cycle**. But a firm 'cannot allow itself to wait every year for the month of February to address its problems'.
Reduces creative initiative	Formal planning discourages **strategic thinking**. Once a plan is locked in place, people are unwilling to question it.
Internal politics	The assumption of 'objectivity' in evaluation ignores political battles between different managers and departments.
Exaggerates power	Managers are not all-knowing, and there are limits to the extent to which they can control the behaviour of the organisation.

BPP PUBLISHING

5.4 Criticism of the rational model in theory

Criticism	Comment
Formalisation	'We have no evidence that any of the strategic planning systems - no matter how elaborate - succeeded in capturing (let alone improving on) the messy informal processes by which strategies really do get developed.'
Detachment: divorcing planning from operations	Managers manage by using 'remote' control. Senior managers at the top 'think great thoughts' while others scurry beneath them. This implies that managers do not really need day-to-day knowledge of the product or market.
Formulation precedes implementation	A strategy is planned - then it is implemented. But **defining** strengths and weaknesses is actually very difficult in advance of **testing** them. 'The detached assessment of strengths and weaknesses may be unreliable, all bound up with aspirations, wishes and hopes.'
Predetermination	Planning assumes that the environment can be forecast, and that its future behaviours can be controlled, by a strategy planned in advanced and delivered on schedule. This is only true of stable environments.

Marketing at Work

This is a classic example of what can go unexpectedly right.

Honda is now one of the leading manufacturers of motorbikes. The company is credited with identifying and targeting an untapped market for small 50cc bikes in the US, which enabled it to expand, trounce European competition and severely damage indigenous US bike manufacturers. By 1965, Honda had 63% of the US market. But this occurred by accident.

On entering the US market, Honda had wanted to compete with the larger European and US bikes of 250ccs and over. These bikes had a defined market, and were sold through dedicated motorbike dealerships. Disaster struck when Honda's larger machines developed faults - they had not been designed for the hard wear and tear imposed by US motorcyclists. Honda had to recall the larger machines.

Honda had made little effort to sell its small 50 cc motorbikes - its staff rode them on errands around Los Angeles. Sports goods shops, ordinary bicycle and department stores had expressed an interest, but Honda did not want to confuse its image in its 'target' market of men who bought the larger bikes.

The faults in Honda's larger machines meant that reluctantly, Honda had to sell the small 50cc bikes just to raise money. They proved very popular with people who would never have bought motorbikes before. Eventually the company adopted this new market with enthusiasm with the slogan: 'You meet the nicest people on a Honda'. The strategy had emerged, against managers' conscious intentions, but they eventually responded to the new situation.

Website address: www.honda.co.uk

Alternatives to planning

No strategic planning: 'freewheeling opportunism'

5.5 The **freewheeling opportunism approach** suggests firms should not bother with strategic plans and should **exploit opportunities** as they arise, judged on their individual merits and not within the rigid structure of an overall corporate strategy.

(a) **Advantages**

    (i) Opportunities can be seized when they arise, whereas a rigid planning framework might impose restrictions so that the opportunities are lost.

    (ii) It might encourage a more flexible, creative attitude among lower-level managers.

(b) **Disadvantages**

    (i) **No co-ordinating framework** for the organisation as a whole.

    (ii) The firm ends up **reacting** all the time rather than acting purposively.

No strategic planning: incrementalism

5.6 Herbert **Simon** suggested that managers do **not optimise (ie get the best possible solution), but instead they satisfice.** Managers are limited **by time,** by the **information** they have and by their own **skills,** habits and reflexes. They do not in practice evaluate **all** the possible options open to them in a given situation, but choose between relatively **few alternatives.** This is called **bounded rationality.**

    (a) Strategy making tends to involve **small scale extensions of past policy - incrementalism** - rather than radical shifts following a comprehensive rational 'search' and evaluation of the alternatives.

    (b) In marketing terms, **small scale adjustments of current marketing programmes may not be enough either to:**

       • **Move** with existing customers and their needs

       • **Identify** new markets or sets of customers

No strategic planning: crafting emergent strategies

5.7 Some strategies do not arise out of **conscious** strategic planning, but result from a number of **ad hoc choices,** perhaps made lower down the hierarchy, which may not be recognised at the time as being of strategic importance. These are called **emergent** strategies. They develop out of **patterns of behaviour,** in contrast to planned strategies which are imposed from above.

Action Programme 4

Aldebaran Ltd is a public relations agency founded by an entrepreneur, Estella Grande, who has employed various talented individuals from other agencies to set up in business. Estella Grande wants Aldebaran Ltd to become the largest public relations agency in North London. Management consultants, in a planning document, have suggested 'growth by acquisition'. In other words, Aldebaran should buy up the other public relations agencies in the area. These would be retained as semi-independent business units, as the Aldebaran Ltd group could benefit from the goodwill of the newly acquired agencies. When Estella presents these ideas to the Board there is general consensus with one significant exception. Livia Strange, the marketing director, is horrified. 'How am I going to sell this to my staff? Ever since we've been in business, we've won business by undercutting and slagging off the competition. My team have a whole culture based on it. I give them champagne if they pinch a high value client. Why acquire these new businesses - why not stick to pinching their clients instead?'

What is the source of the conflict?

5.8 Mintzberg uses the metaphor of **crafting strategy** to help understand the idea. Emergent strategies can be shaped by managers.

Exam Tip

The assumption in many mini-cases is that planning is a 'good thing' - but you need to be aware of the potential limitations of plans, if only to understand what might go wrong or to suggest alternative ways of developing strategy. Where there is high uncertainty, your plans will, inevitably, be tentative, and you may need to develop **contingency plans** – or at least identify the **need** to develop them – in your answer.

6 TACTICAL AND RESOURCE PLANNING

6.1 Tactics involves the deployment of **resources in an agreed strategy**. In implementing a corporate plan, departments and functions in the organisation will be carrying out specific tasks within their areas of expertise.

6.2 It helps to envisage a hierarchy of objectives to show how corporate objectives are communicated to different levels of the organisation. The **hierarchy of objectives** which emerges is as follows.

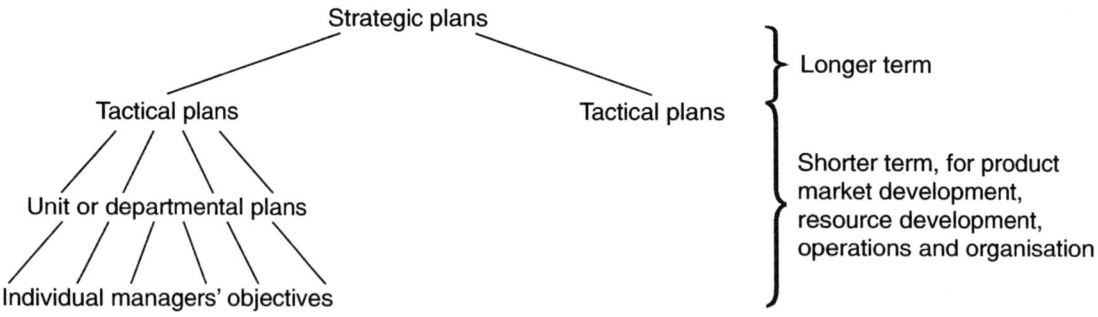

6.3 With this in mind, we can translate corporate strategy into tactical demands, by use of **critical success factors**.

Resources, tactics and CSFs

Key Concepts

(a) **Critical success factors (CSFs)** 'are those factors on which the strategy is fundamentally dependent on its success'.

(b) **Key tasks** are what must be done to ensure each critical success factor is achieved.

(c) **Priorities** indicate the order in which tasks are achieved.

For example, The critical success factor to run a successful mail order business is speedy delivery. Some CSFs are generic to the whole industry, others to a particular firm: a CSF of a parcel delivery service is that it must be quicker than the normal post.

Action Programme 5

Draw up a list of four critical success factors for the strategy of the organisation for which you work.

6.4 EXAMPLE

CSFs can be used to translate strategic objectives into performance targets and tactical plans. Dogger Bank wants to increase profits.

(a) **Business objective**: grow profits.

(b) **Strategy**: increase revenue per customer.

(c) **Tactics**: Increasing revenue per customer might not be possible unless customers buy other services from the bank (eg insurance).

   (i) The **critical success factor** will be the number of extra services sold to each customer.

   (ii) A **key task** might involve developing a **customer database** so that the firm can target customers with information about other services more effectively.

   (iii) The **resources needed** might include the services of a system analyst, hardware etc.

Clarifying the level

6.5 We will see in the next chapter how the corporate strategy and marketing activities interrelate.

6.6 Bear in mind that 'strategy' and 'tactics' are a means to an end, and do not get too worried about definitions and logic chopping.

6.7 In the last section we described the overall corporate planning process. Yet, from the office junior to the managing director, **everyone plans their work and decides how best to allocate their resources** (possibly only time) to **achieve the objectives** which have been set. As a result people **at all levels** of the organisation will talk about their objectives, strategy and tactics. To avoid confusion it is necessary to clarify the level in the organisation at which the individual is working.

6.8 Imagine that you are on a flight of stairs. As you step down from one level to another, the tactics of the higher level becomes the strategy of the lower one.

6.9 **At what management level are you positioned?** This is the first question you need to ask yourself when presented with a new planning project or scenario in the exam.

(a) The **process and framework** of planning is the same whether you are the managing director, marketing manager or sales manager.

(b) The **focus does differ** and it is essential that you keep a clear picture of who you are and what your area of authority is.

Corporate objectives: growth in profit, survival, risk

6.10 At **corporate level** the focus is on the **organisation as a whole**.

    (a) Corporate objectives will be **expressed in financial terms**, for example return on investment or profit. Corporate objectives are often concerned with achieving **growth consistent with limiting risk**. The **stakeholders** in an organisation (ie all those, not only shareholders, who have an interest in what the organisation does) would not normally support high growth objectives which demanded the taking of very high risks.

    (b) **Corporate strategy** directs the functional areas of the business (eg finance, operations and marketing).

6.11 In seeking to grow profitably and reduce risk, **corporate planning will deploy the functional activities of the business to these ends. The functional activities are the resources of the business.**

    • **Marketing** activities can be deployed **to increase (profitable) sales.**

    • The **production** function can be asked to **reduce unit costs.**

    • The **finance function** should **secure funding at lower rates.**

    • **Human resources** will be asked to **increase effectiveness.**

    • The **information technology** function can **enhance the organisation's use of information.**

All these measures could help to increase profit and reduce risk. **Therefore, the functions are deployed strategically to meet corporate objectives since the functions are means to achieve the corporate ends.**

Corporate tactics become marketing strategies

6.12 Once you understand this, we can move on to the next level.

    (a) For a **marketing director,** growth in profitable sales becomes the **marketing objective.** It derives from, and is consistent with but not separate from, the corporate objectives.

    (b) The **marketing strategy** is the way in which the marketing function organises its activities to achieve a profitable growth in sales.

        (i) It could for example seek to do this by introducing new products/services (Ansoff's growth strategy of product development) or by seeking new customers (Ansoff's marketing development).

        (ii) At a **marketing mix level,** sales might be increased profitably by increasing/decreasing prices, by expanding the sales force, investing more money in advertising etc.

6.13 Both **strategy and tactics are means to ends**, in other words, ways of achieving objectives. The difference between **strategy and tactics is simply one of detail** and depends on the level from which you are looking.

(a) To a marketing director, the cleanliness of a room will be a mere detail.

(b) To the office cleaner it will however be an objective and entail a plan.

- Audit (take stock, decide what state of cleanliness the room is currently in)
- Decide objectives (what state the room needs to be in by a given time)
- Decide broad strategies (vacuuming, tidying, dusting)
- Decide tactics (where to start, what to use)
- Schedule the order of actions

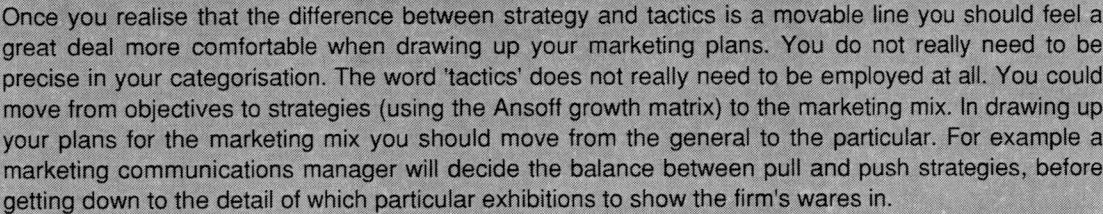

Exam Tip

Once you realise that the difference between strategy and tactics is a movable line you should feel a great deal more comfortable when drawing up your marketing plans. You do not really need to be precise in your categorisation. The word 'tactics' does not really need to be employed at all. You could move from objectives to strategies (using the Ansoff growth matrix) to the marketing mix. In drawing up your plans for the marketing mix you should move from the general to the particular. For example a marketing communications manager will decide the balance between pull and push strategies, before getting down to the detail of which particular exhibitions to show the firm's wares in.

6.14 It is very important to get your thinking clear about this, otherwise your marketing plan and its relationship to the corporate plan will appear confused and your proposals will lose their credibility. To help you further in your thinking please examine and reflect upon the following table.

> Eight ways to distinguish between strategic and tactical decisions
>
> 1 **Importance:** Strategic decisions are significantly more important.
>
> 2 **Level at which conducted:** Strategic decisions usually by more senior management.
>
> 3 **Time horizon:** Strategies = longer term. Tactics = shorter term.
>
> 4 **Regularity:** Strategy formulation is continuous whereas tactics are periodic.
>
> 5 **Nature of problem:** Strategic problems are unstructured and often unique, involving risk and uncertainty. Tactical problems are more structured and repetitive with risks easier to assess.
>
> 6 **Information needed:** Strategies require more external information. Tactics depend more on internally generated information.
>
> 7 **Detail:** Strategy is broad. Tactics are narrower.
>
> 8 **Ease of evaluation:** Strategic decisions are more difficult to make and evaluate.
>
> Source: adapted from 'Strategic Marketing' Weitz and Wensley (ex George Steiner and John Miner)

6.15 To conclude, at **marketing department** level the focus is on the marketing activity.

(a) **Objectives** are developed in line with the corporate objectives and strategy and they are expressed in marketing terms (for example market share or sales volume).

(b) **Marketing strategy indicates how the marketing mix** will be set to achieve these objectives and the marketing tactics include details of their implementation. In turn

these details are expressed in terms of distribution, research, advertising and sales objectives and strategies.

7 CONTINGENCY PLANNING

Key Concept

Contingencies. An event which is not provided for in the main plan. Oil companies assume that they will have uninterrupted supply and plan accordingly. There is a possibility that war in the Middle East could disrupt supply.

7.1 Where contingencies are known about, **contingency plans should be prepared in advance** to deal with the situation if and when it arises. Such plans might be prepared in detail, or in outline only, depending on the likelihood that the contingency will become a reality.

7.2 **Reasons for contingency plans**

(a) **Crisis management.** A contingency might be something like product contamination, the need for a **product recall**. Plans can enable 'crises' of this nature to be dealt with effectively.

(b) **Uncertain outcomes of legal action.** Many supermarket chains have been taken to court over alleged breaches of brand owner's trade marks. The law is still not clear.

Chapter Roundup

- The **process of planning** is similar at all levels, but its **content and scope** differ at each level.

- **Corporate planning** is for the organisation as a whole (eg profit, growth, survival). Individual functions such as marketing and production are deployed to achieve the corporate objectives.

- Each **function** has its own **objectives and activities**, which it deploys to achieve the objectives set for it by the corporate plan. For example, increased profits (corporate objective) can be achieved by increased sales (marketing function) and a reduction in manufacturing costs (production function).

- In addition to their focus on **customers**, marketers who want to have a strategic role must consider **competitors** and the organisation's **other stakeholders**.

- **Planning's function** is to co-ordinate resources to increase the chances of achieving objectives. Planning involves making decisions about what has to be done, how and when it should be done and who should do it. An integral part of the planning process is **control**. If plans are to be successful then systems must be established for their modification in the light of outcomes.

- It is important to recognise the **hierarchical** level of planning and control decisions, because decision makers can only make plans or take control action within the sphere of the **authority** that has been **delegated** to them.

- **Corporate decisions** relate to the scope of a firm's activities, the long-term direction of the organisation, and allocation of resources. The **'planning' model of strategy formation** suggest a logical sequence which involves **analysing** the current situation, **generating** choices (relating to competitors, products and markets) and **implementing** the chosen strategies.

- There are problems with the 'planning' model. Other models of strategy formation include **incrementalism** and **crafting emergent strategies**.

Cont'd

- There is a **hierarchy of objectives**. Corporate objectives are often expressed in financial terms. Corporate strategies deploy the functions of the business. Corporate strategies set marketing objectives.

- **Contingency planning** is necessary in case things happen which undermine the plan and require alternative action to be taken.

Now try illustrative question 2 at the end of the Study Text

Quick Quiz

1 What are the two distinct aspects to management? (see para 2.1)

2 What is the purpose of planning? (3.1)

3 Why are controls important in the planning process? (3.4)

4 What are the distinctions between aims and objectives? (3.9) and strategy and tactics? (3.10)

5 How would you distinguish between the long and short term? (4.13)

6 What are the problems with relying on planning procedures alone in strategic management? (5.3, 5.4)

7 How would you define contingency planning? (7.1-7.2)

8 What is the purpose of tactical planning? (6.1)

9 How can critical success factors be used in operations planning? (6.4)

10 What is the focus of a plan at corporate level? (6.10) and marketing department level? (6.11)

Action Programme Review

1 Mintzberg surveyed senior managers, but many of the roles apply to junior managers too.

2 See paragraph 3.2 for a framework. Needless to say this is expanded in greater detail.

3 The corporate objective is profit growth. The corporate strategy is the decision that this will be achieved by entering new markets, rather than producing new products. The business strategy suggests that those markets include Latin America. The functional strategy involves the decision to invest in new plant (the production function) which is to be financed by shares rather than loans (the finance function).

4 Livia Strange's department has generated its own pattern of competitive behaviour. It is an emergent strategy. It conflicts directly with the planned strategy proposed by the consultants. This little case history also makes the additional point that strategies are not only about numbers, targets and grand plans, but about the organisational cultures influencing a people's behaviour.

5 What would drive your organisation out of business?

BPP
PUBLISHING

3 The Corporate Strategy/Marketing Interface

Chapter Topic List	Syllabus reference
1 Setting the scene	
2 Corporate strategy and marketing strategy	1.2
3 The marketing plan in outline	1.2
4 Strategic intelligence and the MkIS	1.2
5 The organisational context: structure and culture	1.2

Learning Outcomes

- Prepare effective and realistic marketing plans.

- Overcome barriers to effective implementation.

Key Concepts Introduced

- Strategic intelligence
- MkIS
- Organisational structure
- Organisational culture

Examples of Marketing at Work

- British Airways
- Burger King

1 SETTING THE SCENE

1.1 The previous chapter described the overall process of corporate strategy-making. We saw that the planning **process** is similar at many levels, but the **content** of plans differs at each level. We have seen how marketing is one of a number of business functions which is deployed strategically to meet organisational objectives. Marketing is mainly concerned with products and markets and so is intimately concerned with corporate strategy.

1.2 In Section 2 we discuss some of the interrelationships between marketing and other functions: they offer constraints on marketing activity, in particular the finance function, and the production function, as they control key organisational resources.

1.3 In Section 3 we offer an outline of the marketing plan. Marketing objectives and corporate objectives are closely related. Don't get too worried about definitions and logic-chopping - but ensure your marketing plans are appropriate to the level suggested in an exam question. Marketing concerns do have corporate implications and may form the basis for decision-making at corporate level.

1.4 The marketing department is also responsible for obtaining much of the organisation's **strategic intelligence.**

1.5 Culture and structural issues are relevant to an organisation's ability to innovate. Innovation requires the co-operation of the whole organisation. As marketing activities and philosophy become widespread, the organisation must improve its competence at generating ideas - this involves more than just the screening process for new product development, but a whole culture of innovation (Section 5).

Links to other papers

1.6 Planning is relevant everywhere at Diploma level, in every paper.

1.7 The communications plan is developed after the marketing plan and depends on it for its validity.

1.8 Organisation structure issues can be applied to a departmental as well as a corporate level. They are brought into focus particularly in international operations.

1.9 Culture in its environmental sense is a key communications issue.

2 CORPORATE STRATEGY AND MARKETING STRATEGY

How marketing can contribute to the corporate plan

2.1 Marketing makes a particularly important input to the corporate planning decisions. Information inputs from marketing to the **corporate** planning decisions perform a double duty in that they also provide the bases for deciding marketing objectives and strategies. **Marketing research** is vital to **all stages** of the marketing plan hence the need for an effective marketing information system.

Aspect	Comment
The environmental audit	Reviews the organisation's position in relation to changes in the external environment (social/cultural, legal, economic, political and technological) and provides information which directly affects the setting of corporate objectives. The market place is, by definition, part of the 'environment'.
Competitor analysis	Provides competitor intelligence, competitor response models and so on which again influence corporate objectives, strategy and contingency planning.
The customer audit	Assesses the existing and potential customer bases to provide information as to whether to develop new markets.
Product portfolio analysis	Provides input for decisions as to whether to drop particular products and/or add new ones.
The sales forecast	Provides the basis for all other functional activities as well as marketing.

> ### Exam Tip
>
> As indicated in Chapter 2 students often find it difficult to relate marketing objectives clearly to corporate objectives and even more difficult to distinguish clearly marketing objectives from corporate objectives. There can be no corporate plan which does not involve products/services and customers. The following diagram from Kotler clearly expresses the interactive two-way relationship between marketing plans and strategic business planning.
>
>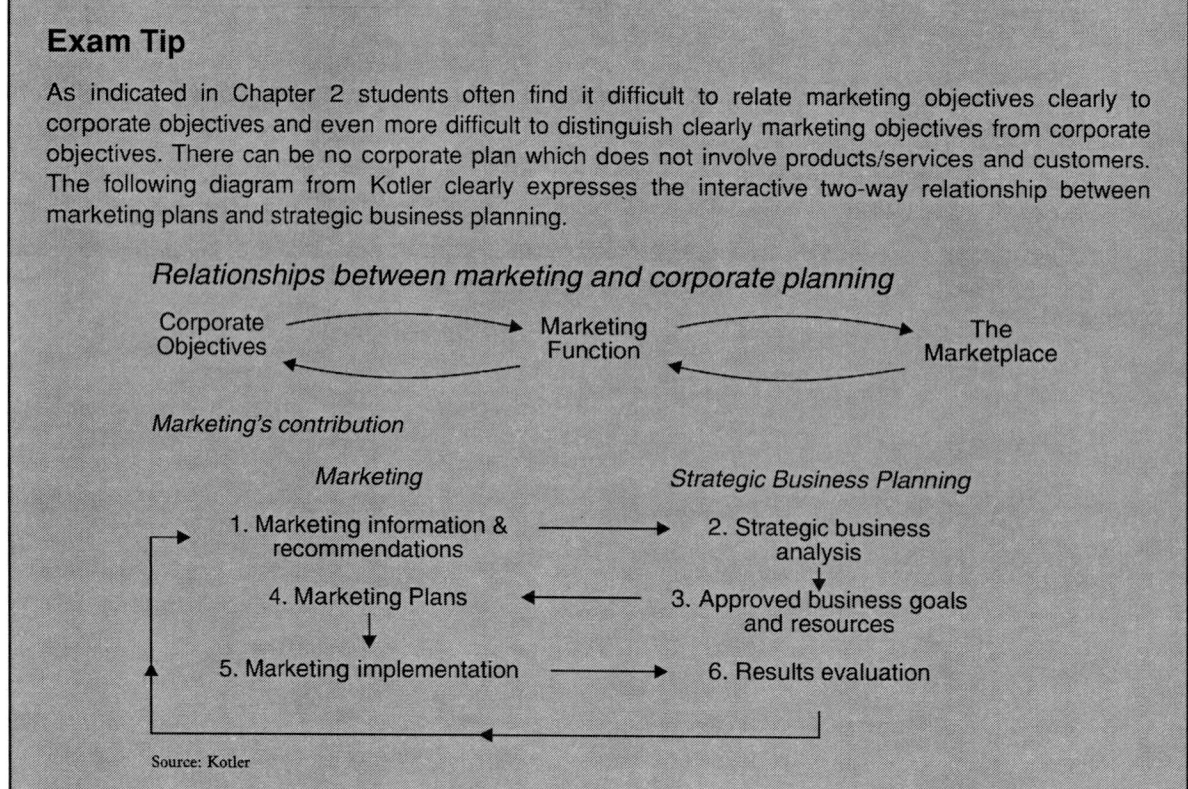

2.2 The **marketing plan** uniquely is concerned with **products** and **markets**.

    (a) These are typically stated in terms of market share, sales volume, levels of distribution and probability.

    (b) Decisions might be taken as to the type of products sold to particular customer groups.

2.3 The marketing manager's plans are often frustrated by other people in the organisation. These 'blockers' can be people in the marketing department but are more likely to be people in other departments. The less an organisation is truly market orientated, the more likely it is that marketing plans are ineffective. Each functional area has its own particular concerns and constraints and, at strategic level, marketers have to take these into account if they want to achieve anything.

2.4 **What other departments do**

Department	Activity
Production	Purchasing, acquiring resources and forming them into products/services the firm can offer.
Human resources	Obtaining the right number of people at the right level of skills. This is vital in **service industries** for successful marketing plans – people are integral to the service marketing mix.
Finance	The need to remain profitable, raising and distributing money and maintaining a healthy cash flow.
Research and development	May be independent of either production or marketing.
IT	In firms where **information** is a key resource, there might be separate plans and strategies for information technology. Financial services firms such as banks pay particular attention to IT. **Database marketing** depends on effective use of IT.

2.5   All these functional plans exist in the wide framework of the corporate plan. In practice all these plans are interrelated. **At strategic level,** marketing cannot be managed in a vacuum. Marketing directors and managers cannot take strategic decisions on their own without reference to the managing director and the directors of other functions - ie corporate management as a team.

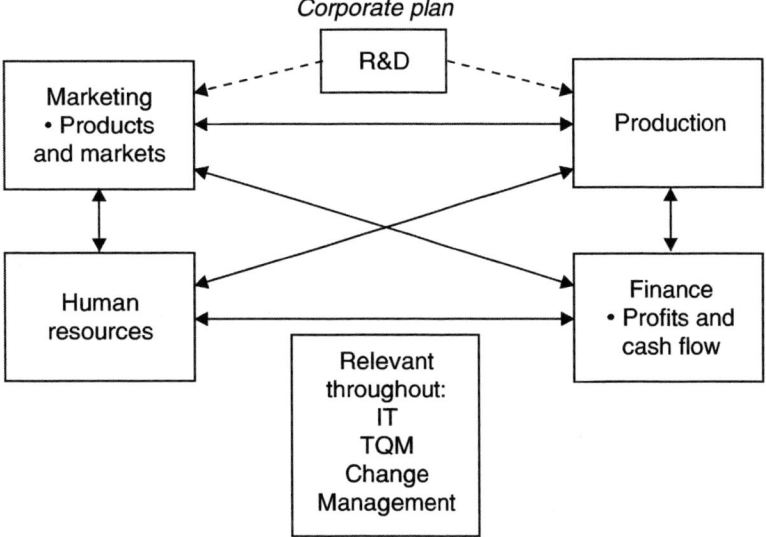

Corporate plan

Action Programme 1

What interrelationships might exist between the marketing plan and the plans for human resources and finance?

The key role of marketing

2.6   Marketing can claim to be the **key** activity in an organisation. Organisations cannot normally survive and **profit** without selling goods or providing services to people (customers) and this involves marketing.

Marketing at Work

From the *Financial Times,* 6 February 2001. (BPP emphasis).

British Airways' recovery appears to be on track, as Rod Eddington, chief executive since May, accelerates the strategy put in place by his predecessor Robert Ayling, ousted in a boardroom coup a year ago. The airline more than doubled operating profits in the nine months to December 31 to £441m (£209m), slightly ahead of expectations.

Mr Eddington said the **strategy of cutting capacity,** switching to **smaller aircraft** and concentrating on **premium traffic** had left it well prepared for any slowdown in the US and the world economy. Along with the **elimination of unprofitable routes** and the **rationalisation of the lossmaking short haul corporate operations** in Europe, he said the strategy would 'continue to **raise margins** over the next few years'.

In the third quarter, it recovered from a pre-tax loss of £60m and an operating loss of £2m last time to a pre-tax profit of £65m and an operating surplus of £80m. Pre-tax profits in the first nine months, inflated a year ago by gains from disposals, rose 19 per cent to £215m. Analysts forecast operating profits for the year to March 31 of £377m, up from £84m a year ago. BA's share price, which has risen sharply from a low in late October of 265p to a 12-month high last Friday of 457½p, fell 8 per cent to 421p yesterday as investors took profits.

After falling into its first loss last year since privatisation 14 years ago, the group's performance has improved strongly with **earnings per share** of 5.4p in the third quarter, up from losses of 6.6p a year ago.

Turnover in the third quarter rose 4.4 per cent to £2.3bn and 4.7 per cent for the nine months to £7.16bn.

BPP PUBLISHING

Mr Eddington said the results showed the group could 'continue to improve profitability by focusing on core activities and the right network'.

Capacity, which has been cut by about 3.5 per cent this year, would be reduced by a further 9 per cent in the year to March 2002. The investment in **product improvements** – including the introduction a year ago of flat beds in long haul business class – is paying off, with improving **yields** and increased **market share of premium passengers. Passenger yields**, or **average fare level**, were 8.3 per cent higher year-on-year in the third quarter, and the improved profits were achieved despite a 46 per cent rise in fuel costs in the three months.

BPP note

Some areas of the 4Ps are identified here: product and price in particular. Note also the role of segmentation: 'premium' passenger offer higher yields.

Website address: british-airways.com

Exam Tip

No direct questions have been set on the relationships between marketing and corporate planning, but the subject certainly may be alluded to, and you will have to decide on which level you are operating. Furthermore, the 6/01 mini-case covered the whole gamut from position analysis to strategy evaluation. Analysing Marks & Spencer, you needed to draw on many of the tools covered in the next few chapters.

3 THE MARKETING PLAN IN OUTLINE

Strategic and tactical decisions in marketing

3.1 It is worthwhile, certainly for exam purposes, deciding the difference between a **strategic marketing plan** and a **tactical marketing plan**.

(a) **Strategic marketing plan**

- Three to five or more years long
- Defines scope of product and market activities
- Aims to match the activities of the firm to its distinctive competences

(b) **Tactical marketing plan**

- One year time horizon
- Generally based on existing products and markets
- Concerned with marketing mix issues

3.2 **Basic elements of the marketing plan.** Although you will be familiar with the marketing **content**, you must be able to produce realistic and credible marketing **plans** for your diploma examinations. The steps involved in developing a **marketing** plan are the same as those already examined in depth for the corporate level.

Step 1. Analysis
Step 2. Objective
Step 3. Strategy
Step 4. Tactics
Step 5. Control

Content of marketing plan

3.3 Kotler identifies the formulation of **marketing plans** as follows.

Section	Content
The executive summary	This is the finalised planning document with a summary of the main goals and recommendations in the plan.
Situation analysis	This consists of the SWOT analysis and forecasts.
Objectives and goals	What the organisation is hoping to achieve, or needs to achieve, perhaps in terms of market share or 'bottom line' profits and returns.
Marketing strategy	This considers the selection of target markets, the marketing mix and marketing expenditure levels.
Action programme	This sets out how these various strategies are going to be achieved.
Budgets	These are developed from the action programme.
Controls	These will be set up to monitor the progress of the plan and the budget.

3.4   We need to see how marketing planning fits into the corporate plan.

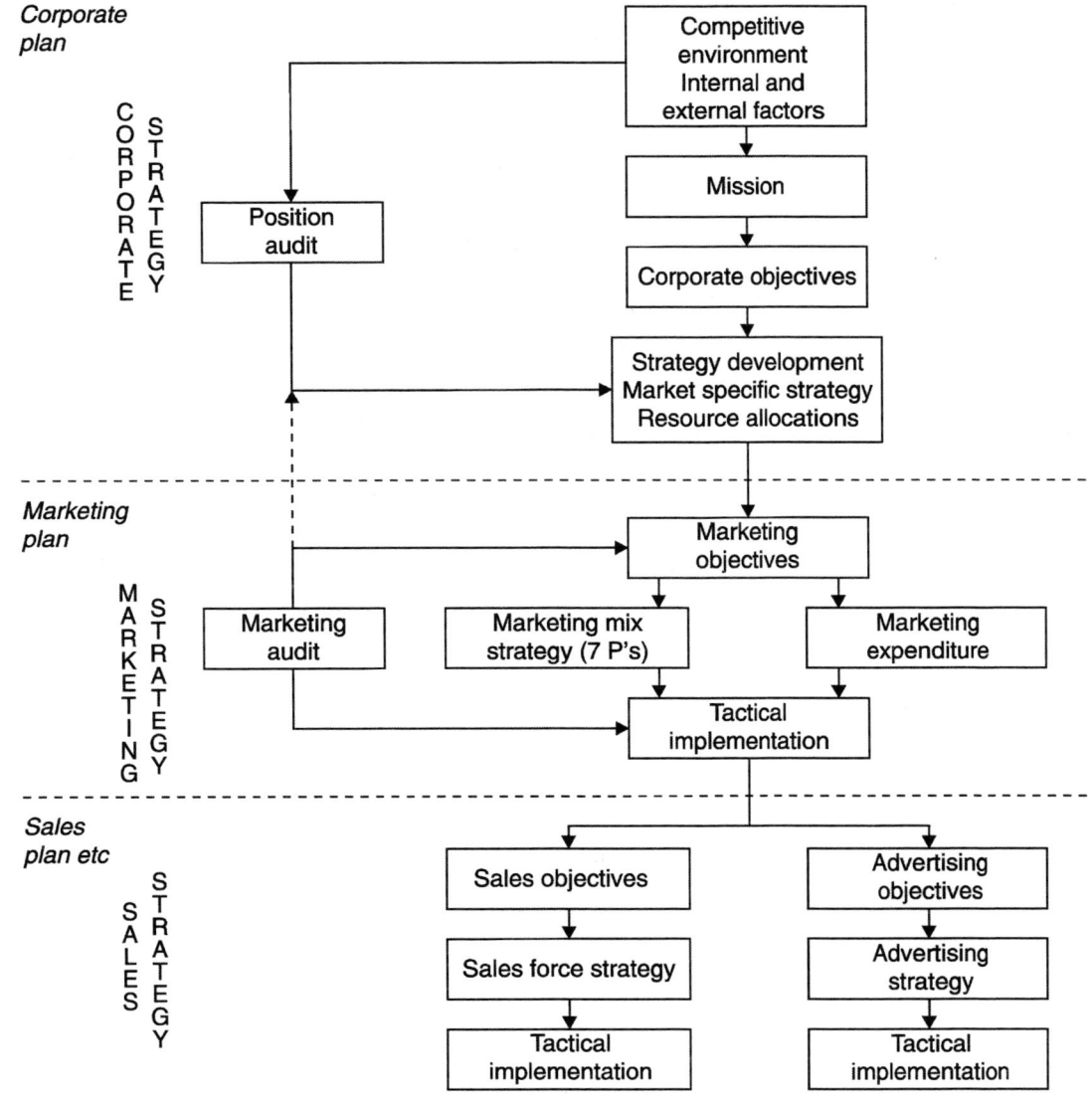

3.5   To support and illustrate the diagram, we can add the following.

(a)   Providing a **link to the overall strategy** illustrates the contribution of the marketing plan.

(b) Marketing objectives must be defined according to **measurable targets**, such as increase in market share or sales volumes.

(c) The **marketing mix strategy** may vary with each market **segment**. The overall direction of the policy is defined, but specific aspects of the mix (7 Ps) may be emphasised for different customers.

(d) With **tactical implementation**, marketing programmes are broken down into individual activities, with details of resource allocation (eg budgets).

(e) The overall plan must be **controlled** and measured following its implementation to make sure that results are as forecast and that corrective action can be taken where necessary.

Formulating marketing strategy

3.6 A **marketing strategy** is a plan to achieve the organisation's objectives by specifying

- What resources should be allocated to marketing
- How those resources should be used to take advantage of opportunities

3.7 In the context of applying the **marketing concept**, a marketing strategy would:

- **Identify target markets** and customer needs in those markets
- Plan products which will **satisfy the needs** of those markets
- **Organise marketing resources**, so as to match products with customers

3.8 The strategic concepts of **segmentation** and **product positioning** should be at the heart of modern marketing planning.

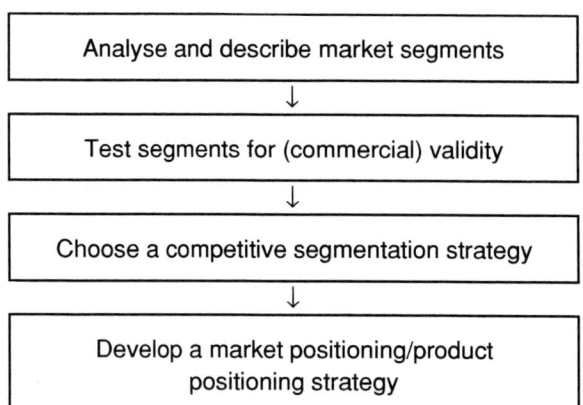

Both these concepts will therefore be given extensive coverage in later chapters.

The marketing action plan: marketing mix proposals

3.9 The link between the formulation and the implementation of marketing strategy is the **marketing action plan**, which identifies how the mix will be deployed. The mix represents the **controlled** use of a firm's resources allocated to the marketing budget.

(a) The marketing mix may be simplified into the four Ps plus three Ps for service.

   (i) **Product:** quality, features, fashion, packaging and branding, after sales service, guarantees, durability, etc.

   (ii) **Price:** the level of price, credit terms, discounts, guarantees.

(iii) **Place**: factors here include the location of sales outlets and the number and type of sales outlets (shops, supermarkets etc), the location of service departments, stock levels and transportation and delivery services.

(iv) **Promotion**: advertising, sales promotion, selling, PR.

(v) **People**: courtesy, competence of the people delivering the service.

(vi) **Processes**: how the service is delivered.

(vii) **Physical evidence**: the environment of the service encounter.

(b) **Different marketing mixes** will appeal to different **market segments** in any particular market.

(c) The marketing mix for a product must be **planned** in advance. It should also be **reviewed** in the light of experience and, if product sales have not been as good as expected, managers might take **control action** by changing the mix, for example, lowering product quality, reducing price and spending more on advertising.

4 STRATEGIC INTELLIGENCE AND THE MKIS

4.1 In the last chapter, we identified the **dual role of marketing** as an input to the corporate planning process and as a distinct function in its own right. This also applies to **information gathering**.

> **Key Concept**
>
> **Strategic intelligence** according to Donald Marchand, can be defined as 'what a company needs to know about its business environment to enable it to anticipate change and design appropriate strategies that will create business value for customers and be profitable in new markets and new industries in the future'. Not only must the firm anticipate the future, but it must have the capability to react to it.

4.2 Each function of the organisation collects information relevant to it, without any wider 'corporate viewpoint'.

- The marketing department identifies customer needs.
- The R&D department identifies new technology.
- The production department suggests process innovation.

4.3 **A model of the process of creating strategic intelligence**

Sensing	Identify appropriate external indicators of change
↓	↓
Collecting	Gather information in ways that ensure it is relevant and meaningful
↓	↓
Organising	Structure the information in the right format
↓	↓
Processing	Analyse information for implications
↓	↓
Communicating	Package and simplify information for users
↓	↓
Using	Apply strategic intelligence

4.4 A source of strategic intelligence is the MkIS.

Key Concept

'A **marketing information system** (MkIS) consists of people, equipment and procedures to gather, sort, analyse, evaluate, and distribute needed, timely and accurate information to marketing decision makers.'

4.5 The marketing information system

The marketing information system

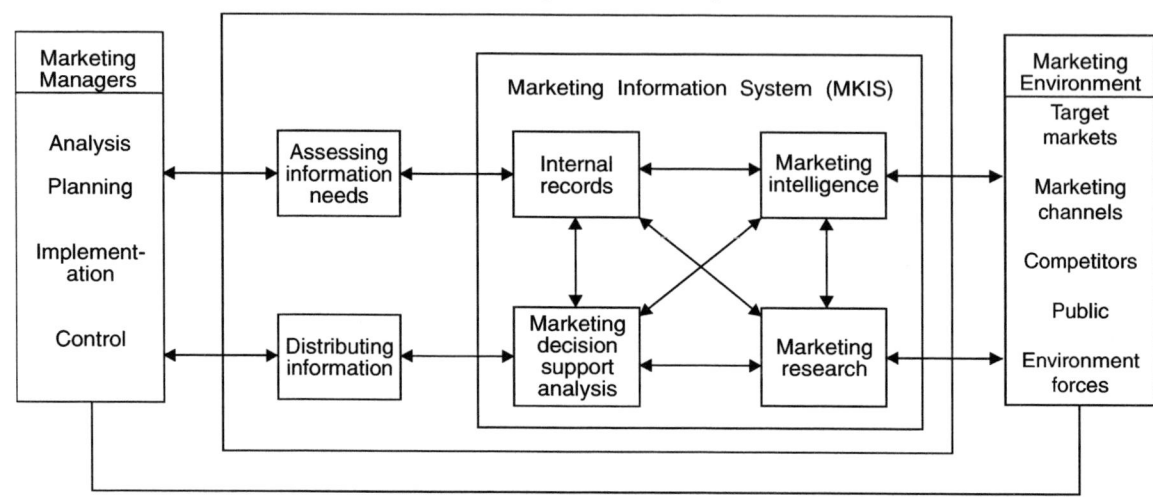

Marketing decisions and communications

Source: Kotler, *Marketing Management Analysis, Planning, Implementation and Control*

(a) **Internal records system**

This includes reports of orders, sales, dispatches, accounts payable and receivable etc which provide a store of historical customer data.

(b) **Marketing intelligence system**

This is the term used for information gathered on the market place by managers on a day-to-day basis. It is derived from **continual monitoring** of the environment to alert managers to new trends.

(c) **Marketing decision support system**

Firms can use regression and correlation analysis, sales forecasting, time series analysis, product design and site selection models.

(d) **Marketing research system**

Marketing research aids management decision making by providing specified information in time for it to be of value.

Exam Tip

Management information systems and marketing research have been covered in earlier modules, for example in Paper 6 Management Information for Marketing Decisions. They are not included in this syllabus, but it is still imperative that you are familiar with these topics at Diploma level.

5 THE ORGANISATIONAL CONTEXT: STRUCTURE AND CULTURE

Organisational structure

> **Key Concept**
>
> **Organisational structure** implies a framework or mechanism intended to:
>
> (a) Link individuals in an established network of relationships so that authority, responsibility and communications can be controlled.
>
> (b) Group together (in any appropriate way) the tasks required to fulfil the objectives of the organisation, and allocate them to suitable individuals or groups.
>
> (c) Give each individual or group the authority required to perform the allocated functions, while controlling behaviour and resources in the interests of the organisation as a whole.
>
> (d) Co-ordinate the objectives and activities of separate units, so that overall aims are achieved without 'gaps' or 'overlaps' in the flow of work required.
>
> (e) Facilitate the flow of work, information and other resources required, through planning, control and other systems.

5.1 We have already touched on the relationship of marketing plans with corporate and other functional plans. We will now briefly cover organisational structure and culture.

(a) **Formal organisations** have an explicit hierarchy of authority in a well-defined structure. Communication channels are also well defined.

(b) An **informal** organisation often exists side by side with the formal one. When people work together, they form social groups and develop informal ways of getting things done.

Different types of structure

5.2 The grouping of organisational activities can be done in different ways. The most common forms of **departmentation** are outlined below.

Grouping	Comment
Function	People are grouped together by the type of work they do (eg marketing department, finance department)
Geography	People are grouped by area or region (eg Northern Region)
Customer	People are grouped by type of customer (eg BT has business and domestic customers)
Product/brand	People are grouped by type of product (eg product or brand manager)

5.3 In practice many organisations are **hybrids,** and contain a variety of these designs.

(a) Sales departments are often organised by territory, although sales is a 'function' within the business.

(b) Certain aspects of marketing management might be organised on a product or brand basis.

(c) Some departments such as R&D might be a central headquarters function.

Matrix and project organisation

5.4 There has been a trend towards **task-centred structures,** for example **multi-disciplinary project teams,** which draw experience, knowledge and expertise together from different functions to facilitate flexibility and innovation.

BPP
PUBLISHING

5.5   This dual authority structure may be shown diagrammatically as a management **grid**.

Matrix

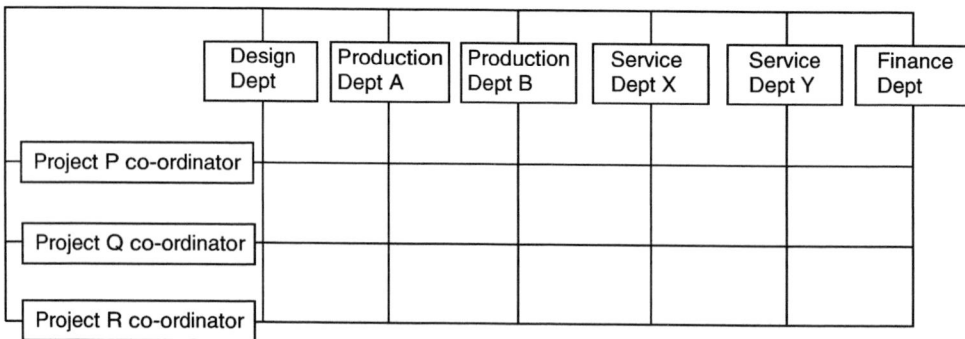

Functional department heads are responsible for the internal organisation of their departments, but **project co-ordinators** are responsible for the aspects of all departmental activity that affects their individual projects.

Exam Tip

Structure has an impact on the culture of the organisation. Attempts to reposition the 'culture' (say from a product to a market orientation) are often best tackled with a new structure, after re-organisation. This need for a new structure is often implicit in major CIM case studies and is something you should look out for.

Action Programme 2

Draw a formal organisation chart for a business with which you are familiar. You may be able to obtain a published one if you work for a large organisation. Now produce a chart of the informal structure and compare the two.

Marketing at Work

Burger King

From *Marketing Week,* 26 April 2001

Burger King is considering a shake-up of its international marketing operations following the appointment of global chief marketing officer and executive vice-president Chris Clouser.

Clouser, who started at the Diageo-owned fast food chain this week, has overall responsibility for creating and implementing international marketing strategies including research, new products, pricing, promotions, sponsorship, corporate communications and community relations.

A restructure of the company's management, overseen by Burger King's recently appointed chief executive John Dasburg, has already led to the departure of Mikel Durham, head of Burger King's North American division. The division has been scrapped as Dasburg **builds a more 'functional', rather than geographical, management structure**.

The restructure will result in more centralised marketing operations, which could lead to ads being brought to the UK from the US.

Website address: www.burgerking.com

Culture

5.6 Every organisation is different, as you will readily appreciate if you have worked in more than one. Why is this so? After all, two organisations such as FMCG manufacturers may be similarly structured and involved in similar activities - and **still** be quite different to work for, or deal with. The most current explanation is **culture**.

> ### Key Concept
>
> **Organisational culture** may be defined as the complex body of shared values and beliefs of an organisation. Handy sums up 'culture' as 'that's the way we do things around here'.

5.7 A culture consists of three elements. Each organisation generates its own culture, either spontaneously or under the more active guidance of a positive managerial strategy.

(a) The **basic, underlying assumptions** which guide the behaviour of the individuals and groups in the organisation, for example **customer orientation,** or belief in quality, trust in the organisation to provide rewards, freedom to make decisions, freedom to make mistakes, and the value of innovation and initiative at all levels. Assumptions will be reflected in the kind of people employed (their age, education or personality), the degree of delegation and communication, whether decisions are made by committees or individuals etc.

(b) **Overt beliefs** expressed by the organisation and its members, which can be used to condition (a) above. These beliefs and values may emerge as sayings, slogans, mottos etc. such as 'we're getting there', 'the customer is always right', or 'the winning team'.

(c) **Visible artefacts:** the style of the offices or other premises, dress 'rules', display of 'trophies', the degree of informality between superiors and subordinates etc.

5.8 **Importance of culture**

(a) The eventual success of their plans when they are implemented will, to a large extent, be influenced by the organisation's culture.

(b) The **motivation and satisfaction of employees** (and possibly therefore their performance) by encouraging commitment to the organisation's values and objectives, making employees feel valued and trusted, fostering satisfying team relationships, and using 'guiding values' instead of rules and controls.

(c) The **adaptability** of the organisation, by encouraging innovation, risk-taking, sensitivity to the environment, customer care, willingness to embrace new methods and technologies etc.

(d) The image of the organisation ('physical evidence' in service marketing). The cultural attributes of an organisation (attractive or unattractive) will affect its appeal to potential employees, **customers** etc.

Marketing at Work

Charles Hampden-Turner describes *British Airways* before it become the 'World's favourite airline', many years ago.

(a) People's job titles, not their names, were on their office doors.

(b) Late one evening, one of the senior directors was overlooking the airport. 'They're all here,' he said. 'The whole fleet, apart from one which is due back from Switzerland in half an hour.' 'What if you wish to fly to Switzerland tonight?' you ask. 'Go by Swiss Airways. None of this lot are leaving until tomorrow morning.'

What does the above tell you about the culture of BA before it changed?

This was not so much a commercial airline, but a military airforce. Hence, the concentration on rank, and the 'I counted them all out, and I've counted them in' mentality. A corporate culture which delighted in, or was relieved by, assets not used and more importantly, potential customers not served, is not really a customer-focused business operation.

5.9   Deal and Kennedy identify four cultures based on their attitude to risk.

High risk

BET YOUR COMPANY CULTURE ('Slow and steady wins the race') Long decision-cycles: stamina and nerve required eg oil companies, aircraft companies, architects	**HARD 'MACHO' CULTURE** ('Find a mountain and climb it') eg entertainment, management consultancy, advertising
PROCESS CULTURE ('It's not what you do, it's the way that you do it') Values centred on attention to excellence of technical detail, risk management, procedures, status symbols eg banks, financial services, government	**WORK HARD/PLAY HARD CULTURE** ('Find a need and fill it') All action - and fun: team spirit eg sales and retail, computer companies, life assurance companies

Slow feedback (left)   *Fast feedback* (right)

Low risk

Source: Deal and Kennedy, *Corporate Cultures*

Exam Tip

Examining the culture of the organisation and understanding its characteristics is an essential first step in successful planning. It will help you to assess the likely reaction of both superiors and subordinates. With this insight you will be able to forecast more accurately the resources required and the time necessary for the implementation of your plans. Case studies will frequently provide you with clues about the organisation and its culture. Recognising these and taking them into account in developing your strategies is an important aspect of the realistic approach the examiners will expect.

For example, a company with a risk averse culture is unlikely to adopt a strategy based on speculative land deals and one with a strong religious base to its culture is unlikely to be happy to diversify into casinos or betting shops.

Issues of 'culture' are often more problematic for the marketer, as cultures are typically resistant to change. Of course, in a service firm you will consider the 7Ps of the service marketing mix. It is here that 'culture' is significant, in that it affects how people relate to each other and to their customers.

Action Programme 3

As a conclusion to Chapters 1 to 3, we will bring together all of the points covered in an example, in the context of a non-profit orientated organisation.

An institution of higher education is concerned at a falling trend in applications. Outline the steps it should take to develop a strategy to halt this trend.

Chapter Roundup

- The specific concerns of the marketing function are **products** and **markets**, as embodied in objectives such as market share, the type of products sold etc.

- Marketing contributes significantly to **corporate planning** and formulating **corporate objectives,** as markets and customers are a key part of the corporate environment and are key to the firm's survival.

- Marketing therefore has a 'lead' role in other business functions. Anticipated sales, for example, determine the **volume** produced by the production function. However, available **production capacity** can lead to constraints on what is produced, and **financial limitations** offer a limit to the resources available.

- The **steps in marketing planning** can be defined as follows.

    ○ **Analysis** of the current situation and **forecasting** based on the current situation.

    ○ **Identification of objectives.**

    ○ The **formulation of strategies and plans** to meet the stated objectives. Marketing strategies should recognise target markets, market segments, target market position, the state of the market (growth, decline etc).

    ○ The setting of **budgets** to cover the costs of implementation.

    ○ **Control** to ensure that plans are achieved.

- **Control** involves reviewing performance with a view to improving it.

- Marketing information provides a great deal of the **strategic intelligence** of the organisation.

- The **marketing function's role** is changing. Project teams are now the preferred norm.

Now try illustrative question 3 at the end of the Study Text

Quick Quiz

1   Give five information inputs which marketing makes to corporate planning. (2.1)

2   Why is marketing a key issue in setting corporate objectives? (2.6)

3   What would be contained in a marketing strategy? (3.3)

4   What two strategic concepts are said to be at the heart of modern marketing? (3.8)

5   What is strategic intelligence? (4.1) How is it created? (4.3)

6   What are the most common forms of organisational departmentation? (5.2)

Action Programme Review

1   (a)   **Human resources** are the 'people' element of the marketing mix for services. Human resources management specialists are involved in recruiting and training marketing personnel and ensuring that staff pursue organisational objectives.

    (b)   **Finance** is all-pervasive. Forecasts for sales revenues affect profit; marketing activities require resources which cost money. Finance is a resource in itself, but also it is the 'language' by which the organisation's performance is reported and controlled.

2   You will probably find that individuals who marketers refer to as 'gatekeepers' (secretaries, personal assistants, reception staff, etc) are important in the informal communication structure of the organisation. They are often the influencers and advisers who it is important to identify in the process of internal marketing.

3   **Step 1: Analysis**

The reasons for the falling trend in applications should be discovered. Possible reasons might be as follows.

(a)   The courses are no longer attractive to students, because their content or quality is not up to the standard expected by them.

(b)   Other institutions of higher education, with a higher academic status, are beginning to offer similar courses.

(c)   The qualifications students obtain are no longer sufficient to guarantee graduates a job at the end of the course.

(d)   The costs of the course are now so high that they deter applicants.

(e)   The size of the target market is falling.

Step 2: Objective

The Institution's objective is assumed to be to improve the appeal of its courses, and so to increase applications by a targeted quantity, ie to maintain next year's enrolments at year x level.

Step 3: Strategy

Having identified the probable reasons for declining applications and an objective for strategic planning, the Institution can begin to develop a strategy to improve the situation, insofar as it has the power to do so (for example the costs of courses might be controlled by government, not by the Institution itself).

(a)   If the courses have an inadequate content or quality, new or improved courses must be designed. Student needs should be investigated.

(i)   What sort of courses do they need? Both the structure of the courses (full time, block release, day release etc) and academic content should be reviewed.

(ii)   What quality of teaching (and teaching equipment) is required? If existing staff are unable to teach the subjects required, some re-planning or re-training of manpower will be necessary.

The product should be capable of satisfying student needs before it can be sold.

(b)   If qualifications are no longer sufficient to guarantee graduates a job, the needs of potential employers should also be investigated. Courses should be designed so as to produce graduates whom employers would prefer to recruit in preference to other people with different qualifications, or even with no qualifications at all.

Any new courses which are designed must conform to the objectives of the Institution, ie to offer education of a particular type and standard. They must be developed to meet the needs of identified segments within the market, for example students may follow a language course to improve their commercial knowledge of the language and may prefer an intensive programme following on from a business course. The business community may prefer breakfast classes or tutors to visit them in their workplace. Those wanting to improve their holiday French will need a different approach to those seeking a formal qualification.

Step 4: More detailed planning

Having identified student needs and employer needs, the next step in a marketing strategy should be as follows.

(a)   Design courses to suit customer needs better.

(b)   Allocate marketing resources to a campaign to attract applicants. Possible elements in a marketing mix would be as follows.

(i)   Better advertising or communication. If students are recruited from schools, better information about courses should be supplied to schools careers advice staff etc.

(ii)   Lower prices.

(iii)   Improving the quality image of the Institution's academic standards, perhaps through the acquisition of new staff or facilities.

Step 5: Control

Any marketing strategy should have a quantified target (for example to raise applications by x% per annum for the next five years) and there should be some procedure or control mechanism whereby actual results are monitored, compared against the strategic plan, and evaluated.

Part B
Analysis

4 External Environment Analysis

Chapter Topic List	Syllabus reference
1 Setting the scene	
2 Environmental influences	2.1
3 The political and legal environment	2.1
4 The economic environment	2.1
5 Social factors	2.1
6 Technological factors	2.1
7 Ecology	2.1
8 Globalisation and hostility to it	2.1

Learning Outcomes

- Conduct and evaluate external aspects of a marketing audit.

- Specify a clear rationale when choosing between strategic alternatives.

Key Concepts Introduced

- Environment
- Demography
- Culture

Examples of Marketing at Work

- Monsanto
- Logistics industry
- Internet

- Gas and electricity deregulation
- Islamic banks
- Cisco Systems

- Film companies
- Eurodisney
- Global hotel chains

1 SETTING THE SCENE

1.1 Business plans cannot be produced in a vacuum. They must be developed within the context of the wider environment in which the organisation is operating. They need to take into account the opportunities and threats which are emerging as these external factors change.

1.2   A key issue to keep in mind is **environmental change**. Some organisations face more complex and changing environments than others; the fashion industry is in a 'fast-moving' environment, but this speed of environmental change does not exist for all industries.

Links with other papers

1.3   The environment is key for all papers at Diploma level.

1.4   In International Marketing Strategy, different PEST factors may apply to each market individually. In marketing communications, the environment provides the context for communications. For example, communications planning that clashes with general election campaign, may be less effective if there are other distractions; cultural factors are most important.

2   ENVIRONMENTAL INFLUENCES

2.1   As we saw in Part A, planning is a central part of the management task wherever you are working in the organisation and the first stage should always be to clarify the current position.

(a)   **Controllable.** Different managers need to review different aspects of the business. The factors which can be controlled by the **marketing** manager can be primarily represented by the 7P's of the marketing mix.

(b)   **Not controllable.** Issues of production capacity and sources of supply are of interest and of indirect importance to the marketing manager, but outside the area of direct control. That said, marketing mix decisions and marketing activities do have a significant impact on these other departments.

Action Programme 1

Choose a business/market with which you are familiar. How has it changed over the last five years? Produce a list of all the external factors (things which the organisation cannot control) which have had a significant impact on the organisation in that time. Refine your list as you work through the rest of this chapter.

Key Concept

The **environment** of an organisation is everything outside its boundaries. All the factors affect the organisation's performance, but the organisation cannot control them.

2.2 Organisations have a variety of relationships with the environment.

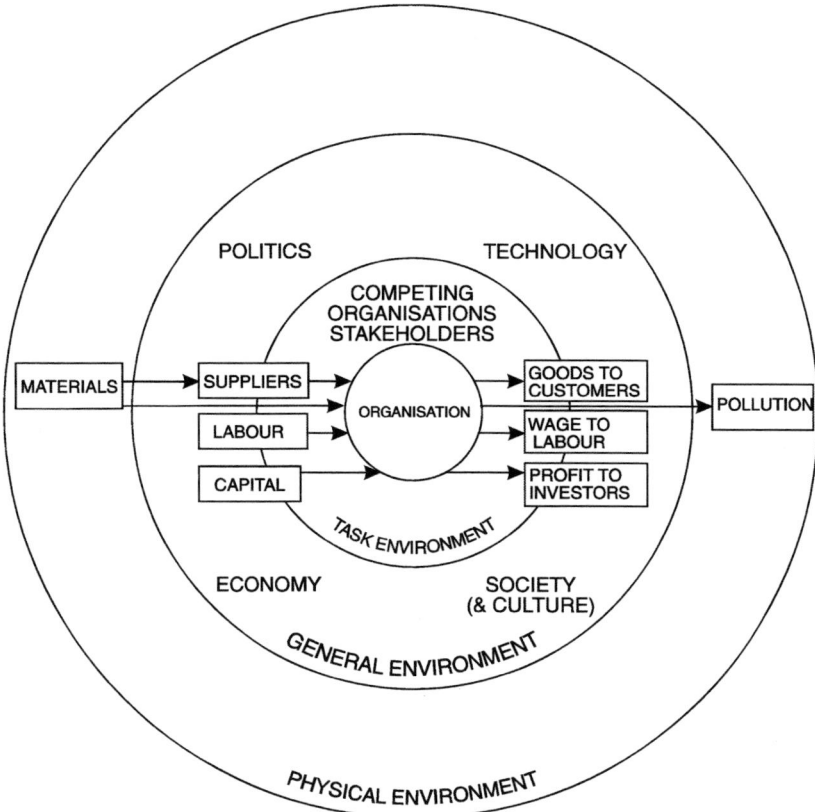

2.3 **Classifying the environment**

(a) The **micro environment** is of immediate concern, and is uniquely configured for each organisation: no organisation has a network of suppliers, customers, competitors or stakeholders identical to another's.

(b) The **macro environment** relates to factors in the environment affecting all organisations.

  - **Political-legal factors**
  - **Economic factors**   } 'PEST'
  - **Social and cultural factors**
  - **Technological factors**

Exam Tip

When you answer an examination question which is a case study problem, you might be expected to think about the specific environmental influences that might be relevant to the particular situation. Although both in mini-cases and in the Analysis and Decision case study you are restricted to using only the information provided, you are expected to bring to bear your general knowledge and general business and marketing awareness. This is particularly evident when dealing with case examples set in an international context.

Marketing at Work

For many years, *Monsanto* has been developing genetically modified foods, and these new substances have been marketed very successfully in the USA, with no public disquiet. In the UK and the EU generally, a combination of factors has led to public concern.

(a) Suspicion of industrial food production processes, especially after the BSE crisis

(b) Concern about ecology

(c) Trends towards 'organic' food

(d) The relative success of the UK's biotechnology industry

(e) Trade friction between the UK and US

Many UK food producers have decided not to use GM foods.

Website addresses

www.monsanto.co.uk

www.which.net/campaigns/gmfood – for reports by The Consumer Association

www.ncbe.reading.ac.uk

Action Programme 2

Choose an industrial product, a consumer durable, a fast moving consumer good and a service business. For each of them identify **how** you think the environmental factors identified in the following paragraphs might affect a business operating in that market.

Environmental analysis

2.4 Johnson and Scholes suggest that a firm should conduct an **audit of environmental influences.** This will identify the environmental factors which have had a significant influence on the organisation's development or performance in the past.

1 Assess the nature of the environment (eg is it changing?)
2 Identify those influences which have affected the organisation in the past or which are likely to do so in future.
3 A structural analysis will be prepared, identifying the 'key forces at work in the immediate or competitive environment'.

↓

These steps should identify important developments. Then the following questions should be asked.

↓

4 What is the organisation's position in relation to other organisations?
5 What threats and/or opportunities are posed by the environment?

2.5 Strategic decisions are made in partial ignorance, as we have seen, because the environment is uncertain. Uncertainty relates to the **complexity and dynamism** of the environment.

(a) **Complexity** arises from:

(i) The **variety of influences** faced by the organisation. The more open an organisation is, the greater the variety of influences. The greater the number of markets the organisation operates in, the greater the number of influences to which it is subject.

(ii) The amount of **knowledge** necessary. All businesses need to have knowledge of the tax system, for example, but only pharmaceuticals businesses need to know about mandatory testing procedures for new drugs.

(iii) The **interconnectedness** of environmental influences. Importing and exporting companies are sensitive to exchange rates, which themselves are sensitive to interest rates. Interest rates then influence a company's borrowing costs.

(b) **Dynamism**. Stable environments are unchanging. Dynamic environments are in a state of change. The computer market is a dynamic market because of the rate of technological change.

2.6   It is not always easy to detect which environmental factors will be relevant in future.

Marketing at Work

CISCO Systems, which provides a lot of the hardware structure of the Internet, announced a 30% drop in quarterly sales to 31/3/2001 – in common with other companies in the industry. This resulted from weak demand and excess optimism that the industry would continue to grow rapidly – only in 2000, orders regularly exceeded forecasts, and long lead times were not uncommon. It has over a year's supply of some components and will have to write off $2.5 billion of stock and reduce its workforce by 8,500. This change has been sudden.

Website address: www.cisco.com

Action Programme 3

How do you consider that Johnson and Scholes model can be easily applied to the scare about genetically modified foods?

2.7   **Types of information collected**

Category	Example
Market tidings	• Market potential • Structural change • Competitors and industry • Pricing • Sales negotiations • Customers
Acquisition leads	• Leads for joint ventures • Mergers or acquisitions
Technical tidings	• New products, processes and technology • Product problems • Costs • Licensing and patents
Broad issues	• General conditions • Government actions and policies

In the past, many companies have collected information in an unsystematic and haphazard way, perhaps because the costs of collecting information were too high. Nowadays with the Internet, there is a problem with **information overload.**

3   THE POLITICAL AND LEGAL ENVIRONMENT

3.1   We will outline in **general** terms some key issues to keep in mind. Laws come from common law, parliamentary legislation and government regulations derived from it, and obligations under EU membership and other treaties.

3.2 Legal factors affecting all companies

Factor	Example
General legal framework: contract, tort, agency	Basic ways of doing business, negligence proceedings
Criminal law	Theft, insider dealing, bribery, deception
Company law	Directors and their duties, reporting requirements, takeover proceedings, shareholders' rights, insolvency
Employment law	Trade Union recognition, Social Chapter provisions, possible minimum wage, unfair dismissal, redundancy, maternity, Equal Opportunities
Health and Safety	Fire precautions, safety procedures
Data protection	Use of information about employees and customers
Marketing and sales	Laws to protect consumers (eg refunds and replacement, 'cooling off' period after credit agreements), what is or isn't allowed in advertising
Environment	Pollution control, waste disposal
Tax law	Corporation tax payment, collection of income tax (PAYE) and National Insurance contributions, VAT

3.3 Some legal and regulatory factors affect **particular industries**, if the public interest is served. For example, electricity, gas, telecommunications, water and rail transport are subject to **regulators** (Offer, Ofgas, Oftel, Ofwat, Ofrail) who have influence over:

- Competition and market access
- Pricing policy (can restrict price increases)

3.4 This is because either:

- The industries are, effectively, monopolies: competition removes the need for regulation

- Large sums of public money are involved (eg in subsidies to rail companies)

Marketing at Work

Gas and electricity deregulation in the UK

Government policy. Gas used to be a state monopoly. The industry was privatised as one company, *British Gas*. Slowly, the UK gas market has been opened to competition.

Regulators. Ofgem regulates the gas and electricity industry. Ofgem has introduced a Code of Conduct requiring gas suppliers to train sales agents, allow for a cooling off period during which customers can change their minds and so on. However as competition intensifies more and more activities are moved out of the regulated environment.

New markets. The government has also deregulated the electricity market. Companies such as British Gas can now sell electricity, and electricity companies can now sell gas.

What happened to the once-monopoly supplier, British Gas? As a result of competition, it demerged some of its operations into two separate companies, Transco and Centrica. These are part of two separate businesses providing services, in Transco's case mainly to other businesses, in Centrica's case to end-users.

- *Transco* is a gas transporter. It does not sell gas itself but does maintain the pipeline infrastructure and some emergency services. Transco is now the principal activity of the *Lattice*, which 'provides, manages and services infrastructure networks'. Lattice is currently investigating how metering services can be supplied to other utilities. Lattice has recently set up **186k**, a telecomms subsidiary. Lattice Energy

Services aims to support other utilities. It is not a gas or energy supplier. *Advantica*, another subsidiary, exports the skills it acquired supporting Transco to overseas markets.

- *Centrica* provides 'energy and other services at home and on the road, through three consumer brands: British Gas, the AA (Automobile Association) and Goldfish (a credit card company). Centrica has a substantial business in the US and Canada. Centrica supplies energy, telecomms, roadside energy and financial services.

Website addresses

www.lattice-group.com
www.centrica.co.uk

3.5 Anticipating changes in the law

(a) The governing party's election **manifesto** is a guide to its political priorities, even if these are not implemented immediately.

(b) The government often publishes advance information about its plans (**green paper** or **white paper**) for consultation purposes.

(c) The **EU's single market programme** indicates future changes in the law.

Political risk and political change

3.6 The political environment is not simply limited to legal factors. Government policy affects the whole **economy**, and governments are responsible for enforcing and creating a **stable framework** in which business can be done. A report by the World Bank indicated that the quality of **government policy is important in providing the right**:

- **Physical infrastructure** (eg transport)
- **Social infrastructure** (education, a welfare safety net, law enforcement)
- **Market infrastructure** (enforceable contracts, policing corruption)

3.7 However, it is **political change** which complicates the planning activities of many firms. Here is a checklist for case study use.

Factor	Example: minimum wage
Possibility of political change	• Concern with social inequality
Nature of impact	• Minimum wage
Consequences	• Level of minimum wage
Coping strategies	• Cash flow planning, increase productivity
Influence on decision making	• Business lobbied to keep it low; trade unions lobbied to keep it high

Political risk

3.8 The political risk in a decision is the risk that political factors will invalidate the strategy and perhaps severely damage the firm. Examples are:

- Wars
- Expropriation ('rationalisation') of business assets by overseas governments
- Other forms of political influence in local decision making
- Local political chaos making business difficult

3.9 **A political risk checklist** was outlined by Jeannet and Hennessey. Companies should ask the following six questions.

1	How **stable** is the host country's political system?
2	How **strong** is the host government's commitment to specific rules of the game, such as ownership or contractual rights, given its ideology and power position?
3	How **long** is the government likely to remain in **power**?
4	If the present government is **succeeded**, how would the specific rules of the game change?
5	What would be the effects of any expected **changes** in the specific rules of the game?
6	In light of those effects, what **decisions and actions should be taken now**?

There are many sources of data. The **Economist Intelligence Unit** offers assessment of risk. Management consultants can also be contacted.

Government policy and the particular industry

3.10 The government may intervene to protect specific sectors.

Marketing at Work

The UK film industry has recently been blessed with tax breaks. Successive lobbying had finally paid off. Business and industries can put their case to government and EU officials.

4 THE ECONOMIC ENVIRONMENT

4.1 The economic environment is an important influence at local and national level.

Factor	Impact
Overall growth or fall in Gross Domestic Product	Increased/decreased demand for goods (eg dishwashers) and services (holidays).
Local economic trends	Type of industry in the area, office/factory rents, labour rates, house prices.
National economic trends:	
• Inflation	Low in most countries; distorts business decisions; wage inflation compensates for price inflation.
• Interest rates	How much it costs to borrow money affects **cash flow**. Some businesses carry a high level of debt. How much customers can afford to spend is also affected as rises in interest rates affect people's mortgage payments.
• Tax levels	Corporation tax affects how much firms can invest or return to shareholders. Income tax and VAT affect how much consumers have to spend, hence demand.
• Government spending	Suppliers to the government (eg construction firms) are affected by spending.

Factor	Impact
• The business cycle	Economic activity is always punctuated by periods of growth followed by decline, simply because of the nature of trade. The UK economy has been characterised by periods of 'boom' and 'bust'. Government policy can cause, exacerbate or mitigate such trends, but cannot abolish the business cycle. (Industries which prosper when others are declining are called **counter-cyclical** industries.)
• Share prices	In the US, an increasing proportion of people's wealth is held in the form of shares. If share prices fall, people perceive they have less money to spend, and thus start saving.

4.2 The **forecast state of the economy** will influence the planning process for organisations which operate within it. In times of boom and increased demand and consumption, the overall planning problem will be to **identify** the demand. Conversely, in times of recession, the emphasis will be on cost-effectiveness, continuing profitability, survival and competition.

4.3 **Key issues for the UK economy**

(a) The **service sector** accounts for most output. Services include activities such as restaurants, tourism, nursing, education, management consultancy, computer consulting, banking and finance. Manufacturing is still important, especially in exports, but it employs fewer and fewer people.

	1981	1998
Men	33	25
Women	18	10

%?

(b) The **housing market** is a key factor for people in the UK. Most houses are owner-occupied, and most people's wealth is tied up in their homes. UK borrowers generally borrow at variable rates of interest, so are vulnerable to changes in interest rates. If house prices rise, people feel wealthier, so they spend more.

(c) **Tax and welfare.** Although headline rates of tax have fallen, people have to spend more on private insurance schemes for health or pensions. The government aims to target welfare provision on the needy and to reduce overall welfare spending by getting people into work.

(d) **Productivity.** An economy cannot grow faster than the underlying growth in productivity, without risking inflation.

(i) UK manufacturing productivity is still lower than that of its main competitors, but in services the UK is relatively efficient.

(ii) UK businesses are high in capital productivity, in other words output earned per £ of capital expenditure.

These measures need to be looked at carefully. For example, countries with high unemployment may have low labour productivity simply because there are more people in work (in less productive jobs). A good measure is GDP per head.

(e) **Inequality.** The government is committed to spending more on health and education, and on reducing presumed inequality, by targeting benefits to those most in need. It has done so by reducing tax breaks for the better off.

(f) **Public spending** as a proportion of GDP is lower in the UK than in some countries. The **private finance initiative** aims to increase public spending by involving the private sector.

4.4 Impact of international factors

Factor	Impact
Exchange rates	Cost of imports, selling prices and value of exports; cost of hedging against fluctuations
Characteristics of overseas markets	Desirable overseas markets (demand) or sources of supply.
Different rates of economic growth and prosperity, tax etc.	
Capital, flows and trade	Investment opportunities, free trade, cost of exporting

Marketing at Work

Growth in trade has affected the logistics industry (transport, warehousing, etc) (worth US $130bn of which $31.6bn is outsourced).

The major problem is congestion. The EU is planning €350bn on trans-European networks (road, rail and air links) with possible extensions into Eastern Europe. Despite the single market, goods are still being held up at national borders. There are particular concerns as to environmental impact of logistics activities.

The single European currency

4.5 Most countries in the EU now account in euros. Interest rates are set by the European Central Bank whose goal is price transparency. Notes and coins will be introduced in 2003. Implications are these.

(a) **Price transparency**: it will be obvious that prices differ in various markets. Cars are known to be priced higher in the UK than elsewhere. Markets may become harder to segment. Even so, the Internet and activities of Consumers Association have publicised 'unjustified' price differentials.

(b) **Interest rates** are now set for the whole of Europe, not by country. What may be suitable for the Netherlands, say, will not be suitable for Portugal. However, this effect should reduce as economic cycles harmonise.

5 SOCIAL FACTORS

Demography

Key Concept

Demography is the study of population and population trends

5.1 The following demographic factors are important to organisational planners. A very good source of information about demography is *Social Trends*, published each year by the *Office of National Statistics*.

Factor	Comment
Growth	The rate of growth or decline in a national population and in regional populations.
Age	Changes in the age distribution of the population. In the UK, there will be an increasing proportion of the national population over retirement age. In developing countries there are very large numbers of young people. • Elderly people have unique needs. • As a segment they will become increasingly powerful.
Geography	The concentration of population into certain geographical areas.
Ethnicity	In the UK, about 5% come from ethnic minorities, although most of these live in London and the South East.
Household and family structure	A household is the basic social unit and its size might be determined by the number of children, whether elderly parents live at home etc. In the UK, there has been an **increase in single-person households** and lone parent families. Obviously, this impacts on the relevance of models such as the **family life cycle**
Social structure	The population of a society can be broken down into a number of subgroups, with different attitudes and access to economic resources. Social class, however, is hard to measure (as people's subjective perceptions vary). • Social classification systems are changing. The old systems based on the registrar-general grades (I, II, III etc) are to be replaced, from the 2001 census. The new grading covers occupations more closely: 1 Higher managerial and professional; 2 Lower managerial and professional; 3 Intermediate; 4 Small employers and own account workers; 5 Lower supervisory craft and related occupations; 6 Semi-routine occupations; 7 Routine occupations. • Social status generally passes from generation to generation, despite evidence of social mobility in individual cases.
Employment	Many people believe that there is a move to a casual flexible workforce; factories will have a group of **core employees**, supplemented by a group of **peripheral employees**, on part-time or temporary contracts, working as and when required. Some research indicates a 'two-tier' society split between **'work-rich'** (with two wage-earners) and **'work-poor'** households. However **most employees are in permanent, full-time employment.**
Wealth	Rising standards of living lead to increased demand for certain types of consumer good. This is why developing countries are attractive as markets.

5.2 **Implications of demographic change**

(a) **Changes in patterns of demand.** An ageing population suggests increased demand for health care services. A 'young' growing population has a growing demand for schools, housing and work.

(b) **Location of demand**: people are moving to the suburbs and small towns.

(c) **Recruitment policies**: there are relatively fewer young people so firms will have to recruit from less familiar sources of labour.

(d) **Wealth and tax.**

Culture

Key Concept

Culture is used by sociologists and anthropologists to encompass 'the sum total of the beliefs, knowledge, attitudes of mind and customs to which people are exposed in their social conditioning.'

Exam Tip

Social change may generate new segmentation possibilities, or changes to the marketing mix. It may be provided in the mini-case data. Bear in mind culture when dealing with buyer behaviour, particularly where overseas markets are concerned.

5.3 Through contact with a particular culture, individuals learn a language, acquire values and learn habits of behaviour and thought.

(a) **Beliefs and values.** Beliefs are what we feel to be the case on the basis of objective and subjective information (eg people can believe the world is round or flat). **Values** are beliefs which are relatively enduring, relatively general and fairly widely accepted as a guide to culturally appropriate behaviour. Beliefs shape attitudes and so create tendencies for individuals and societies to behave in certain ways.

(b) **Customs:** modes of behaviour which represent culturally accepted ways of behaving in response to given situations.

(c) **Artefacts:** all the physical tools designed by human beings for their physical and psychological well-being: works of art, technology, products.

(d) **Rituals.** A ritual is a type of activity which takes on symbolic meaning, consisting of a fixed sequence of behaviour repeated over time.

The learning and sharing of culture is made possible by **language** (both written and spoken, verbal **and** non-verbal).

5.4 **Underlying characteristics of culture**

(a) **Purposeful.** Culture offers order, direction and guidance in all phases of human problem solving.

(b) **Learned.** Cultural values are 'transferred' in institutions (the family, school and church) and through on-going social interaction and mass media exposure in adulthood.

(c) **Shared.** A belief or practice must be common to a significant proportion of a society or group before it can be defined as a cultural characteristic.

(d) **Cumulative.** Culture is 'handed down' to each new generation. There is a strong traditional/historical element to many aspects of culture (eg classical music).

(e) **Dynamic.** Cultures adapt to changes in society: eg technological breakthrough, population shifts, exposure to other cultures.

Marketing at Work

Islamic banking is a powerful example of the importance of culture. The Koran abjures the charging of interest, which is usury. However whilst interest is banned, profits are allowed. A problem is that there is no standard interpretation of the sharia law regarding this. Products promoted by Islamic banks include:

(a) Leasing (the Islamic Bank TII arranged leases for seven Kuwait Airways aircraft)
(b) Trade finance
(c) Commodities trading

The earlier Islamic banks offered current accounts only, but depositors now ask for shares in the bank profits.

5.5 Knowledge of the culture of a society is clearly of value to businesses.

(a) **Marketers** can adapt their products accordingly, and be fairly sure of a sizeable market. This is particularly important in export markets.

(b) **Human resource managers** may need to tackle cultural differences in recruitment. For example, some ethnic minorities have a different body language from the majority, which may be hard for some interviewers to interpret.

5.6 Culture in a society can be divided into **subcultures** reflecting social differences. Most people participate in several of them.

Subculture	Comment
Class	People from different social classes might have different values reflecting their position in society.
Ethnic background	Some ethnic groups can still be considered a distinct cultural group.
Religion	Religion and ethnicity are related.
Geography or region	Distinct regional differences might be brought about by the **past** effects of physical geography (socio-economic differences etc). Speech accents most noticeably differ.
Age	Age subcultures vary according to the period in which individuals were socialised, to an extent, because of the great shifts in social values and customs in this century. ('Youth culture'; the 'generation gap' etc.)
Sex	Some products are targeted directly to women or to men.
Work	Different organisations have different corporate cultures, in that the shared values of one workplace may be different from another.

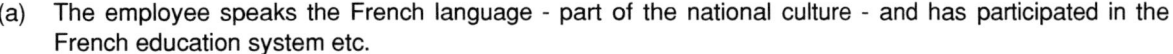

Marketing at Work

Consider the case of a young French employee of *Eurodisney*.

(a) The employee speaks the French language - part of the national culture - and has participated in the French education system etc.

(b) As a youth, the employee might, in his or her spare time, participate in various 'youth culture' activities. Music and fashion are emblematic of youth culture.

(c) As an employee of Eurodisney, the employee will have to participate in the corporate culture, which is based on American standards of service with a high priority put on friendliness to customers.

www.2000.disneylandparis.com

You can look at the employment opportunities on this website to see how a global services firm aims to recruit.

5.7 Cultural change might have to be planned for. There has been a revolution in attitudes to female employment, despite the well-publicised problems of discrimination that still remain.

Action Programme 4

Club Fun is a UK company which sells packaged holidays. Founded in the 1960s, it offered a standard 'cheap and cheerful' package to resorts in Spain and, more recently, to some of the Greek islands. It was particularly successful at providing holidays for the 18-30 age group. What do you think the implications are for Club Fun of the following developments.

(a) A fall in the number of school leavers.
(b) The fact that young people are more likely now than in the 1960s to go into higher education.
(c) Holiday programmes on TV which feature a much greater variety of locations.
(d) Greater disposable income among the 18-30 age group.

Business ethics

5.8 The conduct of an organisation, its management and employees will be measured against **ethical standards** by the customers, suppliers and other members of the public with whom they deal.

5.9 **Types of ethical problem a manager may meet with in practice**

(a) **Production practices.** Attempts to increase profitability by cutting costs may lead to dangerous working conditions, inadequate safety standards in products or reprehensible practices (eg child labour). This is a problem for firms which outsource production to low-cost factories overseas.

(b) **Gifts.** There is a fine line to be drawn between gifts, accepted as part of a way of doing business, and bribes.

(c) **Social responsibility.** Companies are being held to account for pollution and human rights issues.

(d) **Competitive behaviour.** There is a distinction between competing aggressively and competing unethically and illegally.

Action Programme 5

The Heritage Carpet Company is a London-based retailer which imports carpets from Turkey, Iran and India. The company was founded by two Europeans who travelled independently through these countries in the 1970s. The company is the sole customer for carpets made in a number of villages in each of the source countries. The carpets are hand woven. Indeed, they are so finely woven that the process requires that children be used to do the weaving, thanks to their small fingers. The company believes that it is preserving a 'craft', and the directors believe that this is a justifiable social objective. Recently a UK television company has reported unfavourably on child exploitation in the carpet weaving industry. There were reports of children working twelve hour shifts in poorly lit sheds and cramped conditions, with consequent deterioration in eyesight, muscular disorders and a complete absence of education. The examples cited bear no relation to the Heritage Carpet Company's suppliers although children are used in the labour force, but there has been a spate of media attention. The regions in which the Heritage Carpet Company's supplier villages are found are soon expected to enjoy rapid economic growth. What social and ethical issues are raised for the Heritage Carpet Company?

6 TECHNOLOGICAL FACTORS

6.1 Technology refers to:

(a) **Apparatus or equipment:** eg a TV camera.

(b) **Technique:** eg how to use the TV camera to best effect, perhaps in conjunction with other equipment such as lights.

(c) **Organisation:** eg the grouping of camera-operators into teams, to work on a particular project.

6.2 **Technology contributes to overall economic growth.** Technology can increase total output.

- Gains in productivity (more output per units of input)
- Reduced costs (eg transportation technology, preservatives)
- New types of product

6.3 **Effects of technological change on organisations**

(a) **The type of products or services that are made and sold**

(b) **The way in which products are made** (eg robots, new raw materials)

(c) **The way in which services are provided**

Marketing at Work

Mail order/Internet

(a) Companies selling easily transportable goods - for instance, books and CDs - can offer much greater consumer choice and are enjoying considerable success in attracting revenue. However, whether this business is profitably is a different issue entirely, because many e-businesses depended on old economy skills in logistics and distribution.

(b) The financial sector is rapidly going electronic - call centres are now essential to stay in business, Internet banking has taken off, and the Internet and interactive TV are starting to feature in business plans.

A key issue is the role of the website: is it just another promotional tool or a fundamentally new way of doing business?

(d) **The way in which markets are identified.** Database systems make it much easier to analyse the market place. We explore database marketing in brief below.

(e) **The way in which firms are managed.** IT encourages 'delayering' of organisational hierarchies, home-working, and better communication.

(f) **The means and extent of communications with external clients, via Website, e-mail etc).**

Marketing at Work

The Internet has implications for the structure and strategies of some industries and their marketing mixes. Take telecommunications. The telephone tariff system is 'fundamentally a fixed cost system, but we pay for it on the basis of a variable - mainly voice minutes. What is more, where the charges are levied bears no relation to where the costs occur'.

The Internet threatens to undermine this. Access to the Internet is normally charged at local call rates. It will soon be possible to hold conversations over the Internet, which 'will undermine the "price per distance" business model' which allows telephone companies to charge more for long distance calls.

6.4   The impact of **recent** technological change also has potentially important social consequences, which in turn have an impact on business.

   (a)   **Home-working.** Whereas people were once collected together to work in factories, home -working will become more important.

   (b)   **Intellective skills.** Certain sorts of skill, related to interpretation of data and information processes, are likely to become more valued than manual or physical skills.

   (c)   **Services.** Technology increases manufacturing productivity, releasing human resources for service jobs. These jobs require **greater interpersonal skills** (eg in dealing with customers).

Database marketing

6.5   Databases can be compiled of people's spending habits and social profiles enabling more precise targeting of marketing communications.

   (a)   On the **quantitative** side, database marketing is becoming more popular. It is, after all, **real behaviour as opposed to 'simulated' behaviour.**

   (b)   This also makes it more attractive than **qualitative research.** What people say in **focus groups** or to market researchers does not necessarily reflect their actual purchase behaviour.

6.6   Firms use databases to keep up-to-date information on their product lines and the behaviour of customers. The danger with database information is that it can rapidly go out of date. **'Dirty data'** as this is called, is a major problem: some estimates suggest that data 'goes off' by about 30% a year.

6.7   In practice, the data is only as good as firms' use of it. An example of how the different types of data are used is provided below.

Using the Internet

6.8   The Internet enables:

   (a)   New software or information-based products, such as computer games or even distance learning products, to be created or distributed in new ways

   (b)   Firms to sell other types of product more effectively and to mould customer relationships

6.9   **Key implications of the Internet for the market place**

   (a)   **Blurred boundaries** between businesses: a competitor's website is a few mouse-clicks away.

   (b)   **Information is less 'asymmetrical'.** Customers can now compare prices more easily, leading to a greater balance of information than in the past where, typically, the supplier knew more than the customer. The **internet reduces 'search costs'.**

   (c)   It is becoming harder to reach a mass market over the net.

   (d)   Internet shopping operates on a 24-hour basis. Customers can be serviced remotely via e-mail.

   (e)   Competition can appear from anywhere.

   (f)   Marketing can be interactive as a customer 'enters an advert'.

6.10 Within companies

(a) Information is available in **real-time**.

(b) Access to information does not have to be restricted in the organisation.

(c) Innovative businesses can exploit the rich information provided by IT.

Marketing at Work

Supermarket shopping

UK supermarket groups offer two ways of applying Internet technology to their retailing business.

Tesco is one of the world's largest internet supermarket. Customers log on to its website. The goods are picked at the customer's local store and delivered for £5.

Its competitors, such as *ASDA*, have invested heavily in dedicated warehouses and distribution sectors, for Internet orders.

It remains to be seen which will be more profitable. Tesco adds a £5 delivery service: does employing a packer and incurring all the driving and van costs only come to this amount for delivery, or is Tesco's service a means to get a market share?

Website addresses

www.tesco.co.uk
www.asda.co.uk

Exam Tip

A June 1998 exam question gave you a choice of discussing either the Internet or database marketing. However, you need to consider the implications of these developments in other questions.

---

7 ECOLOGY

7.1 The importance of physical environmental conditions

(a) **Resource inputs.** Managing physical resources successfully (eg oil companies, mining companies) is a good source of profits.

(b) **Logistics.** The physical environment presents logistical problems or opportunities to organisations. Proximity to road and rail links can be a reason for siting a warehouse in a particular area.

(c) **Government.** The physical environment is under the control of other organisations.

　　(i) Local authority town planning departments can influence where a building and necessary infrastructure can be sited. Zoning regulations prohibit the siting of commercial developments in some residential districts.

　　(ii) Governments can set regulations about some of the organisation's environmental interactions.

(d) **Disasters.** In some countries, the physical environment can pose a major 'threat' to organisations.

An interrelationship between environmental factors: ecological issues and strategic planning

7.2 Issues relating to the effect of an organisation's activities on the physical environment (which, to avoid confusion, we shall refer to as 'ecology'), have come to the fore in recent years for a number of reasons.

(a) The **entry into decision-making** or political roles of the generation which grew up in the **1960s**.

(b) **Growth in prosperity** might have encouraged people to feel that 'quality of life' is more than just material production and consumption.

(c) Expansion of **media coverage** (eg of famines, global warming) has fuelled public anxiety.

(d) **Disasters** (eg floods, forest fires in Asia, BSE) have aroused public attention.

(e) **Greater scientific knowledge.** The scientific consensus is developing round to the view that 'global warming' is not only a real phenomenon but also is caused by human activity.

7.3 **How issues of ecology will impinge on business**

- **Consumer demand** for products which appear to be ecologically friendly
- Demand for **less pollution** from industry
- Greater **regulation** by government and the EU
- **Polluter pays.** Businesses will be charged with the external cost of their activities
- Possible requirements to conduct **ecology audits**
- Opportunities to develop **products and technologies** which are ecologically friendly

7.4 The consumer demand for products which claim ecological soundness has waxed and waned, with initial enthusiasm replaced by cynicism as to 'green' claims.

(a) **Marketing.** Companies such as Body Shop have exploited ecological friendliness as a marketing tool.

(b) **Bad publicity.** Perhaps companies have more to fear from the impact of bad publicity (relating to their environmental practices) than they have to benefit from positive ecological messages as such.

(c) **Lifestyles.** There may be a limit to which consumers are prepared to alter their lifestyles for the sake of ecological correctness.

(d) Consumers may be **imperfectly educated** about ecological issues. (For example, much recycled paper has simply replaced paper produced from trees from properly managed (ie sustainably developed) forests) In short, some companies may have to 'educate' consumers as to the relative ecological impact of their products.

7.5 As far as pollution goes, there has been a longish history on ecological legislation and it is likely that governments will take an increased interest in this area.

(a) **Government taxes and fees.** A **Landfill Tax** was introduced in the UK from October 1996. Companies can improve their waste handling. The EU has been considering an energy or carbon tax for some time: such a tax would have to be agreed by the member states, however.

(b) **Government regulations.** Fines might be imposed for persistent breach of pollution guidelines, and pollution might be monitored by government inspectors. The UK government has stated **targets** for **recycling** and reducing **carbon dioxide emissions**.

(c) **Tradable pollution permits** (USA). Every year, the government issues pollution permits to relevant firms for a certain price. These permits can be sold. It might be cheaper for a company to reduce its pollution than do nothing, as the cost could be recouped by the revenue gained by selling the permit. There is talk about introducing this scheme globally.

(d) **Commercial opportunities**. Companies can benefit from the commercial opportunities proposed by the new concern for ecological issues. Chemicals companies have been able to benefit from the development of safe alternatives to CFC gases.

(e) Finally, a firm can **relocate** its activities to a country where ecological standards are less strict, or have a lower priority in relation to other economic and social objectives, such as economic growth.

8 GLOBALISATION AND HOSTILITY TO IT

8.1 Globalisation can mean many things.

(a) Relaxation of trade barriers for goods and services
(b) Free flow of investment capital with no restrictions
(c) International co-operation and standardisation

It is covered in detail in your BPP **International Marketing Strategy** Study Text.

8.2 For companies and marketers, globalisation offers the opportunity to enter new markets. Sound marketing principles still apply but there is no doubt that global marketing is more complex (and risky) than marketing at home.

8.3 Conversely, globalisation offers increased competitors to 'domestic' producers.

8.4 **Key issues for marketers**

(a) Characteristics of 'overseas' markets
(b) Can the same segmentation and positioning strategies be adopted?
(c) Is there a global market, or equivalent segments within each country market?
(d) Impact of culture and regulation on resourcing, distribution, advertising and promotion
(e) Management and structure of overseas operations

Marketing at Work

Global hotel chains (extracts from the Guardian, 18 April 2001)

The hotel industry is embracing globalisation. International chains are encircling the world, swallowing local operations on an almost daily basis.

Tom Oliver, chief executive of *Bass Hotels and Resorts*, says: 'Brands are everything – as travel becomes increasingly trans-border, hotels which aren't carrying international brands simply don't deliver the same rate of revenue per room.'

Bass was unwittingly pushed into hotels by trade secretary Margaret Beckett, who thwarted the group's ambitions to become a global brewer by blocking its purchase of Carlsberg-Tetley. Fellow brewer Whitbread realised that it, too, could not go much further in beer, and began building its Travel Inn chain and its British franchise for *Marriott Hotels*, snapping up *Swallow Hotels* for £578m in November 1999.

All these deals have been motivated by a recognition that the **market is changing**. In the US, 75% of hotels have a well-known brand, compared with just 35% in Europe. Lesley Ashplant, a hotels expert at PricewaterhouseCoopers, says: 'Europe is the single largest tourist destination in the world. It has 6m hotel rooms under fragmented ownership. There are clear **opportunities in scale**, in taking advantage of **branding** and **advanced technology**.'

Size is becoming important as **expectations rise** – international business travellers want internet connections, widescreen televisions and push-button blinds in every room, all of which requires investment. They want faxes delivered to their rooms at all hours of the night and the ability to order foie gras at four o'clock in the morning – which means employing more staff than most independent operators can afford.

Hi-tech reservations systems are also emerging as a crucial factor. In an industry where 75% of costs are staff wages, any savings elsewhere are precious.

Between a third and half of hotels' revenue comes from food and drink, but these only contribute 20% to 30% of profit. Attempts to make hotel restaurant more attractive have generally failed.

Much more profitable are the rooms themselves. The main thrust, therefore, for most operators, is on improving **occupancy**. **Loyalty card** schemes are becoming increasingly elaborate.

Even the most ardent advocates of consolidation accept, however, that there will be limits to the creeping internationalisation of European hotels. Mr Abramson says: 'The US is a wide-open country – if you want a hotel, you can just build it. In Europe, there's much less opportunity for new-builds, so you get a lot of conversions. They're harder to fit into the specific model of the US chain.'

It is difficult to turn a 17th century Provençal château into a Holiday Inn, so some independent operators still prosper. This is bad news for the ideal guest of a multinational chain, who likes to wake up anywhere in the world in the knowledge that the bathroom is on the left, the blinds are blue and the phone is on the wall, six and a half inches above the bedside table.

Website address: www.basshotels.com

Hostility to globalisation as a cultural factor

8.5 A number of pressure groups have emerged, linked in their hostility to global capitalism. Thanks, possibly, to better communications and the internet, they are able to co-ordinate their activities on a world-wide scale. These groups participated in recent protests in Seattle (when the global trading was being discussed by members of the World Trading Organisation) and at the Davos economic forum (a regular gathering of the world's business and political elite).

8.6 Indeed, the anti-globalisation brigade has spawned its own anti-marketing literature. *Naomi Klein's* book, *No Logo*, is a key text on the anti-capitalist reading list. In particular she attacks **brands**. Perhaps marketers need to go back to fundamentals as to what brands actually promise.

8.7 Globalisation is blamed for environmental degradation and global inequality, standardisation and the destruction of local cultures – all under the control of multinational firms which, it is said, are greedy and are not democratically accountable.

8.8 Successful global brands such as **McDonald's** or **Starbucks** are subjects of particular hostility.

Chapter Roundup

- Organisations exist in an **environment**. For many firms, this environment is **constantly changing.** These changes can often happen with little warning, as with sudden political unrest and conflicts. Although changes in the external environment are outside the control of managers they must be **monitored** and **responded** to if the organisation is to maximise the **opportunities** and minimise the damaging impact of **threats.**

- The **external environment** is made up of a number of variables. Managers need to know which factors are critical to their own markets and monitor these carefully. A mnemonic is **PEST** (political and legal, economic, social and cultural, technological).

- Uncertainty in this context results from **complexity** and **dynamism.**

- If planners ignore the external influences on the business, they are operating in the dark and the risks of being unprepared for an unexpected **environmental threat** are immense. The ability to produce plans in the context of a realistic **appraisal** of the **current** and **forecasted** business environment is dependent on **adequate information** being available to the planners at the right time and in a usable format. Johnson and Scholes suggest a five stage process.

  - Assess the **environment**
  - Identify **influences**
  - Analysis **key** influences
  - Identify **relative position**
  - Identify **threats and opportunities**

- For your CIM examinations you need to bear in mind that the external factors at **corporate level** influence how the business operates and the nature of the market. At **marketing planning** level the main focus of external changes is on how environmental factors influence and change **consumer demand**.

Now try illustrative question 4 at the end of the Study Text

Quick Quiz

1   What are the main categories of external influences which affect the organisation? (see para 2.3)
2   What is the source of environmental complexity? (2.5)
3   List the types of information that can be collected. (2.7)
4   How does the legal framework potentially affect an organisation? (3.2)
5   Why do planners need to monitor the political environment? (3.5, 3.6)
6   Give two examples of economic change. (4.1)
7   How has the changing age structure affected business plans? (5.2)
8   Why is culture important? (5.5, 5.9)
9   In what three ways does technological change affect business? (6.3)

Action Programme Review

1   You should have identified **specific** examples of how PEST factors affect your business.

2   This exercise requires you to use your imagination. Identify the characteristics of the product and market and then think of the type of influences. You will need to make a similar systematic leap of the imagination in the exam.

3   **Uncertainty** is caused by inadequate knowledge as to risk. The **variety** of influences include technological factors, the animal feed industry, the EU, the media, environmentalists.

4   The firm's market is shrinking. There is an absolute fall in the number of school leavers. Moreover, it is possible that the increasing proportion of school leavers going to higher education will mean there will be fewer who can afford Club Fun's packages. That said, a higher disposable income in the population at large might compensate for this trend. People might be encouraged to try destinations other than Club Fun's traditional resorts if these other destinations are publicised on television.

5   **Many**. This is a case partly about boundary management and partly about enlightened self-interest and business ethics. The adverse publicity, although not about the Heritage Carpet Company's own suppliers, could rebound badly. Potential customers might be put off. Economic growth in the area may also mean that parents will prefer to send their children to school. The Heritage Carpet Company as well as promoting itself as preserving a craft could reinvest some of its profits in the villages (eg by funding a school), by enforcing limits on the hours children worked. It could also pay a decent wage. It could advertise this in a 'code of ethics' so that customers are reassured that the children are not simply being exploited. Alternatively, it could not import child-made carpets at all. (This policy, however, would be unlikely to help communities in which child labour is an economic necessity.)

5 External Situation Analysis

Learning Outcomes

- Conduct detailed marketing audit externally.
- Identify the elements that can be used to create competitive advantage.

Key Concepts Introduced

- Competitive forces
- Market

- Strategic group
- Mobility barriers

Examples of Marketing at Work

- Channel Tunnel
- Ministry of Defence
- Suppliers to supermarkets
- Internet
- Digital jukeboxes

- Argos
- South Western Airlines
- Generation X
- Socio-economic status: alcohol and tobacco
- Audi

1 SETTING THE SCENE

1.1 The general factors in the previous chapter affect all organisations equally. However, each firm is positioned differently in each particular market and in the industry as a whole.

1.2 Each industry contains companies aiming to offer similar satisfaction to customers. However, each company has a unique profile compared to its competitors.

1.3 Market analysis and customer analysis shows what companies and industries are competing for: the managing director of a fast food chain spoke about competing for 'share of stomach'.

1.4 Identifying who your competitors are is easier said than done as competition exists outside any particular industry. While competitors are important, only paying customers can determine which firms have 'competitive advantage'.

Links with other papers

1.5 Marketing communications can be an important differentiation factor for a product – in some cases, communications suggest greater differences than actually exist, by adding an emotional content to a 'product' offering.

1.6 Marketing communications is also a key tool in encouraging customers to buy, hence the importance of behaviour models.

2 INDUSTRY ANALYSIS: THE COMPETITIVE FORCES

2.1 In discussing competition Porter (*Competitive Strategy*) distinguishes between factors which characterise the nature of competition:

(a) **In one industry compared with another** (eg in the chemicals industry compared with the clothing retail industry) and make one industry as a whole potentially more profitable than another (ie yielding a bigger return on investment).

(b) **Within a particular industry.** These relate to the competitive strategies that individual firms might select.

Key Concept

Five **competitive forces** influence the state of competition in an industry, which collectively determine the profit (ie long-run return on capital) potential of the industry as a whole. **Learn them**

(a) The threat of **new entrants** to the industry
(b) The threat of **substitute** products or services
(c) The bargaining power of **customers**
(d) The bargaining power of **suppliers**
(e) The **rivalry** amongst current competitors in the industry

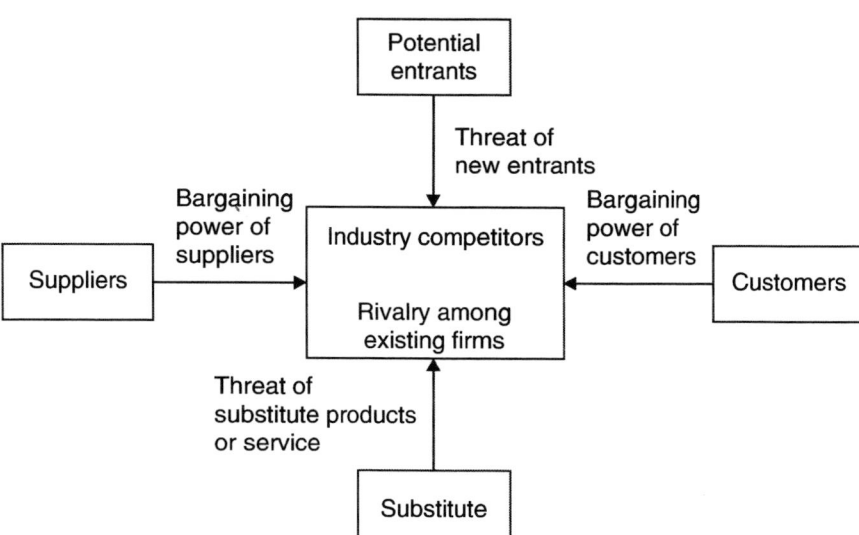

Source: adapted from Porter *(Competitive Strategy)*

The threat of new entrants (and barriers to entry to keep them out)

2.2 **A new entrant into an industry will bring extra capacity and more competition**. The strength of this threat is likely to vary from industry to industry, depending on:

(a) The strength of the **barriers to entry**. Barriers to entry discourage new entrants.

(b) The likely **response of existing competitors** to the new entrant.

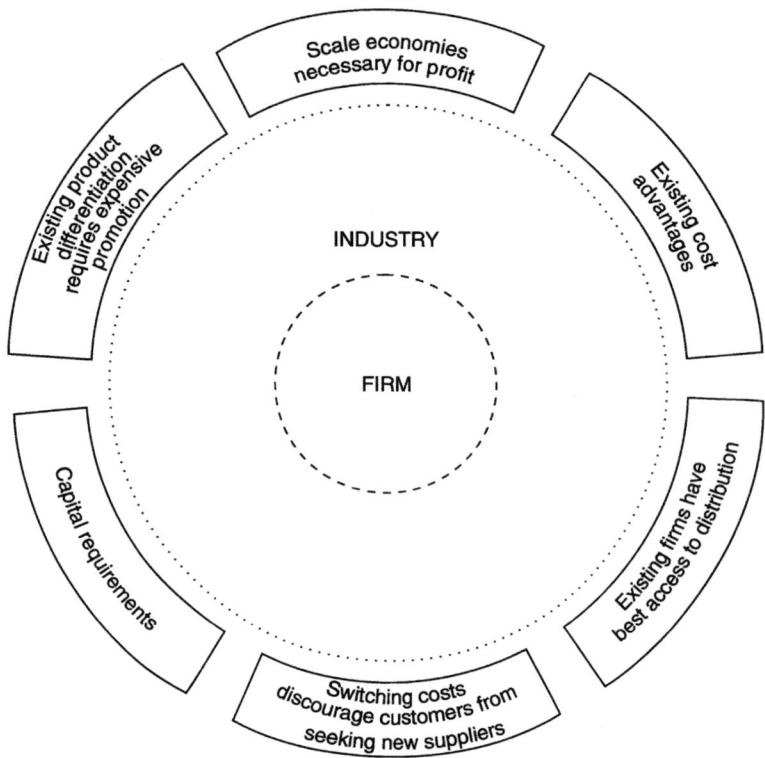

2.3 **Barriers to entry**

(a) **Scale economies.** If the market as a whole is not growing, a new entrant has to capture a large slice of the market from existing competitors, in order to cover its fixed costs. Existing firms, by virtue of their size have an advantage.

(b) **Product differentiation.** Existing firms in an industry may have built up a good brand image and strong customer loyalty over a long period of time. A few firms may promote a large number of brands to crowd out the competition.

(c) **Capital requirements.** When capital investment requirements are high, the barrier against new entrants will be high, particularly when the investment would possibly be high-risk.

(d) **Switching costs.** Switching costs refer to the costs (time, money, convenience) that a customer would have to incur by switching from one supplier's products to another's. Although it might cost a **consumer** nothing to switch from one brand of frozen peas to another, the potential costs for the **retailer or distributor** might be high. As far as consumer marketing is concerned, switching costs can include 'emotional' as well as functional costs.

(e) **Access to distribution channels.** Distribution channels carry a manufacturer's products to the end-buyer. New distribution channels are difficult to establish, and existing distribution channels hard to gain access to.

(f) **Cost advantages of existing producers, independent of economies of scale**

 • Patent rights
 • Experience and know-how (the learning curve)

- Government subsidies and regulations
- Favoured access to raw materials

2.4 Entry barriers might be **lowered** by:

- Changes in the environment
- Technological changes
- Novel distribution channels for products or services

The threat from substitute products

2.5 A **substitute product** is a good/service produced by **another industry** which satisfies the **same customer needs.** Substitutes put a lid on what firms in an industry can charge.

Marketing at Work

The *Channel Tunnel*

Passengers have several ways of getting from London to Paris, and the pricing policies of the various industries transporting them there reflects this.

(a) 'Le Shuttle' carries cars in the Channel Tunnel. Its main competitors are the ferry companies, offering a substitute service. Therefore, you will find that Le Shuttle sets its prices with reference to ferry company prices, and vice versa.

(b) Eurostar is the rail service from London to Paris/Brussels. Its main competitors are not the ferry companies but the airlines. Prices on the London-Paris air routes fell with the commencement of Eurostar services, and some airlines have curtailed the number of flights they offer.

The bargaining power of customers

2.6 Customers want better quality products and services at a lower price. Satisfying this want might force down the profitability of suppliers in the industry. Customer strength depends upon the following.

(a) How much the **customer buys.**

(b) How **critical** the product is to the customer's own business.

(c) **Switching costs (ie the cost of switching supplier).**

(d) Whether the products are **standard items** (hence easily copied) or **specialised.**

(e) The **customer's own profitability:** a customer who makes low profits will be forced to insist on low prices from suppliers.

(f) The customer's **ability to bypass** the supplier or **take over** the supplier.

(g) The **skills** of the customer's **purchasing staff,** or the price-awareness of consumers.

(h) When **product quality** is important to the customer, the customer is less likely to be price-sensitive, and so the industry might be more profitable as a consequence.

Marketing at Work

Although the Ministry of Defence may wish to keep control over defence spending, it is likely as a **customer** to be more concerned that the products it purchases perform satisfactorily than with getting the lowest price possible for everything it buys.

BPP
PUBLISHING

The bargaining power of suppliers

2.7   Suppliers can exert pressure for higher prices, depending upon the following factors.

(a)   Whether there are just **one or two dominant suppliers** to the industry, able to charge monopoly or oligopoly prices.

(b)   The threat of **new entrants** or substitute products to the **supplier's industry**.

(c)   Whether the suppliers have **other customers** outside the industry, and do not rely on the industry for the majority of their sales.

(d)   The **importance of the supplier's product** to the customer's business.

(e)   Whether the supplier has a **differentiated product** which buyers need to obtain.

(f)   Whether **switching costs** for customers would be high.

Marketing at Work

Food products in the UK are largely sold through supermarket chains, and it can be difficult for a new producer to get supermarket organisations to agree to stock its product. As retailers become more powerful, they are placing more and more demands on food producers: failure to comply can mean exclusion from the channel of distribution. Supplier bargaining power is low. Sophisticated marketing firms try to get round this by using advertising, for example, to stimulate customer demand by implementing 'pull strategies'. Such strategies can extend to point of sale advertising. *Safeway* in the UK now features LCD screens in supermarket aisles, which may promote one or more products. For example, the merits of Barilla pasta are forcibly promoted in a short film in the aisle where *Barilla* and other pasta products are being marketed.

Other suppliers try to restrict distribution outlets to maintain high prices, particularly in the case of perfumes and cosmetics, by banning sales of these items in 'undesirable' outlets.

The rivalry amongst current competitors in the industry

2.8   The **intensity of competitive rivalry** within an industry will affect the profitability of the industry as a whole. Competitive actions might take the form of price competition, advertising battles, sales promotion campaigns, introducing new products for the market, improving after sales service or providing guarantees or warranties. Competition can:

(a)   **Stimulate demand**, expanding the market.

(b)   **Leave demand unchanged**, in which case individual competitors will make less money, unless they are able to cut costs.

2.9   **Factors determining the intensity of competition**

(a)   **Market growth.** Rivalry is intensified when firms are competing for a greater market share in a total market where growth is slow or stagnant.

(b)   **Cost structure.** High fixed costs are a temptation for firms to compete on price, as in the short run **any** contribution from sales is better than none at all.

(c)   **Switching.** Suppliers will compete if buyers switch easily (eg Coke vs Pepsi).

(d)   **Capacity.** A supplier might need to achieve a substantial increase in output **capacity**, in order to obtain reductions in unit costs.

(e)   **Uncertainty.** When one firm is not sure what another is up to, there is a tendency to respond to the uncertainty by formulating a more competitive strategy.

(f)   **Strategic importance.** If success is a prime strategic objective, firms will be likely to act very competitively to meet their targets.

(g) **Exit barriers** make it difficult for an existing supplier to leave the industry.

   (i) Fixed assets with a low **break-up value** (eg there may be no other use for them, or they may be old).

   (ii) The cost of **redundancy payments** to employees.

   (iii) If the firm is a division or subsidiary of a larger enterprise, the **effect of withdrawal on the other operations** within the group.

   (iv) The **reluctance of managers** to admit defeat, their loyalty to employees and their fear for their own jobs.

   (v) **Government pressures** on major employers not to shut down operations, especially when competition comes from foreign producers rather than other domestic producers.

Action Programme 1

The tea industry is characterised by oversupply, with a surplus of about 80,000 tonnes a year. Tea estates 'swallow capital, and the return is not as attractive as in industries such as technology or services'. Tea cannot be stockpiled, unlike coffee, keeping for two years at most. Tea is auctioned in London and prices are the same in absolute terms as they were 15 years ago. Tea is produced in Africa and India, Sri Lanka and China. Because of the huge capital investment involved, the most recent investments have been quasi-governmental, such as those by the Commonwealth Development Corporation in ailing estates in East Africa. There is no simple demarcation between buyers and sellers. Tea-bag manufacturers own their own estates, as well as buying in tea from outside sources.

Recently tea prices were described in India at least as being 'exceptionally firm'. The shortage and high prices of coffee have also raised demand for tea which remains the cheapest of all beverages in spite of the recent rise in prices. Demand from Russia, Poland, Iran and Iraq are expected to rise.

(a) Carry out a five forces analysis.

(b) Thinking ahead, suggest a possible marketing strategy for a tea-grower with a number of estates which has traditionally sold its tea at auction.

Information technology and the competitive forces

Marketing at Work

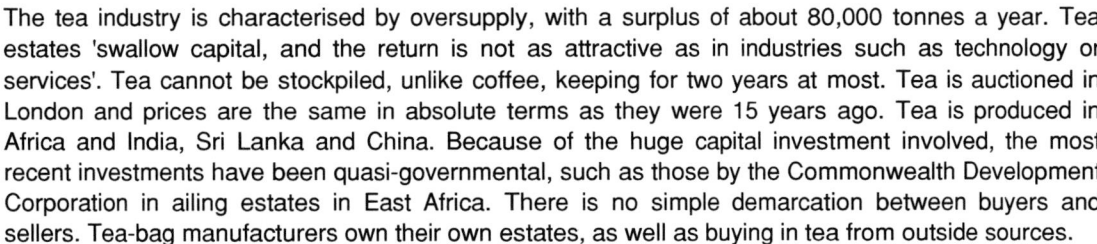

The Internet has had a variety of impacts.

Recently, The Financial Times reported that German companies were losing lucrative niche markets because the Internet made it easier for customers to **compare prices** from other suppliers by obtaining other information over the Internet. High prices made German retailers vulnerable in an age when 'a shopper with a credit card and computer could sit at home and could order from around the world'.

2.10 **Barriers to entry** and IT

   (a) **IT can raise entry barriers** by increasing economies of scale, raising the capital cost of entry (by requiring a similar investment in IT) or effectively colonising distribution channels by tying customers and suppliers into the supply chain or distribution chain by technologies such as **electronic data interchange**.

   (b) **IT can surmount entry barriers.** An example is the use of Internet and telephone banking, which sometimes obviates the need to establish a branch network.

BPP PUBLISHING

2.11 **Bargaining power of suppliers** and IT

   (a) **Increasing the number of** accessible **suppliers.** Supplier power in the past derived from various factors such as geographical proximity and the fact that the organisation requires goods of a certain standard in a certain time. IT enhances supplier information available to customers.

   (b) **Closer supplier relationships.** Suppliers' power can be **shared**. Computer aided design can be used to design components in tandem with suppliers. Such relationships might be developed with a few key suppliers. The supplier and the organisation both benefit from performance improvement, but the relations are closer.

   (c) **Switching costs.** Suppliers can be integrated with the firm's administrative operations, by a system of electronic data interchange.

2.12 **Bargaining power of customers.** IT can 'lock customers in'.

   (a) **IT can raise switching costs.**

   (b) **Customer information systems** can enable a thorough analysis of marketing information so that products and services can be tailored to the needs of each segment. We discussed **database marketing** in the previous chapter.

2.13 **Substitutes.** In many respects, **IT itself is 'the substitute product'.** Here are some examples.

   (a) Video-conferencing systems might substitute for air transport in providing a means by which managers from all over the world can get together in a meeting.

   (b) IT is the basis for new leisure activities (eg computer games) which substitute for TV or other pursuits.

   (c) E-mail might substitute for some postal deliveries.

2.14 **IT and the state of competitive rivalry**

   (a) IT can be used in support of a firm's **competitive** strategy of cost leadership, differentiation or focus. These are discussed later in this text.

   (b) IT can be used in a **collaborative** venture, perhaps to set up new communications networks. Some competitors in the financial services industry share the same ATM network.

Marketing at Work

The music industry: digital jukeboxes

The structure of an industry can be radically changed by technical developments. Music can now be downloaded over the Internet in MP3 files and e-mailed.

The big five record companies command 80% of the global market (£22.6bn). They hope to produce a 'pirate-proof' technical standard to ensure protection of intellectual property.

However, piracy is only one issue. Many bands might bypass the existing record companies altogether: digital jukeboxes enable unsigned acts to post recordings on the net without the support of a big label. In the past, the 'big' five used their commercial clout to enforce dominance. In the new digital market place, size is far less important, as barriers to entry are significantly lower.

'Digital jukeboxes are the online version of independent labels, but with such smaller cost bases that they may prove more resilient. These problems pale beside the risk that established superstars – suppliers, as it were – will bypass record companies and retailers by controlling their own on-line distribution following in the footsteps of Frank Zappa who ran his own mail order catalogue in the 1970s. The big labels are fighting for their contracts.'

The music industry: Napster

More fundamental is technology that allows unlimited digital-to-digital copying on users own PCs. This threatened royalties and earnings of copyright holders, and may have contributed to a 46% fall in sales of CD supplies in the US in 2000 (*Financial Times*, 19 April 2001).

Napster is being sued and forces ongoing demands to shut down its service after failing to comply with a court injunction requiring it to prevent its 72m users downloading copyright material. There was also a marked increase in illegal copying.

Yes, but ...

This implies that all that bands need is a website – what about the marketing support, PR, concert tours?

3 MARKET ANALYSIS

> **Key Concept**
>
> A **market** is a group of actual and potential customers, who can make purchase decisions.

3.1 Businesses also talk about the market 'for' a product (eg the 'confectionery market') as well as other classifications such as 'the youth market'.

3.2 Many firms compete in several markets, if they are diversified or if they have a distinctive competence or brand which can be exploited.

3.3 A **market analysis** will be made up of a range of factors. Here is a checklist (adapted from Dibb and Simkin, 1996).

Statistical data	1999	2000	2001 (forecast)
Company/SBU data Market name Unit sales £ sales Profitability			
Market data Market size Market share No. of main customers No. of dealers/distributors Concentration ratio			
Qualitative data			
Environmental factors			
Critical success factors			
Growing/stable/declining			
Key competitors and their strategies			
Future competitors			
Segmentation opportunities			
Ease of entry			

BPP PUBLISHING

3.4 We can expand upon some elements of the above checklist.

(a) **Market size.** This refers to both actual and potential (forecast) size. A company cannot know whether its market share objectives are feasible unless it knows the market's overall size. Forecasting areas of growth and decline is also important.

(b) **Customers.** The analysis needs to identify who the customers are, what they need, and their buying behaviour (where, when and how they purchase products or services). This will help to point out opportunities.

(c) **Distributors.** The company will need to evaluate its current arrangements for getting goods or services to the customer. Changes in distribution channels can open up new fields of opportunity (eg the Internet).

3.5 Often these factors overlap and PEST factors will affect many areas. For example at the present time the UK government is considering how best to free the country's postal systems from monopoly. Parliamentary bills will eventually need to be passed. Here the major driving force could be said to be political, triggered by economic necessity, facilitated by law. The markets will cease to be a monopoly. They might fragment into public and private sectors.

Marketing at Work

Marketing Week (15 April 1999) reported that *Argos*, the catalogue retailer, is to enter the PC market, 'taking on established players such as *Dixons* and *PC World* and direct sellers such as Time, Tiny and Gateway.

Since 1994, sales volumes in the UK PC sector have grown by 67%, and the market is now valued at £4.6bn. One segment of this market is the small office/home office (Soho) segment, worth £2bn and predicted to grow by 51% (in volume) from 1998 to 2003.

Although Argos does not have the after sales service expertise, first-time buyers go to recognised retailers, and Argos is well known. Prices are falling, and Argos can offer some good deals.

Mintel suggests that the sector will polarise between those who want PCs with bells and whistles and those who require only a very basic model.

4 COMPETITOR ANALYSIS 12/00

4.1 Many firms identify key competitors and plan their strategies with competitors in mind.

4.2 **Key questions for competitor analysis**

- Who are they?
- What are their goals?
- What strategies are they pursuing?
- What are their strengths and weaknesses?
- How are they likely to respond?

Who are our competitors?

Marketing at Work

South Western Airlines is one of the most profitable in the US, partly because it defined its competition carefully.

Most airlines in the US have a 'hub' airport and 'spokes' from it. They compete with each other heavily on matters such as air miles, price and so on.

South Western does not use this arrangement and instead it flies 'point to point' over short distances. It has defined its competitor as the motor car – a substitute product – and has designed its marketing mix so as to minimise the time the customer takes travelling. This has meant flying from smaller, less congested airports, speeded-up check-in times and so on.

4.3 Identifying current competitors is easy. Identifying **potential** competitors is harder as potential competitors might be:

- Smaller companies attacking the market segment
- Companies operating in other markets wishing to expand
- Companies wishing to diversify

4.4 Finally a firm can **define** who its competitors actually are. Coca-Cola, for example, competes against:

- Pepsi in the Cola market

- All other soft drinks

- Tea and coffee

- Tap water: Coca-Cola's chief executive has declared that 'the main competitor is tap water: any other share definition is too narrow'

What are competitors' goals?

4.5 Next, you need to discern what the competitors' goals and objectives are.

(a) **Relevant goals and objectives**

(i) Goals and objectives of the **parent company**, if the competitor is part of a larger group.

(ii) The competitors' assessment of risk; a higher risk will require a higher return from a market.

(iii) The personal goals of key managers. For example, a new chief executive may be brought in to 'turn the company round'. The new chief executive may have made a **public commitment** to one set of goals and may have invested a lot of prestige in achieving these goals.

(iv) A company facing cash flow problems may do anything to maximise cash inflow.

(v) The competitors' history, position and the underlying assumptions of their management. For example, some firms consider themselves to be 'market leaders'.

(vi) **How dependent** the competitor is on the current business? A competitor with one main business will fight much harder to defend it than a competitor exposed to several sectors.

(b) **Types of goals**

- Profit
- Market share
- Cash flow
- Technological leadership
- Service leadership

We cover goal-setting later. Suffice it to say that competitors' goals can be taken into account. Different competitors put different weights on certain goals, particularly with regard to time horizons. Some might sacrifice profit, in the short term, for market share.

Current competitor strategies

4.6 Assessing current competitor strategies is relatively simple, as competitors send out signals to the same customer base. A company's closest competitor is one competing in the same target market.

Strategic group analysis: a constraint on competitive choice

4.7 **Strategic group analysis** tries to show how firms are positioned in a particular market or segment. Porter identifies a number of dimensions in which firms can differ.

- **Specialisation.** (Limited number of segments? Does it have a narrow product range?)
- **Brand.** Does the firm promote a brand or compete on price?
- **Distribution.** What channels are used?
- **Push** or **pull** approach to distribution?
- **Quality**
- Technological **leader** or follower?
- Degree of vertical **integration**
- **Cost structure**
- **Add-on services**
- **Price policy**
- **Indebtedness**
- Degree of **control** by holding company
- **Government involvement**

4.8 Any firm can be defined according to these dimensions. Firms with **low relative prices** are usually **able to control costs**, but **do not have superior product quality**.

Key Concept

In any industry, especially with a large number of firms, some will pursue similar strategies in which case they can be considered a **strategic group**.

4.9 For any two of the attributes in 4.7 above it should be possible to map how firms relate to each other. The number of dimensions of course is very large, so a strategic group is best identified by taking the two most significant dimensions in the industry.

4.10 **Mobility barriers** constrain organisational endeavours and function as barriers to entry.

Key Concept

Mobility barriers make it hard for a firm in one strategic group to develop or migrate to another.

(a) **Market factors**

 (i) Some supermarket chains (eg **Morrisons**) have a low presence in the South-East of England, where there is substantial competition.

 (ii) The brand name may be a mobility barrier, if it is unknown in the particular segment.

 (iii) The product line may not be extensive enough.

 (iv) Other factors include user technologies and selling systems.

(b) **Industry characteristics**. To move into a mass volume end of the market might require economies of scale and large production facilities. To move to the quality end might require greater investment in research and development.

(c) The organisation may lack the **distinctive skills** and competences in the new market area.

(d) **Legal barriers** might exist.

Competitors' strengths and weaknesses

4.11 SWOT analysis is covered in a later chapter, but it is relatively easy to assess a competitor's **strengths** and **weaknesses**. Here are some examples.

- Brand strengths, customer loyalty
- Market share
- Quality of management team
- Resources, financial and otherwise
- Intellectual property
- Distribution network
- Relative cost structure
- Distinctive competence

4.12 In marketing, Kotler suggests the following table for consideration for **marketing strengths and weaknesses**.

- Customer awareness
- Product quality
- Product availability
- Technical assistance
- Sales staff
- Market share
- 'Mind' share (% of customers who had heard about the company)
- Share of benefit

Analysing competitors' costs

4.13 Clearly the strategic response of competitors can vary significantly on the cost profile of the competitor. **Relative costs** are more important than absolute costs: Ward believes that it took Western firms too long to understand that Japanese firms had **sustainable cost advantages,** and hence were able to compete on price on a sustained basis.

4.14 Furthermore, even if the competitor is not competing on price, despite having a lower cost base, the competitor is:

- Under no pressure to raise prices, thus limiting the firm's ability to raise its own
- More profitable, and hence can invest more

Competitor reaction and response

4.15 Kotler identifies the following types of competitor response.

Predictable	Unpredictable
(i) **Laid-back**: competitor does not respond	Stochastic: **impossible to predict** how **competitor will react**
(ii) **Selective**: competitor only responds to certain types of attack	
(iii) **Tiger**: competitor reacts to any attack	

Action Programme 2

Why might a competitor be 'laid-back'?

Action Programme 3

Jot down a list of items of information that might be obtained from an environmental analysis of competitors.

4.16 'Good' competitors

Monopolies are hard to come by, but some competitors are definitely easier to deal with than others. A 'good' competitor:

- Deters new entrants (assuming you are not a new entrant)
- Shares similar assumptions about the industry
- Prefers differentiation and focus to competing on price

Exam Tip

In December 2000, you had to describe how competitor analysis would be carried out by a cosmetics company and how relevant it could be. Branding is probably an issue here.

5 CUSTOMER ANALYSIS

Strategic importance

5.1 This section is all about **understanding** customers. How marketers **use** the information they have gleaned on their customers (in the form of segmentation, targeting and positioning) will be addressed in Chapter 13.

5.2 Marketing is about satisfying customers – but **some customers (or segments) are more important than others**. The factors you should consider in assessing the strategic importance of a customer are outlined below. The list has been adapted from an article by Gary Hamel in the *Harvard Business Review* (July/August 1996).

Strategic importance evaluation guide		High	Medium	Low	N/A
1	Fit between customer's needs and our capabilities, at present and potentially.				
2	Ability to serve customer compared with our major competitor, at present and potentially.				
3	'Health' of customer's industry, currently and forecast.				
4	'Health' of the customer, current and forecast.				
5	Customer's growth prospects, current and forecast.				
6	What can we learn from this customer?				
7	Can the customer help us attract others?				
8	Relative **significance:** how important is the customer compared **with other** customers?				
9	What is the **profitability** of serving the customer?				

5.3 To satisfy customers we need to know how they behave and why they take the purchasing decisions they do.

5.4 A number of models and theories exist to explain the dynamics of the 'not always rational' customer's behaviour. You will probably **already** be familiar with them, but the key aspects are included here for your review. These aspects of behaviour are also critical in the process of segmentation. But first an example.

Marketing at Work

'Generation X'

A segment is a group of customers who might behave in a particular way. In February 1997, Marketing Business identified Generation X. This indicates how buyer behaviour and segmental analysis can be related.

'New consumers, Generation X, call them what you will, youth in the 1990s are a cynical and disillusioned bunch. They eschew eighties-style consumerism, laugh in the face of brands which try to woo them and yet paradoxically remain loyal to brands they deem cool. Tap into this illusive but hugely influential demographic and you are onto a winner. Get it wrong and you will miss a golden opportunity.

In 1991 a novel was published called Generation X. It was by an American - Douglas Copeland - and therefore prone to exaggerated generational claims (the country's favourite pastime since the 1960s). But it touched a nerve: today's young adults, it suggested, were terminally disillusioned and cynical. Unemployed and underexploited, they were wasting away in Mc-jobs, serving burgers instead of bettering themselves. They were the first generation in America to realise that they would not enjoy a higher standard of living than their parents.

Bleak stuff. Whether or not Generation X was fact or fiction, its supposed attributes are certainly an important aspect of today's young consumer. However, the apocalyptic tone is not so accurate.

While young consumers have metamorphosed considerably in recent years, they remain very much consumers. Their cynicism and knowingness cannot be ignored, but it should not be taken as a sign that they have rejected capitalism lock, stock and barrel. Targeting them means recognising their outlook as more than just a passing fad. Marketers must first acknowledge certain fundamental changes which have affected all consumer behaviour, and which will become increasingly part of the mainstream as this generation ages.

First people became brand literate. Then, in the 1980s they became advertising-literate, very much into badges and conspicuous consumption. Now they have become marketing-literate.

"The single most important element of our whole media targeting is attitude", says Simon Soothill, brand manager of top tequila brand Jose Cuervo. His activity centres on the 25-34 age group, who "don't want to be sold to and expect to see very dynamic advertising. We try to find ways of talking to them that they find relevant and involving." Soothill believes this age group has younger tastes than in previous generations.

Just as age is no longer the all-powerful defining factor of consumer behaviour, so gender is not the great divider it once was. This magazine has already commented in detail on the blurring of gender boundaries among younger consumers, as exemplified by the Calvin Klein campaigns.

Marketers climbing the corporate ladder are also managing to find new ways of talking to today's young - and tomorrow's mainstream - consumer.

While young consumers can be said to have some homogenous characteristics, it is not enough to define them by age alone. The concept of the teenager is now looking quite staid and indeed rather 1950s.'

'*Kidults*'

As opposed to this, there is anecdotal comment that older people are not assuming the cultural attributes of their previous generational roles, for example, in terms of music or clothing or even some lifestyle activities.

What influences customer behaviour?

5.5 Understanding customer behaviour assists effective marketing management. However, there are many influences on customer behaviour and so the outcome in terms of purchasing decisions can be very difficult to understand from a rational viewpoint. **Emotional and rational influences** intertwine and lead to purchase outcomes which can seem illogical even to the buyer.

Physiological and psychological influences

5.6 Marketers aim to satisfy customer needs. Maslow's hierarchy of needs is a useful checklist of the needs each person is supposed to have.

Maslow's hierarchy of needs

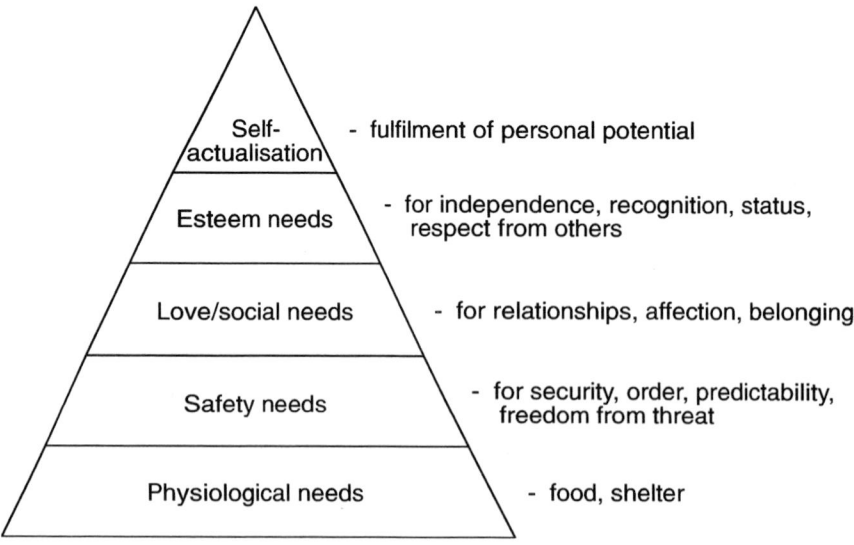

Maslow argued that lower order needs such as physiological needs must be satisfied before higher order ones such as self-actualisation needs (making the most of your potential). These ideas are very appealing, but there are major criticisms in practice.

5.7 **Motives** sit between **needs** and **action**. A need motivates a person to take action. However, motives do not tell us **how consumers choose from the options available** to satisfy needs. Other influences are clearly at work.

Attitudes to risk

5.8 Many purchase decisions involve a degree of risk. People's perceptions of risk differ from 'objective' statistical risks. For example, smoking is a far riskier activity than eating beef on the bone. Examples of risk are **physical risk** (eg BSE in food) and **financial risk** (eg pensions). Some researchers believe that:

(a) **Fear** is a stronger motivator than pleasure.

(b) People's feelings about risk are **irrational**.

(c) Any purchaser of a service runs the **risk of disappointment**.

(d) If marketers understand how consumers perceive risk, then they can design products and services accordingly to reduce risk. For example the 'risk' of wasted time is lessened, in supermarkets, by opening new check-outs if queues longer than a certain length develop.

Cultural influences

5.9 Culture varies widely and has many influences on marketing practice. For example language differences raise obvious marketing implications when brand names have to be translated, often leading to entirely different (and sometimes embarrassing) meanings in the new language. There are many sub-cultures.

5.10 **How cultural and sub-cultural differences affect purchasing**

- **What** is bought (style, colours, types of goods/service)?
- **When** are things bought (for example, is Sunday shopping approved of)?
- **How** are things bought (bartering, haggling about price)?
- **Where** are things bought (type of retail outlet)?
- **Why** are things bought (influence of culture on needs and hence motives)?

Social influences

5.11 Members of specific groups have **similar** lifestyles, beliefs and values which can and do affect their purchasing behaviour.

(a) **Socio-economic status** indicates a person's disposable income and ability to spend.

(b) People can **aspire to a different socio-economic status**, and some products satisfy these aspirations.

(c) **Psychographics** (lifestyle) and **geodemographic segmentation** (ACORN) provide more sophisticated analysis.

Marketing at Work

Socio-economic status can be related to buying patterns in a number of ways, both in the amount people have to spend and what they spend it on.

(a) The wealthier professionals spend less of a proportion of their total income on food and housing, and more on leisure, than do unskilled manuals. This does not imply they spend any less in absolute terms of course: they just have more available to spend on other things.

(b) Interestingly, the consumption of alcohol and tobacco is significantly different: in 1990 only 18% of men and women in the professional category smoked, as opposed to 48% of unskilled manual men and 36% of unskilled manual women.

 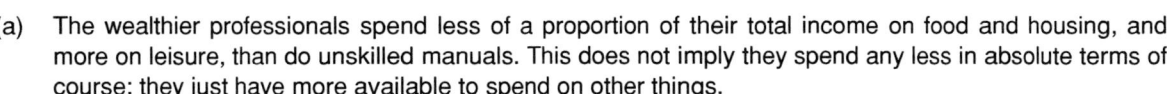

(c)   The effect on social class on leisure and services is an example of how discretionary spending varies from class to class. In 1991 over 80% of members of social class AB took at least one holiday, compared with under 60% of class C2. In classes DE, over half took no holiday at all.

Personal circumstances and reference groups

5.12   Family background is a very strong influence on purchasing behaviour.

(a)   It is in family groups that we learn how to be members of society and how to behave in different settings. Having learnt, it is difficult to forget. Family influences remain strong throughout the rest of our lives.

(b)   The family is important in purchasing behaviour because it is often a 'purchasing unit' with one member (the buyer) buying on behalf of all members (users) but others in the family influencing the decision (influencers). Joint husband and wife purchasing decisions for major items are common.

5.13   A person may identify with or aspire to membership of a reference group of other people. This is particularly true of youth culture and the market for fashion goods.

Marketing at Work

An advertisement for *Audi cars* playing recently profiled members of a reference group (members of an exclusive, backward-looking golf club) that the typical Audi purchaser would not want to belong to, cleverly exploiting the subtle snobberies in the English class system.

Models of buying behaviour

5.14   Buyer behaviour models aim is to help the marketing manager to understand the buying process so as to use a marketing strategy which is most applicable to the specific situation. A simple model might attempt to simplify and clarify the purchase decision process by showing it as a series of sequential steps.

Purchase	Comment	Markets
Step 1.	Felt need	Market research
Step 2.	Pre-purchase activity (eg information search)	Advertising
Step 3.	Purchase decision	Selling, promotion
Step 4.	Usage behaviour	Customer service
Step 5.	Post-purchase feelings and evaluation	Customer service

This type of model is useful to the marketing manager in trying to influence the buying process. For example, advertising and promotional activity is aimed at the **information search** stage and customer service is aimed at the post-purchase evaluation stage.

5.15   Some models try to show the **interrelationship** between the various behavioural and economic factors to give the marketing manager a better understanding of the buying process. The Howard-Sheth model is a good example.

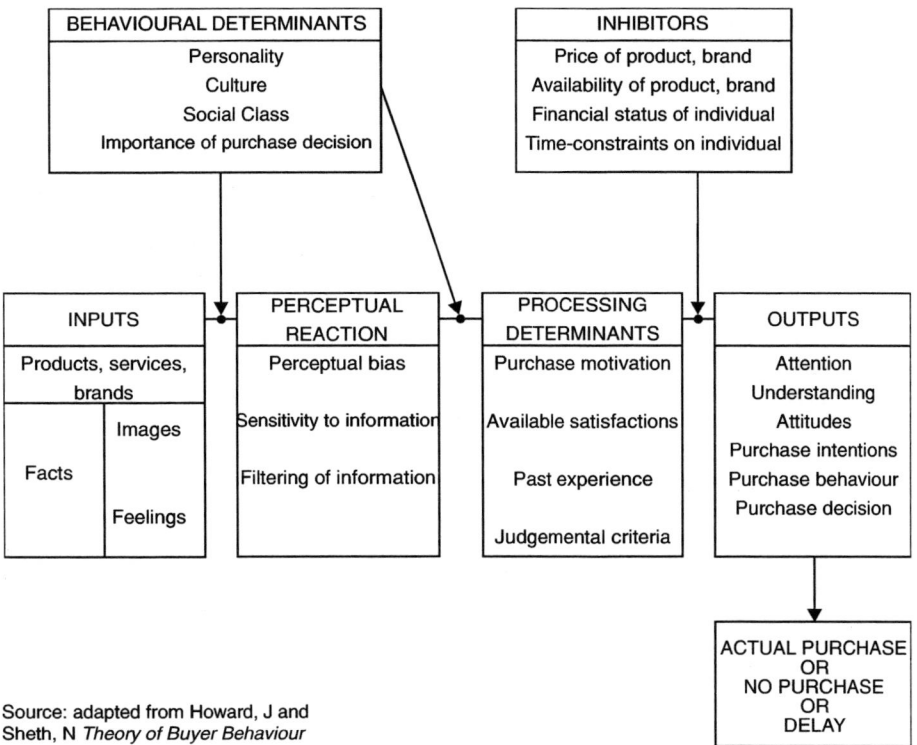

Source: adapted from Howard, J and
Sheth, N *Theory of Buyer Behaviour*

5.16 Elements in the Howard-Sheth model

(a) **Inputs.** Information inputs about the alternative services available include both rational and emotional elements.

(b) **Behavioural determinants.** These elements include the existing predispositions of the purchaser which have been influenced by culture, socio-economic group, family and personality factors, amongst others. This element will have a larger role for big or otherwise significant purchase decisions.

(c) **Perceptual reaction.** Information from inputs is not accepted at face value but interpreted. For example, an individual is likely to value information more highly if it has been actively sought than if it has been passively received (from TV advertisements for example).

(d) **Processing determinants.** These are the factors affecting how the information gathered is evaluated.

(e) **Inhibitors.** There are external constraints on actual or potential purchase behaviour.

(f) **Outputs.** The outcome of the complex process of interacting elements may be a purchase decision, a decision not to buy or a decision to delay buying.

5.17 Advantages of the Howard-Sheth model

(a) It has been **validated** for practical examples of purchases.

(b) It **indicates the complex nature** of the buying process.

(c) It emphasises the need for marketing managers to **analyse the satisfactions** which customers seek in relation to the purchase of goods or services.

(d) It emphasises the need to gain a **clear understanding of individual purchase motivations.**

(e) It points to the importance of **external constraints** on the process.

(f) It suggests that **customer satisfactions occur on a number of levels** and in a number of forms at the same time. For example, both rational and emotional satisfactions are likely to be sought.

Thus the Howard-Sheth model can help the marketing manager to obtain useful and practical insights into customer behaviour.

Action Programme 4

Eleanor Plantagenet works for Mast, Rick, Tree and Tee, an advertising agency which is beginning to fall on hard times. For example, Bill Mast (the MD) has had to make do with a cheaper company car. There are ominous rumours about making the agency 'leaner and fitter', 'optimising the agency's human resources' and 'delayering'. Eleanor assumes that all this means possible redundancy for people like her, although the managing director has denied all such rumours.

Mortgage payments account for 25% of Eleanor's post-tax monthly salary. Her husband is a freelance financial journalist. His earnings are erratic, but he has recently been commissioned to write a book for the non-specialist reader about the single European currency. They have two children. They invested an inheritance of £15,000 in the Carlowe Bowes saving scheme but the scheme was run by a fraudster, and they lost all their money. Both Eleanor and her husband are hard-working individuals with severe demands on their time. Eleanor earns significantly more than her husband.

One evening, Eleanor's husband tells her of a new financial services product offered by the International Bank of Canonbury. It offers redundancy insurance. This means that Eleanor will be paid £100 per month of unemployment (up to 12 months) for every £5 invested per month, to a maximum monthly benefit of £1,000. No benefit will be paid if Eleanor becomes unemployed within six months of taking out the policy.

Identify the behavioural determinants, inhibitors, inputs, possible perceptual reactions processing determinants and outputs (as in the Howard-Sheth model) in the above situation.

Exam Tip

In this exam, questions on buyer behaviour are likely to concern their implications for marketing planning. The implications of culture, social change and so forth are clearly relevant to segmentation, targeting and positioning. They are also relevant to each element of the mix: how can customers be persuaded to part with their money?

The organisational buyer behaviour process

5.18 Organisations are buyers too. Organisational buyer behaviour is more complex than individual buyer behaviour.

(a) There are **many people** influencing the purchase decision.

(b) In theory, organisational purchase decisions are supposed to be driven by **rational** criteria, relating to the **objectives of the business**.

Webster and Wind's model of organisational buyer behaviour

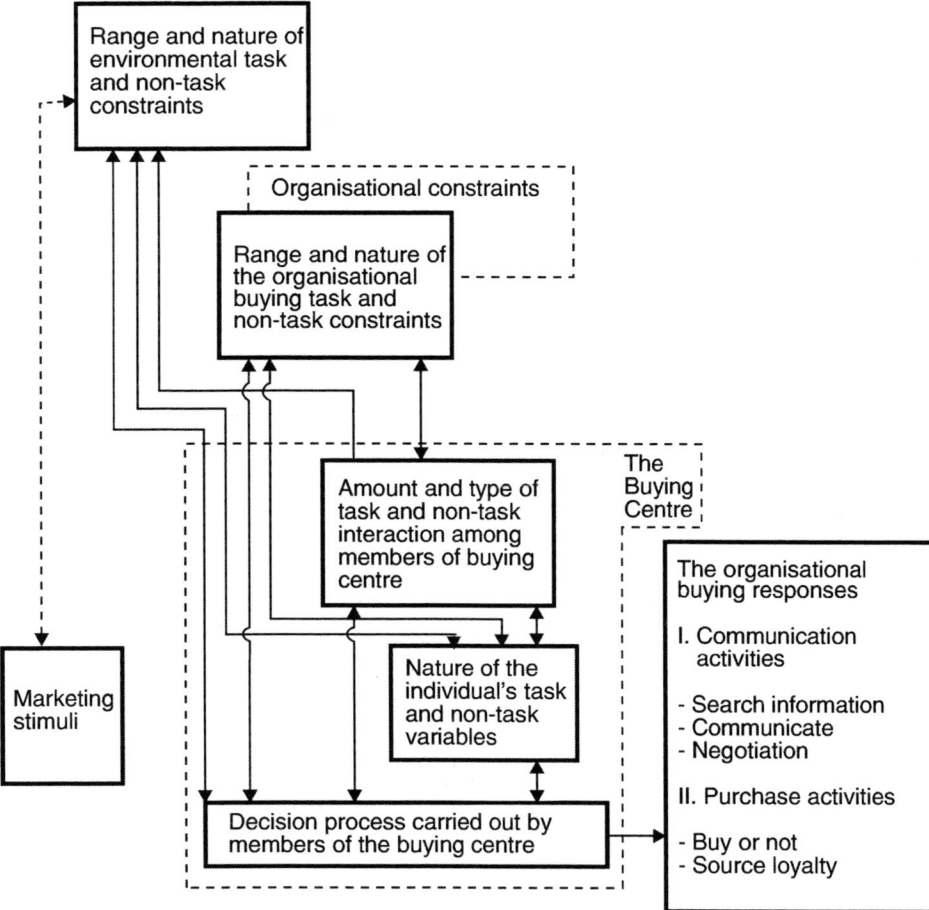

Source: adapted from Webster, F and Wind, Y *Organisational Buyer Behaviour*

5.19 Webster and Wind together see the organisational **buyer (the decision making unit (DMU))** as influenced by a number of sets of variables.

(a) The **individual characteristics** of the members of the DMU, such as personality and preference, are similar to personal buying processes.

(b) The **relationships** between members of the buying centre are also important.

(i) The **user** may have influence on the technical characteristics of the equipment (and hence the cost) and on reliability and performance criteria.

(ii) The **influencer** is particularly useful where the purchase relies on **technical knowledge**.

(iii) The **buyer** or **decider**. These individuals have personal idiosyncrasies, social pressures and organisational and environmental pressures. Thus each has a set of rational factors (task variables) and non-economic factors (non-task variables).

(iv) The **gatekeeper** who controls the flow of information about the purchaser may be senior or junior but is important because he/she influences the communication flow within the organisation.

(c) **Organisational characteristics** include the buying and organisational task, the size and structure of the organisation, the use of technology and so on. The relationships of the buyer within the organisation are particularly important. This post can be senior or junior and can involve power struggles with user departments.

(d) **Environmental factors** such as the physical, technological, economic and legal factors which affect general competitive conditions.

5.20 These four sets of variables interact in the decision process carried out by members of the **decision making unit** (DMU) of the buying organisation. In marketing terms the DMU is a vital target for the supplier's marketing initiatives. The size and structure of the DMU will vary between organisations, over time in the same organisation and for different types of purchase.

5.21 People marketing to corporate clients therefore need to be aware of:

- How buying decisions are made by the DMU
- How the DMU is constructed
- The identities of the most influential figures in the DMU

5.22 The diagram shows the decision process and the role of members of the DMU at each stage. Of course the process will vary according to the type of purchase being made.

A decision process model of industrial purchase behaviour

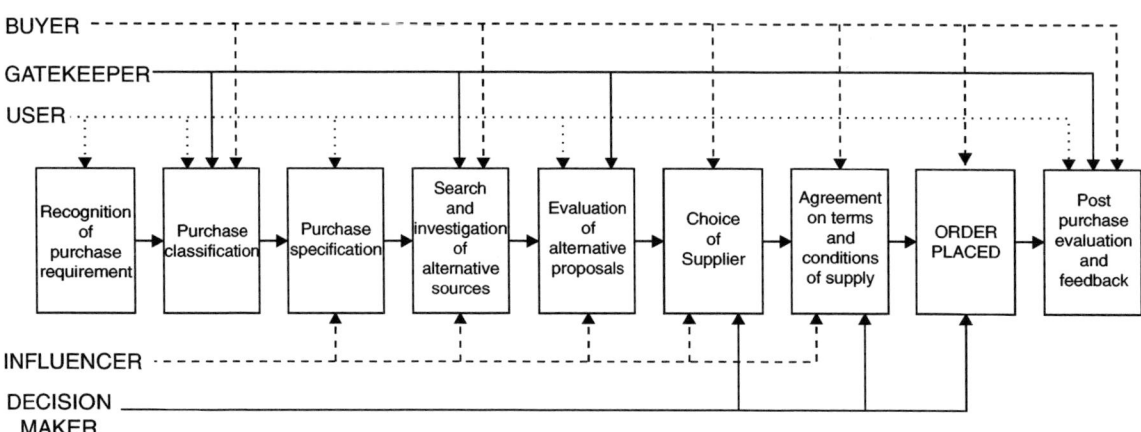

5.23 The organisational buying process is complex and needs careful marketing action if the outcome is to be influenced favourably. Becoming 'close to customers' is an important step towards satisfying and even delighting them.

Exam Tip

Organisational buying has appeared frequently in the Analysis & Decision paper which has featured business-to-business marketing on a number of occasions. Clearly any marketing strategy must take the characteristics and concerns of DMU members into account. However, it has been less common as the scenario in the *Planning & Control* paper under old and new syllabuses: what this space!

Chapter Roundup

- Most companies are **competing** with other companies for customers. They have to identify or create a position in the customer's mind.

- Within the industry there are **five competitive forces**, determining the profitability of the industry as a whole.

    - New entrants
    - Substitute products or services
    - Customer bargaining power

    - Supplier bargaining power
    - Intensity of competition

- Firms also need to analyse the market (or the customer and customer needs that they must satisfy). A **market analysis** covers statistical and qualitative data relating to customers, influences on customers, trends and buying power.

- An **analysis of individual competitors** will cover who they are, their objectives, their strategies, their strengths and weaknesses and how they are likely to respond.

- **Competitor responses** can be classified as laidback, selective, 'tiger' or stochastic (ie unpredictable).

- Models of **buyer behaviour** consider the influences (rational and emotional) on the buying decisions and the process of decision making (eg individual or group as in a DMU).

Now try illustrative question 5 at the end of the Study Text

Quick Quiz

1   List the competitive forces (see para 2.1)

2   What are substitute products? (2.5)

3   How can IT raise barriers to entry? (2.10)

4   What factors would you consider when analysing a market? (3.3)

5   List five key questions in a competitor analysis. (4.2)

6   Identify types of competitor response. (4.15)

7   How can you discriminate between 'important' and 'unimportant' customers? (5.2)

8   Why is the family unit an important influence on behaviour? (5.12)

9   Why are buyer behaviour models useful? (5.14)

10 How should people take the DMU into account? (5.20, 5.21)

Action Programme Review _____

1   (a) Here are some ideas. Barriers to entry are high. There are plenty of substitute products (coffee), competitive rivalry is high because of the difficulty of stockpiling products. Customer bargaining power is high, but supplier power is low: all it needs is capital, the right sort of land and labour.

    (b) Williamson and Magor has begun to switch from tea at auction to consumer marketing. The firm is aiming to build up its own brand image in the UK and Germany, by offering – by mail order – unblended, specialist teas from its Indian estates. It advertised via Barclays Premier Card magazine; replies were used to set up a customer database. When the company's Earl Grey tea was recommended on BBC2's *Food and Drink*, these existing customers were targeted with a letter and a sample.

2   A 'laid back' competitor may be:

    - Unable to respond: lack of capability
    - Unwilling to respond owing to differing assumptions about the segment
    - Unconcerned about the threat, which is does not take seriously

3   (a) Who are the existing competitors? How much of the market do they hold in each segment of the markets (eg in each particular region or country)?

(b) Who are potential competitors? How soon might they enter the market?

(c) How profitable are existing competitors? What is their EPS, dividend yield, ROCE etc?

(d) What do the goals of each competitor appear to be, and what strategies have they adopted so far?

(e) What products/services do they sell? How do they compare with the organisation's own products or services?

(f) How broad is their product line? (eg Are they up-market high quality, or down-market low quality, low price and high volume producers?)

(g) What is their distribution network?

(h) What are their skills and weakness in direct selling, advertising, sales promotions, product design etc?

(i) What are their design skills or R & D skills? Do they innovate or follow the market leader with new product ideas?

(j) What are their costs of sale and operational capabilities, with respect to:

- Economies of scale
- Use of advanced technology equipment
- Patents, trademarks, know-how
- Quality control
- Location
- Transportation costs
- Labour skills and productivity
- Supply advantages (ie special access to raw materials at a low cost)
- Industrial relations and industrial disputes
- Reliability in servicing customers

(k) What are their general managerial capabilities? How do these compare with those of the organisation?

(l) Financial strengths and weaknesses. What is the debt position and financial gearing of each competitor? Do they have easy access to sources of new finance? What proportion of profits do they return in the business in order to finance growth?

(m) How is each competitor organised? How much decentralisation of authority do they allow to operating divisions, and so how flexible or independent can each of the operating divisions be?

(n) Does the competitor have a good spread or portfolio of activities? What is the risk profile of each competitor?

(o) Does any competitor have a special competitive advantage - eg a unique government contract or special access to government authorities?

(p) Does any competitor show signs of changing strategy to increase competition to the market?

4   **Behavioural determinants.** Eleanor and her husband work in service industries. They are used to the concept of investing (even if unsuccessfully), and have financial interests to protect. The family is perhaps slightly unusual in that the female is the breadwinner, and her husband's income is unlikely to be large.

Inputs. Only one product is detailed. As a financial journalist, Eleanor's husband might know of more. He is likely to be interested in the small print, rather than images and feelings.

Inhibitors. If Eleanor feels she is likely to be made redundant within the next six months, she is unlikely to take out the policy as it would not be of much use to her.

Perceptual reaction. Having lost £15,000 in a previous investment, Eleanor and her husband are possibly very risk averse. They will be sensitive to information regarding the status and reputation of the service provider.

Processing determinants. There is a perceived risk that Eleanor will be made redundant, and she is looking for a product which will reduce the financial impact.

Outputs. They will want a benefit which will cover at least the mortgage and regular bills.

6 Internal Situation Analysis

Chapter Topic List	Syllabus reference
1 Setting the scene	
2 Resources and limiting factors	2.2
3 Assets	2.2
4 The marketing audit	2.2
5 Innovation audit	2.2

Learning Outcomes

- Understand and critically appraise a wide variety of marketing techniques, concepts and models.

- Identify the elements that can be used to create competitive advantage.

Key Concepts Introduced

- Limiting factor/key factor
- Efficiency
- Effectiveness
- Distinctive competence

- Marketing asset
- Innovation audit
- The recipe

Examples of Marketing at Work

- Airline alliances

- NXT loudspeakers

1 SETTING THE SCENE

1.1 A look at the internal environment of an organisation is a way of identifying strengths and weaknesses. It therefore covers all aspects of the organisation. This is because the other functions of the organisation effectively act as constraints over what marketing personnel can achieve.

1.2 A company needs to evaluate its ability to compete and satisfy customer needs. The firm's resources, once identified, must be harnessed to a market orientation to ensure that those resources are directed at satisfying those needs.

1.3 There are a number of approaches to be taken with regard to corporate capability. In this chapter we conduct an overview of resources in the context of organisational effectiveness. The key issues are what resources the organisation has and how they are deployed.

1.4 The **marketing audit** is relevant to this chapter, but because the marketing audit is directly relevant to the marketing SWOT, those two topics are treated together in Chapter 8.

1.5 An analysis of corporate/marketing resources covers:

- What the organisation currently has or owns
- What the organisation has access to, even if it currently does not own the resources
- How effectively it **deploys** its resources

2 RESOURCES AND LIMITING FACTORS

2.1 A **resource audit** is a review of the organisation resources which can be grouped into these categories (Hooley, Saunders and Piercy).

Resource	Comment
Technical resources	<ul><li>Technical ability.</li><li>Processes for NPD.</li><li>Ability to convert new technology into new marketing products.</li></ul>
Financial standing	<ul><li>Firms with a good financial standing find it easier to raise money.</li></ul>
Managerial skills	Managerial roles and functions were covered in Chapter 2. An effective management is a key organisation resource in planning activities, controlling the organisation and motivating staff.
Organisation	Organisation structure can be a resource for marketers, for example product divisionalisation or brand management control at brand level. The organisation structure should facilitate communication and decision-making.
Information systems	The strategic role of information systems is covered at various times throughout this Study Text.

2.2 **Resources are of no value unless they are organised into systems**, and so a resource audit should go on to consider how well or how badly resources have been utilised, and whether the organisation's systems are **effective** and **efficient** in meeting customer needs profitably.

Limiting factors

2.3 Every organisation operates under resource **constraints**.

> **Key Concept**
>
> A **limiting factor** or **key factor** is 'a factor which at any time or over a period may limit the activity of an entity, often one where there is shortage or difficulty of supply'.

Examples

- A shortage of production capacity
- A limited number of key personnel, such as salespeople with technical knowledge
- A restricted distribution network

- Too few managers with knowledge about finance, or overseas markets
- Inadequate research design resources to develop new products or services
- A poor system of strategic intelligence
- Lack of money
- A lack of staff who are adequately trained

2.4   Once the limiting factor has been identified, the planners should:

- **Short term,** make best use of the resources available
- **Long term,** reduce the limitation

Resource use

2.5   Resource use is concerned with the **efficiency** with which resources are used, and the **effectiveness** of their use in achieving the planning objectives of the business.

> ### Key Concepts
>
> **Efficiency**: 'how well the resources have been utilised irrespective of the purpose for which they have been employed'.
>
> **Effectiveness**: 'whether the resources have been deployed in the best possible way'.

Distinctive competences

2.6   To recap from Chapter 1, a strategic approach involves identifying a firm's **competences.** 'Members of organisations develop judgements about what they think the company can do well - its core competence.' These competences may derive from:

- **Experience** in making and marketing a product or service
- The talents and potential of individuals in the organisation
- The **quality of co-ordination.**

> ### Key Concept
>
> The **distinctive competence** of an organisation is what it does well, or better, than its rivals.

2.7   **Tests for identifying a core competence**

(a)   It provides potential **access to a wide variety of markets.** GPS of France developed a 'core competence' in 'one-hour' processing, enabling it to process films and build reading glasses in one hour.

(b)   It **contributes significantly to the value enjoyed** by the customer. For example, in GPS in (a) above, the waiting time restriction was very important.

(c)   It should be **hard for a competitor to copy,** if it is technically complex, involves specialised processes, involves complex interrelationships between different people in the organisation or is hard to define.

In many cases, a company might choose to **combine competences**.

2.8   Bear in mind that **relying on a competence is no substitute for a strategy.** However, distinctive competences are an **important support for competitive positioning.**

3 ASSETS

3.1 An asset-based approach matches 'marketing assets' with customer requirements. There are four types of marketing assets (Hooley, Saunders and Piercy).

- **Customer-based** assets
- **Distribution-based** assets
- **Internal** assets
- **Alliance-based** assets

3.2 **Customer-based assets** exist in the customer's mind.

(a) Corporate **image and reputation** can be an asset or a liability, depending on the received wisdom.

(b) **A brand** is an asset. We cover branding in Chapter 9 (the value of brands) and Chapter 14 (in terms of brand building).

(c) **Market domination.** High market share is an asset not only because of economies of scale but also because of 'shelf-space' and so on.

(d) **Better products/services** as perceived by the customer.

3.3 **Distribution-based assets**

(a) **Distribution network.** This covers sites and access to customers. For many years banks regarded their branch networks as an asset, but branches are costly to maintain and Barclays in the UK has recently attracted criticism for its decision to close many of its small local branches.

(b) **Distribution control.** Control of distribution constitutes a barrier to entry to other competitors.

(c) **Pockets of strength.** Where a company cannot serve a wide market, it can build strength in specific regions or through selected distribution outlets.

(d) **Uniqueness.** A unique or hard-to-copy distribution channel is an asset. A good example is **Dell** Computers.

(e) **Lead time.** Rapid response to customer orders is an asset. This can be implemented in a just-in-time system.

(f) **Supplier network.** Further up the supply chain, key suppliers can be a marketing asset if they secure supplies of goods or services.

Marketing at Work

NXT speakers

The difference between a competence and a strategy is illustrated by NXT, a company which 'thinks it has discovered a technology that could change the world. It believes its flat-screen loudspeakers could find their way into everything ... .'

The new speakers came from military research and are based on techniques which show that materials ... radiate sound waves.'

This expertise is the basic competence. But what do they do with it?

They could choose to manufacture speakers themselves, but instead decided to follow *Dolby's* business model by providing its own technology to large companies.

(a)   NXT has 1,500 patents in 70 countries, covering the technical workings and several applications.

(b)   NXT insists its licensees work with it to adapt its ideas, and even vetoes applications it disagrees with.

(c)   NXT aims to ensure its brand name appears on products made by licensees (eg like Dolby or Ontel).

(d)   NXT seeks to develop other ideas.

NXT, unlike Dolby, will not continue in manufacturing, to avoid competing with licensees. The strategy is to develop a relationship marketing approach rather than go into manufacturing.

(*Financial Times*, 6 February 2001)

3.4   Marketing assets internal to the firm

(a)   **Low costs** give a firm the flexibility to choose low prices or to benefit from better margins.

(b)   **Information systems and market intelligence.** Customer databases are built up over time and can enable offers to be targeted.

(c)   The **existing customer base.** Satisfied customers are more likely to be repeat customers.

(d)   Other assets include **technological skills** which can support marketing activities, production **expertise, intellectual property,** partnerships and corporate culture.

3.5   Alliance based assets.
Many firms are expanding through alliances. For example, airlines have code sharing arrangements. Such assets include:

- Market access
- Management skills

- Shared technology
- Exclusivity (eg shutting out competitors)

Marketing at Work

Many airlines have alliances in which they 'share' passengers for flights on certain legs. For example a passenger flying BA might, on certain journeys, be transferred to a Qantas flight.

In theory this can be an asset to both companies, provided that customer expectations are met (ie that BA and Qantas offer similar standards of service quality).

4   THE MARKETING AUDIT   6/00

4.1   A review of marketing effectiveness is carried out in the marketing audit. This important topic is discussed in more depth in a later chapter.

5   INNOVATION AUDIT   6/01

5.1   The chief object of being innovative is to ensure organisational success in a changing world. It can also have the following advantages.

(a)   Improvements in quality of **products** and **service**

(b)   A **leaner structure** - layers of management or administration may be done away with

(c)   Prompt and imaginative **solutions to problems**

(d)   **Less formality** in structure and style, leading to better communication

(e) **Greater confidence** inside and outside the organisation in its ability to cope with change

5.2   Innovation and new product development (NPD) is therefore essential for many firms to survive and prosper. It is an increasingly important area.

Key Concept

Innovation audit: a critical assessment of the firm's innovation record, the internal obstacles to innovation and how performance can be enhanced.

5.3   A firm needs to assess how well it is able to deliver the level and type of innovation necessary to continue to meet customer needs and expectations. Drummond and Ensor (1999) identify **four key areas** for the innovation audit.

- The current **organisational climate**
- Measures of the organisation's **current performance** with regard to innovation
- Review of **policies and practices** supporting innovation and facilitating it
- The balance of **styles** of the management team

Exam Tip

The innovation audit featured in the June 2000 mini-case, in the case of a breakfast cereals producer. Improving the speed and quantity of innovation featured in 6/01.

Organisational climate

5.4   **Barriers to innovation in marketing communications**

(a) **Resistance to change**

Any new method of management thinking can experience some resistance from established managers. This resistance may be due to concern to protect the status quo, or because managers are ignorant of the new thinking. Integrating marketing communications seems so obvious that it may be overlooked or seen as a superficial approach.

(b) **Old planning systems**

Old planning systems have sometimes downgraded promotional decisions to the tactical level. Advertising expenditure is decided on the basis of what the company can afford rather than what is strategically required. Promotion is seen as a series of short-term actions rather than as a long-term investment.

(c) **Old structures/functional specialists**

Complementing traditional planning systems are traditional organisation structures. These structures freeze out new thinking on integrated marketing communications strategy. Individuals have limited specific responsibilities - just for advertising, say, or just for public relations - and this inhibits new thinking on integration.

(d) **Centralised control**

If the chief executive keeps tight control of the organisation and of its planning and is unconvinced either of the benefits of marketing communication or of integrated marketing communications then the new integrated approach will not happen.

(e) **External agencies**

External agencies have formerly been organised in specialist areas such as advertising, public relations, sales promotion and marketing research and are not able to offer a complete and integrated service.

(f) **Cost consideration**

Replacing all old promotional materials with a new integrated set has cost implications.

5.5 **Methods of overcoming these barriers**

(a) **Top management commitment**

The most effective way of overcoming these barriers to change is through the commitment of top management. The chief executive in particular needs to be convinced of the appropriateness of the new thinking and be enthusiastic about its implementation throughout the organisation.

(b) **Marketing reorganisation**

One way in which the chief executive can take advice is through a reorganisation of the marketing function in the organisation. In particular the company should seriously consider the appointment of an individual with overall responsibility for bringing about the adoption of an **integrated marketing communications** program throughout the organisation.

(c) **Training and development**

It is one thing to change attitudes. It is another thing to be in a position to know exactly what to do. The integration of a marketing communications programme is not an easy or a short term task. It needs the services of individuals trained in strategic thinking. Such individuals also need to be aware of the appropriateness of a wide range of promotional tools. The individuals chosen to implement any new programme must be enthusiasts capable of overcoming resistance to change.

(d) **Communications as a competitive advantage**

Those with responsibility for implementing an integrated marketing communications programme must do so with the objective of developing communications as a sustainable, long term competitive advantage.

(e) **Producing the results**

Nothing succeeds like success. Producing the business results as a consequence of effective marketing communications will boost confidence and gain management converts to the new thinking on an integrated approach.

Measures of performance

5.6 This may include measures such as the rate of successful **new product development** and related sales (see Chapter 14) over the past years, or **customer satisfaction ratings**.

5.7 **Customer satisfaction ratings.** An important input to innovation is the degree of customer satisfaction, both from the product itself and service levels.

(a) Customer satisfaction can be measured on a scale (eg from **highly satisfied** to **highly dissatisfied**).

(b) Customers can also be asked to identify which features of a service/product they found most useful.

(c) Firms should **actively measure** customer satisfaction, rather than simply **react to complaints**.

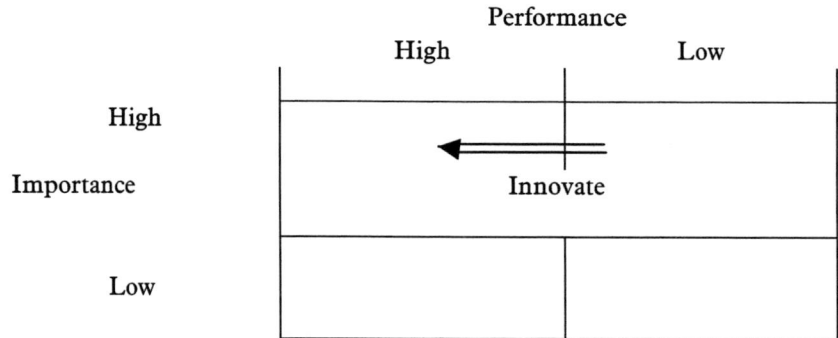

Clearly, a firm should be most concerned about matters of high importance with 'low' performance. Innovation may be necessary to ensure that high performance is achieved on matters of high importance.

5.8 **Innovation/value matrix**

(a) A similar methodology can apply to innovation and its **value** to the customer. Clearly, the best sort of innovation gives highest customer value for the lowest cost or effort. Businesses can be categorised between those that offer the normal level of innovation and market value, those that offer some improvement on the offerings of competition, and finally those that offer significant innovations and value for the customer.

(b) There is a danger that too many innovations can, in fact, confuse the customer. Recent research has encouraged some companies (such as Procter & Gamble) to reduce the variety of goods on offer.

(c) The innovation process should consider both the **technology** and **customer needs**.

(d) For example, once the limitations of the silicon chip are reached, optical computers might be invented. In some cases, instead of technical developments being used to predict future technologies, future social developments can be predicted, in order to **predict future customer needs**. The likely technologies which will satisfy these needs can then be considered.

Policies to encourage innovation

5.9 To encourage innovation the objective for management should be to create a more outward-looking organisation.

- People should be encouraged to look for new products, markets, processes and designs
- People should seek ways to improve productivity

5.10 Thomas Attwood suggests the following steps for creating an innovative culture from one which has previously existed in a cosy, unthreatening world.

- Ensure management and staff know what innovation is and how it happens
- Ensure that senior managers welcome, and are seen to welcome, changes for the better
- Stimulate and motivate management and staff to think and act innovatively
- Understand people in the organisation and their needs
- Recognise and encourage potential 'entrepreneurs'

5.11 An innovation strategy calls for a management policy of **giving encouragement** to innovative ideas.

(a) Giving **financial backing** to innovation, by spending on R & D and market research and risking capital on new ideas.

(b) Giving employees the **opportunity** to work in an environment where the exchange of ideas for innovation can take place. Management style and organisation structure can help here.

    (i) Management can actively encourage employees and customers to put forward new ideas.

    (ii) **Development teams** can be set up and an organisation built up on project team-work.

    (iii) **Quality circles** and brainstorming groups can be used to encourage creative thinking about work issues.

(c) Where appropriate, **recruitment policy** should be directed towards appointing employees with the necessary skills for doing innovative work. Employees should be trained and kept up to date.

(d) Certain managers should be **made responsible for obtaining information** from outside the organisation about innovative ideas, and for **communicating** this information throughout the organisation.

(e) **Strategic planning** should result in targets being set for innovation, and successful achievements by employees should if possible be rewarded.

The management team

5.12 The management team are key in setting the scene for innovation. The management team is also a critical influence on corporate culture. Belbin drew up a list of the characteristics of an ideal team.

Member	Role
Co-ordinator	Presides and co-ordinates; balanced, disciplined, good at working through others.
Shaper	Highly strung, dominant, extrovert, passionate about the task itself, a spur to action.
Plant	Introverted, but intellectually dominant and imaginative; source of ideas and proposals but with disadvantages of introversion.
Monitor-evaluator	Analytically (rather than creatively) intelligent; dissects ideas, spots flaws; possibly aloof, tactless - but necessary.
Resource-investigator	Popular, sociable, extrovert, relaxed; source of new contacts, but not an originator; needs to be made use of.
Implementor	Practical organiser, turning ideas into tasks; scheduling, planning and so on; trustworthy and efficient, but not excited; not a leader, but an administrator.
Team worker	Most concerned with team maintenance - supportive, understanding, diplomatic; popular but uncompetitive - contribution noticed only in absence.
Finisher	Chivvies the team to meet deadlines, attend to details; urgency and follow-through important, though not always popular.

5.13 The dynamics of the management team affects how it perceives the work environment.

> ## Key Concept
>
> The **recipe**, according to Johnson and Scholes, is an evolving set of beliefs, a way of looking at the world, and a way of interpreting information based on **management's shared experience**.

5.14 Although the **environment poses strategic questions**, it is **people who make sense of it** and devise strategies. Whilst the recipe provides cultural coherence it can impede strategic renewal. If the corporate strategy is failing, a company will:

Step 1. Place tighter **controls** over implementation (eg give tougher performance targets to sales staff); but if **this** fails ...

Step 2. Develop a new strategy (eg sell in a new market); but if this fails as well ...

Step 3. Only now will the company abandon the recipe (eg realise that the product is obsolete).

5.15 This is significant if it impacts on the management team's attitude to innovation. A management team might be unbalanced if it has too many 'ideas' people and not enough implementers able to bring projects to fruition.

Stages of an innovation audit

5.16 If asked to describe the innovation **audit**, here is a possible approach.

Step 1. **Benchmark with leading competitors**. For example, many motor firms regard the rate and speed of NPD as something they must emulate.

Step 2. **Assess reactivity: identify performance indicators** for innovation and compare with previous years (Davidson.

- **Rate of NPD**
- Number of innovations
- **Success** rate (more important than quantity)
- Percentage of revenue derived from **innovations** (3M has a target)
- **Incremental** sales resulting from innovation
- Average annual sales per new product/service
- Customer satisfaction ratings
- Staff turnover, if this affects climate of innovation

Note that if a higher percentage of revenue comes from **innovation** then **incremental** products, it looks as if innovatory products are **cannibalising** existing sales.

Step 3. Identify obstacles to innovation which typically reside in the corporate culture of structure.

Step 4. Recommend innovation objectives.

Action Programme

Bowland Carpets Ltd is a major producer of carpets within the UK. The company was taken over by its present parent company, Universal Carpet Inc, in 1995. Universal Carpet is a giant, vertically integrated carpet manufacturing and retailing business, based within the USA but with interests all over the world.

Bowland Carpets operates within the UK in various market segments, including the high value contract and industrial carpeting area - hotels and office blocks etc - and in the domestic (household) market. Within the latter the choice is reasonably wide ranging from luxury carpets down to the cheaper products. Industrial and contract carpets contribute 25% of Bowland Carpets' total annual turnover which is currently £80 million. During the early 1990s the turnover of the company was growing at 8% per annum, but since 1997 sales have dropped by 5% per annum in real terms.

Bowland Carpets has traditionally been known as a producer of high quality carpets, but at competitive prices. It has a powerful brand name, and it has been able to protect this by producing the cheaper, lower quality products under a secondary brand name. It has also maintained a good relationship with the many carpet distributors throughout the UK, particularly the mainstream retail organisations.

The recent decline in carpet sales, partly recession induced, has worried the US parent company. It has recognised that the increasing concentration within the European carpet manufacturing sector has led to aggressive competition within a low growth industry. It does not believe that overseas sales growth by Bowland Carpets is an attractive proposition as this would compete with other Universal Carpet companies. It does, however, consider that vertical integration into retailing (as already practised within the USA) is a serious option. This would give the UK company increased control over its sales and reduce its exposure to competition. The president of the parent company has asked Jeremy Smiles, managing director of Bowland Carpets, to address this issue and provide guidance to the US board of directors. Funding does not appear to be a major issue at this time as the parent company has large cash reserves on its balance sheet.

Required

(a)   To what extent do the distinctive competences of Bowland Carpets conform with the key success factors required for the proposed strategy change?

(b)   Suggest and discuss what might be the prime entry barriers prevalent in the carpet retailing sector.

(c)   In an external environmental analysis concerning the proposed strategy shift, what are likely to be the key external influences which could impact upon the Bowland Carpets' decision?

Chapter Roundup

- The **resource audit** covers technical resources, financial resources, managerial skills, the organisation and information systems.

- Resources should be used **efficiently and effectively** , and this is determined by the organisation's strategy, style, systems, structure, staff, skills and shared values.

- Resources are deployed as **competences** which support a competitive position. A distinctive competence is hard to imitate.

- An **asset-based** approach identifies the types of assets the marketer will use: customer; distribution and internal assets.

- An **innovation audit** identifies a firm's record of innovation and how it can be enhanced. It covers the organisation climate and culture, the value to the customer, the management team and the 'recipe'.

Now try illustrative question 6 at the end of the Study Text

Quick Quiz

1   What is a limiting factor? (2.3)

2   What is a distinctive competence? (2.6) How would you identify one? (2.7)

3   Identify four types of marketing asset (3.1)

4   What are some advantages of being innovative? (5.1)

5   What is an innovation audit? (5.2)

6   What are some organisational barriers to innovation? (5.4)

Action Programme Review

(a)   An organisation's **distinctive competences**, highlighted in its internal analysis, are those features, skills or processes that differentiates an organisation and is performance/products attractively from its competitors and enable it to obtain a special sphere of influence or a strong competitive position. Competences derive from experience, staff skills and the quality of co-ordination.

Key or critical success factors. Organisations need to identify the key success factors, assets and skills needed to compete successfully in a market.

(i)   **Strategic necessities** do not necessarily provide an **advantage,** because others have them, but their **absence** will cause a substantial weakness.

(ii)   **Strategic strengths** (in which the organisation excels), are superior to those of competitors and provide a base of advantage. The market analysis will also be looking at how these will change in the future and how the assets and skills of competitors can be neutralised by strategies.

Key success factors include good distribution networks, advanced office systems and up-to-date marketing intelligence.

Mismatches between competences and success factors

Most organisations doing a SWOT analysis will find a mismatch somewhere. A company may be successful at establishing a strong position during the early stages of market development, only to lose ground later when the key success factors have changed. With consumer products marketing and distribution skills are dominant during the early phases but operations and manufacturing become more crucial as the product moves into the maturity and decline stage.

Bowland's new strategy. The management at the US parent company of Bowland Carpets have come up with a new strategy in an attempt to solve the problem of the declining carpet sales in the UK, mainly in the domestic market. The contract and industrial carpet segment will not be affected radically as the distribution network generally uses direct sales.

Bowland UK's competences are the ability to:

(i)   Offer a wide range of high quality products at **competitive prices**.

(ii)   Sustain **powerful brand names**, presence in different market segments.

(iii)   Sustain **good relationships** with distributors.

Success factors for retailing

The proposed option of vertical integration into retailing will require a set of key success factors which will include some of these competences. However, there are gaps which are a cause for concern.

The key success factors for vertical integration into retail sales which have been developed in the US will not be totally transferable to the UK and the domestic company has no expertise in this field.

(i)   **Distribution.** It is not clear whether the intention is to introduce this strategy as an addition to the current distribution network or instead of it. Both of these options would affect the **relationship with distributors** that has built up over a period and could be very **damaging to sales**. To compensate for this loss, Bowland Carpets would need to have a strong **geographical** presence either in High Street positions or in out-of-town developments. This could be **very costly** in both site selection and development.

(ii)   **Expertise** in **retailing** and **distribution**. Staffing and servicing the retail outlets and training the staff in the skills required will be time-consuming and expensive. When customers buy carpets they expect a measuring, fitting and laying service as well as after-sales support. It may be that the UK company can learn from the USA but the culture of marketing household durables is different in both countries.

(iii) The **ability to provide a choice of products and services for the customer.** If there is insufficient choice, Bowland Carpets will have to find competitive manufacturers to fill the gap. This action may defeat the strategy to raise the sales in the **domestic** carpet market.

Conclusion. Bowland's distinctive competences are not appropriate to the key success factors required for retailing.

(b) **Entry barriers prevalent in the carpet retailing sector**

- The number of established carpet retailers in an already mature market
- The variety of 'own brands' available in dominant department stores
- The cost, availability and maintenance of suitable retail sites
- Suitable suppliers and reasonable terms
- The retailing skills which will need to be developed
- Marketing investments (research, staffing)
- The ability to offer a broad product line
- The level and nature of the service offered
- Brand loyalty

(c) An external environmental analysis identifies emerging trends, **opportunities** and **threats** created by the forces outside the organisation.

(i) Firms must avoid major surprises by anticipating major changes in their business circumstances.

(ii) Firms must make daily responses to changes among their customers, suppliers and workforce. Those who discover the longer-term patterns can decide whether they pose a threat or an opportunity and can gain a headstart on their competitors.

Contents of the analysis

(i) The **competitive** environment. Knowledge of the reactions of the other players in the market, both manufacturers and retailers, could be crucial to the success or otherwise of a new entrant's plan. Established businesses can adopt **retaliation strategies** to make it difficult for new companies to enter the market.

(ii) **Economic** factors include the **rate of growth** and the associated increase/decrease in **disposable income**, the **rate of inflation**, the state of the domestic housing market (house moves are often associated with new refurbishments), unemployment, interest rates and the availability of credit, taxation levels and incentives.

(iii) **Political** factors include laws on the safety of the product, town planning, selling practices adopted and the way a firm treats its employees.

(iv) The **social, demographic and cultural** environment analysis would highlight issues such as: the growth or decline in population; changes in ages when people leave home and start their own household; trends in house refurbishments; trends towards car-centred shopping in superstores and out-of-town shopping 'cities'.

(v) The **technological** environment. Consumers expect modern carpets to have properties which keep stains and insects away. The manufacturing environment is undergoing rapid changes with the growth of advanced manufacturing technology. Retail outlets are using point of sale equipment which can be used for stock control and to analyse the customer trends. **Some DIY stores allow customers access to large cutting machines to avoid expensive cutting and laying services.**

Part C
Techniques for Analysis and Strategy Development

7 *Auditing tools*

Learning Outcomes

- Understand and critically appraise a wide variety of marketing techniques, concepts and models.

Key Concepts Introduced

- Product class, form and brand
- Adoption process
- Economies of scale

- Market share
- Portfolio
- Activities; value activities

Examples of Marketing at Work

- Glaxo
- Airbus and Boeing
- Japanese firms: target costing

- Reebok, Timberland
- Unilever and Nestle
- Tesco and Amazon

1 SETTING THE SCENE

1.1 The tools discussed in this chapter can be used at many stages in the process of strategic marketing planning. None of the models can be used uncritically as we shall see.

1.2 In **international marketing,** you may find that the product is at a different stage of the life cycle in each market. However such timing differences may shrink with speedier communications and growing prosperity in some customer segments.

2 THE PRODUCT LIFE CYCLE

Specimen paper, 6/01

2.1 Many firms make a number of different products or services. Each product or service has its own financial, marketing and risk characteristics. The combination of products or services influences the profitability of the firm.

Marketing at Work

Note the difference between the life cycle of the product and its value to the company. **Copyrights** and **patents** are only granted for a restricted time period to enable the holders of intellectual property to benefit from their investment.

2.2 The profitability and sales of a product can be expected to change over time. The **product life cycle** is an attempt to recognise distinct stages in a product's sales history. Marketing managers distinguish between product class, form and brand.

Key Concept

(a) **Product class:** this is a broad category of product, such as cars, washing machines, newspapers, also referred to as the generic product.

(b) **Product form:** within a product class there are different forms that the product can take, for example five-door hatchback cars or two-seater sports cars, twin tub or front-loading automatic washing machines, national daily newspapers or weekly local papers etc.

(c) **Brand:** the particular type of the product form (for example Ford Escort, Vauxhall Astra; Financial Times, Daily Mail, Sun etc).

2.3 The product life cycle applies in differing degrees to each of the three cases. A product-class (eg cars) may have a long maturity stage, and a particular make or brand **might** have an erratic life cycle (eg Rolls Royce) or not. Product forms however tend to conform to the 'classic' life cycle pattern, commonly described by a curve as follows.

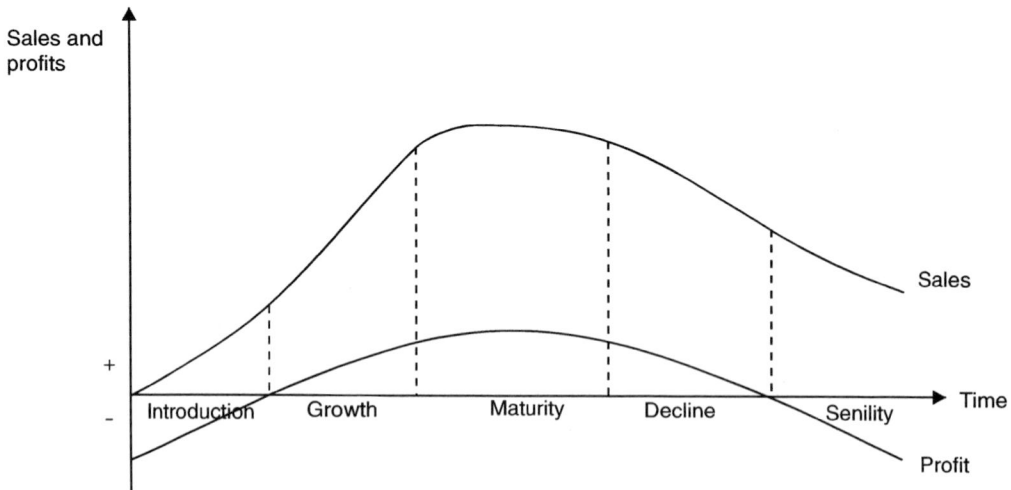

2.4 **Introduction**

- A new product takes time to find acceptance by would-be purchasers and there is a slow growth in sales. Unit costs are high because of low output and expensive sales promotion.

- There may be early teething troubles with production technology.

- The product for the time being is a loss-maker.

2.5 Growth

- If the new product gains market acceptance, sales will eventually rise more sharply and the product will start to make profits.

- Competitors are attracted. As sales and production rise, unit costs fall.

2.6 **Maturity.** The rate of sales growth slows down and the product reaches a period of maturity which is probably the longest period of a successful product's life. Most products on the market will be at the mature stage of their life. Profits are good.

2.7 **Decline.** Some products reach a stage of decline, which may be slow or fast. Eventually, sales will begin to decline so that there is over-capacity of production in the industry. Severe competition occurs, profits fall and some producers leave the market. The remaining producers seek means of prolonging the product life by modifying it and searching for new market segments. Many producers are reluctant to leave the market, although some inevitably do because of falling profits.

The relevance of the product life cycle to strategic planning

2.8 In reviewing outputs, planners should assess the following.

(a) The **stage of its life cycle** that any product has reached

(b) The **product's remaining life**, ie how much longer the product will be able to contribute significantly to profits

(c) How **urgent is the need to innovate**, to develop new and improved products in time?

Difficulties of the product life cycle concept

2.9 (a) **Recognition.** How can managers recognise where a product stands in its life cycle?

(b) **Not always true.** The traditional S-shaped curve of a product life cycle does not always occur in practice. Some products have no maturity phase, and go straight from growth to decline. Some never decline if they are marketed competitively (eg certain brands of breakfast cereals).

(c) **Changeable.** Strategic decisions can change or extend a product's life cycle.

(d) **Competition varies** in different industries. The financial markets are an example of markets where there is a tendency for competitors to copy the leader very quickly, so that competition has built up well **ahead** of demand.

Exam Tip

Problems in using and applying the PLC were covered in the specimen paper. You may have to discuss a particular stage of the plc. It's overall value was examined in June 2001.

Marketing at Work

Airbus is now, by some measures, the world's second largest manufacturer of aircraft - it is a consortium of four partners, and commands about 30% of the airliner market outside the EU. Airbus has launched a range of aircraft which compete with Boeing in every sector of the market, save the Boeing 747, and it is now going to build a 'super-jumbo', and has firm orders for it.

BPP PUBLISHING

Airbus is expected to be very profitable. 'It has a relatively modern range of aircraft in an industry with product life cycles of 25 years or more.'

The 'carrot' Airbus offers to potential partners is that it will be able to introduce new technology. Almost as a spoiler, Boeing, whose offer of a 'stretched' 747 has not got down well with purchasers, has suggested an oxygen-burning plane flying at supersonic speeds.

The PLC and cash generation

2.10 It is essential that firms plan their portfolio of products to ensure that new products are generating positive cash flow before existing 'earners' enter the decline stage.

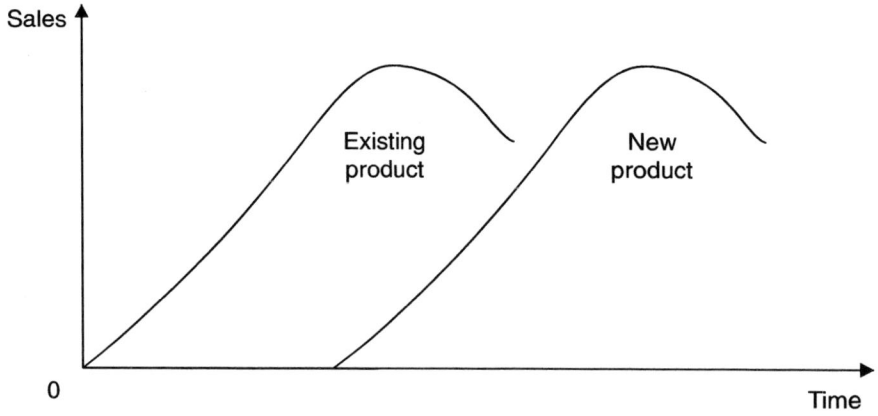

In the situation above the company is likely to experience cash flow problems.

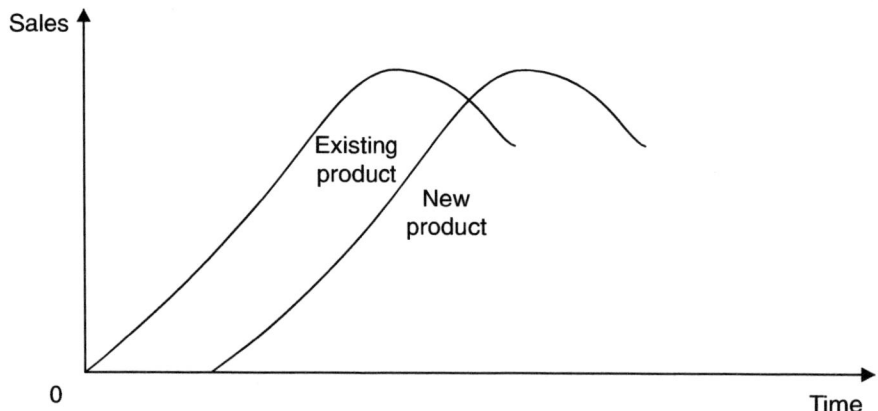

By considering the product life cycle of the existing product when planning the timing for launch of a new product cash flow problems can be avoided.

2.11 It is perhaps easy enough to accept that products have a life cycle, but it is not so easy to sort out how far through its life a product is, and what its expected future life might be.

(a) There ought to be a **regular review** of existing products, as a part of marketing management responsibilities.

(b) **Sources of PLC predictions**

- An analysis of past sales and profit trends
- The history of other products
- Market research
- If possible, an analysis of competitors
- A review of technological developments

(c) The future of each product should be estimated in terms of both sales revenue and profits.

2.12 Decisions for each product

- **Continue selling**, with no foreseeable intention yet of stopping production
- **Prolong the product's life**, perhaps by adjusting the mix or finding new customers
- **Stop producing** the product

Possible implications of each stage are on the following page.

The product life cycle and the marketing orientation

2.13 Does the PLC promote a 'product orientated' focus when in fact a 'market orientated' focus is necessary? Ansoff follows Levitt's thinking in extending the PLC concept to encompass the **demand/technology life cycle** (DLC), and the technology life cycle (TLC). The diagram below illustrates how a **demand life cycle** is made up of a number of **technology life cycles** which in turn are composed of PLCs.

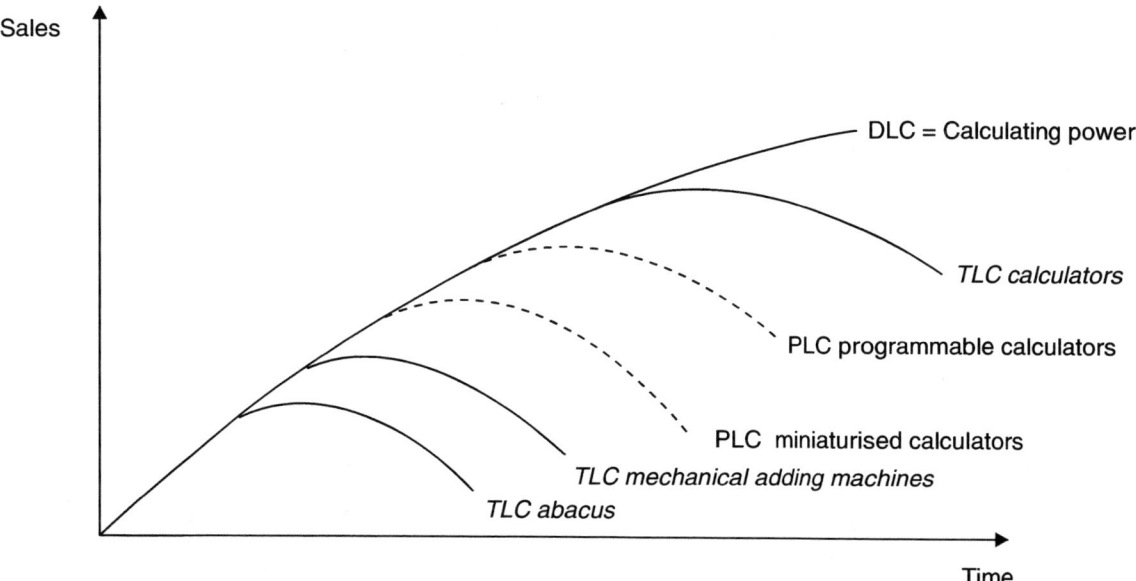

2.14 For example, 'calculating power' represents a human demand that is probably in the growth stage of the DLC. This has been composed of a number of TLCs - finger counting, abacuses, slide rules, adding machines, calculators, computers. Each new technology usually satisfies the **generic need** in a **superior way**.

2.15 The TLC indicates that for many products, death will eventually transpire through **technology** and **competitive innovation**.

Marketing at Work

Going back to the Airbus example, Airbus assumed continued demand for long-haul air travel and believes that this is best satisfied by large planes flying to major destination hubs. Much of this is deemed accounted for by the growth in long-haul tourism.

		Phase		
	Introduction	*Growth*	*Maturity*	*Decline*
1 *Products*	Initially, poor quality. Product design and development are a key to success. No standard product and frequent design changes (eg microcomputers in the early 1980s).	Competitors' products have marked quality differences and technical differences. Quality improves. Product reliability may be important.	Products become more standardised and differences between competing products less distinct.	Products even less differentiated. Quality becomes more variable.
2 *Customers*	Initial customers willing to pay high prices. Customers need to be convinced about buying.	Customers increase in number.	Mass market. Market saturation. Repeat-buying of products becomes significant. Brand image also important.	Customers are 'sophisticated' buyers of a product they understand well.
3 *Promotion*	High advertising and sales promotion costs.	High advertising costs still, but as a % of sales, costs are falling.	Markets become segmented. Segmentation and extending the maturity phase of the life cycle can be key strategies.	Less money spent on advertising and sales promotion.
4 *Competition*	Few or no competitors.	More competitors enter the market. Barriers to entry can be important.	Competition at its keenest: on prices, branding, servicing customers, packaging etc.	Competitors gradually exit from the market. Exit barriers can be important.
5 *Prices and costs*	High prices but losses due to high fixed costs.	High prices. High contribution margins, and increasing profit margins. High P/E ratios for quoted companies in the growth market.	Falling prices but good profit margins due to high sales volume. Higher prices in some market segments.	Still low prices but falling profits as sales volume falls, since total contribution falls towards the level of fixed costs. Some increase in prices may occur in late decline stage.
6 *Manufacturing*	Over-capacity. High production costs.	Under-capacity. Move towards mass production and less reliance on skilled labour.	Optimum capacity. Low labour skills.	Over-capacity because mass production techniques are still used.
7 *Distribution*	Few distribution channels.	Distribution channels flourish and getting adequate distribution channels is a key to marketing success.	Distribution channels fully developed, but less successful channels might be cut.	Distribution channels dwindling.

Action Programme 1

Try to apply some of your knowledge of the PLC consumer electronics equipment in recent years.

2.16 The product life cycle concept probably has more value as a **control tool** than as a method of **forecasting** a product's life. Control can be applied to speeding up the growth phase, extending the maturity phase and recognising when to cease making a product altogether.

Exam Tip

Exam questions are likely to concentrate on the marketing strategies relevant to **individual** stages of the life cycle, as each stage involves different strategic choices. Each stage involves configuring the marketing mix in a particular way, to meet the firm's objectives.

The examiner is unlikely to want mere descriptions of the model. In the past exam questions have focused on **specific** stages of the life cycle and their implications for marketing strategy.

(a) **Introduction and launch**

    (i) Does the firm lead in NPD or copy competitors?

    (ii) Penetration or skimming: should the firm seek to get as much market share as early as possible or should it seek to recoup as much profit as possible?

(b) **Growth stage**

    (i) What competitive strategy is most appropriate in the market place? Will the firm have to differentiate its offer?

    (ii) How long should the firm continue the intense marketing support needed at this stage to build a market?

(c) **Maturity**. Higher profits can be achieved by segmenting the market and modifying the product. Market share objectives and distribution are strategically important. Should you rejuvenate a mature product or finish it off? If so, what strategies can you use for rejuvenation: product enhancement, segmentation and so on?

(d) **Decline** is probably the hardest to negotiate.

    (i) Manage decline. Sales will be falling, so costs should be cut to maintain dealer loyalty. Decline needs to be managed slowly and smoothly, so that the firm can redirect its resources elsewhere.

    (ii) Rejuvenation involves 'finding new needs or uses for the product and fitting the product to them to produce new sales.' This involves modifying the mix, producing new versions of the product or positioning the product for another group. For example Campbell's condensed soups have been additionally positioned as ingredients for cooking sauces.

(e) As a general rule, any answers about the PLC should cover its drawbacks as well as its merits.

Control

2.17 The management of a product should fit its prevailing life cycle stage, as each stage has different financial characteristics.

    (a) **Development**. Money will be spent on market research and product development. Cash flows are negative and there is a high business risk.

    (b) **Launches** require expensive promotion campaigns.

    (c) **Growth**. The market grows, as does the demand for the product. Risks are competitor action.

(i)   The market price mix might turn out to be inappropriate for the product (eg the price is set too high).

(ii)   Competitors will enter, thereby reducing the profits that can be earned.

(d) **Maturity.** Few new competitors will enter the market. Risk is low, so the concentration is on profit.

2.18   At all stages, the **risk and return profile** of the product can be managed.

(a)   Appropriate product-market strategies, such as innovation, new advertising, changing the product, finding new markets

(b)   Raising entry barriers.

Increased marketing expenditure may have the effect of reducing risk, commensurate with the decreased return.

2.19   **Information and financial control needs of different stages of the product life cycle.**

	Launch	Growth	Maturity	Decline
Characteristics	High business risk. Negative net cash flow. DCF evaluation for overall investment	High business risk. Neutral net cash flow	Medium business risk. Positive cash flow	Low risk. Neutral-positive cash flow
Critical success factors	Time to launch	Market share growth. Sustaining competitive advantage	Contribution per unit of scarce resource. Customer retention.	Timely exit
Information needs	Market research into size and demand	Market growth, share. Diminishing returns. Competitor marketing strategies	Comparative competitor costs. Limiting factors	Rate of decline; best time to leave; reliable sale values of assets
Financial and other controls	Strategic 'milestones'. Physical evaluation. Mainly non-financial measures owing to volatility (eg rate of take up by consumers)	Discounted cash flow Market share Marketing objectives	ROI Profit margin Maintaining market share	Free cash flow (for investment elsewhere)

3   NEW PRODUCTS AND THE DIFFUSION PROCESS

3.1   An important issue to planners is how quickly a new product will be adopted by the market, in other words what sort of time scale is expected along the horizontal axis of the PLC.

3.2   **Factors influencing the speed at which new ideas and product innovations will spread or be diffused through the marketplace**

(a)   The **complexity** of the new product

(b)   The **relative advantages** it offers

(c) The degree to which the innovation fits into **existing patterns** of behaviour/needs

(d) The **ability to try** the new product, samples, test drives or low value purchases entailing little risk

(e) The ease with which the product's benefits can be **communicated** to the potential customer

3.3 The market segments attitude to change, accessibility to channels of communication and the time frame involved in the **adoption process** are all critical factors in assessing the diffusion process.

> ### Key Concept
>
> The **adoption process**, sometimes referred to as the decision-making process refers to the stages a customer goes through before making a purchase decision, or a decision not to purchase or repurchase. The five stages identifiable in most models of this process are: awareness → interest → evaluation → trial → adoption. There can be a considerable time lag between awareness and adoption.

3.4 In *Consumer Behaviour* Schiffmann and Kanuk offer a modified analysis of Everett Rogers' earlier *Sequence and Proportion of Adopter Categories*.

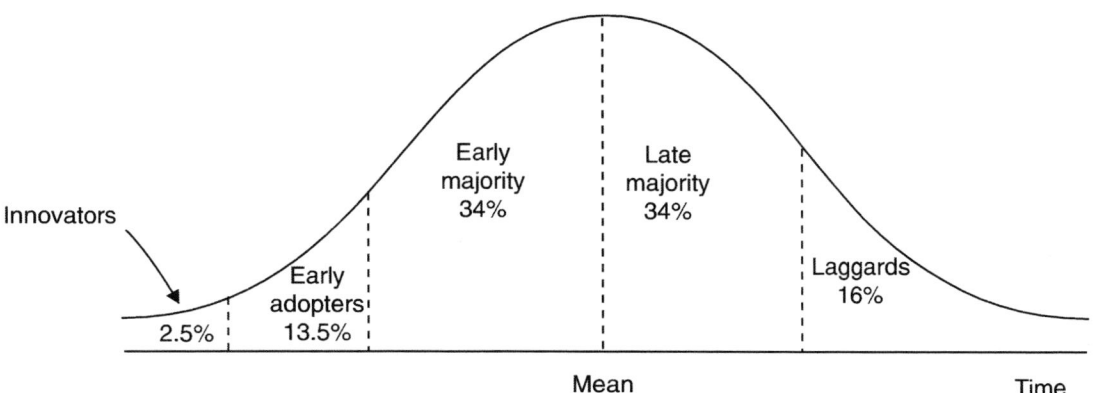

3.5 The characteristics of consumers in these adopter categories varies and so the marketing planner wishing to get the best from a new product, encourage its diffusion and avoid wasting budget, will focus market attention on these different segments, as the product passes through the life cycle.

(a) **Innovators**   These are eager to try new ideas and products and often in close contact with change agents like sales staff and other opinion leaders. Often perceived to be risk takers, prepared to try and willing to pay often premium prices for 'being the first'.

(b) **Early adopters**   They too are willing to change and are often opinion leaders themselves. They are likely to have greater exposure to the mass media than later adopters and certainly more willing to change. They are likely to seek out information actively about new products in specialist journals etc.

(c) **Early majority**   A more conservative segment who tend to purchase a new product just ahead of the average time, but who will have given it some thought before the purchase.

(d) **Late majority**   These are slower than the average and sceptical about new products. They are very cautious purchasers likely to need some persuading.

(e) **Laggards**   These are the smaller group of traditionalists actually unwilling to change. They may actually be forced to change only when their previous choice is obsolete and no longer available.

3.6   **Diffusion and marketing strategy.** Marketers usually want to ensure a rapid diffusion or rate of adoption for a new product. This allows them to gain a large share of the market prior to competitors responding.

(a) A **penetration strategy** associated with low introductory pricing and promotions designed to facilitate trial are associated with such a strategy.

(b) However in some markets, particularly where R & D cost has been high, where the product involves 'new' technology or where it is protected from competition perhaps by patent, a **skimming** policy may be adopted. Here price is high initially usually representing very high unit profits and sales can be increased in steps with price reductions, in line with available capacity or competitors' responses.

Speed of diffusion

3.7   Needless to say, different products get adopted at different speeds. The marketer will want rapid acceptance, to forestall competition. Here is a list of issues which influence the speed of market penetration.

Issue	Comment
Network externalities	The product is only of value if other people have it – such as telephones, the internet
Common standards	CD players operate to a common standard owned by Phillips. For DVD (the successor to CDs), acceptance will be delayed because of disputes over standards. Mobile phones operate to two standards globally. Digital TV in the UK is delivered by competing intermediaries
Complementary products	Computer games consoles need computer games to play on them
Switching costs	It will cost a lot to change to certain products
Experimentation	For groceries, it is easy to try something new, as the expense is small. Film companies introduce 'trailers' as part of a marketing campaign to give potential audiences a feel for the film.

4   EXPERIENCE CURVES, MARKET SHARE AND PIMS

Economies of scale

4.1   There is a relationship between the quantity of products produced and the cost per unit.

Key Concept

Economy of scale. The more you produce, the cheaper each successive unit will be (up to a certain amount).

4.2 EXAMPLE

Let us take an example of a publisher contracting with a printer to print Study Texts. (Note: the prices below are notional only. Printers' charges vary according to paper prices, paper quality, turnaround times, volume of work and so on.)

Quantity printed	Cost	Cost per book
100	£500	£5.00
1,000	£2,500	£2.50
2,000	£4,720	£2.36

The reason for the difference is that there are the same **fixed costs** incurred (for example, in setting up the press) no matter how many or few books you print.

4.3 This shows that the quantity produced affects the cost per unit. From the above example, if customers were unwilling to pay more than £3 for their books, and the publishers wanted to make £0.50p profit on top of print cost, then the publisher would have to sell **at least** 1,000 books.

4.4 How is this relevant to market share? It shows that high market share can, by spreading fixed costs over many units of production, be more profitable. Higher sales volumes can mean lower costs per unit, hence higher profits. The Boston Consulting Group estimated that as production volume doubles, cost per unit falls by up to 20%. **High market share therefore gives cost advantages.**

Experience curves

4.5 The experience curve takes this further. The more units **over time** that a firm produces, the cheaper will each unit be to produce. Why?

(a) **Economies of scale**, as identified above.

(b) **Learning**: the more people do a task, the more efficient they become (up to a point), and it takes them less time.

(c) **Technological** improvements: firms can improve their production operations and make better use of equipment.

(d) **Simplifying products can cut costs**. For example, car manufacturers are cutting costs by ensuring that the same components can be used in different marques.

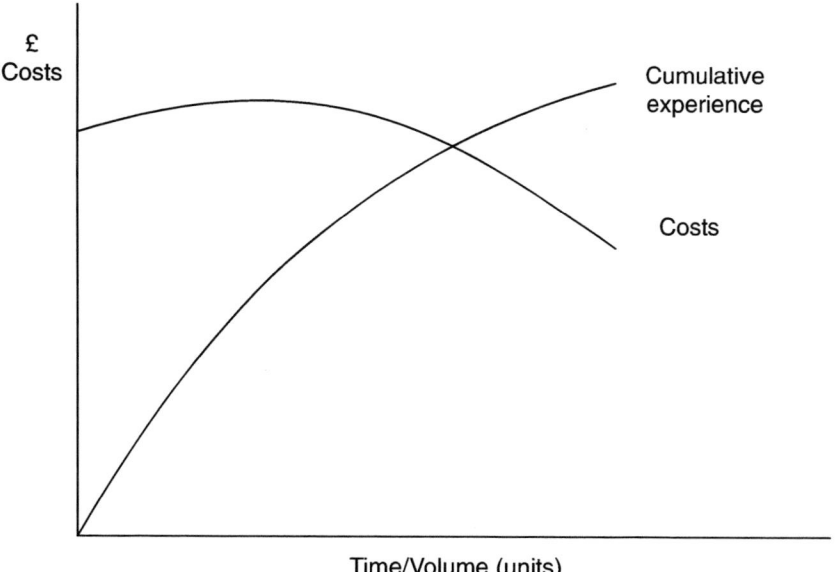

4.6 Working with the experience curve

(a) The experience curve is not automatic.

(b) Technological changes can render a particular process obsolete.

(c) Low costs do not have to mean lower prices, although many firms have used the experience curve to buy market share.

(d) Marketing people should focus on the customer not on the process, and so the experience curve should not detract from **customer focus**.

Marketing at Work

Japanese firms pioneered target costing. They identified a customer need and specified a product to satisfy that need.

The production department and its accountants then worked out:

- How the product could be built
- The volume needed to reach the market price
- How quickly costs could be driven down.

Market share and PIMS   6/01

Key Concept

Market share is 'one entity's sales of a product or service in a specified market expressed as a percentage of total sales by all entities offering that product or service'. Thus, a company may have a 30% share of a total market, meaning that 30% of all sales in the market are made by that company.

4.7 **Relative market share** as the share of the market relative to that of the manufacturer's largest competitor.

(a) An evaluation of market shares helps to identify **who the true competitor really is**, and avoids trying to outdo the wrong competitor.

(b) The approach serves as a basis for marketing strategy, with a firm seeking as a target to build up an x% share of a particular market.

Profit Impact of Market Strategies (PIMS)

4.8 **PIMS analysis** attempts to establish the profitability (ie return on capital) of various marketing strategies, and identifies a link between the size of **return on capital** and **market share** so that companies in a strong competitive position in the markets for their base products would be earning high returns.

4.9 In general, profits increase in line with market share.

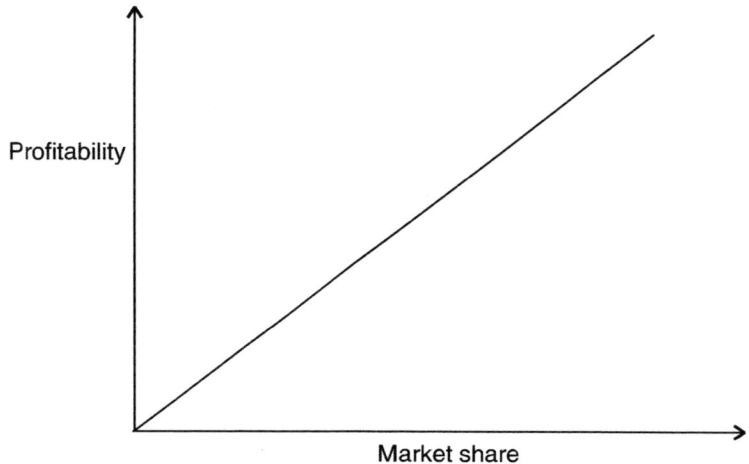

Three possible reasons were put forward for this correlation.

(a) **Economies of scale** and experience curve effects enable a market leader to produce at lower unit costs than competitors, and so make bigger profits. A company with the highest market share, especially if this company is also the innovator with the longest experience, will enjoy a considerable competitive advantage. This is referred to as the experience curve.

(b) **Bargaining power**. A strong position in the market gives a firm greater strength in its dealings with both buyers and suppliers.

(c) **Quality of management**. Market leaders often seem to be run by managers of a high calibre.

4.10 The linear relationship above does not always hold true. Some industries display a V-shaped relationship.

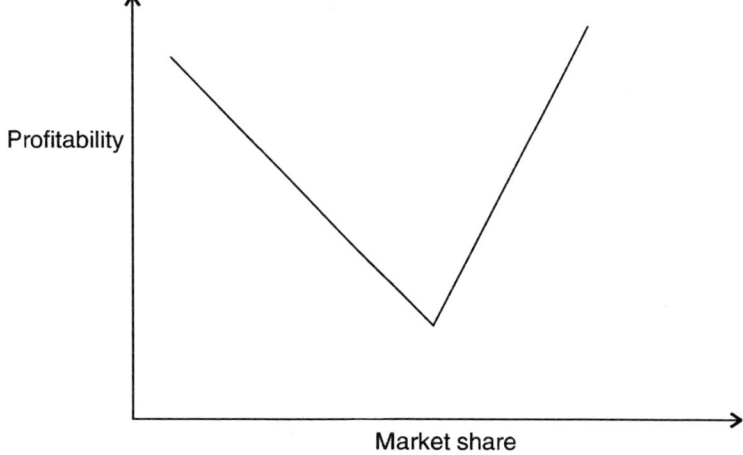

Profitability falls until a certain critical market share is reached, which makes it more likely that there will be a polarisation between large firms and small players. SME's (small and medium sized enterprises) find it very difficult to maintain their position.

4.11 PIMS researchers would argue that since profitability is a key objective, and since profitability depends on market share, companies should formulate market share objectives. There are four broad groups of market share strategies.

- Building
- Holding
- Harvesting
- Withdrawal

Low market share

4.12 Low market share does not **inevitably** mean poor returns. If this were so, small businesses would always make low returns, and this is simply not true. However, certain **conditions must exist for a low market share to be compatible with high returns.**

(a) **Niche marketing.** Create new market segments which are a small but profitable proportion of the total market.

(b) **Premium price strategy.** Emphasising product quality, and charging higher prices. (Efficient use would have to be made of R & D in manufacturing industries.)

(c) Strong management.

(d) When there is a **large, stable market,** where product innovations and developments are uncommon, and where **repeat-buying by customers is frequent,** a company can earn good profits with only a low market share.

Problems with PIMS

4.13 (a) **Identifying each market segment properly.** An up-market producer is in a different market segment to a down-market cheap-goods producer, and it would be wrong to classify them as competitors in the same market. In Porter's terminology, they may not exist in the same **strategic group**

(b) **Measuring the actual size of the market,** and so the company's own market share in proportional terms.

(c) **Establishing what returns** are available from a particular market share.

It has also been argued that **PIMS analysis is more relevant to industrial goods markets** than to consumer goods markets, where the correlation between high market share and high returns is not as strong.

Exam Tip

An old syllabus question asked why market share is important and when it might not be appropriate as an objective. Consider for example market leaders with near monopolies. Increasing market share and driving out competitors would lead to government action and regulation. Furthermore, the cost of increasing market share might exceed its value in profit terms.

PIMS was examined in 6/01. You were asked to say why assuming a clear correlation between market share and profitability is dangerous and simplistic.

Strategic implications of market share

4.14 Implications of market share should be considered in product-market development planning.

(a) **How easy will it be to build up a market share?** This will depend on the rate of sales growth in the market. Obviously, it is easier to penetrate a growing market than a static one.

(b) **What share of the market will be needed to earn the target profit and return on capital?** Depending on costs, sales prices and total sales volume in the market, the size of market share needed to make a profit will vary.

Marketing at Work

Reebok

Reebok in 1986 was a best-selling trainer brand but competition from *Nike* and *Adidas* saw its market share plummet and its share price fall from over $50 in 1997 to $7 at the start of 2001.

In 1990 in the UK Reebok has a 16% share, Nike 15%, Adidas 9%. Reebok has not maintained this position.

Reebok is seeking to bounce back as a 'sports brand that operates' in a fashion market, and has designed advertising to appeal to 16-24 year olds.

Other 'outdoor' brands, such as Timberland and Caterpillar, have also eaten away Reebok's market share. In 2000, Timberland had 2.9% of the US trainer market (2.1% in 1999). Fashion brands such as Hermes and DKNY have also entered the market.

---

5 PORTFOLIO ANALYSIS   Specimen paper

5.1   **Portfolio planning** analyses the current position of an organisation's products on SBUs in their markets, and the state of growth or decline in each of those markets. Several matrices have been developed over the years to analyse market share, market growth and market position.

> ### Key Concept
>
> **Portfolio:** A collection of products/SBUs reporting to one entity. Each product SBU can be separately identified for decision-making and performance measurement.

Market share, market growth and cash generation: the Boston classification

5.2   The **Boston Consulting Group** (BCG) developed a matrix, based on empirical research, which classifies a company's products in terms of potential cash generation and cash expenditure requirements. This is related to **market share relative to competitors**.

5.3   You should also note that BCG analysis can be applied to:

- Individual products
- Whole strategic business units (SBUs)

5.4   EXAMPLE

To illustrate how to evaluate a portfolio a simulated company example will be provided. An industrial equipment company has five products with the following sales and market characteristics.

Product	Sales £m	£m sales Top 3 firms			Market growth rate %	Relative share
A	0.5	0.7	0.7	0.5★	15%	0.71
B	1.6	1.6	1.6★	1.0	18%	1.0
C	1.8	1.8★	1.2	1.0	7%	1.5
D	3.2	3.2★	0.8	0.7	4%	4.0
E	0.5	2.5	1.8	1.7	4%	0.2

★ Company sales within the market

This information can then be plotted on to a matrix. The circles indicate the contribution the product makes to overall turnover. The centre of circles indicates their position on the matrix:

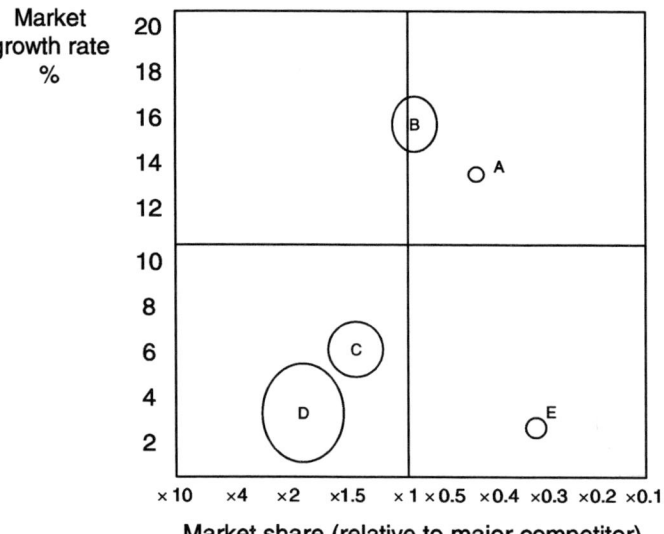

5.5 This growth/share matrix for the classification of products into cash cows, cash dogs, stars and question marks is known as the **Boston classification** (or the **Boston Matrix**).

(a) **Stars** are products with a high share of a high growth market. In the short term, these require capital expenditure in excess of the cash they generate, in order to maintain their market position, but promise high returns in the future.

(b) In due course, stars will become **cash cows**, with a high share of a low-growth market. Cash cows need very little capital expenditure and generate high levels of cash income. Cash cows generate high cash returns, which can be used to finance the stars.

(c) **Question marks** are products in a high-growth market, but where they have a low market share. Do the products justify considerable capital expenditure in the hope of increasing their market share, or should they be allowed to 'die' quietly as they are squeezed out of the expanding market by rival products? Because considerable expenditure would be needed to turn a question mark into a star by building up market share, question marks will usually be poor cash generators and show a negative cash flow.

(d) **Dogs** are products with a low share of a low growth market. They may be ex-cash cows that have now fallen on hard times. Dogs should be allowed to die, or should be killed off. Although they will show only a modest net cash outflow, or even a modest net cash inflow, they are 'cash traps' which tie up funds and provide a poor return on investment, and not enough to achieve the organisation's target rate of return.

There are also **infants** (ie products in an early stage of development), **warhorses** (ie products that have been cash cows in the past, and are still making good sales and earning good profits even now) and even **cash dogs,** which are dogs still generating cash.

5.6 The evaluation and resulting strategic considerations for the company in the diagram above paragraph 5.5 are these.

(a) There are two cash cows, thus the company should be in a cash-positive state.

(b) New products will be required to follow on from A.

(c) A is doing well (15%) but needs to gain market share to move from position 3 in the market - continued funding is essential. Similar for B.

(d) C is a market leader in a maturing market - strategy of consolidation is required.

(e) D is the major product which dominates its market; cash funds should be generated from this product.

(f) E is very small. Is it profitable? Funding to maintain the position or selling off are appropriate strategies.

Action Programme 2

The marketing manager of Juicy Drinks Ltd has invited you in for a chat. Juicy Drinks Ltd provides fruit juices to a number of supermarket chains, which sell them under their own label. 'We've got a large number of products, of course. Our freshly squeezed orange juice is doing fine - it sells in huge quantities. Although margins are low, we have sufficient economies of scale to do very nicely in this market. We've got advanced production and bottling equipment and long-term contracts with some major growers. No problems there. We also sell freshly squeezed pomegranate juice: customers loved it in the tests, but producing the stuff at the right price is a major hassle: all the seeds get in the way. We hope it will be a winner, once we get the production right and start converting customers to it. After all the market for exotic fruit juices generally is expanding fast.'

What sort of products, according to the Boston classification, are described here?

5.7 The **product life cycle** concept can be added to a market share/market growth classification of products, as follows.

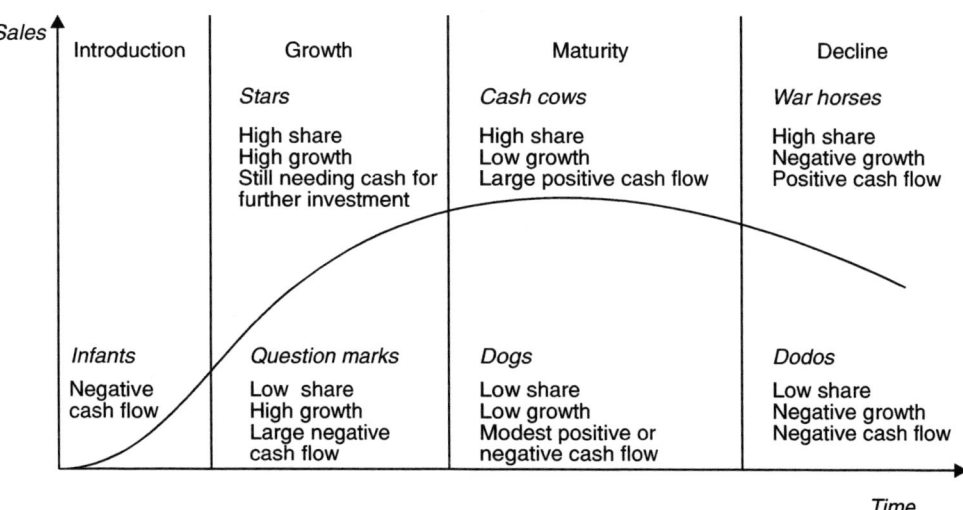

The BCG portfolio analysis is useful because it provides a framework for planners to consider and forecast potential market growth and to evaluate the competitive dimension through an evaluation of market share and the likely changes in cash flow.

5.8 Shortcomings of BCG

(a) **Factors besides market share and sales growth affect cash flow.**

(b) Many firms still use **return on investment when assessing the attractiveness of a business opportunity,** despite the opportunity it gives for accounting manipulation and the fact that it ignores the time value of money.

(c) The model provides **no real insight into how to compare one opportunity with another** when considering which opportunity should be allocated investment resources, eg how does a star compare with a question mark?

(d) As we have seen **in the right conditions a firm can profit from a low share of a low-growth market.**

(e) The techniques do not tell you how to generate new businesses.

(f) A tendency to invest too heavily in dogs.

(g) An over-concentration on turning question marks into stars, as opposed to managing the cash cows effectively. In other words, cash cows do not get the money they need.

(h) Expenditure needed to maintain cash cows is not provided.

Competitiveness of products

5.9 As a result of some of these weaknesses in the BCG model variations have evolved. Johnson and Scholes cite **General Electric's Business Screen**

(a) This compares **market attractiveness** with **business strength.**

   (i) **Determinants of industry/market attractiveness**

   - Market factors (eg size, growth)
   - Competitors
   - Investment factors
   - Technological change
   - Other PEST factors

   (ii) **Determinants of business strength**

   - Product quality
   - Distribution
   - Brand reputation
   - Production capacity
   - Management skill

   (iii) These factors can then be scored and weighted. For example, a market with a low size and intense competition based on price might receive a lower weighting than a market with high growth and limited competition. The **GE matrix** is based on Return on Capital Employed.

   (iv) Business strengths and market attractiveness are thus plotted on a grid, and a strategy appropriate to each can be considered.

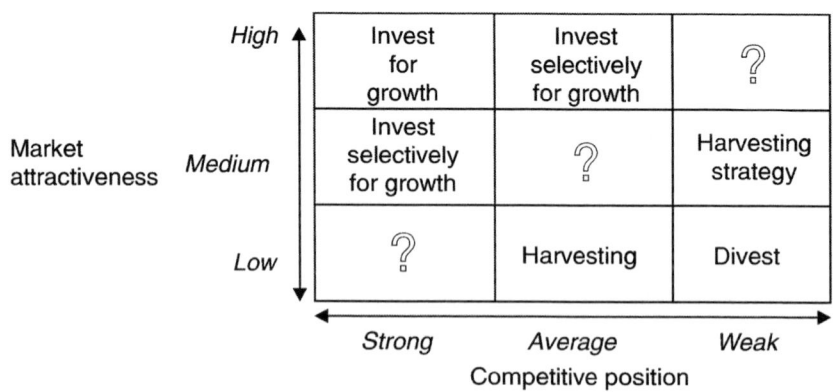

(b) Each 'cell' requires a different management approach.

   (i) Each SBU can be plotted in one of the cells and the appropriate management approach adopted.

   (ii) It is possible that SBUs might move around the matrix. Changes in PEST factors may change an industry/market's attractiveness.

   (iii) The matrix ignores the possibility of **knowledge generation** and **competence** sharing between SBUs. Applications in one SBU may be of value elsewhere.

Shell Directional Policy Matrix

5.10 Another example is the Shell Directional Policy Matrix (Shell) which comprises:

- Prospects for sector profitability
- The enterprise's competitive capabilities

Prospects for sector profitability

Enterprise's competitive capabilities		Unattractive	Average	Attractive
	Weak	Disinvest	Phased withdrawal	Double or quit
	Average	Phased withdrawal	Custodial Growth	Try harder
	Strong	Cash generation	Growth Leader	Leader

5.11 **Contrasts between BCG and 'policy matrices'**

(a) The BCG looks at individual products and markets in a portfolio

(b) The other matrices look at a company's competences in market sectors, without reference to individual products.

The advantages and disadvantages of portfolio planning

5.12 Portfolio planning provides an excellent framework for analysis, and a starting point for developing a product-market mix strategy.

5.13 **Drawbacks**

(a) Portfolio models are simple: they do not reflect the uncertainties of decision-making.

(b) BCG analysis, in particular, does not really take risk into account.

(c) They ignore opportunities for creative segmentation or identifying new niches.

(d) They assume a market is 'given' rather than something that can be created and nurtured. After all, markets may be 'unattractive' because customer needs have not been analysed sufficiently.

(e) A lot of complicated analysis is needed to come up with relevant data. How do you decide whether an industry is attractive or not?

Exam Tip

The weakness of the BCG model is that it only covers products and markets.

Marketing at Work

The *Pearson Group*

This shows how the portfolio approach can be applied to 'businesses' as much as products. Pearson has four main divisions.

- Pearson Education is an educational publisher (with a variety of imprints – or sub brands) and it provides on-line learning. It also includes FT knowledge, which has invested heavily in the Internet.

  In 1999 Pearson Education made a profit of £265m, but FT knowledge a loss of £8m.

- Penguin group. The Penguin brand, chiefly known for books has sub brands (eg rough guides). It is a book publisher. The Penguin Classics brand extends to CDs (and may go on-line so that 'Penguin Classic readers' become a virtual community linked by the Internet).

- Pearson Television produces programmes.

- Financial Times is a business newspaper, building a pan-European network of other business papers.

Cutting across these businesses are Pearson's internet activities. In 1999, for example, the Financial Times division's profits of £150m were offset in part by a loss of £36m on internet enterprises, a clear example of an 'old economy' business supporting a 'new economy' business.

---

6 THE VALUE CHAIN

12/99, 6/00

Exam Tip

The value chain is a key model.

(a) In June 2000 (question 2 of the exam), you had to describe the value chain and how it would be used.

(b) In the December 1999 mini-case, you had to apply the value chain to a low-cost airline.

We recommend you look at these two questions, both reproduced in the BPP Practice & Revision Kit: they also provide a **useful contrast** between **describing a theory** and **applying it**: application is a key exam skill.

6.1 The **value chain** model of corporate activities, developed by Michael Porter, offers a bird's eye view of the firm and what it does. Competitive advantage, says Porter, arises out of the way in which firms organise and perform **activities**. (In other words, this describes **how** an organisation uses its inputs and transforms them into the outputs that customers pay for.)

Activities

Key Concept

Activities are the means by which a firm creates value in its products. (They are sometimes referred to as **value activities**.)

6.2 Activities incur costs, and, in combination with other activities, provide a product or service which earns revenue. 'Firms create value for their buyers by performing these activities.'

6.3 EXAMPLE

Let us explain this point by using the example of a **restaurant**. A restaurant's activities can be divided into buying food, cooking it, and serving it (to customers). There is no reason, in theory, why the customers should not do all these things themselves, at home. The customer however, is not only prepared to **pay for someone else** to do all this but also **pays more than the cost of** the resources (food, wages etc). The ultimate value a firm creates is measured by the amount customers are willing to pay for its products or services above the

cost of carrying out value activities. A firm is profitable if the realised value to customers exceeds the collective cost of performing the activities.

(a) Customers **'purchase' value,** which they measure by comparing a firm's products and services with similar offerings by competitors.

(b) The business **'creates' value** by carrying out its activities either more efficiently than other businesses, or combine them in such a way as to provide a unique product or service.

Action Programme 3

Outline different ways in which the restaurant can 'create' value.

6.4 Porter (in *Competitive Advantage*) grouped the various activities of an organisation into a **value chain.** Here is a diagram.

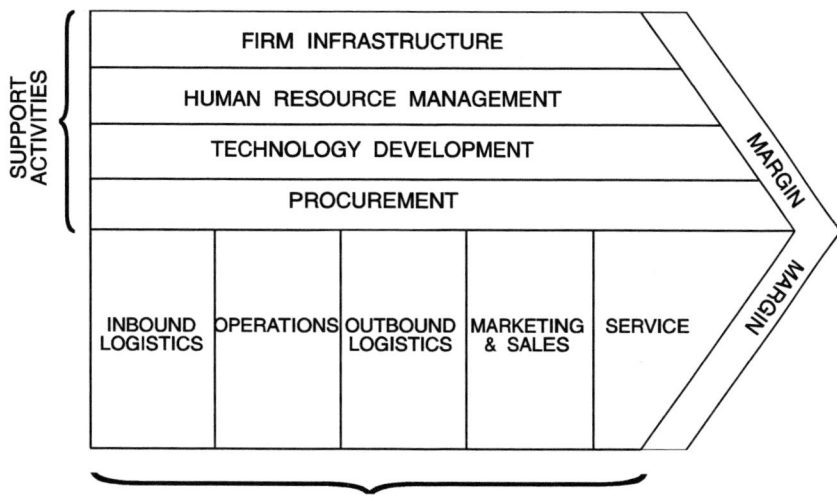

The **margin** is the excess the customer is prepared to **pay** over the **cost** to the firm of obtaining resource inputs and providing value activities.

6.5 **Primary activities** are directly related to production, sales, marketing, delivery and service.

Activity	Comment
Inbound logistics	Receiving, handling and storing inputs to the production system (ie warehousing, transport, stock control etc).
Operations	Convert resource inputs into a final product. Resource inputs are not only materials. 'People' are a 'resource' especially in service industries.
Outbound logistics	Storing the product and its distribution to customers: packaging, warehousing, testing etc.
Marketing and sales	Informing customers about the product, persuading them to buy it, and enabling them to do so: advertising, promotion etc.
After sales service	Installing products, repairing them, upgrading them, providing spare parts and so forth.

6.6 **Support activities** provide purchased inputs, human resources, technology and infrastructural functions to support the primary activities.

Activity	Comment
Procurement	Acquire the resource inputs to the primary activities (eg purchase of materials, subcomponents equipment).
Technology development	Product design, improving processes and/or resource utilisation.
Human resource management	Recruiting, training, developing and rewarding people.
Management planning	Planning, finance, quality control: Porter believes they are crucially important to an organisation's strategic capability in all primary activities.

6.7   **Linkages** connect the activities of the value chain.

   (a)   **Activities in the value chain affect one another.** For example, more costly product design or better quality production might reduce the need for after-sales service.

   (b)   **Linkages require co-ordination.** For example, just-in-time requires smooth functioning of operations, outbound logistics and service activities such as installation.

Value system

6.8   Activities that add value do not stop at the organisation's **boundaries**. For example, when a restaurant serves a meal, the quality of the ingredients - although they are chosen by the cook - is determined by the grower. The grower has added value, and the grower's success in growing produce of good quality is as important to the customer's ultimate satisfaction as the skills of the chef. A firm's value chain is connected to what Porter calls a **value system**.

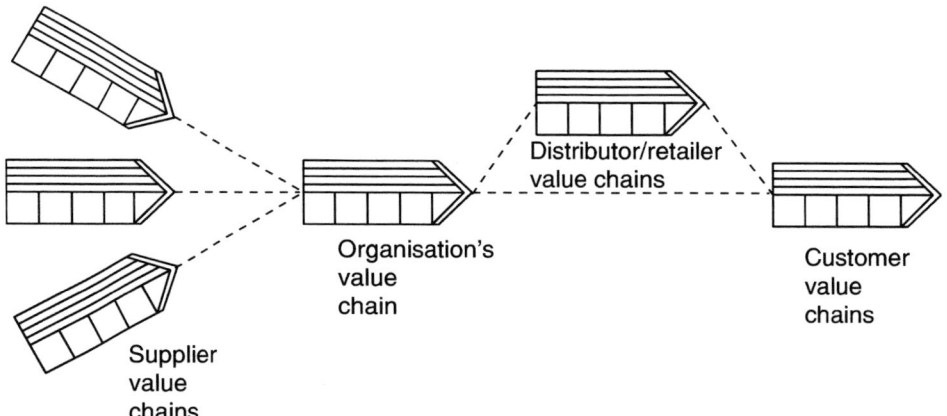

6.9   **Using the value chain.** A firm can secure competitive advantage by:

   •   Inventing new or better ways to do activities
   •   Combining activities in new or better ways
   •   Managing the linkages in its own value chain
   •   Managing the linkages in the value system

Action Programme 4

Sana Sounds is a small record company. Representatives from Sana Sounds scour music clubs for new bands to promote. Once a band has signed a contract (with Sana Sounds) it makes a recording. The recording process is subcontracted to one of a number of recording studio firms which Sana Sounds uses regularly. (At the moment Sana Sounds is not large enough to invest in its own equipment and studios.) Sana Sounds also subcontracts the production of records and CDs to a number of manufacturing companies. Sana Sounds then distributes the disks to selected stores, and engages in any promotional activities required.

What would you say were the activities in Sana Sounds' value chain?

6.10 The examples below are based on two supermarket chains, one concentrating on low prices, the other differentiated on quality and service. See if you can tell which is which.

(a)

	INBOUND LOGISTICS	OPERATIONS	OUTBOUND LOGISTICS	MARKETING & SALES	SERVICE
Firm infrastructure	Central control of operations and credit control				
Human resource management	Recruitment of mature staff	Client care training	Flexible staff to help with packing		
Technology development		Recipe research	Electronic point of sale	Consumer research & tests	Itemised bills
Procurement	Own label products	Prime retail positions		Adverts in quality magazines & poster sites	
	Dedicated refrigerated transport	In store food halls. Modern store design. Open front refrigerators. Tight control of sell-by dates	Collect by car service	No price discounts on food past sell-by dates	No quibble refunds

(b)

	INBOUND LOGISTICS	OPERATIONS	OUTBOUND LOGISTICS	MARKETING & SALES	SERVICE
Firm infrastructure	Minimum corporate HQ				
Human resource management		De-skilled store-ops	Dismissal for checkout error		
Technology development	Computerised warehousing		Checkouts simple		
Procurement	Branded only purchases big discounts	Low cost sites			Use of concessions
	Bulk warehousing	Limited range. Price points. Basic store design		Low price promotion. Local focus	Nil

6.11 The two supermarkets represented are based on the following.

(a) The value chain in 6.10(a) is based on a firm, which seeks to differentiate on quality and service. Hence the 'no quibble' refunds, the use of prime retail sites, and customer care training.

(b) The value chain in 6.10(b) is similar to that of Lidl, a 'discount' supermarket chain which sells on price, pursuing a cost leadership, or perhaps more accurately, a cost-focus strategy. This can be seen in the limited product range and its low-cost sites.

Marketing at Work

Caterpillar is the world's biggest manufacturer of diesel detecting generators. Owing to problems in California's electricity supply market, demand has been growing.

- Technology development: Caterpillar is investing in innovative **energy technology (ET)** such as fuel cells, for the long term.

- Caterpillar is moving into after sales service, to **operate** and service generators on-site.

Website address: www.cat.com

IT and the value chain

6.12 IT can be used at each stage in the value chain.

6.13 **Operations.** IT can be used to **automate and improve physical tasks** in the operating core. It also **provides information** about operational processes.

(a) **Inbound and outbound logistics**

(i) **Warehousing. Parcelforce** uses IT to track the progress of different parcels through the system.

(ii) Create **virtual warehouses** of stock actually held at **suppliers.** For example an organisation with several outlets might have each connected to a system which indicates the total amount of stock available at different sites.

(iii) Planning procedures to schedule production such as MRPII.

(a) **Marketing and services**

(i) **Internet websites** can be used as an advertising medium and to gather information about customers.

(ii) **Customer databases** enable firms to monitor consumers' buying habits and to identify new segments.

(iii) Supermarkets use **EPOS** systems to give them a precise hour-by-hour idea of how products are selling to enable speedy ordering and replenishments.

Chapter Roundup

- This chapter contains analytical and planning tools which can be used throughout the planning process.

- The **product life cycle** assumes that the marketing and financial characteristics of a product change over time, in relation to the market and in relation to other products.

- Market characteristics partly determine the speed by which **innovations** are diffused and adopted, and buyers can be segmented by their attitudes to innovation.

- Increasing **market share** is a desirable objective as there is sometimes a correlation between market share and profit, owing to **economies of scale** and the **experience curve** effect.

- **Portfolio analyses** compare the marketing and financial performance of a firm's products and/or SBUs with a view to decision-making. BCG analyses products according to market growth and relative market share.

- The **value chain** models how an organisation creates 'value' through managing value activities and the linkages between them. These can be deployed to give distinct customer benefits.

Now try illustrative question 7 at the end of the Study Text

Quick Quiz

1   Distinguish between product class, form and brand. (see para 2.2)

2   What are the problems of the PLC? (2.9)

3   How is the product life cycle related to marketing orientation? (2.13)

4   Identify five market segments with different attitudes to innovation. (3.5)

5   What impedes diffusion? (3.7)

6   Identify four strategies for market share. (4.11)

7   How do question marks differ from stars? (5.5)

8   List some drawbacks to portfolio planning. (5.8, 5.12)

9   What is the value chain? (6.4)

10 How might a firm use the value chain? (6.10)

Action Programme Review

1   The compact disc player, and its almost total replacement of the turntable, is in part indicative of the product life cycle. Initial high prices meant that it took a while to be accepted, but its benefits have led to considerable growth in sales. CD players have come down considerably in price and the market is reaching maturity. Consequently, turntables and vinyl records are in decline although vinyl is important in the 'club' scene.

Interestingly, the relative performance of CD players and turntables varied for a while according to market segment. CDs dominated the market for classical music earlier than they did for popular music. CDs have had less success in replacing tapes, as tapes are recordable. The Sony mini-disc has had some, limited, success. Furthermore the whole future of recorded music might be threatened by MP3.

In the video market, DVD offers higher quality reproduction, but until these are easily recordable, they will not replace home video.

2   (a)   Orange juice is a cash cow.

(b)   Pomegranate juice is a question mark, which the company wants to turn into a star.

3   Here are some ideas.

(a)   It can become more efficient, by automating the production of food, as in a fast food chain.

(b)   The chef can develop commercial relationships with growers, so he or she can obtain the best quality fresh produce.

(c)   The chef can specialise in a particular type of cuisine (eg Nepalese, Korean).

(d)   The restaurant can be sumptuously decorated for those customers who value 'atmosphere' and a sense of occasion, in addition to a restaurant's purely gastronomic pleasures.

(e)   The restaurant can serve a particular type of customer (eg celebrities).

Each of these options is a way of organising the activities of buying, cooking and serving food in a way that customers or chosen customers will value.

4   Sana Sounds is involved in the record industry from start to finish. Although recording and CD manufacture are contracted out to external suppliers, this makes no difference to the fact that these activities are part of Sana Sounds' own value chain. Sana Sounds earns its money by managing the whole set of activities. If the company grows then perhaps it will acquire its own recording studios. A value chain of activities is not the same as an organisation's business functions.

8 Marketing Audits and SWOT

Chapter Topic List	Syllabus reference
1 Setting the scene	
2 Marketing audits and marketing effectiveness	2.2
3 SWOT analysis	3.2
4 The marketing SWOT	3.2

Learning Outcomes

- Conduct and evaluate a detailed marketing audit.

- Identify the elements that can be used to create competitive advantage.

- Compare and contrast strategic options.

Key Concepts Introduced

- Marketing audit
- Efficiency

- Effectiveness
- Corporate appraisal

Examples of Marketing at Work

- Co-op

1 SETTING THE SCENE

1.1 Having moved from the external environment, we now move to pulling all the information together.

1.2 The marketing audit contributes to the marketing SWOT which itself contributes to the corporate SWOT.

Links to other papers

1.3 A review of the 'current position', together with the SWOT tool, can help in any Diploma exam. Note, however, that a 'strong' product can be undermined by 'weak' communications and vice versa; strengths and weaknesses cannot be considered in isolation.

2 MARKETING AUDITS AND MARKETING EFFECTIVENESS

Marketing audits

> ### Key Concept
>
> 'A **marketing audit** is a comprehensive, systematic, independent and periodic examination of a company's - or business unit's - marketing environment, objectives, strategies and activities with a view to determining problem areas and opportunities and recommending a plan of action to improve the company's marketing performance.'   (Kotler, Gregor and Rodgers, 1977)

2.1 A marketing audit does not exist in the compulsory formal sense that an external financial audit does. For proper strategic control, however, a marketing audit should have the following features.

   (a) **Regular.** It should be conducted **regularly,** for example once a year.

   (b) **Comprehensive.** It should take a **comprehensive** look at every product, market, distribution channel, ingredient in the marketing mix etc. It should not be restricted to areas of apparent ineffectiveness (for example an unprofitable product, a troublesome distribution channel, low efficiency on direct selling etc).

   (c) **Systematic.** It should be carried out according to a set of predetermined, specified procedures.

   (d) **Independence.** A consultant might be appointed, or someone else within the organisation.

The audit procedure

2.2 A marketing audit should consider the following areas, according to Kotler.

   • The market environment, macro and micro
   • Marketing strategies
   • Marketing systems
   • Marketing organisation
   • Marketing function

2.3 **The marketing environment**

   (a) **Micro.** What are the organisation's major markets, and what is the segmentation of these markets? What are the future prospects of each market segment?

   (i) Who are the customers, what is known about customer needs, intentions and behaviour?

   (ii) Who are the competitors, and what is their standing in the market?

   (b) **Macro.** Have there been any significant developments in the broader environment (for example economic, or political changes, population or social changes etc)?

2.4 **Marketing strategy audit**

   (a) What are the organisation's marketing objectives and how do they relate to overall objectives? Are they reasonable?

   (b) Are enough (or too many) resources being committed to marketing to enable the objectives to be achieved? Is the division of costs between products, areas etc satisfactory?

2.5 **Marketing systems.** What are the procedures for formulating marketing plans and management control of these plans? Are they satisfactory?

2.6 **Marketing organisation.** Does the organisation have the structural capability to implement the plan?

2.7 **Marketing functions.** A review of the effectiveness of each element of the mix (eg advertising and sales promotion activities) should be carried out.

    (a) A review of sales and price levels should be made (for example supply and demand, customer attitudes, the use of temporary price reductions etc).

    (b) A review of the state of each individual product (ie its market 'health') and of the product mix as a whole should be made.

    (c) A critical analysis of the distribution system should be made, with a view to finding improvements.

2.8 **Marketing productivity.** How profitable and cost-effective is the marketing programme?

Exam Tip

You may have to explain the purpose, focus and components of a marketing audit. Show how it can be made relevant to the firm, how it can be conducted, and how the results might be used.

2.9 **Advantages of a marketing audit**

- It should reduce the need for crisis management
- It should identify information needs
- A formal process forces people to think

Efficiency and effectiveness

Key Concepts

(a) **Efficiency**: gaining maximum output for a minimum input and is normally used relatively (ie in comparison to a standard or norm, to competitors, to industry norms, or the PIMS database).

(b) **Effectiveness**: doing the right things rather than doing things right. A firm can be incredibly efficient in producing widgets at the lowest cost but if no one will buy them it is all to no effect and it will soon be out of business.

2.10 A company that is both efficient and effective will prosper. A company that is inefficient but effective will survive, at least in the short term. A company that is both inefficient and ineffective will die quickly. Let us put this on a grid.

Effectiveness

		High	Low
Efficiency	High	THRIVE	DIE SLOWLY
	Low	SURVIVE	DIE QUICKLY

Source: Wilson, Gilligan, Pearson

Marketing at Work

In *Marketing Week*, David Benadly described some of the long-term problems facing the *Co-op*.

'The *Co-operative Bank* has shown that it can be done. Tesco demonstrates that supermarkets can do it. But whether the 500-strong Co-operative Retail Society grocery chain can carry it off is by no means assured. "It" is nothing less than staging the complete relaunch of a flagging brand, turning round consumer perceptions and giving a real point of difference to rivals.

The problems of CRS, a rag-tag portfolio of 500 stores under three different facias - Leo's, Pioneer and Stop & Shop - are profound and difficult. Its market share in the grocery trade has fallen from nearly nine per cent in the late 1980s, to less than six per cent today (1998).

The stores are now being rebranded under two names - the larger stores as Co-operative Pioneer and the convenience stores as Co-operative Local. The variation in store sizes and poor location of some stores means different stores offer different ranges, opening hours and standards of service.

Many CRS customers are older and less affluent than those of Sainsbury's and Tesco, so another objective is to make the stores appeal to a broader, more representative, group of customers.

The problems at CRS have been accentuated by the technical advances made by the other multiples in stock replenishment, electronic point of sale, loyalty and customer service. It is not so much what CRS has been doing wrong, but what the competition has been doing right.

Yet CRS, and the Co-operative movement in general, have some important saving graces. 'The Co-op is one of the best known brands in the UK. It has got latent heritage and there are a lot of things people think are good about the brand - but it has become tarnished in recent years."

CRS needs more efficient organisation, and is implementing a new management structure and redefining lines of responsibility and reporting. There is also work to do on product ranges, which are seen as too diffuse. Ranges are decided locally rather than nationally. While this means local tastes can be targeted accurately, it can lead to confusion in relations with suppliers and in the negotiation of discounts.

The importance of marketing effectiveness

2.11 Although it is obviously true that marketing effectiveness is a vital component of organisational effectiveness, it is not always easy to measure precisely, especially as marketing 'assets' are hard to measure and value.

The marketing excellence framework

2.12 In *Manufacturing: the Marketing Solution,* the CIM has developed a framework for evaluating companies' marketing operations. A sample of 44 companies from the UK's manufacturing sector was taken, and each company's marketing activities were assessed and scored on a

marketing excellence framework. Then, the marketing excellence score was compared with financial results.

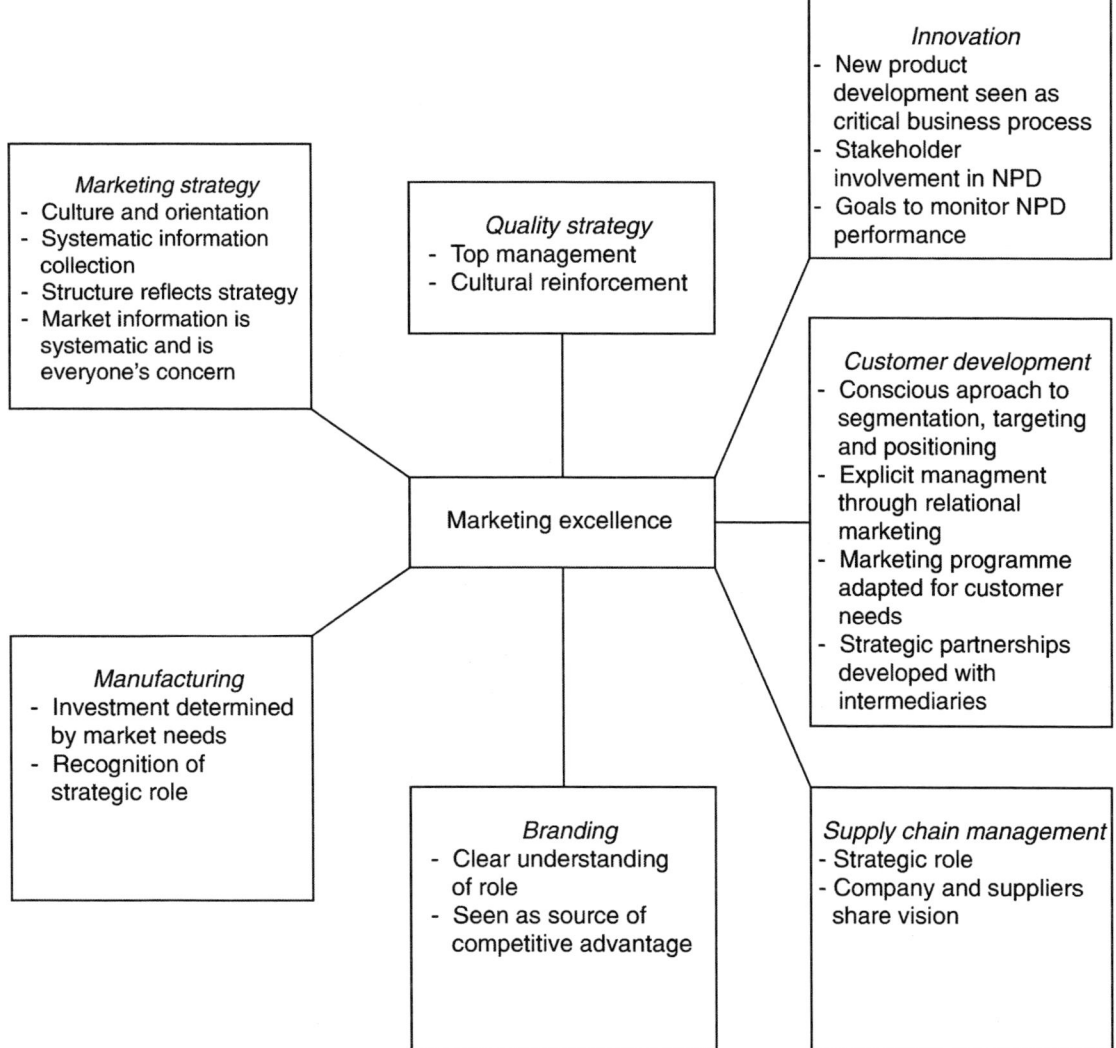

2.13 Most companies in the sample scored badly. The better scorers tended to be large companies. **Correlation with financial performance is not entirely straightforward.**

(a) For many firms, there **is** a link between total score on the marketing excellence framework and profitability and return on capital.

(b) It appears that some companies in particularly demanding markets have 'to run fast to stand still'.

(c) No company earns a high return on capital if it scores **badly** on the framework.

Measuring marketing capability

2.14 Kotler has developed the thinking on marketing effectiveness into a general purpose rating tool based upon the following fifteen questions, as adapted in the table below.

Marketing effectiveness rating

Customer philosophy

1   To what extent does management recognise the need to organise the company to satisfy specific market demands?

2   To what extent is the marketing programme tailored to the needs of different market segments?

3   Does management adopt a systems approach to planning, with recognition being given to the interrelationships between the environment, suppliers, channels, customers and competitors?

Marketing organisation

4   To what extent does senior management attempt to control and integrate the major marketing functions?

5   What sort of relationship exists between marketing management and the management of the R&D, finance, production and manufacturing functions?

6   How well organised is the new product development process?

Marketing information

7   How frequently does the company conduct market research studies of customers, channels and competitors?

8   To what extent is management aware of the sales potential and profitability of different market segments, customers, territories, products and order sizes?

9   What effort is made to measure the cost-effectiveness of different levels and types of marketing expenditure?

The strategic perspective

10   How formalised is the marketing planning process?

11   What is the quality of the thinking that underlies the current marketing strategy?

12   To what extent does management engage in contingency thinking and planning?

Operational efficiency

13   How well is senior management thinking on marketing communicated and implemented down the line?

14   Does marketing management do an effective job with the resources available?

15   Does management respond quickly and effectively to unexpected developments in the market-place?

2.15   Each question can be answered on three levels.

(a)   Question 1 could have answers:

> 1.1   To no extent
> 1.2   To some extent
> 1.3   To a very high extent

(b)   Question 5 could have answers:

> 5.1   Extremely poor, antagonism exists, marketing regarded as being too demanding
>
> 5.2   Normally satisfactory although there is an underlying attitude that each department is basically self-serving
>
> 5.3   Extremely good with all departments working together to serve the customer

(c) Each of these three levels is then allocated a score of 0, 1, or 2:

Poor = 0
Satisfactory = 1
Excellent = 2

(d) Each manager works his way through the fifteen questions in order to arrive at a score. The scores are then aggregated and averaged. The overall measure of marketing effectiveness can then be assessed against the following scale.

0 - 5	=	None	Firm's survival in doubt
6 - 10	=	Poor	
11 - 15	=	Fair	Opportunity to improve
16 - 20	=	Good	
21 - 25	=	Very good	
26 - 30	=	Superior	Beware complacency

2.16 The beauty of the Kotler approach is that it can be adapted to suit the purposes of any organisation. Extra questions can be posed as thought fit. For example, if **marketing planning** was considered to be a key attribute of marketing effectiveness than this could be audited and scored using the following schematic approach.

AUDITING THE MARKETING PLAN - SCHEMATIC APPROACH	
Planning	*Auditing*
Corporate mission	Correct? Understood?
Corporate objectives	Feasible? Being achieved?
Corporate strategies	Appropriate? Have environmental factors changed? What are competitors doing?
Marketing objectives	Feasible? Being achieved?
Marketing strategies	Appropriate? Working? Competitors? (Direct, indirect)
Marketing mix plans	Harmonised? Tailored for each segment? Positioning OK? Check price, place, product/service and promotion. Internal audits, customer audits.
Marketing research plan	Is the right data provided at the right time in the right format?
Budgets/performance measures	Appropriate? Being achieved?
Organisation, integration, co-ordination	Working harmoniously? Is the organisation effective?
Overall	How do we compare with last year and the years before? How do we compare with competitors?

Other more general questions on planning could be devised, for example:

Marketing planning

16 To what extent is marketing planning being conducted?

   (a) For the short term
   (b) For the medium term
   (c) For the long term

17 To what extent are marketing plans communicated to other departments?

18 To what extent are marketing plans considered realistic by other departments?

2.17 **Other more obvious ways of reviewing marketing effectiveness and measuring marketing capability**

(a) The extent to which the company has consistently increased **market share.**

(b) **Customer audits**, ideally subcontracted to a marketing research agency to establish objectively the company's standing relative to competitors with regard to:

- Product-service mix
- Pricing policies
- Promotional strategies, in particular customer support and personal selling
- Distribution service including deliveries, stocks etc
- Marketing knowledge/image

(c) **Interfirm comparisons.**

(d) **PIMS database** (comparisons of company's overall product, market and financial effectiveness relative to similar companies).

(e) **Competitor audits** (checking published accounts, competitor intelligence etc).

(f) **Internal audits** of all resources.

3 SWOT ANALYSIS

3.1 The purpose of **corporate appraisal** (SWOT analysis) is to **combine** the assessment of the environment and the analysis of the organisation's internal resources and capabilities.

Key Concept

Corporate appraisal: 'a critical assessment of the strengths and weaknesses, opportunities and threats in relation to the internal and environmental factors affecting the entity in order to establish its condition prior to the preparation of a long-term plan.'

3.2 A **strengths and weaknesses** analysis expresses which areas of the business have:

- Strengths that should be exploited
- Weaknesses which should be improved

It therefore covers the results of the position audit.

3.3 **Opportunities**

- What opportunities exist in the business environment?
- Their inherent profit-making potential
- The organisation's ability to exploit the worthwhile opportunities

3.4 **Threats**

- What threats might arise?
- How will competitors be affected?
- How will the company be affected?

The opportunities and threats might arise from PEST and competitive factors.

Bringing the SWOT elements together

3.5 The internal and external appraisals will be brought together, and perhaps shown in a cruciform chart.

3.6 EXAMPLE

Strengths	**Weaknesses**
£10 million of capital available	Heavy reliance on a small number of customers
Production expertise and appropriate marketing skills	Limited product range, with no new products and expected market decline. Small marketing organisation.

Threats	**Opportunities**
A major competitor has already entered the new market	Government tax incentives for new investment
	Growing demand in a new market, although customers so far relatively small in number

The company is in imminent danger of losing its existing markets and must diversify its products and/or markets. The new market opportunity exists to be exploited, and since the number of customers is currently small, the relatively small size of the existing marketing force would not be an immediate hindrance. A strategic plan could be developed to buy new equipment and use existing production and marketing to enter the new market, with a view to rapid expansion. Careful planning of manpower, equipment, facilities, research and development would be required and there would be an objective to meet the threat of competition so as to obtain a substantial share of a growing market. The cost of entry at this early stage of market development should not be unacceptably high.

3.7 The SWOT technique can also be used for specific areas of strategy such as IT and marketing.

3.8 Effective SWOT analysis does not simply require a categorisation of information, it also requires some **evaluation of the relative importance** of the various factors under consideration.

(a) These features are only of relevance if they are **perceived to exist by the customers.** Listing corporate features that internal personnel regard as strengths/weaknesses is of little relevance if customers do not perceive them as such.

(b) In the same vein, threats and opportunities are conditions presented by the external environment and they should be independent of the firm.

3.9 The SWOT can now be used to guide strategy formulation. The two major options are **matching** and **conversion**.

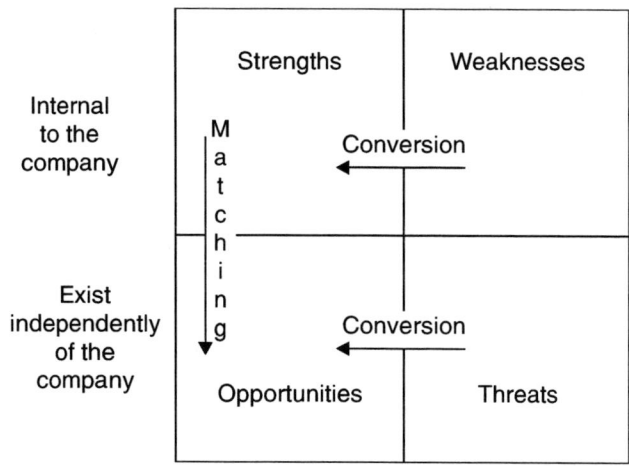

BPP PUBLISHING

(a) **Matching**

This entails finding, where possible, a match between the strengths of the organisation and the opportunities presented by the market. Strengths which do not match any available opportunity are of limited use while opportunities which do not have any matching strengths are of little immediate value.

(b) **Conversion**

This requires the development of strategies which will convert weaknesses into strengths in order to take advantage of some particular opportunity, or converting threats into opportunities which can then be matched by existing strengths.

Action Programme 1

Hall Faull Downes Ltd has been in business for 25 years, during which time profits have risen by an average of 3% per annum, although there have been peaks and troughs in profitability due to the ups and downs of trade in the customers' industry. The increase in profits until five years ago was the result of increasing sales in a buoyant market, but more recently, the total market has become somewhat smaller and Hall Faull Downes has only increased sales and profits as a result of improving its market share.

The company produces components for manufacturers in the engineering industry.

In recent years, the company has developed many new products and currently has 40 items in its range compared to 24 only five years ago. Over the same five-year period, the number of customers has fallen from 20 to nine, two of whom together account for 60% of the company's sales.

Give your appraisal of the company's future, and suggest what it is probably doing wrong.

3.10 In practice - and indeed in the Analysis and Decision case study - it helps if you rank the items of the SWOT in order of **importance** and **urgency**. Marketers have to concentrate their limited resources on the essentials.

4 THE MARKETING SWOT

4.1 Having looked at corporate level SWOT analysis we should now turn our attention to the marketing level. It is important to remember that the concept and approach remains the same, it is only the factors which we are considering which vary. Corporate SWOTs are concerned with everything. Marketing SWOTs concentrate more specifically on **markets** and the mix.

Strengths and weaknesses

4.2 The marketing department is probably the most important source of 'bottom up' information, opinions and views which influence the development of the corporate strategy. But the marketing audit also represents the starting point for developing the **marketing** plan, answering the 'where are we now' question in terms of marketing controllables.

4.3 A **marketing audit** as we have seen earlier, should involve a thorough 'taking stock' of the complete marketing activity.

Action Programme 2

Jot down some of the elements of the marketing audit which you might consider useful inputs to the marketing SWOT.

4.4 A prime objective as far as the marketing manager is concerned of this internal marketing analysis is to be able to log the company's current market position on a **positioning map**.

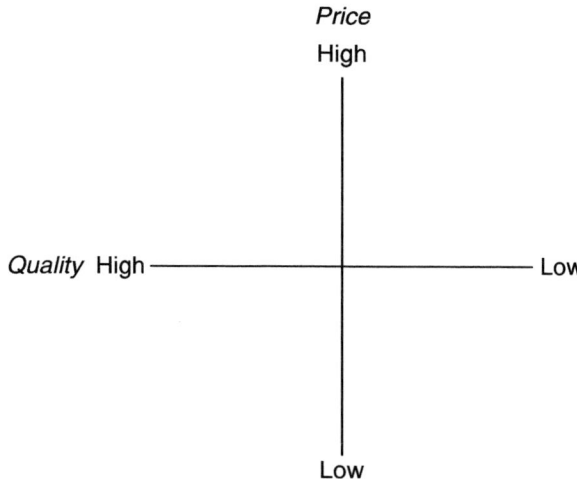

4.5 The variables used on this positioning map are dimensions of the marketing mix. You may need several such maps to consider the real position of a complex product, but the variables you should focus on are those recognised as having the greatest influence on purchasing decisions.

Action Programme 3

Use the positioning maps above and below to log the positions of your company and its key competitors.

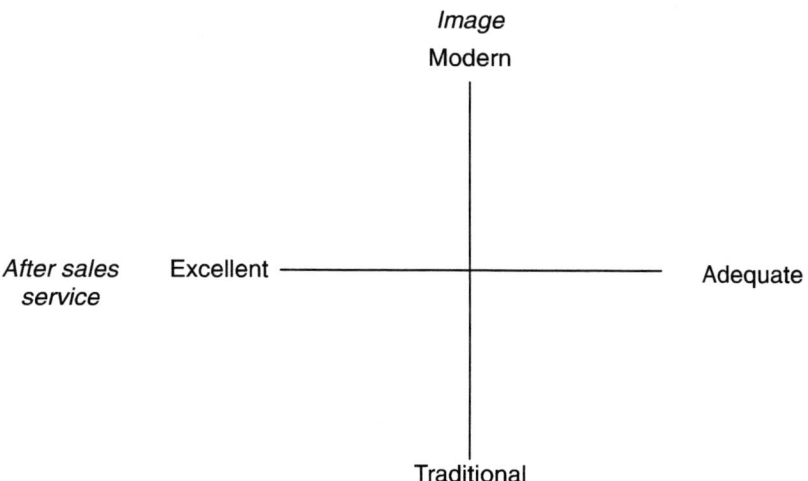

Opportunities and threats

4.6 The external aspects of the marketing SWOT are the product/market opportunities and threats which evolve from changes in the macro environment identified at the corporate level. For example a demographic shift increasing the proportion of older customers for overseas holidays may have been identified in the environmental analysis of a package holiday company. At **marketing** level this translates into a number of possibilities.

(a) An opportunity to sell existing holidays to this new target market.

(b) An opportunity to develop new products specifically developed to meet the needs of this emerging segment.

(c)   The possible option of switching resources away from segments which are showing less growth potential.

4.7   At marketing level, opportunities can be considered and communicated using the **Ansoff matrix** which provides the alternative product/market options available to a company. (*Note*. Although not specifically shown by implication the threats at this level are factors which reduce the viability or potential of any of the product/market possibilities.)

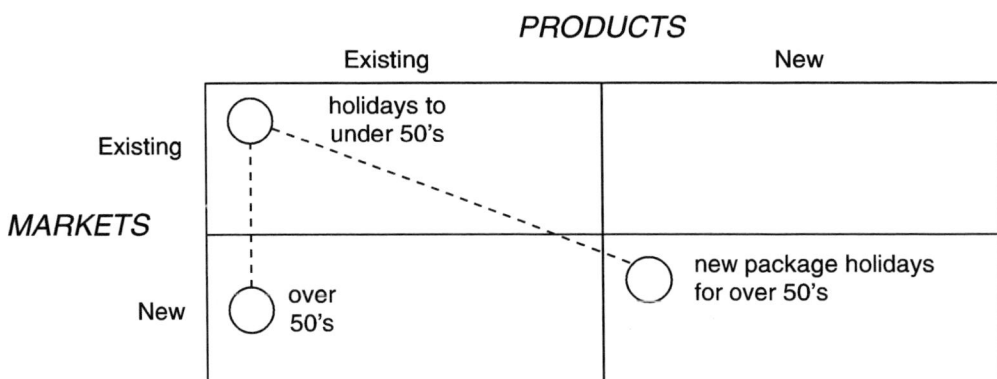

4.8   To summarise the marketing SWOT:

Strengths	Weaknesses
These are **internal** factors controllable by marketing managers; they are the 7P's	
Opportunities	Threats
These are **external** uncontrollable factors related to an appraisal of changing product/market position	

A note on the SWOT technique

4.9   In this chapter we have seen SWOT used at both corporate and marketing level to help sort information and clarify the picture.

4.10   As a management tool you should use SWOT whenever you have to get to grips with a large volume of data, when you are evaluating alternatives, or when you are faced with a mini-case study or scenario.

4.11   However, you should recognise that without further analysis and work your SWOT will only provide a 'broad brush' picture and you should take care not to read too much into it. Your weaknesses may be identified, but not ranked in order of priority. Your threats are noted, but which are the most significant? (You may score highly compared to your competitors for speedy delivery, but how important is that in the customer's decision making?)

4.12   As at corporate level, to get the most from your SWOT analysis the factors identified need **ranking** in order of significance, and **quantifying** against criteria based on your broader knowledge of the business and the market place.

Action Programme 4

Adventure Travel is a travel agent with 20 town-centre offices in one region of the country. Its head office is inside its largest office. Adventure Travel was founded by an entrepreneur who still owns what she considers to be a small business. She believes that 'My customers should receive the best possible service from us and also enjoy their travel'. She manages the head office herself.

Adventure Travel employs three senior managers who control the 20 offices. Each office sells to the general public and to small business customers. The number of customers at each office varies from 2,500 to 6,000, although 4,000 is typical. Managers have to work within an expenditure budget. They are responsible for new business development, promotion and advertising and customer service. The owner also expects them to achieve certain goals, for example, number of new customers booking a holiday. Managers do not participate in setting the size of their budgets or their goals.

Recently, Adventure Travel's owner carried out a SWOT analysis for her business. Her conclusions are summarised below.

Strengths

- Well-established and financially secure.
- Good town-centre locations.

Weaknesses

- Staff in the offices who deal with the public are not always friendly.
- Staff do not always provide the customer with the cheapest means of travel.
- The three senior managers appear to be demotivated.

Opportunities

Expenditure on personal travel is expected to rise by 5% (in real terms) each year for the next eight years.

Threats

- An increasing number of airlines are opening their own town-centre travel offices.

Required

Describe the contribution which marketing personnel could have made to the SWOT analysis carried out by Adventure Travel's owner.

Exam Tip

SWOT is a valuable tool but must be used carefully. To answer some questions, you must do a SWOT, even though it does not form part of your answer. SWOT is not the right tool for every question.

Chapter Roundup

- The **marketing audit** is a comprehensive review of a firm's marketing activities.

- The marketing audit also contributes to the **corporate SWOT.**

- **SWOT analysis** is a useful technique for organising information about an organisation's strengths and weaknesses (**internal** appraisal) and the opportunities and threats (**external** appraisal) which it encounters.

- SWOT can be enhanced by **ranking** items in order of significance, and it is always important not to confuse the level at which the analysis is conducted (eg corporate SWOT and marketing SWOT).

- The SWOT can be used to identify possible **strategies.**

Now try illustrative question 8 at the end of the Study Text

Quick Quiz

1   What is a marketing audit? (see para 2.1)

2   List the steps in a marketing audit. (2.2)

3   How would you measure marketing capability? (2.14)

4   What is SWOT analysis and when would you use it? (3.1)

5   What would be considered in an analysis of strengths and weaknesses? (3.2)

6   What are the two major strategy options outlined on a SWOT chart? (3.9)

7   What matters are covered in the marketing SWOT? (4.3)

8   What are the main variables on a firm's positioning map? (4.5)

9   What are the main elements of the marketing SWOT? (4.8)

10   How should you most benefit from the SWOT? (4.12)

Action Programme Review

1   A general interpretation of the facts as given might be sketched as follows.

(a)   Objectives: the company has no declared objectives. Profits have risen by 3% per annum in the past, which has failed to keep pace with inflation but may have been a satisfactory rate of increase in the current conditions of the industry. Even so, stronger growth is indicated in the future.

(b)

Strengths	Weaknesses
Many new products developed.	Products may be reaching the end of their life and entering decline.
Marketing success in increasing market share.	New product life cycles may be shorter.
	Reduction in customers.
	Excessive reliance on a few customers.
	Doubtful whether profit record is satisfactory.
Threats	*Opportunities*
Possible decline in the end-product.	None identified.
Smaller end-product market will restrict future sales prospects for Hall Faull Downes.	

(c)   Strengths: the growth in company sales in the last five years has been as a result of increasing the market share in a declining market. This success may be the result of the following.

- Research and development spending
- Good product development programmes
- Extending the product range to suit changing customer needs
- Marketing skills
- Long-term supply contracts with customers
- Cheap pricing policy
- Product quality and reliable service

(d)   Weaknesses:

(i)   The products may be custom-made for customers so that they provide little or no opportunity for market development.

(ii)   Products might have a shorter life cycle than in the past, in view of the declining total market demand.

(iii)   Excessive reliance on two major customers leaves the company exposed to the dangers of losing their custom.

150

(e)   Threats: there may be a decline in the end-market for the customers' product so that the customer demands for the company's own products will also fall.

(f)   Opportunities: no opportunities have been identified, but in view of the situation as described, new strategies for the longer term would appear to be essential.

(g)   Conclusions: the company does not appear to be planning beyond the short term, or is reacting to the business environment in a piecemeal fashion. A strategic planning programme should be introduced.

(h)   Recommendations: the company must look for new opportunities in the longer term.

   (i)   In the short term, current strengths must be exploited to continue to increase market share in existing markets and product development programmes should also continue.

   (ii)   In the longer term, the company must diversify into new markets or into new products and new markets. Diversification opportunities should be sought with a view to exploiting any competitive advantage or synergy that might be achievable.

   (iii)   The company should use its strengths (whether in R & D, production skills or marketing expertise) in exploiting any identifiable opportunities.

   (iv)   Objectives need to be quantified in order to assess the extent to which new long-term strategies are required.

2   (a)   Marketing strategy - quality and effectiveness of marketing plans in the past.

       (b)   The marketing organisation - marketing systems, organisation structure, degree of market orientation in the corporate philosophy and the quality of marketing information available.

       (c)   The strengths and weaknesses of the organisation's marketing mix (ie operational effectiveness).

          (i)   Products: range, quality, competitive advantage, stage of the life cycle and technical reputation etc.

          (ii)   Price: perceived value for money compared with competitors and price position in the market place.

          (iii)   Promotion: image and reputation of the organisation and various products and brands in the market place. Brand loyalty and corporate image.

          (iv)   Place: availability of the product, channels of distribution used, waiting lists and the availability of distribution services like credit for end users etc.

          (v)   After sales service: reputation for after sales customer care, provision of spare parts, servicing etc.

          These are the controllable factors.

3   You can change the dimensions on the grid if it makes sense.

4   Here are some ideas. The main marketing issues are products and markets.

       Products. What precisely is Adventure Travel's product? Not the holidays themselves, but the service. A marketing department would have reviewed the service and identified strengths and weaknesses in comparison with other services.

       Markets. The owner has not really thought about customers at all. The SWOT shows the various assumptions the owner has made. Despite her statement that customers receive the best possible service and enjoy their travel, she assumes that customers are necessarily interested in getting the cheapest means of travel. The appropriate performance measure is the number of new customers booking a holiday, whereas for many service businesses, the level of repeat business is more important: it costs more to recruit new customers than to retain existing ones. Finally, some town centres are in decline, so her strength may be less of a strength than she thinks.

       A marketing department could identify customer segments (eg business vs holiday travel) and the success the firm has in promotion and advertising. These have not appeared in the owner's SWOT.

9 *Financial Analysis*

Chapter Topic List	Syllabus reference
1 Setting the scene	
2 The role of finance in marketing	3.2
3 The balance sheet	3.2
4 Profit or cash?	3.2
5 The profit and loss account	3.2
6 Ratio analysis	3.2
7 Segmental analysis and customer profitability	3.2
8 Productivity	3.2

Learning Outcomes

- Understand and critically appraise a wide variety of marketing techniques, concepts and models.

- Initiate control systems for marketing planning.

- Specify a clear rationale when choosing between strategic alternatives.

Key Concepts Introduced

- Assets
- Liability
- Capital
- Liquidity

- Profitability
- Customer/segment profitability
- Productivity

Examples of Marketing at Work

- British Steel
- Post Office

- Coutts Bank
- Coca Cola

1   SETTING THE SCENE

1.1   Finance is a common language of business, enabling the costs and benefits of different courses of action to be quantified and compared. You may be expected to demonstrate your

understanding of the financial implications of the marketing strategies which you propose. (You will have studied financial issues in previous CIM modules, notably *Management Information for Marketing Decisions*. This chapter recaps the fundamental principles of financial analysis.)

Links with other papers

1.2 In Analysis & Decision, there is frequently a financial component in that you are given financial statements of a company or division to read. You may also have to prepare a budget.

2 THE ROLE OF FINANCE IN MARKETING

2.1 Those developing marketing strategy should:

(a) **Understand the impact of their decisions on the finances** of the business

(b) Be able to **work effectively with the finance professionals** in the business

(c) Be **competent in the use of financial techniques** necessary in the day-to-day management and planning for their own departments

2.2 **Financial comparisons can aid decision-making**

(a) **Past comparisons and trends.** Looking back at the organisation's financial history and records can identify similar situations and help draw conclusions and trends from the information.

(b) **Competitor analysis.** Examining published information of other organisations, such as competitors, for any indicators may aid decision-making.

(c) **Forecasting** the future based on assumptions.

(d) **Modelling.** Using financial data as a means of modelling the effect of different decisions.

The finance department relative to marketing

2.3 The finance department has three important accounting roles, and produces three different forms of output, all of which are relevant to the marketing department.

(a) **Financial accounting.** For public limited companies (plcs), the financial statements are published in a document called the **annual report and accounts**. This is a legal requirement, to let shareholders know how their business is doing.

(i) It will include a **balance sheet**, a **profit and loss account** and a **cash flow statement**. These must follow certain rules laid down by law and by Financial Reporting Standards.

(ii) The annual report also includes a **directors' report** and a **chairman's report** which talk about the past and future of the company in general terms.

(iii) Financial accounting is **important to marketing activities** because the financial effects of marketing activities must be recorded properly and accurately.

(iv) The financial statements are an important communication to outsiders, and thus have a **PR impact**.

(b) **Management accounting.** Management accounts will be produced, usually on a monthly or quarterly basis. These accounts are intended to help the decision-making process within the company.

(c) **Corporate finance**. Sometimes called 'treasury management', it is concerned with ensuring that sufficient **funds** are available to the business in order for it to pursue its objectives. For example, a £25m advertising campaign requires the organisation to have these funds to spend.

Action Programme 1

Obtain some company reports which contain published accounts. These can be obtained from a variety of sources, including via the Financial Times annual report service. Examine the content of the accounts.

Marketing at Work

The history of the *dot.coms* in 2000 is a salutary lesson of failure to observe financial fundamentals.

Investors piled in huge amounts of money, and dot.coms were rewarded by high share prices, enabling them to raise more money.

A number of different valuation models were adopted, and investors (and stock brokers) abandoned 'boring' performance indicators such as profitability. Internet start-ups raised large capital sums from investors and their corporate performance was assessed on the basis of:

- Market share, bought at whatever expense) or number of subscribers. In January 2001, *amazon.com* announced it was to lay off staff in a bid to return to operating profitability.

- 'Cash burn' – effectively, the rate of cash outflows. Obviously a lower burn rate was 'healthier'. Companies like boo.com invested heavily in the website and promotion but did not have enough cash. It was noted that they failed to appoint a finance director until too late.

Few business-to-consumer dot.coms survived. On a more positive note, look at *Ebookers* below.

Shares in *Ebookers.com* rose 19 percent yesterday after the online travel company said it was on track to achieve positive cash flows by the fourth quarter of this year or first quarter of 2002 at the latest. (*Financial Times*, 1 May 2001)

The company said its cash burn would fall from $3m (£2m) to less than $1.5m a month in the second half, helping its transition to positive cash flows.

Ebookers also reported sales in the first quarter to March 31 above analysts' expectations. Pre-tax losses were $12m ($22m).

'Our focus right now is on cash flow profitability,' said Navneet Bali, finance director. 'Real profitability should follow through soon thereafter because we don't have many fixed assets.'

Ebookers.com operates in one of the few areas where business-to-consumer e-commerce is still regarded as a promising market.

Ebookers is already present in 11 European countries and has built strong relationships with airlines over nearly 20 years through its offline subsidiary Flightbookers. Analysts are predicting a $31.7m loos this year. But after next year's transition to profits of $2.3m, the company is expected to generate profits of $20m and earnings per share of 78 cents in 2003. Hence the significance of yesterday's reiteration of the company's cash flow goals and subsequent share price rise. Nevertheless, investors should be packed for a long haul.

2.4 The following fundamental concepts need to be borne in mind.

(a) **Accruals**: revenue and costs are matched in the period when incurred.

(b) **Consistency**: similar items are treated in a similar way from year to year.

(c) **Prudence**: don't count your chickens!

(d) **Going concern**: the business is not expected to collapse and will carry on for the foreseeable future.

3 THE BALANCE SHEET

The accounting equation

> ### Key Concepts
>
> The **assets** of a business are the things it owns which offer an economic benefit.
>
> A **liability** is money owed by a business, for whatever reason. For example, at anyone time, it might owe money to suppliers for goods it has purchased but not yet paid for (trade creditors). It might owe tax.
>
> The **capital** is the amount invested by the owners in the business. Arguably the business 'owes' it to the owners (in a similar way to owing money to creditors).

3.1 We can put assets together and this gives us the **accounting equation**:

$$\text{Capital} + \text{Liabilities} = \text{Assets}$$

This could equally well be written:

$$\text{Capital} = \text{Assets} - \text{Liabilities}$$

Since the second part of this equation is what we call **net assets**, we can write, even more simply:

$$\text{Capital} = \text{Net assets}$$

The balance sheet

3.2 The accounting equation explains why the 'net assets' and the total of 'capital and reserves' are both equal to £16,100,000 in 20X1 in the balance sheet shown below.

ARC LIMITED
BALANCE SHEETS AT 31 DECEMBER 20X1

	20X0		20X1	
Fixed assets	£'000	£'000	£'000	£'000
Intangible assets	100		100	
Tangible assets	7,900		12,950	
Investments	100		100	
		8,100		13,150
Current assets				
Stocks	5,000		15,000	
Debtors	8,900		27,100	
Cash at bank and in hand	600		-	
	14,500		42,100	
Creditors: amounts falling due within one year				
Bank loans and overdrafts	-		16,200	
Trade creditors	6,000		10,000	
Accruals and deferred income	800		1,000	
Other creditors including taxation	6,200		11,200	
	13,000		38,400	
Net current assets		1,500		3,700
Creditors: amounts falling due after more than one year				
15% debenture stock		600		750
Net assets		9,000		16,100

	20X0		*20X1*	
	£'000	£'000	£'000	£'000
Capital and reserves				
Called up share capital				
Ordinary shares of £1 each		6,000		6,000
Profit and loss account reserve		3,000		10,100
		9,000		16,100

3.3   Particular aspects to note about the balance sheets shown above are as follows.

    (a) **Date**. The balance sheet is headed up 'as at 31 December 20X1'. This is telling the user that it is a picture of the affairs of the company **at a point in time**. Over time this picture will change.

    (b) **Comparative figures** (figures for the previous period) are always given to indicate movement. They should be prepared on a consistent basis and usually refer to the balance sheet one year ago.

    (c) **Equation balances. In the example, capital and reserves (or shareholders' funds) equal net assets.**

3.4   We will now briefly discuss each heading.

Fixed assets

3.5   A **fixed asset** is any asset, tangible or intangible, acquired for retention by a **business** to give continuing economic benefits (ie it must be in use for over one year) by **the business**, and not held for resale in the normal course of trading.

    (a) A **tangible** fixed asset is a physical asset. A salesman's car is a tangible fixed asset.

    (b) An **intangible** fixed asset does not have a physical existence. The expense of acquiring **patent rights** and some NPD costs on occasions would be classified as an intangible fixed asset. The value of a **brand name** also comes under this category although this is a matter of considerable dispute. (We deal with this later in this section.)

    (c) **Investments** held for the long term would be classified as fixed assets.

3.6   Fixed assets, except freehold land, **wear out or lose their usefulness in the course of time**. The accounts of a business try to recognise this by gradually writing off the asset's cost in the **profit and loss account** over several accounting periods to reflect the loss in value in the balance sheet. This is called **depreciation**.

Current assets

3.7   **Current assets** are either:

    (a) **Items owned** by the business (or owed to the business) which will be turned into cash within one year

    (b) **Cash**, including money in the bank, owned by the business

These assets are 'current' as that they are **continually flowing** through the business.

Stock

3.8   **Stock** comprises **goods for use or resale**. They can exist either in their original form (for example as the component parts which when assembled make up the product), or as **work in**

progress or as **finished goods** awaiting resale. The basic rule of stock valuation is that stock should be valued at the **lower of cost or net realisable value.**

(a) **Cost** is the amount **paid** for the stock in cash terms to bring it to its current location and condition: raw materials, manufacturing time, labour costs etc.

(b) **Net realisable value** (NRV) is defined as the expected selling price, less any costs still to be incurred getting the stock ready for sale and then selling it.

Debtors

3.9 A debtor is a person, business or company who **owes money to the business.** When the debt is finally paid, the debtor 'disappears' as an asset, to be replaced by 'cash at bank and in hand', another asset. **Most debtors are customers who have bought on credit but have not yet paid.**

3.10 This is why many firms have **credit control departments.** They assess the creditworthiness of new customers, and monitor their payments record. They chase any late-payers and employ **debt collectors. The purpose of any sale is to make a profit, and offering credit has a cost and a risk.**

Current liabilities

3.11 A **liability** is owed **by** a business **to** another person or organisation (eg to the bank or government). Examples of current liabilities are:

* Loans repayable within one year
* A bank overdraft is normally payable 'on demand'
* A **trade creditor** (owed money for debts incurred in the course of trading)
* Taxation payable
* 'Accrued charges' (expenses incurred, for which no bill has yet been received)

Long-term liabilities

3.12 Long-term liabilities include:

* Loans which are repayable after one year, such as a bank loan
* A mortgage loan, which is a loan specifically secured against a freehold property
* Debentures (securities issued at a fixed rate of interest repayable by a specified date)

Capital and reserves

3.13 The **capital and reserves** figures in the balance sheet represent the **shareholders' funds.**

(a) The original **capital** contributed by the 'ordinary' shareholders (the cost of the shares).

(b) The **profits** the business has **retained** over the years **which** are accumulated in the profit and loss account balance.

Brand valuation

3.14 **Companies expect to derive long-term future economic benefit from the value of their brands.** Some have wished to reflect the value of the brands on their balance sheets, since they would then most truly reflect the worth of the company.

(a) What **valuation methodology** should be adopted?

(b) Should brands be treated as an **intangible fixed asset,** like patents, in the **published financial statements?**

(c) **How should brands be treated in the internal decision-making processes of the company?**

3.15 **Carrying out a brand valuation exercise**

(a) A **brand audit** identifies the strength of the brand.

(b) The **current earnings** and **future prospects** are assessed

(c) The brand is given a 'capital' value. **Discounted cash flow (DCF) analysis** might be used.

3.16 **Sources of brand strength (Guilding and Moorhouse)**

Source	Weighting	Comment
Leadership	25%	How dominant is the brand in its sector? High scores are earned for dominance.
Market	10%	What are the growth characteristics of the market?
Stability	15%	'Well established brands that enjoy consumer loyalty will receive higher strength scores.'
Internationality	25%	International brands are generally worth more than national ones, as they are not vulnerable to one market, and a brand might be in another stage of its life cycle in an overseas market.
Trend	10%	A trend indicates a brand's ability to sustain itself. Reductions in sales volume reduce profit, but also make price increases harder to justify.
Support	10%	Marketing expenditure can support a brand, but it must be of the right quality (eg a successful re-positioning).
Protection	5%	(eg Patent protection, copyright, imitation etc)

Exam Tip

Brand valuation is a means of 'strengthening' a company so that it would appear too expensive for the acquirer. High brand values enable firms to raise money, by issuing shares.

4   PROFIT OR CASH?

4.1   Businesses aim to make a profit. We can define profit in very simple terms as follows.

$$P = S - E$$

Where   P = Profit
S = Sales value (or revenue)
E = Expenses (or costs)

4.2 EXAMPLE

(a) As a very simple example, suppose that you buy a cheap jacket for £8. You then sell it to a friend for £10. Obviously, you are now £2 better off, and this £2 represents your profit.

(b) The relationship between profit and cash in the example above is simple and direct. The £2 profit was represented by £2 in cash.

(c) But what if your friend had given you an IOU for the £10, to be paid in one month's time? You have still made a **profit** of £2 on the sale of your jacket, but you are £8 worse off in terms of **cash** than you were before you touched the jacket.

(d) **Profit and cash are not the same in the short term.**

> ### Key Concepts
>
> **Liquidity.** The firm can pay its bills as they fall due. Liquid assets are cash or assets which can be converted quickly and easily into cash. Limited companies are **not** allowed to continue trading if they cannot pay bills as they fall due. Liquidity is therefore very important to them.
>
> **Profitability.** The excess of revenue over costs.

4.3 We can demonstrate the significance using a diagram.

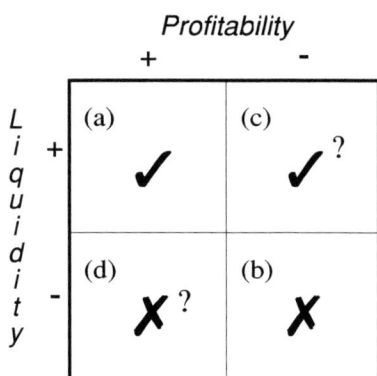

(a) **Profitable and liquid.** Such a firm will survive as it can pay its bills as they fall due and it can attract investment because it is profitable.

(b) **Neither liquid nor profitable.** Such a firm cannot pay bills as they become due and it cannot attract investment because it is not profitable and it therefore will not give a good return to the investor. It will not survive.

(c) **Not profitable but still liquid.** The company has money to pay bills in the short term but it is unprofitable and therefore would not be expected to survive in the long term.

(d) **Profitable but not liquid.** The company in this situation would have difficulty surviving in the **short term** as it cannot pay its bills. However, its profitability should attract **long-term** investment.

Sales volume versus profit

4.4 A business which is **increasing its sales revenue**, perhaps as a result of increased sales effort, is **not necessarily increasingly profitable. If new sales are won on the basis of substantially increased costs, or by offering significant discounts**, it is possible to **increase revenue without increasing profits.**

(a) **Period 1.** For example, a business sells its products for £10 each and in **period 1** sales = 10 units and total expenses £80.

$$\text{Profit} = \text{revenue} - \text{expenses}$$
$$£20 \qquad £100 \qquad £80$$

(b) **Period 2**

After an increased expenditure on marketing support, costs increase by £20 and sales increase to 12 units.

$$£20 = £120 - £100$$

Although revenue has increased by 20% the profit has stayed the same.

4.5 Alternatively if the additional sales are earned by offering significant **discounts** so that the sales price per unit becomes £8 each, it can be seen that **both** revenue **and** profit can actually fall, despite **sales volume** rising to 12 units each.

$$£16 = £96 - £80$$

Action Programme 2

Why do you think many small firms are asking for the government to make it a legal requirement that firms pay their debts within a specified time period?

5 THE PROFIT AND LOSS ACCOUNT

5.1 We now turn to the profit and loss account. Once again, as an example, let us look at the accounts of ARC Ltd.

ARC LIMITED
PROFIT AND LOSS ACCOUNTS FOR THE
YEARS ENDED 31 DECEMBER

	20X0	20X1
	£'000	£'000
Turnover	53,470	98,455
Cost of sales	40,653	70,728
Gross profit	12,817	27,727
Distribution costs	2,317	4,911
Administrative expenses	1,100	2,176
Profit on ordinary activities before interest	9,400	20,640
Interest receivable	100	40
Interest payable	-	(280)
Profit for the financial year	9,500	20,400
Tax on profit on ordinary activities	3,200	5,200
Profit on ordinary activities after taxation	6,300	15,200
Dividends		
Ordinary: interim (paid)	1,100	2,100
final (proposed)	3,000	6,000
Retained profit for the financial year	2,200	7,100

5.2 The profit and loss account is a statement in which **revenues and expenditure** are compared to arrive at a figure of **profit or loss**.

5.3 Most of the **marketing expenses** will appear in this section.

(a) **Distribution costs**. These are expenses associated with the process of selling and delivering goods to customers and in published accounts they will **include marketing expenses**.

- Salaries of marketing and sales directors and management
- Salaries and commissions of sales staff
- Travelling and entertainment expenses of sales people
- Marketing costs (eg advertising, market research, sales promotion)
- Costs of running and maintaining delivery vans
- Discounts allowed to customers for early payment of their debts
- Bad debts written off

(b) **Administration expenses**

- Salaries of directors, management and office staff
- Rent and rates
- Insurance
- Telephone and postage
- Printing and stationery
- Heating and lighting

Capital and revenue items

5.4 **Distinction between capital and revenue items**

(a) **Capital items** are related to financing decisions, such as the purchase of a fixed asset and how the purchase is to be financed.

(b) **Revenue items** are related to trading decisions, that is the sale, purchase and expense, transactions associated with normal trading.

(c) (i) The type of decision-making involved will be very different for revenue and capital items.

(ii) The accounting treatment for capital items is different to that of revenue items.

6 RATIO ANALYSIS

6.1 The financial statements provide sources of useful information about the condition of a business. They are in the **public domain** and can be an important feature in a **competitor analysis**. A company which is losing money and has borrowed heavily may behave quite differently in marketing terms than one which has many sources of cash.

6.2 The analysis and interpretation of these statements can be carried out by calculating certain ratios and then **using the ratios for comparison**.

(a) **One year and the next** for a particular business, in order to identify any trends, or significantly better or worse results than before.

(b) **One business and another**, to establish which business has performed better, and in what ways. You should be very careful, when comparing two different businesses, to ensure that the accounts have been prepared in a similar way.

6.3 Below we identify some typical ratios used.

Profitability and performance ratios

Profit margin

6.4 **Profit margin** is the **ratio of profit before interest and tax over sales turnover**. For example in 20X0, ARC's profit margin was 17.6% (hence costs as a percentage of sales were 82.4%). **Profit Before Interest and Tax** (PBIT), is also known as the operating profit. In the accounts of ARC Ltd, the PBIT for 20X1 is £20,640,000 and for 20X0, £9,400,000. The profit margins for the two years are:

$$\begin{array}{cc} \textit{20X0} & \textit{20X1} \\ \dfrac{9,400}{53,470} = 17.6\% & \dfrac{20,640}{98,455} = 21\% \end{array}$$

If the ratio of costs to sales goes down, the profit margin will automatically go up. For example, if the cost:sales ratio changes from 80% to 75%, the profit margin will go up from 20% to 25%. What does this mean?

- A **high margin** indicates costs are controlled and/or sales prices are high.
- A **low margin** can mean **high costs** or **low prices**.

Asset turnover

6.5 **Asset turnover** is the ratio of sales turnover in a year to the amount of **net assets** which should equate to the amount invested in the business. In the accounts of ARC Ltd, the asset turnover for 20X1 and 20X0 is:

$$\begin{array}{cc} \textit{20X0} & \textit{20X1} \\ \dfrac{53,470}{9,000} = 5.9 \text{ times} & \dfrac{98,455}{16,100} = 6.1 \text{ times} \end{array}$$

This means that for every £1 of assets employed in 20X0, the company generated sales turnover of £5.90 per annum. To utilise assets more efficiently, managers should try to create a higher volume of sales and a higher asset turnover ratio.

Return on capital employed (ROCE)

6.6 **Return on capital employed** (ROCE) is the amount of profit as a percentage of capital employed (net assets). If a company makes a profit of £30,000, we do not know how good or bad the result is until we look at the amount of capital which has been invested to achieve the profit. £30,000 might be a good sized profit for a small firm, but this would not be good enough for a 'giant' firm such as Marks and Spencer. For this reason, it is helpful to measure performance by relating profits to capital employed. The ROCE of ARC Ltd for 20X1 and 20X1 is:

$$\begin{array}{cc} \textit{20X0} & \textit{20X1} \\ \dfrac{9,400}{9,000} = 104.4\% & \dfrac{20,640}{16,100} = 128\% \end{array}$$

6.7 You may already have realised that there is a mathematical connection between return on capital employed, profit margin and asset turnover:

$$\frac{\text{Profit}}{\text{Capital employed}} = \frac{\text{Profit}}{\text{Sales}} \times \frac{\text{Sales}}{\text{Capital employed}}$$

$$\text{ie ROCE} = \text{Profit margin} \times \text{Asset turnover}$$

This is important. If we accept that ROCE is the single most important measure of business performance, comparing profit with the amount of capital invested, we can go on to say that

business performance is dependent on two separate 'subsidiary' factors, each of which contributes to ROCE, **profit margin** and **asset turnover**.

6.8 EXAMPLE

Company A and Company B both sell electrical goods. Both have £100,000 capital employed (net assets) and both want to make a target ROCE of 20%. Company A is a specialist retailer and Company B is a discount warehouse.

(a) **Specialist Company A** might decide to sell its products at a fairly high price and make a profit margin on sales of 10%. It would then need an asset turnover of 2.0 times to achieve a ROCE of 20%. It would therefore need annual sales of £200,000.

(b) **Discount warehouse Company B** might decide to cut its prices so that its profit margin is only 2½%. Provided that it can achieve an asset turnover of 8 times a year, attracting more customers with its lower prices, it will **still make a ROCE of 2½% × 8 = 20%**. It would need annual sales of £800,000.

Action Programme 3

What might be the implications for marketing mix decisions of the two approaches to achieving a target ROCE in 6.8 above?

Action Programme 4

Suppose that Swings and Roundabouts Ltd achieved the following results in 20X6:

Sales	£100,000
Profit	£5,000
Capital employed	£20,000

The company's management wish to decide whether to raise its selling prices. They think that if they do so, they can raise the profit margin to 10% and by introducing extra capital of £55,000, sales turnover could be increased to £150,000. You are required to evaluate the decision in terms of effect on ROCE, profit margin and asset turnover.

6.9 A single ratio is nearly meaningless. What is important is the movement in that ratio over time and the comparison of that ratio with other companies in a similar business.

6.10 **Earnings per share** shows the return due to the ordinary shareholders. This simply divides profit after tax by the average number of ordinary shares in issue whilst the profit was generated.

6.11 The **price/earnings (P/E) ratio** reflects the investors' view of the future prospects of a share. Share prices depend on expectations of future earnings.

$$P/E = \frac{\text{The market price of a share (in pence)}}{\text{Earnings per share}}$$

Gearing

6.12 **Gearing** is a method of comparing how much of the long-term capital of a business is provided by **equity** (ordinary shares and reserves) and how much is provided by long-term **loan capital**.

6.13 **Why is gearing important?**

(a) If a company's gearing is **too high** (say over 50%), **we might find that it is difficult to raise more loans.**

(b) **Loan capital is cheaper,** because the interest cost diminishes in real terms if secured on company assets and attracts tax benefits.

(c) Interest **must** be paid, whereas the directors of a company can decide **not** to pay a dividend.

(d) High gearing might be considered **risky** for lenders is that the more loan capital a business has, the bigger becomes the size of profit before interest and tax (PBIT) which is necessary to meet demands for interest payments.

Operational ratios

6.14 **Operational ratios relate to the cash cycle of a business.**

(a) A business which cannot pay its debts as they fall due is insolvent. **Liquidity** is a critical and urgent issue, which is why working capital is monitored thoroughly. A company facing crises in liquidity has few options.

(b) Often external parties, such a banks, will provide extra funds, but in extreme cases **marketing strategies must be devised to raise as much cash as possible.**

6.15 Consequently the finance function will monitor **turnover periods**. These ratios, usually expressed in days, measure how long or how many times the business is exchanging cash over a period of time.

6.16 **Debtors turnover period**, or **debt collection period**: the length of the credit period taken by customers or the time between the sale of an item and the receipt of cash for the sale from the customer.

(a) This describes the level of debtors compared with the sales turnover. So the ratio for ARC Ltd is:

	20X0	*20X1*
$\dfrac{\text{Debtors}}{\text{Sales}}$	$\dfrac{8,600}{53,470} = 16\%$	$\dfrac{26,700}{98,455} = 27\%$

(b) This can be expressed in days. By multiplying our ratio by 365 we recognise that the debtors are on average:

20X0	*20X1*
$\dfrac{8,600}{53,470} \times 365 = 59 \text{ days}$	$\dfrac{26,700}{98,455} \times 365 = 99 \text{ days}$

6.17 We can, of course, do similar turnover calculations for **stock turnover period**. This is the length of time an item stays in stores before use.

$$\frac{\text{Average finished goods stocks (use closing stock)}}{\text{Total cost of goods sold in the period}} \times 365 \text{ days}$$

	20X0	*20X1*
Stock turnover period	$\dfrac{5,000}{40,653} \times 365 = 45 \text{ days}$	$\dfrac{15,000}{70,728} \times 365 = 77 \text{ days}$

6.18 Similarly, the **creditors turnover period**, or period of credit taken from suppliers, is the length of time between the purchase of materials and the payment to suppliers.

$$\frac{\text{Average trade creditors (use closing creditors)}}{\text{Total purchases in the period} \star} \times 365 \text{ days}$$

	20X0	*20X1*
Creditors payment period	$\frac{6,000}{40,653} \times 365 = 54 \text{ days}$	$\frac{10,000}{70,728} \times 365 = 52 \text{ days}$

$\star$ Cost of sales can be substituted as an approximation

Again these can be expressed in days or months.

6.19 The **importance** of turnover ratios is their impact on **cash requirements**. An increase in the **stock turnover ratio** or in the **debtor turnover ratio** means that more money is being tied up in funding **working capital** and this may not be desirable.

Liquidity ratios

6.20 Liquidity as we have seen is an organisation's ability to convert its assets into cash to meet all the demands for payments when they fall due. They are particularly important for **credit control.**

6.21 **Current liabilities** are items which must be paid for in the near future. When payment becomes due, enough cash must be available to make the payment.

6.22 Let us see how some ratios apply.

Ratio	*Current ratio* $\frac{\text{Current assets}}{\text{Current liabilities}}$	*Quick ratio* $\frac{\text{Current assets less stock}}{\text{Current liabilities}}$
ARC 20X0	$\frac{14,500}{13,000} = 1.1{:}1$	$\frac{14,500 - 5,000}{13,000} = 0.7{:}1$
ARC 20X1	$\frac{42,100}{38,400} = 1.1{:}1$	$\frac{42,100 - 15,000}{38,400} = 0.7{:}1$

6.23 The best way to judge liquidity would be to look at the current ratio at different dates over a period of time. If the trend is towards a **lower current ratio,** we would judge that the **liquidity position is getting steadily worse.**

Action Programme 5

Calculate liquidity and working capital ratios from these accounts of a manufacturer of products for the construction industry.

	2000	1999
	£m	£m
Turnover	2,065.0	1,788.7
Cost of sales	1,478.6	1,304.0
Gross profit	586.4	484.7
Current assets		
Stocks	119.0	109.0
Debtors (note 1)	400.9	347.4
Short-term investments	4.2	18.8
Cash at bank and in hand	48.2	48.0
	572.3	523.2
Creditors: amounts falling due within one year		
Loans and overdrafts	49.1	35.3
Corporation taxes	62.0	46.7
Dividend	19.2	14.3
Creditors (note 2)	370.7	324.0
	501.0	420.3
Net current assets	71.3	102.9
Notes		
1 Trade debtors	329.8	285.4
2 Trade creditors	236.2	210.8

Exam Tip

Many of the analytical techniques in this chapter can be used in evaluation of strategies.

7   SEGMENTAL ANALYSIS AND CUSTOMER PROFITABILITY

7.1   **One of the most important tools for market analysis is that of segmentation.** We can approach this firstly by examining what market segments we currently market in and how big a contribution each segment is making to total turnover and profit. Finally we should consider whether each market segment is in growth or decline.

7.2   A segmental analysis might therefore look as follows.

Market segment	Turnover	Proportion of total turnover	Profit	Proportion of total profit
	£k		£k	
A	500	14%	50	9%
B	1,000	28%	200	36%
C	1,500	44%	150	27%
D	500	14%	150	27%

7.3   The following return on sales apply to each segment.

Market segment	Turnover	Profit	Profit as a % of turnover
	£k	£k	
A	500	50	10
B	1,000	200	20
C	1,500	150	10
D	500	150	30

7.4 You will note that each segment offers different profit opportunities.

How to calculate profits on a segmental basis

7.5 Identifying total turnover is easy. A segment is a collection of customers, and revenue streams from them are fairly easy to identify.

7.6 Identifying costs is much harder. Here are some different types of cost.

(a) **Fixed vs variable**

    (i) **Fixed costs:** you will incur these however many or however few items you produce or sell. Factory rent is an example.

    (ii) **Variable costs:** these relate directly to the number of units produced. For example, a variable cost in producing books is paper.

(b) **Controllable vs uncontrollable**

    (i) Controllable costs are at management discretion, such as an advertising campaign.

    (ii) Uncontrollable costs are those which, in the short run at least, management are committed to.

(c) **Direct vs indirect**

    (i) A direct cost relates to a unit of production (eg the amount of material).

    (ii) Indirect costs or overheads **cannot** be tied specifically to a unit of production. However, new management accounting techniques such as activity based costing try to set up the link.

(d) **Avoidable vs unavoidable**

    (i) Avoidable cost: this cost is affected by a decision.
    (ii) Unavoidable cost: this cost will not be affected by a decision.

For example, the cost of the managing director's salary will not be affected by a decision not to serve an individual customer.

7.7 **Typical marketing costs**

Cost	Comment
Direct selling expense	Personal calls by salesperson
Indirect selling	Sales admin, supervision
	Marketing research
Advertising	Media costs
Sales promotion	Consumer, trade etc
Transport	Carriage costs
Storage	
Order processing	Checking, billing, bad debts

7.8 These can be allocated, in different ways, to products, customer groups, and sales territories. We are currently interested in segments.

Step 1. Identify revenue derived from a segment

Step 2. Identify direct product costs (eg materials)

Step 3. Identify marketing costs

Step 4. Allocate **avoidable** costs to the segment (ie those costs which would be saved if the segment were not serviced)

Customer profitability

Marketing at Work

Take the Post Office. A uniform price is paid for a first class stamp irrespective of whether it is to be delivered to an address five miles away or five hundred (in the UK), despite the significant differences in transport costs. Of course the advantages of a uniform price are that there are savings on the costs of administering a wide range of prices, and that people are encouraged to use the postal services.

7.9 It is the case in many industries that the total costs of servicing customers can vary depending on **how** customers are serviced. Here are two examples.

(a) **Volume discounts.** A customer who places **one large order** is given a discount, presumably because it benefits the supplier to do so.

(b) The **different rates** charged by power utilities to domestic as opposed to business users. This reflects the administrative cost of dealing with individual customers.

Key Concept

Customer or segment profitability is the 'total sales revenue generated from a customer or customer group, less all the costs that are incurred in servicing that customer or customer group.'

7.10 EXAMPLE

Seth Ltd supplies shoes to Narayan Ltd and Kipling Ltd. Each pair of shoes has a list price of £50 each; as Kipling buys in bulk, Kipling receives a 10% trade discount for every order over 100 shoes. It costs £1,000 to deliver each order. In the year so far, Kipling has made five orders of 100 shoes each. Narayan Ltd receives a 15% discount irrespective of order size, because Narayan Ltd collects the shoes, thereby saving Seth Ltd any distribution costs. The cost of administering each order is £50. Narayan makes ten orders in the year, totalling 420 pairs of shoes. Which relationship is the most profitable for Seth?

7.11 SOLUTION

You can see below that the profit earned by Seth in servicing Narayan is greater, despite the increased discount.

	Kipling	*Narayan*
Number of shoes	500	420
	£	£
Revenue (after discount)	22,500	17,850
Transport	(5,000)	-
Administration	(250)	(500)
Net profit	17,250	17,350

7.12 **Customer profitability analysis (CPA)** focuses on profits generated by customers and suggests that profit does not automatically increase with sales revenue.

(a) The benefits of CPA are that a **company can focus its efforts on customers which promise the highest profit**, or at least it can **rationalise its approach to those which do not**. Note that the concern is **relative** differences in profitability.

(b) The obvious problem with CPA is identifying which customers or customer groups generate the most profit.

(c) This is a consideration that must be brought into **market segmentation** decisions. The firm's **existing customer groupings may reflect administrative measures (eg sales force convenience) rather than their strategic value or market realities.**

7.13 It is necessary to focus on the right costs for comparison.

(a) Costs **common to all customers** (eg sales director's basic salary) would not be avoided by failing to serve **one** of them.

(b) Furthermore, you have to be careful that you **choose the 'right' product cost**. The 'cost' of a product as revealed by the accounting system might include an amount of marketing overhead, which may **not** be avoided by ceasing to serve a customer. Therefore only **avoidable costs** should be taken into account.

7.14 Ward suggests the following format for a statement of customer or segment profitability.

		£'000
Sales revenue		X
Less direct product cost		(X)
		X
Customer or segment-specific variable costs:		
- distribution	X	
- rebates and discounts	X	
- promotion etc	X	
		(X)
		X
Other costs		
- sales force	X	
- customer service	X	
- management cost	X	
		(X)
		X
Financing cost		
- credit period	X	
- customer-specific inventory	X	
		(X)
Customer or segment profitability		X

7.15 Such a report can highlight the differences between the cost of servicing different individuals or firms. This information can be used for the following purposes.

(a) Directing management effort to cutting **customer or segment specific costs**. Installing an EDI system can save the costs of paperwork, data input and so forth.

(b) **Identifying those customers who are expensive to service**, thereby suggesting action to increase profitability.

(c) Using this as part of a **comparison with competitors' costs**. A firm which services a customer more cheaply than a competitor can use this cost advantage to offer extra benefits to the customer.

(d) CPA can indicate cases where **profitability might be endangered**, for example by servicing customers for whom a firm's core competence is not especially relevant.

Marketing at Work

Pareto's law, or the 80:20 rule applies here. In retail banking, wealthier customers account for a significant proportion of bank's profits. Hence many banks are targeting the 'new affluent' by setting up private bank subsidiaries for customers with assets of over £50,000.

Market performance ratios

7.16 An organisation should study information not only about its share of a particular market, but also the performance of the market as a whole.

(a) **Some markets are more profitable than others**. The reasons why this might be so (rivalry among existing firms, the threat of new entrants, the bargaining power of buyers, the bargaining power of suppliers and the threat from substitute products or services) were discussed in an earlier chapter.

(b) Some markets will be new, others growing, some mature and others declining. The stage in the product's life cycle might be relevant to performance analysis.

Information about market performance is needed to enable an organisation to plan and control its product-market strategy.

7.17 We can, of course, now make projections for these segments to determine where we are likely to be in the future and whether we need to consider moving into **new segments**.

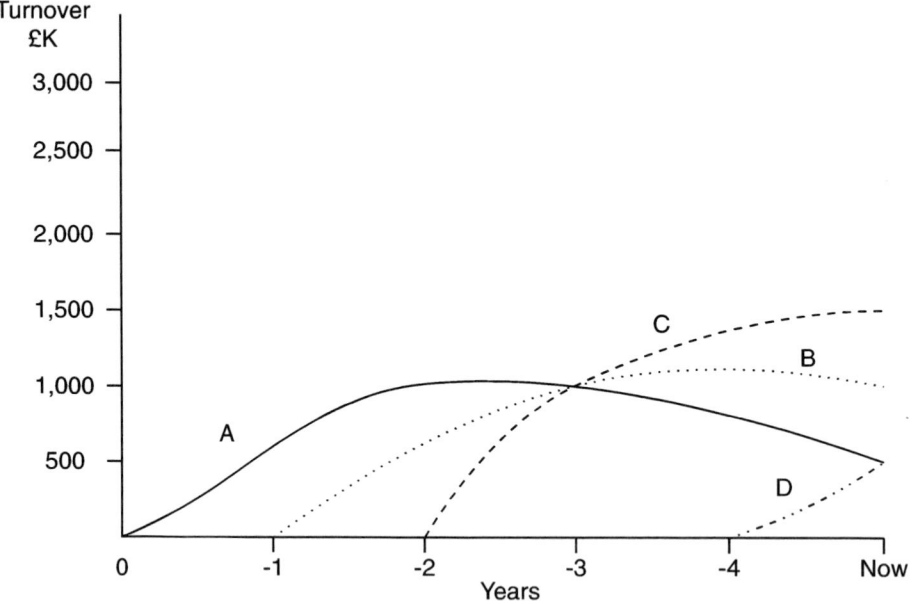

(a) Segment A is in decline and a relatively low contributor to profit.

(b) Segment B is contributing well to turnover and is the major contributor to profit.

(c) Segment C is growing. This is the major contributor to turnover and a relatively high contributor to profit.

(d) Segment D is a relatively new segment for us. Sales to this segment are likely to rise, and so could become our future major contributor to profit.

8 PRODUCTIVITY

> **Key Concept**
>
> **Productivity** is the ratio of $\dfrac{\text{Outputs}}{\text{Inputs}}$ or $\dfrac{\text{Output units}}{\text{Input units}}$

8.1 For example, a measure of productivity might be revenue/profit per employee.

	Revenue	*Profits*	*Employees*
Deutsche Telecom	$41.8bn	$2.5bn	179,000
TeleKom Italia	$27.3bn	$2.2bn	127,000
BT	$25.7bn	$2.8bn	124,000

In this example, BT appears to be most productive generating $22,000 profit per employee compared with $17,000 for TeleKom Italia and $14,000 for Deutsche Telecom.

8.2 Productivity can be targeted to marketing measures too.

8.3 **Examples of 'productivity' relating to marketing costs**

- Increases in customer recognition of a brand name per £ of advertising.
- Number of sales leads generated by an exhibition.
- Response rate to direct mailshots.
- Number of 'hits' on a website converted into purchases per cost of website.

Marketing at Work

Coca-Cola (*Economist* 24 April 1999)

Coca-Cola enjoyed volume growth of 7 - 8% pa in the 15 years to 1998, with profits rising 18% pa. However, on 21/4/99, it revealed a 13% fall in profits, and a return to shareholders of only 1.4%. The share price fell. Most worrying, unit-case volumes of syrup (the firm's preferred underlying measure of growth) fell by 1% Jan-March 1999, the first fall for a long time. Coca-Cola blamed the world economy.

Coke's recent growth was due to a unique set of circumstances. It had rationalised its bottling operations and Pepsi had not performed well. There is now market resistance to price increases. Selling expenses are $6.6bn, compared to net profit of $3.5bn. In 1997, a 4% rise in selling expenses produced a 10% rise in sales volumes. In 1998 a similar rise only increased volumes by 6%.

Update

Since that time, Coca-Cola has faced a public relations crisis in Belgium and two changes of chief executive. It is still successful, but is facing yet more changes in direction, and is investing in more brands.

In India, Coca-Cola markets itself and an Indian sub-brand *Thumsup*

Chapter Roundup

- The **published accounts** are relevant in understanding the basic **financial health** of a company and may provide some insight into fundamental trends and strategies being adopted. This is especially relevant to competitor analysis.

- A firm's **management accounting** function can provide valuable information to the marketer.

- **Profit** is sales revenue less costs. It is not the same as **liquidity**, which denotes a firm's ability to pay its bills on time, and to have access to cash. It is possible to have high profitability but low liquidity. A sale is not recognised until the customer has accepted the goods. It is not secure until the customer has paid. It is **timing differences** like this which differentiate profitability and liquidity.

- A **balance sheet** is a snapshot of the financial position of a business at a point in time.

- A **profit and loss account** measures the operational performance of the company over a period of time.

- Capital items are concerned with financing decisions. Revenue items are concerned with trading decisions.

- The **cash flow statement** is an analysis of where a business gets its cash and how cash is used.

- Financial terms have been defined in this chapter and you should be able to reproduce these definitions to enable you to communicate effectively with financial staff. The main definitions are given briefly here.

  ○ **Assets** are things of value that a business owns or has use of. **Fixed assets** are assets which are acquired for use within a business with a view to facilitating the generation of revenue (and consequently profits). **Current assets** are assets which are owned by the business which are intended to be turned into cash within one year. **Debts** are financial obligations **to** us. **Brands** are problematic.

  ○ **Liabilities** are financial obligations to someone else. **Creditors** are people to whom the business has a financial obligation. **Capital** is the money put into a business by the owners and it is therefore owed by the business to the owners.

  ○ **Gross profit** is the profit shown after the purchase or production cost of the goods sold is deducted from the value of sales.

  ○ **Net profit** is the gross profit, plus any other income from sources other than the sale of goods, minus other expenses of the business which are not included in the cost of goods sold.

- The **interpretation of financial data** is the key to the understanding of any business, either in a practical application or during your studies. Companies as large as GEC have been effectively managed for many years simply by ensuring that the ratios relevant to their businesses were kept within acceptable limits. These are the important to be lessons learned.

  ○ **Ratios** are a useful measure when in comparison with something else: either the company's history, or a competitor or an industry norm.

  ○ **Consistency in calculation** and in the base data is important otherwise we could end up comparing apples and oranges.

  ○ **Return on capital employed** is the product of two other ratios.

    ROCE = profit margin × asset turnover

  ○ **Gearing** is a measure of how funds have been generated to buy assets.

  ○ Proper control of cash is vital to the continued financial strength of any company. Marketing managers should be aware of the **debt collection periods** (also known as the debtor turnover or day sales outstanding) and other tests of liquidity such as stock turnover.

- Different **segments** and different **customers** offer different levels of **profit**.

Now try illustrative question 9 at the end of the Study Text

Quick Quiz

1 Why is accounting useful to the marketing manager? (see para 2.1)

2 What are the three main roles of the accounting function in relation to marketing activities? (2.3)

3 Give a definition of a fixed asset. (3.5)

4 What is a liability? (3.11)

5 What is the purpose of giving a financial value to brands? (3.14)

6 What is a simple definition of profit? (4.1, 4.2)

7 How is liquidity defined? (4.2)

8 Write down a list of the items which appear in the profit and loss account. (5.1)

9 How can ratios be used? (6.2)

10 What ratios would you use to determine whether a business could pay its liabilities as they fall due? (6.22)

11 Draw up a report to show customer or segment profitability. (7.14)

Action Programme Review

1 Do not be concerned with some of the more technical aspects of financial information but look at the **layout of the accounts**. It would be useful if you could obtain copies of similar documents from a couple of your major competitors or customers and compare the basic layout and information available. You may also note how useful this report has become as a means of communicating a **public relations** message to the shareholders and potential shareholders, to banks and to other users.

2 Many small firms sell to large companies. Large firms have higher bargaining power, as their suppliers **depend** on the sales. **Small firms have fewer financial resources**.

3 (a) Company A - low volume of sales, but high margin on each unit sold. To justify the high profit margin, the firm might have to differentiate its offer in some way, for example, by superior service or another differentiating factor, or by effective segmentation.

  (b) Company B - high volume, low margin. This might be similar to the 'Every Day Low Pricing' policy adopted by B&Q. Its explicit aim was to increase sales volume by lowering prices. It is unlikely that A or B would sell exactly the same product/service. Of course, they might sell the same equipment, but augmentation to the product might be made.

Furthermore, Company A and Company B may have little option but to pursue their different strategies, because of the characteristics of the industry and their existing position within it. This is relevant to **strategic group analysis.**

4 Is the increased profit figure necessarily a good thing?

  (a) At present, ratios are:

Profit margin	5%
Asset turnover	5 times
ROCE (5/20)	25%

  (b) With the proposed changes, the profit would be 10% × £150,000 = £15,000, and the asset turnover would be:

$$\frac{£150,000}{£75,000} = 2 \text{ times}, \text{ so that the ratios might be:}$$

Profit margin	× Asset turnover	=	ROCE		
10%	× 2 times	=	20%	ie	$\dfrac{15,000}{75,000}$

  (c) In spite of increasing the profit margin and raising the total volume of sales, the extra assets required (£55,000) only raise total profits by £(15,000 − 5,000) = £10,000. The return on capital

employed **falls** from 25% to 20% because of the sharp fall in asset turnover from 5 times to 2 times. In other words, the new investment is not used efficiently.

(d) This does not mean that the management of the company would not raise its prices. However, the financial analysis has provided them with another piece of the decision-making jigsaw. It may be that this is a weakness because the owners of the business, although very happy with the increased profitability, may not be happy with the reduced ROCE. The management must judge which aspect is most acceptable.

5

	2000	*1999*
Current ratio	$\dfrac{572.3}{501.0} = 1.14$	$\dfrac{523.2}{420.3} = 1.24$
Quick ratio	$\dfrac{453.3}{501.0} = 0.90$	$\dfrac{414.2}{420.3} = 0.99$
Debtors' payment period	$\dfrac{329.8 \times 365}{2,065.0} = 58$ days	$\dfrac{285.4 \times 365}{1,788.7} = 58$ days
Stock turnover period	$\dfrac{119.0 \times 365}{1,478.6} = 29$ days	$\dfrac{109.0 \times 365}{1,304.0} = 31$ days
Creditors' turnover period	$\dfrac{236.2 \times 365}{1,478.6} = 58$ days	$\dfrac{210.8 \times 365}{1,304.0} = 59$ days

10 *Techniques for Developing a Future Orientation*

Chapter Topic List	Syllabus reference
1 Setting the scene	
2 The future orientation	3.1
3 Gap analysis	3.1
4 Forecasting	3.1
5 Scenario planning	3.1
6 Market sensing	3.1

Learning Outcomes

- Understand and critically appraise a wide variety of marketing techniques, concepts and models.

- Prepare effective and realistic marketing plans.

Key Concepts Introduced

- Gap analysis
- Forecasting
- Projection
- Extrapolation
- Model

- Market forecast
- Sales potential
- Scenario
- Scenario planning
- Market sensing

Examples of Marketing at Work

- Virgin
- The Body Shop
- Paper merchants: UPM Kymenne

- Internet fiction
- Encyclopaedia Britannica

1   SETTING THE SCENE

1.1 A marketing plan is an attempt to '**control**' the future, based on assumptions as to how people will continue to behave and how trends will develop.

1.2 This chapter completes the 'analytical' section of this text. Thinking about the future is necessary for creation of strategic intent, and this chapter covers some of the ways in which thinking about the future can be systematised.

2   THE FUTURE ORIENTATION

2.1   'Some management teams were simply more foresightful than others. Some were capable of imagining products, services and entire industries that did not exist and then giving them birth. These managers seemed to spend less time worrying about how to position the firm in existing competitive space and more time creating fundamentally new competitive space.' (Hamel and Prahalad, 1994)

2.2   According to this view, there are two 'approaches' to the future.

- The future will be incrementally similar to the present.
- The future will be radically different.

2.3   Hamel and Prahalad suggest that:

- The future is not just something that 'happens' to organisations
- Organisations can 'create' the future

2.4   In practice, there is truth in both perspectives.

(a)   Some trends are likely to continue indefinitely. In the physical environment, global warming will continue for the long term. In terms of demography, other than wars or famine, it is relatively easy to predict population trends. Forecasting techniques cover this.

(b)   Other developments are harder to determine.

(i)   In 1900, a long-term investor would have invested in railway shares.

(ii)   In 1947, it was assumed that demand for computers would be no more than five worldwide.

(iii)   Even now, nobody really knows which inventions or innovations will succeed.

2.5   Hamel and Prahalad suggest, however, that **some companies are more 'prepared' to shape the future** than others, and that this **future-orientated stance is somehow embodied in the corporate culture.** Hamel and Prahalad offer a 'diagnostic' to indicate how future-orientated a company is.

Diagnostic statement	Protect the past	Create the future
Senior management's viewpoint about the future is ...	Conventional, reactive	Distinctive, far-sighted
Senior management spend most of their time on ...	Re-engineering current processes	Regenerating core strategies
Within the industry, the company ...	Follows the rules	Makes the rules
The company is better at ...	Operational efficiency	Building new businesses
To what extent does the company pursue competitive advantage by ...	Catching up with competitors?	Creating new sources of competitive advantage?
How is the company's agenda for change actually set?	By competitors	By a vision of the future
Are managers	Engineers of the present?	Architects of the future?
Are employees	Anxious?	Hopeful?

Action Programme 1

Undertake this diagnostic test for your own company. Carry it out alone and then get another member of staff to do it - from another department, say.

---

3   GAP ANALYSIS

3.1   Strategic planners must think about the extent to which new strategies are needed to enable the organisation to achieve its **objectives**. One technique whereby this can be done is **gap analysis**. Gap analysis is based on establishing:

(a)   What are the **organisation's targets for achievement** over the planning period?

(b)   What would the organisation be expected to achieve if it **did not** develop any new strategies, but **simply carried on in the current way** with the same products and selling to the same markets?

There will be a difference between the targets in (a) and expected achievements in (b). New strategies will then have to be developed which **will close this gap**, so that the organisation can expect to achieve its targets over the planning period.

Key Concept

Gap analysis is 'the comparison of an entity's ultimate objective with the sum of projections and already planned projects, identifying how the consequent gap might be filled'.

A forecast or projection based on existing performance: F_0 forecasts

3.2   The F_0 **forecast** is a forecast of the company's future results assuming that it **does nothing new**. The company is expected to continue to operate as at present without any changes in its products, markets, organisation, assets, human resources, research spending, financial structure, purchasing and so forth. Preparation of an F_0 forecast entails the following.

- The analysis of revenues, costs and volumes
- Projections into the future based on past trends
- Other factors affecting profits and return (eg in the environment, strikes, competitors)
- Finalising the forecast

3.3   The purpose of the F_0 forecast and gap analysis is to determine the **size of the task** facing the company if it wishes to achieve its target profits.

3.4   Forecasts can never be completely accurate. If possible, the error should be quantified in either of the following two ways.

(a)   **Estimating likely variations.** For example 'in 2001 the forecast profit is £5 million with possible variations of plus or minus £2 million'.

(b)   **Providing a probability distribution for profits.** For example 'in 2001 there is a 20% chance that profits will exceed £7 million, a 50% chance that they will exceed £5 million and an 80% chance that they will exceed £2½ million. Minimum profits in 2001 will be £2 million.'

The profit gap

3.5 The **profit gap** is the difference between the target profits (according to the overall corporate objectives of the company) and the profits on the F_0 forecast. Other forms of gap analysis (eg for sales revenue) can be developed.

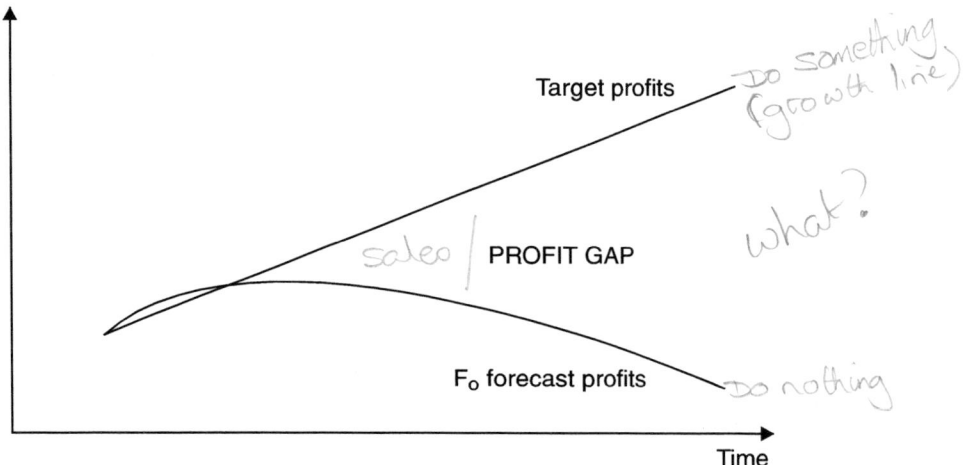

3.6 It is now that the company must decide what the **options are for bridging the gap**. This gap represents the extra task facing the company, in addition to just continuing the existing business. It indicates how much extra profit **has to be** generated by the decisions and the commitments to be made over the next few years. In deciding the size of the gap that must be closed, allowance must be made for errors in the forecast.

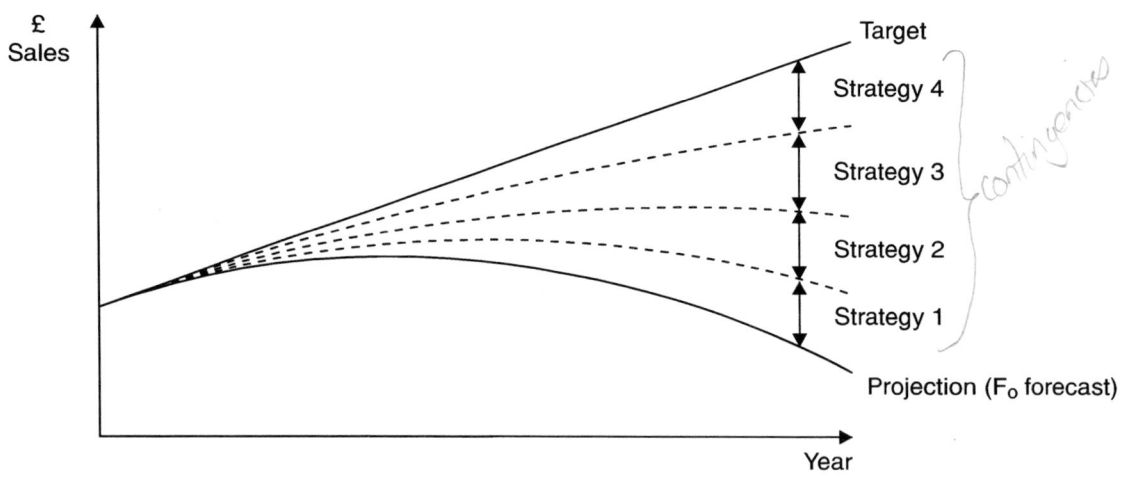

3.7 A key issue, however, is whether it is possible to forecast accurately.

4 FORECASTING

Types of forecast

Key Concepts

(a) **Forecasting** is 'the identification of factors and quantifications of their effect on an entity, as a basis for planning'.

(b) **Projection**. A projection is 'an expected future trend pattern obtained by extrapolation. It is principally concerned with quantitative factors whereas a forecast includes judgements'.

(c) **Extrapolation** is 'the technique of determining a projection by statistical means'.

Statistical forecasts

4.1 Statistical forecasts take past data and endeavour to direct it to the future, by **assuming** that **patterns or relationships which held in the past will continue to do so**. Many statistical techniques aim to reduce the uncertainty managers face. In **simple/static conditions the past is a relatively good guide** to the future.

4.2 **Statistical forecasting techniques for static conditions**

(a) **Time series analysis.** Data for a number of months/years is obtained and analysed. The aim of time series analysis is to identify:

- Seasonal and other cyclical fluctuations
- Long term underlying trends

For example, the UK's monthly unemployment statistics show a 'headline figure' and the 'underlying trend'.

(b) **Regression analysis** is a quantitative technique to check any underlying correlations between two variables (eg sales of ice cream and the weather). Remember that the relationship between two variables may **only hold between certain values**. (You would expect ice cream consumption to rise as the temperature becomes hotter, but there is a maximum number of ice creams an individual can consume in a day, no matter how hot it is.)

(c) **Econometrics** is the study of economic variables and their interrelationships, using computer models. Short-term or medium-term econometric models might be used for forecasting.

(i) **Leading indicators** are indicators which change **before** market demand changes. For example, a sudden increase in the birth rate would be an indicator of future demand for children's clothes. Similarly, a fall in retail sales would be an indicator to manufacturers that demand from retailers for their products will soon fall.

(ii) The firm needs the ability to **predict the span of time between a change in the indicator and a change in market demand.** Change in an indicator is especially useful for demand forecasting when they reach their highest or lowest points (when an increase turns into a decline or vice versa).

(d) **Adoptive forecasts** change in response to **recent** data.

4.3 **Problems with statistical forecasts**

(a) **Past relationships do not necessarily hold for the future.**

(b) Data can be misinterpreted, and **relationships assumed where none exist**. For example, sales of ice cream rise in the summer, and sales of umbrellas fall - the link is the weather, not any correlation between them.

(c) Forecasts do not account for special events (eg wars), the likely response of competitors and so on.

(d) The variation and depth of business cycles fluctuate.

(e) In practice statistical forecasters **underestimate uncertainty**.

Judgemental forecasts

4.4 Judgemental forecasts are used principally for the long term, covering several decades. However, because of the limitations of short-term forecasting they are used for the short

term too. Effectively, they are based on **hunches or educated guesses**. Sometimes, these prove surprisingly accurate. At other times they are wide of the mark.

Modelling

4.5 At various points in this text, you have been given frameworks or models to structure your thinking.

> ### Key Concept
>
> A **model** is anything used to represent something else.
>
> - Descriptive: describing real-world processes
> - Predictive: attempting to predict future events
> - Control: showing how action can be taken

4.6 A model is a simplified representation of reality, which enables complex data to be classified and analysed.

4.7 **Examples of models**

Type of model	Example	
Descriptive	Value chain	Buyer behaviour
	BCG analysis	
	Five competitive forces	
Predictive	Product life cycle	
	Cost-volume profit analysis	
Control	Input-process-output-feedback	
	Sensitivity analysis	
	Discounted cash flow	

4.8 Their relevance to building a 'future orientation' depends on **how well they are used** and a **recognition of their limitations**.

4.9 **Individual forecasting**

(a) A company might forecast sales on the basis of the judgement of one or more executives.

   (i) **Advantages**

   - Cheap
   - Suitable if demand is stable or relatively simple

   (ii) **Disadvantages**

   - Swayed most heavily by **most recent** experience rather than trend

(b) **Genius forecasting**

An individual with expert judgement might be asked for advice. This might be the case with the fashion industry; although demand might be hard to quantify, an ability to understand the mind of the customer will be very useful.

(c) In practice, 'forecasts' might be prepared by an interested individual who has read the papers, say, and has promoted an item for management attention.

Consensus forecasts

4.10 Jury forecasts

A panel of experts and/or executives prepare their own forecasts and a consensus forecast emerges from this.

(a) **Advantages**: expert opinions are sought and obtained.

(b) **Disadvantages.** The jury might **dilute** the best. The **group dynamics** will interfere with the decision. Each expert might differ and, in a face-to-face situation, the more forceful or confident would win the argument.

4.11 Delphi method. This was developed to overcome problems relying on **known** experts or personalities in the jury.

(a) Participants remain **anonymous**, known only to the organiser.

(b) Participants respond to a **questionnaire** containing tightly-defined questions. The Delphi technique **retains anonymity**. The results are collated and statistically analysed, and are defined by the organiser to each expert. The experts respond again.

(c) The Delphi technique is **time consuming**.

(d) In practice, it seems to be the case that experts are **universally optimistic.**

Statistical versus judgemental and consensus forecasts

4.12 David Mercer (1998) identifies the relative advantages and disadvantages of each method.

Use of forecasts	Statistical	Judgement
Changes in established patterns	Past data is no guide	Can be predicted but could be ignored
Using available data	Not all past data is used	Personal biases and preferences obscure data
Objectivity	Based on specific criteria for selection	Personal propensity to optimism/pessimism
Uncertainty	Underestimated	Underestimated, with a tendency to over-optimism
Cost	Inexpensive	Expensive

4.13 Using both methods

Judgemental forecasting is **speculative**. However, speculation may be necessary to identify changing patterns in data or 'weak signals' reflecting or presaging social changes.

Marketing at Work

Many small enterprises lack even the most basic marketing skills, with seven out of ten start-ups failing to identify their market and potential customers. But simple marketing techniques can make the difference between failure and runaway success.

Some of Britain's most innovative entrepreneurs started their businesses as little more than cottage industries. Richard Branson founded his business empire - which now stretches from air travel to personal equity plans - by selling records to his school friends, and Anita Roddick started The *Body Shop* by bottling potions and lotions on her kitchen table. Both have eschewed the text book marketing techniques and the jargon favoured by their competitors because they are intuitive marketers and, crucially, they carefully identified their target markets.

BPP
PUBLISHING

Inevitably, not all those starting up a new enterprise have the innate talent of a Branson or a Roddick and some fail to embrace even the most basic marketing principles. John Stubbs, chief executive of the Marketing Council, says: 'Marketing for some remains obscure and is perceived as an expensive luxury.' Recent research from Barclays Bank and The Chartered Institute of Marketing indicates that only three in ten start-up businesses carry out initial research to identify their market and potential customers, increasing the likelihood of one of the most common causes of business failure: loss of market and sales.

Market forecasts and sales forecasts

4.14 Market forecasts and sales forecasts complement each other. The market forecast should be carried out first of all and should cover a longer period of time.

> ### Key Concept
>
> **Market forecast.** This is a forecast for the market as a whole. It is mainly involved in the assessment of environmental factors, outside the organisation's control, which will affect the demand for its products/services.

   (a) **Components of a market forecast**

   (i) The **economic review** (national economy, government policy, covering forecasts on investment, population, gross national product, etc).

   (ii) **Specific market research** (to obtain data about specific markets and forecasts concerning total market demand).

   (iii) Evaluation of **total market demand** for the firm's and similar products, for example profitability, market potential etc.

   (b) **Sales forecasts** are estimates of sales (in volume, value and profit terms) of a product in a future period at a given marketing mix.

Research into potential sales

> ### Key Concept
>
> **Sales potential** is an estimate of the part of the market which is within the possible reach of a product.

4.15 **Factors governing sales potential**

   • The price of the product
   • The amount of money spent on sales promotion
   • How essential the product is to consumers
   • Whether it is a durable commodity whose purchase is postponable
   • The overall size of the possible market
   • Competition

4.16 Whether sales potential is worth exploiting will depend on the cost which must be incurred to realise the potential.

Example

Market research has led a company to the opinion that the sales potential of product X is as follows.

	Sales value	*Contribution earned before selling costs deducted*	*Cost of selling*
either	£100,000	£40,000	£10,000
or	£110,000	£44,000	£15,000

In this example, it would not be worth spending an extra £5,000 on selling in order to realise an extra sales potential of £10,000, because the net effect would be a loss of £(5,000 – 4,000) = £1,000.

Estimating market demand

4.17 Estimating market demand is not necessarily as straightforward as you might at first think. Imagine you are the marketing manager of a company producing sports footwear. What is your market demand? Is it the volume of shoes purchased in the UK, or Europe, or the whole world? Should you be considering tennis shoes as well as running shoes? Shoes for children or only adults? And should you be forecasting demand for next year or over the next five years? The permutations seem endless. Kotler identifies 90 possible combinations of market demand definitions based on product level, geographic area and time horizon.

4.18 **A demand function** is simply an expression which shows how sales demand for a product is dependent on several factors. These demand variables can be grouped into two broad categories.

   (a) **Controllable variables or strategic variables.** These are factors over which the firm's management should have some degree of control, and which they can change if they wish. Controllable variables are essentially the marketing mix.

   (b) **Uncontrollable variables.** These are factors over which the firm's management has no control.

       (i) **Consumer variables** depend on decisions by consumers, or the circumstances of consumers (for example their wealth).

       (ii) **Competitor variables** depend on decisions and actions by other firms, particularly competitors.

       (iii) **Other variables.** These include decisions by other organisations (for example the government) or factors which are outside the control of anyone (for example weather conditions, or the total size of the population).

4.19 A demand function can be set out as follows.

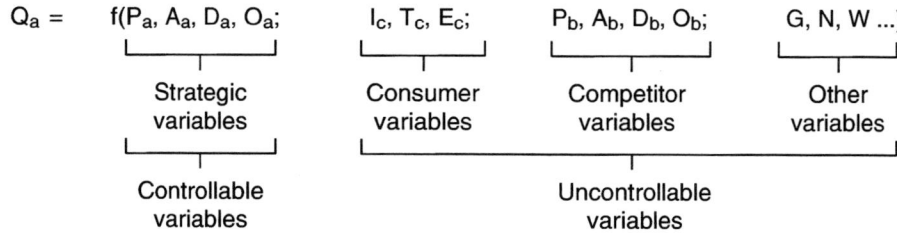

where

Q_a is quantity demanded of a product A per period
P_a is price of product A
A_a is advertising and sales promotion for product A
D_a is the design or quality of product A
O_a is the number of retail outlets or other outlets for distribution of product A

183

I_c is incomes of consumers/customers

T_c is the tastes and preferences of consumers

E_c is the expectation of consumers about future prices etc

P_b is the prices of related goods (substitutes, complements)

A_b is advertising/promotion for related goods

D_b is design and quality of related goods

O_b is the number of outlets for distribution of related goods

G   is government policy

N   is the number of people in the economy/potential market

W   represents the weather conditions

4.20   The demand function set out above is little more than common sense. But what firms should want to estimate or forecast is what future demand is likely to be. To do this, **an attempt should be made to quantify the relationship between demand for a product and the significant demand variables.** For example a demand function might be measurable as

$$Q_a = 3{,}000 - 0.032\,P_a + 240\,A_a + 0.05\,O_a + 0.35\,P_b - 320\,A_b - 0.02\,O_b + 36\,I_b$$

There are two problems with measuring a demand function in this way.

(a) **Measurement.** There is the problem of deciding how to measure variables, especially qualitative variables such as product design, and consumer tastes.

(b) **Valuation.** Then there is the mathematical problem of putting values to the 'constants' or coefficients for each variable (as in 4.19 above). This might be done using **regression analysis**.

5   SCENARIO PLANNING   6/00

5.1   Because the environment is so complex, it is easy to become overwhelmed by the many factors. Firms therefore try to model the future and one technique is **scenario building**.

> **Key Concepts**
>
> - A **scenario** is 'an internally consistent view of what the future might turn out to be'. (Porter)
> - **Scenario planning** is the development of a number of different views of the future to aid management decision-making

Macro scenarios

5.2   **Macro scenarios** use macro-economic or political factors, creating alternative views of the future environment (eg global economic growth, political changes, interest rates). Macro scenarios developed because the activities of oil and resource companies (which are global and at one time were heavily influenced by political factors) needed techniques to deal with uncertainties.

Building scenarios

5.3   Keeping the scenario process simple is the way to get most out of scenarios.

(a) Normally a **team** is selected to develop scenarios, preferably from diverse backgrounds. The team should include **'dissidents',** who challenge the consensus, and some **reference outsiders** to offer different perspectives.

(b)   Most participants in the team draw on general reading and specialist knowledge.

5.4   **Steps in scenario planning**

Step 1.   **Decide on the drivers for change**

- Environmental analysis helps determine key factors

- **At least** a ten year time horizon is needed, to avoid simply extrapolating from the present

- Identify and select the **important** issues and **degree of certainty**

Step 2.   **Bring drivers together into a viable framework**

- This relies almost on an intuitive ability to make patterns out of 'soft' data, so is the hardest stage.

- Items identified can be brought together as mini-scenarios.

- There might be many possible trends, but these can be grouped together.

Step 3.   **Produce seven to nine mini-scenarios. The underlying logic of the connections between the items can be explored.**

Step 4.   **Group mini-scenarios into two or three larger scenarios containing all topics.**

- This generates most debate and is likely to highlight fundamental issues.

- More than three scenarios will confuse people.

- The scenarios should be complementary not opposite. They should be equally likely. There is no 'good' or 'bad' scenario.

- The scenarios should be tested to ensure they hang together. If not, go back to Step 1.

Step 5.   **Write the scenarios**

- The scenarios should be written up in the form most suitable for managers taking decisions based on them.

- Most scenarios are qualitative rather than quantitative in nature.

Step 6.   **Identify issues arising**

- Determine the most **critical outcomes,** or **branching points** which are critical to the long term survival of the organisation

- Role play can be used to test what the scenarios mean to 'key actors' involved in the future of the business.

Industry scenarios

5.5   Porter believes that the most appropriate use for scenario analysis is if it is restricted to an industry. An **industry scenario** is an internally consistent view of an **industry's** future structure.

5.6   A set of industry scenarios is selected to reflect a range of possible futures. The **entire range**, not the most **likely** 'future', is used to design a competitive strategy. The process is as follows.

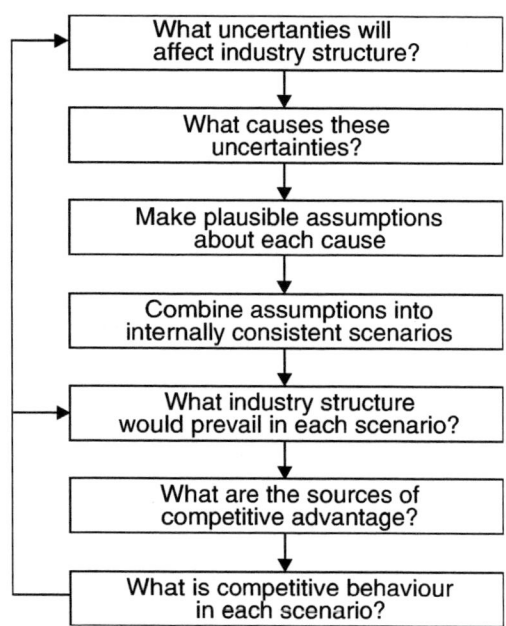

5.7 Using scenarios to formulate competitive strategy

(a) A strategy built in response to only **one scenario is risky**, whereas one supposed to cope with them **all might be expensive**.

(b) **Choosing scenarios as a basis for decisions about competitive strategy**

Approach	Comment
Assume the most probable	This appears to be common sense, but this choice puts too much faith in the scenario process and guesswork. A less probable scenario may be one whose **failure** to occur would have the **worst** consequences for the firm.
Hope for the best	A firm designs a strategy based on the scenario most attractive to the firm: wishful thinking.
Hedge	The firm chooses the strategy that produces **satisfactory** results under **all** scenarios. **Hedging, however, is not optimal**. The **low risk** is paid for by a **low reward**.
Flexibility	A firm taking this approach plays a 'wait and see' game. This means that the firm waits to follow others. It is more secure, but sacrifices first-mover advantages.
Influence	A firm will try and influence the future, for example by influencing demand for related products in order that its favoured scenario will be realised in events as they unfold.

Exam Tip

The June 2000 exam asked you to advise how **scenario planning** could help an academic publishing company. Note you were not asked to develop the scenario itself but show how the process could benefit the firm.

Marketing at Work

Scenario planning in *The paper industry*

Extracts from the *Financial Times*, 21 March 2001

If there is one thing managers are confident they understand, it is their business. So imagine the shock when they discover their assumptions about its future are probably wrong.

That was the experience of senior managers from *UPM-Kymmene*, one of the world's largest papermakers, when they embarked on a scenario-planning project led by the University of Strathclyde Graduate School of Business.

What could change things most radically was the **internet**, which was little understood when the project began in 1997. As managers drew up possible scenarios for the paper industry, the internet emerged as a serious threat to future demand.

To add value to the project, UPM invited IPC Media, the biggest customer of its Caledonian mill, to join in. IPC, then part of Reed Elsevier, publishes UK magazines ranging from TV Times to Woman's Own, Country Life and New Musical Express. Seven managers from UPM and three from IPC were interviewed about their perception of outside forces and concerns about the industry. The researchers synthesised the interviews into broad themes and presented them to the managers, whose overriding preoccupation then was the **volatile price of paper**.

This preoccupation was challenged as they spent two days developing three scenarios, naming them 'The Godfather', 'The Party of Invaders' and 'The new constellations'.

The first examined what would happen if industry consolidation gave fewer, larger companies greater control over how quickly paper capacity expanded. This scenario has been at least partially realised with the merger of Stora of Sweden and Enso of Finland in 1998 and more recent acquisitions by European groups in the Americas and Asia.

The Invaders scenario examined how the internet would affect consumers and demand for paper. The New Constellations considered how tense relationships between paper manufacturers and publishers, based on price and volume, might be replaced by greater co-operation.

One thing that has changed is UPM's approach to its customers, says Mr Borthwick. 'We've recognised very clearly and are very focused on delivering value, rather than just using the traditional commodity-type selling approach.

This shift led to the concept of 'synergy bank' through which UPM and its customers could benefit by helping each other. The paper manufacturer now offers customers advice on supply chain management, and they provide feedback on sales and readers.

Mr Burt is convinced, from his work with UPM and subsequently with a whisky company and a consulting firm in Scotland, that scenario planning leads to major changes in thinking.

Peter Barber, manufacturing director of IPC Media, says the publisher has reduced paper costs in a number of ways, partly thanks to the Strathclyde work. But he believes the big issues raised would have been better aimed at board directors.

Mr Borthwick does not expect demand for paper to slump in the foreseeable future. But he can imagine there might be a generational shift when children who have grown up with computers become decision-makers.

Website address: www.paperX.com

6 MARKET SENSING

12/99

Key Concept

Market sensing: 'how those ..... inside the company understand and react to the market place and the way it is changing' (Piercy, 1997)

6.1 **Market sensing** does **not** relate to the gathering and processing of information (**market research**) but how the information is **interpreted** and **understood** by decision makers in the company. It is related, therefore, to Johnson & Scholes' concept of the **recipe**.

Exam Tip

The difference between market sensing and market research came up in December 1999 in an essay question.

Marketing at Work

- Piercy cites the *Encyclopaedia Britannica*. Its managers simply did not believe that a small CD-ROM would replace the traditional book. In Autumn 1998, Encyclopaedia Britannica announced it was going to put its entire output on CD-ROM and abandon paper.

- In contrast, the horror novelist *Stephen King* decided in 2000 to publish a novel, chapter by chapter, on the Internet, for a 'voluntary' fee of $1. King abandoned the experiment because many people downloading the material did not pay, and there was not huge demand.

In short, market sensing failed. For reference, such as a dictionary or encyclopaedia, the ability to search is most important. People treat novels and narrative fiction in a different way, perhaps.

6.2 Piercy identifies the **myths of marketing information.**

- We need more information
- We need it quicker
- We can learn everything
- We know what our information needs are
- We know what we do **not** need to know
- We measure what matters
- We know what we know (and do not first accept what we are told)
- We know **who** decides what we know
- We know what this information means

6.3 These 'myths' are countermanded by practical organisational realities.

(a) **Organisational culture controls how information is interpreted and how the company's 'picture of the world' is treated.**

(b) 'Knowledge is power'; **information is a weapon** in organisational politics.

(c) Defining the 'market' and forecasting sales is often a matter for **negotiation**. Marketing information can produce a lot of conflicting evidence. Where does a 'niche' end and the 'market' begin?

(d) The significance of information depends in part on the choices managers make.

6.4 Market sensing is a process in which managers can be drawn in to challenge their preconceptions and improve their understanding. Ideally, the process is one of discovery.

6.5 **Process of market sensing**

Step 1. **Capture** information by identifying the **environment** (eg five forces), the dimension (eg **substitute** products), the **time frame** and the **market**.

Step 2. '**Brainstorm**' the events in the environment that are currently developing and assess the probability of their occurrence and their likely effect (on a scale).

Step 3. **Categorise** the event on the basis of probability and effect.

Utopia:	likely, desirable
Dreams:	unlikely, desirable
Danger:	likely, undesirable
Future risks:	unlikely, undesirable
Things to watch:	medium likelihood, neutral effect

Probability of event

		High		Low
	7	Utopia		Field of dreams
Effect of event			Things to watch	
	1	Danger		Future crises

Step 4. Answer the following questions

- Where are we planning for Utopia?
- Where are we planning for dangers?
- Where are we monitoring the factors in the MKIS?

It may be quite possible that managers have not made plans to deal with these eventualities or that the information systems do not report on these key issues.

Step 5. **Link** conclusions from the sensing approach explicitly to **marketing plans**.

Step 6. Encourage **participation** across **functions** and across **levels**. (Customer service staff have a very different perspective from the Board of Directors.)

Step 7. Where necessary, change information provision to provide a richer or more relevant picture of the world, whilst avoiding:

- Information overload
- Confusion as the existing model appears outdated
- Fear of making any decisions at all
- Creating conflict between groups who may have shared a sense of direction

Chapter Roundup

- **Future orientated** firms see the future as something that can be influenced and, in cases of industry transformation, created. A firm's activity to influence its future in part depends on the outlook of its management.

- Conventionally, **forecasting techniques** can be used to predict demand in the short to medium term. However, such techniques depend on the reliability of past data. The uncertainties in using statistical forecasting to predict the future are considerable.

- **Intuitive** or **judgemental forecasting** is sometimes used. The Delphi technique aims to ensure that group dynamics do not take over from consideration of the issues.

- **Scenario building** is a more structured approach to developing views of the future. A scenario has to be internally consistent.

- Some 'market signals' are hard to pick up, even though they may be of long-term significance. Managers thus need to be skilled in **market sensing**.

Now try illustrative question 10 at the end of the Study Text

Quick Quiz

1 Identify two views of the future (see para 2.2)

2 What is gap analysis? (3.1)

3 What do statistical forecasts do? (4.1)

4 What problems underlie using a panel of experts to develop a forecast? (4.10)

5 What is sales potential? (4.15)

6 What is a model? (4.5)

7 What is a scenario? (5.1)

8 Outline a step process for building scenarios. (5.4)

9 What is market sensing? (6.1)

Action Programme Review

1 The benefit of having someone from another department fill out the diagnostic is that you will get a different perspective on the business; Hamel and Prahalad talk about creating industries not markets.

Part D
Strategy Formulation and Selection

11 Strategic Intent

Chapter Topic List	Syllabus reference
1 Setting the scene	
2 Vision, mission and strategic intent	4.1
3 Goals and objectives: introduction	4.1
4 Commercial goals and objectives	4.1
5 Stakeholders' goals and objectives	4.1
6 The balanced scorecard	4.1
7 Marketing objectives	4.1
8 Customer, competitor and stakeholder orientation	4.1

Learning Outcomes

- Students should be able to understand and critically appraise a wide variety of marketing techniques, concepts and models.

Key Concepts Introduced

- Mission
- Goals
- SBU
- Stakeholders

Examples of Marketing at Work

- Co-op
- British Airways
- Marks & Spencer
- Oracle
- Mars
- Philip Morris

1   SETTING THE SCENE

1.1 In Section 2 we discuss mission: 'what business are we in?' Most of the time, the mission should not change, but you may find that the mission often needs to be rewritten to remain relevant to the needs of the organisation.

Links with other papers

1.2 For the *Analysis and Decision* paper, BPP's Tutorial Text suggests that you draft a mission statement from scratch or amend the existing mission statement - but changing a mission too often ends in mere sloganising.

1.3 Objectives (Section 3) are generally quantified targets as to what the organisation hopes to achieve. Corporate objectives often relate to the financial performance of the organisation as a whole. This financial performance generally reflects the expectations of shareholders, who balance the return on investment with the risk that it might all go sour. Corporate objectives cascade down to marketing objectives and then objectives for each element of the mix.

Exam Tip

Mission and objectives are implicit in many questions, as you may often be given targets as the context for the advice you must offer.

In December 1999, the examiner asked a specific question about:

* Influences on objectives
* Trade-offs between them

You can consider corporate as well as marketing objectives.

In June 2000, the examiner asked a question on the balanced scorecard (see Section 6) – a simple question about its usefulness.

In December 2000 and June 2001, you had to advise a company of the issues they should consider when **developing** mission, goals and objectives, the process as much as the content. (You were asked in particular to address the company's unique situation: this shows the importance of application.)

2 VISION, MISSION AND STRATEGIC INTENT 12/99, 12/00, 6/01

Key Concept

Mission 'describes the organisation's basic function in society, in terms of the products and services it produces for its clients'. (Mintzberg)

Marketing at Work

The *Co-operative* movement is a good example of the role of mission.

Being owned by their suppliers/customers rather than external shareholders, Co-op have always, since its foundation, had a wider social concern.

The Co-op has been criticised by some analysts on the grounds that it is insufficiently profitable, certainly in comparison with supermarket chains such as Tesco.

The Co-op has explicit social objectives. In some cases it will retain stores which, although too small to be as profitable as a large supermarket, provide an important social function in the communities which host them.

Of course, the Co-op's performance as a retailer can be improved, but judging it on the conventional basis of profitability ignores its social objectives.

Elements of mission

2.1 **Purpose**

Why does the company exist, or why do its managers and employees feel it exists?

(a) To create wealth for shareholders?

(b) To satisfy the needs of all stakeholders (including employees, society at large)?

(c) To reach some higher goal ('the advancement of society' and so forth)?

2.2 Strategy

Mission provides the commercial logic for the company, and so defines:

- The business the company is in, and the products/services it offers
- The competences by which it hopes to prosper, and its way of competing

2.3 Policies and standards of behaviour

The mission needs to be converted into **everyday performance**. For example, a service firm that wishes to be the best in its market must aim for standards of service at least as good as those offered by its competitors: this includes simple matters such as politeness to customers, speed at which phone calls are answered and so forth.

2.4 Values

Mission is a 'cultural glue that enables the organisation to function as a unity'. Values relate to the organisation's culture and are the basic, perhaps unstated, beliefs of the people who work in the organisation.

(a) Values can include **principles of business**:

- Commitment to suppliers and staff
- Social policy eg on non-discrimination or ecology
- Commitments to customers

(b) **Loyalty and commitment.** A sense of mission may inspire employees to sacrifice their own personal interests for the good of the whole. This however has to be reciprocated by company loyalty to its staff (eg long-term staff retention).

(c) **Guidance for behaviour.** A sense of mission helps create a work environment where there is a sense of **common purpose**.

2.5 A sense of mission within an organisation requires that the values of the business as a **collective entity** are in tune with the **personal values** of the individuals working for it. In conflicts of ethics, clashes between organisational and personal values are hard to resolve if someone's principles disagree with what the organisation wants.

2.6 For there to be a strong, motivating sense of mission, the four elements above must be mutually reinforcing.

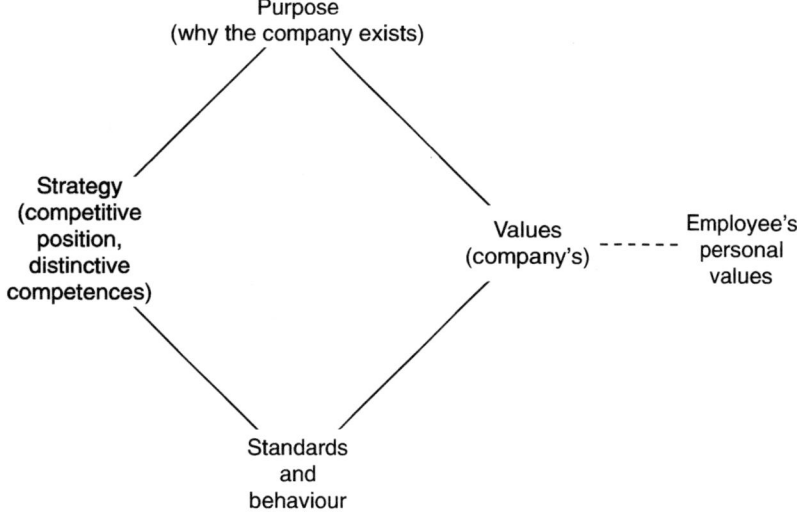

BPP PUBLISHING

Influences on mission statements

2.7 Johnson and Scholes (1999) see four major influences on an organisation's mission statement.

(a) **Corporate governance.** Voluntary and legal regulations act to constrain the management of a company and protect stakeholders from any abuse of power. Guidelines exist on such matters as the appointment and removal of directors and the length of their service contracts. The accountability of directors and managers to the shareholders (the owners of the business) influences strategic direction.

(b) **Stakeholders.** We look at these in section 5. Broadly speaking, they are the groups or individuals whose interests are directly affected by the activities of a firm or organisation. Organisations must ensure that they have regard to such interests when formulating strategy.

(c) **Business ethics.** This mainly refers to questions of social responsibility. Businesses must recognise that strategic options have varying effects on the wider community. One concern might be the sustainability of resources, or the effect of certain operations on a local community. As well as external factors, this area also brings in internal considerations, such as job design and working conditions for employees.

(d) **Cultural context.** Any business operates in a cultural environment, and this will influence strategic choices. Culture is manifested both at broad, national levels and within the organisation itself, where staff operating at functional levels may devise their own informal ways of getting things done.

The importance of mission

2.8 Mission is taken seriously by many firms.

(a) Values and feelings are integral elements of **consumers' buying decisions**, as evidenced by advertising, branding and market research. Therefore, there is no reason to exclude these matters from a company's decision-making processes further up the line. Customers not only ask 'What do you sell?' but 'What do you stand for?'

(b) It is an important communication mechanism **internally** (internal marketing) and **externally** (to various publics).

(c) Studies into organisational behaviour suggest that employees are **motivated** by more than money. A sense of mission and values can help to motivate employees.

(d) Many firms take mission seriously in strategic management.

2.9 **Mission statements** are formal statements of an organisation's mission. They might be reproduced in a number of places (eg at the front of an organisation's annual report, on publicity material, in the chairman's office, in communal work areas etc). There is no standard format, but they should be:

- **Brief** - easy to understand and remember
- **Flexible** - to accommodate change
- **Distinctive** - to make the firm stand out

Vision

2.10 A strategic thinker should have a **vision** of:

- What the business is now
- What it could be in an ideal world
- What the ideal world would be like

Marketing at Work

At the moment there is a debate in the computer industry about the future of the PC.

(a) Other challengers to the PC include enhanced games consoles, from a different market segment entirely.

2.11 A vision gives a general sense of direction to the company, even if there is not too much attention to detail. A vision, it is hoped, enables **flexibility** to exist in the context of a guiding idea. 'Like the North Star, a manager's vision is not a goal. Rather, it is the orientation point that guides the company in a specific direction. A vision should be clear.

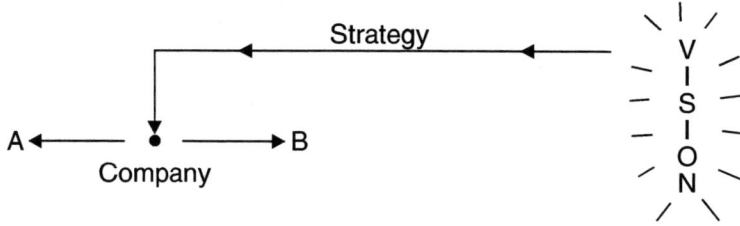

A company with two choices would move to 'B' rather than 'A'. The strategy draws on the vision. A vision might provide the 'boundaries' for the firm's direction.

2.12 **Problems with vision**

- It ignores real, practical problems.

- It can degenerate into wishful thinking on the part of managers, blinding them to reality.

2.13 **Differences between mission and vision**

(a) Mission is about the here and now, whereas vision refers to the future.

(b) A vision which is too vague will fail to motivate, whereas a mission is designed to motivate.

(c) A vision, when achieved, might lose motivating power unless it can be reinvented.

Marketing at Work

Beyond petroleum

Vision: *Then*

In the **early 1990's**, BP articulated its 'vision' as follows:

'With our bold, innovative strategic agenda, BP will be the world's most successful oil company in the 1990's and beyond.

In 2001, BP has effectively rebranded itself, with an advertising campaign with the strapline 'beyond petroleum'. Although petrol is the world's principal source of global warming, BP is trying to promote an 'environmentally conscious' message, by repositioning itself as an energy company and investing more in alternative or renewable sources of energy such as solar power.

Vision: *Now*

Arguably, the 'vision' has changed. From the stated desire to be the world's most successful oil company, BP has moved to a state 'beyond' petroleum.

BPP PUBLISHING

Mission

But what about **mission**? Mission describes the **purpose** of the company, in other words why it exists at all. Many organisations interpret their mission in terms of stakeholders, typically the owners or shareholders and customers.

BP once described itself as follows

'BP is a family of businesses principally in oil and gas exploration and production, refining and marketing, chemicals and nutrition. In everything we do we are committed to **creating wealth**, always with integrity, to reward the stakeholders in BP – our shareholders, our employees, our customers and suppliers and the community.' (BPP emphasis)

Website address: www.bpamoco.com

Strategic intent

2.14 **Strategic intent** is similar to the 'strategy' concept of mission as outlined above and to vision. Strategic intent as defined by **Hamel and Prahalad** involves the following.

(a) 'A **dream** that energises a company' (Hamel and Prahalad). It has an **emotional** core.

(b) It implies a '**stretch**' for the organisation, even if current resources will not satisfy the aspirations of the vision. It is more than just matching resources with objectives.

(c) Sense of **direction**. It is a long-term ambition, which enables the integration of complex skills within the firm.

(d) Sense of **discovery**: strategic intent offers a new destination for employees to work towards.

(e) It gives **coherence** to strategic plans.

2.15 'Strategic intent' aims to enthuse employees with the company's business goals, as if they are fighting a war. (**Values** in the long term are possibly more motivating.)

Action Programme 1

Spend a little time producing a short mission statement for each of the following organisations. Make clear any differences between what you think their current mission statement is and what you think it should be.

(a) The local library
(b) Your local college
(c) Your GP's practice

Vision, mission and planning

2.16 Although the mission and vision might be seen as a set of abstract principles, they can play an important **role in the planning process**.

(a) **Plans should outline the fulfilment of the organisation's mission**. To take the example of a religious organisation, the mission of 'spreading the gospel' might be embodied in plans to send individuals as missionaries to various parts of the world, plans for fund-raising activities, or even targets for the numbers of new converts.

(b) **Evaluation and screening**. Mission also acts as a yardstick by which plans are judged.

(i) Take the example of a financial services organisation which runs a number of 'ethical' investment funds. 'Ethical' investment funds exclude from their

investment portfolios shares in firms involved in alcohol, tobacco and armaments. Therefore, if a new fund manager proposed as part of an investment strategy to invest in shares of a diversified company involved in several product market areas, the company would be examined to see if its activities included those which the investment fund considered 'unethical'. The investment strategy would be assessed with reference to the investment fund's mission.

 (ii) Mission helps to ensure consistency in decisions.

(c) **Implementation.** Mission also affects the implementation of a planned strategy, in terms of:

- The ways in which the firm carries out its business
- The culture of the organisation.

In other words, mission can be embodied in the policies and behaviour standards of the firm.

3 GOALS AND OBJECTIVES: INTRODUCTION

3.1 From the mission, **goals** are derived.

> ## Key Concept
>
> **Goals** are 'the intentions behind decisions or actions, the states of mind that drive individuals or collectives of individuals called organisations to do what they do.' Mintzberg *(Power In and Around Organisations)*

(a) **Operational goals** can be expressed as **objectives**. Mintzberg says that an objective is a goal expressed in a form by which its attainment can be **measured**. Here is an example.

 (i) **Mission**: deliver a quality service

 (ii) **Goal**: enhance manufacturing quality

 (iii) **Objectives**: over the next twelve months, reduce the number of defects to 1 part per million

(b) **Non-operational goals** or **aims** on the other hand cannot be expressed as objectives. Mintzberg quotes the example of a university, whose goal might be to 'seek truth'. This cannot really be expressed as a quantified objective.

3.2 Objectives should meet the **SMART** criteria. They should be:

- **S**pecific
- **M**easurable
- **A**ttainable
- **R**esults-orientated
- **T**ime-bounded

3.3 However, not all goals, as we have seen, can be measured, or can ever be attained completely. **Customer satisfaction** is a goal, but satisfying customers and ensuring that they remain satisfied is a **continuous process** that does not stop when one target has been reached.

4 COMMERCIAL GOALS AND OBJECTIVES

4.1 **Objectives** are normally **quantified statements** of what the organisation actually intends to achieve over a period of time.

4.2 Uses of objectives

(a) Objectives **orientate the activities** of the organisation towards the fulfilment of the organisation's mission, in theory if not always in practice.

(b) In business organisations, a paramount consideration is **profitability**. The mission of a business, whether this is stated or not, must be to carry on its activities at a profit.

(c) Objectives can also be used as standards **for measuring the performance** of the organisation and departments in it.

Corporate and unit objectives

4.3 **Corporate objectives** concern the firm as **a whole**, for example:

- Profitability
- Market share
- Growth
- Cash flow
- Return on capital employed
- Risk

- Customer satisfaction
- Quality
- Industrial relations
- Added value
- Earnings per share

4.4 Similar objectives can be developed for each **strategic business unit (SBU)**.

Key Concept

A strategic business unit **(SBU)** is a part of the company that for all intents and purposes has its own distinct products, markets and assets.

4.5 **Unit objectives** are objectives that are specific to individual units of an organisation. Some examples are as follows.

Primary and secondary objectives

4.6 Some objectives are more important than others. There is a **primary corporate objective** (restricted by certain constraints on corporate activity) and other **secondary objectives** which are strategic objectives which should combine to ensure the achievement of the primary corporate objective.

(a) For example, if a company sets itself an objective of growth in profits, as its primary objective, it will then have to develop strategies by which this primary objective can be achieved.

(b) Secondary objectives might then be concerned with sales growth, continual technological innovation, customer service, product quality, efficient resource management (eg labour productivity) or reducing the company's reliance on debt capital etc.

Ranking objectives and trade-offs   12/99

4.7   Where there are multiple objectives a problem of ranking can arise.

(a)   **There is never enough time or resources** to achieve all of the desired objectives.

(b)   **There are degrees of accomplishment.** For example, if there is an objective to achieve a 10% annual growth in earnings per share, an achievement of 9% could be described as a near-success. When it comes to ranking objectives, a target ROI of, say, 25% might be given greater priority than an EPS growth of 10%, but a lower priority than an EPS growth of, say, 15%.

4.8   Some objectives might be achieved only **at the expense of others**. For example, a company's objective of achieving good profits and profit growth might have adverse consequences for the cash flow of the business, or the quality of the firm's products.

4.9   There will be a **trade-off** between objectives when strategies are formulated, and a choice will have to be made. For example, there might be a choice between the following two options.

Option A   15% sales growth, 10% profit growth, a £2 million negative cash flow and reduced product quality and customer satisfaction.

Option B   8% sales growth, 5% profit growth, a £500,000 surplus cash flow, and maintenance of high product quality/customer satisfaction.

If the firm chose option B in preference to option A, it would be trading off sales growth and profit growth for better cash flow, product quality and customer satisfaction. The long-term effect of reduced quality has not been considered.

4.10   One of the tasks of strategic management is to ensure **goal congruence**. Some objectives may not be in line with each other, and different stakeholders have different sets of priorities.

Marketing at Work

There are plenty of examples of 'primary' objectives throughout this book.

For businesses, these are long-term profits; note the constant concern about the share price. To what extent, however, is this profit/shareholder orientation a peculiarity of the UK?

Look at Marks & Spencer in 2001.

(a)   In the short term, for managers the primary objectives is survival.

(b)   For investors, the primary objective is profitability and shareholder wealth

(c)   These objectives translate into

- Increased sales, for store managers
- More attractive designs, for designers
- Lower costs for buyers

Website address: www.marksandspencer.com

Long-term and short-term objectives

4.11   Objectives may be long-term and short-term.

(a)   A company that is suffering from a recession in its core industries and making losses in the short term might continue to have a primary objective in the long term of achieving a steady growth in earnings or profits, but in the short term, its primary objective might switch to survival.

(b) Secondary objectives will range from short-term to long-term. Planners will formulate secondary objectives within the guidelines set by the primary objective, after selecting strategies for achieving the primary objective.

5 STAKEHOLDERS' GOALS AND OBJECTIVES

5.1 Johnson and Scholes (*Exploring Corporate Strategy*) argue that although 'economic' objectives are an important influence on strategy formulation, 'strategies tend to evolve in organisations within a cultural and political system'.

Stakeholders

> **Key Concept**
>
> **Stakeholders:** groups or individuals whose interests are directly affected by the activities of a firm or organisation.

5.2 Here are the main stakeholder groups.

Stakeholder group	Members
• Internal stakeholders	Employees, management
• Connected	Shareholders, customers, suppliers, lenders
• External	The government, local government, the public

5.3 Stakeholder groups can exert influence on strategy. The greater the power of a stakeholder group, the greater its influence will be on strategy.

5.4 Each stakeholder group has different expectations about what it wants, and the expectations of the various groups will conflict.

Stakeholders' objectives

5.5 Here is a checklist of stakeholders' objectives. It is not comprehensive.

(a) **Employees and managers**

- Job security (over and above legal protection)
- Good conditions of work (above minimum safety standards)
- Job satisfaction
- Career development and relevant training

(b) **Customers**

- Satisfaction of expectations
- After sales service
- Consistent quality

(c) **For suppliers**: to offer regular orders in return for reliable delivery and good service.

(d) **For shareholders**: to provide an appropriate return.

(e) **For society as a whole**

- Control pollution
- Financial assistance to charities, sports and community activities
- Co-operate with the government in minimising health risks in the product

We will return to stakeholder analysis in Chapter 15. However, this goes to show that satisfying customers cannot be achieved in isolation from other objectives.

Marketing at Work

British Airways publicity once indicated the following corporate goals.

- Safety and security
- Strong and consistent financial performance
- Global reach
- Good neighbourliness

- Superior services
- Good value for money
- Healthy working environment

'Overall, our aim is to be the best and most successful company in the airline industry.'

---

6   THE BALANCED SCORECARD   6/00

6.1   The balanced scorecard is a technique designed to ensure that the different functions of the business are integrated together in order that they work to achieve the corporate goals.

> ### Key Concept
>
> The **balanced scorecard** is 'a set of measures that gives top managers a fast but comprehensive view of the business. The balanced scorecard includes financial measures that tell the results of actions already taken. And it complements the financial measures with operational measures on customer satisfaction, internal processes, and the organisation's innovation and improvement activities - operational measures that are the drivers of future financial performance.' (Robert Kaplan, January-February 1992, *Harvard Business Review.*)

6.2   'Traditional financial accounting measures like return on investment and earnings per share can give misleading signals for continuous improvement and innovation'. The balanced scorecard allows managers to look at the business from **four important perspectives**.

- **Customer**
- **Financial**

- **Internal business**
- **Innovation and learning**

Customer perspective

6.3   **'How do customers see us?'** The balanced scorecard translates this into specific measures.

(a) **Time.** Lead time is the time it takes a firm to meet customer needs, from receiving an order to delivering the product.

(b) **Quality.** Quality measures not only include defect levels - although these should be minimised by TQM - but accuracy in forecasting.

(c) **Performance** of the product. (How often does the photocopier break down?)

(d) **Service.** How long will it take a problem to be rectified? (If the photocopier breaks down, how long will it take the maintenance engineer to arrive?)

6.4 To view the firm's performance through customers' eyes, firms hire market researchers to assess how the firm performs. Higher service and quality may cost more at the outset, but savings can be made in the long term.

Internal business perspective

6.5 Findings from the **customers'** perspective need to be **translated into the actions the firm must** take to meet these expectations. The **internal business perspective** identifies the **business processes that have the greatest impact on customer satisfaction,** such as quality and employee skills.

   (a) Companies should also attempt to identify and measure their **distinctive competences** and the critical technologies they need to ensure continued leadership. Which processes should they excel at?

   (b) To achieve these goals, **performance measures must relate to employee behaviour,** to tie in the strategic direction with employee action.

   (c) An information system is necessary to enable executives to measure performance. An **executive information system** enables managers to drill down into lower level information.

Innovation and learning perspective

6.6 The question is '**Can we continue to improve and create value?**' Whilst the customer and internal process perspectives identify the **current** parameters for competitive success, the company needs to learn and to innovate to **satisfy future needs.** This might be one of the hardest items to measure.

   (a) How long does it take to develop new products?

   (b) How quickly does the firm climb the experience curve to manufacture new products?

   (c) What percentage of revenue comes from new products?

   (d) How many suggestions are made by staff and are acted upon?

   (e) What are staff attitudes? Some firms believe that employee motivation and successful communication are necessary for organisational learning.

   (f) Depending on circumstances, the company can identify measures for training and long-term investment.

   Continuous improvement measures might also be relevant here.

Financial perspective

6.7 From the financial perspective, the question to be asked is: '**How do we appear to shareholders?**' Financial performance indicators indicate 'whether the company's strategies, implementation, and execution are contributing to bottom line management.'

6.8 Some analysts consider that financial issues take care of themselves, and that they are only the **result** of the customer, internal process, and innovation and learning issues discussed earlier. This view is rather naive for a number of obvious reasons.

   (a) Money is a resource, and financial measures will ultimately effect a firm's ability to obtain that resource (eg by raising the firm's cost of capital, if shareholders perceive greater risk).

(b) Well designed financial control systems can actually assist in TQM programmes (eg by identifying variances).

(c) The balanced scorecard **only measures** strategy. **It does not indicate that the strategy is the right one.** 'A failure to convert improved operational performance into improved financial performance should send executives back to their drawing boards to rethink the company's strategy or its implementation plans.'

Linkages

6.9 **Disappointing results** might result from a **failure to view all the measures as a whole.** For example, increasing productivity means that fewer employees are needed for a given level of output. Excess capacity can be created by quality improvements. However these improvements have to be exploited (eg by increasing sales). The **financial element** of the balanced scorecard 'reminds executives that improved quality, response time, productivity or new products, benefit the company only when they are translated into improved financial results', or if they enable the firm to obtain a sustainable competitive advantage.

6.10 **EXAMPLE: A BALANCED SCORECARD**

Balanced Scorecard

Financial Perspective

GOALS	MEASURES
Survive	Cash flow
Succeed	Monthly sales growth and operating income by division
Prosper	Increase market share and ROCE

Customer Perspective

GOALS	MEASURES
New products	Percentage of sales from new products
Responsive supply	On-time delivery (defined by customer)
Preferred supplier	Share of key accounts' purchases
	Ranking by key accounts
Customer partnership	Number of cooperative engineering efforts

Internal Business Perspective

GOALS	MEASURES
Technology capability	Manufacturing configuration vs competition
Manufacturing excellence	Cycle time
	Unit cost
	Yield
Design productivity	Silicon efficiency
	Engineering efficiency
New product introduction	Actual introduction schedule vs plan

Innovation and Learning Perspective

GOALS	MEASURES
Technology leadership	Time to develop next generation of products
Manufacturing learning	Process time to maturity
Product focus	Percentage of products that equal 80% sales
Time to market	New product introduction vs competition

6.11 From a marketing point-of-view, the balanced scorecard enables all the vital perspectives - not just the financial ones - to be taken into account. In fact two of the main perspectives - customer and innovation - relate directly to marketing

7 MARKETING OBJECTIVES

7.1 To take an example, let's say that middle managers have been faced with a corporate objective of increasing profitability by x% over three years.

   (a) In pursuit of this, **production** could cut costs, reduce stockholdings and trim back production levels.

   (b) **Marketing** could be implementing strategies to increase revenue, through higher sales. These two departments would clearly be working **against each other**, although both aiming to contribute to the stated corporate goal.

7.2 It is only when armed with clear, quantified corporate objectives and the co-ordinating influence of a corporate strategy that unit managers can develop their own functional plans. The first step is to generate unit objectives.

7.3 We can outline a hierarchy as follows.

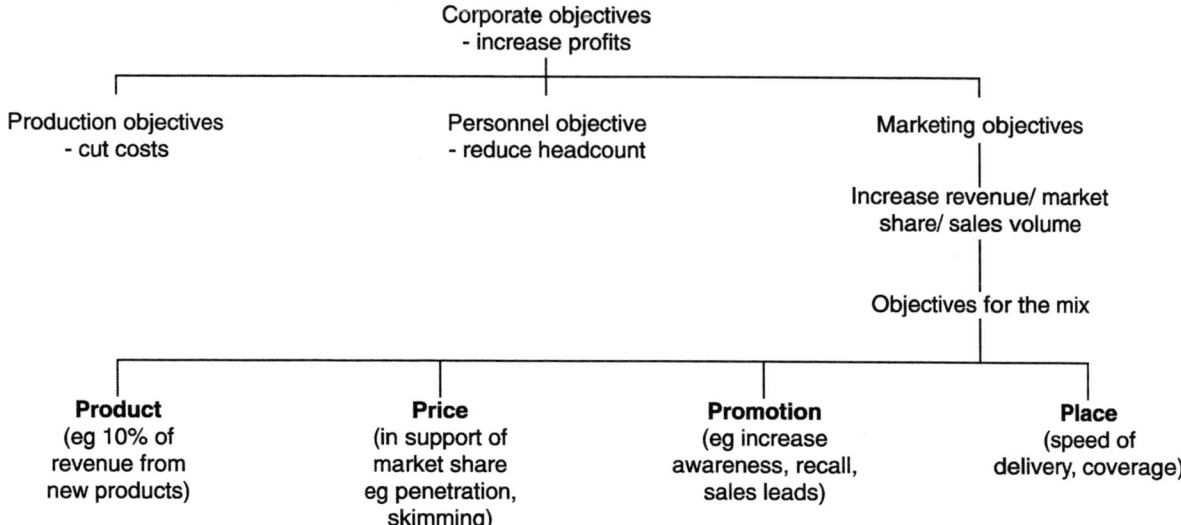

7.4 EXAMPLE

Marketing objectives are often expressed in **sales terms**, for example, market share or revenue or sales volume.

   (a) For example A Ltd wishes to increase **market share** to 43% by 2005.

   (b) This objective can then be further developed by the sales manager who can forecast that 43% in 2005 will equal 1 million cases. In turn the sales manager can then develop the next level of objectives into terms which mean something to those in the sales team: to sell 1,000 more cases per month by 2005.

   (c) The individual sales targets or objectives can be set from this. With a salesforce of 20, each salesperson needs to be selling 50 extra cases per month by 2005.

7.5 Objectives can be set for other elements of the mix and for marketing activities.

Mix element	Comment
Product	Although 'marketing' deals with products and markets, marketing objectives for products require the co-operation of the production department and R&D. Marketing can suggest that a percentage (eg 10%) of revenue should come from **new products.**
Pricing	**Distribution** pricing has market share implications (eg penetration or skimming pricing). Distribution can be considered a marketing tool - an objective might be to reduce the time from when the order is received to when the goods are delivered: 'By March 2007, reduce delivery lead times from 5 to 3 days'.
Promotion	Advertising and promotion objectives can be set to shape customer awareness and expectations of the product as well as to generate sales leads. • Recall: How many remember an ad? • Awareness • Interest (eg % of people replying to a mailshot) • 'Share of voice' (compared to other companies' promotions)
Service marketing mix	• People - staff training • Processes - efficiency • Physical evidence (cleanliness of sites).
Customers	• For many firms, repeat business is more profitable than new business - this is the justification behind **relationship marketing,** discussed in a later chapter. • A firm might **reposition** its offer to attract a new segment.

7.6 Finally, a firm's marketing activities might relate to **crisis management**, which might be the objective of a public relations department.

Marketing at Work

The American tobacco company *Philip Morris* advertised scientific studies which revealed that the dangers of passive smoking (ie inhaling other people's cigarette smoke) have been much exaggerated.

This campaign was widely controversial. Allegedly, the tobacco industry funded the research, but importantly, other research studies contradicted its conclusions. Most people don't understand the niceties of a scientific procedure and are unaware of much of the material on the topic.

What do you think the objective of the campaign was, in terms of the firm's wider strategy?

8 CUSTOMER, COMPETITOR AND STAKEHOLDER ORIENTATION

8.1 A competitor orientation involves a firm comparing its performance with a competitor and designing its marketing programmes accordingly.

8.2 A purely customer orientation views this as secondary, but companies cannot get away from the problem that the customer is always **comparing** the offers made by competitors.

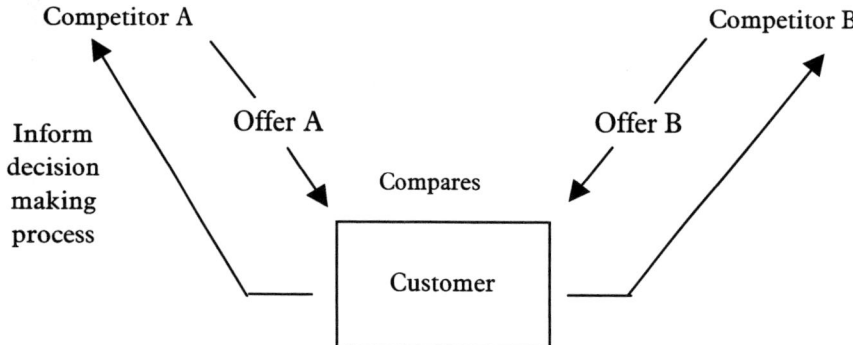

8.3 No matter how focused a firm is on the customer's needs, the space in the customer's mind is always important and competitors are always fighting for it.

8.4 A **competitor focus** is necessary for the reason that competitors can and do undermine your own strategy if they are powerful. In the long term, the survival of the business is at stake.

8.5 The importance of the competitors is underlined in an article in *Marketing Business* (July/August 1996) by Sean Meeham and Patrick Bourse. They argue that 'competition' is an underestimated aspect of the marketing process.

    (a) **The 'battleground' is the customer's mind**. 'One component which appears to distinguish winners is the amount of time senior managers spend talking to real customers, defectors and prospects.'

    (b) Firms should aim to '**understand the competition better than themselves**', in other words competitor assumptions, strategies, weaknesses and problems.

    (c) Firms should really **differentiate the product**: 'a winning positioning is not one that just sounds good, it is one that customers believe achieves a genuine differentiation of your offering'.

8.6 **Porter** (*Harvard Business Review*, Nov - Dec 1996) highlights the importance and danger of taking a competitive viewpoint. Porter suggests that over the past twenty years, firms have been learning to play by a new set of rules, using benchmarking, outsourcing and the nurture of a few basic core competences. However, **many companies are now competing destructively** with each other in a state of **hyper-competition**. 'As managers push to improve on **all** fronts, they move further away from viable competitive positions'.

8.7 **Creating a sustainable strategic position**

Task	Comment
Operational effectiveness is not the same as strategy	Organisational effectiveness involves doing the **same** things better than other firms. Managers' use of TQM is geared towards operational effectiveness - improvements here can be imitated.
Strategy rests on unique activities	Competitive strategy is about being **different** ... choosing to perform activities differently or to perform different activities than rivals.

Task	Comment
A sustainable strategic position requires trade-offs	• Trade-offs limit what a company does. Trade-offs occur: ○ When activities are not compatible (eg an airline can offer a cheap no-meals service, or offer meals. Doing both results in inefficiencies). ○ Where there will be inconsistencies in image and reputation. ○ Where an activity is over or under designed for its use (eg overqualified staff in menial positions).
Strategy is about combining activities, and the way in which activities fit and reinforce one another	• This is hard to imitate. (Operational effectiveness is about being good at **individual** activities.)
Strategy is about choices, not blindly imitating competitors	Of course, many firms operate inefficiently, and so can benefit by improving operational effectiveness, but those at the productivity frontier need to make choices and trade-offs.

Exam Tip

Strategic positioning and competitor response was the subject of the June 2000 mini-case, which described Weetabix facing a concerted price war conducted by Kelloggs, which also has a reputation for innovation.

Other stakeholders

8.8 Marketers are meant to look outwards, not inwards. However, an ability to satisfy the customer profitably sometimes means that marketers must look internally at the company, its **resources** (human and otherwise) its **processes** and its **competences**.

(a) **The organisation's competences and resources can be deployed in a number of different ways to satisfy customers.** Marketers cannot afford to live in an ivory tower if they want a strategic role. The **value chain** model indicates how the organisation's resources can be arranged in different ways to add value.

(b) **The company puts constraints** on what the marketer can achieve. Such constraints might relate to finance, time, technological expertise, experience and competences.

(c) **The company has to satisfy (to different degrees) all stakeholders**, not just customers. There is the need for profit (for shareholders), respect for the law (the government, the public). Although the marketer is not directly involved, normally, in communicating with shareholders, the marketer's understanding of the needs of wider stakeholder groups will help to satisfy customers in an **appropriate** way.

Approaching the customer

8.9 Of course, the customer is the centre of any marketer's concerns, but there is a dispute as to **how.** Kotler, in an article in *Marketing Business* (February 1997) takes issue with some thinking about customers, particularly regarding an excessive concentration on niche marketing. **Niche marketing is, to some extent, a means of avoiding competition**, in the short term at least.

Proposition	Yes, but . . .
'Mass marketing is dead': this featured - Single market - 4Ps - Large volume output	'The vast markets in the developing countries and former planned economies are taking to mass marketing as a godsend.'
'Niche marketing is only the way forward'	Niches are indeed very profitable, but there are dangers. 'Some critics charge that companies are in danger of slicing a market too fine.'

Customer-specific marketing

8.10 Kotler notes that some companies are 'slicing the market further and further and, ultimately defining and pursuing segments of one'.

8.11 Kotler suggests that 'smart companies' can practise marketing at all these levels, from mass marketing to customer-specific marketing.

Marketing at Work

Kotler cites the example of *Mars*.

'Thus today the Mars company, in its pet food business, practises a mix of mass marketing and customer-specific marketing. In its cat food market, it has accumulated the names of most cat owners in Germany and relates to them on a direct marketing, database approach. Mars sends a birthday card to each cat on its birthday, congratulating the cat and presenting the family with some cost-saving coupons or a sample.'

Chapter Roundup

- **Mission** describes an organisation's **purpose** (ie its **basic function in society**). Mission directs strategy, embodies values, and influences policies and standards of behaviour.

- Mission may be embodied in a **mission statement**, which should be brief, flexible and distinctive.

- The mission has to be translated into actual business practice. According to the rational model, this is achieved by **goals** covering all areas of the business and most, if not all, stakeholder groups.

- People use the words **goal and objective interchangeably**, it is useful to keep in mind the difference between those goals which can be expressed as **objectives** (quantitative and SMART) and **aims**, which are not quantitative.

- An organisation has many goals and objectives. A business has **profitability** or **return** as an overriding goal. However each **stakeholder group** has its own expectations of the business. Managers have to satisfy stakeholders, but this depends on the power different stakeholders have.

- Marketing objectives are derived from corporate objectives and support them.

- Firms are essentially competing for a space in the customer's mind. A competitor orientation can underpin a positioning strategy.

Now try illustrative question 11 at the end of the Study Text

Quick Quiz

1   What is the role of mission in organisations? (see paras 2.1 - 2.4)

2   What are the four influences on mission statements? (2.7)

3   What is vision? (2.10)

4   What do you understand by 'strategic intent'? (2.14)

5   What is the distinction sometimes drawn between aims and objectives? (3.1)

6   Draw up a list of corporate objectives of a business. (4.3)

7   Draw up a list of stakeholders. (5.2)

8   What sort of expectations might employees have of a business? (5.5)

9   Identify specific marketing objectives (7.3)

10   Why is a competitor orientation useful? (8.2)

Action Programme Review

1   You may be surprised at how difficult this task actually is and the important choices included in writing a mission statement.

    (a)   Is the library in the sole business of lending books? What about other media, videos, software and records etc? Is the library in the business of leisure - providing popular materials, or the business of education - giving priority to the purchase of classics and reference materials?

    (b)   Many colleges have had long debates as to whether they are in the business of training (giving skills) or education (providing knowledge). If you are attending college, should your tutors be in the business of teaching you about marketing or helping you to pass an examination? The two are not always the same.

    (c)   The current changes to the funding of general practices have been centred very much on the 'what business are we in' debate. Should your GP be in the business of making you well, or preventing you from getting ill? The targets, organisation and services provided will be very different according to which you have selected.

12 *Approaches to Creating Strategic Advantage*

Chapter Topic List	Syllabus reference
1 **Setting the scene**	
2 **Strategic choices**	4.2
3 **Competitive strategy: how to compete**	4.2
4 **Sustainable competitive advantage**	4.2
5 **Competitive positions**	4.2
6 **Products and markets (Ansoff)**	4.2
7 **Method of growth: alliances and networks**	4.2
8 **Hostile and declining markets**	4.2
9 **Wear-out and renewal**	4.2

Learning Outcomes

- Understand and critically appraise a wide variety of marketing techniques, concepts and models.

- Specify a clear rationale when comparing strategic options.

Key Concepts Introduced

- Competitive strategy
- Cost leadership
- Differentiation
- Focus
- Product/market mix

- Related diversification
- Unrelated diversification
- Synergy
- Wear-out

Examples of Marketing at Work

- Category killers
- Organic food, soya beans
- Ratners
- Cinema
- Air miles

- Horizontal and vertical integration
- easyGroup, Daimler-Chrysler
- SGS - Thompson
- Pirelli
- Mint, Itallo

1 SETTING THE SCENE

1.1 Having established **where we are now** through the environmental, situation and SWOT analysis, and **where we are going** via the statement of corporate objectives, the next step in the planning process is deciding on the best route.

1.2 For a business, the purpose of any strategy should be to seize competitive advantage in the long term. Three overall strategies (Section 3) are: **cost leadership** and product **differentiation**, which address the whole market, and **focus** which addresses only a segment.

Links to other papers

1.3 **Competitive strategy** features in the Analysis and Decision paper, but it is also relevant in International Marketing, given segmentation opportunities in the global market and in individual country markets. Products and companies are often differentiated by branding, the key to which is marketing communications.

1.4 The next two chapters discuss where a firm chooses to compete and with what products.

2 STRATEGIC CHOICES

2.1 Having determined the extent of the gap that needs to be filled, we can now turn our attention to the strategies needed to fill it. The important point to recognise is that there will almost always be **alternatives**. Identifying these alternatives and carefully evaluating the options is an essential part of the planning process.

2.2 We identified three categories of strategic choice.

(a) The **competitive strategies** are the strategies an organisation will pursue for competitive advantage (a condition which is proof against 'erosion by competitor behaviour or industry evolution'). They determine **how you compete.**

(b) **Product-market strategies** (which markets you should enter or leave, which products you should sell) determine **where you compete** and the direction of growth.

(c) Institutional strategies (ie relationships with other organisations) determine the **method of growth**.

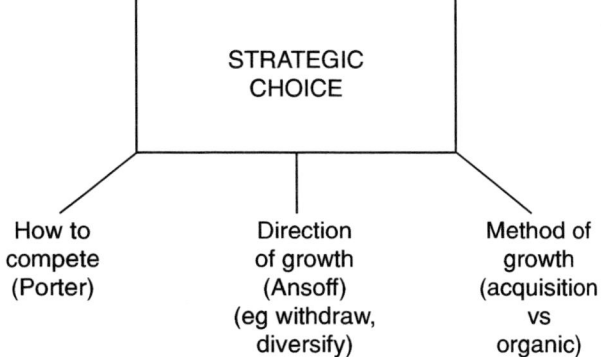

2.3 In some instances you might find it difficult to distinguish between **corporate strategy** and **marketing strategy**.

(a) **Corporate strategy** will ultimately involve decisions and direction for all functions of the operation.

(b) **Marketing strategy** incorporates decisions relating to the positioning of the marketing mix to exploit and develop product/market opportunities.

3 COMPETITIVE STRATEGY: HOW TO COMPETE Specimen paper

3.1 **Competitive advantage** is anything which gives one organisation an edge over its rivals in the products it sells or the services it offers.

3.2 A firm should adopt a **competitive strategy** to secure a **competitive advantage**.

Key Concept

Competitive strategy means 'taking offensive or defensive actions to create a defendable position in an industry, to cope successfully with ... competitive forces and thereby yield a superior return on investment for the firm. Firms have discovered many different approaches to this end, and the best strategy for a given firm is ultimately a unique construction reflecting its particular circumstances'. (Porter)

The choice of competitive strategy

3.3 Porter believes there are **three generic strategies** for competitive advantage.

Key Concepts

(a) **Cost leadership** means being the lowest-cost producer in the industry as a whole.

(b) **Differentiation** is the exploitation of a product or service which the **industry as a whole** believes to be unique.

(c) **Focus** involves a restriction of activities to only part of the market (a segment) through:

- Providing goods and/or services at lower cost to that segment (**cost-focus**)
- Providing a differentiated product or service to that segment (**differentiation-focus**)

3.4 **Cost leadership and differentiation are industry-wide strategies. Focus involves segmentation** but involves pursuing, **within the segment only,** a strategy of cost leadership or differentiation.

Cost leadership

3.5 A cost leadership strategy seeks to achieve the position of lowest-cost producer in the **industry as a whole**. By producing at the lowest cost, the manufacturer can compete on price with every other producer in the industry, and earn higher unit profits, if the manufacturer so chooses.

3.6 **How to achieve overall cost leadership**

(a) Set up production facilities to obtain **economies of scale**

(b) Use the **latest technology** to reduce costs and/or enhance productivity (or use cheap labour if available)

(c) In high technology industries, and in industries depending on labour skills for product design and production methods, exploit the **learning curve effect**. By producing more

items than any other competitor, a firm can benefit more from the learning curve, and achieve lower average costs.

(d) Concentrate on **improving productivity**

(e) **Minimise overhead costs**

(f) **Get favourable access to sources of supply**

(g) **Relocate to cheaper areas**

Marketing at Work

Large out-of-town stores specialising in one particular category of product are able to secure cost leadership by economies of scale over other retailers. Such shops have been called *category killers*, an example of which is PC World.

Differentiation

3.7 A differentiation strategy assumes that competitive advantage can be gained through **particular characteristics** of a firm's products. Products may be categorised as:

(a) **Breakthrough products** offering a radical performance advantage over competition, perhaps at a drastically lower price.

(b) **Improved products** which are not radically different from their competition but are obviously superior in terms of better performance for a similar price.

(c) **Competitive products** which derive their appeal from a particular compromise of cost and performance. For example, cars are not all sold at rock-bottom prices, nor do they all provide immaculate comfort and performance. They compete with each other by trying to offer a more attractive compromise than rival models.

3.8 **How to differentiate**

- **Build up a brand image**
- **Give the product special features** to make it stand out
- **Exploit other activities of the value chain.**

Marketing at Work

Differentiation and food

We all know about branding and product modification in food. *Organic food* is increasing in popularity, as it is differentiated on the basis of:

- Possible health benefits (disputed by some nutritionists)
- Kindliness to the environment (and to animals)

The end product may be the same (eg pasta) but the ingredients and process by which it is made are a source of differentiation. Retailers and manufacturers of branded goods charge more for organic variants of standard products.

The Economist (21 April 2001) reported that Japanese buyers of American soya beans 'are willing to pay a premium for quality – and for knowing exactly where their food came from. By preserving [the] crop's identity [farmers] can fetch over 25% more per bushel.' A number of companies provide tracking services.

Ultimately this is about differentiating a commodity – in short decommodifying it. The advantage for retailers is that, with 25,000 new food products introduced to US supermarkets in 1998, the right agricultural pedigree provides further differentiation.

BPP PUBLISHING

3.9 **Advantages and disadvantages of industry-wide strategies**

Advantages	Cost leadership	Differentiation
New entrants	Economies of scale raise entry barriers	Brand loyalty and perceived uniqueness are entry barriers
Substitutes	Firm is not so vulnerable as its less cost-effective competitors to the threat of substitutes	Customer loyalty is a weapon against substitutes
Customers	Customers cannot drive down prices further than the next most efficient competitor	Customers have no comparable alternative
Suppliers	Flexibility to deal with cost increases	Higher margins can offset vulnerability to supplier price rises
Industry rivalry	Firm remains profitable when rivals go under through excessive price competition	Brand loyalty should lower price sensitivity

Disadvantages	Cost leadership	Differentiation
New entrants	Technological change will require capital investment, or make production cheaper for competitors	New entrants can differentiate too
Substitutes		Sooner or later, customers become price sensitive
Customers	Cost concerns ignore product design or marketing issues	Customers may not value the differentiating factor
Suppliers	Increase in input costs can reduce price advantages	Differentiation might require specialist inputs
Industry rivalry	Competitors can benchmark their processes or cut costs	Competitors can copy

Focus (or niche) strategy

3.10 In a focus strategy, a firm concentrates its attention on one or more particular segments or niches of the market, and does not try to serve the entire market with a single product.

(a) A **cost-focus strategy:** aim to be a cost leader for a particular segment. This type of strategy is often found in the printing, clothes manufacture and car repair industries.

(b) A **differentiation-focus strategy:** pursue differentiation for a chosen segment. Luxury goods are the prime example of such a strategy.

3.11 **Advantages of focus**

- A niche is more secure and a firm can insulate itself from competition.
- The firm does not spread itself too thinly.

3.12 **Drawbacks of a focus strategy**

(a) The firm **sacrifices economies of scale** which would be gained by serving a wider market.

(b) **Competitors can move into the segment,** with increased resources (eg the Japanese moved into the US luxury car market, to compete with Mercedes and BMW).

(c) The **segment's needs may eventually become less distinct** from the main market.

Exam Tip

The December 2000 exam examined niche strategies in the car industry. The example of Rover springs to mind.

Which strategy?

3.13 Although there is a risk with any of the generic strategies, Porter argues that a firm **must** pursue one of them. A **stuck-in-the-middle** strategy is almost certain to make only low profits. 'This firm lacks the market share, capital investment and resolve to play the low-cost game, the industry-wide differentiation necessary to obviate the need for a low-cost position, or the focus to create differentiation or a low-cost position in a more limited sphere.'

Action Programme 1

The managing director of Hermes Telecommunications plc is interested in corporate strategy. Hermes has invested a great deal of money in establishing a network which competes with that of Telecom UK, a recently privatised utility. Initially Hermes concentrated its efforts on business customers in the South East of England, especially the City of London, where it offered a lower cost service to that supplied by Telecom UK. Recently, Hermes has approached the residential market (ie domestic telephone users) offering a lower cost service on long-distance calls. Technological developments have resulted in the possibility of a cheap mobile telecommunication network, using microwave radio links. The franchise for this service has been awarded to Gerbil phone, which is installing transmitters in town centres and stations etc.

What issues of competitive strategy have been raised in the above scenario, particularly in relation to Hermes Telecommunications plc?

3.14 In practice, it is rarely simple to draw hard and fast distinctions between the generic strategies as there are conceptual problems underlying them.

   (a) **Problems with the 'cost leadership' concept**

      (i) **Internal focus.** Cost refers to internal measures, rather than the market demand. It can be used to gain market share: but it is the **market share which is important,** not cost leadership as such.

      (ii) **Only one firm.** If cost leadership applies cross the whole industry, only one firm will pursue this strategy successfully.

      (iii) **Higher margins can be used for differentiation.** Having low costs does **not** mean you have to charge lower prices or compete on price. A cost leader can choose to 'invest higher margins in R & D or marketing'. Being a cost leader arguably gives producers more freedom to choose **other** competitive strategies.

   (b) **Problems with the differentiation concept**

      Porter assumes that a differentiated product will always be sold at a **higher price.**

      (i) However, a **differentiated product** may be sold at the same price as competing products in order to **increase market share.**

      (ii) **Choice of competitor.** Differentiation from whom? Who are the competitors? Do they serve other market segments? Do they compete on the same basis?

BPP PUBLISHING

(iii) **Source of differentiation**. This can include **all** aspects of the firm's offer, not only the product. Restaurants aim to create an atmosphere or 'ambience', as well as serving food of good quality.

3.15 **Focus** probably has fewer conceptual difficulties, as it ties in very neatly with ideas of market segmentation. In practice most companies pursue this strategy to some extent, by designing products/services to meet the needs of particular target markets.

3.16 'Stuck-in-the-middle' is therefore what many companies actually pursue quite successfully. Any number of strategies can be pursued, with different approaches to **price** and the **perceived added value** (ie the differentiation factor) in the eyes of the customer.

Marketing at Work

Pirelli

Pirelli, the tyre and fibre-optics firm, has introduced a new automated tyre production system (called MIRS) which is more efficient – and cost effective – than traditional tyre making. This allows Pirelli to pursue 'quality' and growing sectors in the market for high-tech components.

Pirelli invests significantly in R & D. The company has net profits in 2000 of €3,626m, compared to a loss of $501m in 1991.

3.17 Section summary

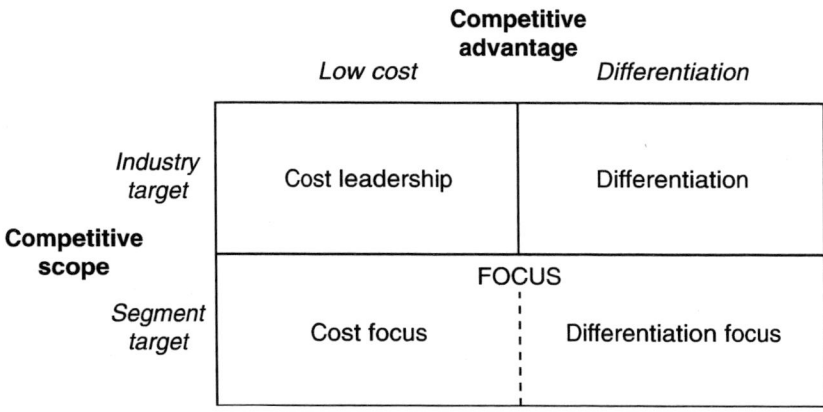

4 SUSTAINABLE COMPETITIVE ADVANTAGE

4.1 A key issue in competitive advantage is ensuring it is **sustained**.

(a) Competitive advantage only really exists in the customer's mind.

(b) Competitive advantage can be **lost easily** as a result of **market changes** or **new ways of doing business**. The advantage of Marks & Spencer (covered in more detail later in this text) comes to mind.

4.2 In an earlier chapter, we identified some key issues regarding competitor orientation.

- Operational effectiveness is not the same as strategy
- Strategy rests on unique activities
- A sustainable strategic position requires trade-offs
- Strategy involves making choices not blindly imitating competitors

4.3 Different types of advantage (Davidson)

Competitive advantage	Example/comment
Better product in some way	Renault - safest car in its class
Perceived advantage or psychic benefit	Exclusivity (eg Harrods)
Global skills	BA
Low costs, via high productivity or focus	Discount retailers or supermarkets such as Lidl or Aldi
Better **competences**	Some firms are 'better' at marketing or aligning technologies to markets than others
Superior assets	Property, cash or brands
Economies of scale	Size can be a source of competitive advantage
Attitude	This is partly related to culture and management abilities
Superior **relationships**	Companies can exploit business alliances and develop personal relationships

4.4 The most important competitive advantages depend on the market and existing competitors. Davidson suggests that the best advantages are the hardest to copy.

Marketing at Work

Ratners sold low-cost jewellery, cleverly developing a 'low cost' position for a luxury indulgent item tied up with people's self-image.

Ratners destroyed this advantage when its managing director publicly announced that the products were 'crap'.

---

5 COMPETITIVE POSITIONS

5.1 The broad generic strategies outlined above have some flaws, as we have seen. We suggested a number of approaches to price and value. In this section we describe how marketing activities can be used against **competitors.**

5.2 Considering strategic options from a competitor rather than customer orientation is referred to as **competitive marketing strategy.** Kotler and Singh in the McKinsey Quarterly (1981) identified **five offensive** and **six defensive** competitive strategies named after military strategies.

Offensive warfare

5.3 Offensive strategies can be used by all companies. In order to ensure success, a company must be able to gain an advantage over the competition in the segment or area of attack. Kotler (1997) describes the following **attack strategies.**

Strategy	Comment
Frontal attack	This is the direct, head-on attack meeting competitors with the **same product line, price, promotion and so on**. Because the attacker is attacking the enemy's strengths rather than weaknesses, it is generally considered the riskiest and least advised of strategies.
Flanking attack	The aim is to engage competitors in those product markets where they are weak or have no presence at all. Its overreaching goal is to build a position from which to launch an attack on the major battlefield later without waking 'sleeping giants'.
Encirclement attack	Multi-pronged attack aimed at diluting the defender's ability to retaliate in strength. The attacker stands ready to block the competitor no matter which way he turns in the product market.
	(i) An attacker can encircle by **product proliferation** as Seiko did in the watch market, supplying 400 watch types in the UK out of 2,300 models worldwide.
	(ii) **Market encirclement** consists of expanding the products into **all** segments and distribution channels.
Bypass attack	This is the most indirect form of competitive strategy as it **avoids confrontation** by moving into new and as yet uncontested fields. Three types of bypass are possible; develop **new products**, diversify into **unrelated products** or diversify into **new geographical markets**.
Guerrilla warfare	Less ambitious in scope, this involves making small attacks in different locations whilst remaining mobile. Such attacks take several forms: law suits, poaching personnel, interfering with supply networks and so on. The overriding aim is to **destabilise** by prods rather than blows.

Defensive warfare

5.4 It is generally agreed that **only a market leader** should play defence in an attempt to hold on to its existing markets in the face of competitive attack.

Strategy	Comment
Position defence	Static defence of a current position, retaining current product-markets by consolidating resources within existing areas. **Exclusive reliance** on a position defence effectively means that a business is a **sitting target** for competition.
Mobile defence	A high degree of **mobility prevents the attacker's chances of localising defence** and accumulating its forces for a decisive battle. A business should seek market development, product development and diversification to create a stronger base.
Pre-emptive defence	**Attack is the best form of defence.** Pre-emptive defence is launched in a segment where an attack is **anticipated** instead of a move into related or new segments.

Strategy	Comment
Flank position defence	This is used to occupy a position of **potential** future importance in order to deny that position to the opponent. Leaders need to develop and hold secondary markets to prevent competitors using them as a spring board into the primary market. (For example, Japanese manufacturers used the upper end executive and coupe market to break into the volume car sector in the US.)
Counter-offensive defence	This is attacking where one is being attacked. This requires **immediate response** to any competitor entering a segment or initiating new moves. Examples are price wars, where firms try to undercut each other.
Strategic withdrawal	

5.5 The five attacking strategies for challenging market leaders and the six defensive strategies used to fight off challenges are not mutually exclusive. As contingent factors change, a successful company will reconsider and revise its core strategies.

Action Programme 2

Hester Bateman plc (HB plc) is a manufacturing cutler: that is, the company makes knives, forks and spoons. HB is based in Sheffield in the United Kingdom which has been the centre of the UK cutlery industry for at least one hundred years. When the industry was first established, it was very fragmented and there were many small entrepreneurial businesses making cutlery. Often, these businesses were organised around a family and they usually employed between six and ten people. Hester Bateman was one such entrepreneur. The industry began to consolidate, in the late nineteenth century and early twentieth century, as a series of mergers were effected.

HB plc was constituted in its present form in the 1920s when it obtained its market listing on the Stock Exchange. It now consists of a large factory which employs 500 people and a Head Office employing 200 people. These are both in Sheffield.

In 1987 HB plc made a rights issue to finance a modernisation programme in its factory. At that time the Board reviewed the company's objectives. A statement was issued by the Board which said:

'HB plc is a UK manufacturing cutler based in Sheffield, the home of the cutlery industry. Our success is due to harnessing local skills in production and design and using these to deliver the finest quality product to our customers across the world. They know that the finest cutlery in the world is stamped "Made in Sheffield". We intend to continue with our fine traditions.'

HB plc has always made all its cutlery in Sheffield and attaches great importance to the fact that it can, therefore, be marked 'Made in Sheffield'.

HB plc usually spends approximately £150,000 a year on research and development. 5% of this spending is on new designs for the export market and the remainder is evenly split on designs for the home market and on improvements in production systems.

BQ plc

There is another UK manufacturing cutler of a similar size to HB plc, BQ plc, which is based in Birmingham.

Since 1988 BQ plc has followed a different production policy to HB plc. Approximately half of its cutlery is made in Korea and imported to the UK and marketed under BQ plc's brand names.

Markets

From the date of its formation until the mid 1980s HB plc did very good business with countries across the world.

Since 1987 HB plc has experienced increasing competition from countries of the Pacific Rim - Korea, Taiwan, Hong Kong and Singapore. This competition has been conducted on the basis of cost. This has been possible because the production technology involved in making cutlery is a mature one. It is also comparatively cheap and readily available. Further, for many users cutlery has become a generic product.

Generics are unbranded, plainly packaged, less-expensive versions of products, purchased in supermarkets, such as spaghetti, paper towels and canned peaches.(Kotler, *Marketing Management*, Prentice-Hall).

HB plc has experienced a growing loss of market share in the UK to imports from the Pacific Rim. HB plc's export markets have largely disappeared. The only export business which it does is an annual sale of about £200,000 of very high quality cutlery to a department store in New York. HB plc makes a gross margin of 45% on this business.

Estimated market data at December 1999:

	UK market share	
	by quantity %	by value %
HB plc	35	45
BQ plc*	30	35
Imports	35	20

* These percentages include all cutlery sold by BQ plc whether made in the UK or in Korea.

Financial performance

The increasingly competitive environment has had a marked effect on HB plc's profitability and stock market performance. After the publication of its latest annual results the following comment was made in an influential UK financial newspaper:

HB plc's latest results which show a profit after tax of £2.25 million look deceptively good. However, these are flattered by the fact that HB plc has not made any major investments since the 1980s.

Its ROCE is about 4% and this could be beaten by any fixed return risk-free deposit investment. There seems to be little prospect of growth in any direction. These shares are really only a HOLD for the sentimental; otherwise SELL.

Required

(a) How can Porter's classification of generic strategies be used by HB plc to analyse its current competitive position?

(b) Discuss the extent to which you believe that the statement of objectives made in 1987 is still applicable in 2000.

(c) Recommend possible marketing strategies for HB plc. Discuss the advantages and disadvantages of your recommendations.

5.6 We can apply these strategies to firms with different positions in the market.

- Leaders
- Followers
- Challengers
- 'Nichers'

5.7 Strategies for leaders

- Position defence
- Mobile defence
- Flanking defence
- Contraction defence (withdrawal)
- Pre-emptive defence
- Counter-offence

5.8 Strategies for challengers

Challenges can either attack lenders accept the status quo, or try and win market share from other smaller companies in the market.

- Frontal attack
- Flank attack
- Encirclement attack
- Bypass attack
- Guerrilla attack

5.9 Strategies for followers

Many firms succeed by imitating the leaders. This is common in financial services markets where the basic functionality of a product is similar. Given that there are controls over monopoly status, most markets will have at least two 'players'. Followers can follow:

- **Closely**, by imitating the marketing mix, and targeting similar segments
- **At a distance**, with more differentiating factors
- **Selectively** to avoid direct competition.

5.10 Kotler makes the important point that 'followership is not the same as being passive or a carbon copy of the leader'. The follower has to define a path that does not invite competitive retaliation. He identifies three broad followership strategies.

(a) **Cloner**. This is a 'parasite' that lives off the investment made by the leader in the marketing mix (such as in products or distribution).

(b) **Counterfeiter**. This is an extreme version of the cloner, who produces fakes of the original (eg fake Rolex watches for sale in the Far East).

(c) **Imitator**. This strategy copies some elements but differentiates on others (such as packaging).

(d) **Adapter**. This involves taking the leader's products and adapting or even improving them. The adapter may grow to challenge the leader.

5.11 Market nichers

This is associated with a **focus** strategy and relies partly on segmentation, and partly on specialising. Accordingly to Kotler, there are several specialist roles open to market nichers.

(a) **End user specialist**, specialising in one type of customer

(b) **Vertical-level specialist**, specialising at one particular point of the production/ distribution chain

(c) **Specific-customer specialist**, limiting selling to one or just a few customers

(d) **Geographic specialist** selling to one locality

(e) **Product or service specialist**, offering specialised services not available from other firms

(f) **Quality/price specialist** operating at the low or high end of the market

(g) **Channel specialist**, concentrating on just one channel of distribution

6 PRODUCTS AND MARKETS (ANSOFF)

6.1 Ansoff drew up a **growth vector matrix**, describing a combination of a firm's activities in current and new markets, with existing and new products.

Key Concept

Product-market mix is a short-hand term for the products/services a firm sells (or a service which a public sector organisation provides) and the markets it sells them to.

Ansoff's product-market growth matrix

	Existing products	*New products*
Existing markets	*Market penetration strategy* 1 More purchasing and usage from existing customers 2 Gain customers from competitors 3 Convert non-users into users (where both are in same market segment)	*Product development strategy* 1 Product modification via new features 2 Different quality levels 3 'New' product
New markets	*Market development strategy* 1 New market segments 2 New distribution channels 3 New geographic areas eg exports	*Diversification strategy* 1 Organic growth 2 Joint ventures 3 Mergers 4 Acquisition/take-over

Current products and current markets: market penetration

6.2 **Market penetration.** The firm seeks to:

(a) **Maintain or to increase its share** of current markets with current products, eg through competitive pricing, advertising, sales promotion

(b) Secure dominance of growth markets

(c) Restructure a mature market by driving out competitors

(d) Increase usage by existing customers (eg airmiles, loyalty cards)

Marketing at Work

Good examples of strategies for market penetration are air miles and 'frequent flier' services. A decision to fly with an airline gives the customer air miles, which can be redeemed on later flights, and which will encourage the customer to fly again.

Present products and new markets: market development

6.3 **Market development** is when the firm seeks new markets for its **current** products or services. It is appropriate when its products are strengths which can be matched by opportunities in new markets. Ways of developing markets include:

(a) **New geographical areas** and export markets (eg a radio station building a new transmitter to reach a new audience).

(b) **Different package sizes** for food and other domestic items so that both those who buy in bulk and those who buy in small quantities are catered for.

(c) **New distribution channels** to attract new customers (eg organic food sold in supermarkets not just specialist shops).

(d) **Differential pricing policies** to attract different types of customer and create **new market segments**. For example, travel companies have developed a market for cheap long-stay winter breaks in warmer countries for retired couples.

New products and present markets: product development

6.4 Product development is the launch of new products to existing markets.

(a) **Advantages**

- Product development forces competitors to innovate
- Newcomers to the market might be discouraged

(b) The **drawbacks** include the expense and the risk.

New products: new markets (diversification)

6.5 **Diversification** occurs when a company decides to make **new products for new markets**. It should have a clear idea about what it expects to gain from diversification. There are two types of diversification, related and unrelated diversification.

(a) **Growth.** New products and new markets should be selected which offer prospects for growth which the existing product-market mix does not.

(b) **Investing surplus** funds not required for other expansion needs: but the funds could be returned to shareholders.

(c) The firm's strengths match the opportunity if:

(i) Outstanding new products have been developed by the firm's research and development department

(ii) The profit opportunities from diversification are high.

Related diversification

> **Key Concept**
>
> **Related diversification** is 'development beyond the present product market, but still within the broad confines of the industry ... [it] ... therefore builds on the assets or activities which the firm has developed' (Johnson and Scholes). It takes the form of vertical or horizontal integration'.

6.6 **Horizontal integration** refers to 'development into activities which are competitive with or directly **complementary** to a company's present activities. *Sony*, for example, started to compete in computer games, building on its presence in consumer electronics.

6.7 **Vertical integration** occurs when a company becomes its own:

(a) **Supplier** of raw materials, components or services (**backward vertical integration**). For example, backward integration would occur where a milk producer acquires its own dairy farms rather than buying raw milk from independent farmers

(b) **Distributor** or sales agent (**forward vertical integration**), for example where a manufacturer of synthetic yarn begins to produce shirts from the yarn instead of selling it to other shirt manufacturers.

6.8   **Advantages of vertical integration**

(a)   A **secure supply of components** or raw materials with more control. Supplier bargaining power is reduced.

(b)   **Strengthen the relationships** and contacts of the manufacturer with the 'final consumer' of the product.

(c)   Win a share of the **higher profits**

(d)   Pursue a **differentiation strategy** more effectively

(e)   Raise **barriers to entry**

6.9   **Disadvantages of vertical integration**

(a)   **Overconcentration.** A company places 'more eggs in the same end-market basket' (Ansoff). Such a policy is fairly inflexible, more sensitive to instabilities and increases the firm's dependence on a particular aspect of economic demand.

(b)   The firm **fails to benefit from any economies of scale or technical advances** in the industry into which it has diversified. This is why, in the publishing industry, most printing is subcontracted to specialist printing firms, who can work machinery to capacity by doing work for many firms.

Related diversification

```
  ┌──────────────┐   ┌──────────────┐   ┌──────────────┐
  │ Raw material │   │  Components  │   │  Machinery   │
  │  production  │   │ manufacture  │   │ manufacture  │
  │              │   │  and supply  │   │  and supply  │
  └──────────────┘   └──────────────┘   └──────────────┘
        ▲                  ▲                    ▲              Backward
  ┌──────────────┐   ┌──────────────┐                         integration
  │ Raw material │◄──│  Transport   │
  │    supply    │   │              │
  └──────────────┘   └──────────────┘
- - - - - - - - - - - - - - - - - - - - - - - - - - - - - -
  ┌──────────────┐                            ▲
  │ Competitive  │◄──────────────┐
  │   products   │                │
  └──────────────┘                │
                          ┌──────────────┐                    Horizontal
                          │ MANUFACTURER │                    integration
  ┌──────────────┐        └──────────────┘
  │Complementary │◄────────┘     │
  │   products   │               │
  └──────────────┘               │
- - - - - - - - - - - - - - - - -│- - - - - - - - - - - - - -
  ┌──────────┐  ┌──────────┐  ┌──────────┐  ┌──────────────┐
  │Distribution│ │Marketing │  │Transport │  │ After-sales  │  Forward
  │  outlets  │  │ research │  │          │  │service, repairs│ integration
  └──────────┘  └──────────┘  └──────────┘  │and maintenance│
                                            └──────────────┘
```

Source: Johnson and Scholes

Marketing at Work

(a)   An example of horizontal integration has been cited earlier in this text. In the UK, deregulation of energy supplies means that gas suppliers can sell electricity and electricity suppliers can sell gas. They are complementary and also, when it comes to heating, competitive products.

(b) Two good examples of forwards vertical integration are *Laura Ashley* and *Benetton*, both clothing manufacturers with dedicated retail outlets and a distinct brand identity. Vertical integration does not only apply to the retail sector, even though these are two easy examples.

An example of backwards vertical integration is from the pharmaceuticals sector, when big pharmaceuticals have acquired small-product biotech companies.

Unrelated diversification

> **Key Concept**
>
> **Unrelated or conglomerate diversification** 'is development beyond the present industry into products/ markets which, at face value, may bear no close relation to the present product/market.'

6.10 Conglomerate diversification is now very unfashionable. However, it has been a key strategy for companies in Asia, particularly South Korea.

6.11 **Advantages of conglomerate diversification**

(a) **Risk-spreading.** Entering new products into new markets offers protection against the failure of current products and markets.

(b) **High profit opportunities.** An improvement of the **overall profitability and flexibility** of the firm through acquisition in industries which have better economic characteristics than those of the acquiring firms.

(c) **Escape** from the present business. For example, Reed International moved away from paper production and into publishing.

(d) **Better access to capital** markets.

(e) **No other way to grow.** Expansion along existing lines might create a monopoly and lead to government investigations and control. Diversifications offer the chance of growth without creating a monopoly.

(f) **Use surplus cash.**

(g) **Exploit under-utilised resources.**

(h) **Obtain cash,** or other financial advantages (such as accumulated tax losses).

(i) **Use a company's image and reputation** in one market to develop into another where corporate image and reputation could be vital ingredients for success.

6.12 **Disadvantages of conglomerate diversification**

(a) The **dilution of shareholders' earnings** if diversification is into growth industries with high P/E ratios.

(b) **Lack of a common identity and purpose** in a conglomerate organisation. A conglomerate will only be successful if it has a high quality of management and financial ability at central headquarters, where the diverse operations are brought together.

(c) **Failure in one of the businesses will drag down the rest,** as it will eat up resources. **British Aerospace** was severely damaged by the effect of a downturn in the property market on its property subsidiary, **Arlington Securities.**

(d) **Lack of management experience** in the business area. **Japanese steel companies** have diversified into areas completely unrelated to steel such as personal computers, with limited success.

(e) **No good for shareholders.** Shareholders can spread risk quite easily, simply by buying a diverse portfolio of shares. They do not need management to do it for them.

Action Programme 3

A large organisation in road transport operates nation-wide in general haulage. This field has become very competitive and with the recent down-turn in trade, has become only marginally profitable. It has been suggested that the strategic structure of the company should be widened to include other aspects of physical distribution so that the maximum synergy would be obtained from that type of diversification.

(a) Name three activities which might fit into the suggested new strategic structure, explaining each one briefly.

(b) Explain how each of these activities could be incorporated into the existing structure.

(c) State the advantages and disadvantages of such diversification.

Exam Tip

Arguably, vertical integration is the opposite of **outsourcing** some activities – do you buy them in or make your own? A problem with the 'integration' model is that it is focused on a simple manufacturer rather than the service sector.

Withdrawal

6.13 It might be the right decision to cease producing a product and/or to pull out of a market completely. This is a hard decision for managers to take if they have invested time and money or if the decision involves redundancies.

6.14 **Exit barriers** make this difficult.

(a) Cost barriers include redundancy costs, the difficulty of selling assets.

(b) Political barriers include government attitudes. Defence is an example.

(c) Marketing considerations may delay withdrawal. A product might be a 'loss-leader' for others, or might contribute to the company's reputation for its breadth of coverage.

(d) Psychology. Managers hate to admit failure, and there might be a desire to avoid a 'bloodletting'. Furthermore, people might wrongly assume that carrying on is a low risk strategy, especially if they (wrongly) feel bound to carry on, as they have spent money already.

6.15 **Reasons for exit**

(a) The **company's business** may be in buying firms, selling their assets and improving their performance, and then selling them at a profit.

(b) **Resource limitations** mean that less profitable businesses have to be abandoned. A business might be sold to a competitor, or occasionally to management (as a buy-out).

(c) A company may be forced to quit, because of **insolvency**.

(d) **Change of competitive strategy**. In the microprocessor industry, many American firms have left high-volume DRAM chips to Asian firms so as to concentrate on high value added niche products.

(e) **Decline in attractiveness of the market**

(f) **Funds can earn more elsewhere.**

6.16 Section summary

Product-market strategy can be:

- **Penetration**: same products, same markets
- **Product development**: new products, same markets
- **Market development**: same products, new markets
- **Diversification**: new products, new markets
- **Withdrawal**
- Any **combination** of the above, depending on the product portfolio

7 METHOD OF GROWTH: ALLIANCES AND NETWORKS

7.1 **Growth** can involve:

(a) **Building up new businesses** from scratch and developing them (sometimes called organic growth)

(b) **Acquiring** already existing businesses from their current owners via the purchase of a controlling interest in another company

(c) A **merger** is the joining of two or more separate companies to form a single company

(d) Spreading the costs and risks (**joint ventures, alliances** or other forms of **co-operation**)

Acquisitions

7.2 **The purpose of acquisitions**

(a) **Marketing advantages**

   (i)   Buy in a new product range

   (ii) Buy a market presence (especially true if acquiring a company with overseas offices and contacts that can be utilised by the parent company)

   (iii) Unify sales departments or to rationalise distribution and advertising

   (iv) Eliminate competition or to protect an existing market

(b) **Production advantages**

   (i)   Gain a higher utilisation of production facilities and reap economies of scale by larger machine runs

   (ii) 'Buy in' technology and skills

   (iii) Obtain greater production capacity

   (iv) Safeguard future supplies of raw materials

   (v)   Improve purchasing by buying in bulk.

(c) **Finance and management**

   (i)   Buy a high quality management team, which exists in the acquired company

   (ii) Obtain cash resources where the acquired company is very liquid

(iii) Gain undervalued assets or surplus assets that can be sold off ('asset stripping')

(iv) Obtain tax advantages (eg purchase of a tax loss company).

(d) **Risk-spreading**

(e) **Independence**. A company threatened by a take-over might take over another company, just to make itself bigger and so a more expensive 'target' for the predator company.

(f) **Overcome barriers to entry**

Organic growth

7.3 Organic growth (sometimes referred to as internal development) is the primary method of growth for many organisations, for a number of reasons. Organic growth is achieved through the development of internal resources.

7.4 **Reasons for pursuing organic growth**

(a) **Learning**. The process of developing a new product gives the firm the best understanding of the market and the product.

(b) **Innovation**. It might be the only sensible way to pursue genuine technological innovations, and exploit them. (Compact disk technology was developed by Philips and Sony, which earns royalties from other manufacturers licensed to use it.)

(c) There is **no suitable target for acquisition**.

(d) Organic growth can be **planned more meticulously** and offers little disruption.

(e) It is often **more convenient** for managers, as organic growth can be financed easily from the company's current cash flows, without having to raise extra money on the stock market (eg to fund an acquisition).

(f) The **same style of management and corporate culture** can be maintained.

(g) **Hidden or unforeseen losses are less likely** with organic growth than with acquisitions.

(h) **Economies of scale** can be achieved from more **efficient use of central head office** functions such as finance, purchasing, personnel, management services etc.

7.5 **Problems with organic growth**

(a) **Time** - sometimes it takes a long time to climb a **learning curve**.

(b) **Barriers to entry** (eg distribution networks) are harder to overcome: for example a brand image may be built up from scratch.

(c) The firm will have to **acquire the resources independently**.

(d) Organic growth may be **too slow for the dynamics of the market**.

Marketing at Work

Stelios Haji-Ioannou, *easyGroup* chairman, has launched easyRentacar.com, an Internet-only car rental business aimed at the private consumer, charging lower prices thanks to a low cost base.

To the surprise of industry watchers, the company will not offer a down-market product but instead will offer just one model, the small Mercedes A-class. Stelios signed the deal for 5,000 cars with *Daimler-Chrysler* at the Geneva Motor Show. The first outlets will be in the London area, Glasgow and Barcelona, with Amsterdam, Geneva, Malaga and Nice set to follow.

Alliances   6/00

7.6   **Alliances are becoming more popular.** An alliance is a business arrangement whereby firms share data, resources and activities to achieve mutually beneficial objectives. Alliances can take a number of forms.

- Agreements to co-operate on various issues
- Shared research and development
- Joint ventures, in which the partners create a separate business unit
- Supply chain rationalisation
- Licensing and franchising
- Purchase of minority stakes

Alliances and synergy

> ### Key Concept
>
> **Synergy** is the 2 + 2 = 5 effect, where a firm looks for combined results that reflect a better rate of return than would be achieved by the same resources used independently as separate operations. Synergy is used to justify the diversification.

7.7   **Obtaining synergy from alliances**

(a)   **Marketing synergy:** use of common marketing facilities such as distribution channels, sales staff and administration, and warehousing. Petrol stations can double as burger outlets.

(b)   **Operating synergy:** arises from the better use of operational facilities and personnel, bulk purchasing, a greater spread of fixed costs whereby the firm's competence can be transferred to making new products.

(c)   **Investment synergy:** the joint use of plant, common raw material stocks, transfer of research and development from one product to another - ie from the wider use of a common investment in fixed assets, working capital or research.

(d)   **Management synergy:** the advantage to be gained where management skills concerning current operations are easily transferred to new operations because of the similarity of problems in the two industries.

7.8   Hooley et al (1998) give an overview of some of the environmental factors that are stimulating the need for alliances.

- Scarce resources
- Increased competition
- Higher customer expectations
- Pressures from strong distributors
- Internationalisation of markets
- Changing markets and technologies
- Turbulent and unpredictable markets

Marketing at Work

Iceland (the country!), with a population of 280,000, has several million surplus telephone numbers. *Mint* is a British company pioneering technology enabling mobile phone users to logon from network to network when abroad. Mint has acquired 50% of *Itallo*, an Icelandic mobile phone firm, in order to issue Mint's customers

with an Icelandic mobile phone number, using Iceland as a hub from which to track users. (On arriving at their destination, users swap their usual SIM card for an Icelandic one: their calls are diverted via Iceland at a cheaper flat rate.)

> ### Exam Tip
>
> The June 2000 exam asked about strategic choices. The partnership was between a bank and a mobile phone company, to provide customers with home banking, bill paying and smart cards.

Consortia

7.9 **Consortia:** organisations co-operate on specific business prospects. **Airbus** is an example, a consortium including British Aerospace, Dasa, Aerospatiale and Casa (of Spain). However, it does have an unusual financial structure, and it will soon turn into a normal company.

Joint ventures

7.10 Two firms (or more) join forces for manufacturing, financial and marketing purposes and each has a share in both the equity and the management of the business. A joint venture is a separate business unit set up for the reasons outlined below.

(a) **Share funding.** As the capital outlay is shared, joint ventures are especially attractive to smaller or risk-averse firms, or where very expensive new technologies are being researched and developed (such is the civil aerospace industry).

(b) **Cut risk.** A joint venture can reduce the risk of government intervention if a local firm is involved (eg Club Méditerranée pays much attention to this factor).

(c) Participating enterprises **benefit from all sources of profit.**

(d) **Close control** over marketing and other operations.

(e) Overseas, a joint venture with an indigenous firm provides **local knowledge, quickly.**

(f) **Synergies.** One firm's production expertise can be supplemented by the other's marketing and distribution facility.

(g) **Learning** can also be a 'learning' exercise in which each partner tries to learn as much as possible from the other.

(h) **Technology.** New technology offers many uncertainties and many opportunities. Such alliances provide funds for expensive research projects, spreading risk.

(i) **The joint venture itself can generate innovations.**

(j) The alliance can involve **'testing' the firm's core competence** in different conditions, which can suggest ways to improve it.

7.11 **Disadvantages of joint ventures**

(a) Conflicts of interest between the different parties.

(b) Disagreements may arise over profit shares, amounts invested, the management of the joint venture and the marketing strategy.

(c) One partner may wish to withdraw from the arrangement.

Marketing at Work

SGS-Thompson's semiconductor manufacturing facility in Shenzhen, China (cost US$110m) was a joint venture. There were many problems, including the unsuitable site, selected by the Chinese partner. By 1996, according to The Economist, 'morale was at rock bottom and the partners did not trust each other'. "Vendors were ripping us off, the government was robbing us blind, key employees were on the take." The situation has now improved.

Licensing

7.12 A **licensing agreement** is a commercial contract whereby the licenser gives something of value to the licensee in exchange for certain performances and payments. The licenser may provide, in return for a royalty:

- Rights to produce a patented product or use a patented production process
- Manufacturing know-how (unpatented)
- Technical advice and assistance
- Marketing advice and assistance
- Rights to use a trademark, brand etc

7.13 **Subcontracting** is also a type of 'alliance'. Co-operative arrangements also feature in supply chain management, JIT and quality programmes.

Franchising   Specimen paper

7.14 **Franchising** is a method of expanding the business on less capital than would otherwise be possible. For suitable businesses, it is an **alternative business strategy to raising extra capital** for growth. Franchisers include Budget Rent-a-car, Dyno-rod, Express Dairy, Holiday Inn, Kall-Kwik Printing, KFC, Prontaprint, Sketchley Cleaners, Body Shop and even McDonald's.

(a) The **franchiser** offers its:

- Name, and any goodwill associated with it
- Systems and business methods
- Support services, such as advertising, training, help with site decoration etc

(b) The **franchisee**:

- Provides capital, personal involvement and local market knowledge
- Pays the franchiser for being granted these rights and services
- Has responsibility for the running and profitability of his franchise

The virtual firm

7.15 An extreme example of an alliance is the so-called **virtual firm**. A virtual firm is created out of a **network of alliances** and subcontracting arrangements: it is as if most of the activities in a particular value chain are conducted by different firms, even though the process is loosely co-ordinated by one of them. It is outsourcing taken to its greatest extent.

7.16 For example, assume you manufacture small toys. You could in theory **outsource**:

- The design to a consultancy
- Manufacturing to a subcontractor in a low-cost country
- Delivery arrangements to a specialist logistics firm

- Debt collection to a bank (factoring)
- Filing, tax returns, bookkeeping to an accountancy firm

7.17 Virtual corporations effectively put market forces in all linkages of the value chain - this has the advantage of creating **incentives** for suppliers, perhaps to take risks to produce a better product, but can lead to a loss of control.

Vertical marketing systems (VMS)

7.18 These have been developed to offer an alternative to traditional distribution channels. A VMS approach aims to integrate all the members in a chain of distribution into one cohesive and co-operative unit, all with a common objective and the ability to solve problems jointly.

7.19 Accordingly to Drummond and Ensor (1999) VMS arrangements may be:

(a) **Corporate**, with all parties having ownership

(b) **Administrative**, with independent companies signing up to common systems and standards (eg car dealerships)

(c) **Contractual**, signing up to centralised agreements (eg on buying)

7.20 The following diagram illustrates some of the various types of collaborative relationships that a company may get into. It may even be involved in several at once.

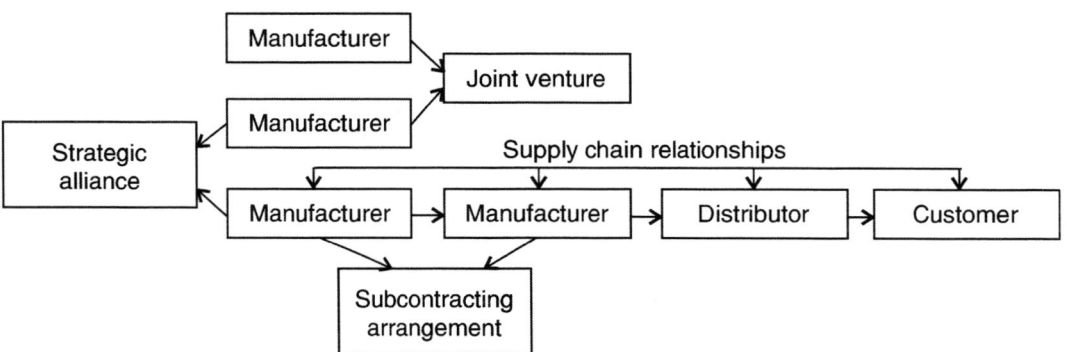

(*Source:* Hooley et al, *Marketing Strategy and Competitive Positioning, 1998*)

8 HOSTILE AND DECLINING MARKETS

8.1 Many of the portfolio models assume that markets are growing. However, this is certainly not the case in many markets and firms within them still have to survive.

Declining markets

8.2 **Why do markets decline?**

- Obsolete technology
- Change in customer needs, leading to fall in demand
- Alternative satisfactions

8.3 **Strategic alternatives** include:

- Revitalising the market
- Becoming a profitable survivor
- Harvest and withdraw

234

8.4 Revitalising the market

- Identify new market segments or 'submarkets'
- Introduce new products
- Introduce new applications of existing products
- Change the market

Marketing at Work

Since the 1950s, *cinema attendances* were in virtual decline in the 'moving pictures' market, having competed unsuccessfully with TV. However, cinema reinvented itself in the 1980s and 1990s.

(a) New action-packed features, such as 'Star Wars', supported by intensive marketing campaigns, brought in a new audience. Similarly, the digital technology makes for enhanced special effects such as shown in 'Gladiator'.

(b) In the UK, the 'experience' of cinema-going has been revolutionised with easily accessible multiplex cinemas open all day, in complexes with a variety of leisure activities, bars and restaurants.

(c) New formats, such as IMAX, are now available.

(d) Merchandising has significantly improved profits.

8.5 Becoming a profitable survivor

(a) Make a visible commitment to the market, as a signal to other competitors.

(b) Encourage competitors to leave by aggressive competition or by making it easier for them to quit.

(c) Purchase the competitor's capacity, close it down and carry on in a smaller niche.

8.6 'Harvest' and withdraw. Reduce investment and operating resources in order to make a graceful exit. Profits may still be made. However employees and customers may fear the lack of commitment and go elsewhere. A 'milking or harvesting' strategy can be reversed, as the firm still has a market presence.

Hostile environments

8.7 Aaker (1995) denotes a 'six-phase' cycle for hostile markets.

Phase 1: Margin pressure	Overcapacity leads to predatory pricing, benefiting large customers
Phase 2: Share shift	Each year, up to 5% of market share will shift under price pressure
Phase 3: Product proliferation	Firms create 'excess value' by adding new lines
Phase 4: Self-defeating cost reduction	Firms cut costs but, in doing so, weaken themselves
Phase 5: Shakeout	Closures, mergers
Phase 6: Rescue	Some markets recover with fewer companies competing

8.8 Winning in hostile markets

- Focus on **large customers,** to benefit from economies of scale
- **Differentiate on intangible factors** such as reliability and 'relationships'
- Offer a broad **array of products** at a variety of prices

- Turn price into a commodity by **removing price from the customer's buying criteria**
- **Control cost** structures

9 WEAR-OUT AND RENEWAL

Key Concept

Strategic and tactical **wear-out** is the problem that any organisation will face if it retains its current strategies and tactics without any review or consideration of change.

9.1 Davidson identifies the following factors giving rise to wear-out.

(a) **Market changes**

- Customer requirements
- Distribution requirements

(b) **Competitor innovations**

(c) **Internal factors**

- Poor cost control
- Lack of consistent investment
- Ill-advised tinkering with successful strategies

9.2 Some organisations still continue to pursue marketing programmes long after their effectiveness has diminished. Many reasons can be put forward to explain this.

Reason	Comment
Fear of change	Most people are afraid of change, preferring to stay in their own 'comfort zone'.
Change is becoming harder to forecast	Many organisations opt to stay with what is familiar.
'If it ain't broke, don't fix it!'	Market leaders, having developed a successful strategy, are understandably reluctant to change it.
Change too late	The need for change often only becomes apparent when the gap between what a company is doing and what it should be doing increases to a point at which performance suffers in an obvious way.
Failure to learn	Companies fail because managers' 'theory of the business' no longer works. A theory of the business contains the assumptions (about markets, technology etc) that 'shape any organisation's behaviour.
The 'wrong' customers	Keeping **too** close to existing customers, rather than thinking about future customers, can also result in strategic wearout: 'an industry's leaders are rarely in the forefront of commercialising new technologies that do not initially meet the functional demands of mainstream customers'. **New technologies** are developed and take industry leaders unawares.
Failure to look	Some organisations do not have environmental monitoring and strategic review procedures embedded within their marketing planning systems.

9.3 In order to avoid strategic wear-out a multi-functional perspective is required. A combination of strategic, organisational and cultural change is required. Companies are likely to be unsuccessful in maintaining change unless five demanding criteria are met.

- **Coherence** of direction, actions and timing
- **Environmental** assessment of competitors, customers and regulatory climate
- Leading change by creating the correct climate
- **Linking** strategic with operational change (communication and reward systems)
- Treating people as assets and investments rather than costs

Exam Tip

Companies need to recognise the danger of strategic wear-out, to plan for it, to be constantly on their guard against it. From an examination viewpoint, be able to point to examples of it in the marketplace. When were your company's systems last reviewed? How long have these systems been in place? Do you frequently review your marketing strategies and those of your major competitors and, having reviewed them, are they changed?

The December 199 exam offered a straightforward question – to be answered in report format – about the dangers, causes and preventative measures of strategic wearout.

Marketing at Work

Marks & Spencer, an icon of British retailing, had 'lost its way' and appointed a new MD, Luc Vandeveld, to turn it round.

When M&S's profitability started to fall, there were hints that this was to do with positioning and product designs.

- A number of other retailers had set up offering competitive or lower prices (ie better and value for money) with different designs

- *Matalan* stores offered designer goods at low cost (eg even mannequins are too expensive for Matalan)

- M&S took a number of control actions

    ◦ New advertising (based on 'real' sizes for women)
    ◦ New designers
    ◦ Concept stores

More radical steps were then taken – to close overseas stores to concentrate on the UK.

Website addresses

www.marks-and-spencer.co.uk
www.marksandspencer.com

Action Programme 4

The Smalltown Horticulture Society is a non-profit-making organisation with 300 members. It is owned by its members who each pay an annual subscription of £7 a year, and it has £12,000 in the bank. It has no debts and its only assets are an old PC and printer and some stationery. It rents its premises. The society's purpose is to 'promote a greater understanding of Horticulture'.

Note. Horticulture: 'the art or science of cultivating gardens' *(Collins English Dictionary)*

The society has held an annual flower show since 1905. Until 1980 the show was very well supported. It was held on the Wednesday and Thursday of the final week in September and attracted an attendance of around 8,000 people. Such a level of attendance enabled the society to cover the costs of the show and also to make a surplus. It used the surplus to finance its other activities, for instance providing free seeds to local elderly people.

Since 1980 the attendances have declined, and in 2000 the show was put on to a single-day basis as the admission receipts were insufficient to pay for the hire of the premises for two days. However attendances have continued to decline and the latest show was 'very disappointing' (Society Chairman).

Following this, the chairman made a statement in which he called for 'the ladies of Smalltown to become involved with the show like they used to be'. He observed that at the same time as the Smalltown show was being held, another society held a much bigger show in a town some sixty miles away. This show made a profit and was very well attended. Some Smalltown residents travelled to the other show but did not attend the Smalltown one.

The chairman concluded that 'unless we get better support in future, we will not be able to continue with the show and the people of Smalltown will lose out'.

Required

(a) Comment on the extent to which the marketing concept has been utilised effectively, if at all, by the Society.

(b) Recommend strategies which would enable the society to fulfil its purpose in the future.

Chapter Roundup

- Strategic choice relates to **how** to compete, **where** to compete and **method of growth.**

- **Competitive strategies** require actions to create a defendable position. They include cost leadership, differentiation and focus.

- **Competitive advantage** has to be sustained. It can come from better products, customer perceptions, costs, competencies, assets, economies of scale, attitudes and relationships, offensive and defensive.

- Firms can choose a variety of strategies to **attack or defend** their position. Different strategies are appropriate to challengers, followers, leaders and nichers.

- **Product-market strategy** includes market penetration, market development, product development and diversification.

- Many firms are growing by **alliances** with other firms, short of a full scale merger or acquisition. These are supposed to offer synergies and mutual benefits.

- Markets decline because of **environmental factors**. Some can be revitalised. In others, a firm has to choose whether it wants to stay in the market or withdraw.

- **Strategic wear out** occurs when firms continue with old strategies that are no longer viable.

Now try illustrative question 12 at the end of the Study Text

Quick Quiz

1   Identify three categories of strategic choice. (2.2)

2   What is competitive strategy? (3.2)

3   Where can firms obtain competitive advantage? (4.3)

4   Identify offensive and defensive strategies. (5.2)

5   Identify strategies for challengers. (5.8)

6   Identify possible approaches to market penetration, market development, product development and diversification. (6.2 - 6.5)

7   What are exit barriers? (6.14)

8   Why do firms pursue organic growth rather than get involved with other firms? (7.4)

9   What is synergy? (7.7)

9   How can growth be created in declining markets? (8.4)

10   What is wear-out? (9.1)

Action Programme Review

1   (a)   Arguably, Hermes initially pursued a cost-focus strategy, by targeting the business segment.

    (b)   It seems to be moving into a cost leadership strategy over the whole market although its competitive offer, in terms of lower costs for local calls, is incomplete.

    (c)   The barriers to entry to the market have been lowered by the new technology. Gerbil phone might pick up a significant amount of business.

2   (a)   In Hester Bateman's (HB's) case, the issues are not particularly clear cut. The size of the market is changing. From being strictly demarcated on national lines, the market has become global. This trend is certain to continue. In this new global market, what strategies can HB pursue?

        (i)   Cost leadership would seem out of the question, in the short term at least. This is because cutlery making technology can be easily imitated by countries in the Pacific. At the moment, their labour costs are much lower; how long this will remain is a different question.

        (ii)   Differentiation. HB could differentiate the product on a global basis, on the basis of quality (by using special alloys) or by designing products that are attractive to users, or by introducing a range of new designs.

        (iii)   Focus. HB could decide to serve the UK or European market only, but it will still be vulnerable to cheaper competition. On the other hand it could position itself as a luxury brand to serve wealthier consumers.

        Clearly, differentiation or focus are the way forward, as HB will always be vulnerable to lower cost competition, from Pacific rim countries first of all, and then from other countries as they industrialise.

    (b)   Statement of objectives

        The statement of objectives contains remarkably few of them! Nothing has been quantified. As a mission statement it addresses the past not the future, on the assumption that past traditions can be preserved as a guarantee for future success.

        The date at which the statement was drawn up, 1981, throws an interesting light on the problem. Many UK manufacturing firms closed down in the recession that characterised the first years of the Thatcher administration. The value of the pound sterling on foreign exchange markets was very high, pricing UK exporters out of their markets, and sucking in cheaper imports. Yet HB was confident enough, in the depth of that recession, to make a rights issue, and investors supported it. Clearly, managers saw their survival as a result of concentrating on their existing skills.

        To some extent, having survived the recessions of the early 1980s and 1990s, HB is in a strong position, having obviously taken steps to maintain its competitiveness. It is still able to trade on is quality image, as it has 45% of the market by value, as opposed to only 35% by volume. This is

still significantly more than its competitors from overseas, suggesting that they are fighting over a niche that is relatively unprofitable for UK companies. Concentrating on the higher end of the market, rather than battling over market share for cheap generic items has been a sound strategy.

However, can this strategy be continued? It is possible that competitors will do their best to raise quality and HB's premium position will no longer be secure. Furthermore, the lack of investment will begin to tell. Finally, although the firm has maintained its market position in the short term, it has lost the confidence of investors in its ability to deliver long-term improvements.

HB therefore needs to update its objectives with a proper mission statement to satisfy the needs of its various stakeholders.

- To what extent can it continue to trade on its quality image?
- What customers is it looking to satisfy?
- What does it intend to do to address the concerns of its investors?

Clearly, the survival of the firm itself as an independent entity is in doubt. Investors are being advised to sell, yet the firm is still profitable and has a large share of the UK market. An argument perhaps is that it has failed to capitalise on the competitive strengths it has. If it is exporting to a New York department store, it is clear that there might be further export opportunities, which are not being satisfied, in the luxury goods market.

HB's position is therefore confused. On the one hand, it has survived two recessions, no mean feat. It has a commanding position in the British market, and its designs satisfy choosy US customers. Investors however have another viewpoint. The firm seems vulnerable to a take-over.

(c)   Marketing strategies

HB must first of all decide which generic strategy it is to pursue. We have suggested that cost leadership is out of the question, and so either differentiation or focus should be pursued. Once this is decided, a suitable marketing mix must devised. We can suggest a focus strategy, exploiting product differentiation (ie a differentiation-focus strategy). HB already produces cutlery of a different quality (g the highest quality is exported to the US). In order to improve profits, HB first of all needs to identify which product markets are the most profitable, and deal with them in a suitable way. Different strategies might be suggested for different market niches to ensure profit streams.

Furthermore, the firm needs to undertake a programme of market research to find out what its customers (both retailers such as the New York department store, and the end-consumer or user) think about HB, and how it can better satisfy their needs.

Product

'Made in Sheffield' goods enable the firm to charge a premium price. The firm should concentrate on exploiting the international luxury market for high quality 'designer' goods. For example, scotch whisky is exported to Japan, and HB can skew its R and D towards producing a variety of innovative designs that can combine premium prices at the high end of the market.

At the same time it needs to enhance the profits earned from the UK market where it is facing cheap generic competition. It has little scope for cutting prices, and so it might be a good idea to maintain its position but at a lower price. It could set up, therefore, a brand of cheap imported cutlery, to compete with BQ and the other importers. This would release resources to concentrate on higher quality premium-priced products which could still have the Made in Sheffield tag. HB can therefore set up two brands. There are obviously profits to be earned from the generic end of the market, and HB still has the opportunity to deliver.

Many firms sell low and high-quality versions of a product under different brand names. It is not so much the company that has to be positioned appropriately in the market, as its brands.

The firm could also use its expertise in quality metal work to expand its product range (using Ansoff's product development strategy) into the same market. Suggestions might include:

- Related products such as silver (soup tureens, trays, silver goblets)
- Less plausibly, perhaps, ornaments, jewellery, even cufflinks

Price

The price element of the mix is implicit in the product. To increase its profitability, HB is to manufacture premium products at premium prices. This is in order to increase the ROCE: the New York business earns a gross margin of 45%.

Under a different brand name, HB is to import cheap generic products from Pacific Rim or cheaper countries, and use its existing networks to take on the competition. This will hopefully

generate more profits, or at least cover costs, as the expensive manufacturing capability will be directed elsewhere. HB will be able to compete more effectively.

Place

The distribution system is an important element of the marketing mix. HB has obviously no problem in the UK, but perhaps it needs to consider whether it is as effective and efficient as it could be. We are told little about HB's existing distribution and logistics systems.

However, the twin pronged strategy does require some new expertise.

(i) If the company is importing its generic products from overseas, it will need to have suitable warehousing and storage facilities, and to have systems which can predict likely demand, so customers do not have to wait too long.

(ii) It is hoped that many of the premium priced products will be exported. The US department store is a model for strategies that can be adopted in other countries in the EU and over the world. HB will need assistance, perhaps from one of the UK government's export advisory services, to find distributors for its product. The distributors will inevitably have a significant say in how the goods are to be positioned and sold. In a market such as Japan, HB will need a suitable partner to negotiate the thickets of the distribution system; in a country that uses chopsticks, demand for cutlery will be limited, but it can be sold as a luxury item.

However, the main markets would be the US where further expansion is obviously possible and the EU.

The company might consider offering an enhanced service to customers, for example a **just-in-time** delivery system.

Promotion

Promotional strategies will be an essential feature of HB's repositioning itself as a premium priced quality product. This means finding a suitable advertising agency, and researching the communications messages the company wishes to pursue. It might mean advertising in media it has not used before (eg magazines promoting luxury goods, or lifestyle magazines such as The World of Interiors).

Finally the firm needs to promote itself to another audience: investors, who have to be convinced that the new strategy will work. At the moment they are critical, and will sell to a bidder. To keep their jobs, the existing managers must work to convince investors that the company's existing and potential strengths can be better exploited in future.

3   The first step in a suggested solution is to think of how a company operating nation-wide in general road haulage might diversify, with some synergistic benefits. Perhaps you thought of the following.

- Moving from nation-wide haulage to international haulage.

- Moving from general haulage to 'speciality' types of haulage (eg large items).

- Providing a despatch service for small items (although this too is a very competitive business).

- Hiring smaller vehicles to customers for 'self-drive'.

- Moving into warehousing.

Only three suggestions are required by the question. You may have thought of different ideas to those in the list. You should appreciate however, that the principles of diversification need to be applied in a specific situation and there are no obvious ready-made and off-the-peg answers to such problems.

(a) To move from nation-wide to international haulage, the company might be able to use its existing contacts with customers to develop an international trade. Existing administration and depot facilities in the UK could be used. Drivers should be available who are willing to work abroad, and the scope for making reasonable profits should exist. However, international road haulage might involve the company in the purchase of new vehicles (eg road haulage in Europe often involves the carriage of containerised products on large purpose-built vehicles). Since international haulage takes longer, vehicles will be tied up in jobs for several days, and a substantial investment might be required to develop the business. In addition, in the event of breakdowns, a network of overseas garage service arrangements will have to be created. It might take some time before business builds up sufficiently to become profitable.

(b) The same broad considerations apply to speciality types of haulage. Existing depot facilities could be used and existing customer contacts might be developed. However, expertise in specialist work will have to be 'brought in' as well as developed within the company and special vehicles might need to be bought. Business might take some time to build up and if the initial investment is high, there could be substantial early losses.

In the same way, you should be able to consider the other means of diversification suggested earlier in the solution. Although items (a) and (b) above do not cover all of the following items, the factors which need to be considered in a policy of diversification are as follows.

- Potential synergy.
- The size of the initial investments.
- The potential for growth and profits.
- Facilities required.
- Manpower required and expertise needed.
- The difficulties in building up customer contacts.
- Contingency planning: what happens if things do not go as well as expected?
- Risk.
- To what extent are the products and services new, and to what extent are the markets new?

4   (a)   Background

There is considerable public interest in horticulture and gardening generally, as witnessed by the variety of television programmes on the subject, and the success of flower shows generally. The Society should be able to flourish in such a setting, as there appears to be no dearth of public interest.

Although the Society should be flourishing, it has not succeeded in tapping the wealth of public interest. This is shown in the slow decline of people attending the annual flower show.

This decline has prevented the Society from pursuing some of its traditional activities in the local community, such as providing seeds for the elderly. The club is not paying its way.

Possible causes

There have been significant social changes since the Society was founded. One significant change, identified by the Chairman's plea to the ladies of the town, is the changing role of women. Perhaps women are just not available to carry out the Society's functions any more. Reasons for this might include the increase in female employment.

Another significant change is the overall increase in car ownership. This has meant it is a easier than before for people to travel the distance to the next town with its competing flower show. This means that the catchment area of any show has grown larger, and people's activities may not be restricted to the strictly local environment.

The marketing concept

Although the Society is not a business seeking to make a profit, the marketing concept is still relevant to the past and future of the society. There has been no decline in public interest in horticulture, but it is clear that the Society is failing to tap the interest that does exist in the subject.

It is clear that the marketing concept has not applied to any significant degree.

(i)   The Chairman believes the Society is of benefit to the local townsfolk, but the declining interests and attendances would indicate that this is definitely not the case. Fewer people are attending the shows, and this implies that people are being put off.

(ii)   The Chairman is simply trying to carry on with the existing practices. This is at best a sales or a production orientation.

(b)   *Suggested strategies*

In order to address the slow decline in public interest, first of all an analysis should be carried out as to why there is a decline in interest.

(i)   Existing members of the society should be asked for their views, as those who are not on the committee of the society may have their own ideas on the situation.

(ii)   The society should conduct a survey to identify the population profile of Smalltown, how this relates to the Association's traditional membership, interest in horticulture amongst residents, and residents' knowledge of and opinions about the society and its activities.

The research is quite important. It may suggest that the society is simply not publicising itself or the show properly; perhaps it needs to arrange advance coverage in the local news media or local BBC or commercial radio station.

On the other hand, the society may have a poor but unjustified image; perhaps people perceive it as being run by a clique, who are out of touch with current demand. Certainly the Chairman's plea to the ladies of the town to perform their traditional duties suggests he is out of touch.

The study might reveal **other** activities that the society could carry out (eg evening classes).

The Society should also consider how to promote the annual flower show more effectively, as this is its main source of funds.

(i)   Ensure that the show does not clash with larger ones held elsewhere.

(ii)   Give proper notice in local papers, or indeed by leafleting local people, or buy advertising at local garden centres, DIY stores.

(iii)   Try and obtain sponsorship from local businesses. Such funds might be used for advertising.

(iv)   Most importantly, address the identified deficiencies in the show, so that people are not disappointed.

(v)   Try to reach out to new, younger members, eg by a simple web page.

13 Developing a Specific Competitive Position

Chapter Topic List	Syllabus reference
1 Setting the scene	
2 Aligning assets and competences	4.3
3 Segmentation	4.3
4 Segment validity and attractiveness	4.3
5 Target markets	4.3
6 Positioning	4.3

Learning Outcomes

- Identify the elements that can be used to create competitive advantage.

Key Concepts Introduced

- Market segmentation
- Conjoint analysis
- Target market
- Positioning

Examples of Marketing at Work

- Airport cafes
- Attitudes to technology
- Credit card companies
- Levis
- European car makers

1 SETTING THE SCENE

1.1 This chapter and Chapter 14 outline the ways in which companies can develop and exploit a specific competitive advantage. In this chapter we cover how a firm can align its assets with its competences, in order to deploy them to target customers. we also show how a firm can segment its market and then prioritise which segments to go for.

Links to other papers

1.2 Segmentation, targeting and positioning are key to Analysis and Decision, and provide context for promotional decisions.

2 ALIGNING ASSETS AND COMPETENCES

2.1 The structure of this section draws on Davidson *Even More Offensive Marketing* (1997).

2.2 In order to market successfully, a company should use its assets and competences and align them with the needs of the customer. This is similar to the approach adopted in SWOT analysis, where strengths are matched with opportunities.

2.3 The steps in the process are these.

Step		Comment
Step 1.	Identify exploitable assets	For example property, patents, systems, brand names, distribution
Step 2.	Identify exploitable competence	For example: <ul><li>Skill at NPD (marketing)</li><li>Skill at customer service (selling)</li><li>Skill at operations (eg project management)</li></ul>
Step 3.	Identify and rank business areas in order of priority	Effectively, this means choosing markets and segments on the basis of their attractiveness
Step 4.	Match assets and competences to real opportunities	This is like matching strengths to opportunities in the SWOT. Some attractive markets may be unattainable
Step 5.	Identify assets and competences to be strengthened	This is similar to dealing with the weaknesses and threats element in the SWOT

2.4 The marketer can try to match the **cost of producing a particular customer benefit with the value to the customer.** Ideally, the marketer should identify benefits of most value to the customer which cost least to produce.

2.5 In the short term, however, there may not be time for such a fundamental analysis. The trick is to identify measures of cutting costs without cutting quality.

3 SEGMENTATION
Specimen paper, 12/00, 6/01

Exam Tip

The purpose of segmentation is to identify target markets in which the firm can take a position.

The whole process of segmentation, targeting and positioning was covered in the December 2000 mini-case – interestingly, the firm's initial segmentation, targeting and positioning strategy was not borne out by actual experience, so re-segmentation was necessary. Repositioning also came up in the same exam.

Geodemographic and psychodemographic segmentation were covered in June 2001 in the context of a new consumer service – positioning chocolate houses as an alternative to 'coffee houses' such as Starbucks.

3.1 A market is not a mass, homogeneous group of customers, each wanting an identical product. Market segmentation is based on the recognition that every market consists of potential buyers with different needs, and different buying behaviour. It is relevant to a **focus strategy.**

Key Concept

Market segmentation may therefore be defined as 'the subdividing of a market into distinct and increasingly homogeneous subgroups of customers, where any subgroup can conceivably be selected as a target market to be met with a distinct marketing mix'. (Kotler)

3.2 There are two important elements in this definition of market segmentation.

(a) Although the total market consists of widely different groups of consumers, each group consists of people (or organisations) with **common needs and preferences**, who perhaps react to 'market stimuli' in much the same way.

(b) Each market segment can become a **target market for a firm**, and would require a unique marketing mix if the firm is to exploit it successfully.

3.3 **Reasons for segmenting markets**

Reason	Comment
Better satisfaction of customer needs	One solution won't satisfy **all** customers
Growth in profits	Some customers will pay more for certain benefits
Revenue growth	Segmentation means that more customers may be attracted by what is on offer, in preference to competing products
Customer retention	By targeting customers, a number of different products can be offered to them
Targeted communications	Segmentation enables clear communications as people in the target audience share common needs
Innovation	By identifying unmet needs, companies can innovate to satisfy them
Segment share	Segmentation enables a firm to implement a focus strategy successfully

3.4 **Steps in segmentation, targeting and positioning identified by Kotler**

Step 1. Identify **segmentation** variables and segment the market ⎫
Step 2. Develop segment profiles ⎭ Segmentation

Step 3. Evaluate the attractiveness of each segment ⎫
Step 4. Select the **target** segment(s) ⎭ Targeting

Step 5. Identify **positioning** concepts for each target segment ⎫
Step 6. Select, develop and communicate the chosen concept ⎭ Positioning

Action Programme 1

Jot down possible segmentation variables for adult education, magazines, and sports facilities.

3.5 Identifying segments

(a) **One basis will not be appropriate in every market,** and sometimes **two or more bases might be valid** at the same time.

(b) One basis or 'segmentation variable' might be 'superior' to another in a hierarchy of variables. Here are thus **primary and secondary segmentation variables.**

Marketing at Work

An airport cafe conducted a segmentation exercise of its customers. It identified a number of possible segments.

- Business travellers
- Airport employees
- Groups
- Single tourists

However, further analysis revealed that running through each of these categories was the same fault line.

- Those 'in a hurry'
- Those with time to spare

For marketing purposes, this latter segmentation exercise was more useful, and the firm was able to develop an 'express menu' for those in a hurry.

Geography

3.6 At its simplest, this involves dividing the market into regions and tailoring the marketing mix accordingly.

(a) An example is **commercial radio stations,** which broadcast local news.

(b) The market for educational material in the UK segments geographically: Scotland has a different system to England.

Demography

3.7 Demographic segmentation involves classifying people according to objective variables about their situation.

Geodemographic segmentation

3.8 The ACORN system divides the UK into 17 groups which together comprise a total of 54 different types of areas, which share common socio-economic characteristics.

(a)   The 17 ACORN groups are as follows.

The ACORN targeting classification: abbreviated list		% of population
A	*Thriving (19.7%)*	
A1	Wealthy achievers, suburban areas	15.0
A2	Affluent greys, rural communities	2.3
A3	Prosperous pensioners, retirement areas	2.4
B	*Expanding (11.6%)*	
B4	Affluent executives, family areas	3.8
B5	Well-off workers, family areas	7.8
C	*Rising (7.8%)*	
C6	Affluent urbanites, town and city areas	2.3
C7	Prosperous professionals, metropolitan areas	2.1
C8	Better-off executives, inner city areas	3.4
D	*Settling (24.1%)*	
D9	Comfortable middle agers, mature home-owning areas	13.4
D10	Skilled workers, home-owning areas	10.7
E	*Aspiring (13.7%)*	
E11	New home-owners, mature communities	9.7
E12	White collar workers, better-off multi-ethnic areas	4.0
F	*Striving (22.7%)*	
F13	Older people, less prosperous areas	3.6
F14	Council estate residents, better-off homes	11.5
F15	Council estate residents, high unemployment	2.7
F16	Council estate residents, greatest hardships	2.8
F17	People in multi-ethnic, low-income areas	2.1

(b)   As an example of a more detailed breakdown, group E ('Aspiring') contains the following groups.

E	*Aspiring (13.7% of population)*	
E11	*New home-owners, mature communities (9.7%)*	
11.33	Council areas, some new home-owners	3.8
11.34	Mature home-owning areas, skilled workers	3.1
11.35	Low rise estates, older workers, new home-owners	2.8
E12	*White collar workers, better-off multi-ethnic areas (4.0%)*	
12.36	Home-owning multi-ethnic areas, young families	1.1
12.37	Multi-occupied town centres, mixed occupations	1.8
12.38	Multi-ethnic areas, white collar workers	1.1

3.9   Unlike geographical segmentation, which is fairly crude by area, geodemographics enables similar groups of people to be targeted, even though they might exist in different areas of the country. These various classifications share certain characteristics, including:

- Car ownership
- Unemployment rates
- Purchase of financial service products
- Number of holidays
- Age profile

The family life cycle

3.10 The **family life cycle (FLC)** is a summary demographic variable that combines the effects of age, marital status, career status (income) and the presence or absence of children. It is able to identify the various **stages through which households progress**. The table on the next page shows features of the family at various stages of its life cycle. Particular products and services can be target-marketed at specific stages in the life cycle of families.

3.11 It is important to remember that the model of the family life cycle shown in the table displays the **classic route** from young single to older unmarried. In contemporary society, characterised by divorce and what may be the declining importance of marriage as an institution, this picture can vary. It is possible and not uncommon to be young, childless and divorced, or young and unmarried with children. Some people go through life without marrying or having children at all. Individuals may go through the life cycle belonging to more than one family group. At each stage, whether on the classic route or an **alternative path**, needs and disposable income will change. Family groupings are, however, a key feature of society.

3.12 There has been some **criticism** of the traditional FLC model as a basis for market segmentation in recent years. (See, for example, Rob Lawson, 'The Family Life Cycle: a demographic analysis', *Journal of Marketing Management* (Summer 1988).)

(a) It is modelled on the **demographic patterns of industrialised western nations** - and particularly America. This pattern may not be universally applicable.

(b) As noted in paragraph 3.11 above, while the FLC model was once typical of the overwhelming majority of American families, there are now **important potential variations** from that pattern, including:

(i)	Childless couples	- because of choice, career-oriented women and delayed marriage
(ii)	Later marriages	- because of greater career-orientation and non-marital relationships: likely to have fewer children
(iii)	Later children	- say in late 30s. Likely to have fewer children, but to stress 'quality of life'
(iv)	Single parents	- (especially mothers) because of divorce
(v)	Fluctuating labour status	- not just 'in labour' or 'retired', but redundancy, career change, dual-income etc
(vi)	Extended parenting	- young, single adults returning home while they establish careers/financial independence; divorced children returning to parents; elderly parents requiring care; newly-weds living with in-laws
(vii)	Non-family households	- unmarried (homosexual or heterosexual) couples
		- divorced persons with no children
		- single persons (mainly women, or older products of delay in first marriage)
		- widowed persons (especially women, because of longer life-expectancy)

BPP PUBLISHING

I	II	III	IV	V	VI	VII	VIII	IX
Bachelor Stage	*Newly married couples*	*Full nest I*	*Full nest II*	*Full nest III*	*Empty nest I*	*Empty nest II*	*Solitary survivor in labour force*	*Solitary survivor(s) retired*
Young single people not living at home	Young, no children	Youngest child under six	Youngest child six or over	Older married couples with dependent children	Older married couples, no children living with them, head of family still in labour force	Older married couples, no children living at home head of family retired		
Few financial burdens.	Better off financially than they will be in the near future.	Home purchasing at peak.	Financial position better.	Financial position still better.	Home ownership at peak.	Significant cut in income.	Income still adequate but likely to sell family home and purchase smaller accommodation.	Significant cut in income.
Fashion/ opinion leader led.	High levels of purchase of homes and consumer durable goods.	Liquid assets/ savings low.	Some wives return to work.	More wives work.	More satisfied with financial position and money saved.	Keep home.	Concern with level of savings and pension.	Additional medical requirements. Special need for attention, affection and security.
Recreation orientated.		Dissatisfied with financial position and amount of money saved.	Child dominated household.	School and examination dominated household.	Interested in travel, recreation, self-education.	Buy medical appliances or medical care, products which aid health, sleep and digestion.	Some expenditure on hobbies and pastimes.	May seek sheltered accommodation.
Buy basic kitchen equipment, basic furniture, cars, equipment for the mating game, holidays.	Buy cars, fridges, cookers, life assurance, durable furniture, holidays.	Reliance on credit finance, credit cards, overdrafts etc.	Buy necessities foods, cleaning material, clothes, bicycles, sports gear, music lessons, pianos, holidays etc.	Some children get first jobs; others in further / higher education.	Make financial gifts and contributions.	Assist children. Concern with level of savings and pension. Some expenditure on hobbies and pastimes.	Worries about security and dependence.	Possible dependence on others for personal financial management and control.
Experiment with patterns of personal financial management and control.	Establish patterns of personal financial management and control.	Child dominated household.		Expenditure to support children's further / higher education.	Children gain qualifications; move to Stage I.			
		Buy necessities washers, dryers, baby food and clothes, vitamins, toys, books etc.		Buy new, more tasteful furniture, non-necessary appliances, boats etc holidays.	Buy luxuries, home improvements e.g. fitted kitchens etc.			

3.13 An alternative or modified FLC model is needed to take account of consumption variables such as:

(a) Spontaneous **changes** in brand preference when a household undergoes a **change of status** (divorce, redundancy, death of a spouse, change in membership of a non-family household)

(b) **Different economic circumstances** and extent of consumption planning in single-parent families, households where there is a redundancy, dual-income households

(c) **Different buying and consumption roles** to compensate/adjust in households where the **woman works**. Women can be segmented into at least four categories - each of which may represent a distinct market for goods and services:

- Stay-at-home homemaker
- Plan-to-work homemaker
- 'Just-a-job' working woman
- Career-oriented working woman

Psychographic segmentation

3.14 Psychographic segmentation is not based on 'objective' data so much as how people see themselves and their **subjective** feelings and attitudes towards a particular product or service, or towards life in general.

Lifestyle dimensions			
Activities	*Interests*	*Opinions*	*Demographics*
Work	Family	Themselves	Age
Hobbies	Home	Social issues	Education
Social events	Job	Politics	Income
Vacation	Community	Business	Occupation
Entertainment	Recreation	Economics	Family size
Club membership	Fashion	Education	Dwelling
Community	Food	Products	Geography
Shopping	Media	Future	City size
Sports	Achievements	Culture	Stage in lifecycle

Source: Joseph Plummer,
'The Concept and Application of Lifestyle Segmentation',
Journal of Marketing (January 1974), pp 33-37

3.15 Riesman identified three **distinct types of social behaviour.**

- **Tradition directed** behaviour is easy to predict and changes little
- **Other directness** is behaviour influenced by the action and views of peer groups
- **Inner directness** is behaviour uninfluenced by views of others

3.16 **Taylor Nelson** also identifies three main groups with sub groups.

(a) **Sustenance driven group**

(i) **Belongers.** What they seek is a quiet undisturbed family life. They are conservative, conventional, rule followers. Not all are sustenance driven.

(ii) **Survivors.** Strongly class-conscious, and community spirited, their motivation is to 'get by'.

BPP
PUBLISHING

        (iii)   **Aimless.** Comprises two groups, (a) the young unemployed, who are often anti-authority, and (b) the old, whose motivation is day-to-day existence.

    (b) **Outer directed group**

        (i)   The balance of the belongers.

        (ii)   **Conspicuous consumers.** They are materialistic and pushy, motivated by acquisition, competition, and getting ahead. Pro-authority, law and order.

    (c) **Inner directed group**

        (i)   **Self-explorers.** Motivated by self-expression and self-realisation. Less materialistic than other groups, and showing high tolerance levels.

        (ii)   **Social resistors.** The caring group, concerned with fairness and social values, but often appearing intolerant and moralistic.

        (iii)   **Experimentalists.** Highly individualistic, motivated by fast moving enjoyment. They are materialistic, pro-technology but anti-traditional authority.

Exam Tip

A December 1998 question covered lifestyle segmentation in a global market. To what extent is this valid?

(1)   The assumption is that, despite culture and demographic differences, certain lifestyle categories can be identified across borders.

(2)   The question then arises whether they are suitable variables for segmentation.

(3)   Acting on such segmentation variables is hampered cultural differences.

3.17   Variations on the lifestyle or psychographic approach have been developed, analysing more precisely people's attitudes towards **certain goods or services**. The value of this approach is that it isolates potential consumer responses to particular product offerings.

Marketing at Work

The Henley Centre for Forecasting has outlined four different kinds of consumers in the market for technological and media products.

(a)   *Technophiles* (24% of the population) 'are enthusiastic about technology in a general sense and also show a high level of interest in applications of new technology. They are concentrated among the under-35s, are more likely to be male than female, and are more likely to belong to social grade C1 than AB'.

(b)   *Aspirational technophiles* (22% of the population) 'are excited in a general sense about technology but are much less interested in its applications. They are more likely to be male than female, and are concentrated in the AB social grade'.

(c)   *Functionals* (25% of the population) 'claim to be uninterested in technology but are not hostile to its applications, especially those areas which offer an enhancement of existing services. These consumers are more likely to be family ... and are most numerous among the over 45s'.

(d)   *Technophobes* (28% of the population) 'are hostile to technology at all levels and are sceptical about whether technology can offer anything new. Technophobes are concentrated in the over-60 age group, are more likely to be female than male, and are distributed fairly evenly through the social grades'.

Exam Tip

Lifestyle and geographic segmentation has featured in past questions. There are connections between the two. Some lifestyle segmentation approaches suggest that there are connections between demographic characteristics and lifestyles. Geodemographic segmentation extends this further to particular geographic areas.

The VALs framework

3.18 This framework was the result of a survey in the USA, identifying nine lifestyle groups in the population passing through various developmental stages. It is presented below.

Developmental stage	Grouping (% of US population)
Need-driven	**Survivors**. This is a disadvantaged group who are likely to be withdrawn, despairing and depressed (4%).
	Sustainers are another disadvantaged group, but they are working hard to escape poverty (7%).
	These groups have relatively little purchasing power.
Outer-directed	**Belongers** are characterised as being conventional, nostalgic, reluctant to try new ideas and generally conservative (33%).
	Emulators are upwardly mobile, ambitious and status conscious (10%).
	Achievers. This group enjoys life and makes things happen (23%).
	These groups are affluent and interested in status products.
Inner-directed	**'I-am-me'** tend to be young, self engrossed and act on whims (5%).
	Experientials wish to enjoy as wide a range of life as possible (7%).
	Societally conscious have a clear sense of social responsibility and wish to improve society (9%).
	These groups are more concerned with individual needs.
Nirvana	**Integrateds** are completely mature psychologically and combine the positive elements of outer and inner directedness (2%). Very few individuals reach this stage.

Social class

3.19 Age and sex present few problems but social class has always been one of the most dubious areas of marketing research investigation. 'Class' is a highly personal and subjective phenomenon, to the extent that some people are 'class conscious' or class aware and have a sense of belonging to a particular group. JICNAR's social grade definitions (A-E), which correspond closely to what are called Social Classes I-V on the Registrar General's Scale, are often used in quota setting.

Registrar General's Social classes	JICNAR Social grades	Social status	Characteristics of occupation (of head of household)
I	A	Upper middle class	Higher managerial/professional eg lawyers, directors
II	B	Middle class	Intermediate managerial/administrative/ professional eg teachers, managers, computer operators, sales managers
III (i) non-manual	C_1	Lower middle class	Supervisory, clerical, junior managerial/ administrative/professional eg foremen, shop assistants
(ii) manual	C_2	Skilled working class	Skilled manual labour eg electricians, mechanics

Registrar General's Social classes	JICNAR Social grades	Social status	Characteristics of occupation (of head of household)
IV	D	Working class	Semi-skilled manual labour eg machine operators
V			Unskilled manual labour eg cleaning, waiting tables, assembly
	E	Lowest level of subsistence	State pensioners, widows (no other earner), casual workers

3.20 From 2001 UK Office for National Statistics used a new categorisation system, reflecting recent changes in the UK population.

New social class	Occupations	Example
1	Higher managerial and professional occupations	
1.1	Employers and managers in larger organisations	Bank managers, company directors
1.2	Higher professional	Doctors, lawyers
2	Lower managerial and professional occupations	Police officers
3	Intermediate occupations	Secretaries/PAs, clerical workers
4	Small employers and own-account workers	
5	Lower supervisory, craft and related occupations	Electricians
6	Semi-routine occupations	Drivers, hairdressers, bricklayers
7	Routine occupations	Car park attendants, cleaners

Behavioural segmentation

3.21 Behavioural segmentation segments buyers into groups based on their attitudes to and use of the product, and the **benefits** they expect to receive.

Benefit segmentation of the toothpaste market

Segment Name	Principal benefit sought	Demographic Strengths	Special behavioural characteristics	Brands dis-proportion-ately favoured	Personality character-istics	Lifestyle character-istics
The sensory segment	Flavour, product appearance	Children	Users of spearmint flavoured toothpaste	Colgate, Stripe	High self-involvement	Hedonistic
The Sociables	Brightness of teeth	Teens, young people	Smokers	Macleans, Ultra-Brite	High sociability	Active
The Worriers	Decay prevention	Large families	Heavy users	Crest	High hypochon-driasis	Conserva-tive
The Independent Segment	Price	Men	Heavy users	Brands on sale	High autonomy	Value-oriented

254

Risk reduction

3.22 A benefit of a product is that it **reduces risk**. Toothpaste reduces the risk of tooth decay, for example. This is relevant to the worriers in the table above. **Perceptions** of risk are often very subjective. **Attitudes to risk** are useful in that they **offer segmentation opportunities.**

(a) Research has indicated high, medium, and low risk segments for producers of professional services by organisations such as consultants and market research agencies.

(b) **Risk can also affect how a product is positioned.** According to *Marketing Business* (January 1997), certain 'food studies identified the feminine image of wine as a risk inhibiting the drinking of wine in certain segments'. Hence the repositioning of Bulgarian wines such as 'Bull's Blood'.

Occasion

3.23 Buyers can be segmented according to the occasion, when they use a product. The best example is business and 'leisure' travel packages. Kellogg's has been trying to increase consumption of cornflakes by suggesting that cornflakes can be eaten at any time of the day, not only breakfast.

User status

3.24 The markets can be segmented according to types of users.

- Heavy users
- Medium users
- Rare users

3.25 In addition, the degree of loyalty can be estimated. Some customers are more 'loyal' than others. Many firms mistake inertia for loyalty, however.

Marketing at Work

The credit card market in the UK is becoming increasingly fragmented. Newcomers such as BankOne offer lower interest rates than mainstream competitors such as Barclaycard. The newcomers target or cherry-pick certain groups of customers with good credit history and who are motivated mainly by price.

Other card operators offer different customer benefits, by linking their cards to charitable organisations, so that some of the on each transaction goes to charity: Beneficial Bank is an example of this.

Segmentation of the industrial market

3.26 Segmentation may apply more obviously to the consumer market, but it can also be applied to an industrial market.

3.27 Industrial markets can be segmented with many of the bases used in consumer markets such as geography, usage rate and benefits sought. Additional, more traditional bases include customer type, product/technology, customer size and purchasing procedures.

(a) **Geographic location.** Some industries and related industries are clustered in particular areas. Firms selling services to the banking sector might be interested in the City of London.

BPP PUBLISHING

(b) **Type of business** (eg service, manufacturing)

    (i) **Nature of the customers' business.** Accountants or lawyers, for example, might choose to specialise in serving customers in a particular type of business. An accountant may choose to specialise in the accounts of retail businesses, and a firm of solicitors may specialise in conveyancing work for property development companies.

    (ii) **Components manufacturers specialise in the industries of the firms to which they supply components.**

(c) **Use of the product.** In the UK, many new cars are sold to businesses, as benefit cars. Although this practice is changing with the viability of a 'cash alternative' to a company car, the varying levels of specification are developed with the business buyer in mind (eg junior salesperson gets an Escort, Regional Manager gets a Ford Mondeo).

(d) **Type of organisation.** Organisations in an industry as a whole may have certain needs in common. Employment agencies offering business services to publishers, say, must offer their clients personnel with experience in particular desk top publishing packages. Suitable temporary staff offered to legal firms can be more effective if used to legal jargon. Each different type of firm can be offered a tailored product or service.

(e) **Size of organisation.** Large organisations may have elaborate purchasing procedures, and may do many things in-house. Small organisations may be more likely to subcontract certain specialist services.

3.28 **Wind and Cardozo** developed a two-stage framework.

(a) *Stage 1* calls for the formation of macrosegments based on organisational characteristics such as size, SIC (Standard Industrial Classification) code and product applications.

(b) *Stage 2* involves dividing these macrosegments into microsegments based on the distinguishing characteristics of decision making units. They identify five general segmentation bases moving from the outer next towards the inner in the following sequence: demographic, operating variables, purchasing approaches, situational factors and personal characteristics of the buyer.

3.29 Less research has been carried out in industrial markets as compared with consumer markets. Moreover, consumer goods companies have, generally, applied marketing theory more rigorously in practice.

Conjoint analysis

3.30 Conjoint analysis is a tool for implementing segmentation strategies, in NPD, repositioning exercises and pricing.

> **Key Concept**
>
> **Conjoint analysis** describes each product/service as a series of attributes, to which consumers ascribe different values. Consumers choose the offer that has the highest total value to them from the product attributes.

3.31 This involves developing a picture of a product in terms of its **attributes** and the **level** of each attribute. For example, motor cars have attributes of speed, safety, comfort, interior space, driving experience, price, style and reliability. Customers will ascribe different values to these attributes.

Trends in segmentation techniques

3.32 In Mastering Marketing (FT), the following trends have been identified.

- Greater use of 'softer' variables (eg lifestyles, attitudes).
- The segmentation variables are used for different purposes.
- Data-mining: patterns in statistical data speak for themselves.
- Greater use of primary and secondary segmentation variables.
- A close connection between segmentation and NPD.
- Computer modelling to discern the optimal addition to product lines.
- Consideration of the segment's response to competitors' products.

Exam Tip

The CIM is keen to internationalise the paper, and so you may have to consider segments in overseas markets.

- To what extent are these segments equivalent to their buying behaviour to the segments in the home market?

- How much adaptation to the mix will be needed?

Do not consider the 'Russian market', say, or the 'Sri Lankan market' or the UK market to be any more or less complex than each other.

4 SEGMENT VALIDITY AND ATTRACTIVENESS

Segment validity

4.1 A market segment will only **be valid if it is worth designing and developing a unique marketing mix for that specific segment.** The following questions are commonly asked to decide whether or not the segment can be used for developing marketing plans.

Criteria	Comment
Can the segment be measured?	It might be possible to conceive of a market segment, but it is not necessarily easy to measure it. For example for a segment based on people with a conservative outlook to life, can conservatism of outlook be measured by market research?
Is the segment big enough?	There has to be a large enough potential market to be profitable.
Can the segment be reached?	There has to be a way of getting to the potential customers via the organisation's promotion and distribution channels.
Do segments respond differently?	If two or more segments are identified by marketing planners but each segment responds in the same way to a marketing mix, the segments are effectively one and the same and there is no point in distinguishing them from each other.
Can the segment be reached profitably?	Do the identified customer needs, cost less to satisfy than the revenue they earn?
Is the segment suitably stable?	The stability of the segment is important, if the organisation is to commit huge production and marketing resources to serve it. The firm does not want the segment to 'disappear' next year. Of course, this may not matter in some industries.

Steps in the analysis of segmentation

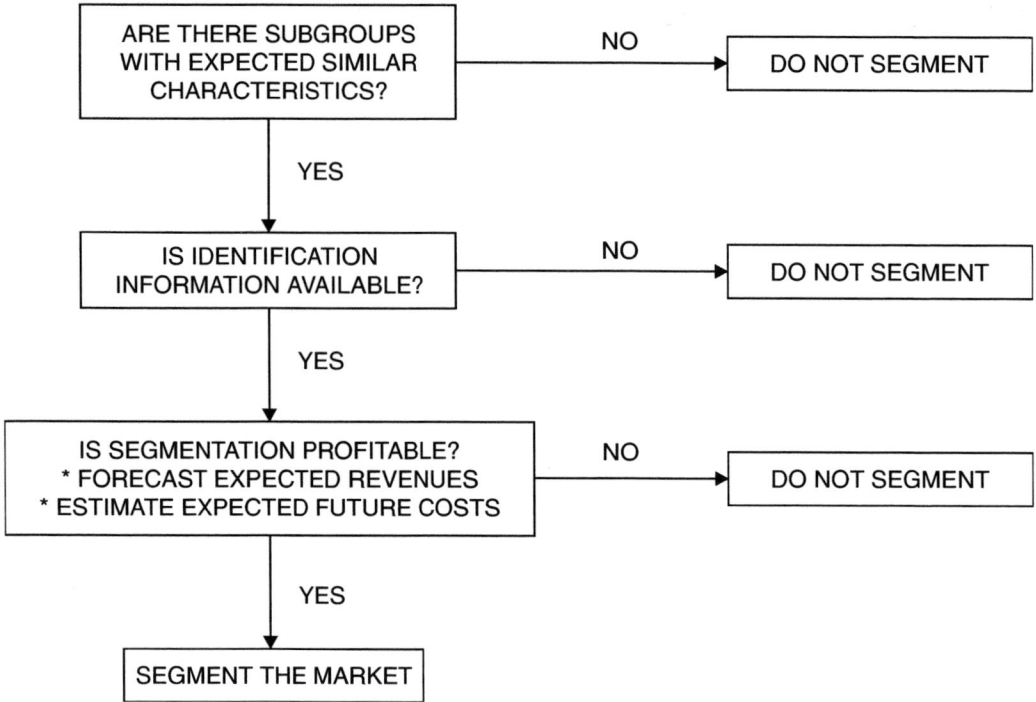

Segment attractiveness

4.2 A segment might be valid and potentially profitable, but is it potentially **attractive?**

   (a) A segment which has **high barriers to entry** might cost more to enter but will be less **vulnerable to competitors.**

   (b) For firms involved in **relationship marketing,** the segment should be one in which **viable relationship** between the firm and the customer can be established.

4.3 Segments which are most attractive will be those whose needs can be met by building on the company's strengths and where forecasts for demand, sales profitability and **growth** are favourable.

Exam Tip

You may be required to identify new segments and to take a strategic approach to positioning your offer to them.

A checklist of factors to consider when evaluating segment attractiveness

4.4 Hooley et al give a comprehensive list of factors for evaluating market attractiveness.

Factors	Characteristics to examine
Market factors	• Size of the segment
	• Segment growth rate
	• Stage of industry evaluation
	• Predictability
	• Price elasticity and sensitivity
	• Bargaining power of customers
	• Seasonality of demand

Factors	Characteristics to examine
Economic and technological factors	• Barriers to entry • Barriers to exit • Bargaining power of suppliers • Level of technology • Investment required • Margins available
Competitive factors	• Competitive intensity • Quality of competition • Threat of substitution • Degree of differentiation
Environmental factors	• Exposure to economic fluctuations • Exposure to political and legal factors • Degree of regulation • Social acceptability

4.5 It is important to assess company strengths when evaluating attractiveness and targeting a market. This can help determine the appropriate strategy, because once the attractiveness of each identified segment has been assessed it can be considered along with relative strengths to determine the potential advantages the organisation would have. In this way preferred segments can be targeted.

Market segment attractiveness →

Current and potential company strengths in serving the segment		Unattractive	Average	Attractive
	Weak	Strongly avoid	Avoid	Possibilities
	Average	Avoid	Possibilities	Secondary targets
↓	*Strong*	Possibilities	Secondary targets	Prime targets

Exam Tip

The June 2000 exam asked about evaluating target markets. Your answers could have covered Sections 4 and 5.

You could have extended your answer to cover the competences and assets determining the attractiveness of the market to a company.

The December 2000 mini-case covered targeting in the wider context of segmentation and positioning.

5 TARGET MARKETS   6/00, 12/00

5.1 Having analysed the attractiveness of a segment, the firm will now choose one or more **target markets**.

> **Key Concept**
>
> A **target market** is a market or segment selected for special attention by an organisation (possibly served with a distinct marketing mix).

5.2 The marketing management of a company may choose one of the following policy options.

Policy	Comment
Undifferentiated marketing	This policy is to produce a single product and hope to get as many customers as possible to buy it; segmentation is ignored entirely. This is sometimes called **mass marketing**.
Concentrated marketing	The company attempts to produce the ideal product for a single segment of the market (for example Rolls Royce cars, Mothercare mother and baby shops).
Differentiated marketing	The company attempts to introduce several product versions, each aimed at a different market segment (for example the manufacture of different styles of the same article of clothing).

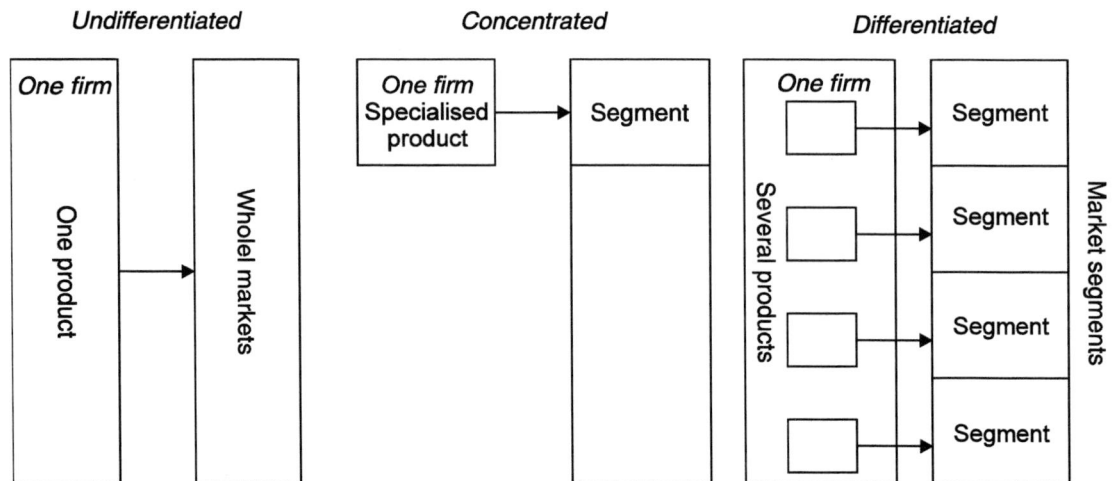

5.3 The major **disadvantage of differentiated marketing** is the additional costs of marketing and production (more product design and development costs, the loss of economies of scale in production and storage, additional promotion costs and administrative costs etc). When the **costs of further differentiation of the market exceed the benefits** from further segmentation and **target marketing**, a firm is said to have '**over-differentiated**'.

5.4 The major **disadvantage of concentrated marketing** is the business risk of relying on a single segment of a single market. On the other hand, specialisation in a particular market segment can give a firm a profitable, although perhaps temporary, competitive edge over rival firms.

5.5 The choice between undifferentiated, differentiated or concentrated marketing as a marketing strategy will depend on the following factors.

(a) The extent to which the product and/or the market may be considered **homogeneous**. **Mass marketing** may be 'sufficient' if the market is largely homogeneous (for example, for safety matches).

(b) The **company's resources** must not be over extended by differentiated marketing. Small firms may succeed better by concentrating on one segment only.

(c) The product must be sufficiently **advanced in its life cycle** to have attracted a substantial total market; otherwise segmentation and target marketing is unlikely to be profitable, because each segment would be too small in size.

Micromarketing

5.6 Segmentation, as part of target marketing, looks certain to play an even more crucial role in the marketing strategies of consumer organisations in the years ahead. The move from traditional mass marketing to **micro marketing** is rapidly gaining ground as marketers explore more cost-effective ways to recruit new customers. This has been brought about by a number of trends.

(a) The **ability to create large numbers of product variants without the need for corresponding increases in resources** is causing markets to become overcrowded.

(b) The **growth in 'minority' lifestyles** is creating opportunities for niche brands aimed at consumers with very distinct purchasing habits.

(c) The **fragmentation of the media** to service ever more specialist and local audiences is denying mass media the ability to assure market dominance for major brand advertisers.

(d) The **advance in information technology** is enabling information about individual customers to be organised in ways that enable highly selective and personal communications.

Such trends have promoted the developments in benefit, lifestyle and geodemographic segmentation techniques outlined. Consumer market segmentation has developed so much in the last few years that the vision of multinational marketers accessing a PC to plan retail distribution and supporting promotional activity in cities as far apart as Naples, Nottingham and Nice is now a practical reality.

Mass customisation

5.7 Micro-marketing is made possible by **mass customisation**, which features:

- The huge economies of scale of mass production
- The tailoring of products precisely to the customer's requirements

5.8 New manufacturing technology makes this possible. There is less need for a 'standard' or 'average' product if people's individual preferences can be catered for.

Marketing at Work

Levi Jeans in the US has offered a service whereby customers' measurements are fed through to an automated garment cutting process.

---

6 POSITIONING

Key Concept

Positioning is the act of designing the company's offer and image so that it offers a distinct and valued place in the target customer's mind.

Marketing at Work

In 2001, the *car industry* faces 4 challenges (*Economist*, 31 March 2001).

- A slump in demand (down perhaps by 20%) in the US and Europe, the two biggest markets
- Financial weakness
- Falling prices
- 21% overcapacity

In Europe, the biggest losers have been GM, Pood, Toyota, Nissan and Honda.

- GM – 'quality problems and tired designs' exacerbated by having four bosses in three years
- Japanese firms' 'product weakness' aggravated by exchange rate difficulties

The three American manufacturers are vulnerable because their profits have come from too narrow a model range. 'Car makers must dream up some exciting new vehicles to entice jaded and cautious consumers to open their wallets in a downturn.'

The article suggests that the 'recent success of European companies such as Volkswagen, Renault and PSA Peugeot Citroen, all of which have bounced back from near-death experiences, is instructive.'

Although they have improved efficiency, 'the secret of their success has been innovative products ... . It is ironic that the Europeans, notably the French, are showing the way as the car market fragments and branding becomes crucial ... . Today the cut is to have engineering skills and product development combined with a flair for brand management Europeans only *deploy for luxury goods*.'

In the past, 'with five body styles, you could cover all of Europe's product segments in 1989. Now that would only reach 50%.

Problems with positioning

6.1 How much do people remember about a product or brand?

(a) **Many products are, in fact, very similar,** and the key issue is to make them **distinct in the customer's mind.**

(b) People remember 'number 1', so the product should be positioned as 'number 1' in relation to a valued attribute.

(c) **Cosmetic changes** can have the effect of repositioning the product in the customer's mind. To be effective, however, this **psychological positioning** has to be **reinforced by 'real' positioning.**

6.2 As **positioning is psychological as well as real,** we can now identify **positioning errors.**

Mistake	Consequence
Underpositioning	The brand does not have a clear identity in the eyes of the customer
Overpositioning	Buyers may have too narrow an image of a brand
Confused positioning	Too many claims might be made for a brand
Doubtful positioning	The positioning may not be credible in the eyes of the buyer

6.3 **Positioning strategy checklist**

Positioning variable	Comment
• Attributes	• Size, for example
• Benefit	• What benefits we offer
• Use/application	• Ease of use; accessibility
• User	• The sort of person the product appeals to
• Product category	• Consciously differentiated from competition
• Quality/price	

Action Programme 2

Identify examples of positioning strategies in the table above.

Perceptual maps

6.4 One simple perceptual map that can be used is to plot brands or competing products in terms of two key characteristics such as price and quality.

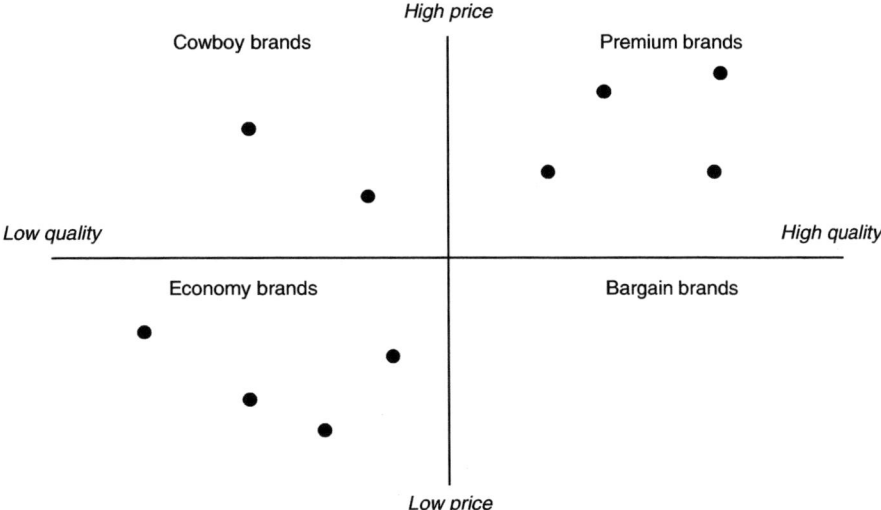

6.5 A perceptual map of market positioning can be used to **identify gaps in the market**. This example might suggest that there could be potential in the market for a low-price high-quality 'bargain brand'. A company that carries out such an analysis might decide to conduct further research to find out whether there is scope in the market for a new product which would be targeted at a market position where there are few or no rivals.

Mapping positions

6.6 Kotler identified a 3 × 3 matrix of nine different competitive positioning strategies.

Product quality	Product price		
	High price	*Medium price*	*Low price*
High	Premium strategy	Penetration strategy	Superbargain strategy
Medium	Overpricing strategy	Average-quality strategy	Bargain strategy
Low	Hit-and-run strategy	Shoddy goods strategy	Cheap goods strategy

6.7 Once selected, the needs of the targeted segment can be identified and the marketing mix strategy developed to provide the benefits package needed to satisfy them. Positioning the product offering then becomes a matter of matching and communicating appropriate benefits.

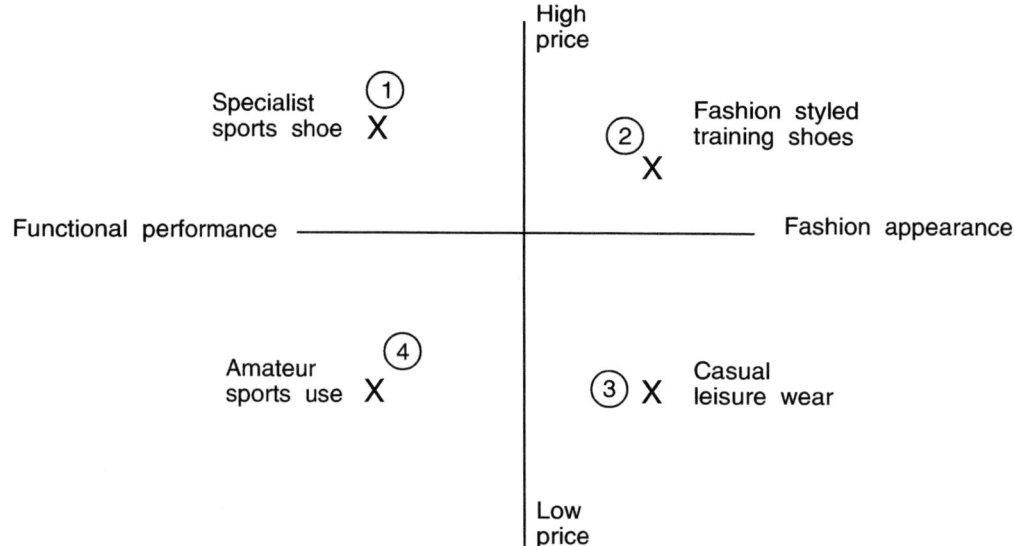

6.8 Steps in positioning

Step 1. Identify differentiating factors in products or services in relation to competitors

Step 2. Select the most important differences

Step 3. Communicate the position to the target market

6.9 The value of positioning is that it enables **tactical marketing mix decisions to be made.**

Exam Tip

The 'position map' approach can be applied to a number of areas, to brands for example, as in the December 2000 exam, in a question that also touched on non-profit marketing.

Chapter Roundup

- The foundation of a **positioning strategy** is to align what the company can do with what customers want.

- **Segmentation** enables firms to identify customer needs and products can be positioned to appeal to each segment.

- **Market segmentation** is based on different needs and different buying behaviour. Different products (eg fast cars or economical cars) are not segments in themselves, rather it is consumer needs for fast cars, commercial needs for cars which are cheap to run etc which determine segments.

- Each market segment, providing it is large and profitable enough, can become a **target market** for a firm.

- Market segmentation is increasing because marketing, economic and technological advances have made it possible to address a greater variety of customer needs.

- More and more **segmentation variables** are being added as marketing becomes more sophisticated (eg lifestyle and VALS).

- **Segment validity** depends upon size, availability, measurability and differentiation.

- **Segment attractiveness** can be assessed by analysing marketing, competitive and financial factors. Sometimes sales and markets forecasts can be used to assess the attractiveness of a market.

- Companies competing in any segment normally adopt a **differentiated marketing mix**. They 'position' themselves on price-quality spectrums and other marketing mix variables relative to competitors. Firms pursuing a focus strategy concentrate on a particular segment.

- **Positioning** can be 'psychological' and 'real'. **Perceptual maps** enable users to identify positioning options.

Now try illustrative question 13 at the end of the Study Text

Quick Quiz

1   List the steps identified by Davidson in aligning competences with customer needs. (see para 2.3)

2   To which competitive strategy is segmentation particularly relevant? (3.1)

3   What is the importance of having a number of segmentation bases? (3.5)

4   Suggest some ways in which markets could be segmented (section 3)

5   What categories have been traditionally used to segment industrial customers? (3.27)

6   What criteria must be satisfied if a market segment is to be valid? (3.32)

7   What factors might you consider in assessing segment attractiveness? (4.4)

8   What are the three policy options in selecting target markets? (4.2)

9   What is positioning? (6.1)

Action Programme Review _____

1   (a)   Adult education

- Age
- Sex
- Occupation
- Social class
- Education
- Family life cycle
- Lifestyle
- Leisure interest and hobbies

(b)   Magazines and periodicals

- Sex (Woman's Own)
- Social class (Country Life)
- Income and class aspirations (Ideal Home)
- Occupation (Marketing Week, Computer Weekly)
- Leisure interests (Railway Modeller)
- Political ideology (Spectator, New Statesman)
- Age

(c)   Sporting facilities

(i)   Geographical area (rugby in Wales, skiing in parts of Scotland, sailing in coastal towns)

(ii)   Population density (squash clubs in cities, riding in country areas)

(iii)   Occupation (gyms for office workers)

(iv)   Education (there may be a demand for facilities for sports taught at certain schools, such as rowing)

(v)   Family life cycle or age (parents may want facilities for their children, young single or married people may want facilities for themselves)

2

Positioning strategy	Example
Attributes	Ads for PCs emphasise 'speed', what sort of chip they have (eg Pentium III)
Benefit	Holidays are advertised as offering relaxation or excitement
Use/application	'Easy to use' products (eg hair tints that can be 'washed' in).
Competitor	
Product category	The Natural History Museum is fundamentally educational, but is moving towards a 'theme park' image for the schools market
Quality/price	'Value for money' advertisements

14
The Marketing Mix

Chapter Topic List	Syllabus reference
1 **Setting the scene**	
2 **An overview of the mix elements**	4.3
3 **Services and the service marketing mix**	4.3
4 **Branding strategy**	4.3
5 **Innovation and NPD**	4.3
6 **Customer care and customer relationships**	4.3

Learning Outcomes

- You will be reminded of the main elements of the marketing mix for products and service.

- You will have grasped some of the planning and organisational issues underlying NPD, branding and customer relationships.

Key Concepts Introduced

- Marketing mix
- Product
- Brand
- Brand equity

- Brand identity and image
- Brand extension/stretching
- Learning company
- Relationship marketing

Examples of Marketing at Work

- Holiday firms
- Drugs pricing
- Direct Line insurance
- Levi's jeans and Tesco
- Airlines
- Virgin
- Mercedes
- EasyJet

- Marlboro
- Sunny Delight
- Penguin books, Mills & Boon, Folio Society
- Television formats
- Daiichi
- Coca Cola
- Mobile phones
- Unofficial internet sites

BPP
PUBLISHING

1 SETTING THE SCENE

1.1 If you have sat any of the CIM's exams at previous levels, the elements of the marketing mix will be as familiar to you as they will if you come to this qualification with a career background in marketing. In this chapter, therefore, we do not go into detail about each area of the mix.

1.2 We provide you with an overview and then concentrate on:

- Areas specific to the syllabus
- The mix from a strategic viewpoint, highlighting key issues

Links with other papers

1.3 For Planning & Control, you need to think **strategically,** and so you cannot consider the mix in isolation, a key issue for Analysis and Decision. Don't get drawn into doing tactical plans.

2 AN OVERVIEW OF THE MIX ELEMENTS

Key Concept

Kotler defines the mix as follows. '**Marketing mix** is the set of controllable variables and their levels that the firm uses to influence the target market.'

2.1 The **marketing plan** is made up of decisions relating to the marketing mix for a product or service. In turn, each of these mix elements would be turned into a plan, at a more tactical level within the organisation. Each of these plans is prepared using the same basic framework that we have identified at both corporate and marketing level.

- Where are we now? (audit)
- Where are we going? (objectives)
- What are the alternative ways of getting there?
- Choosing the best option
- Developing an action plan (tactics)
- Implementation and control

You need to be prepared to understand and produce plans for these marketing mix elements in Diploma examinations.

2.2 The balance is often between a 'push' and a 'pull' strategy.

(a) A **push strategy** is concerned with moving goods out to wholesalers and retailers who then have the task of selling to customers, **ie getting dealers to accept goods.**

(b) A **pull strategy** is one of influencing final consumer attitudes so that a **consumer demand is created which dealers are obliged to satisfy.** A pull policy usually involves heavy expenditure on advertising, but holds the promise of stimulating a much higher demand.

(c) A proper balance between 'push' and 'pull' is necessary to optimise sales.

2.3 Stages in the formulation of a marketing mix

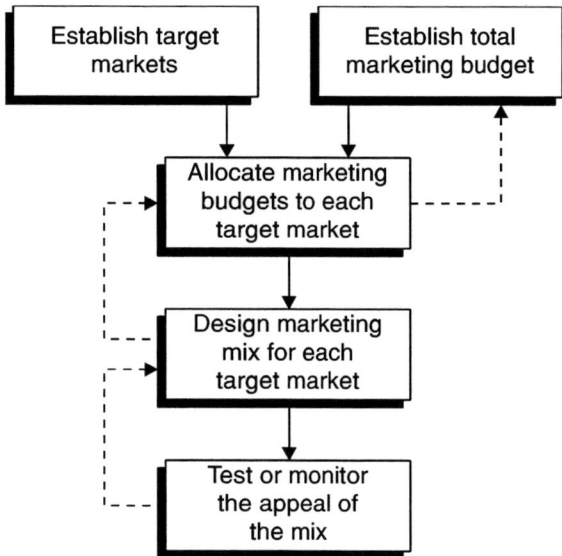

Design issues for the marketing mix

2.4

Issue	Comment
Profit/volume	The sales response function shows how different areas of the mix affect volume sales and **profits.** All other things being equal, the mix design should maximise profits.
Brand value	The mix should, where relevant, support the brand value, if a strong brand is important. Not all firms depend on branding.
Customers and distribution, segmentation	The mix should satisfy customer needs, but note in many cases there are two customers to consider: the end-user and the intermediary or reseller.
Life cycle	The appropriate mix changes over the life cycle of the product. For example a firm might adopt **penetration** or **skimming** prices at launch.
Marketing environment	This affects the optimal mix, but should be taken into account earlier in the planning process.
Seasonality	Clothes retailers are seasonally based, hence 'sales' after Christmas.
Integration	The elements of the marketing mix must support each other. There is no point promising the earth (promotion) if this cannot be delivered.
Push/pull	The mix can pull demand through the distribution chain or push it down.
Competitive strategy	The mix will support the competitive strategy.

Marketing at Work

You might like to contrast the marketing mix of these holiday firms. Each has been designed to appeal to a particular market segment.

(a) *British Museum Tours.* These are tours with an archaeological or cultural interest, and are accompanied by a leading academic. The tours are expensive and might include destinations such as Iran and

Ethiopia. Hotels are the most comfortable available. Advertising is not high profile, and is often directed to those who are already members of the British Museum Society.

(b) *Explore.* This firm offers escorted holidays to small groups, in a variety of locations, which may involve some trekking and camping. Locations might include isolated villages in northern Thailand. The firm advertises itself on the basis of 'You'll see more'. The firm advertises in newspapers, but also likes to generate repeat business and word of mouth recommendation. Poster or TV advertising is not used.

(c) *Club 18-30.* Targeted at a specific age group, these promise 'fun' or 'activity' holidays in or around beach resorts. Holidays are fairly cheap.

Combining the marketing mix in practice

2.5   For high-selling products some firms prepare a demand function showing the relationship between price and quantity of demand. This is not always possible.

(a) It may not be possible to establish, scientifically, how the different elements of the mix might interact.

(b) Many smaller businesses do not have the resources to prepare complicated models in this way.

(c) Another problem, especially true of business-to-business markets, is that there might be relatively **few customers**, who might be able to dictate, quite precisely, product specifications and other arrangements. The price may be negotiated after the sort of hard bargaining rarely encountered in consumer markets.

2.6   We will now briefly identify some issues regarding each element of the mix. This section is partly revision and partly to get you thinking about key issues of each element of the mix, including the marketing mix for services. In the **UK and most of the developed world, services account for greater economic output than manufacturing**, so we will take a 7P rather than a 4P approach to this issue.

- Product
- Place
- Price
- Promotion

- People
- Processes
- Physical evidence

Key issues for a product

2.7   **What is a product?**

> ### Key Concept
>
> A **product** is a 'package of benefits' meeting particular needs. It is anything that can be offered to a market, for attention, acquisition, use or consumption that might satisfy a want or need.

Aspect	Example
Physical aspect: what the product is	Bank account
Functional aspect: what the product does	Keeps your money safe
Symbolic aspect: what the product means	If you bank with Coutts, you are a member of an exclusive set of people

2.8 Levels of a product (Kotler)

Level	Comment
Core benefit	A hotel offers rest and sleep away from home
Generic product	Any hotel is a building with rooms to rent
Expected product	Must expect cleanliness and quiet
Augmented product	Additional benefits (eg taxi service)
Potential product	Possible augmentations in the future (for example fax machines for business travellers)

(a) The augmented product in one country may, in a more prosperous country, be the expected product in a poor country.

(b) Most **competition** in the developed world is based around the **augmented product**.

2.9 Strategic issues for product

(a) **Defining the product.** Product/service is key in differentiation strategy, as the product can be manipulated to satisfy the needs of different market segments.

(b) **Selecting the product range,** in terms of **width** (how many segments) and **depth** (variety of options in each segment).

(c) Building a **brand**.

(d) Managing the **product portfolio** with new launches and deletions.

(e) **Quality**: this is 'fitness for use' and can be analysed as quality of design, and quality of conformance (the product has been manufactured without defects).

Price

Exam Tip

Many firms avoid competing on price if possible, but sometimes there is no alternative. Before responding on price alone, you should assess:

- Is the competitor offering the same combination of price and service?
- Is the price cut significant?
- What was the competitor's underlying justification for cutting the price?
- Effect on profitability
- Effect on overall marketing strategy

You are then offered a choice between maintaining prices, matching the lower prices, raising perceived quality and so on.

2.10 Price represents the revenue earning side of the mix. Influences on pricing policy are:

- The customer
- Competitors and the environment
- The company

Pricing involves a set of trade-offs between these three elements, more so, perhaps, than other aspects of the mix.

BPP PUBLISHING

The customer

2.11 'Price' is the sacrifice the customer has to pay for the package of benefits, real or psychological, that the company has to offer.

(a) Traditional economics suggest a link between **pricing** policy and **quantity** ordered. For example, by lowering the price you would expect customers, within reason, to buy more. **Elasticity of demand** is where the extent to which demand is sensitive to price. If elasticity is low, raising or lowering the price will make little difference to the quantity bought.

(b) **Price sensitivity** affects elasticity. Price is only one influence on the buying decision. Piercy (1997) argues that **many firms under-price,** on the mistaken assumption that competitors will do the same and that consumers are highly price sensitive.

(c) **Raising prices and enhancing value** may be as **easy a way to raise profits** as **cutting prices to increase volumes.**

(d) Different price/value propositions succeed in different market segments.

(e) **Distributors and intermediaries** also have pricing objectives, so the price to the consumer may have to be set with the distributor's objectives in mind.

(f) Many customers have limited price awareness of prices in general, but they may notice sudden **fluctuations.**

(g) Many people think that pricing is an **ethical** issue.

Marketing at Work

Developing *drugs to combat AIDS* has been expensive. The prices charged put the treatment way out of reach of sufferers in poorer countries where AIDS is prevalent. Some say that this pricing strategy is unethical. Others say that the money spent researching into drugs for AIDS could be spent on dealing with other life-threatening illnesses in poorer countries. Price does have 'ethical' connotations.

This has been highlighted very recently by events in South Africa, where there is a substantial problem with HIV.

The South African government intended to import cheap 'generic' copies of anti-AIDS drugs, as the price charged by the major *pharmaceuticals companies* was regarded as prohibitive.

The pharmaceuticals companies went to court, arguing that this breached their intellectual property rights and they needed to recover the development costs.

The court action turned into a PR disaster for the pharmaceuticals firm. They were perceived to have 'backed down' from the court action – especially when pressure groups started to ask difficult questions. They were portrayed in the (Western) media as being greedy and exploitative. However, the key issue for pharmaceuticals companies – getting a return on risky investments – will not go away.

The company

2.12 Pricing is a key decision as it can very easily affect margins and profits.

	A	B
	£	£
Price	10	9.50
Cost	8	8.00
Profit	2	1.50

B is priced at 5% cheaper than A, but is 25% less profitable. In other words, a 5% cut in price leads to a 25% cut in profits. Clearly more of the unit will have to be sold to make up the shortfall.

2.13 The problem is that the **cost of producing something is not determined by the price** charged. As firms aim to make profits for shareholders, prices are often set with costs in mind, as a floor. The marketer thus does not have complete freedom to determine prices.

Competitors   **Specimen paper**

2.14 Price is also set by reference to other firms in the industry. Price can act as a differentiating factor, in line with other aspects of the mix.

(a) In **commodity** markets, where differentiation is difficult, **price may be the only competitive tool.**

(b) In some markets, a **firm acts as price leader**. Other firms follow the price leader if the leader raises, lowers or maintains the price level for a product.

2.15 Generally, price cuts to increase market share will be matched by competitors in some way. **If a rival firm cuts its prices in the expectation of increasing its market share**, a firm has the following options.

Maintain its existing prices	This will work if only a little market share would be lost. Eventually, the rival firm may drop out of the market or be forced to raise its prices. However, this strategy may fail if the price cutter has a long-term advantage and can sustain lower prices.
Maintain prices but responding with a non-price counter-attack	The firm will be securing or justifying its current prices with a product change, advertising, or better back-up services, etc.
Reduce prices	This should protect the firm's market share so that the main beneficiary from the price reduction will be the consumer.
Raise prices and respond with a non-price counter-attack	The extra revenue from the higher prices might be used to finance an advertising campaign or product design changes. A price increase would be based on a campaign to emphasise the quality difference between the rival products.

Current trends in pricing

2.16 Some trends in the **retail market** are worthy of note.

(a) Consumers want **high quality at lower prices**. 'Own-label' brands are improving their quality.

(b) Relatively **slow growth in consumer spending** means **greater competition** and **shrinking margins**.

(c) National **brand owners** have to offer more benefits to the **retailer**.

(d) The entry of US chains such as Wal-mart to Europe will put downward pressure on retail prices.

Marketing at Work

Air travel for corporate executives

There are two main alternatives: one is business- and first-class tickets, priced at several thousand pounds, which account for the mass of corporate executive travel; the other is corporate jets, which cost tens of millions of pounds and capture minuscule market share.

Executive Jet, a subsidiary of Berkshire Hathaway, came up with a breakthrough pricing model: instead of selling jets, it sold shares of time in using a jet. This allowed it to price jets per year at roughly the amount a

company would spend on business- and first-class tickets. It won orders from business-class customers and from executives who preferred a relatively cheap time-share in Executive Jet to full ownership of a Gulfstream or Learjet that would spend much of its time sitting idle on the tarmac.

Place

2.17 Distribution or place refers to the 'availability' of the product to the customer and involves:

- Logistics (warehouses, lorries)
- The distribution channel, other companies (wholesalers etc)

2.18 **Logistics** is a significant problem for many companies, particularly if they provide 'just-in-time' services. Logistics, however, is something that it increasingly outsourced to specialist delivery firms such as **Eddie Stobart** (a brand in its own right) and specialist warehousing firms.

(a) The Channel Tunnel has changed some of the economics of long-term distribution.

(b) The UK and European governments would wish to encourage more use of rail on ecological grounds.

2.19 The **distribution channel** dilemma facing management is that of the trade-off between cost and control. The shorter the distribution channel the more control managers have over the marketing of the products, but the higher their distribution costs. Long distribution channels cut the costs but also reduce the firm's control. The various channels are outlined in the diagram below.

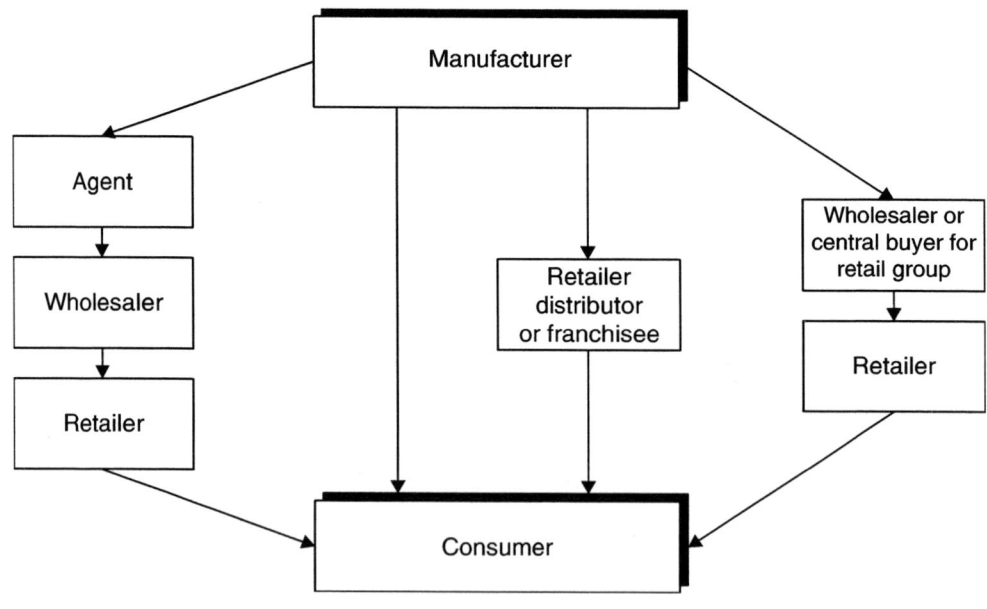

Marketing at Work

In the US, a pair of *Levis jeans* costs £30. In the UK, you might pay £45. In the US, Levi's jeans are a standard commodity, not a premium product (the positioning in the UK).

Tesco has obtained Levis from elsewhere, selling them for £25, nearer the American price. Levi has taken them to court, owing to exclusive distribution.

The EU has pursued a policy supporting exclusive distributor arrangements, largely at the behest of luxury goods manufacturers. Some EU states are trying to outlaw them.

As consumers travel more, there may be a 'leaking' of perceptions of brand quality. With alcoholic drinks, a key price difference is caused by taxes.

Choosing or designing the distribution channel

2.20 Key issues relating to the choice of distribution channel

- Number of intermediaries
- Support given to distributors (eg technical advice)
- Control of distribution
- Integration of marketing effort throughout this chain
- Positioning of the product: the distribution should be aligned with this
- Possibility of direct marketing

2.21 Why do firms use intermediaries?

- Geography: customers may live too far away to be reached directly, or may be too dispersed
- Consolidation of small orders into large ones
- Better use of resources elsewhere
- Lack of retailing know-how
- Segmentation, with different segments for each market being reached by different distribution channels

Current strategic developments in distribution

2.22 According to Peter Drucker, in the near future: 'The greatest change will be in distribution channels, not in new methods of production and consumption'. The spurs to change are these.

(a) **Physical distribution costs** are increasing **relative** to other costs (ie as production costs fall). Sometimes these amount to 50% of the price the end-consumer pays.

(b) **Changing consumer lifestyles:** 'one small example is that those in work are time-poorer but money richer ... no wonder there's been a rapid rise in home delivery, from pizzas to wine to potatoes'.

(c) 'Long established discrete **distribution channels are beginning to 'leak'** (eg beer-buyers can go to France and stock up with lower-taxed drinks).

(d) Offering EDI (**electronic data interchange**) enables a firm to cut lead times for orders. This can be a source of differentiation.

(e) **Distribution has a 'branding effect'.** 'Distribution can be a central and, explicit part of a brand's identity, such as First Direct (Midland Bank's telephone banking subsidiary).

(f) **Distribution channels' generation of customer information opens the door to marketing insight and power.** Retailers (through using EPOS) probably know more about customers than manufacturers. Distribution might become 'essentially an information system'.

(g) There has been a move towards a **concentration of retailer power** with large **retailers** tending to gain **power over the manufacturers in the distribution channel**. This shift in the balance of power has two consequences. **Large multiples** are able to **dictate product specifications,** and drive much harder bargains on matters of price and delivery. The large multiples' **own-label brands** are increasingly the major competition against branded goods.

(h) **Just-in-time** is a philosophy which applies to the whole production chain, but it is increasingly relevant to distribution, in satisfying the needs of demanding customers, particularly in business-to-business markets.

(i)   Manufacturers are seeking to reduce their stocks of components and raw materials, to eliminate stock holding costs and wasteful activities.

(ii)   Consequently they expect their suppliers to deliver in very small batches as and when demanded.

2.23 **Mail order,** in which goods are sold by catalogue, over the Internet, delivered by post or directly, is common in some markets.

(a) **Retailers do not have to be offered a mark-up.** This is why **book clubs** and internet bookshops such as **Amazon.com** are able to offer discounts on recommended retail prices.

(b) **Customers can be reached** who might not normally be able to purchase the product **from a shop.**

(c) This makes it easier to sell to customers who **cannot do their shopping in normal shopping hours.**

(d) **No large and expensive display area** in a shop.

(e) Mail-order facilities can be **combined with an Internet web-site.**

Action Programme 1

What social trends do you think might increase home delivery?

Exam Tip

You may be asked to identify direct marketing's contribution to marketing strategy. Do not just concentrate on the distribution aspect. Direct marketing also enables users to build up customer profiles, so information gleaned from successful direct marketing exercises can be input to the MkIS.

Promotion

2.24 Kotler identifies four **categories of promotional activity**

Promotional	Comment
Advertising	Any **paid** form of non-personal presentation and promotion of ideas, goods or services by an identified sponsor.
Sales promotion	Encourage through incentives, over a short-term period, the purchase of the good or service.
Personal selling	The oral presentation of the goods or services, either to make a sale, or to create goodwill to improve the prospects of sales in the future.
Public relations	Unlike advertising, publicity cannot be bought and it might be thought of as unpaid advertising. Although organisations will spend large sums of money on publicity, they do not formally buy space in a newspaper or time on television or radio. Nor do they usually control the content of the publicity message, and so some publicity can be bad rather than good. However, they often try to manage publicity through the use of public relations.

2.25 Marketing communications convey information about the product and the company. Recently, the trend is towards **integrated marketing communications**. In other words, the

marketing communications should be integrated with the business strategy, the other elements of the marketing mix, and with each other. Few organisations practise an integrated communications approach in any systematic way. The various tools of marketing communications have traditionally been the exclusive preserve of different groups within the organisation.

2.26 **Promotion is the element of the mix most under control of the marketing department.** Piercy suggests that, as far as managers are concerned, there are a number of issues which must be considered strategically for each form of communication.

Issue	Comment
Role	**Each form of communication has a different target.** Media advertising is direct to the end user, whereas personal selling may be preferred for distributors.
Objectives	Each form of communication needs specific objectives: • Advertising: raising awareness, repositioning • Public relations: favourable press exposure • Personal selling: sales targets, client relationships • Sales promotion: sample rates
Process management	This covers relationships with external suppliers, budgeting, recruiting and personnel
Integration	The elements of the mix should be integrated so that all customers get the appropriate message, and the different elements of the mix do not conflict with each other.

2.27 **Key strategic developments in promotion**

Development	Consequence
Database marketing and data mining	This enables targeting of promotional messages.
Digital TV, many channels	It will be harder to reach a single audience: rather like the trade magazine sector, fragmentation may cut advertising rates.
Internet	Internet advertisements are generally **sought** out by 'surfers', **banner ads** possibility of **interactive marketing,** concerns about junk e-mail, concerns about low profitability of Internet firms.
Call centres	Telephone call centres are mushrooming over the country. They provide sales and customer support activity. They tend to be rigid and bureaucratic in style.
Sponsorship	Sports and cultural organisations are seeking sponsors. Like all forms of activity, the sponsor has objectives to fulfil. This can be a difficult relationship. Sponsorship is not intrusive.
Personal advice and loyalty	As service industries develop, there will be greater scope for personal service such as financial services.
Lobbying	Some decisions regarding product standardisation and safety will be taken at EU level. Expertise in this area is necessary.

Marketing at Work

Unofficial Internet sites

The Internet offers firms the opportunity to create 'virtual' communities. But it also offers dissatisfied customers or employees the chance to set up 'bulletin boards' to discuss exactly what they think of the company, to publicise information companies would rather keep quiet, or to forward confidential price-sensitive information.

Specific 'anti-corporate' websites have been set up to knock household names. McSpotlight, a site founded by Greenpeace, average 1.5m hits a month. A large amount of the information may be biased, distorted or false.

From a PR point of view what should you do?

(a) Libel is hard to prove especially when people log on under assumed names, but some firms feel that suing is the only solution

(b) Threats to close down a site would be seen as a threat to free speech, and anyhow would be hard to enforce

3 SERVICES AND THE SERVICE MARKETING MIX

The importance of services

3.1 Importance of services

(a) The service sector accounts for most economic activity in the UK accounting for more employment than manufacturing, although many services cannot be exported.

(b) Competition has been introduced to service industries.

(c) Many 'products' contain a service element.

(d) Service can be a differentiating factor in a firm's offer to the market.

(e) **Bad service is costly.**

Marketing at Work

Bank accounts

A study by the Henley Centre indicated that 17% of a typical company's customers were affected by a range of service problems, such as poor information or inefficiency. 15% of people who switched bank account cited poor service as the reason. An unhappy customer tells up to nine others about bad service received.

Elements of services

3.2 Services differ from physical goods.

Intangibility	A service cannot be seen, touched or displayed. The service is often difficult for the consumer to understand.
Inseparability	In general, it is impossible to separate the production and consumption of a service. (For example, a theatrical event is consumed when it is produced.)
Perishability	Services are perishable. They cannot be stored, they must be produced on demand and often can only be produced in the presence of the customer. Transport is a sort of service industry. A bus journey cannot be 'stored'.
Variability	The quality of the service product is typically highly dependent on the quality of the personnel conducting the transaction.

Products and services combined

3.3 Many offers to the market have **both a product and a service element** to them.

- Teaching is almost entirely a service
- A restaurant meal is part product and part service
- A 'house' is almost entirely a product, but it is acquired with the help of service firms

3.4 Dimensions of service quality

(a) **Technical quality** of the service encounter (what is received by the customer). For example, a customer is going to a bank about a pension. The quality of financial advice received can sometimes be evaluated by a customer. The dimension is based on the technical product training of the staff and their knowledge of the bank's services. It can be backed up by a range of sales aids, such as brochures and even computer based product illustrations which feed the customer's specific requirements into an interactive programme when then produces a customised quotation.

(b) **The functional quality** of the service encounter is how the service is provided. The dimension relates to the psychological interaction between the buyer and seller and is typically perceived in a very subjective way. It includes elements such as the following: the attitudes and behaviour of the employees, how they appear, how accessible the service is, the interrelationships between employees and customers.

(c) The **corporate image** dimension of service quality is a result of how consumers perceive the firm. This dimension can be affected by many factors including advertising and past experience with the firm.

3.5 Determinants of service quality

Determinant	Quality
Tangibles	The physical evidence, such as the quality of fixtures and fittings of the company's service area, must be consistent with the desired image.
Reliability	Getting it right first time is very important, not only to ensure repeat business, but, in financial services, as a matter of ethics, if the customer is buying a future benefit.
Responsiveness	The staff's willingness to deal with the customer's queries must be apparent.
Communication	Staff should talk to customers in non-technical language which they can understand.
Credibility	The organisation should be perceived as honest, trustworthy and as acting in the best interests of customers.
Security	This is specially relevant to medical and financial services organisations. The customer needs to feel that the conversations with bank service staff are private and confidential. This factor should influence the design of the service area.
Competence	All the service staff need to appear competent in understanding the product range and interpreting the needs of the customers. In part, this can be achieved through training programmes.
Courtesy	Customers (even rude ones) should perceive service staff as polite, respectful and friendly. This basic requirement is often difficult to achieve in practice, although training programmes can help.

Determinant	Quality
Understanding customers' needs	The use of computer-based customer databases can be very impressive in this context. The service personnel can then call up the customer's records and use these data in the service process, thus personalising the process. Service staff need to meet customer needs rather than try to sell products. This is a subtle but important difference.
Access	Minimising queues, having a fair queuing system and speedy but accurate service are all factors which can avoid customers' irritation building up. A pleasant relaxing environment is a useful design factor in this context.

Deploying the marketing mix in services

3.6 As services differ from manufactured products, this causes potential **marketing problems.**

(a) The degree of **complexity** which characterises, for example, many financial products.

(b) **Inseparability**: the difficulty for consumers to distinguish between the service itself and its delivery system. The delivery system will be inextricably linked with the service itself and will often be considered as a component of that product. In this sense, there will be some aspects of the delivery system which must be seen as components of the core or tangible product while others may usefully be characterised as part of the augmented product.

3.7 **Marketing services**

(a) **Poor service quality in one case** (eg lack of punctuality of trains, staff rudeness, a bank's incompetence) **is likely to lead to widespread distrust of everything the organisation does.**

(b) If the service is intangible and offers a complicated future benefit, or is consumed 'on the spot', then attracting customers means promoting an attractive image and ensuring that the **service lives up to its reputation, consistently.**

(c) The **pricing of services is often complicated,** especially if large numbers of people are involved in providing the service.

(d) **Human resources management, not just customer care, is a key ingredient in the services marketing mix,** as so many services are produced and consumed in a specific social context. The human element cannot always be designed out of a service.

3.8 Service marketing involves three additional 'P's: people, processes and physical evidence.

People

3.9 That **employees** are relevant as an element in the marketing mix is particularly evident in service industries. After all, if you have had poor service in a shop or restaurant, you may not be willing to go there again. An American retailing firm estimated that there was an identifiable relationship between low staff turnover and repeat purchases. Managing front-line workers (eg cabin-crew on aircraft), who are the lowest in the organisational hierarchy but whose behaviour has most effect on customers, is an important task for senior management. It involves corporate culture, job design and motivational issues.

- Appearance
- Attitude
- Commitment
- Behaviour

- Professionalism
- Skills
- Numbers
- Discretion

Processes

3.10   **Processes involve the ways in which the marketer's task is achieved.** Efficient processes can become a **marketing advantage** in their own right. For example, if an airline develops a sophisticated **ticketing system**, it can encourage customers to take connecting flights offered by allied airlines. Efficient processing of purchase orders received from customers can decrease the time it takes to satisfy them. Efficient procedures in the long term save money.

- Procedures
- Policies
- Mechanisation
- Queuing

- Information
- Capacity levels
- Speed/timing
- Accessibility

Physical evidence

3.11   **Physical evidence.** Again, this is particularly important in service industries, for example where the ambience of a restaurant is important. Logos and uniforms help create a sense of corporate identity.

Environment	Facilities	Tangible evidence
• Furnishings • Colours • Layout • Noise levels • Smells • Ambience	• Vans/vehicles/ aeroplanes • Equipment/tools • Uniforms • Paperwork	• Labels • Tickets • Logos • Packaging

Marketing at Work

Telecommunications is a service, and an important aspect of physical evidence in telecommunications is the public phone box. BT replaced its old, expensive-to-maintain red phone boxes and introduced nondescript metallic kiosks, in which the phones actually worked. Scrapping the red phone boxes caused outrage.

4   BRANDING STRATEGY   12/99

What is a brand?

> ### Key Concept
>
> - A '**brand**' is a collection of attributes which strongly influence purchase. (Davidson)
>
> - 'A name, term, sign, symbol or design or combination of them, intended to identify the goods or services of one seller or group of sellers and to differentiate them from those of competitors.' (Kotler)

4.1   Branding and a firm's reputation are linked. The important thing to remember is that a brand is something **customers** value: it exists in the customer's mind. A brand is the link between a company's marketing activities and the customer's perception.

Marketing at Work

Virgin is a brand that covers airlines, pensions, bank accounts, record stores, coca-cola and, notoriously, railways.

There is clearly little in common with the services on offer. Virgin Trains have a poor reputation, whereas the airline has a good reputation for service. Virgin Train's aspiration however is towards providing excellent service, even though the execution has some way to go.

4.2 What makes up a brand?

- Effective product
- Distinctive identity
- Added values

} supported by {

Visible: Symbol, advertising, presentation (eg packaging)

Invisible: assets and competences, strong R&D, supply chain, effective selling, costs

(Sources: Doyle, Davidson)

4.3 Benefits of branding

Beneficiary	Benefit of branding
Customers	• Branding makes it easier to choose between competing products, if brands offer different benefits. Brands help consumers cope with information overload • Brands can support 'aspirations' and self image • Branding (eg Nike) can confer membership of reference groups
Marketers	• Enables extra value to be added to the product • Creates an impression in the consumer's mind; encourages re-purchase • Differentiates the product, especially if competing products are similar • Reduces the importance of price • Encourages a 'pull' strategy • Other products/services can exploit the brand image (eg Virgin)

Shareholders	• A brand is an intangible asset; even though it is not on the financial statements, a strong brand promises to generate future cash inflows and profits. This is called **brand equity**.
	
	• Brands build market share, which can generate high profits through:
	   ◦ Higher volume
	   ◦ Higher value (higher prices)
	   ◦ Higher control over distributors

Key Concept

Brand equity is the asset the marketer builds to ensure continuity of satisfaction for the customer and profit for the supplier. The asset consists of consumer attitudes, distribution.

4.4 Evolution of brands.

Brands have evolved over time, to the extent that they satisfy customer needs.

(a) **Classic brands** (post World War II) were linked to a single goal (eg cleaner clothes).

(b) **Contemporary brands** meet functional needs but give associated benefits (eg Volvo and 'safety').

(c) **Post-modern brands?** Consumers use brands to attain a broad array of goals, as a result of 'time famine'.

    (i) Some marketers suggest that brands have an 'emotional' content. Certainly, this might be the case for fashion items (eg trainers) where they confer status.

    (ii) Strangest of all is Mercedes (a subsidiary of Daimler Chysler), previously known for upmarket luxury cars. Current (2001) advertising suggests that a whole range of people might want Mercedes: identifying 'difference' and 'adaptability' as the heart of the brand. Mercedes now has product offering that embraces small cars.

Brand strategies

4.5 Different types of brand strategy

(a) **Company brand.** The company name is the most prominent feature of the branding (eg Mercedes).

(b) **The company brand combined with an individual brand name** (eg Kelloggs - Corn Flakes, Rice Krispies). This option both legitimises (because of the company name) and individualises (the individual product name). It allows **new 'names' to be introduced quickly and relatively cheaply.** Sometimes known as **umbrella branding,** firms might use this approach as a short-term way to save money.

(c) **Range brand.** Firms group types of product under different brands. For example, Sharwoods is a brand owned by *RHM Foods.* Sharwoods offers pickles, poppadums, sauces etc.

(d) **Individual name.** Each product has a unique name. This is the option chosen by *Procter & Gamble* for example, who even have different brand names within the same product line, eg Bold, Tide. The main advantage of individual product branding is that an unsuccessful brand does not adversely affect the firm's other products, nor the firm's reputation generally.

Marketing at Work

Penguin Books, Mills & Boon, the *Folio Society*

Penguin is one of the oldest brands in UK paperback publishing and over the years has introduced brand extensions (Puffin for children, Pelican for academic) and sub-brands (Penguin Classics, Penguin Modern Classics) and indeed other products (Penguin Classic CDs).

A key issue for publishing is to identify the core of the brand.

(a) The imprint or publisher?
(b) The author? It appears to go without saying that people will buy a book by a recognised author, and that the author is at the heart of the brand.

In contrast, people buy '*Mills & Boon*' books - the core of the brand is the publisher, not the author.

The *Folio Society* publishes versions of classic literature, but markets its books partly as art objects, owing to the quality of the binding and paper, and the specially-commissioned illustrations.

4.6   **Choice of brand strategy**

(a)   **Company and/or umbrella brand name**

Advantages	Disadvantages
• Cheap (only one marketing effort)	• Not ideal for segmentation
• Easy to launch new products under umbrella brand	• Harder to obtain distinct identity
• Good for internal marketing	• Risk that failure in one area can damage the brand
	• Variable quality

For example, **Virgin** is a company brand name, supported by advertising, PR and the 'celebrity' status of Richard Branson. (To what extent will the problems of Virgin Trains adversely affect the other brands?)

(i)   Service industries use 'umbrella' marketing as customer benefits can cross product categories. Marks & Spencer diversified from clothes, to food and to financial services. Tesco and Asda have followed suit.

(ii)   Communication media are more diffuse and fragmented.

(iii) One brand is supported by integrated marketing communications.

(iv)   Umbrella branding supports **database marketing** across the whole product range.

(v)   Distributor/retailer brands are 'umbrella' brands in their own right, so **brand owners** have to follow suit.

(d)   Range brands offer some of the advantages of an umbrella brand with more precise targeting.

(c)   Individual brand name

Advantage	Disadvantages
• Ideal for precise segmentation	• Expensive
• Crowds out competition by offering more choice	• Risky
• Damage limitation to company's reputation	

Brands/values

4.7   'Added values - the **subjective beliefs of customers** - are at the heart of building **brands**' (Doyle). These added values are largely subjective. In 'blind testing' many consumers cannot tell the difference between different products; however, they will exhibit a preference for a strong brand name when shown it.

4.8   **Most consumer buying decisions, therefore, do not depend on the functionality of the product.**

(a)   Products are bought for 'emotional reasons'. For example, most sports trainers are 'fashion' products.

(b)   Branding reduces the need to choose.

Marketing at Work

Early in 1993, it was announced that the price of Marlboro cigarettes was to be cut in some of its US markets. Marlboro had been one of the USA's most heavily supported brands, but was losing ground to cheap discounted competitor brands. What do you think might be the significance of this?

The purpose of a brand is, in part, to reduce the consumer's sensitivity to price. It might promise an income stream in future and hence be worth valuing as a fixed asset. However, the price cut of Marlboro cigarettes sends a significant message to many brand-based businesses. US analysts believed that Marlboro was one of the strongest brands ever promoted, recognised world wide and supported by consistently heavy investment. Cutting the price of Marlboro indicated the fact that some brands are never impervious to price competition. The price cut led to a fall in the share price of companies dealing heavily in branded goods, indicating that the value of their main asset, their brand, was less than supposed.

4.9 Sources of brand values

Source	Comment
Experience	Customer's actual usage of a brand can give positive or negative associations.
User associations	Brands get an image from the type of people using them; brands might be associated with particular personalities.
Belief	This might be a 'placebo' effect; **belief** in a brand may enhance its effectiveness.
Appearance	Design appeals to people's aesthetic sensibilities.
Manufacturer's name	The company reputation may support the brand.

4.10 Brand identity

> **Key Concept**
>
> **Brand identity**: 'the message sent out by the brand through its product form, name, visual signs, advertising. This is not the same as **brand image** which is how the target market perceives the brand.

4.11 Three aspects to a brand (Doyle)

Aspect	Comment
Core	Fundamental, unchanging aspect of a brand. (Cider is an **alcoholic** drink made from applies.)
Style	This is the brand's culture, personality, the identity it conveys and so on. Compare the: • 'Rustic' personality of 'Scrumpy Jack' • Almost club-orientated personality of 'Diamond White'
Themes	These are how the brand communicates through physical appearance of the product.

Clearly, the **themes** are more easy to change than the **style**, which is more easy to change than the **core**.

Exam Tip

A June 2000 question asked about introducing a UK brand of soft drinks – with a distinct personality – into the Russian market. It showed how branding and segmentation can be applied to more complex problems.

How to build brands

4.12 The process for building the brand is similar to that of building a product (core product, an expected product, an augmented product and a potential product). However, a product is, in some respects, purely functional, whereas a brand offers more.

4.13 **A step approach to designing brands**

Step 1. **Have a 'quality' product** - but remember quality means 'fitness for use' not 'the maximum specification'. Functionality is only a starting point.

Step 2. **Build the basic brand.** These are the marketing mix criteria.

- They should support product performance
- They should differentiate the brand
- They should be consistent with positioning
- The basic brand delivers the core product in an attractive way.

Step 3. **Augmentations** include extra services, guarantees and so on. (Expensive guarantees provide evidence that the firm takes quality seriously.)

Step 4. **Reaching its potential,** so that customers will not easily accept substitutes.

Step 5. Maintain **brand value** by using the marketing mix to persuade customers to re-buy.

Step 6. **Build brand loyalty.** Customers who rebuy and are loyal are valuable because:

- Revenue from them is more predictable
- Existing customers are 'cheaper' than new customers

Step 7. **Know where to stop in developing the brand. (For example, an alcohol-free version of 'alcoholic lemonade' would be pointless.)**

Implementing the brand strategy

4.14 Brands that **reach their potential** have five key characteristics (Doyle).

- A quality product underpinning the brand
- Being first to market, giving early mover advantages
- Unique positioning concept: in other words they are precisely positioned
- Strong communications underpinning the brand
- Time and consistency

4.15 **The brand planning process**

Brand strategy is one of the steps in the brand planning process just as marketing strategy is one step in the marketing planning process. Arnold (1992) in *The Handbook of Brand Management* offers a five stage brand planning process.

Stage	Description
Market analysis	An overview of trends in the macro and micro environment and so includes customer and competitor analysis and the identification of any PEST factors which may affect our brand. For soft drinks, the explosion of competitive activity, particularly by own label, and new product introductions, such as Fruitopia, will be important.
Brand situation analysis	Analysis of the brand's personality and individual attributes. This represents the internal audit and questions such as, 'Is advertising projecting the right image?', 'Is the packaging too aggressive?', 'Does the product need updating?' need asking. This is a fundamental evaluation of the brand's character.
Targeting future positions	This is the core of brand strategy. Any brand strategy could incorporate what has been learnt in steps (i) and (ii) into a view of how the market will evolve and what strategic response is most appropriate. Brand strategy can be considered under three headings. (1) Target markets (2) Brand positions (3) Brand scope
Testing new offers	Once the strategy has been decided the next step is to develop individual elements of the marketing mix and test the brand concept for clarity, credibility and competitiveness with the target market.
Planning and evaluating performance	The setting of the brand budget, establishing the type of support activity needed and measurement of results against objectives. Information on tracking of performance feeds into step (i) of the brand management process.

Marketing at Work

Sunny Delight

This is an example of what can go well – and – not to well in planning, introducing and managing a new product. (Extracts from the *Guardian*, 11 April 2001.)

Sunny Delight burst upon Britain with its sunshine logo in April 1998. **By August 1999, it was the country's third-largest-selling soft drink**. Yet only **three years** later, sales are down 36% by value and 28% by volume (moving annual totals to February 2001).

It was a textbook **launch**. Delight had been available in the US since 1964, it was sold as a downmarket drink competing for space alongside squashes and long-life drinks on ordinary shelves. The approach in the UK was to be different. P&G, one of the world's most powerful grocery manufacturers, had acquired it at the end of the 80s and in 1996 began a long and thorough process of test marketing it for the UK in Carlisle.

Delight is 5% citrus juice, and a lot of sugar and water, with vegetable oil, thickeners, added vitamins and flavourings, colourings and other additives that make it **look** like fresh orange juice but appeal to the immature tastebuds of young children.

The **ingredients were cheap but the price was set at a premium**. P&G invested in a new filling plant costing about £12m, according to industry estimates, so that the drink could be **packaged** in the short of frosted plastic bottles that fresh orange juice is usually sold in chill cabinets, next to fresh fruit juices.

P&G is one of the handful of companies that has the muscle to dictate where products are sold in supermarkets. All this was backed up by a huge direct marketing campaign and a £9.2m advertising campaign.

P&G's brands include Pampers and it is thought to have built up a powerful **database** from offers over the years which tells the company who we are and how old our children are ... also reported to have worked with retailer's data from loyalty cards to identify young, lower-income families. Teenagers were targeted with sponsorship of basketball.

This combined onslaught led to instant success. But the backlash came equally fast. The Food Commission condemned Sunny Delight as a con, accusing P&G of putting it in chill cabinets to mislead. Newspapers, the BBC's Watchdog programme and Radio 4 all carried attacks on the brand and dubbed it 'The unreal thing'.

Then came the comic twist in the drama. In December 1999, a paediatrician, Dr Duncan Cameron, reported a new and alarming condition in the medical journals: Sunny Delight syndrome. A girl of five had turned bright yellow and orange after drinking 1.5 litres of the stuff a day. She was overdosing on betacarotene, the additive that gives the sugar-and-water drink its orange colour.

By a marketing man's nightmare of coincidence, the TV ads for the brand at the time showed two white snowmen raiding the fridge for Sunny Delight and turning bright orange. To add to the embarrassment, a leading consultant dermatologist, Professor John Hawks, said too much betacarotene could cause tummy upsets and farting. As if to confirm its status as spawn of the devil, P&G was forced to join that happy band of cigarette manufacturers who put voluntary warnings on their products.

'A brand needs to have some genuine advantage over rivals and to inspire trust. In an age where the link between producers and consumers is largely broken, brands become our shorthand – they represent a substitute kind of trust.'

Last month, P&G announced it would be hiving off Sunny D into a new joint venture company with Coca-Cola.

Specific strategies for brands 12/99

Brand stretching

> ### Key Concept
>
> '**Brand extension** involves using the same brand name, successfully established in one market or channel, to enter other' (Doyle). It is often termed **brand stretching** when the markets are very different.

4.16 Examples of brand extension

- **Retailers** such as *Dixons* and *Tesco* launching themselves as **Internet Service Providers**
- *Penguin Books* launching its own 'brand' of compact discs
- *Swatch* becoming involved in motor vehicles

4.17 Conditions for brand stretching/extension

(a) The **core values** of the brand must be **relevant to the new market**. EasyJet has transferred to car rental and internet cafes.

(b) The new market area must not affect the core values of the brand by association. Failure in one activity can adversely affect the core brand.

4.18 Advantages of brand extension

Advantage	Comment
Cheap	It is less costly to extend a brand then to establish a new one from scratch.
Customer-perception	Customer expectations of the brand have been built up, so this lower risk for the customer encourages 'trial'.
Less risky	Failure rate of completely new brands.

4.19 Disadvantages of brand extension

Disadvantage	Comment
Segments	The brand personality may not carry over successfully to the new segment. The brand values may not be relevant to the new market.
Strength	The brand needs to be strong already.
Perception	The brand still needs a differential advantage over competitors.
Over-dilution	Excessive extensions can dilute the values of the brand.

Revitalising brands

4.20 At times, the performance of a brand will falter and managers will attempt to rectify the situation by:

- Enhancing sales volume
- Improving profits in other ways

4.21 **Revitalisation** means increasing the sales volume through:

- New markets (eg overseas)

- New segments (eg personal computers are being sold for family, as opposed to business, use)

- Increased usage (encouraging people to eat breakfast cereals as a snack during the day)

4.22 **Repositioning is more fundamental**, in that it is a **competitive strategy** aimed to change position to increase market share.

Type of position	Comment
Real	Relates to actual product features and design
Psychological	Change the buyer's beliefs about the brand
Competitive	Alter beliefs about competing brands
Change emphasis	The emphasis in the advertising can change over time

Success criteria for branding

4.23 **Beneficial qualities of a brand name**

(a) Suggest **benefits,** eg Schweppes' 'Slimline' tonic

(b) Suggest qualities such as **action** or **colour** (eg easyJet, with an orange colour)

(c) Be **easy to pronounce**, recognise and remember

(d) Be **acceptable in all markets** both linguistically and culturally (eg Kodak).

(e) Be **distinctive**

(f) Be **meaningful** (eg South American countries, research found that there was no recognised Spanish translation for dental tartar)

Marketing at Work

Compare the following mobile phone brands.

- Orange
- Vodafone
- Cellnet
- One-to-One

Orange appropriates the colour orange, whereas Vodafone and Cellnet suggest aspects of the product, and One-to-One suggests the actual consumer benefit.

Global or local brand?

4.24 The key differences between a standardised global brand approach and an approach based upon identifying and exploiting global marketing opportunities are as described below.

(a) The **standardised global brand approach** requires:

(i) A standardised product offering to market segments which have exactly similar needs across cultures

(ii) A common approach to the marketing mix and one that is as nearly standardised as may be, given language differences

(b) An approach based upon **global marketing opportunities** reflects:

(i) A recognition that the resources of the company may be adapted to fulfil marketing opportunities in different ways taking into account local needs and preferences but on a global basis

(ii) A willingness to sub-optimise the benefits of having a single global brand (eg advertising synergy) in order to optimise the benefits of meeting specific needs more closely

4.25 For the international company marketing products which can be branded there are two further policy decisions to be made. These are:

(a) The problem of deciding if and how to protect the company's brands (and associated trademarks)

(b) Whether there should be one global brand or many different national brands for a given product

Marketing at Work

Television formats

- *Who wants to be a Millionaire?*

  Developed in the UK, this format has been successfully exported to the US and India (as *Crorepati*?). In the Indian version, the programme is in Hindi and hosted by a major film star (Amitabh Bachhan); otherwise the music and lighting is very similar. Is this a global brand?

- *The Weakest Link* vs *AbFab*

  When Absolutely Fabulous was remade for the US market, cigarettes and excess alcohol consumption were deemed not appropriate and so these offensive features were removed, perhaps destroying the programmes appeal.

  With The Weakest Link, however, the 'rudeness' and aggression of the British presenter, Ann Robinson, has been replicated in the American version, with successful impacts on audience share.

4.26 The most successful examples of worldwide branding occur where the brand has become **synonymous with the generic product** (eg Sellotape, Aspirin).

5 INNOVATION AND NPD

12/99

New products

5.1 New products feature in a firm's competitive and marketing strategies.

(a) New and innovatory products can **lower entry barriers** to existing industries and markets, if new technology is involved.

(b) The market for any product changes over time and its life. The interests of the company are therefore best met with a **balanced product portfolio.** Managers therefore must plan when to introduce new products, how best to extend the life of mature ones and when to abandon those in decline.

5.2 A firm should identify its **strategy underlying new product development.**

(a) **Leader strategy.** Will the firm gain competitive advantage by operating at the leading edge of new developments? If yes, there are significant implications for the R&D activity and the likely length of product life cycles within the portfolio.

(b) **Follower strategy.** Will the firm be more pro-active, adopt a follower strategy, which involves lower costs and less emphasis on the R&D activity? It sacrifices early rewards of innovation, but avoids its risks. A follower might have to license certain technologies from a leader (as in the case with many consumer electronics companies).

What are new products?

5.3 The term **new product development** encompasses a wide range of different types of activity ranging form the development of completely new products and technologies to repackaging of existing ones.

(a) Bear in mind that new products can be:

- New to the market
- New to the company

(b) Booz, Allen and Hamilton identified the following categories, in a survey of 700 firms.

• New to the world: new market	10%
• New product lines to enable a firm to enter a new sector	20%
• Additions to product line	26%
• Repositionings to new segments	7%
• Improvements/revisions	26%
• Cost reductions	11%

The process of NPD in overview

5.4 **Key factors for NPD success.** A systematic NPD process is outlined in the diagram on the following page

Step 1. **Idea generation** requires the maximum number of new ideas to be generated. This necessitates an active search of the environment and for no suggestion to be rejected out of hand. Sources include employees, scientists, competitors, customers.

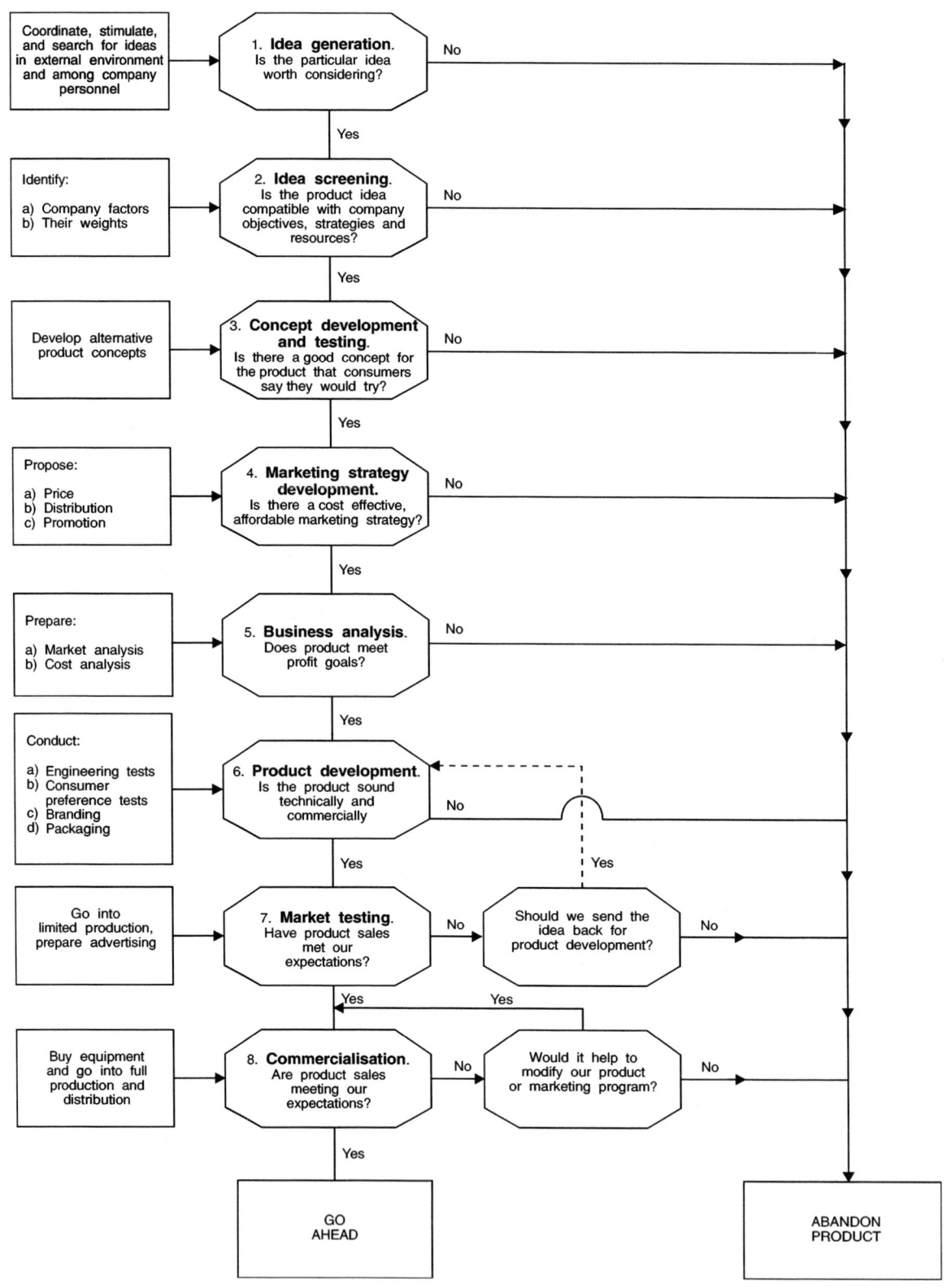

Coordinate, stimulate, and search for ideas in external environment and among company personnel	→	**1. Idea generation.** Is the particular idea worth considering?	No →
Identify: a) Company factors b) Their weights	→	**2. Idea screening.** Is the product idea compatible with company objectives, strategies and resources?	No →
Develop alternative product concepts	→	**3. Concept development and testing.** Is there a good concept for the product that consumers say they would try?	No →
Propose: a) Price b) Distribution c) Promotion	→	**4. Marketing strategy development.** Is there a cost effective, affordable marketing strategy?	No →
Prepare: a) Market analysis b) Cost analysis	→	**5. Business analysis.** Does product meet profit goals?	No →
Conduct: a) Engineering tests b) Consumer preference tests c) Branding d) Packaging	→	**6. Product development.** Is the product sound technically and commercially	No
Go into limited production, prepare advertising	→	**7. Market testing.** Have product sales met our expectations?	No → Should we send the idea back for product development?
Buy equipment and go into full production and distribution	→	**8. Commercialisation.** Are product sales meeting our expectations?	No → Would it help to modify our product or marketing program?

GO AHEAD

ABANDON PRODUCT

Step 2. **Screening** sorts the ideas for compatibility with organisational strategy, resources, distribution channels, competitive advantage etc.

Step 3. **Concept development and testing** is focused on customer needs. Can we find a concept that wraps the idea up into a package that will be adopted by enough consumers? Conceptual **positioning maps** are often used.

Step 4. **Marketing strategy.** The next stage is to draft a marketing plan including short and long-term sales, profit and market share objectives and the structure of the marketing mix.

Step 5. **Business analysis** is focused on determining whether the product will meet the plan's objectives. Sales forecasting is used with estimates firstly on the level and speed of first-time sales and secondly the level of replacement sales. Costs and profits are also estimated.

Step 6. **Product development** involves the physical development of the product in the form of a prototype and a substantial increase in commitment and investment. Tests are then conducted (eg food, for taste and shelf life).

Step 7. **Market testing.** Test marketing is often used to arrive at a more reliable sales forecast and to pre-test marketing plans. Store tests are often used in consumer markets with product use tests and trade shows used more in industrial markets.

Step 8. **Commercialisation.** Often, market testing is omitted and full scale product launch occurs. The questions to ask at this stage are: when to launch? Where to launch? Which groups should be targeted? How should the product be launched?

5.5 Identifying innovations likely to succeed

Arguably, the NPD process can start with looking at how an innovation can benefit the customers. One way of doing so is looking at customer benefits or buyer utility. (Wichai Kim & Renée Mauborgne, *Financial Times*, 25 January 2001.)

Item	Comment
Customer productivity	Does the innovation save time and effort?
Simplicity	Does the innovation reduce the complexity a customer faces? ('because life's complicated enough')
Convenience	Does innovation reduce the inconvenience the customer goes through? (eg speedier or automated check ins)
Risk	Does the innovation reduce risk?
'Fun' image	Can the innovation be enjoyed?
Environmental friendliness	

All these together add up to a 'utility proposition'. Clearly the firm has to price strategically, and deal with barriers to communication.

Responsibility for NPD

5.6 At strategic level, NPD is ultimately the responsibility of the **board**. NPD requires, at different stages, the co-operation of R&D, marketing and production departments.

- The **marketing** department should identify the opportunity.
- The **designers** should, ideally, develop the product so that it satisfies customers' need.
- The **products** should be designed also to be produced in the most cost-effective way.

5.7 The ideal management structure for the NPD process involves:

- **Clear, realistic planning targets**
- A **project manager** to drive the project, perhaps with a sponsor at Board level

5.8 A key relationship is that between marketing personnel and R&D. The **danger** is that **NPD will be 'owned' by R&D,** so technically perfect products are produced which do not meet customer needs profitably.

5.9 The relationship of the R&D department with marketing personnel is sometimes problematic.

   (a) **Cultural.** The R&D department may have an 'academic' or university atmosphere, as opposed to a commercial one.

   (b) **Organisational.** If R&D consumes substantial resources, it would seem quite logical to exploit economies of scale by having it centralised.

   (c) **Work.** Marketing work and R&D work differ in many important respects. R&D work is likely to be more open ended than marketing work.

5.10 **Why R&D should be more closely co-ordinated with marketing**

   (a) If the firm operates the **marketing concept,** then the 'identification of customer needs' should be a vital input to new product development.

   (b) The R&D department might identify possible changes to product specifications so that a **variety of marketing mixes** can be tried out and screened.

Marketing at Work

Nestlé once had a central R&D function, with regional development centres. The central R&D function was involved in basic research. 'Much of the lab's work was only tenuously connected with the company's business... When scientists joined the lab, they were told "Just work in this or that area. If you work hard enough, we're sure you'll find something".' The results of this approach were:

* The research laboratory was largely cut off from development centres
* Much research never found commercial application

Nestlé reorganised the business into strategic business units (SBUs). Formal links were established between R&D and the SBUs. This means that research procedures have been changed so that a commercial time horizon was established.

Exam Tip

You may be asked to improve the 'sequential' process of NPD as suggested in the December 1999 question. Suggestions include:

* Small product modifications more often than big one-off changes
* Improved MkIS and the use of focus groups early on
* Outsourcing some NPD work
* Use licensing arrangements
* Re-engineer the process, perhaps by using some of the project management techniques described at the end of the text
* Involving customers
* Drawing together a profit or venture team from elsewhere in the organisation
* Appoint managers dedicated to new products
* NPD development

5.11 The purpose of **test marketing** is to obtain information about how consumers react to a new product - ie will they buy it, and if so, will they buy it again?

- The total market demand for the product can be made
- The product/service can be amended
- Other aspects of the marketing mix can be changed

5.12 A test market involves testing a new consumer product in selected areas which are thought to be '**representative**' of the total market. In the selected areas, the firm will attempt to distribute the product through the same types of sales outlets it plans to use in the full market launch, and also to use the advertising and promotion plans it intends to use in the full market.

5.13 **Characteristics of a good test marketing exercise**

Size of market	The test market area should be **large enough** to be representative of how the 'full' market might behave, but not so large as to be almost as expensive as a full national market launch.
Time	The test period should be sufficiently long to give customers time to become aware of the product, and to monitor not only initial sales demand but also 'repeat buying' habits.
Representative	The test market must be as closely representative of the national market as possible.
Promotional facilities	One of the television regions could be used as a test area.

5.14 **Benefits of test marketing**

(a) The company **can pre-test a planned marketing mix**. For example, they may be able to identify product faults not identified at the development stage, or they may discover potential distribution problems.

(b) Expensive product failure may be avoided.

(c) **Results** from the test market may enable the company to prepare more accurate **sales forecasts**.

(d) The costs and risks of a full time launch are postponed.

5.15 **Disadvantages of test marketing**

(a) Unless the test market area is **typical** of the market as a whole, the information obtained about potential demand will be **biased** and misleading.

(b) A lengthy test market will **alert competitors** to what the firm is planning to do, and give them time to prepare their own response to the new product.

(c) Only a **small sample** will be used, which raises statistical problems.

(d) Consumers may be aware of the test and **distort their answers** accordingly.

(e) Estimates for the future cannot reliably be based on results recorded today.

(f) **Competitors** may decide to **sabotage** the test, for example by flooding the area with increased advertising activity.

(g) It is difficult to translate national media plans into local equivalents.

(h)   Some goods, for example consumer goods such as household furniture, have lengthy repurchase cycles which would make test marketing far too lengthy to be of any practical forecasting value.

5.16   **Other forms of experimentation** (other than test marketing).

(a)   **Simulated store technique (or laboratory test markets).** In these tests, a group of shoppers are invited to watch a selection of advertisements for a number of products, including an advertisement for the new product. They are then given some money and invited to spend it in a supermarket or shopping area. Their purchases are recorded and they are asked to explain their purchase decisions (and non-purchase decisions).

(b)   **Controlled test marketing.** In these tests, a research firm pays a **panel of stores to carry the new product for a given length of time.** This test helps to provide an assessment of 'in-store' factors.

New product pricing: market penetration and market skimming

5.17   There are **three elements in the pricing decision for a new product.**

-    Getting the product accepted
-    Maintaining a market share in the face of competition
-    Making a profit from the product

5.18   When a firm launches a new product on to the market, it must decide on a pricing policy which lies between the two extremes of market penetration and market skimming.

5.19   **Market penetration** pricing is a policy of low prices when the product is first launched in order to gain sufficient penetration into the market. It is therefore a policy of sacrificing short-term profits in the interests of long-term profits.

5.20   **In favour of a penetration policy**

(a)   The firm wishes to **discourage rivals** from entering the market.

(b)   The firm wishes **to shorten the initial period of the product's life cycle,** in order to enter the growth and maturity stages as quickly as possible. (This would happen if there is high elasticity of demand for the product.)

(c)   A firm might therefore deliberately build excess production capacity and set its prices very low; as demand builds up, the spare capacity will be used up gradually, and unit costs will fall; the firm might even reduce prices further as unit costs fall.

(d)   In this way, early year losses will enable the firm to dominate the market and have the lowest costs.

5.21   **Market skimming.** The aim of market skimming is to gain **high unit profits very early** on in the product's life.

(a)   The firm charges **high prices** when a product is **first launched.**

(b)   The firm **spends heavily on advertising** and sales promotion to win customers.

(c)   As the product moves into the later stages of its **life cycle** (growth, maturity and decline) **progressively lower prices will be charged.** The profitable 'cream' is thus 'skimmed' off in progressive stages until sales can only be sustained at lower prices.

(d) **Conditions suitable for a skimming policy**

(i) Where the **product is new and different**, so that customers are prepared to pay high prices.

(ii) **Where demand elasticity is unknown**. It is better to start by charging high prices and then reducing them if the demand for the product turns out to be price elastic than to start by charging low prices and then attempting to raise them substantially when demand turns out to be price inelastic.

(iii) High initial prices might not be profit-maximising in the long run, but they generate **high initial cash flows**. A firm with liquidity problems may prefer market-skimming for this reason.

(iv) Skimming may also enable the firm to identify **different market segments** for the product, each prepared to pay progressively lower prices.

(e) The firm may lower its prices in order to attract more price-elastic segments of the market; however, these price reductions will be gradual. Alternately, the entry of competitors into the market may make price reductions inevitable.

5.22 **Introductory offers** may be used to attract an initial customer interest. Introductory offers are temporary price reductions, after which the price is then raised to its normal 'commercial' rate.

Success and failure

5.23 New products can fail in the short-term or in the long-term. The NPD process should improve success rates, but success is never guaranteed.

5.24 A successful new product or brand satisfies corporate objectives by:

- Gaining/sustaining market share
- Meeting profit targets
- Generating cash inflows
- Doing (a), (b) and (c) above in the right time.

5.25 **Reasons for failure**

Reason	Comment
Poor commitment	NPD is a sideline; managers want to do NPD, but are unwilling to risk the resources to develop the competences necessary
Poor thinking	Designers and promoters of NPD within the organisation have their own interests to pursue and downplay potential problems
Poor execution	Many NPD processes involve uncertain outcomes but the product is wanted in an unrealistic timescale
Poor management	The research process for NPD may not be run properly
Poor marketing	The product might fail because of poor marketing research or by poor marketing
Poor analysis	Both the process of NPD and the product can be more time consuming and expensive than anticipated

Enhancing innovation   **Specimen paper**

5.26 **The need to speed up innovation is a key issue**

'Innovation has become the religion of the late 20th century' (*Economist*, 20 February 1999). Commonly cited spurs to innovation are:

- Shorter product life cycles
- Increasing prosperity
- New technology enabling new services

5.27 A *Marketing Business* survey of UK marketers (March 1996), offers the following findings.

(a) 71% of respondents 'considered innovation to be more important then marketing existing products and services'.

(b) Whilst 59% of respondents believe strongly that innovation is 'key to British business surviving the millennium', only 31% believe their companies share this view.

(c) When asked to consider what would improve the potential for innovation, 71% said that 'the key to making their own companies more innovation-driven lay in **management initiatives**... The need for a **risk taking culture** and **better communications** were also mentioned.' Two-thirds identified lack of time as a constraint.

5.28 **Seven types of 'opportunity' for innovation** (Drucker)

- The 'unexpected success': exploit it
- The difference between what did happen and what was supposed to happen: find out why
- Inadequacy in an underlying process: reforms to process
- Changes in industry or market structure
- Demographic changes
- Fashion
- New knowledge and technology

5.29 **Many businesses only concentrate on new technology** (in other words, option (g) in the list above) rather than the other opportunities ((a) to (f))to innovate. Many businesses feel that their future survival is at stake if they do not innovate. Companies are keen to find out a more **predictable way of emerging with winners**. There is no systematic way to encourage innovation but the Economist suggests these steps.

Step 1. **Imagining**: the initial insight about a market opportunity for a particular technology

Step 2. **Incubating**: nurturing the technology to gauge whether it can be commercialised.

Step 3. **Demonstrating**: building prototypes and getting feedback from potential customers

Step 4. **Promoting**: persuading the market to adopt the invitation

Step 5. **Ensuring** the product or process has as **long a life as possible**

5.30 Steps 1, 2 and 3 cannot be managed in a conventional way. Firms could:

- Create a culture in which **innovation and learning exist** throughout the organisation
- Designate separate teams, or individuals to come up with ideas.

5.31 An innovation culture can be considered in the context of a **learning organisation**.

Creativity and innovation

5.32 Creative ideas can come from anywhere and at any time, but if management wish to foster innovation they should try to provide an organisation structure in which innovative ideas are encouraged to emerge.

(a) **Innovation requires creativity**. Creativity may be encouraged in an individual or group by establishing a climate in which free expression of abilities is allowed. 'Hot water thought sessions' (brainstorming etc) could be used.

(b) Creative ideas must then be **rationally analysed** (in 'cold water thought sessions') to decide whether they provide a viable (commercial etc) proposition.

5.33 In an article in *Marketing Business* (April 2000), Ty Francis exposes ten myths about innovation.

(a) Extensive **market research** is not essential: creativity is more important than collecting more data.

(b) **Creative leaps** into the unknown are needed. They may change the entire company (there is no place in today's business environment for 'steady-as-she-goes incrementalism').

(c) **The responsibility of the entire enterprise**. Focusing on existing products and customers will achieve nothing. Functional responsibilities need to be disregarded: 'if you do what you've always done you'll get the results you've always had'.

(d) More than simply **intellectual** endeavour. **Core creative competencies** are needed, and a creative culture needs to be stimulated.

(e) **Not just about NPD**. Innovation may simply mean a new process or a new component material for an existing product. The biggest returns came from **innovative strategy**.

(f) **'The future is happening now'**. Organisations need to get away from a problem solving orientation, and become more involved in **creating their future** rather than simply planning for it.

(g) **'Not just in a crisis'**. Innovation should not just occur quickly and under duress when a company is **desperate**. Real innovative breakthroughs need proper consideration and thought.

(h) **'Not one best way'**. There is no such thing as a foolproof or faddish **toolkit** for innovation. Commercially viable innovations only come from a **proper knowledge** of the company's abilities and its industry.

(i) **'Not a mechanistic business process'**. Innovation is a way of working that should colour everything the company does. 'In a very real sense, innovation is better approached as an art form rather than a science.'

(j) Innovation does not live off **existing brands and products**. Companies must move on. Strong brands can actually stifle innovation, and in any case some competitors are always going to be able to copy what you do.

Organisational learning

5.34 Ikujiro Nonaka holds that the successful creation of **ideas**, as opposed to the mere processing of information, depends on a number of organisational factors.

(a) 'Creating new knowledge is not simply a matter of processing objective information. Rather it depends on tapping the highly subjective insights, intuitions, and hunches and making those insights available for testing and use by the company as a whole'. Basically, this means that:

    (i) no one individual or group of individuals can, even in principle, be the source of all knowledge about a firm's activities;

    (ii) there must be a way whereby all individuals can communicate their insights to other members of the organisation, so that these insights flow into a pool of knowledge from which the whole company can draw.

(b) Furthermore, there is the idea that a company is 'a living organism'. This means that it can learn.

5.35 Peter **Senge** (in *The Fifth Discipline - The Art and Practice of the Learning Organisation*) argues that to create a learning organisation, individuals and groups should be encouraged to learn five disciplines.

Discipline	Comment
Systems thinking	This is the ability to see particular problems as part of a wider whole, and to devise appropriate solutions to them.
Personal learning and growth	Individuals should be encouraged to acquire skills and knowledge.
Mental models	These are deeply ingrained assumptions which determine what individuals think. This can be about the best way of managing people, about products (eg how a car looks is more important than how comfortable it is to drive) or marketing (price is more important than quality). Learning organisations can use a number of group techniques to make these models explicit, and to challenge them. An inability to question mental models can lead to strategic wear-out.
Shared vision	but not so forceful as to discourage organisational learning.
Team learning	Some tasks can only be done in groups. Teams, however, must be trained to learn, as there are factors in group dynamics which impede learning.

Key Concept

'A **learning company** is an organisation skilled at creating, acquiring, and transferring knowledge, and at modifying its behaviour to reflect new knowledge and insights.'

5.36 **Characteristics of the learning company**

Characteristic	Comment
The learning approach to strategy	The strategy process is designed as a learning process with experimentation and feedback loops built into a system. Pedler, Burgoyne and Boydell cite as an example Shell, where a senior executive from another plant and/or country is invited to review the operation of a plant, to discover its hidden fundamentals and ways of doing business. As much information as possible is brought to bear on a problem.

Characteristic	Comment
Participative policy making	All 'members' of a learning company have the chance to participate in the learning process. In practice it means that a variety of stakeholder influences are accepted.
Informating	'Informating' is the use of information as a resource for the whole organisation to exploit in order to develop new insights.
Formative accounting	Accounting and budgeting systems should be structured for the benefit of all their internal users to assist learning. Such systems might encourage individuals or departments to act as 'small businesses treating internal users as customers'.
Internal exchange	Internal exchange develops the idea of the internal customer. Each unit regards the other units as customers, whose needs must be identified and satisfied, in the context of the company as a whole.
Reward flexibility	In a learning company, there is a flexible approach to remuneration. The underlying principles of the salary remuneration system should be brought out into the open. Changing the reward system might result in a change in the distribution of power within the company. 'Rewards' are not only financial but relate to the pleasure, enjoyment, and social life that people get out of work.
Enabling structures	The notion of 'enabling structures' implies the features of the organic organisation with indeterminate roles which alter to allow for growth. Organisation structures are temporary arrangements that must respond to changed conditions and opportunities.
Boundary workers as environmental scanners	In a learning organisation, environmental monitoring is not restricted to specialists or managers. All employees dealing with the boundary should try and monitor the environment.
Intercompany learning	**Benchmarking** is an example of intercompany learning.
Learning climate	Managers must encourage learning.
Self development opportunities for all	A variety of training resources should be offered, initiating courses, seminars, counselling, work experience. Training and development has a high priority in a learning organisation, as it increases the flow of information and ideas, and develops the skills which can make use of them.

Marketing at Work

Daiichi, a Japanese electronics appliance firm, offers three year warranties on its products. Before the warranty expires, it sends a repairman to service the customer's machine. Before he leaves, the repairman offers to check other appliances, whether or not the customer acquired them from Daiichi. This is a means of gathering product and market information. When the repairman returns to the office, he fills out a detailed report on the types of products in the home, their models and ages. This information is made available to Daiichi's sales force, who can offer the customer an appropriate mix of products.

6 CUSTOMER CARE AND CUSTOMER RELATIONSHIPS

Customer care

6.1 In deciding strategic direction and formulating marketing strategy, any company needs to address issues of customer care, because of:

(a) **Legal** constraints

(b) Industry **codes of conduct**

(c) The recognition that keeping existing customers happy is cheaper than acquiring new ones.

(d) The **value chain**. Customer care is part of after-sales service and offers an opportunity for differentiation. It is also a valuable source of information.

6.2 **Customer care strategy**

Stage	Content
Corporate strategy and objectives	Objectives for customer loyalty and customer care
	A strategy for caring for customers
External environmental analysis	Analyse what makes customers loyal and how well they respond to different policies aimed at encouraging them to do so.
Internal environmental analysis	Analyse suppliers' capabilities in relation to keeping customers
Marketing objectives and strategy	Marketing objectives and strategy should focus on long-term impact on customer loyalty as well as profit sales and market share
Action plans - marketing operations	Focus on effect on customers, not just procedural efficiency
Results	Track customer inventory movements (ie new customers, repeat business) not just sales and profit

Relationship marketing

Key Concept

Relationship marketing focuses the firm's attention on customer retention with a view to building up a long-term relationship with a customer. A sale is not an end of a process but the beginning of a relationship.

6.3 **Importance of relationships: the cost of lost customers**

Kotler identified the lifetime value of a customer. If a company loses customers unnecessarily, it sacrifices the lifetime profits. This is known as **lifetime customer value**. 'A 5% increase in customer retention can increase the total company operating profits by 50%' (Davidson).

Existing, loyal customers are valuable because:

- They do not have to be acquired
- They buy a broader range of products
- They cost less to service as they are familiar with the company's ways of doing business
- They become less sensitive to price over time
- They can recommend by word of mouth

6.4 Building up customer relationships requires a change of focus from the 'transaction-based approach' to the relationship approach. The contrast is shown in the table below.

TRANSACTION MARKETING (mainly one-way communication)	RELATIONSHIP MARKETING (mainly two-way communication)
• Focus on single sale • Orientation on product features • Short time-scale • Little customer service • Limited customer commitment • Moderate customer contact • Quality is the concern of production	• Focus on customer retention • Orientation on product benefits • Long time-scale • High customer service • High customer commitment • High customer contact • Quality is the concern of all

6.5 The process of retaining customers for a lifetime is an important one and one in which integrated marketing communications has an important role to play. Instead of one-way communication aimed solely at gaining a sale it is necessary to develop an effective two-way communication process to turn a **prospect into a lifetime advocate**. This is shown in the following ladder of customer loyalty.

Ladder of customer loyalty

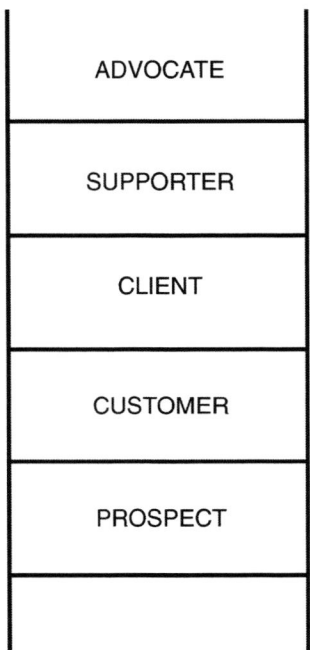

6.6 The purpose of relationship marketing is to establish, maintain and enhance relationships with customers and other parties so that the objectives of both parties involved are met.

(a) Because **service and industrial companies** have direct, regular and often multiple contacts with their customers (for example the regular hotel guest who interacts with reception), the importance of what Gummerson calls 'part-time' marketers is increased. Customer contact with all employees is vital.

(b) **Trust and keeping promises.** To have an ongoing relationship, both parties need to trust each other and keep the promises they make. Marketing moves from one-off potentially manipulative exchanges towards co-operative relationships built on financial, social and structural benefits.

(c) **Network of exchange partners.** Customer relationships are important but so too are the relationships which organisations have with other parties such as suppliers, distributors, professional bodies, banks, trade associations etc.

'Customers are assets'

6.7 You might already be familiar with the concept of the customer as a current asset - a customer is a debtor. Goodwill - or a company's reputation - is also considered an asset.

6.8 However, it will sometimes help you in evaluating strategic marketing decisions and persuading sceptical management accountants of your case if you consider the customer base as an asset worth 'investing' in. After all, if you are looking for repeat business, you will expect future benefits from customers.

Action Programme 2

What do you think are the differences between:

(a) Loyal customers with whom you have a long-term 'relationship'
(b) Captive markets

Even if you can tell the difference, will your customers be able to?

6.9 Recently there has been a **backlash** against relationship marketing especially as applied to the consumer sector. Not all 'customers' want a relationship and resent the potential for intrusion. Furthermore, many firms practise relationship marketing purely as an information gathering exercise. Does the **customer** benefit from the relationship?

Implementing relationship marketing programmes

6.10 Kotler suggests five steps, suitable for business-to-business or service markets.

Step 1. Identify key customers: this has been covered in an earlier chapter
Step 2. Assign a 'relationship manager' to each
Step 3. Develop clear job descriptions
Step 4. Appoint a manager to supervise the relationship managers
Step 5. Develop long-term plans for developing relationships

6.11 **Sustaining the relationship.** George Day says that relationship marketing will succeed if it is founded on the principles below.

(a) Offer **superior customer value** by personalising the interaction, involving two-way communication. This is essential for service industries such as life assurance. Hotels have systems that 'remember' guests' preferences.

(b) Be trustworthy and **reliable**, for example by offering a replacement.

(c) **Tighten the connection.** Once the relationship is established, it must be nurtured to make it harder for the customer to defect.

(d) **Co-ordinating capabilities.** The more successful the relationship, the greater the risk of imitation.

6.12 Kotler's approach is suitable for business-to-business markets or personal services such as financial advice. Some firms, however, have sought through data mining techniques to get a long-term view of the customer.

6.13 **Loyalty cards** are designed to reward customers for repeat purchase. They:

- Collect information about customer purchasing habits, enabling targeted marketing communication

- Reward customers for repeat purchase, to encourage sales volumes.

6.14 Loyalty schemes vary in the benefit they offer.

(a) Recent UK research indicates that owners of 'loyalty' cards spend more, but they are not necessarily loyal.

(b) Furthermore, most customers still shop around and have one or more loyalty cards.

(c) **Loyalty cards may prove to be an expensive failure.** Safeway in the UK has abandoned its UK loyalty card, preferring to invest in others promotional activities determined by stores individually.

Chapter Roundup

- In this chapter we have reviewed the concept and role of the **marketing mix** as a set of **controllable variables** which management can alter to influence demand.

- The exact components of the marketing mix need to be put together with judgement and creativity. Every product, market and every stage in the product's life will require a different balance of the marketing mix ingredients.

- **Over time** the demand for a product changes and the external environment changes. Therefore the marketing mix needs to be **adjusted** throughout the product's life.

- By now you should be thoroughly aware of the **mix elements**

    ° **Product**. quality; differentiation; suitable NPD process; 'service' element.

    ° **Price**: determined by what the customer will pay, the cost of the product (and the need to make a profit) and what competitors are doing.

    ° **Place**: essential for customers to acquire the product.

    ° **Promotion**: the need for integrated communications.

    ° **People**

    ° **Processes**

    ° **Physical evidence**

- Much of the marketing mix activity goes to the development of **brands**, which are what the customers identify. Brands embody a set of expectations about the product. A brand image exists in the customer's mind.

- In recent times emphasis has increased on building and maintaining good long-term **relationships** with customers. This is because such relationships are more profitable than constantly searching for new customers owing to repeat purchasing, ease of service and so on.

- **Innovation and NPD** are key strategic issues. Most new products fail, but a properly-planned NPD process, with appropriate test marketing, can reduce the risk of failure. Nurturing innovation requires attention to the culture of the organisation.

- There is a move away from 'transactions' to **relationship marketing**. Firms aim to build loyalty.

Now try illustrative question 14 at the end of the Study Text

BPP PUBLISHING

Quick Quiz

1   Explain the marketing mix. (see para 2.1)

2   What is meant by the terms 'push and pull strategy'? (2.2)

3   What is a product, defined from the customer's point of view? (2.7)

4   Identify the basic influences on price. (2.10)

5   What is the main concept underpinning integrated marketing communications? (2.25)

6   What are the four characteristics distinguishing most services from most products? (3.2)

7   What constitutes a brand? (4.1)

8   Who benefits from branding? (4.3)

9   Identify two strategies for NPD. (5.2)

10   Distinguish between penetration and skimming strategies. (5.20, 5.21)

11   What are the commonly cited factors stimulating innovation? (5.26)

12   What is relationship marketing? (6.3)

Action Programme Review

1   (a)   Ageing population: people may be physically incapable of trawling the supermarkets

(b)   Increased traffic congestion: people may resent taking longer to drive to the shops

(c)   More time at work: less time for shopping

(d)   Once Internet shopping takes off, mail order will have the benefits of email. Tesco currently has around 400,000 customers for its Internet shopping service

15 *Strategic Choice Evaluation*

Chapter Topic List	Syllabus reference
1 Setting the scene	
2 The application of financial and non-financial criteria to choice evaluation	4.3
3 Financial analysis techniques	4.4
4 Risk evaluation and feasibility studies	4.5
5 Issues of responsibility and stakeholder response	4.3

Learning Outcomes

- Compare and contrast strategic options.

- Specify a clear rationale when choosing between strategic alternatives.

Key Concepts Introduced

- Suitability
- Feasibility
- Acceptability
- Fixed costs

- Variable costs
- Societal marketing concept
- Risk
- Discounted cash flow

Examples of Marketing at Work

- Shell
- CIM's Code of Professional Standards

- Pharmaceuticals

1 SETTING THE SCENE

1.1 Careful evaluation of all the alternative strategies identified is important at both the corporate and marketing levels of planning.

1.2 In this chapter we examine some of the techniques which might be used to evaluate strategies. No one technique can provide the perfect answer: some decisions are easier to quantify than others.

1.3 In Section 2 we give an overview of the sort of basic questions that need to be asked of any strategy: is it suitable, appropriate and feasible? **These questions can be asked of any strategy.**

1.4 In Section 3 we describe how financial analysis techniques can help the marketer evaluate the profit and cash flow impact of strategic choices. Using such techniques will help marketers justify these strategies in financial terms.

1.5 Many strategies involve risk. Although not always easy to quantify there are a number of techniques managers can use to make informed choices.

1.6 We discuss the stakeholder view, and the need to evaluate strategies in terms of their effect on stakeholders.

2 THE APPLICATION OF FINANCIAL AND NON-FINANCIAL CRITERIA TO CHOICE EVALUATION 6/01

Exam Tip

In June 2001 you were asked very simply to evaluate some strategic options posed by Marks & Spencer. The company featured significantly in the business press, courting controversy by closing branches outside the UK and the by nature of its management bonus schemes.

2.1 Strategies are examined according to a number of different criteria to enable a choice. Johnson and Scholes narrow these down to three broad categories: **suitability**, **feasibility** and **acceptability**.

Suitability

Key Concept

Suitability. Does the strategy fit the situation of the firm?

2.2 • Does it exploit company strengths and distinctive competences?
 • Does it rectify company weaknesses?
 • Does it neutralise or deflect environmental threats?
 • Does it help the firm to seize opportunities?
 • Does it satisfy the goals of organisation?
 • Is the strategy consistent with other activities of the organisation?

Feasibility

Key Concept

Feasibility. Can the strategy be implemented?

2.3 • Is there enough money?
 • Can the company deliver the goods/services specified in the strategy?
 • Can the company deal with the likely responses that competitors will make?
 • Does the company have access to technology, materials and resources?
 • Is there enough time to implement the strategy?
 • Is the strategy preferable to other, mutually exclusive strategies?

2.4 **Strategies which do not make use of the existing competences,** manpower skills and technical expertise of the company, and which therefore call for new skills to be acquired, **might not be feasible** for the following reasons.

(a) **Acquiring expertise** and experience through organic growth, say, would **take too long** to process.

(b) If a **takeover of another company** is therefore necessary for faster entry into a new product-market area, the **disadvantages of an acquisition policy** might outweigh the advantages.

(c) **Time** must be allowed for **new organisational and communication patterns** to develop and operate freely, and for personal abilities and relationships to mature.

Acceptability

> **Key Concept**
>
> **Acceptability**: a strategy should be acceptable to stakeholders – inasmuch as they have a legitimate interest in the organisation.

2.5 The acceptability of a strategy relates to people's expectations of it. It is here that stakeholder analysis can be brought in. **Stakeholders** are able to exercise different degrees of power.

(a) **Financial considerations.** Strategies will be evaluated by considering how far they contribute to meeting the dominant objectives, for return on investment, profits, growth, EPS and cash flow. These measures of wealth serve to satisfy shareholders. The public sector equivalent might be cost/benefit analysis.

(b) **Customers** may object to a strategy if it means reducing service, but on the other hand they may have no choice. Other stakeholders include banks and the government.

(c) A strategy involving a takeover may be prohibited under **monopolies and mergers legislation.**

(d) Similarly, the **environmental impact** may cause key stakeholders to withhold consent - out of town superstores are now frowned upon by national and local government.

(e) **Risk.** Different shareholders have different attitudes to risk. A strategy which changes the risk/return profile, for whatever reason, may not be acceptable.

A summary

2.6 Strategies are evaluated to decide whether they will help to **achieve the organisation's objectives** and so whether they are desirable. The final list of desirable strategic opportunities, if it is not empty, will be a list for ranking in order of priority. Kotler summarises the stages in evaluating a marketing opportunity as follows.

Evaluating Market Opportunities

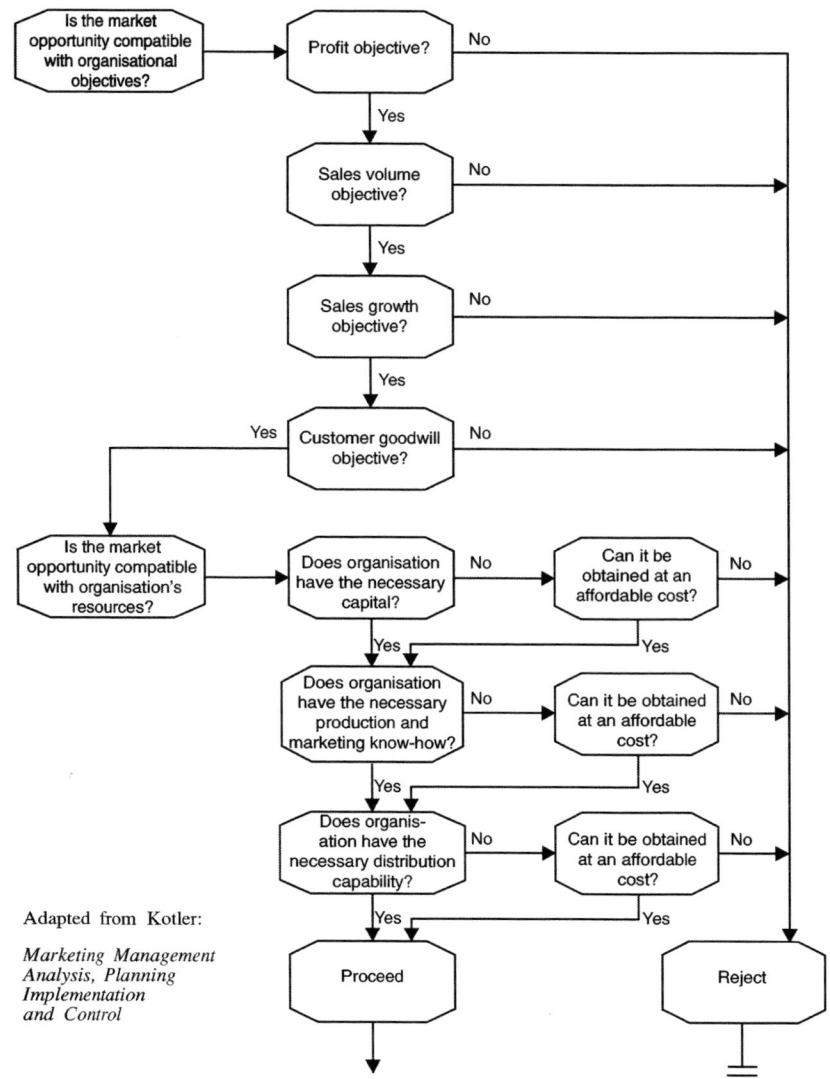

Adapted from Kotler:

*Marketing Management
Analysis, Planning
Implementation
and Control*

Ranking and scoring

2.7 **Ranking and scoring methods** are used to evaluate strategies to the extent that they satisfy corporate objectives.

2.8 EXAMPLE

The **objectives** are weighted in relative importance (so that minimising competitive threats is the most important). Assume that the strategic options cannot be realistically combined.

Objectives Strategic option	Growth in profit by over 10%	Reduce dependence on suppliers	Minimise competitive threats	Score	Rank
Do nothing	X	X	X	-	
Cut costs by subcontracting	✓	X	X	4	3rd
Expand product range	✓	X	✓	9	1st
Offer discounts to customers for fixed term contract	X	X	✓	5	2nd
Objective weighting	4	3	5		

In the example, expanding the product range would be chosen as the firm believes this will enhance profits and minimise competitive threats. Note that this is a deliberately simple example. In many cases, the strategies may not be mutually exclusive, and it might be possible to implement all the strategic options above. The example indicates the following.

- The relative importance given to different commercial objectives
- The assessment of how well a strategy conforms with commercial objectives

3 FINANCIAL ANALYSIS TECHNIQUES

3.1 Earlier, we suggested that strategies will be compared and evaluated in **financial terms**.

CVP analysis

3.2 **CVP analysis** (cost-volume-profit or **breakeven analysis**) is used to assess the level of sales needed to make a profit.

> ### Key Concept
>
> **Fixed costs** do not change with the volume of production.
>
> **Variable costs** change directly with the volume of production.

(a) For example, firms have to pay the **Uniform Business Rate** on their premises, irrespective of how many products they actually sell. This is a fixed cost.

(b) A firm making cars will use so many tonnes of material for each car. Making **two** cars requires twice as much material as making **one** car. Other variable costs relate to labour, sales admin etc.

(c) The **contribution** is sales **revenue** less **variable costs**.

(d) Breakeven occurs where **contribution** exceeds **fixed costs**.

(e) For example:

	£	£
Sales	500	1,000
Variable costs	300	600
Contribution	200	400
Fixed costs	200	200
Profit	-	100

The firm breaks even when sales revenue is £500, as fixed costs are covered. The contribution/sales ratio in this example is $\frac{£400}{£1,000}$ or 40%.

3.3 **Uses of CVP analysis**

(a) What **level of sales** would be needed to break even each year?

(b) What **market share** is needed for the level of sales required to break even?

(c) What is the **margin of safety**? This is the difference between the forecast actual level of sales and the level needed to break even.

Example: cost-volume-profit analysis

3.4 Snapper Flatt Ltd makes and sells a single product.

(a) The **variable cost** of production is £3 per unit, and the variable cost of selling is £1 per unit.

(b) Fixed costs total £6,000.

(c) The unit sales price is £6.

(d) The company budgets to make and sell 3,600 units in the next year.

You can draw a breakeven chart or do arithmetic.

3.5 A **breakeven chart** records the amount of fixed costs, variable costs, total costs and total revenue at all volumes of sales, and at a given sales price.

(a)

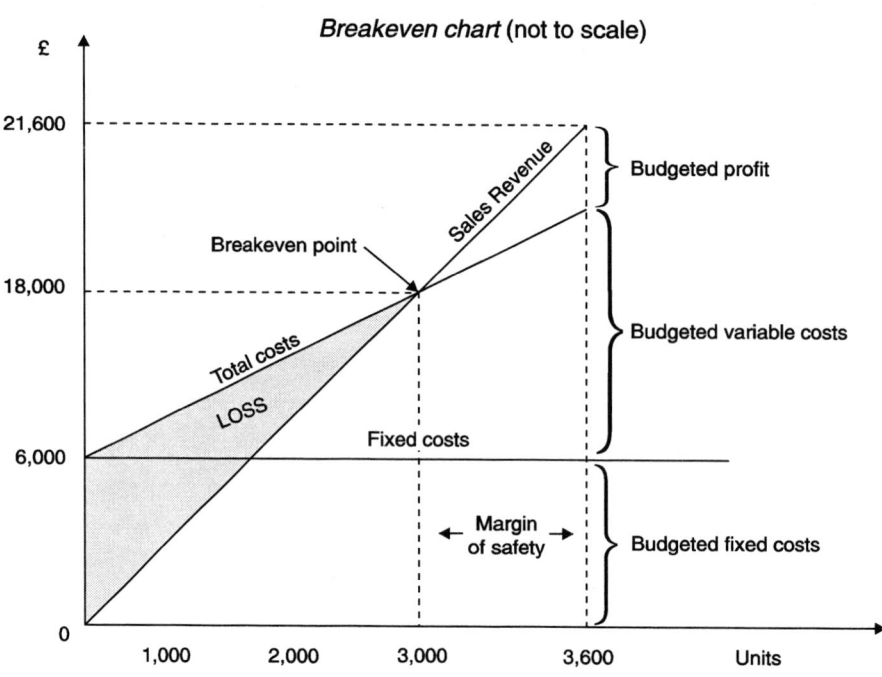

(b) The breakeven point can also be calculated arithmetically as follows.

$$\frac{\text{Fixed costs (required contribution)}}{\text{Contribution per unit}} \quad = \quad \frac{£6,000}{£(6-3-1)}$$

$$= \quad £6,000 \div £2 \text{ per unit}$$

$$= \quad 3,000 \text{ units}$$

In other words, the firm needs to sell 3,000 units to cover its costs.

3.6 There are several **assumptions normally applied in CVP analysis.**

(a) The **sale price per unit is constant** over the entire relevant range of output.

(b) **Stock levels do not vary significantly,** so that production output and sales volumes are the same.

(c) The **mix of products sold is constant** at all levels of activity, where more than one product is included in the analysis. In other words, the same proportion of each product will be sold whether total sales are, say, 100 units, or 1,000 units.

(d) **Variable cost** per unit does not change, in the short run.

(e) **Fixed costs are constant.** In practice many 'fixed cost' items are **step** cost in nature over a wide range of activity. For example, to increase output a new factory might have to be built. Fixed costs estimates should therefore apply within the relevant range of activity only.

(f) **It ignores risk.**

(g) It generally assumes that there are no **limiting factors** on production.

Investment appraisal: cash flows

> ### Key Concept
>
> **Discounted cash flow** (DCF) operates on the principle that money has a time value. £100 received now is worth more than £100 received in a year's time.

3.7 Apart from inflation, why does money have a **time value**?

(a) If you were to invest £100 received now at an **interest** rate of 10% for a year, in a year's time it would be worth £110 (ie £100 × 1.10).

(b) Put another way, if you invested £90.91 now at 10% interest for one year you would get £100.

(c) Therefore £100 received in a **year's** time is worth, at a discount rate of 10%, £100 × 1/1.10 (**discount factor**) = **£90.91 if you were given it now.**

(d) What is £100 received in **two** years time worth **now**? Assume a discount rate of 10%.

$$£100 \times \frac{1}{1.10} \times \frac{1}{1.10} = £100 \times \frac{1}{1.10^2} = £82.65 \text{ today.}$$

3.8 DCF concentrates on **cash flows** rather than profits and can be applied to investments.

3.9 **Strategic investment appraisal using DCF**

Step 1. **Identifying all the cash flows** arising from a project, investment or strategy.

Step 2. Identifying **when** these cash flows will take place.

Step 3. Applying the appropriate **discount factor** to these cash flows. Normally this will be how much it **costs the firm to get capital** (eg the interest rate on a long-term loan, or the anticipated size of the dividend shareholders require).

Step 4. Aggregating these discounted cash flows, and arriving at a **net present value** (NPV). This means that **all the cash flows have been converted into today's money.**

Step 5. Comparing the net present value of one project, investment or strategy with another. Normally, **projects with higher NPVs will be preferred.**

3.10 There are other variants on DCF analysis which we won't go into here. However, **review** the example below to see how DCF analysis can be used to evaluate a particular strategy.

3.11 EXAMPLE

Ballard Ltd can choose between two competing projects, both of which produce future benefits. Project 'A' involves investing in a new product, the Magma, which is expected to last three years. Project 'B' involves investing in a loyalty scheme, expected to expire after three years. The company's cost of capital is 10%.

	Year	Project A cash flows	Project B cash flows	Discount factor	A	B
Initial investment	0	(1,000)	(1,500)	1	(1,000)	(1,500)
Net cash flows	1	500	400	0.91	455	364
Net cash flows	2	500	1,000	0.83	415	830
Net cash flows	3	400	600	0.75	300	450
Net cash flows		400	500	NPV	170	144

(a) Both products have positive NPVs. In other words, if shareholders expect a 10% return they will be more than satisfied as both profits have positive net present values.

(b) Because of the timing and nature of the cash flows, Project A is a better bet than B as it has a higher net present value (NPV), even though the cash flows of Project B look more attractive.

3.12 **DCF analysis can be applied to brand values.**

Step 1. Predict future brand sales, costs and cash flows.

Step 2. The discount rate applied can take account of the risks of each brand in each market. For example cash flows which are high risk might be discounted at a rate of 15%. Low risk cash flows might be discounted at a rate of 10%.

Step 3. The net present value is therefore the 'brand value'.

3.13 Armed with this information the marketer can at least begin to meet finance and other specialists on their own ground.

3.14 **DCF and repositioning**

(a) Assume the marketing department chooses to spend £10m on re-positioning a product.

   (i) How can a link between **future sales** and the **£10m expenditure** be established?

   (ii) **What would happen if the money was not spent?** Would market share fall? Or would competitors find an opening?

   (iii) Would an alternative use of £10m be more valuable?

(b) The benefits from marketing expenditure might sometimes be much less easy to quantify than, say, the cost savings on new equipment.

4 RISK EVALUATION AND FEASIBILITY STUDIES

Types of risk

Key Concept

Risk relates to uncertainty about the future. Any forward looking strategy is risky, because events might not turn out as anticipated.

4.1 (a) **Physical risk**, such as fire, earthquakes, computer failure.

(b) **Economic risk.** The strategy might be based on assumptions as to the economy which might turn out to be wrong.

(c) **Financial risk** relates to the type of financial arrangement in the decision, and the quality of the cash flows.

(d) **Business risk.** These risks relate to commercial and industry factors. In other words, there is the possibility that the strategy will fail because of new technology, competitors, customer reaction, operational failures.

(e) **Political or country risk** includes nationalisation, sanctions, civil war, political instability, if these have an impact on the business.

(f) **Exchange risk.** Changes in exchange rates affect the value of a transaction in a foreign currency.

(g) **Information risk.** The data may not be reliable.

Risk appraisal in strategy evaluation

4.2 **Some strategies will be more risky than others.** One of the problems arising when evaluating alternative strategies is the reliability of the data used. Since the figures are compiled on estimates of the future, there must be considerable uncertainty about the final accuracy of the figures. Business planners frequently use the following.

- Operational research techniques to measure the degree of uncertainty involved
- Probability theory to express the likelihood of a forecast result occurring.

4.3 **Risk and evaluating strategies**

(a) If an individual strategy involves an **unacceptable amount of risk** it should be eliminated from further consideration in the planning process.

(b) However, the risk of an **individual strategy** should also be considered in the context of the **overall 'portfolio' of investment strategies** and products adopted by the company.

4.4 **Risk can be quantified in statistical terms.** In decision trees, a variety of possible outcomes are developed. Each is given an **expected value (EV),** based on probabilities. The EVs at each decision point are then aggregated to produce an EV for the decision as a whole. However, the EVs do not deal in the relative riskiness of each project.

(a) Project A might offer **profits** of £1,000,000 and **losses** of £500,000. If the probability of each is 50:50, the EV is $(£1,000,000 \times 50\%) - (£500,000 \times 50\%) = £250,000$.

(b) Project B offers a 75% probability of a £300,000 profit and a 25% probability of a loss of £100,000. The EV is thus £200,000 ie $(£300,000 \times 0.75\%) - (£100,000 \times 25\%)$

Project A would be favoured, on a basis of EV **alone**, which is £250,000. There is a much higher prospect of **large** profits or **large** losses compared to project B. However, A is much more **risky** as the spread of outcomes is diverse.

4.5 **Sensitivity analysis involves asking 'what if?' questions.** By changing the value of different variables in the model, a number of different **scenarios** for the future will be produced. Price rises can be altered to 10% from 5%, demand for a product can be reduced from 100,000 to 80,000, the introduction of new processing equipment can be deferred by six months, on the revised assumption that there will be delays, and so on. Sensitivity analysis can be formalised by identifying **key variables** in the model and then changing the value of each, perhaps in progressive steps. For example, prices might be increased in steps by 5%, 7½%, 10%, 12½% and 15% and the effect on demand, profits and cash flows under each of these assumptions can be tested.

4.6 Sensitivity analysis would show which were the **key variables**.

BPP PUBLISHING

4.7 EXAMPLE

A company is producing a new product and a key variable is time to market. If it launches on time, it will sell 1,000 units at £10 each. If it is a month late, demand will fall by 50%. Each unit costs £5 to make. The company has learned that a material supplier has gone out of business. It can get the material for the same price, at the expense of being a month late, or it can pay £1 per unit more for the material and keep to the original deadline.

	Original plan £	Month delay £	Pay more for material £
Revenue	10,000	5,000	10,000
Costs	5,000	2,500	6,000
Profit	5,000	2,500	4,000

In this example we can see that profits are more sensitive to **demand** than to costs, so the firm would pay more for the new material.

4.8 A firm has a choice.

- Apply the most stringent controls to the most critical variables
- Alter the plans so that the most critical variables are no longer as critical
- When different planning options are available, choose a lower-risk plan

Feasibility studies

4.9 Very little appears to have been written specifically on this aspect in marketing literature. The following guidelines should therefore be found useful in the event of a future question on this matter. The guidelines are based on a specimen answer to a specific question on feasibility in a previous CIM case study.

The form and content of a feasibility (viability) study

1 *Corporate audit*

- Objectives, five year plan
- Key criteria for project appraisal/evaluation

2 *The scenario or project*

3 *Assumptions*

4 *Feasibility research*

(a) *Experimental/technical research*
Design studies, performance specification, timings, costs.

(b) *Market research*
Demand analysis, competition, buying motives, pricing etc.

(c) *Commercial potential* (to include analysis of the feasibility research in terms of timing, cost, human resource needs). Outline income and expenditure analysis.

- DCF projections over 5 years, prices, break-even analysis
- Venture capital required
- Cost of capital at current interest rate
- Working capital
- Short-term loans/overdraft requirements
- Cash flow projections - funding periods
- Contingencies
- Payback periods and net gains

5 ISSUES OF RESPONSIBILITY AND STAKEHOLDER RESPONSE

Stakeholder response

5.1 **Stakeholder analysis** identifies the interest groups in an enterprise. Different stakeholders will have their own views as to strategy. As some stakeholders have **negative power,** in other words power to impede or disrupt the decision, their likely response might be considered. An analysis of **stakeholder risk** has two elements.

(a) The risk that any particular strategic option poses to the **interests of the different stakeholders.**

(b) The **risk that stakeholders might respond** in such a way as to make a proposed strategy less attractive.

5.2

Stakeholder	Interests at stake	Response risk
Management	Pay, status, power, promotion	Subtle sabotage, procrastination, internal politics
Employees	Pay, security, expertise	Strike action, resignation
Shareholders	Return on investment	Sell shares, leaving the firm vulnerable to take over; refuse to invest more
Bankers	Loan security; profits	Refusal to continue lending arrangements; call in liquidator
Customers	Product	Switch to another supplier
Suppliers	Business	Will fail to deliver
Government	The public interest; election success; tax	Will regulate or tax

The strategic value of stakeholders

5.3 **The firm can make strategic gains from managing stakeholder relationships.** This was highlighted by a recent report by the Royal Society of Arts on **Tomorrow's Company.** 'Failure to manage such relationships can carry heavy penalties.' Studies have revealed:

(a) **Correlation between employee retention and customer loyalty** (eg local staff turnover in service firms generally results in more repeat business).

(b) **Continuity and stability** in relationships with employees, customers and suppliers is important in enabling organisations to **respond to certain types of change.**

5.4 These 'soft' issues are particularly pertinent for industries where creativity is important and for service businesses. 'Knowledge' based and service industries are likely to be the growth industries of the future.

The societal marketing concept

5.5 Kotler suggested that a **societal marketing concept** should replace the marketing concept as a philosophy for the future.

Key Concept

'The **societal marketing concept** is a management orientation that holds that the key task of the organisation is to determine the needs and wants of target markets and to adapt the organisation to delivering the desired satisfactions more effectively and efficiently than its competitors in a way that preserves or enhances the consumers' and society's well-being.'

Ethics

5.6 In general, ethical issues - how companies behave - have become of more importance recently. Many companies are exploiting new found public concern with **ethical behaviour**. The Co-operative Bank developed a whole advertising campaign around avoiding investment in countries with oppressive regimes. For some companies, copying Body Shop and the Co-operative Bank is not really an option (eg tobacco firms, drinks firms).

5.7 Responses to ethical concerns

- Introducing codes of **conduct** (eg to help and guide employees in difficult situations)
- Inviting outsiders to review ethical performance in some way.

Marketing at Work

- In 1997 Shell announced that it was to invite environmental and human rights groups to participate in some of its more sensitive projects in the developing world. This comes after criticism of its activities in Nigeria and the North Sea.

- Pharmaceuticals firms have, after some pressure, offered cheaper drugs to third world markets.

5.8 Ultimately, however, 'ethics' comes down to the individual behaviour of managers and employees. Acting ethically is often good business. *Which?* magazine alleged that BT employees had given misleading or inaccurate information about telephone services offered by cable firms. The poor publicity can hardly have helped BT's campaign to win back 'cable' customers.

Ethical issues and marketing

5.9 An August 1996 edition of *Marketing Success* briefly covered some issues of ethics which might be of relevance to marketers, using the 4Ps of the marketing mix as a framework.

(a) **Product/service**

  (i) Failure to inform customers about risks associated with the use of the product: **dishonesty**. Currently, there are lawsuits in the US in which people are suggesting that the tobacco companies, despite their denials, have known for some time that nicotine is addictive.

  (ii) Using materials of a poorer quality in a bid to cut costs.

  (iii) Does manufacture involve an unacceptable environmental cost?

(b) **Pricing.** In economic terms, price is a matter of supply and demand and, in the pursuit of profit, prices are 'what the market will bear'. Ethics come into the discussion when:

  - Cartels attempt to 'fix' prices by rigging the market
  - Consumers are sometimes charged extras, not officially disclosed

(c) **Promotion**

- Advertising: honest, legal, decent and truthful
- Tastefulness of imagery (eg violence, sexual stereotyping)

(d) **Place.** Ethical concerns regarding relationships with intermediaries can involve the use of power, or delays in payment.

5.10 Of course, ethics concerns many non-marketing issues.

- Employees: keeping to terms of the contract and avoiding discrimination
- Suppliers: paying on time.

5.11 Some of the 'ethical' issues are backed up by law (eg against price fixing and unfair contracts). The firm also has an ethical duty to its investors not to squander their money. A wider issue relating to stakeholders is a business's whole stance toward **social responsibility** especially with regard to pollution.

Marketing at Work

The Chartered Institute of Marketing's *Code of Professional Standards* is reproduced below.

1 A member shall at all times conduct himself with integrity in such a way as to bring credit to the profession of marketing and The Chartered Institute of Marketing.

2 A member shall not by any unfair or unprofessional practice injure the business, reputation or interest of any other member of the Institute.

3 Members shall, at all times, act honestly in their professional dealings with customers and clients (actual and potential), employers and employees.

4 A member shall not, knowingly or recklessly, disseminate any false or misleading information, either on his own behalf or on behalf of anyone else.

5 A member shall keep abreast of current marketing practice and act competently and diligently and be encouraged to register for the Institute's scheme of Continuing Professional Development.

6 A member shall, at all times, seek to avoid conflict of interest and shall make prior voluntary and full disclosure to all parties concerned of all matters that may rise to any such conflict. Where a conflict arises a member must withdraw prior to the work commencing.

7 A member shall keep business information confidential except: from those persons entitled to receive it, where it breaches this code and where it is illegal to do so.

8 A member shall promote and seek business in a professional and ethical manner.

9 A member shall observe the requirements of all other codes of practice which may from time to time have any relevance to the practice of marketing insofar as such requirements do not conflict with any provisions of this code, or the Institute's Royal Charter and Bye-laws; a list of such codes being obtainable from the Institute's head office.

10 Members shall not hold themselves out as having the Institute's endorsement in connection with an activity unless the Institute's prior written approval has been obtained first.

11 A member shall not use any funds derived from the Institute for any purpose which does not fall within the powers and obligations contained in the Branch or Group handbook, and which does not fully comply with this code.

12 A member shall have due regard for, and comply with, all the relevant laws of the country in which they are operating.

13 A member who knowingly causes or permits any other person or organisation to be in substantial breach of this code or who is a party to such a breach shall himself be guilty of such breach.

14 A member shall observe this Code of Professional Standards as it may be expanded and annotated and published from time to time by the Ethics Committee in the manner provided for below.

BPP PUBLISHING

5.12 Transgressions of morality or ethics will quite rightly invoke the wrath and retaliation of **consumer watchdogs, ombudsmen** and last but by no means least, unfavourable **publicity in the media.** Gratifying needs and wants at the expense of others has become commercially if not politically incorrect. Matters such as smoking, litter, pollution, waste and noise have been issues of public concern.

5.13 There is increasing debate on the subject of '**ethical marketing**' and we are reading of the possibility of banks conducting 'environmental accounting' before agreeing to fund companies in industries which might have to conduct punitive environmental cleansing in response to future European legislation. In strategic marketing planning, therefore, ethical issues are of increasing concern.

5.14 The extended Action Programme below covers many of the issues raised in this chapter. It could take you about an hour.

Action Programme

Organisational background

SJM is a long-established retail organisation operating 227 supermarkets nationally. It is a listed company which has expanded over its 60-year history. The company has attained distinctive competitive advantage by stocking and selling only high-quality products. SJM plc has enjoyed profitable trading and now ranks as one of the leading retailers in the country. It has not been affected by restructuring of the retailing industry and its Board is intent on maintaining the company's independence.

The Board of the company has set a clear aim of achieving profitability with efficient consumption of resources, whilst maintaining the sale of high-quality goods and delivering a courteous and efficient service to customers. This overall aim has been incorporated within the mission statement and forms a central part of the company's promotional advertising.

Financial characteristics of the company

The following information is supplied in respect of SJM plc for the last financial year.

	£million
Turnover,	2,400
Earnings attributable to ordinary shareholders	220

There were 1,200 million ordinary shares in issue at the end of the last financial year and the company's share price was £4.03.

SJM plc has established that its cost of capital is 12% per annum. Over the last year, the company's share price has varied between £3.30 and £4.05. SJM plc paid a dividend of £0.12 (12 pence) per share in the last financial year and has achieved steady dividend growth of 8.4% per annum over the last five years.

'Out-of-town' stores

The company has recognised that its customers are increasingly using personal transport and value the convenience of 'out-of-town' locations. 'Out-of-town' means that a store is located on a city's fringes rather than in the centre. The object of building stores in such a location is to provide customers with easier access to shopping facilities as this is often difficult within the busy city environment. Typical of the out-of-town location is a large car parking facility and good public transport links.

SJM plc established a plan five years ago to build a number of out-of-town superstores to an original design near four major cities. The first of these superstores has now been in operation for one year. The other superstores are in various stages of completion.

SJM has followed its competitors in developing out-of-town sites and is considering a partnership initiative with another retailer whose merchandise would not be a competitive threat. This would involve joint development of superstores on out-of-town sites. The only commitment to this initiative by SJM plc, so far, is a feasibility study of a single joint project with the other retailer. This will be completed before entering any contractual obligations.

The superstore strategy

SJM aims to provide a satisfactory return to its shareholders. The superstore which is already operational has achieved a high level of profitability in its first year of operation. The company has also experienced a simultaneous reduction in return obtained from other stores which it operates within the vicinity of the superstore. SJM plc is aware of growing governmental concern at the impact out-of-town developments are having on city centre retailing. These two factors have caused the company planners to pause before approving any other out-of-town developments. In addition, public transport provision has been established to service the operational superstore, but the transport providers are now objecting that there is insufficient demand to maintain frequent services as most customers travel to and from the site by car.

Superstore developments

The superstore developments are all built to a standard specification which comprises 40,000 square metres. The life of the project is fifteen years. Typically, the development takes place over a three-year period from planning stage to final commissioning. Each superstore is assumed, for investment appraisal purposes, to have a life of 12 years following completion. The cost of the first superstore development was £25 million with approximately 20% being incurred in the first year. The remaining costs are split evenly over the second and third years. Included within these costs was £500,000 for architects' fees which have reduced by half in subsequent developments. The architects' fees can be assumed to fall due for payment in direct proportion to the building costs.

The superstore developments are targeted to achieve a net cash inflow of £250 per square metre per annum from the commencement of operations. Experience has shown that the first superstore has achieved this target during the first year of operation. A total reduction in net cash inflow over the same period has occurred in other SJM plc stores which trade within the surrounding areas. This has been calculated as having the effect of reducing the superstore net cash inflow by £40 per square metre per annum.

Each superstore is assumed to have a net residual value of zero. All cashflows can be assumed to occur at the end of the year to which they relate. The cashflows and discount rate are in real terms (ie they have been adjusted for inflation).

Financial appraisal of the first superstore

Year			Discount factor @ 12%	Present value
		£'000		£'000
Cost of development				
1	£25m × 20%	5,000	0.893	(4,465)
2	(£25m – £5m) × 50%	10,000	0.797	(7,970
3	(£25m – £25m) × 50%	10,000	0.712	(7,120)
Total		25,000		(19,555)
			Cumulative discount factor	
Revenue over 12 years		£'000		
Gross £250 × 40,000 sq metres		10,000		
Less £40 × 40,000 sq metres		(1,600)		
Net annual revenue per annum		8,400	4.409	37,035
Net present value				17,480

Required

(a) Comment on the financial appraisal which justified the investment in the first superstore.

(b) Identify the market opportunities and threats which SJM plc will confront if it develops more out-of-town superstores.

(c) Describe and comment on the impact of the out-of-town developments by SJM plc on each of five groups of stakeholders.

(d) Discuss whether SJM plc should pursue other out-of-town developments completely on its own or jointly with the other retailer. Pay particular attention to potential planning and operational difficulties which may arise from these initiatives.

Chapter Roundup

- Potential strategies need to be carefully **evaluated** to identify those which will fill the identified planning gap within the limits of the resources and strengths of the organisation.

- A number of **financial and marketing tools** are available to help managers make their strategic evaluations.

- Marketing models include **buyer behaviour** and **competitor analysis**. These are used at all stages in the planning processes.

- **Financial models** include CVP analysis - relevant to planning unit sales and market share, and DCF analysis which can be used to evaluate strategic marketing expenditure.

- Much strategy evaluation is involved with reducing the **risk** of a particular course of action, or assessing what that risk is. Risk can sometimes be quantified.

- **Sensitivity analysis** is a way of analysing the degree to which a strategy is vulnerable to changes in certain variables.

- A strategy can be perceived differently by management and various **stakeholder groups**. Some stakeholder groups have the power to influence strategic decisions.

- For major marketing projects involving new products, new markets or strategic alliances, **feasibility studies** are imperative.

Now try illustrative question 15 at the end of the Study Text

Quick quiz

1   Suggest three criteria for testing strategic options. (see para 2.1)

2   What are the stages in evaluating a marketing opportunity? (2.6)

3   What is the use of CVP analysis? (3.3)

4   Give at least three assumptions of CVP analysis. (3.6)

5   What are the underlying principles of DCF? (3.7)

6   How can DCF analysis be used in marketing evaluation? (3.9 - 3.14)

7   Give examples of risk. (4.1)

8   How should risk be dealt with in strategic decisions? (4.3)

9   What are two aspects of stakeholder risk? (5.1)

10   Identify stakeholder responses. (5.2)

Action Programme Review

(a)   The financial appraisal does justify the investment. However, it has a number of deficiencies.

    (i)   It is unlikely that a superstore would have a residual value of nil. The land alone would be worth something for redevelopment, and its value might be high. Of course, this increases the attractiveness of the project still further.

    (ii)   As the cash flows and discount rates have been expressed in real terms, inflation has presumably been considered. The problem lies not so much in the discount rate but the fact that net cash inflow in real terms is supposed not to change. In fact, inflation rates differ on retail products, and so the sales mix of the superstore will have a significant impact. Is this likely to change?

(iii)   The calculation seems to take no account of the **risk** that revenue might be less than expected. Were a competitor to open a similar store nearby, the sales per square metre could fall significantly. Many UK supermarkets have faced competition from discounters recently, which has forced price cutting. Political factors have been mentioned in the question; possible curbs on car usage suggested might reduce the stores' attractiveness as destinations. With current plans to revitalise high streets, customers might want a number of stores to visit.

(iv)   No account has been taken of major changes in retail formats, and additional construction costs.

(v)   As an exercise in strategic management there seems little external orientation or consideration of wider issues of the business environment. A scenario building approach could have integrated strategic and financial issues.

(vi)   How will the development affect investors' view of the company over the next few years? Shareholders are expecting consistent dividend growth. The firm has to ensure sufficient resources of cash for this, as well as to fund its investment programmes, with dividend cover of 1.5 (£220 million earnings ÷ £144 million total dividend).

(b)   **Market opportunities and threats**

Opportunities

Supermarkets make their profits on a high volume of transactions. (Earnings of £220m are 10% of revenue.) Any increase in the volume of transactions will bring significantly increased profits. The new superstores have been designed to increase the volume of transactions. They hope to attract new customers (market development):

(i)   Who have cars and who like to do all their shopping in one go

(ii)   From competitors with no out-of-town stores in the area

(iii)   From the city centre (in the USA, where out-of-town shopping has become more developed, some suburbs are said to have developed into 'edge cities' of their own)

(iv)   From other outlying areas, as the store's location will be convenient for people who are further afield

(v)   In other parts of the country, if SJM's geographical coverage is not evenly spread

The firm can generate additional sales to existing customers

(i)   Extend the range of products on offer (product development eg ASDA, who are selling books)
(ii)   Provide services which make shopping convenient (eg a crèche or a tea shop)

The superstores will enable the firm to retain its existing customers, who might otherwise go over to competitors. (This is a reason why many supermarkets now have loyalty card schemes.)

It is possible that there will be knock on effect. Some customers may visit the superstores only rarely but, if they are favourably impressed, they might use SJM's other stores at other times.

SJM's new stores offer an opportunity to save money, in that the logistics of stocking them are probably better than the city centre sites. They are probably more profitable. SJM already seems quite large; any increase in market share might enable the firm to strike even better bargains with suppliers.

Threats

In the UK, supermarkets have been expanding at the expense of smaller grocers and butchers, and against weaker chains, but there might come a point when the market is unable to support any more stores.

The danger is that SJM and its competitors may thus saturate the market, in which case SJM will be left with a large fixed capital investment with limited opportunity for growth.

However, competition in any area is partly restricted by planning regulations, in that most local authorities would not want too many out-of-town developments next to each other. Paradoxically, better transport links, especially roads, would enable customers to go even further afield, thus increasing competition.

New firms can enter the industry. In the UK, discount retailers have established useful niches, by concentrating on price. SJM might have to segment its stores differently. For example, people might change their habits and go to discount stores for essentials and specialist stores for other items.

BPP PUBLISHING

The government is hoping to revive the city centres, although it is not clear what form this policy will take. If city centre shopping becomes more attractive, for whatever reason, out-of-town developments will suffer. (A number of the supermarket chains have returned to city centre sites; an example is **Tesco Metro**.) A problem might be that customers will visit a site with a **number** of stores, not just one.

The heavy use of funds might mean that other ways of increasing profitability (eg by investing in IT or making other service improvements) are not exploited.

Any curtailment on car usage (eg through road pricing, whereby people pay per mile travelled) will decrease the centre's attractiveness. Furthermore decreased bus service will discourage some shoppers (eg the elderly) from using the centre.

(c) **Impact on stakeholders**

A stakeholder is a person or group with an interest in the activities of a business. The affect on stakeholder groups (five only required) is outlined below.

(i) **Shareholders**

Shareholders expect dividend growth, and they probably hope that the 8.4% annual growth will be continued. In this they may be disappointed in the long term, as there are government restrictions on out-of-town shopping developments and there is the risk that the market will be saturated and that cheaper stores will take over. This might restrict profits growth. Furthermore, any investment programmes will need more resources. However, given management's track record so far, they should have no cause for concern. The short-term prospects seem bright, and given slow rises in living standards, customers will have more to spend.

The higher the P/E ratio, the greater investors' confidence. The prospect of enhanced profits and cash flows should raise the share price, and might enable SJM to raise more capital more cheaply to fund its programme.

(ii) **Customers**

Serving customers more effectively is the rationale for the whole business. Their interests will be served by the convenience the store offers, its size and range of goods, the easy parking, and the possibility of one-stop shopping.

However, if city centre shops close, customers might feel forced to use the out-of-town site. The problems with public transport suggest that some customers might eventually be disadvantaged by the move. SJM must hope that the increased business deals with this problem.

(iii) **Suppliers.** The out-of-town developments affect two groups of suppliers.

(1) The investment will be a boon to construction firms which will be building the new developments. Firms which provide infrastructure (eg electricity and water) can expect increased revenue from the development.

(2) Suppliers of the goods that SJM retails will welcome the opportunity for increased sales. Much of the immediate impact will depend on delivery arrangements: most supermarkets have central warehouses from which deliveries are made. The new store programme might involve improvements to SJM's existing logistics networks.

Suppliers might be concerned at increased concentration of bargaining power in the hands of a smaller number of large retailers, and to this extent such developments may not be entirely welcome in the long term. Retailers can more or less dictate terms to suppliers (especially small firms).

(iv) Employees as suppliers of labour will benefit from available jobs, and the new sites may be more pleasant places to work. However, such jobs are not paid too well, and employees may have to rely on a decreasingly reliable public transport service. That said, if the firm was consistently loss making they'd lose their jobs anyway, whereas if the firm expands, this gives further opportunities for promotion.

Many firms have employee share ownership schemes (ASDA is an example); if SJM has one, employees will benefit from increased profits.

(v) **The local community.** Local people will benefit from a major employment opportunity nearby, and better shops. It is local government's job to ensure that planning regulations are adhered to, but there may be drawbacks.

(1) A massive change in traffic patterns may result, causing inconvenience and noise in previously quiet areas, and pressure on existing infrastructure

(2)   A loss of 'countryside' (although this is in theory protected by green belt policies), which spoils the environment

(3)   Some local businesses will suffer, both competitors and other firms in the city centre which benefited from passing trade

(vi) **Central government**

The government aims to promote economic growth, and this economic activity will be welcome, as will the concomitant tax policy. Government policy covers many areas, however, including transport and the environment, and central government does not always speak with one voice.

(d) **Joint ventures**

The first store was effectively an experiment which has succeeded well. If all future developments are going to do as well, why share the benefits with another firm?

(i)   We noted that the initial financial appraisal ignored risk. A joint venture is a way of sharing risk.

(ii)   Sites are not always easy to find, and will become more difficult if new developments are becoming less acceptable. A joint venture might afford more flexibility.

(iii)   Customers are probably familiar with shopping malls which contain a large number of major stores. Both stores would benefit from trade from each other's customers. In other words, as well as customers who drove specifically to shop at SJM, customers of the partner firm might also drop in.

(iv)   Costs might be saved on construction and legal costs. For example, the firms would share the costs of any roads that had to be built. There would be other economies of scale in managing the development.

If a joint venture with a supplier of non-competing products is attractive to SJM's customers, it should be attractive to SJM, in its search to maximise sales per square metre. Whether SJM should go ahead or not will depend on the results of the feasibility study.

(i)   The relationship between the partners' business should be genuinely complementary for both to benefit. The mere fact that they do not compete is not enough. A clothes retailer and a food retailer might go together. A food retailer and, say, a firm selling car spares is a less logical mix if both hope to benefit from their mutual proximity.

(ii)   Both will have to agree on the joint management of the site, and this includes things such as delivery times (so their respective delivery lorries do not get in each others' way).

(iii)   They need to agree common policies for security, fire safety and so forth, which become more pressing the larger the site. In addition, there needs to be a clear agreement as to running the site. They may appoint a site manager to look after the entire operation.

(iv)   Joint marketing arrangements might be needed to entice people to the site. For this to have maximum effectiveness, the partners will need to co-ordinate promotions. This implies that any incompatibilities in their business aims should be kept to a minimum. Furthermore, colour schemes, signage and so forth need to be acceptable to both parties. SJM might have to give the site a separate identity of its own.

Part E
Implementation and Control

16 *Implementation*

Chapter Topic List	Syllabus reference
1 Setting the scene	
2 Implementing plans	5.1
3 Strategic marketing orientation	5.1
4 Managing change	5.1
5 Internal marketing	5.1
6 Leadership and power	5.1
7 Project management	5.1

Learning Outcomes

- Understand and evaluate the processes that can be used to overcome barriers to effective implementation of marketing strategies and plans.

Key Concepts Introduced

- Marketing orientation
- Internal marketing
- Project

Examples of Marketing at Work

- Medicines and e-commerce
- Sega Dreamcast

1 SETTING THE SCENE

1.1 Many marketing plans fail to be implemented effectively. In part this is a result of the generic problems in planning. There are specific problems relating to marketing plans which need to be addressed. Internal marketing and change management are two useful approaches.

329

2 IMPLEMENTING PLANS

2.1 Having determined objectives, appraised strategy and formulated plans, it is time to put the corporate plan into action. Everyone involved should know what is required and when, and should be committed to the successful accomplishment of the plan.

2.2 Senior management cannot just leave it to their middle managers to finish off the work by putting the plans into effect.

(a) Senior managers have the **ultimate responsibility** for ensuring that the organisation achieves its objectives. Monitoring actual results is thus an essential ingredient of the control cycle.

(b) Senior management need to remain committed to the wider picture. Middle management almost invariably, when left to themselves, spend their time on short term or pressing issues, rather than dealing with the less immediate problems of the corporate plan.

(c) The performance appraisal of middle and junior management is based on achieving short-term or budgeted tasks and targets.

2.3 **Implementation of the corporate or marketing plan**

(a) **Converting strategic plans into action plans,** ie operations plans and budgets.

(b) **Allocating responsibilities** and giving authority to individual managers to use resources, for example spend sufficient money to allow them to achieve their individual targets.

(c) **Establishing checkpoints** to monitor activities, such as:

(i) Have deadlines been met and are future deadlines going to be met?

(ii) Are any targets in danger of being missed?

(iii) Will the required resources be available to make the products/services?

(iv) Will the products be available in sufficient numbers to achieve the aims of the marketing plan?

(d) **Exerting pressure for control action** where necessary, to ensure that things get done according to the aims of the plan.

(e) **Modifying the plan** in the light of changing circumstances.

2.4 There are always **unforeseen** events to deal with, some of them controllable and others uncontrollable and unavoidable.

Problem areas and organisational considerations

2.5 Problems in both implementation and control of marketing plans arise from a variety of sources internal and external.

External factors

2.6 By now you should have a thoroughly realistic idea of external environmental factors which affect marketing, both in PEST/SLEPT terms, and in the actions of competitors, suppliers and customers.

Internal factors

2.7 As problematic are the internal factors. The marketing department is only one of many, and competes with others for resources. Moreover, the marketing department **depends** on other business functions to deliver the marketing mix.

Implications of mix decisions; e-marketing example

2.8 The example below describes some of the issues that have to be addressed to satisfy a particularly demanding customers in the business-to-business market with the need to improve profitability.

(a) **Mix issues**

- Product: new products
- Place: distribution of drugs by choosy intermediaries
- Price: the need to stay profitable
- Promotion: personal selling replaced by e-marketing

(b) **Resource implications**

- Extra resources being devoted to new drugs and new marketing mechanisms
- Improving the internal communication systems
- The need for the internal marketing of change
- Improved @!!??!!@

Marketing at Work

Extracts from *The Economist*, 14 April 2001

Medicines and e-commerce

In America, an army of 63,000 drug-firms sales reps pound the pavement in an attempt to persuade doctors to prescribe their company's products. Last year, such doctor 'detailing' accounted for almost half of the $15.5 billion that drug companies spent on product marketing.

According to Health Strategies Group, a consultancy, only 60% of such visits result in a meeting with a doctor, which is anyway usually only a brief encounter: almost 90% of such meeting least less than two minutes.

A solution may lie in electronic marketing or 'e-detailing'. A dozen firms have sprung up to pitch drugs to doctors over the web and via other remote channels, giving them easy access to such information at times that are convenient.

Many doctors would welcome meetings with sales reps if only they could take place at a better moment. This is what iPhysicianNet, based in Arizona, hopes to facilitate. The firm has installed computers, with high-speed phone lines and video-conferencing equipment, in the offices of almost 7,000 of America's highest-prescribing doctors. In exchange for this free set-up, doctors agree to participate in one video-detailing session per month with each of the nine drug makers – among them Merck and GlaxoSmith Kline – that pay for the service.

Because the session takes place at the doctor's convenience, it lasts on average four times longer than typical sales visits. Moreover, the video format allows sales reps to show data and other visual aids that make the session more informative – something that a rushed meeting in the doctor's surgery rarely permits.

iPhysicianNet claims that each video session costs $110, compared with almost $200 for a real-life encounter. It also says that pilot trials have shown that its service boosts new prescriptions by 14% compared with the knock-on-the-door approach.

BPP
PUBLISHING

2.9 Frequently encountered implementation problems

Problem	Comment
Weak support from the chief executive and top management	Without this support it is unlikely that other functional managers will take the marketing manager's initiatives very seriously.
Lack of a plan for planning	It is naive to assume that once a marketing planning system has been designed that it will operate smoothly from day one. The evidence indicates that a period of around three years is required in a large company to overcome resistance to the change that planning inevitably brings. Internal marketing is required.
Lack of line management support	Operational managers are often unwilling to participate fully because of hostility, lack of skills, lack of information, lack of resources and an inadequate organisational structure without a fully integrated marketing function.
Confusion over planning terms	The initiators of the system often use academic planning terminology which line managers see as meaningless jargon.
Numbers in lieu of written objectives and strategies	Prior to a planning system, often all that is used is sales forecasts and financial projections. Making explicit the route to achieving these objectives is a new and difficult skill. It requires managers to express the logic of their objective and in this sense is a creative process requiring qualitative rather than quantitative information.
Too much detail, too far ahead	Overplanning is often associated with too much information and ends with piles of paperwork which confuses and demotivates rather than promoting positive participation. Marketing auditing can result in far too many issues demanding management attention. Key issues need to be identified - the wood needs to be drawn from the trees.
Once a year ritual	This is a common barrier to effective implementation, when the task is seen as just another job to do which gets in the way of the really pressing day-to-day activities. Plans which are written and then filed away until next year do not work. Planning needs to be an integral part of the manger's job with progress towards objectives being reviewed and discussed on a regular basis.
Separation of operational planning from strategic planning	Strategic plans need to be built up from sound analysis at grass-roots level, and all managers need to consider not just continuing in the same direction but what longer term changes may be required.
Failure to integrate marketing planning into a total corporate planning system	Unless marketing plans are considered in relation to the plans of finance, production and personnel it becomes impossible to resource accurately the plan's product/market requirements.
Delegation of planning to a planner	When planning is divorced from the reality of operations, and the people who are expected to put the ideas into action are not involved, it is not surprising that resistance and lack of commitment can exist.

3 STRATEGIC MARKETING ORIENTATION

3.1 There are many doubts as to whether the marketing concept is followed in practice and the degree to which firms are in fact market orientated.

Key Concept

Marketing orientation: 'the process by which an enterprise's target customers' needs and wants are effectively and efficiently satisfied within the resource limitations and long-term survival requirements of that enterprise' (Wilson, Gilligan and Pearson)

3.2 **The marketing orientation checklist** (adapted from Wilson, Gilligan and Pearson) shows how a firm can assess how far it has a marketing orientation.

		High	Medium	Low
1	Understanding of customer needs throughout the organisation			
2	Profit-maximising, not sales-volume chasing			
3	Chief executive is the voice of the customer			
4	Market-driven mission			
5	Strategies reflect the market			
6	Marketing seen as more important than other functions			
7	Responsiveness to marketing opportunities			
8	Good MkIS			
9	Use of marketing research			
10	Analysis of marketing revenues/costs			
11	Link between marketing and NPD			
12	Are marketing staff market-orientated, not just sales orientated?			
13	Marketing seen as everyone's responsibility			
14	Co-ordinated and integrated marketing decisions			

A model of organisational effectiveness

3.3 A useful model which will help integrate various aspects of the internal functioning of the organisation is the 7S framework, developed by McKinsey.

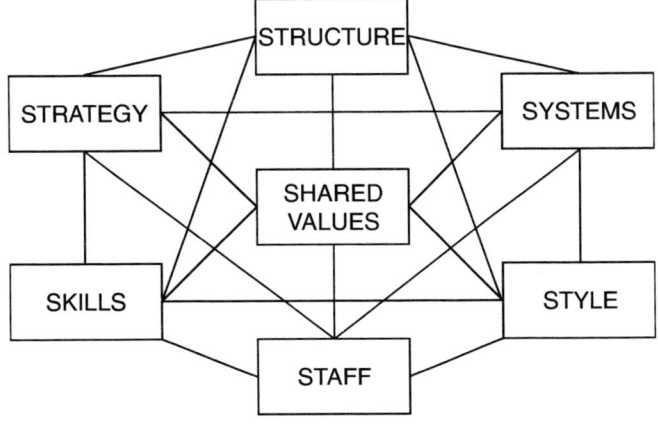

Source: McKinsey

BPP
PUBLISHING

'S'	Description
Structure	How the organisation is arranged into departments
Systems	How the organisation carries out its operations and processes information. As is shown elsewhere in this Study Text, information systems are a key marketing tool
Style	Organisation culture, how it presents itself to the world
Staff/Skills	How individual skills are deployed to meet corporate objectives
Strategy	The organisation's business and competitive strategies
Shared values	How people feel about the organisation and its mission

3.4   Structure, strategy, systems are relatively 'hard' in that they are easy to define and quantify. The other 'S's - shared values, skills, style and staff - are harder to quantify.

3.5   Developing a strategic marketing orientation can involve **changing the culture** of the organisation and requires the support of top management.

Step 1.   Get top management commitment to introducing strategic marketing orientation (SMO)

Step 2.   Specify mission, objectives and resources for introducing SMO

Step 3.   Set up a task force

- Identify current orientation
- Identify **needs analysis** to change orientation
- Implement training and management development programmes

Step 4.   Monitor marketing effectiveness to maintain momentum

4   MANAGING CHANGE

4.1   It is management's responsibility to prepare the organisation for the future. We have also seen that the future will inevitably bring change. Organisations have to adapt and modify if they are to survive in the environment of the future. We have already seen how **strategic management** and corporate planning are essential in identifying and meeting needs, both **for** change and those brought about **by** change. Change in the environment creates opportunities and threats: the organisation must respond with internal change in order to maximise its strengths and minimise its weaknesses.

4.2   **Aspects of change**

Aspect	Comment
The environment	These could be changes in what competitors are doing, what customers are buying, how they spend their money, changes in the law, changes in social behaviour and attitudes and economic changes.
The products the organisation makes, or the services it provides	These are made in response to changes in customer demands, competitors' actions and new technology.

Aspect	Comment
How products are made (or services provided), by whom, working methods	These changes are also in response to environmental change, for example new technology and new laws on safety at work.
Management, working relationships and corporate culture	These include changes in leadership style, and in the way that employees are encouraged to work together. Changes in training and staff development are also relevant here.
Organisation structure or size	These might involve creating new departments and divisions, greater delegation of authority or more centralisation, changes in the way that plans are made, management information is provided and control is exercised.

4.3 **Evaluating the effectiveness of change management**

(a) The **impact of the change on organisational goals**: has the change contributed to the overall objectives of the organisation as defined by the corporate plan?

(b) The success of the change in meeting its **specified objective** (and short-term targets set for progress measurement): has the change solved the problem?

(c) The **behaviour of people in the organisation**: has the change programme resulted in the behavioural changes planned (for example higher output, better teamwork, more attention to customer care)?

(d) The **reaction of the people** in the organisation: has the change programme been implemented without arousing hostility, fear, conflict, and its symptoms (absenteeism, labour turnover etc)?

4.4 **Reasons why an organisation might fail to manage change successfully**

(a) **Failure to identify the need to change** (typically a failure to pay attention to change in the environment).

(b) **Failure to identify the objectives of change,** so that the wrong areas are addressed.

(c) **Failure to identify correctly the strategy required,** out of all the options, to achieve the objectives. The result is that change takes place, but not in the relevant direction. New technology, for example, is sometimes regarded as a universal solution to organisational problems, but it will not necessarily improve productivity or profitability if the product/market strategy or the workforce is the real problem.

(d) **Failure to commit sufficient resources** to the strategy.

(e) **Failure to identify the appropriate method of implementing change,** for the situation and the people involved (typically, failing to anticipate resistance to change).

(f) **Failure to implement the change in a way that secures acceptance,** because of the leadership style of the person managing the change (typically, failure to consult and involve employees).

4.5 The first four of the above reasons for failure are to do with strategic planning generally: they are potential shortcomings in any planning exercise. The **peculiar difficulties of introducing change, however, are human factors**. When implementing plans or changes, managers must never lose sight of the fact that their success depends on people. **Before commencing their internal marketing of plans, managers must recognise the behavioural factors** which might influence people to welcome or resist change.

335

4.6 **Reasons for resisting change**

(a)	Fear of personal loss

- Security
- Money (eg travelling costs to work, when a change of office location is proposed)
- pride and job satisfaction
- friends and contacts
- freedom
- responsibility
- authority/discretion
- good working conditions
- status

(b) Cannot see the need for change

(c) Believes change will do more harm than good

(d) Lack of respect for the person initiating the change

(e) Objection to the manner in which the planned change was communicated

(f) No participation 'We weren't asked'

(g) Negative attitude to the job

(h) Belief that the change is a personal criticism of what the individual has been doing

(i) The change requires effort

(j) The change comes at a bad time 'We have enough on our plate already'

(k) Challenge to authority in the act of resisting change

Reasons for welcoming change

(a) Expectations of personal gain

(b) Change provides a new and welcome challenge

(c) Change will reduce the boredom of work

(d) Likes/respects the source of the change

(e) Likes the manner in which the change was suggested

(f) Participation in the decision

(g) Wants the change

(h) The change improves the employee's future prospects

(i) The change comes at a good time

4.7 Good managers should ensure they are in a position to plan for it. In this way they are able to market change to their staff so that it is welcomed and not resisted. Internal marketing and leadership are useful in this respect.

5 **INTERNAL MARKETING** Specimen paper

Key Concept

Internal marketing is the use of a marketing approach in the internal environment of organisation, whose employees are seen as 'customers' and have to be persuaded to buy into management ideas.

5.1 Internal marketing is particularly important in introducing strategic marketing organisation or in any change. In service industries, the employee is the deliverer of the

336

service (interactive marketing). Kotler identifies a **marketing triangle**, which is adapted below.

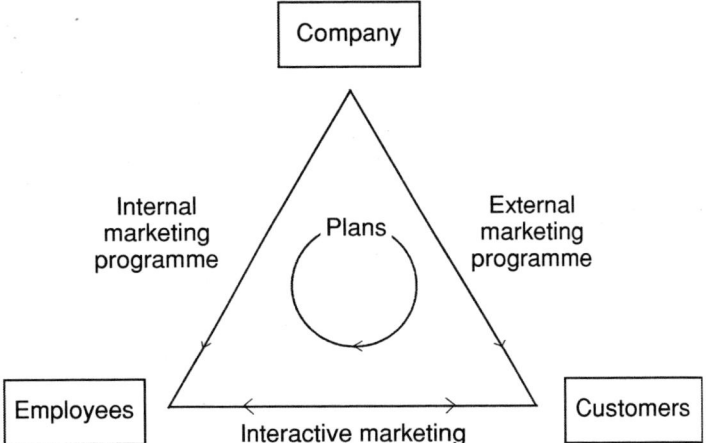

This shows that the external customer and employees need to be marketed to, but that in a marketing-oriented company the natural planning cycle considers the needs of the external customer first.

Implementing internal marketing

5.2 A similar step approach can be taken to planning internal marketing as in external marketing.

Step 1. **Internal marketing objectives and strategy**

The internal marketing programme should be designed to achieve the external marketing strategy. Research may be needed to assess the implications of the external marketing programme for the internal customer.

Step 2. **Segment the internal market, identifying** (Piercy):

- Influential supporters of the strategy
- Influential opponents of the strategy (how do we win them over?)
- Non involved supporters of the strategy (how do we increase their influence?)
- Non involved opponents

Step 3. **Develop an internal marketing mix.**

(a) **Product:** this is the plan or change which management wants to implement.

(b) **Price:** there will be a price tag. The **costs and benefits to staff** need to be clearly assessed. As with any product there may need to be negotiation, but managers must be clear what the costs and benefits are. For example a move to a new office block may entail a longer journey to work, but offers improved working conditions. A change in the sales commission package may depress potential earnings in exchange for a higher average salary.

(c) **Place:** in marketing, place represents when and where the product is available. The timing of the announcement of plans can have a dramatic effect on the way they are received and this needs careful consideration. The **distribution** of internal marketing is perhaps an issue for human resources management. Appropriate appraisal systems need to be devised, in which customer commitment is seen as core. Some firms employ 360° appraisal techniques whereby customer input is used to measure performance.

(d) **Promotion:** poor communication is probably the biggest single failure when evaluating internal company problems. The grapevine tends to work quickly and not always very accurately. Communication should be two way and meetings and discussions to take account of staff's views and thoughts at an early stage will help implementation later.

Step 5. Gain commitment: monitor the success of the internal marketing programme

5.3 **Key skills** in implementing internal marketing

Marketing personnel have to communicate to other people in the company who control key resources (production) and who are directly concerned with key stakeholders (finance function).

(a) **Persuasion.** Marketers must persuade other company decision-makers of the business case. The Finance Director will be particularly concerned with profit.

(b) **Negotiation.** A negotiation occurs when two parties with different objectives agree on a mutually acceptably outcome. Negotiation is at the heart of relationship with outsourcers (over price, delivery and so on) but is also relevant internally. Each business alliance must benefit both parties.

(c) **Politics.** People in organisations have their own personal and departmental goals. Different individuals compete for resources, promotions. Building **coalitions of support** is a necessary skill, especially for those without direct control over other functions.

5.4 Internal marketing is about the manner in which plans and change are 'sold' to those they affect. The right manner is important in creating a motivated and successful team at whatever level the plan is being implemented.

Action Programme 1

Some time ago, those who travelled by train were referred to as 'passengers': recently, the word has changed to 'customers'. What do you think the significance of this might be?

Exam Tip

Internal marketing has to consider:

- Organisation structure and internal communication systems
- Employee attitudes to management
- Segmenting the workforce

Internal marketing is vitally important where change is concerned.

6 LEADERSHIP AND POWER

6.1 A **marketing executive** has to persuade other members of the board at similar levels, but also **provide leadership**, especially in times of change. The marketer has to lead the team and motivate them.

Leadership and change

6.2 In the context of change and the top management team we can identify specific leadership roles.

(a) **Charismatic leaders** lead by force of personality, which will only be exercised in difficult situations.

(b) **Transformational leaders** not only have charisma, but use it to some purpose.

- To create a new vision for the organisation
- To gain acceptance of the new vision
- To force through and 'refreeze' the change

6.3 Increasing attention is being paid to the notion of the **visionary leader,** who is capable of transforming the organisation by taking it on to even greater success or by turning it round from imminent collapse.

Characteristics	Comment
Imaginative and experienced, intuitive and analytical	The visionary takes 'mental leaps' from 'what is' into 'what could or should be'. It draws on a deep understanding of what already is and how it could be modified or revolutionised.
Excellence	A key visionary insight is often one which sees mismatches between how things are done currently and how things might be done more effectively.
Orientated towards action	They prefer doing rather than planning, talk rather than writing. Their common management style is one of MBWA (management by wandering about), talking, listening, observing: as Richardson says, 'The classical, planner/manager view of the leader does not reflect the reality' of visionary leadership.
Brilliant communicators	This enables deeply thought-out visions to quickly become shared meanings. They operate as role models, leading by example and their actions can be summarised in just six words: 'Do anything you see me doing'.
Practices empowerment	Managers are allowed to lead their departments and feel some ownership for the effectiveness of the organisation as a whole.
Calculated risk-taker	The leader checks out the acceptability of the vision before becoming publicly committed to it. In this way the leader ensures that he or she is never too far adrift from the wishes and inclinations of those who will act as 'followers'.
Independent	Capable of making up their own minds. This autocratic side to their characters is necessary for the single-minded commitment required to instil vision and to get things done.
Passionate about achievement	With a capacity for hard work which is greater than that of most other people. This is matched by a dogged determination to overcome setbacks and to find ways round obstacles.
Desire to make things happen	They have a strong need to be in charge of their destinies and to be the 'boss' of the organisation. Further, they are optimistic, believing that the world is full of opportunities and that most things are possible.

Leading the team

6.4 More mundanely, many managers need leadership skills to deal with the teams, particularly sales teams, under their control.

Tells/sells/consults/joins

6.5 The Research Unit at Ashridge Management College distinguished four different management styles. They are outlined on the table on the next page.

(a) Subordinates preferred the **consults style of leadership**. Those managed in that way had the most favourable attitude to work, but managers were most commonly thought to be exercising the **tells or sells** style.

(b) The least favourable attitudes were found amongst subordinates who were **unable to perceive a consistent style** of leadership in their boss.

6.6 There are a wide variety of leadership theories, but keep in mind the key issues.

- The task
- The needs of the individuals
- The needs of the team
- The context
- The leader's own needs, style and personality

Marketing at Work

Sega Dreamcast

For Sega, competing with Sony and Nintendo, the Dreamcast was supposed to guarantee its survival. Its Saturn console had been upstaged by the Sony Playstation. 'Everybody ... could agree that Sega needed a successful product. But the problem then and for most of the next five years was that nobody could agree on much else.'

- Launch: US or Japan?

- Include modem or not? (to do so would have raised the retail price)

- Chip specifications (70% of the console costs). While executives bickered, memory prices jumped 30-40%

According to the Financial Times (28 April 2001), the long debates reflected a management undergoing a lot of change.

Senior management was split. Three company presidents oversaw the project. A leading shareholder got involved – who disagreed significantly with the management. Executives from Honda and Nomura were imported – they disagreed on everything.

Finally, because Sega gave NEC its chip specifications three months late, the product hit the market with too few games (4, not 15) and too few consoles (200,000 not 600,000).

'In the games industry, a product's destiny is decided within one month of launch.' Dreamcast was over.

Since then, Sega has pulled out of making video consoles, and is now focused in games software for other hardware producers. It failed because of management, and poor implementation.

Website address: www.sega.com

Style	Characteristics	Strengths	Weaknesses
Tells (autocratic)	The manager makes all the decisions, and issues instructions which must be obeyed without question.	(1) Quick decisions can be made when speed is required. (2) It is the most efficient type of leadership for highly-programmed routine work.	(1) It does not encourage the sub-ordinates to give their opinions when these might be useful. (2) Communications between the manager and sub-ordinate will be one-way and the manager will not know until afterwards whether the orders have been properly understood. (3) It does not encourage initiative and commitment from subordinates.
Sells (persuasive)	The manager still makes all the decisions, but believes that subordinates have to be motivated to accept them in order to carry them out properly.	(1) Employees are made aware of the reasons for decisions. (2) Selling decisions to staff might make them more committed. (3) Staff will have a better idea of what to do when unforeseen events arise in their work because the manager will have explained his intentions.	(1) Communications are still largely one-way. Sub-ordinates might not accept the decisions. (2) It does not encourage initiative and commitment from subordinates.
Consults	The manager confers with subordinates and takes their views into account, but has the final say.	(1) Employees are involved in decisions before they are made. This encourages motivation through greater interest and involvement. (2) An agreed consensus of opinion can be reached and for some decisions consensus can be an advantage rather than a weak compromise. (3) Employees can contribute their knowledge and experience to help in solving more complex problems.	(1) It might take much longer to reach decisions. (2) Subordinates might be too inexperienced to formulate mature opinions and give practical advice. (3) Consultation can too easily turn into a facade con-cealing, basically, a sells style.
Joins (democratic)	Leader and followers make the decision on the basis of consensus.	(1) It can provide high motivation and commit-ment from employees. (2) It shares the other advantages of the con-sultative style (especially where subordinates have expert power).	(1) The authority of the manager might be under-mined. (2) Decision-making might become a very long process, and clear decisions might be difficult to reach. (3) Subordinates might lack enough experience.

7 PROJECT MANAGEMENT

> ### Key Concept
>
> A **project** is 'an undertaking that has a beginning and an end and is carried out to meet established goals within cost, schedule and quality objectives' (Haynes, *Project Management*).

7.1 Characteristics of projects

- Specific start and end points
- Well-defined objectives
- The project endeavour is to a degree unique
- The project usually contains costs and time schedules
- A project cuts across many organisational and functional boundaries

7.2 Examples of projects

Project	Comment
Management	• Development of MkIS • The mounting of a major trade exhibition.
Marketing	• Developing and launching a new product • Implementing a promotional campaign with defined objectives

7.3 Special management problems with projects

Problem	Comment
Teambuilding	The work is carried out by a team of people usually assembled for one project, who must be able to communicate effectively and immediately with each other.
Expected problems	There can be many novel **expected** problems, each one of which should be resolved by careful design and planning prior to commencement of work.
Unexpected problems	There can be many novel **unexpected** problems, particularly with a project working at the limits of existing and new technologies. There should be mechanisms within the project to enable these problems to be resolved during the time span of the project without detriment to the objective, the cost or the time span.
Delayed benefit	There is normally no benefit until the work is finished. The 'lead in' time to this can cause a strain on the eventual recipient who feels deprived until the benefit is achieved (even though in many cases it is a major improvement on existing activities) and who is also faced with increasing expenditure for no immediate benefit.
Specialists	Contributions made by specialists are of differing importance at each stage. Assembling a team working towards the one objective is made difficult due to the tendency of specialists to regard their contribution as always being more important than other people's and not understanding the interrelationship between their various specialities in the context of the project.
Stakeholders	If the project involves several parties with different interests in the outcome, there might be disputes between them.

7.4 The objectives of project management

Objective	Comment
Quality	The end result should conform to the proper specification. In other words, the result should achieve what the project was supposed to do.
Budget	The project should be completed without exceeding authorised expenditure.
Timescale	The progress of the project must follow the planned process, so that the 'result' is ready for use at the agreed date. As time is money, proper time management can help contain costs.

The project life cycle

7.5 A typical project has a **project life cycle**.

- Conceiving and defining the project
- Planning the project
- Carrying out the plan (project implementation) and control
- Completing and evaluating the project

The role of the project manager

7.6 The project manager has resources of time, money and staff. These have to be co-ordinated effectively. The project manager's duties are summarised below.

Duty	Comment
Outline planning	Project planning (eg targets, sequencing) • Developing project targets such as overall costs or timescale needed (eg project should take 20 weeks). • Dividing the project into activities (eg questionnaire design, review etc), and placing these activities into the right sequence, often a complicated task if overlapping. • Developing a framework for the procedures and structures, managing the project (eg decide, in principle, to have weekly team meetings, performance reviews etc).
Detailed planning	Work breakdown structure, resource requirements, network analysis for scheduling.
Teambuilding and delegation	The project manager has to meld the members into an effective team.
Communication	The project manager must let superiors know what is going on, and ensure that members of the project team are properly briefed.
Co-ordinating project activities	Between the project team and users, and other external parties (eg suppliers of hardware and software).
Monitoring and control	The project manager should estimate the causes for each departure from the standard, and take corrective measures.
Problem resolution	Even with the best planning, unforeseen problems may arise, and it falls upon the project manager to sort them out, or to delegate the responsibility for so doing to a subordinate.

BPP PUBLISHING

Duty	Comment
Quality control	This is a problematic issue, as there is often a short-sighted trade-off between getting the project out on time and the project's quality.

Project planning tools

7.7 The project manager thus needs to **schedule the activities** in the most efficient way given:

(a) The **dependency** of some activities on others (the foundations of a house are **always** laid before the roof is constructed). Alternatively, some tasks may be carried out in **parallel** to save time.

(b) **Constraints on resources.** Some resources will not be available at the ideal time or at the lowest price.

7.8 The project manager will have been given a broad-brush time estimation for any activity. For this you need:

- The **duration** of each sub-unit of work
- The **earliest time** work in a particular unit must be started
- The **latest time** it must be started

Gantt charts

7.9 A simple plan for a project can use a **bar line chart** (sometimes called a **Gantt chart**).

(a) It can be used as a **progress control chart** with the lower section of each bar being completed as the activity is undertaken.

(b) A delay in a particular piece of work and its 'knock on' effect on other work can be shown in a **linked bar chart**. This shows the links between an activity and preceding activities which have to be completed before this particular activity can start.

7.10 Here is an example of a progress control chart.

No.	DESCRIPTION OF WORK OR ACTIVITY	TIME (DAYS)													
		1	2	3	4	5	6	7	8	9	10	11	12	13	14
1	Excavate for foundations and services (drainage)														
2	Concrete foundations														
3	Build walls and soakaways for drainage														
4	Construct roof														
5	Fit garage doors														
6	Provide services (electric)														
7	Plaster														
8	Decorate														

- **Advantage:** easy to understand

- **Disadvantage:** limited when dealing with complex projects. They only display a restricted amount of information and the links between activities are fairly crude.

Chapter Roundup

- Plans cannot be forgotten by senior managers once they have been prepared. The **implementation of plans** requires the continued interest of senior managers and their involvement in the progress.

- **Marketing planning** in particular is beset by a variety of problems emanating from both within and outside the organisation. Within the organisation, other departments also are accountable to powerful stakeholders and have their own resource problems.

- The effective implementation of plans requires that they are marketed to staff. The process of **internal marketing** is the same as marketing to external customers and should be taken as seriously.

- Internal marketing is particularly relevant to the **management of change**, given that change can positively or adversely affect individuals.

- Some change can involve developing a **strategic marketing orientation**, in which all organisational activities are aligned around the customer.

- **Plans involve change** and managing that process of change is an important responsibility.

Now try illustrative question 16 at the end of the Study Text

Quick Quiz

1 Why should senior managers not simply leave the implementation of plans to subordinates? (see para 2.2)

2 Give three particular problems affecting marketing plan implementation and control. (2.8, 2.9)

3 Identify the factors showing if a firm has a strategic marketing orientation. (3.2)

4 What kind of organisation and management changes might be necessary? (4.2)

5 How would you judge the effectiveness of the management of change? (4.3)

6 Why might organisations fail to manage change successfully? (4.4)

7 List five reasons why change may be resisted. (4.6)

8 List five reasons why change may be welcomed. (4.6)

9 What is internal marketing? (5.1)

10 What three skills are needed for implementing plans, where the implementer has limited control? (5.3)

11 Identify four leadership styles. (6.5)

12 What is a project? (7.1)

13 What is a typical project life-cycle? (7.5)

Action Programme Review

1 This might be a crude form of internal marketing, trying to promote a marketing orientation within the rail system to railway staff, to persuade their staff that they are competing for people's custom. The effect of the change on passengers is not known.

17 *Control*

Chapter Topic List

		Syllabus reference
1	Setting the scene	
2	Effective marketing feedback and control systems	5.2
3	Basic control concepts	5.2
4	Strategic control	5.2
5	Benchmarking and the market environment	5.2
6	Targets, budgets and ratios	5.2
7	Marketing mix effectiveness	5.2
8	The auditing process as a control mechanism	5.2

Learning Outcomes

- Initiate control systems for marketing planning.

Key Concepts Introduced

- Benchmark
- Budget

Examples of Marketing at Work

- Financial services
- Life insurers
- BA
- ONdigital
- Research study

1 SETTING THE SCENE

1.1 Control in a planning system has two aspects. It monitors and corrects current performance. Also, it feeds into the next planning cycle. Control in effect asks 'Where are we now?', the starting point of the planning process. Similarly, the measures used for control do bear some relationship with, and might be identical to, the detailed objectives and critical success factors determined earlier. Control involves a review of what we have achieved, or what we anticipate achieving in the light of our plans.

1.2   Performance measures include financial performance (as expressed in budgets), strategic performance (as monitored by strategic control systems - Sections 4 and 5) and various other measures (eg market share) and the effectiveness of the mix generally.

Links with other papers

1.3   Control is often neglected in exam answers and Analysis and Decision answers. It is harder to exercise in widely-dispersed, global markets. In marketing communications, the control measures (eg recall) should be developed from the communications objectives.

2   EFFECTIVE MARKETING FEEDBACK AND CONTROL SYSTEMS

2.1   In contrast to, say, mechanistic production processes, **marketing feedback and control systems need to recognise the volatile nature of human beings.** After all, **markets are people** or rather people's wants and needs, modified by affordability and availability. Problems of unsatisfactory feedback and control can occur.

(a)   People change.

(b)   Reasons for change are not always apparent or identifiable.

(c)   The same product can be bought by the same person for different purposes eg champagne to celebrate a win on the 3.30, or to drown sorrows after a loss on the 4.00.

(d)   Delays occur in the system due to suppliers being remote from consumers.

(e)   Competitor actions can seriously affect the systems.

(f)   Rarely is complete information affordable so that inadequacies occur in feedback.

(g)   Distortions inevitably occur in the data transfer between people. The more often the data is transcribed the more distortion will occur.

2.2   We have already seen the need for **marketing information feedback at each stage of the planning process.**

(a)   Only if marketing managers are kept informed of what is happening and what is likely to happen, can they make sensible decisions. For example, **contingency planning depends upon 'what if' scenarios.** Only when managers receive information indicating a particular scenario is taking place can the right contingency plan be invoked. The information in this case acts as an identifier, a selector and a trigger.

(b)   The dimensions of marketing feedback and control systems are in fact wide-ranging and flexible. One of the most important marketing planning philosophies is to avoid a laissez-faire, complacent attitude to 'good news'. It is all too easy to adopt the 'if it ain't broke, don't fix it' attitude. We need to remember that **good sales figures these represent the past situation,** so we need to worry about the future longer-term survival and growth.

2.3   Some items have greater immediacy than others. Failure to act on a serious complaint could lead to the loss of an important customer, adversely affecting future sales and profitability.

Exam Tip

A question might ask about financial and other information in a marketing control system. A four stage model is suggested.

(1) Set targets
(2) Measure achievement
(3) Examine reasons
(4) Take corrective action

This is similar to the control model we outline below.

3 BASIC CONTROL CONCEPTS

3.1 A good starting point in thinking about basic control concepts is to take the example of driving a car. In doing this we receive various **feedbacks** eg visual feedback to tell us if we are driving in the right direction, in the correct position on the road, at the right speed etc. Instruments such as the speedometer and our senses - eyes, touch (vibration) provide the basic data. We measure this data against **standards** such as the speed limit, the highway code/laws etc and where necessary take **corrective action** using control devices like the steering wheel and the accelerator.

3.2 The marketing planning and implementation process follows similar precepts. We cannot implement a plan in the first place until we know where we are going. In planning where we are going we need to know where we are now. It also helps if we know where we have come from.

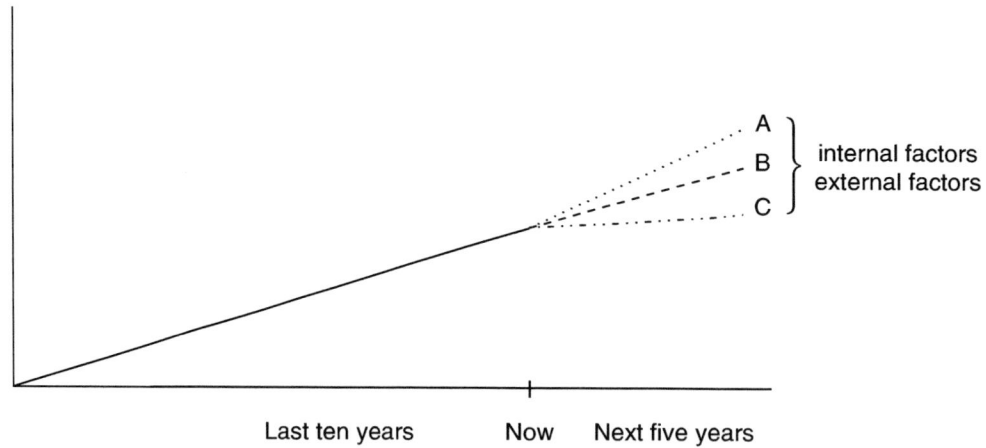

The past determines not only where we are now relative to it but out **future direction** (extrapolation of past trend assuming no change = position B). **Control is, however, only partial in marketing.**

(a) We can change internal factors (the 7 Ps) positively so as to aim for position A.

(b) However, external factors (political, economic, sociological, technological and competition) might act positively or negatively, in the latter case dragging us down to position C.

(c) Nevertheless, the more information we have about the so called uncontrollable external factors, the more we can anticipate, ride or avoid the blows.

3.3 Basic control concepts are often depicted diagrammatically as follows.

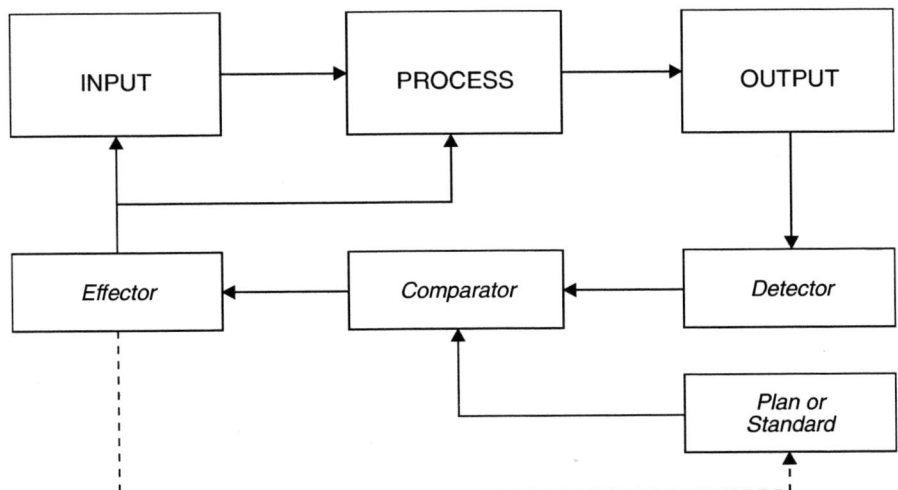

In marketing's case, the **input** could be **money and people**, the **process** could be **implementation of the marketing mix** and the **output** could be **profitable sales**. However, in the above diagram there is very little control. The process could go wrong ie the marketing mix could fail to deliver sufficient sales to be profitable. Finally we need a warning device. In the above diagram companies often reduce input (ie cut costs) in the event of decreased output which may not be the best (most productive) reaction.

3.4 The operation of a control system involves the activities below.

Control activity	Description
Target setting	To have a control system, there has to be a plan, standard, budget, target or guideline towards which the system as a whole should be aiming.
Measuring and feedback	A sensor or detector is the device by which data is collected and measured, or the person who does the collection and measuring.
Comparing performance with standards	A comparator is the person or means (eg computer) by which the actual results of the system are measured against the pre-determined plans or standards.
An effector initiates control action	In a production department, an effector may be a component in some automatic equipment which regulates the functioning of the equipment (for example a thermostat). An effector may also be a manager's instruction and a subordinate's action.
Feedback	In a business organisation, it is **information** produced from within the organisation (for example management control reports) with the purpose of helping management and other employees with control decisions.
Single loop feedback	Results in the system's behaviour being altered to meet the plan.
Double loop feedback	Results in changes to the plan itself. If a system is to react to a changing environment, which it must do to survive, then double loop feedback is essential.
Feedforward	This is based on comparing original targets or actual results with a current forecast of future results. Control action is taken in advance.

BPP PUBLISHING

3.5 EXAMPLES

Feedback	Standards	Control actions
Sales figures	Against budget plus or minus	Stimulate/dampen down demand
Complaints	Number, frequency, seriousness	Corrective action
Competitors	Relative to us	Attack/defence strategies
Market size changes	Market share	Marketing mix manipulation
Costs/profitability	Ratios	Cost cutting exercises
Corporate image	Attribute measures	Internal/external communications
Environmental factors	Variances from norm	Invoke strategic alternatives

Action Programme 1

Sally Keene works for a large department store, as a manager.

(a) At the beginning of each year she is given a yearly plan, subdivided into twelve months. This is based on the previous year's performance and some allowance is made for anticipated economic conditions. Every three months she sends her views as to the next quarter to senior management, who give her a new plan in the light of changing conditions.

(b) She monitors sales revenue per square foot, and sales per employee. Employees who do not meet the necessary sales targets are at first counselled and then if performance does not improve they are dismissed. Sally is not unreasonable. She sets what she believes are realistic targets.

(c) She believes there is a good team spirit in the sales force, however, and that employees, whose commission is partly based on the sales revenue earned by the store as a whole, discourage slackers in their ranks.

What kind of control, control system or control information can you identify in the three cases above?

4 STRATEGIC CONTROL

4.1 The **control measures and analytical techniques** that might be relevant for control at a strategic level are as follows.

Type of analysis	Used to control
1 *Financial analysis*	
Ratio analysis	Elements of profitability
Variance analysis	Costs or revenue
Cash budgeting	Cash flow
Capital budgeting and Capital expenditure audit	Investment
2 *Market/sales analysis*	
Demand analysis	Competitive standing
Market share or penetration	
Sales targets	Sales effectiveness
Sales budget	Efficiency in use of resources for selling
3 *Physical resource analysis*	
Capacity fill	Plant utilisation
Yield	Materials utilisation
Product inspection	Quality

Type of analysis	*Used to control*
4 *Human resources analysis*	
Work measurement	Productivity
Output measurement	
Labour turnover	Workforce stability
5 *Analysis of systems*	
Management by objectives	Implementation of strategy
Network analysis	Resource planning and scheduling

4.2 Features of basic strategic control systems

Control must influence the behaviour of individuals and groups towards the implementation of the corporate strategy and towards progressive change.

(a) **Distinguish between control at different levels** in the management hierarchy (strategic, tactical, operational). Is the control measure intended to have an immediate impact (for example 'firefighting' at an operational control or budgetary level) or will it take time for the measure to have a tangible effect?

    (i) Define **strategic objectives** (ie the organisation's eventual objectives in terms of competitive strategy).

    (ii) Identify **strategic milestones** on the way to achieving strategic objectives. These could be the specific tasks by which strategic objectives are achieved. These are short-term steps along the way to long-term goals.

    (iii) The **key assumptions** on which the strategy is based must also be monitored. A strategy drawn up from a position of limited competition (eg a protected national market) would have to be changed if the market was opened to foreign companies.

(b) **Individual managers** should be identified as having the responsibility for certain matters, and authority to take control measures.

(c) The **key factors for control** should be identified. Managers responsible for taking control action must be informed about what the key factors are, and why they are critical.

(d) **Control reporting should be timed sensibly.** Depending on the level of control control reports should vary from occasional to regular and frequent.

(e) **Apply targets and standards**

    • Targets for market share, in absolute and relative terms, compared with competitors
    • Targets for relative product quality
    • Timetables for strategic action programmes
    • Targets for costs relative to the competitors' costs

(f) Control reports should only contain **relevant information** for the manager receiving the report.

(g) **Selective reporting.** Selective reporting means identifying **key points for control**.

    (i) The **position of each product** in the product-market matrix or in its life cycle will suggest how much close watching the product needs.

    (ii) A product which performs **inconsistently** might need close watching and control.

    (iii) **Information and control reporting costs money.**

(iv) The **key item might be 'qualitative'**. For example within the marketing function it might be considered vitally important that there should be a rapid and significant improvement in employee commitment and enthusiasm. Control reporting at the corporate planning level should therefore emphasise these points, and shift back to other matters when appropriate.

4.3 EXAMPLE

Date: March 2002

Source: January 1998 planning document

Mission: Market share

1. *Long term targets, to be achieved by 2007*
   (a) X% value of market share
   (b) Y% profitability over the decade

   Status: March 2002. Market share lower than anticipated, owing to unexpected competition. Profits lower than expected because of loss of scale economies and increased marketing costs.

   Outlook. Profit will be improved thanks to cost-cutting measures. Market share target might be missed.

2. *Critical assumptions*
   The home market is growing only slowly, and is becoming mature. There are limited opportunities for segmentation.
   Overseas markets are likely to expand by Z% as some are reducing tariffs.

   Status March 2002. The home market has matured more quickly than expected. Overseas market growth can compensate for this.

3. *Critical success factors*
   - Exports increased by W%
   - Secure distribution arrangements

4. *Key tasks*
   - Launch of budget products for overseas markets
   - Setting up of a computerised distribution system to enhance speedy response to demand and to cut warehousing costs
   - Get ISO 9000 certification

4.4 Note the use of **critical success factors**. We discussed them briefly in the context of resource planning but they are also relevant to control.

4.5 **Day and Wensley** relate these to **advantages** and **outcomes** as follows.

(a) **Sources of advantage**

- Superior skills
- Superior resources

(b) **Positional advantages**

- Superior customer value
- Lower relative costs

(c) **Performance outcomes**

- Customer satisfaction
- Customer loyalty
- Higher market share
- Higher profits

Marketing at Work

Freund relates CSFs with strategies and performance indicators for a life insurance company as follows.

CSF	Strategies	Performance indicators
Able to achieve critical mass volumes via existing brokers/agents.	Develop closer ties with agents. Telemarket to brokers. Adjust agents' compensation.	Number of policies in force. Number of new policies written. Percentage of business with existing brokers.
Able to introduce new pro ducts within six months of industry leaders.	Underwrite strategic joint ventures.	Time taken to introduce. Percentage out within six months. Percentage of underwriters having extra certification.
Be able to manage product and product lines, profitably.	Segment investment portfolio. Improve cost accounting. Closely manage loss rate.	Return on portfolio segments. Actual product cost revenue versus budget. Loss ratio relative to competitors.

4.6 CSFs which cover both financial and non-financial criteria are outlined below.

Sphere of activity	Critical factors
Marketing	Sales volume
	Market share
	Gross margins
Production	Capacity utilisation
	Quality standards
Logistics	Capacity utilisation
	Level of service

4.7 **CSFs which relate to specific elements of the marketing mix**

Activity	CSF
New product development	Trial rate
	Repurchase rate
Sales programmes	Contribution by region, salesperson
	Controllable margin as percentage of sales
	Number of new accounts
	Travel costs
Advertising programmes	Awareness levels
	Attribute ratings
	Cost levels
Pricing programmes	Price relative to industry average
	Price elasticity of demand
Distribution programmes	Number of distributors carrying the product

The trade off between short term and long term for control action

4.8 It is often the case that in order to rectify short-term results, control action will be at the expense of long-term targets. Similarly, controls over longer-term achievements might call for short-term sacrifices.

4.9 **Examples of the reasons for S/L trade-offs** are as follows.

(a) **Short-term losses.** A company has a target of building up its market share for a new product to 30% within four years. It has decided to do this with a low price market penetration strategy. As a short-term target, it wants the product to earn a small profit (£100,000) in the current year. Actual results after three months of the year indicate that the market share has already built up to 18%, but that the product will make a £50,000 loss in the year.

The S/L trade off involves a decision about what to do about short-term profitability (raise prices? cut back on advertising? reduce the sales force?) without sacrificing altogether the long-term market share target.

(b) **Capital expenditure.** K Bhattacharya has written as follows.

> 'This is one of the most vulnerable areas for detrimental S/L trade-offs. The horizon for returns is most certainly more than a year off, yet costs associated with the implementation of the programme can easily reduce short-term profits. Postponements can almost always release capital and manpower resources needed to generate immediate operating profit.'

(c) **Research and development.** This is another area where short-term profitability is boosted, by cutting back on R & D expenditure at the expense of the longer-term need to continue to develop new products.

(d) **Behaviour.** Very often managers are under pressure to produce good short-term results (for example immediate profitability) in order to get their next promotion.

4.10 **Ensuring that the S/L trade off is properly judged and well balanced**

(a) Managers should **recognise** whether or not S/L trade-offs in control action could be a serious problem.

(b) **Managers should be aware** that S/L trade-offs take place in practice.

(c) Controls should exist to prevent or minimise the possibility that short-term controls can be taken which damage long-term targets.

(d) Senior management must be given **adequate control information** for long-term as well as short-term consequences.

(e) The planning and review system should **motivate** managers to keep long-term goals in view.

(f) **Short-term goals should be realistic.** Very often, the pressure on managers to sacrifice long-term interests for short-term results is caused by the imposition of stringent and unrealistic short-term targets on those managers in the first place.

(g) **Performance measures should reflect both long-term and short-term targets.** There might be, say, quarterly performance reviews on the achievement of strategic goals.

Marketing at Work

From *The Observer*, 29 April 2001

ONdigital is a UK TV company offering digital TV via the terrestrial TV network. As a digital TV service, it competes with satellite BSkyB and cable TV. Marketing activities are linked in with the fundamental financial objectives of the business.

Gerry Murphy, chief executive of Carlton Communications announced a restructuring of ONdigital. The decision was taken to satisfy shareholders, who had always been sceptical about Carlton and Granada's ambition to create a digital channel to rival BSkyB.

Costs of £20 million a year will be saved by integrating the management of the digital and conventional ITV channels under Stuart Prebble, who is currently ONdigital's chief executive.

Currently ONdigital takes around £220 from every customer it signs up, but it costs the company £200 or so to give – or lend, as it prefers to say – them a set-up box to receive the signal, advertising, promotion and programming. So Carlton and Granada have to pump in £150m a year to keep the service going.

Although the figures for subscribers, at just under 1.1 million, were better than the City had feared, ONdigital is not now expecting to break even until 2004, a couple of years later than it had originally hoped.

The break-even target requires 1.7 million subscribers spending at least £300 apiece. Yet even Carlton admits that the easy targets have already been converted to digital and that it will take a lot to persuade the rest of us that it is worth paying up for a diet of repeats, soaps and special-interest services.

5   BENCHMARKING AND THE MARKET ENVIRONMENT

> **Key Concept**
>
> **Benchmark:** an external target of performance against which a firm measures its activities.

5.1   **Benchmarks** can be set against say the leading competitor on a variety of key performance indicators, as an objective form of control. In this case, marketing research and competitor intelligence would be needed to establish benchmarks and to monitor progress.

5.2   The practice of benchmarking is becoming increasingly popular. There are two principal approaches.

(a)   **Process benchmarking**, where data is exchanged between companies with similar administrative and manufacturing processes. For example, one of the factors affecting aircraft turnaround away from the home is the availability of spare parts required for routine maintenance. This process is very similar to the provision of field maintenance for office systems such as photocopiers and computers.

(b)   **Competitor benchmarking** focuses on the performance and relative strengths of direct competitors using information from customer and supplier interviews and published data from any source available. A firm tries to be as good as its competitors.

Monitoring competitor performance

5.3   When an organisation operates in a competitive environment, it should try to obtain information about the financial performance of competitors, to make a comparison with the organisation's own results. It might not be possible to obtain reliable competitor information, but if the competitor is a public company it will publish an annual report and accounts.

5.4   **Financial information which might be obtainable about a competitor.**

(a)   Total profits, sales and capital employed.

(b)   ROCE, profit/sales ratio, cost/sales ratios and asset turnover ratios.

(c)   The increase in profits and sales over the course of the past twelve months (and prospects for the future, which will probably be mentioned in the chairman's statement in the report and accounts).

(d)   Sales and profits in each major business segment that the competitor operates in.

(e)   Dividend per share and earnings per share.

(f)   Gearing and interest rates on debt.

(g)   Share price, and P/E ratio (stock exchange information).

5.5   Advantages of benchmarking

(a)   The comparisons are carried out by the managers who have to live with any changes implemented as a result of the exercise.

(b)   Benchmarking focuses on improvement in key areas and sets targets which are challenging but 'achievable'. What is really achievable can be discovered by examining what others have achieved: managers are thus able to accept that they are not being asked to perform miracles.

5.6   Disadvantages of benchmarking

(a)   Benchmarking is reactive; rather than imitating a competitor, another competitive strategy may be more focused.

(b)   It is not focused on the customer. The firm should set itself targets that customers value.

Market share performance

5.7   When a market manager is given responsibility for a product or a market segment, the product or market segment will be a profit centre, and measures of performance for the centre will include profits and cost variances etc. However, another useful measure of performance would be the **market share** obtained by the organisation's product in the market. A market share performance report should draw attention to the following.

(a)   The link between **cost and profit** and market performance in both the short term and the long term.

(b)   The performance of the **product or market segment** in the context of the product life cycle.

(c)   Whether or not the product is gaining or losing ground, as its market share goes up or down.

Changes in market share have to be considered against the change in the **market as a whole**, since the product might be increasing its share simply when the market is declining, but the competition is losing sales even more quickly. (The reverse may also be true. The market could be expanding, and a declining market share might not represent a decline in absolute sales volume, but a failure to grab more of the growing market.)

Monitoring customers

5.8   In some industrial markets or reseller markets, a producer might sell to a small number of key customers. The performance of these customers would therefore be of some importance to the producer: if the customer prospers, he will probably buy more and if he does badly, he will probably buy less. It may also be worthwhile monitoring the level of profitability of selling to the customer. **Key customer analysis** calls for six main areas of investigation.

(a)   **Key customer identity**

- Name of each key customer
- Location
- Status in market
- Products they make and sell
- Size of firm (capital employed, turnover, number of employees)

(b) **Customer history**

- First purchase date
- Who makes the buying decision in the customer's organisation?
- What is the average order size, by product?
- What is the regularity/ periodicity of the order, by product?
- What is the trend in size of orders?
- What is the motive in purchasing?
- What does the customer know about the firm's and competitors' products?
- On what basis does the customer reorder?
- Were there any lost or cancelled orders? For what reason?

(c) **Relationship of customer to product**

- Are the products purchased to be resold? If not, why are they bought?
- Do the products form part of the customer's service/product?

(d) **Relationship of customer to potential market**

- What is the size of the customer in relation to the total end-market?
- Is the customer likely to expand, or not? Diversify? Integrate?

(e) **Customer attitudes and behaviour**

- What interpersonal factors exist which could affecting selling processes?
- Does the customer also buy competitors' products?
- To what extent may purchases be postponed?
- What emotional factors exist in buying decisions?

(f) **The financial performance of the customer**

How successful is the customer in his own markets? Similar analysis can be carried out as with competitors.

(g) **The profitability of selling to the customer**

6 TARGETS, BUDGETS AND RATIOS

6.1 In terms of strategic marketing management, **planned** results often comprise:

(a) Targets for the overall **financial objective**, for each year over the planning period, and other financial strategy objectives such as productivity targets.

(b) Subsidiary **financial targets**

(c) Financial targets in the annual budget (including the sales budget and marketing expenditures budget)

(d) Product-market strategy targets

(e) Targets for each element of the **marketing mix**

Setting targets

6.2 **The organisation's objectives provide the basis for setting targets and standards.** Each manager's targets will be directed towards achieving the company objectives. Targets or standards:

(a) Tell managers what they are **required to accomplish**, given the authority to make appropriate decisions

(b) Indicate to managers how **well their actual results** measure up against their targets, so that control action can be taken where it is needed

6.3 It follows that in setting standards for performance, **it is important to distinguish between controllable or manageable variables and uncontrollable ones.** Any matters which cannot be controlled by an individual manager should be excluded from their standards for performance.

Budgets as a feedforward control device

> ### Key Concept
>
> A **budget** is a consolidated statement of the resources required to achieve objectives or to implement planned activities. It is a planning and control tool relevant to all aspects of management activities.

6.4 Purposes of a budget

(a) **Co-ordinates** the activities of all the different departments of an organisation; in addition, through participation by employees in preparing a budget, it may be possible to motivate them to raise their targets and standards and to achieve better results.

(b) **Communicates** the policies and targets to every manager in the organisation responsible for carrying out a part of that plan.

(c) **Control** by having a plan against which actual results can be progressively compared.

Preparing budgets

6.5 Procedures for preparing the budget are contained in the **budget manual**, which indicates:

- People responsible for preparing budgets
- The order in which they must be prepared
- Deadlines for preparation
- Standard forms

6.6 The preparation and administration of budgets is usually the responsibility of a **budget committee.** Every part of the organisation should be represented on the committee.

6.7 The preparation of a budget may take weeks or months, and the budget committee may meet several times before the master budget is finally agreed. Functional budgets and cost centre budgets prepared in draft may need to be amended many times over as a consequence of discussions between departments, changes in market conditions, reversals of decisions by management, etc during the course of budget preparation.

The budget period

6.8 A budget does not necessarily have to be restricted to a one year planning horizon. The factors which should influence the **budget period** are as follows.

(a) **Lead times.** A plan decided upon now might need a **considerable time** to be put into operation. Many companies expect growth in market share to take a number of years.

(b) **In the short-term some resources are fixed.** The fixed nature of these resources, and the length of time which must elapse before they become variable, might therefore determine the planning horizon for budgeting.

(c) All budgets involve some element of **forecasting and even guesswork,** since future events cannot be quantified with accuracy.

(d) Since **unforeseen events** cannot be planned for, it would be a waste of time to plan in detail too far ahead.

(e) Most budgets are prepared over a one-year period to enable managers to plan and control **financial results for the purposes of the annual accounts.**

6.9 **The principal budget factor**

The first task in budgeting is to identify the principal (key, limiting) budget factor. This is the factor which puts constraints on growth. The principal budget factor could be:

(a) Normally, sales demand, ie a company is restricted from making and selling more of its products because there would be no sales demand for the increased output at a price which would be acceptable/profitable to the company.

(b) Resources machine capacity, distribution and selling resources, the availability of key raw materials or the availability of cash etc.

(c) Once this factor is defined then the rest of the budget can be prepared.

Action Programme 2

What do you think is the crucial difference between the principal budget factors of an organisation producing confectionery and a non-profit orientated organisation such as a hospital?

6.10 **Budgets and forecasts**

(a) A **forecast is an estimate of what might** happen in the future.

(b) In contrast, a **budget is a plan of what the organisation would like** to happen, and what it has set as a target, although it should be realistic and so it will be based to some extent on the forecasts prepared.

(c) However, in formulating a budget, **management will be trying to establish some control over the conditions** that will apply in the future. (For example in setting a sales budget, management must decide on the prices to be charged and the advertising expenditure budget, even though they might have no control **over other** market factors.)

(i) Management might be able to take **control action** to bring forecasts back into line **with the budget.**

(ii) Alternatively, management will have to accept that the budget will not be achieved, or it will be exceeded, depending on what the current forecasts include.

6.11 Budgets perform a dual role.

(a) They **incorporate forecasting** and planning information.

(b) They **incorporate control measures,** in that they plan how resources are to be used to achieve the targets, and they can be flexed for corrective action.

6.12 **Problems in constructing budgets**

(a) Difficulties in identifying **principal budget factors**

- Sales demand may not be known
- Resources may not be known

(b) **Unpredictability** in economic conditions or prices of inputs

(c) Because of **inflation**, it might be difficult to estimate future price levels for materials, expenses, wages and salaries.

(d) **Managers might be reluctant to budget accurately**.

(i) **Slack.** They may overstate their expected expenditure, so that by having a budget which is larger than necessary, they will be unlikely to overspend the budget allowance. (They will then not be held accountable in control reports for excess spending).

(ii) They may **compete** with other departments for the available resources, by trying to expand their budgeted expenditure. Budget planning might well intensify inter-departmental rivalry and the problems of 'empire building'.

(e) **Inter departmental rivalries** might ruin the efforts towards co-ordination in a budget.

(f) Employees might resist budget plans either because the plans are not properly communicated to them, or because they feel that the budget puts them 'under pressure' from senior managers to achieve better results.

Exam Tip

You will have come across budgets and budgeting in your earlier studies or work experience. It is important to recognise that CIM examiners are increasingly requiring that Diploma students demonstrate their appreciation of financial aspects and their implications for both marketing and business. You must be prepared to support plans with budgets both in the context of mini-cases and major case study exercises. These should:

- Indicate your awareness of the process of budgeting and its significance
- Identify key headings and inclusions.

6.13 **Sales budget**

(a) **A preliminary sales estimate**

- A study of normal business growth
- A forecast of general business conditions
- A knowledge of potential markets for each product
- The practical judgement of sales and management staff
- A realisation of the effect on sales of basic changes in company policy

(b) The **adjustment of the above preliminary sales estimate**

- Seasonal nature of the business
- The viewpoint of optimum selling prices
- Overall production or purchasing capacity
- Viewpoint of securing even manufacturing loads
- Overall selling expenses and net profits
- The financial capacity of the business

(c) The adjusted anticipated sales by value and quantity contained in the sales budget should then be classified by commodities, departments, customers, salesmen,

countries, terms of sale, methods of sale, methods of delivery and urgency of delivery (rush or normal).

6.14 The expense budgets related to marketing

(a) *Selling expenses budget*
- Salaries and commission
- Materials, literature, samples
- Travelling (car cost, petrol, insurance) and entertaining
- Staff recruitment and selection and training
- Telephones and telegrams, postage
- After sales service
- Royalties/patents
- Office rent and rates, lighting, heating etc.
- Office equipment
- Credit costs, bad debts etc

(b) *Advertising budget*
- Trade journal - space
- Prestige media - space
- PR space (costs of releases, entertainment etc)
- Blocks and artwork
- Advertising agents commission
- Staff salaries, office costs, etc
- Posters
- Cinema
- TV
- Signs

(c) *Sales promotion budget*
- Exhibitions: space, equipment, staff, transport, hotels, bar etc
- Literature: leaflets, catalogues
- Samples/working models
- Point of sale display, window or showroom displays
- Special offers
- Direct mail shots - enclosure, postage, design costs

(d) *Research and development budget*
- Market research - design and development and analysis costs
- Packaging and product research - departmental costs, materials, equipment
- Pure research - departmental costs materials, equipment
- Sales analysis and research
- Economic surveys
- Product planning
- Patents

(e) *Distribution budget*
- Warehouse/deposits - rent, rates, lighting, heating
- Transport - capital costs
- Fuel - running costs
- Warehouse/depot and transport staff wages
- Packing (as opposed to packaging)

A note on marketing communication

6.15 The theory behind setting an advertising budget is the theory of diminishing returns, ie for every extra £1 of advertising spent, the company will earn an extra £x of profit. Further expenditure on advertising is justified until the marginal return £x diminishes to the point where £x < £1. Unfortunately, the marginal return from additional advertising cannot be measured easily in practice for the following reasons.

(a) Advertising is only one aspect of the overall marketing mix, and only one element of the promotions mix.

(b) Advertising has some long-term effect, which goes beyond the limits of a measurable accounting period.

(c) Where the advertising budget is fixed as a percentage of sales, advertising costs tend to follow sales levels and not vice versa.

6.16 **Methods of setting the marketing budget**

Method	Comment
Competitive parity	Fixing promotional expenditure in relation to the expenditure incurred by competitors. (This is unsatisfactory because it presupposes that the competitor's decision must be a good one.)
The task method (or objective and task method)	The marketing task for the organisation is set and a promotional budget is prepared which will help to ensure that this objective is achieved. A problem occurs if the objective is achieved only by paying out more on promotion than the extra profits obtained would justify.
Communication stage models	These are based on the idea that the link between promotion and sales cannot be measured directly, but can be measured by means of intermediate stages (for example increase in awareness, comprehension, and then intention to buy).
All you can afford	Crude and unscientific, but commonly used. The firm simply takes a view on what it thinks it can afford to spend on promotion given that it would like to spend as much as it can.
Investment	The advertising and promotions budget can thus be designed around the amount felt necessary to maintain a certain brand value.
Rule-of-thumb, non-scientific methods	These include the percentage of sales, profits etc.

Variance analysis

6.17 It is fine to have a set of budgets and standards, but how do you apply them in practice? The use of budgets as a control device is often achieved through **variance analysis**. Quite complex variance analysis systems are applied to production costs: these need not concern us here, but a brief description of the technique might help, as it is relevant to marketing costs.

6.18 **EXAMPLE**

Assume that, in a month, **budgeted** sales revenue amount to £1m. Actual sales amount to £960,000. The total **sales variance** is thus £40,000 (ie £1m – £960,000). It is adverse as we have sold less than planned. So far so good. But with a little bit more information we can find out a lot more.

6.19 Let us assume that, in our original budget, the £1m sales revenue was to result from selling 100,000 units at £10 each. However the cost of a key component rose suddenly, so we had to increase the selling price to £12 a unit. We sold only 80,000 units: total sales revenue amounted to £960,000. There is a total negative sales variance of £40,000 as actual sales are less than we anticipated (£1,000,000). This variance of £40,000 can be analysed into two elements.

(a) **Price variance.** We put up the prices to receive extra revenue from the actual sales

$(£12 - £10) \times 80,000 = £160,000$, a positive or **favourable** price variance

(b) **Volume variance.** We sold fewer, so in volume terms, at the budgeted/standard price of £10 we have a negative or **adverse** volume variance of $(100,000 - 80,000) \times £10$ or £200,000.

(c)

	£
Budgeted sales revenue	1,000,000
Price variance	160,000
Volume variance	(200,000)
Actual sales revenue	£960,000

6.20 Other applications of sales variances include the **sales mix variance**. A firm might sell more of one product in a range and less of another than you anticipated, or there might have been some difference in prices. Variances can also be used in analysing other marketing costs, such as distribution expenditure.

Tolerance limits for variances at planning level

6.21 No corporate plan has the detail or 'accuracy' that a budget has. Consequently, the tolerance limits giving 'early warning' or deviations from the plan should be wider. For example if tolerance limits in budgetary control are variance ± 5% from standard, then corporate planning tolerance limits might be set at ± 10% or more from targets.

6.22 Whatever the tolerance limits are, the reporting of results which go outside (either favourably or adversely) the limits must be prompt. If sales have dropped well below target, the reasons must be established quickly and possible solutions thought about. For example if a company's products unexpectedly gain second highest market share, the questions that should be asked are as follows.

- How did it happen?
- Has profit suffered?
- Can second place be made secure, and if so, how?
- Can the market leader be toppled? (And if so, is this profitable?)

Ratio analysis

6.23 We covered ratio analysis in the chapter on finance, but we can broaden it when discussing control. A ratio takes two variables (eg profit/sales) and compares them with other measures for the same variable.

6.24 **Corporate ratios**

Chapter 9 discussed ROCE and P/E ratios and profitability. Marketing strategies **contribute** towards these, but they are at **too high a level of control** to be useful as control measures over marketing activities in particular.

(a) **Profitability.** Marketing personnel have little direct control over the cost structure of the company, and so while they do contribute to profitability, they cannot control it.

(b) **ROCE,** as conventionally measured, is a control measure for the company as a whole.

6.25 **Marketing relevant ratios** are a **mix of financial ratios and non-financial ratios.** For example:

(a) **Financial ratio only**

(i) Sales revenue or marketing expenditure can be compared: **over time,** against **budget** or against **competition.**

	1999	2000
Revenue	£10m	£15m

2000/1999 gives an increase of 1.5:1.

(ii) There may be relationships between different variables. For example

	1999	2000
Revenue	£10m	£15m
Bad debts	0.5m	1.2m
Bad debts/revenue	1:20 or 5%	2:25 or 8%

Comparing these over time suggests that while **income has increased,** the **quality of sales** (in terms of **creditworthiness**) has fallen, as bad debts are 8% of revenue rather than 5%. Perhaps the sales force has been too generous.

(b) **A mixture of financial ratios and non-financial data**

	1999	2000
Revenue	£10m	£15m
Sales personnel	50	60

Revenue has increased by 50% whereas the sales force has increased by 20%.

	1999	2000
Revenue per sales employee	£0.2m	£0.25m

The sales force is more productive in 2000 then 1999.

(c) **Non-financial data only**

This can refer to almost any aspect of a company's operations. We are concerned with marketing.

	1999	2000
Sales orders	250	300
Sales leads	1,000	1,025
Sales personnel	50	60

In 1999, 25% of leads turned into orders, whereas in 2000 this has increased to 29%, so the sales force is more effective. The number of orders by sales person has stayed the same.

6.26 The next section identifies some ways you can apply performance measures in the marketing mix.

7 MARKETING MIX EFFECTIVENESS

7.1 Marketing managers are responsible for monitoring their progress towards the agreed targets and objectives. To do this it is necessary to evaluate the marketing mix effectiveness. This section will consider ways of controlling the effectiveness of four of the mix elements.

- Personal selling

- Advertising and sales promotions
- Pricing
- Channels of distribution

Personal selling

7.2 The effectiveness of personal selling can be measured for:

- The sales force as a whole
- Each group of the sales force (eg each regional sales team)
- Each individual salesperson

If there are telephone sales staff, their performance should be measured separately from the 'travelling' sales staff.

7.3 Measures of performance would compare actual results against a target or standard.

- Sales, in total, by customer, and by product
- Contribution, in total, by customer and by product
- Selling expenses (budget versus actual) in relation to sales
- Customer call frequency
- Average sales value per call
- Average contribution per call
- Average cost per call
- Average trade discount
- Number of new customers obtained
- Percentage increase in sales compared with previous period
- Average number of repeat calls per sale
- Average mileage travelled per £1 sales

7.4 It is not an easy task to decide what the standards should be. It is important not to assume that the 'efficient' sales person who makes ten calls a day is doing a better job than the colleague who makes fewer calls but wins more orders.

7.5 There can be a big difference between (a) net sales (ie sales after returns and discounts) and (b) profits or contribution. The costs of selling and distribution can be a very large proportion of an organisation's total costs, and so the performance of a sales force should be based on productivity and profitability, rather than sales alone.

The effectiveness of advertising

7.6 **Performance measures for advertising**

(a) **Exposure.** Exposure can be measured in terms of frequency (eg the number of times a TV advertisement is screened) and the number of potential customers reached. One TV advertisement might reach two million people; by repeating the advertisement, the intention would be to reach people who missed the advertisement previously, but also to reinforce the message through repetition to people who have seen it before.

(b) **Awareness.** Awareness of the existence of a product, or awareness of certain particular features of a product. Awareness could be measured by recall tests or recognition tests.

(c) **Sales** (volume and/or revenue). Advertising is often intended to increase sales, the effect of advertising on sales is not easy to measure. Why?

(i)   Advertising is only one part of a marketing mix. Other factors influencing sales might be price changes, whether intermediaries have stocked enough of the products to meet an increase in demand, and competitors' actions.

(ii)   Advertising might succeed in **maintaining** a firm's existing market share, without actually increasing sales.

(d) **Profits**. The difficulties of measuring the effect of an advertising campaign on profits are therefore the same as those described in (c) above. Breakeven analysis might be used to calculate the volume of extra sales required to cover the (fixed) costs of the advertising. In monitoring the effects of a campaign, management might be able to judge whether this minimum increase in sales has or has not, in all probability, been achieved. However, advertising might be necessary to 'build' a brand or for management to 'invest' in it.

(e) **Attitudes**. The aim of a campaign might be expressed in terms of 'x% of customers should show a preference for Product A over rival products'.

(f) **Enquiries**. Advertising might be aimed at generating extra enquiries from potential customers. Where possible, enquiries should be traced to the advertisement. For example, a customer reply coupon in a magazine advertisement should be printed with an identification number or label, identifying the magazine and date of its issue.

7.7   It is difficult to measure the **success of an advertising** campaign, although volume of sales may be a short-term guide.

(a) A campaign to launch a new product, however, may have to be judged over a longer period of time (ie to see how well the product establishes itself in the market).

(b) Advertising's main purpose in the communication mix is to create **awareness** and **interest**.

(c) The effectiveness of advertising is therefore usually measured by marketing researchers in terms of **customer attitudes** or **psychological response**. Most of the money is spent by agencies on **pre-testing** the given advertisement or campaign before launching it into national circulation. Relatively less tends to be spent on **post-testing** the effect of given advertisements and campaigns.

Post-testing involves finding out how well people can **recall** an advertisement and the product it advertises, and whether (on the basis of a sample of respondents) attitudes to the product have changed since the advertising campaign.

Marketing at Work

New financial service brands including Virgin Direct and Goldfish failed to convert high levels of awareness into new business.

'The brands, supported by estimated ad budgets of about £5m and £10m respectively and featuring Richard Branson and Billy Connolly, were ever-present on TV at the end of 1996, with Goldfish securing 30 per cent brand awareness for its credit card and Virgin 13 per cent for its products. But neither converted that awareness into new business, according to exclusive research on new financial service and loyalty schemes conducted by the RSL Strategic Initiatives Monitor.

Its survey showed that less high-profile brands such as MBNA's credit card, which had an awareness of only ten per cent, achieved a holding of two per cent - outstripping its higher spending rivals.

Significantly the reasons for changing suggest that credit card holders are looking for immediate benefits rather than the promise of rebates in the future from their cards. Over a third of new cardholders mention low APR (annual percentage rate - broadly, interest rate) and a quarter 'no annual fee' as reasons for taking new cards. In contrast only six per cent were attracted by points or tokens offered, while five per cent claim to have switched because they banked with the card issuer.

Justifying advertising

7.8 It would seem sensible too, to try to consider the effectiveness of advertising in terms of **cost, sales and profit**, but only if the aim of an advertising campaign was directed towards boosting sales. If there is a noticeable increase in sales volume as a result of an advertising campaign, it should be possible to estimate the extent to which advertising might have been responsible for the extra sales and contribution, and the extra net profit per £1 of advertising could be measured.

7.9 Marketers face continual problems in justifying advertising expenditure (according to *Marketing Business*, July/August 1996).

> 'Marketers continue to face an uphill struggle to win the confidence of finance directors and main boards, new research by the Institute of Practitioners in Advertising reveals.
>
> The IPA survey indicates that from board representation through budget setting processes to effectiveness measurement, marketing and advertising comes a poor second or third to other disciplines in finance directors' eyes.
>
> While 58% of finance directors believe marketing and advertising is a long-term investment it is not seen to be as necessary as training, IT, human resources, and R&D, all of which get thumbs-up ratings of 70 per cent or more.
>
> Finance directors' scepticism about advertising's contribution is underlined by their attitudes towards effectiveness. While over two thirds try to measure advertising effectiveness, just 34 per cent try measuring the effectiveness of R&D and 28 per cent bother judging human resources' contribution.'

Marketing at Work

The UK advertising industry has introduced a Marketing Effectiveness Awards, based on key criteria.

We are all aware of ads which are **not** effective.

The effectiveness of sales promotions

7.10 There is often a direct link between below-the-line advertising (sales promotions) and short-term sales volume.

    (a) The **consumer sales response** to the following is readily measurable.

- Price reductions as sales promotions (for example introductory offers)
- Coupon 'money-off' offers
- Free sendaway gifts
- On-pack free gift offers
- Combination pack offers

    (b) It might also be possible to measure the link between sales and promotions for industrial goods, for example special discounts, orders taken at trade fairs or exhibitions and the response to trade-in allowances.

    (c) However, there are other promotions where the effect on sales volume is **indirect** and not readily measurable, for example sponsorship, free samples, catalogues, point-of-sale material and inducements.

    (d) Promotions may go hand in hand with a direct advertising campaign, especially in the case of consumer products, and so the effectiveness of the advertising and the sales promotions should then be considered together.

7.11 A manufacturer can try to control sales promotion costs by:

(a) Setting a **time limit** to the campaign (for example money off coupons, free gift offers etc must be used before a specified date).

(b) **Restricting the campaign** to certain areas or outlets.

(c) Restricting the campaign to **specific goods** (for example to only three or four goods in the manufacturer's product range, or only to products which are specially labelled with the offer).

Pricing

7.12 Aspects to pricing

(a) **Discount policy should be directed** towards: encouraging a greater volume of sales, and/or obtaining the financial benefits of earlier payments from customers, which ought to exceed the costs of the discounts allowed.

(b) Sales prices are set with a view to the total **sales volume** they should attract.

   (i) **New product pricing policy** might be to set high 'skimming' prices or low 'penetration' prices.

   (1) For skimming prices, whether they have been too high, because the market has grown faster than anticipated, leaving the organisation with a low market share because of its high prices.

   (2) For penetration prices, whether the price level has succeeded in helping the market to grow quickly and the organisation to grab its target share of the market.

   (ii) Decisions to raise prices or lower prices will be based on assumptions about the **elasticity of demand**. Did actual increases or decreases in demand exceed or fall short of expectation?

(c) An aspect of **product-market strategy** and positioning is the mixture of product quality and price. An organisation might opt for a **high price and high quality** strategy, or **a low price and average quality** strategy etc. Actual price performance can be judged:

   (i) By comparing the organisation's prices with those of competitors, to establish whether prices were comparatively low, average or high, as planned

   (ii) By judging whether the mix of product quality and price appears to have been effective

---

Marketing at Work

Some of the most familiar ways to market consumer goods are proving to be costly failures (extracts from *The Economist,* 14 March 1998).

Recent research has begun to tell the makers of consumer goods which types of marketing actually work. Marketing is not about to become a science, but it will henceforth be easier to tell one half of the marketing budget from the other.

One surprise concerns price cuts. Packaged-goods firms spend some $70 billion a year on various promotions. Among marketing men, however, price cuts remained as popular as ever. It is an article of faith that they both reward loyal customers and woo new ones. Now even this is in question.

(a) For a start, consumers say they prefer incentives other than price.

(b)   Price cuts also appear to have little lasting effect on sales volumes. In an unpublished study, a team at Purdue University led by Doug Bowman spent eight years scrutinising how almost 1,600 households in America bought a typical household product such as detergent. The study found that consumers exposed to repeated price cuts learnt to ignore the 'usual' price.

(c)   Neither do price cuts attract new customers. The unexpected explanation for this was that almost all the customers buying the discounted product had tried it before. It seems that brands are built in other ways: price cuts are simply a gift to loyal customers. Little wonder that only a third of all promotions pay for themselves.

Another trick is to dazzle the jaded consumer with variety. At one time, Procter & Gamble was selling 35 variations of Crest toothpaste and different nappies for girls and boys. The average supermarket in America devotes 20ft of shelving to medicine for coughs and colds. Most of this choice is trumpery.

In fact, more choice does not translate into more sales. Ravi Dhar, of Yale University, examined how students decided what to buy, based on the number of versions of each product-category on offer. As the choice increased, so did the likelihood that students would not buy anything at all. John Gourville at Harvard Business School believes that some types of choice are more troublesome than others. His - as yet incomplete - research suggests that consumers like to be offered choices in a single dimension: different sizes of cereal packet, say. if they are asked to make too many trade-offs, such as whether to buy a computer with a modem or speakers, consumers start to feel anxious or even irritated.

The custom in marketing departments of moving managers off a brand within two years has rewarded those who boost sales, even if their favoured marketing strategy achieves no lasting good. Some firms, such as Coca-Cola and AT&T, now employ brand equity managers to oversee the long-term health of their brands.

There are also new ways of using detailed information to target promotions. Buzzwords abound - relationship marketing, key-account management, and in the world of packaged goods, efficient consumer response (ECR), which has become a marketing mantra in America in the past few years.

Channels of distribution

7.13   Some organisations might use channels of distribution for their goods which are unprofitable to use, and which should either be abandoned in favour of more profitable channels, or made profitable by giving some attention to cutting costs or increasing minimum order sizes.

7.14   It might well be the case that an organisation gives close scrutiny to the profitability of its products, and the profitability of its market segments, but does not have a costing system which measures the costs of distributing the products to their markets via different distribution channels.

7.15   A numerical example might help to illustrate this point. Let us suppose that Biomarket Ltd sells two consumer products, X and Y, in two markets A and B. In both markets, sales are made through the following outlets.

- Direct sales to supermarkets
- Wholesalers

BPP
PUBLISHING

Sales and costs for the most recent quarter have been analysed by product and market as follows.

	Market A			Market B			Both markets		
	X	Y	Total	X	Y	Total	X	Y	Total
	£'000	£'000	£'000	£'000	£'000	£'000	£'000	£'000	£'000
Sales	900	600	1,500	1,000	2,000	3,000	1,900	2,600	4,500
Variable production costs	450	450	900	500	1,500	2,000	950	1,950	2,900
	450	150	600	500	500	1,000	950	650	1,600
Variable sales costs	90	60	150	100	100	200	190	160	350
Contribution	360	90	450	400	400	800	760	490	1,250
Share of fixed costs (production, sales, distribution, administration)	170	80	250	290	170	460	460	250	710
Net profit	190	10	200	110	230	340	300	240	540

7.16 This analysis shows that both products are profitable, and both markets are profitable. But what about the channels of distribution? A further analysis of market A might show the following.

		Market A	
	Supermarkets	Wholesalers	Total
	£'000	£'000	£'000
Sales	1,125	375	1,500
Variable production costs	675	225	900
	450	150	600
Variable selling costs	105	45	150
Contribution	345	105	
Direct distribution costs	10	80	90
	335	25	360
Share of fixed costs	120	40	160
Net profit/(loss)	215	(15)	200

7.17 This analysis shows that although sales through wholesalers make a contribution after deducting direct distribution costs, the profitability of this channel of distribution is disappointing, and some attention ought perhaps to be given to improving it.

8 THE AUDITING PROCESS AS A CONTROL MECHANISM

8.1 It should be clearly understood that establishing 'where we are now' by means of a thorough **marketing audit** performs a dual role in checking where we have come from. In other words marketing planning is a cyclical or iterative process. Perhaps the following diagram will help to demonstrate this more clearly.

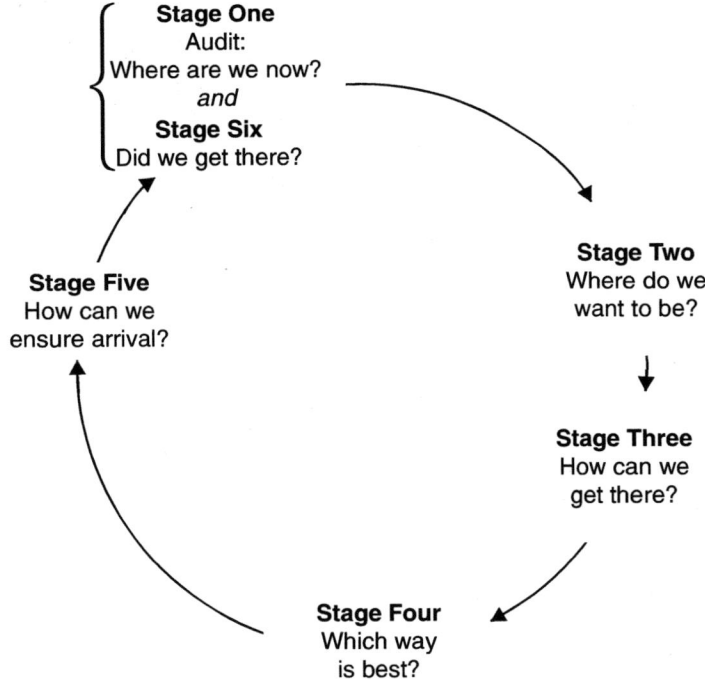

Source: adapted from Wilson, Gilligan, Pearson

Chapter Roundup

- Special problems occur in marketing **feedback and control systems** because of the 'people' element.

- **Basic control systems** comprise inputs, processes and outputs, governed by a control device, actioned by feedback.

- **Planning** is not just an extension of **budgeting**, but there is a close link between them.

- A **budget** is a plan expressed in money terms, representing the resources needed to achieve the objective.

- The **principal budget factor** should be identified at the beginning of the budgetary process. It is often sales volume and so the sales budget has to be produced before all the others.

- **Controls** are essential to ensure that planning targets are achieved and much of this information is provided internally in the form of feedback.

- The control signposts can be easily identified from the quantified objectives. To prevent managers being swamped with data, they need to establish a system of **exception reporting** where only results which vary by more than agreed tolerance levels are brought to their attention for corrective actions.

- **Control information** should also be used to inform strategic planners of the need to revise longer term forecasts.

- At marketing management level controls are equally important to ensure **efficient and effective use of the marketing budget**. Marketing practitioners need to be familiar with measures appropriate for evaluating the elements of the marketing mix, whilst recognising that it is how the variables are used in combination which brings about changes in demand.

Now try illustrative question 17 at the end of the Study Text

Quick Quiz

1   What special problems occur in marketing with regard to feedback and control systems? (see para 2.1)

2   Draw a diagram of a basic control system. (3.3)

3   Identify characteristics of a strategic control system? (4.2)

4   What financial information might be obtainable about a competitor? (5.4)

5   What areas should be investigated when undertaking an analysis of key customers? (5.8)

6   How are targets or standards derived? (6.1)

7   What is the purpose of a budget? (6.4)

8   How long is the budget period? (6.8)

9   How are marketing budgets fixed? (6.16)

10 List eight measures of performance which could be used to evaluate the effectiveness of personal selling. (7.3)

11 What are possible aims of discount pricing? (7.12)

Action Programme Review

1   The plan has to be altered as a result of feedback.

(a)   This is a **standard**, in other words, a measure of expected performance.

(b)   Counselling is control action to improve the individual's performance. Dismissal is control action too, if the employee is replaced by someone who performs better, thus raising the performance of the department as a whole.

(c)   This is feedforward control based on culture.

2   A sweet company's principal budget factor is likely to be demand, as expressed in sales forecasts. A hospital's principal budget factor is almost certainly going to be the funding allocation from the government.

Part F
The Examination

18

Mini-cases in the Examination

Chapter Topic List

1	**Setting the scene**
2	**What is a mini-case?**
3	**An approach to mini-cases**
4	**Other questions in the examination**

---

1   SETTING THE SCENE

1.1   This chapter offers detailed guidance on how to tackle mini-cases. After you have done this chapter, do the specimen paper case in the question bank at the end of the Study Text. Further question practice can be found in the BPP Practice & Revision Kit for this subject - an order form can be found at the end of the Study Text.

2   WHAT IS A MINI-CASE?

2.1   A mini-case in the examination is a 500-800 word long description of an organisation at a moment in time. You first see it in the examination room and so you have a maximum of 72 minutes to read, understand, analyse and answer the mini-case.

2.2   The mini-case is a feature of all the Diploma examinations, with the exception of *Analysis and Decision*, which is of course a major case study exercise in itself. It is therefore worth spending some time mastering the technique of the mini-case. The approach is the same for all the subjects and so practice in one area will benefit your other Diploma subjects.

2.3   The mini-case (Part A of the paper) carries 40% of the available marks in the examination. Students who fail a Diploma paper are often found to have had difficulties with the mini-case. It is worth noting that a good result on the mini-case can be used to compensate for a weaker performance in part B of the paper.

2.4   As mini-cases are fundamental to your exam success, you should be absolutely clear about what mini-cases are, CIM's purpose in using them, what the examiners seek and then, in context, to consider how best they should be tackled.

The purpose of the mini-case

2.5 Diploma examiners require students to demonstrate not only their knowledge of marketing management, but also their ability to use that knowledge in a commercially credible way in the context of a 'real' business scenario.

2.6 You cannot pass this part of the paper by regurgitating theory. You must be able to apply the theory to real problems. The mini-case is included to test your competence in analysing information and making clear and reasonable decisions.

The Examiner's requirements

2.7 The examiners are the 'consumers' of your examination script. You should remember first and foremost that they need a paper which makes their life easy. That means that the script should be well laid out, with plenty of white space and neat readable writing. All the basic rules of examination technique must be applied, but because communication skills are fundamental to the marketer, the ability to communicate clearly is particularly important.

2.8 The examination is your opportunity to market yourself to the examiner, in this case as a marketing professional competent in the skills of planning and control. As actions speak louder than words, a candidate who has failed to plan the answers or who has run out of the resource time, is unlikely to impress.

2.9 Management skills are commonly ignored by candidates who fail to recognise their importance. Management is more about thinking than knowing, more about decision than analysis. It is about achieving action through persuasive communication. It is about meeting deadlines. It is therefore about clear, logical analysis under time pressure, which leads to decisive recommendations presented in simple, clear Business English.

2.10 The six key factors from the above paragraph are:

- Thinking
- Logical analysis
- Decision
- Action
- Persuasive communication
- Business English

All must be demonstrated to the examiners, especially in the case and mini-case study elements of the Diploma examinations.

2.11 If you are entering the Diploma by exemption, take particular note of the examiner's requirements. Certificate holders will have encountered mini-cases before. They should note the change in emphasis from the learning of marketing to its management.

2.12 Examiners' reports note the reasons why candidates fail. It makes depressing reading to go back over a series of reports because year after year the examiners make the same points and year after year many candidates ignore them! No examiner can understand why candidates refuse to take notice of their requirements. In everyday life we do what our manager instructs, or we leave the job (one way or another). If candidates would only think of the examiners as senior managers at work, and address them accordingly, the pass rate would shoot up.

Examiners' comments

2.13 Examiners' reports on mini-cases repeatedly stress the same points.

(a) Relate the time allocated to the answer to the marks available.

(b) Answer the question asked. Never use a question as a pretext to answer a different one.

(c) Time planning is crucial to success.

(d) Quality and insight are worth more than quantity and detail.

(e) It is essential to write in role.

(f) Intelligently apply knowledge of theory to a marketing problem.

(g) Do not repeat chunks of the mini-case in the answer.

(h) Do not show any analytical work (for example SWOT) unless specifically requested.

(i) Presentation must be of management quality. Spelling and grammar are important, only a certain laxity will be allowed for the pressures of the exam room.

2.14 Direct quotes from examiners' reports reinforce the points made in the previous paragraph.

(a) 'The commonest 'self-destruct' faults

- Bad time management
- Using the question as a pretext to answer a different one
- Poor presentation'

(b) 'Your examiners regard badly constructed and unrealistic case solutions as a particularly serious failing among candidates for the professional diploma of a chartered institute.'

(c) 'The gap between question answering and case solving abilities continues to be very marked.'

(d) 'A wider spread of up-to-date knowledge (greater than Coca-Cola and McDonald's) would give the examiner greater confidence in your competence.'

(e) 'Management of any sort, and particularly marketing management, is about thinking rather than knowing. It is for example about selecting the best strategy rather than simply knowing the range of options available.'

(f) 'Preparation time should be spent in practising techniques as much as in learning content.'

(g) 'Diploma candidates not only need to demonstrate their ability to communicate succinctly as a subsidiary test of marketing awareness but in their own interests of scoring higher marks by getting more valid points across in the limited time available in the exam situation.'

(h) 'It is a shame that such basic mistakes mar what are often otherwise diligent and enthusiastic efforts.'

The expectations of examiners

2.15 Examiners are experienced marketing managers. They know that mini-cases give only limited information and that candidates are working under a tight time constraint. They do not, therefore, require considered, fully rounded answers. There is insufficient data and time. The successful candidate learns to work with what is available, to make reasonable assumptions that help in the decision making process, and to present an answer cogently and concisely.

2.16 The examiner can only mark within the criteria that have been established. The requirements are set out very clearly. It is not difficult to satisfy them. The well prepared candidate should not fail the mini-case. Since the information is limited, the time is very constrained, and the examiner is looking for evidence of a managerial approach, any candidate that makes reasonable assumptions about the case, takes clear and sensible decisions, and communicates these succinctly must pass.

2.17 Also remember that mini-cases are set for all candidates. Some will know absolutely nothing about the industry, some will work in it and be expert. Candidates take the examinations in centres across the world. Therefore the examiner will not ask technical questions about the industry, nor any tied to a specific culture or economy. Questions have to be more general, more open, less specific. However, you will be expected to have acquired a level of business appreciation and marketing knowledge from your other studies.

2.18 Summary

The requirements are as follows.

Quality		Quantity
Insight		Detail
Decision	**NOT**	Analysis
Report		Essay

Management reports in CIM mini-cases

2.19 A management report is a specialised form of communication. It is the language used in business. It is not difficult to learn to write in report style, but it does require practice to become fluent. Mini-cases must always be answered in report style.

2.20 Management reports are action planning documents and are generally written in the third person. Their role is to make positive recommendations for action. Situational analysis is included only if it is needed to clarify an ambiguity. Examiners complain that many candidates do little more than produce a SWOT analysis as their response to a mini-case. Support material is often included, but as appendices to the body of the report. In CIM mini-case work it is exceptional to include an appendix.

2.21 Management reports: the basic rules

- Always head a report with the name of your organisation.
- State to whom it is addressed, from whom it comes, and give the date.
- Head the report (for example 'Marketing research plan for 2000/01').
- Number and sub-number paragraphs. Head them if appropriate.
- Present the contents in a logical order.
- Include diagrams, graphs, tables only if they have positive value.
- Include recommendations for action that are written as intention against time.

2.22 If you are forced to use appendices there are two further rules to remember.

- Refer to them within the body of the report (eg 'See Appendix A').
- Indicate when the report concludes (.../ends).

2.23 Management reports are written in crisp, no-nonsense business English. There is no room for superlatives, flowery adjectives nor flowing sentences. You are not trying to entertain, simply to present facts as clearly as possible. Think about the style you would adopt if writing a report to senior managers at work.

2.24 As we have already said, presentation is of key importance in CIM examinations. The rules are as follows.

- Use a black or a blue pen, never red or green.
- Start your first answer on the facing page of the answer book, never inside the cover.
- Make the first three pages as neat and well laid out as possible, to impress.
- Use plenty of space. Do not crowd your work.
- Number your questions above your answers. Never write in either margin.
- Leave space (four or five lines) between sections of your report.

3 AN APPROACH TO MINI-CASES

3.1 Mini-cases are easy once you have mastered the basic techniques. The key to success lies in adopting a logical sequence of steps which with practice you will master. You must enter the exam room with the process as second nature, so you can concentrate your attention on the marketing issues which face you.

3.2 Students who are at first apprehensive when faced with a mini-case often come to find them much more stimulating and rewarding than traditional examination questions. There is the added security of knowing that there is no single correct answer to a case study.

3.3 You will be assessed on your approach, style, creativity and commercial credibility, but you will not be judged against a single 'correct' answer. Treat the mini-case as though it were happening in real life, at work or at a social meeting with a friend. Most of the mini-case is narrative; it tells a story or paints a picture. If a friend says over a drink 'I've got a problem at work' the most usual answer is 'Tell me about it'. The listener will need background information to establish frame reference and to understand the problem. That is what the case narrative is doing. Most of it is background, and it should be read just to grasp the context and flavour of the situation.

3.4 It helps to pretend to yourself that the examiner needs your advice. The questions posed indicate the advice which is being sought.

(a) Just as your friend would not be impressed if you spent half an hour pontificating on how he or she got themselves into this situation, neither will the examiner reward you for analysis of how the situation arose.

(b) Neither will the examiner be impressed with a long list of 'you could do this ....' 'but on the other hand....' Identify the alternatives, but make a clear recommendation if you want to win friends and influence examiners.

3.5 You will be faced with limited information, less than would be available to you in the real world. This is one of the limitations of case study examinations, but everyone is faced with the same constraint. You are able to make assumptions where it is necessary.

3.6 A reasonable assumption is logically possible and factually credible. You may need to make and clearly state two or three assumptions in order to tackle a case.

3.7 Some students feel uncomfortable that there is no bedrock (an easy, well defined question) on which to build. They feel all at sea and panic.

BPP
PUBLISHING

3.8 Preparation is the answer. It is important to practise the technique of handling a mini-case. There are three later in this chapter, and they should be taken individually. For each there are careful instructions and a time guide is given. After you have completed these it will still be necessary for you to develop speed, but the principles needed for success in the examination will have been established. Mini-case scenarios are also included as one of the data sheets in the CIM's *Marketing Success* and these will provide you with regular new material on which to practise.

An example of a mini-case

3.9 This mini-case example is worked through stage by stage to show you the process. This shows you the methodology. Another mini-case is at the end of this text.

Direct Lounge Furniture Ltd (DLF)

3.10 DLF is owned by two entrepreneurs each of whom built up a separate direct marketing business, one in the East Midlands and one in the West Midlands over a period of some 15 years, before merging three years ago. The main advantages of the merger were joint advertising, wider product ranges, more flexible production and less reliance upon one person. The two owners are good friends and work well together, meeting at least once a week.

3.11 Both the two constituent businesses comprise showrooms mainly featuring upholstered three-piece suites finished in Dralon cloth, in a wide variety of styles and colours. This furniture is manufactured in two small factories, each of which has an adjoining showroom.

3.12 Sales are achieved by advertising in free newspapers delivered to Midlands households. These advertisements illustrate the furniture on offer, strongly emphasise the lower prices available to the public by buying direct from the manufacturers and of course invite readers to visit the showrooms without obligation.

3.13 Upon visiting the showroom the public can look around the products on offer, discuss their individual requirements with a salesperson and be shown round the factory to emphasise the quality of the workmanship, wooden frames etc.

3.14 This marketing formula works very well and sales/profits are booming. Customers feel they are involved in the design of their own furniture and that they are getting good value. DLF enjoy high proportions of recommendations and repeat sales.

3.15 Buying behaviour patterns are however changing. People are tending to buy individual items rather than the standard three-piece suite (two armchairs plus a 2/3/4 seater settee) and to seek co-ordination with curtains, carpet etc. In partial response to this the East Midlands showroom offers made-to-measure curtains in Dralon to complement or match the upholstery. Another change in the industry is in the foam used for upholstering which was formerly highly flammable and when on fire gave out dense black smoke causing many deaths. Legislation has now been passed enforcing the use of safer foam.

3.16 The media exposure of the fire hazard has caused the public to be more careful when choosing furniture and increasing affluence has also resulted in a move up-market by more households.

3.17 DLF are well aware that their formula appeals mainly to the more price-conscious households, who have been tolerant of the somewhat less than sophisticated showroom and factory conditions associated with direct marketing of this nature.

Question

3.18 You have been called in by DLF as a consultant to advise on expansion options. After conducting a marketing audit and a SWOT analysis you are now evaluating the options for:

- Product development only
- Market development only
- A combination of both product and market development

Submit your report giving the advantages and disadvantages of each of these three options in more detail, stating what control techniques you would recommend in each case.

Analysis

3.19 You should immediately identify the following characteristics about the business.

- DLF is a small business.
- They operate in a local market.
- They specialise in the direct marketing of consumer durables.

3.20 These characteristics should start to inform your thinking about the case and the nature of the business, for example you can now make the following connections.

(a) *Small business:* may mean limited resources.

(b) *Local market:* local communication media.

(c) *Direct marketing:* control over marketing mix but cost of storage and delivery, credit provision etc.

(d) *Consumer durables:* infrequent purchase, influenced strongly by style, colour, not brand names etc.

3.21 The secret of case study questions is to really play the role you have been given. You need to be able to picture this business, its products and showrooms. As soon as you have a mental picture you will be able to fit easily into the role of marketing consultant.

3.22 Now read through the case again and identify the key points, strengths, weaknesses etc. You can do this on the examination paper to save time. You need to really think about the narrative and what it is telling you.

3.23 Alternatively, or in addition, you can convert the information onto a SWOT chart to help clarify the picture. Remember that you are not presenting this to the examiner, so use a page at the back of your answer book and do not waste too much time on it.

> Remember that weaknesses can always be converted into strengths and that threats can usually be turned to opportunities. Do not waste time worrying about how to categorise an element. It is usually more important that you have identified it.

3.24   *SWOT of Direct Lounge Furniture Ltd*

Strengths	*Weaknesses*
• Owners are friends	Could be a weakness if they fall out; may imply informal systems and procedures
• Established	Resources for expansion limited for a small business
• Financially strong; sales and profits high	Perceived as bottom end of market

• Good reputation
   -price
   -workmanship
	• Limited geographic market
	• Two unsophisticated showrooms
	• Product oriented
	• Limited product portfolio
	• Little marketing activity

Opportunity	*Threats*
• Higher customer incomes	• Legislation
• Safety awareness pushing demand towards higher value products	• Changing customer needs and attitudes
• New materials and production techniques which may become available	• Increased standard of living amongst current customers • Possibility of increased competition

3.25   Marketing audit is an assessment of the current marketing activity of DLF. We have uncovered some clues when developing the corporate SWOT.

(a) The company is product oriented not marketing oriented.

(b) There is advertising activity but no evidence of a co-ordinated marketing function, therefore no marketing procedures, plans etc.

(c) We can do a SWOT on the marketing mix.

    (i)   *Product*

        Strength: good workmanship, low prices, range of suites

        Weakness: not a varied product portfolio, one material used, traditional ideas of customer needs

    (ii)   *Promotion*

        Weakness: limited to local advertising, not targeted or controlled. Product oriented by featuring pictures of products.

        Strengths: good local image and reputation for value for money.

    (iii)   *Place*

        Weakness: limited to two showrooms. No information on waiting lists etc.

    (iv)   *Price*

        Strength: current pricing policy is a strength while market is price conscious, but the market is changing.

3.26   Marketing opportunities do exist and some have been identified for us.

(a) To diversify into new products

    •   Curtains

    •   Other furniture

(b)   To develop a wider market

(c)   To develop new segments in the current geographic market

(d)   To reposition DLF as a quality product provider

3.27   Review the question carefully. We have done the SWOT and the marketing audit. Our response should be based on our analysis of the company. It should not be just a presentation of the analysis.

3.28   We are required to evaluate three options and to submit a report indicating the advantages, disadvantages and control techniques in each case.

> It is important that you attempt all parts of this question if you want a chance to gain the maximum marks. In this case the question requirements give you an automatic structure to your report.

Before going further you will find it useful to spend 55 minutes preparing your own answer to the question. Compare it with the suggested solution we have provided. Remember that there is no single right answer. Use our solution only as a guide and as an indicator of the process involved.

Solution

3.29

Report to:	Managing Directors
	Direct Lounge Furniture Ltd
From:	A Consultant
Date:	5 April 20XX
Subject:	Evaluation of product/market opportunities for DLF Ltd.

1   Background

1.1   Following our initial analysis of DLF's current situation we have found that although the company is in a secure financial position, with no doubt about short-term survival, the medium-term picture is rather bleak.

1.2   The DLF product range is limited to lounge suites, traditionally configured and covered in one fabric, Dralon. This type of lounge furniture is probably in the mature stage and possibly in the decline stage of its life cycle. The DLF position has been weakened by the following macroenvironmental changes.

- Changing customer needs and expectations in home furnishings.
- Higher incomes making demand increasingly price inelastic.
- Safety fears encouraging customers to trade up.

1.3   We would therefore confirm your personal assessment that for DLF to thrive in the medium and long term, positive action must be taken to develop new product/market strategies. It is important that this action is undertaken before declining demand has an adverse impact on profitability and erodes the resources necessary for exploiting a new opportunity.

The options

2   Product development only

2.1   Product development could cover any activity from modification of the existing product (lounge suites), to adding new products to the range. We will assume that the option is basically the former.

2.2   *Advantages*

(a)   This would be a market oriented development, allowing products to be designed to meet identified customer needs.

(b)   You are experienced in the business, its production and operational requirements,

BPP PUBLISHING

materials etc.

(c)   You have an established reputation in the business of lounge furniture.

(d)   Product development would allow ranges and lines to be developed to meet the needs of a variety of market segments and would provide a number of opportunities to develop and enhance the business. The workmen have the skills to develop a quality 'made to order' package.

2.3   *Disadvantages*

(a)   You are positioned at the 'value for money' end of the market. Repositioning for a new segment of the market would require a considerable marketing effort and may be easier with a new kind of product, for example dining room furniture.

(b)   Proliferation of product choice would increase the costs of stockholding, requiring a greater variety of raw materials etc.

(c)   Existing showrooms may be unsuitable for attracting a different group of customers.

(d)   Product portfolio is limited. Recession and declining demand for lounge furniture affects the whole business.

2.4   *Controls*

(a)   Enquiry and sales data by product line would be important to assess the profitability of new products offered.

(b)   If the product range was extended to provide all lounge furnishings, for example curtains, cushions, and tables, it would be important to measure the scale of 'value added' sales, by customers purchasing additional items.

(c)   Information on customers would help to identify whether target markets are being attracted. As most products will be delivered, it should be relatively easy to monitor geographic locations and possibly develop a simplified process for classifying residential neighbourhoods.

(d)   There should be controls on production activities such as average stock levels. Order times etc would also be important to monitor efficiency of the operations as a more customer oriented product policy was developed.

3   **Market development only**

3.1   This would involve looking for new customers for the existing product range. It would imply increasing the geographic spread of the business.

3.2   *Advantages*
(a)   It would require no change to the existing operation at production level.

(b)   It would allow the profitable 'value for money' target customer base to be extended. These are customers who DLF already know well.
(c)   It would require no additional investment in the production resources.

3.3   *Disadvantages*
(a)   It would leave the company product oriented, looking for customers for products, instead of developing products for customers. In the long run this approach will make DLF very vulnerable to competition.
(b)   Although this strategy may boost sales in the short run, we know that customer needs and wants are changing and that this low price, traditional product is in decline.
(c)   It would require investment in distribution to set up either showrooms or agencies in new areas. These may prove difficult to control.

3.4   *Controls*
(a)   Controls would need to focus on any new distribution channels and salespeople established. Cost of sales and conversions of enquiries would help DLF establish the rate at which the new market became aware of their products.
(b)   Given the indicators of general decline in DLF's market, control information would be needed to monitor average customer purchases (two sofas and no chairs), demand for matched curtains, average spend and other purchase patterns. This would provide valuable control information for sales forecasting.

4   Product and market development

4.1   At its extreme, for example moving into high quality kitchen units, product and market developments could be a major diversification, involving not only products but also customers with whom DLF is unfamiliar. However, diversifying into TV cabinets and coffee tables for a made to measure premium market would involve less risk.

4.2   *Advantages*

(a)   It allows DLF to have an effective new start, researching the market to identify product/market opportunities which could be developed.

(b)   Assuming that the current cash cow business will be retained at least in the short run, this strategy would diversify the business and so reduce the risk of sudden changes in demand caused by external variables.

(c)   A product/market development would allow DLF to completely reposition themselves in the furniture market.

4.3   *Disadvantages*

(a)   The strategy would be risky. The extent of the diversification would indicate how much risk is involved.

(b)   It would be expensive, involving investment in both marketing and production.

(c)   There is a danger of attempting to develop too many opportunities simultaneously, losing sight of the core business and over-extending resources.

4.4   *Controls*

(a)   Such a major shift in strategy would require close control. New product sales levels would need to be monitored as would the value of business from new market segments.

(b)   New distribution channels and promotional activities would probably be needed and these would also require evaluating to assess their effectiveness.

(c)   Plans and budgets for the separate parts of the business would need establishing, together with administrative systems and procedures. These are unlikely to exist in the current small scale operation.

5   Conclusions and recommendations

(a)   Action is needed to ensure the medium term survival of DLF.

(b)   The business has the strengths to extend its product range to meet the needs of new customer segments, in particular high quality, made to order products at premium prices. This extension of the product portfolio should be developed after careful research of the target market.

(c)   The company should clearly review its mission and should establish financial objectives for the operation. Corporate and marketing plans must be developed as well as a management information system.

A Consultancy will be happy to offer any further assistance to DLF in this activity.

BPP
PUBLISHING

3.30 DLF was set under the old Marketing Planning and Control syllabus. The specimen case study for the current syllabus, The Lens Shop, is in the bank of illustrative questions at the end of this text. More mini-cases for you to practise on are provided, with full suggested solutions, in the BPP Practice and Revision Kit: an order form can be found at the end of this Study Text.

4 OTHER QUESTIONS IN THE EXAMINATION

4.1 Although the questions in section B are of the more 'traditional' examination style, you must still make certain that you do not answer them in a purely academic manner.

4.2 Ensure that you support theory with real world examples and illustrations, use the introductions and conclusions to comment on the value of the concept in question, disadvantages of a technique and so on. You should evaluate every question in terms not only of its content, but also the context in which it is being asked.

4.3 Most students will have the knowledge to pass the exam, it is using that information in the 'context' of the question which causes the downfall. A question about the role of planning in the public sector should be answered differently from the same question set in a private sector context.

4.4 Make sure you answer the questions set out and watch out for variations in mark allocation made within a question.

4.5 These suggested solutions which follow are just that. There is no single correct answer, but use them as a comparison for your own work and an example of the style, approach and the depth needed in the exam.

4.6 Remember to practise answers in exam conditions. You will have only 30 minutes per question in the exam room. After allowing planning and review time allow a little over 20 minutes writing time per question. Quality not quantity is required.

Chapter Roundup

- This chapter has explained the nature and purpose of a mini-case. We have used examples from past examination papers to demonstrate how to use our recommended technique and extracts from examiners' reports have illustrated the examiners' requirements and common mistakes made by candidates.

- Future mini-cases require you to use tabulated data such as that illustrated in The Lens Shop at the end of the illustrative questions. Go back and try to produce an answer for The Lens Shop related to the answer guidelines provided by the Senior Examiner.

Now try illustrative question 18 at the end of the Study Text

Quick Quiz

1 What are the six key management skills that you must demonstrate to the examiner? (see para 2.10)

2 Summarise the requirements of a mini-case examination answer. (2.18)

3 What are the basic rules for management reports? (2.21)

Illustrative Questions and Suggested Answers

1   MARKETING TASK   *32 mins*

As markets fragment and life cycles get shorter and less predictable, the nature of the marketing task is changing. Identify the causes of these changes and how a marketing manager might possibly respond.

(20 marks)

2   MARKETING PLAN   *32 mins*

Outline the major stages in the development of a marketing plan. Draw up a hypothetical plan showing the likely features to be considered at each stage for a national tourist board.   **(20 marks)**

3   MARKETING AND CORPORATE STRATEGY   *32 mins*

What are the characteristics of strategic decisions at the corporate and marketing level, and how can a strategic perspective at the marketing level be developed?   **(20 marks)**

4   SOCIAL CHANGE   *32 mins*

Societies are changing in a wide variety of ways. Identify the nature and significance of two such changes that are taking place within your own society and discuss their implications for the marketing planning and control process.   **(20 marks)**

5   INFORMATION ABOUT COMPETITORS   *32 mins*

Your company's markets are becoming increasingly competitive. Explain how you would develop an effective competitive information system in these circumstances, the nature of the inputs that the system would require and how the outputs from the system might be used to improve the strategic marketing process.   **(20 marks)**

6   INTERNAL CAPABILITIES   *32 mins*

For a number of years a small group of friends have pursued their interest in building and flying model aircraft. The combination of their design and mechanical skills has resulted in many requests for custom built aeroplanes from other members of their club. More recently they have built remote control cars for friends' children. Others have encouraged them to go into business full-time, pointing out that a significant opportunity exists for 'custom made' remote control models. In the role of a small business adviser, produce a report which analyses the likely strengths and weaknesses of this new company's internal capabilities relative to this marketing opportunity.   **(20 marks)**

7   FLEXIBLE MATRIX   *32 mins*

Several models have been developed to provide a more flexible approach to portfolio analysis than that developed by the Boston Consultancy Group Matrix (BCG). What are the weaknesses of the BCG approach? Using an alternative model of your choice show how it tries to overcome the limitations of the BCG.   **(20 marks)**

8   SWOT: NEED FOR RIGOUR   *32 mins*

It has been suggested that the majority of SWOT analyses are far too bland and of little real planning value. Explain how you would go about conducting a rigorous SWOT analysis and how the results might then be used strategically.   **(20 marks)**

9   FINANCIAL ANALYSIS   *32 mins*

As a newly appointed marketing manager with profit responsibility for a wide range of consumer durables that are sold though several types of distribution network, draft a memorandum to the financial director explaining types of financial analysis you require and how the results will be used.

(20 marks)

BPP PUBLISHING

10 FORECASTING OF SALES
32 mins

You have been given the task of coordinating the forecasting of sales for your firm's budget preparation. Last year the sales forecast was overstated by more than thirty per cent against actual sales. As a result some profit centres budgeted to spend more than they actually achieved in revenue.

Required

Write a memo to the sales department which:

(a) explains the importance of having accurate forecasts

(b) discusses and evaluates the importance of having meaningful budgetary control information in the context of this example. **(20 marks)**

11 MISSION AND OBJECTIVES
32 mins

Illustrate the essential differences between an organisation's mission, policies, aims and objectives.

(20 marks)

12 FRANCHISE
32 mins

Your Taiwan based organisation has been approached by a major UK clothing retailer with a view to franchising their operation in your home market. Write a report outlining the information that is needed in order to make a management decision on this proposal. Show how you would acquire this data.

(20 marks)

13 DISCOUNT ORIENTED COMPETITOR
32 mins

A major bank has declared that it is going to enter an already very competitive motor insurance market and offer highly competitive prices to customers. You have been asked to provide a briefing paper advising a financial services company, which is a well established direct insurer, on the options open to them when faced by this new discount orientated competitor. **(20 marks)**

14 BRAND STRETCHING
32 mins

As a Marketing Planner for a financial services company, identify the key elements of a brand strategy and the criteria which should be used in brand stretching decisions. **(20 marks)**

15 CRITERIA FOR A NEW PROPOSAL
32 mins

Identify the financial and marketing criteria which should be used to evaluate a new service proposal and how these criteria might be applied. **(20 marks)**

16 IMPLEMENTATION PROBLEMS
32 mins

'Marketing planning is a generally straightforward exercise; the marketer's real problems are those of effective implementation.' (Anonymous). Identify the barriers to effective implementation that marketers typically encounter. **(20 marks)**

17 FEEDBACK AND CONTROL SYSTEM
32 mins

What factors should be taken into account in the development of a marketing feedback and control system? In what ways might the information possibly be used? **(20 marks)**

18   THE LENS SHOP

The Lens Shop Ltd (TLS) is a camera retailer based in the UK. It currently has 15 outlets based in the major centres of population.

There are two types of retailers selling cameras in the UK. On the one hand stores that sell a limited range of cameras amongst a range of other electrical and domestic appliances. These are mainly large department stores and electrical retailers that sell computers, hi-fi's, televisions and cameras, then there are specialist camera stores that only sell photographic products. TLS is one of the major retailers in this more specialist camera sector.

TLS sells the majority of the leading brands, it also is the largest and most well established outlet for discontinued products, used by all the distributors to clear their shelves of 'old' product lines. These products are discounted heavily by TLS. TLS are able to buy in bulk and as a result can negotiate extra discounts.

All TLS stores are small and are located on less expensive secondary sites in the city centre but away from the main, high rent, shopping centre locations. The outlets are small they need less stock for display purposes and have very limited stock room space. Management feel that small stores have a better atmosphere, are less formal, hectic, yet friendly.

TLS's main promotional vehicle is a colour catalogue, which is described as '16 great pages of bargains'. This is very much seen as a 'fun' brochure promoting products in a positive light-hearted way by mixing illustrations, technical details and humour. The catalogue is distributed in a number of ways: to people coming into the stores, from racks outside the store, by 'freephone' telephone hotline and via a database of past customers. Media advertising is also used. Typically camera magazines will carry a five-page advertisement which highlights current bargains and often contains a promotional voucher for discounts or free accessories.

Prices are highly competitive, often discounted below recommended retail levels. The customer is provided with a price guarantee that TLS will beat any current local price by £10 for a similar brand of camera. TLS also offer a three year warranty at an extremely low price. Additionally, their warranty offers a unique guaranteed buy-back service for customers wishing to upgrade their photographic equipment. Management sees this as a genuine customer service which will hopefully encourage customer loyalty. All goods are subject to a 14-day exchange.

The company also aims to give high levels of customer service. Members of staff have a high degree of product knowledge. Sales assistants are particularly helpful, advising on the best purchases for any given budget. Staff are also happy to demonstrate the equipment. Selections of recent reviews from camera magazines are also available in the store to provide further information to customers.

To maintain required levels of customer service all customers are given a short questionnaire and asked to return them to the Managing Directors of TLS by freepost. The Managing Director reviews all comments relating to customer service, and responds where appropriate.

As the new Marketing Manager for 'TLS' you have been asked to:

(a)   Identify and explain the sources of the organisation's competitive advantage and whether their current position is sustainable.   **(20 marks)**

(b)   The Managing Directors of 'TLS' has heard that internal marketing might be a useful approach to adopt in her business. You have been asked to write a report illustrating how an internal marketing programme could be implemented. This report should also highlight the benefits of such a programme and the potential problems.   **(20 marks)**

(40 marks total)

Suggested answers

1   MARKETING TASK

> *Examiner's comments: summary/extracts.* Better answers focused on a spectrum of issues accelerating the pace of change including demographics, global business and greater competition. Some candidates saw the words, 'product life cycle' and simply talked about the four stages of this model and consequently were awarded very few marks.

Marketers are facing a number of new *strategic challenges* as the environment changes. These include increasing pressure from governments to take a greater account of '*green*', *consumer and community relations* issues, the growing power of *global companies* and concentration of power within industries, changing social and cultural trends which bring about fragmentation of markets and innovation based on new technologies and emergent industries which stem from this. The focus of this question will be on the last two of these issues; *market fragmentation* and shorter/less predictable *life cycles*, the cause of these changes and how they affect the practice of marketing.

(a)   *Market fragmentation*

People eat both health food and junk food and have a repertoire of brands depending upon the occasion. A few years ago, accessing daily news was something you did by listening to the BBC's 9 O'Clock News. Now you can listen to any of the hundreds of celestial, satellite and cable channels, read any one of hundreds of newspapers or magazines, listen to any of the myriad of radio stations or search for a particular topic on the Internet.

(b)   Shorter and less predictable product *life cycles* are a characteristic of high technology products and services. New technology and innovations have escalated over the last 30 years, with new products, concepts, channels and technology being launched at a massive rate. High technology products almost have a built in obsolescence, as technology development never stays still. Predicting the diffusion of innovation rate is very difficult.

Causes of market fragmentation and lack of predictability of life cycles

(a)   *Social change*

The CIM/Henley Centre report, '*Metamorphosis in Marketing*' details how consumer behaviour and attitudes are changing. Traditional *consumer life stages* are changing. Wells and Guber's traditional family life cycle model which depicts a staged progression from youth to marriage and family to empty nesters is now a much less predictable path. A career for life is no longer the norm, redundancy and self-employment are rising, growing work and affluence of women, so too divorce, caring for elderly parents and middle age inheritances - all of these factors disrupt the pattern and lead to more consumer segments in many markets. The growth in 'minority' lifestyles is creating opportunities for niche brands aimed at consumers with very distinct purchasing habits.

(b)   *Technological innovation* is bringing the ability to create large numbers of product variants without corresponding increases in resources. This is causing markets to become overcrowded. The fragmentation of the media to service ever more specialist and local audiences is denying mass media the ability to assure market dominance for major brand advertisers. This creates *space for niche players* and speeds up the diffusion of *innovation thus shortening life cycles*. The advance in information technology is enabling information about individual customers to be organised in ways that enable highly selective and personal communications. It also fuels *quicker 'me-too' product launches* which potentially shorten product life cycles.

How should the marketing manager respond to these challenges?

Finer segmentation, in response to market fragmentation, looks certain to play an even more crucial role in the marketing strategies in the years ahead. The move from traditional mass marketing to 'micro marketing' is rapidly gaining ground as marketers explore the incremental profit potential of niche markets.

Tyrrell from Henley, advises marketers to 'forget people' and think of *occasions* and, in a branding sense, to think about creating and 'owning' those occasions. An example of this leading edge approach to market segmentation is Bass Brewers' new product development focus. New alcoholic drinks categories are much more quickly being developed to satisfy different drinking occasions, Hooch as a punctuation, refreshing drink in the middle of a session, Red as a stimulant based drink to help ravers keep going, Snapshots to start the evening or help latecomers catch up.

Perhaps the most important response has to come in relation to *long-term marketing strategy*. With less predictable life cycles, marketing managers must redefine the guidelines provided by the traditional PLC. In order for PLC theory to be relevant, some kind of reliable method for *projecting lifespans* of the product is needed. With technology advancing so rapidly, historical data is no longer sufficient to be a useful predictive tool. Popper and Buskirk (1992) suggest that the concept of the Technology Life Cycle is superior to the PLC concept. A key difference in thinking is that high-tech firms must make a critical decision regarding focus. A company can attempt to follow a technology through its life cycle or specialise in one stage. Whichever is chosen, speed of response becomes vital.

Hooley and Saunders (1993) suggest that in fragmented markets, success depends on finding *niches* where particular product specifications are needed, as in the computer software market. As each niche provides little opportunity for growth, a firm needs to find a number of niches with some degree of commonality to allow economies to be achieved. In contrast to niche players, brands such as Marks and Spencer and McDonald's over-arch social differences and appeal to standard needs on an international scale. As such marketers are having to stretch their vision to encompass the details and speed of micro-marketing and rapid new product development and the grand strategy of global branding, the cost pressures of tertiary brands and the image and service pressures of the differentiated offering.

As a recent article in Marketing Business concluded, marketers are having to become innovators, not only of brands and products, but of marketing itself.

2   MARKETING PLAN

(a)   The question does not indicate whether the plan is a long-term plan or an annual budget. The solution which follows incorporates the approach to developing both.

The first stage in a marketing plan should be to identify the separate products or product lines for which separate plans will be prepared. For each product, management must then analyse the current and prospective market situation. This 'situation analysis' will consider the trend of sales in recent years, the growth or decline in market share for the product, changes in the unit selling price and variable costs over the same period, together with turnover, gross contribution, advertising, sales promotion and distribution costs. Together with a consideration of 'threats' or 'opportunities' in the market which offer the prospect of a decline or an expansion of the total market and product sales, management should then be able to assess where the product stands and what its future is likely to be.

The situation analysis for each product in the company's range can then be brought together, so that management can assess the total sales, gross contribution, selling and distribution costs etc based on the current situation. This assessment should be compared with the long-term objectives of the company, which should be stated in terms of return on shareholder capital, or market share etc. If there is any discrepancy between strategic objectives and the forecast derived from the situation analysis, management must consider ways of improving product performance or developing new products quickly.

An 'action programme' can then be developed in which individual managers are given strategic tasks to accomplish (for example to raise the sales of product X, to achieve a 20% share of the market for product Y etc). This action programme must then be converted into a budget for short-term planning and control.

For each product or new product development, management must now consider the marketing mix, in order to produce a budget for sales volume and turnover, gross contribution, selling and distribution costs (analysed into budgets for direct selling, advertising, promotions etc).

The budget for each product, as developed in accordance with the action programmes, should then be sufficient, in combination, to enable the company to plan to achieve its strategic objectives.

(b)   A marketing plan could be developed by a national tourist board in the way described above, as follows.

For each tourist region of the country, and for each major resort within each region, a situation analysis would consider trends over recent years in the number and type of hotels, the number of beds in hotels, the number and capacity of caravan sites and camping sites, the actual 'occupancy' of hotels, caravan and camping sites, the amount of foreign exchange and travellers' cheques spent by foreign visitors to the country, attendances at major tourist attractions, the amount of money spent on advertising at home and abroad by the tourist board etc.

An analysis of threats and opportunities might concern the economic aspects of a world recession on the tourist trade in general. As another example, it appears that the chaos at Britain's airports during the summer of 1988, when thousands of holiday-makers faced long delays to their flights abroad, led to a much stronger demand for holidays in the UK in 1989.

The situation analysis for each resort or region can then be brought together to provide a picture of the expected situation in the tourist industry in the immediate and longer-term future. This should be compared with the strategic objectives of the tourist board (for example to raise the money spent on tourism to an amount equivalent to x% of the GNP etc).

An action programme can then be developed which attempts to improve performance in the tourist industry or to develop new tourist areas. Individual managers may be given the tasks, for example, of increasing hotel accommodation in the South West region by 10% in the next five years, increasing the number of visitors to the North by 20% next year, increasing the number of Japanese visitors by 20% over the next two years etc.

These action programmes must then be converted into a detailed plan, ideally within the framework of an annual budget. The tourist board will need to consider, within the limitations of its budget and available resources, how to produce a marketing mix which will enable it to achieve its targets. The marketing mix will consist of advertising expenditure at home and in overseas countries, expenditure on tourist offices, tourist literature and guides, advisory services to hotels etc.

The plan will be finalised as a series of expenditure budgets and achievement targets. Means of monitoring and controlling performance should, if possible, be built into the plan.

3   MARKETING AND CORPORATE STRATEGY

Planning occurs at different management levels.

Level		Management	Time Scale
1	Corporate	Top	Long term
2	Business/Functional	Middle	Medium term
3	Operational/Action	Junior/staff	Short term

Clarifying the level of analysis within the overall framework of a business plan causes some students and managers alike difficulty. Confusion arises because there are a number of different terms used in the literature for the same thing.

To help understand these levels imagine you are on a staircase, as you move up from one level to another the strategy of the lower level is the tactics of the higher. So for example, marketing strategy is part of corporate tactics. Similarly, sales strategy is marketing tactics.

A strategic perspective centres around planning for the future, either planning for the whole organisation or just for the marketing aspects of the organisation.

Johnson and Scholes in *Exploring corporate strategy* outline the characteristics associated with the word strategy and strategic decisions at the corporate or 'company wide' level.

(a)   *The scope of an organisation's activities.* Does it focus on one area of activity or many? For example should BAe focus on defence?

(b)   *The matching of the activities of an organisation to its environment.* In Europe, defence firms are seeking to collaborate to compete internationally, not just serve the home government.

(c)   *The matching of an organisation's activities to its resource capability:* strategies need to be rooted in an adequate resource base.

(d)   *The allocation of major resources* (often to do with major acquisitions or disposal of resources). BAe significantly rationalised its operations and workforce.

(e)   *Affecting operational decisions.* Strategic decisions set off waves of lesser decisions. BAe's decision to rationalise the operation resulted in human resource issues for personnel, revised product and manufacturing plans which inevitably resulted in changes to the sorts of day-to-day problems faced by a production manager or a sales manager.

(f)   *The values and expectations of those who have power.* Strategy can be thought of as a reflection of the attitudes and beliefs of those who have most influence in the organisation, this being related to the mission of the organisation. The expectations of the Government to maintain BAe as a major international competitor are influential in its mission.

(g)   *The long term direction of the organisation.* The decision to privatise BAe affected its long-term future.

(h)   *Implications for change are thus are likely to be complex in nature.* This arises for three reasons: strategic decisions usually involve *a high degree of uncertainty*, require *an integrated approach* to managing the organisation (including a cross-functional perspective) and thirdly, *involve change*, not only planning change but also in implementing it.

Marketing planning represents the strategic approach to marketing. Lancaster and Massingham (*Marketing Management* (1993)), outline three key reasons for what they see as an increasing need for a strategic approach to marketing.

(a)   The pace of change and environmental complexity - environmental issues, technological change, social change etc.

(b)   Increasing organisation size and complexity - a move from functionally structured to matrix and strategic business units, internationalisation.

(c)   Increased competition (deregulation, globalisation, technology).

Kotler (in *Marketing Management*) highlights the characteristics of a strategic perspective in his definition of marketing management:

'The marketing *management process* consists of analysing market opportunities, researching and selecting target markets, designing marketing strategies, planning marketing programmes and organising, implementing and controlling the marketing effort.'

At the strategic level we see that marketing involves four processes.

(a)   *Analysis:* the antecedent of decision-making and plan formulation.

(b)   *Planning:* analysis forms basis of plans, plans represent decision-making.

(c)   *Implementation:* having made plans they need to be put into action.

(d)   *Control:* this completes the cycle of functional management as it feeds into the analysis and planning stages and the cycle starts again.

The tangible outcome of a strategic perspective to marketing is the marketing plan which outlines the current marketing situation, sets marketing objectives, strategies and tactics and outlines how the plan will be controlled.

Empirical research by Greenley (1987) and McDonald (1990) indicates that very few firms actually have formally written marketing plans, and this is particularly the case within the small business and not-for-profit sectors. Many organisations find it difficult to develop a strategic approach to marketing because of a lack of resources, marketing knowledge, skills, time and probably most importantly a lack of marketing orientation or culture.

Many prescriptive approaches have been developed, often as a checklist of activities needed to be done to write a marketing plan. However, changing an organisation's culture is not a simple or quick task. It requires top management support, internal communications and training on an on-going basis related to marketing skills and cross-function co-ordination.

However, the reality is that many organisations still do not adopt marketing planning practices at all. Therefore the first challenge for marketers working in these types of companies will be to introduce successfully a simple planning system which has the support of senior management.

4   SOCIAL CHANGE

> *Examiner's comments: summaries/extracts.* Reasonable answers, with most candidates focusing on demography and new technology - but many ignored the implications for planning and control.

A key stage in the marketing planning and control process is an analysis of the current situation, or marketing audit. The audit should consist of an analysis of the wider macro environment, the more specific micro environment and an internal analysis of the organisation. The reason for conducting an audit is to ensure that the strategies, tactics and controls implemented are in line with the current needs, wants, behaviours and contexts of the target market. In this sense as societies change, so too should the way we market our products and services. Less than twenty years ago in the UK it was acceptable to market Supersoft shampoo with an image of a rather amused woman being forcibly taken away on the shoulder of a Viking. Equally the idea of a product designer being able to work together with a client hundreds of miles away via an Internet connection was not a possibility.

Societies constantly change. Doyle, in *Marketing Management and Strategy*, looks ahead to the year 2000 and offers ten environmental changes which appear to be accelerating:

(a) *Fashionisation:* goods affected by annual model changes, rapid obsolescence and unpredictable demand. New models and new services are becoming the key to enhancing margins.

(b) *Micro-markets:* customers expect customisation of goods to their specific needs. Technology permits ever-finer market segmentation and product range expansion.

(c) *Rising expectations:* brought about by higher quality products and services.

(d) *Technological change:* brought about both product and process improvements together with a society much more receptive to diffusion of technological innovation.

(e) *Competition:* market barriers have fallen with declining tariffs, lower transport costs and speed of information about market opportunities.

(f) *Globalisation:* rising incomes for travel and access to international media have created common demands and opportunities for common suppliers.

(g) *Service:* product advantages are difficult to gain and defend, often competition is based on service augmentation.

(h) *Commoditisation:* today's speciality products are tomorrow's commodities, unless companies can move the goalposts through faster innovation, profit margins decline.

(i) *Erosion of brands:* the fractionisation of previously homogenous markets, together with the growth in own label reliability is reducing the power of the big brands.

(j) *New constraints:* new regulations from the EU in terms of the environment and the raising of ethical standards brings offending companies under increasing scrutiny.

Mitchell, reporting in Marketing Business (1994), adds a number of additional ways in which society is changing: an ageing of the population in Europe; a growing social divide between relatively prosperous 'knowledge' workers and the rest; the fragmentation of traditional consumer lifestages due to fractured career paths, redundancy, self-employment, rising divorce, caring for parents, middle age inheritances and single parent families.

Of all these changes the two which will be selected for further discussion are *demographic change* and *technological change*.

Demography

At the beginning of the 1990s people aged over fifty were 17.8m or 31% of the UK population. By 2025 this will rise to 23m representing a significant increase in the proportion of old to young people, non-working to working people in the UK Currently, approximately 30% of the over fifties have no mortgage left to pay and they represent the inheritance generation with £10bn inherited in 1987 rising to £17bn in 1997. In the UK the over sixty-fives can be divided into three segments:

- 20% well-off
- 30% property rich but cash poor
- 50% state pension

Clearly with the growth in the older consumers and the related reduction in younger people, this brings significant implications for the planning and control for specific product groups. The demand for financial services, medical products, retirement housing and holidays is likely to increase whilst the demand for nightclubs, alcohol, starter homes and jeans is likely to fall. More specifically, the product manager of Thomson Holidays' 'Young at Heart' brand markets to 'JOLLies'; Jet-Setting Oldies with Loads of Loot, or the 20% well-off. At the beginning of the 1990s this represented 60,000 holidays and the market is increasing. When marketing the brand a number of key points emerge.

(a) Good service is vital to repeat purchase.

(b) This segment is responsive to sales promotions which take time to redeem, involve collection and reward rather than competitions, free draws or lotteries.

(c) Media choice is skewed towards the Daily Telegraph and Daily Mail and retirement magazines such as Saga, Yours and Choice.

(d) This group watches a lot of TV. Good audience profiles include 'This Is Your Life' and 'Coronation Street'.

(e) This segment tend to identify with their children rather than with their parents and so think of themselves as 20 years younger.

For those organisations which find themselves in declining markets they will experience growing competition. Those that remain will need to more closely segment and position their products, consider expanding their product/market focus through market and product development strategies and closely control their cost and profit performance.

Technology

Perhaps even more significant than demographic changes is the influence exerted by changing technology on society. The convergence of computing and telecom technologies is significantly changing work, leisure and marketing planning practice. As the cost of IT falls and computer speeds increase the resultant information revolution is beginning to change how we learn and work. Consumers' acceptance of new technologically based products has also increased; the use of mobile telephones, faxes, home multi media systems, virtual shopping malls and interactive terminals is common. But what are the specific implications for marketing planning and control processes? Some examples of how technology is being applied will help to answer this question.

(a) *Sales.* The salesperson with a portable PC can run interactive sales demonstrations and automatic order processing.

(b) *Distribution.* The videobooth allows customers to talk directly to staff such as accounts personnel and forms can be signed and transmitted. Electronic data interchange has reduced the costs and speed of the grocery supply chain.

(c) *Product development.* The designer can have video clips of customers' reactions to prototypes from focus groups, designs can be viewed anywhere in the world, amended or approved in minutes rather than days through the post.

(d) *Market research.* Researchers can use software to tailor questions depending on the previous answer. Results can be downloaded for immediate analysis. Real time sales data can be merged, cut and presented in striking visual form and communicating direct to the marketing director.

(e) *Communications.* Companies can produce interactive infomercials such as Sainsburys recipe book and if linked to a home shopping system, purchases can be made. The logistics and costs of advertising are being re-worked due to the ability to send ads. from computer to computer down ISDN phone lines.

(f) *Control.* As the data gathering for the results of product launches moves from months to weeks this feedback is leading to more reactive, time-sensitive, accountable marketing strategies. Retailers can use scanning data to determine which lines should be delisted and which to carry.

Often changes in society are afforded too much significance in relation to the nature and speed of their affects on marketing practice. For example, many writers talked about how consumers would be prepared to pay vast extra amounts for environmentally friendly products. Then we all heard about the caring, sharing, stakeholding nineties. Whilst the ageing population, new technologies, environmentalism and a growing focus on social responsibility are all changes which are taking place, most marketers have kept their balance and not over responded, but adjusted gradually in-line with the pace of change. As Mitchell (1994) points out, the microwave, like the video recorder, patented just after world war two was not commercialised until the sixties and took twenty years to achieve wide scale consumer acceptance. That stated, those organisations which practise marketing planning and control successfully, will be those which anticipate and respond to changing societal needs.

5   **INFORMATION ABOUT COMPETITORS**

> *Examiner's comments: summary/extracts.* The better answers discussed the structure of a competitive information system, the nature of the inputs and how the outputs could then be fed into the strategic marketing process.

A competitive information system is an integral element of a marketing information system. The importance of this element is heightened when a company is faced with increasingly competitive market conditions. In this situation, information obtained from the system is invaluable when formulating competitive marketing strategy.

When establishing a competitive information system it is important to consider the operational set-up. Lancaster and Massingham (1993) suggest that the entire process should be considered in detail. The type of information required should be specified and sources of data and methods for collection considered. Procedures should then be formulated for gathering and reporting the information and responsibility for information gathering assigned. Finally, procedures for analysing and distributing the information are needed.

The nature of the inputs to the competitive information system would be as follows.

(a) *Marketing intelligence*

This constitutes information gathered on the marketplace on a day to day basis forming continual monitoring to identify trend, change and unexpected event data.

Sources

- Trade journals, publications and press articles
- Exhibitions and industry contacts
- Competitor promotional literature and price lists
- Competitors annual reports
- Industry reports e.g. Mintel, Euromonitor etc
- Trade Associations
- Sales representative reports
- Reports from marketing channels eg distributors and retailers
- 'Off the peg' research data eg AGB Superpanel

(b) *Marketing research*

Where information is needed on an 'ad-hoc' basis to make a specific marketing decision. Information of this type is obtained from two methods.

(i) *Secondary (desk) research*

Where data gathered for another purpose is applied to the problem at hand. A number of sources from the above list would be appropriate in this area eg Industry Reports.

(ii) *Primary (field) research*

Surveys, customer panels and observation research of this type could produce information on issues such as:

- Customer care
- Service/product quality

The *outputs from the system* need to be evaluated, analysed and disseminated to appropriate departments within the company. Information of this type can be used, for example, to build a profile on current and potential market competitors, their market positioning and comparative strengths and weaknesses. Strategically, this information would be invaluable when making decisions in areas such as segmentation and positioning, product and market development as well as building competitor response models. Overall, competitive information systems are invaluable to formulating marketing strategy, particularly in increasing competitive marketplaces.

6 INTERNAL CAPABILITIES

(a) *Introduction.* This report reviews the company's perceived strengths and weaknesses with regard to its internal capabilities of exploiting the opportunity for custom-built remote control models.

(b) *Strengths and weaknesses analysis*

Area	Strengths	Weaknesses
Corporate management and organisation	• Friends with a common interest • Some years' experience of working together • Flexible, innovative, responsive • Willing to seek advice	• No MD • No formal structure • No corporate objectives
Financial	• None apparent	• Need capital investment • High risk borrowers • Lack of expertise
Personnel	• Enthusiastic/motivated • Work well as a team	• Assumed lack of business and marketing experience • No formal relationships
Production	• Possess necessary skills • Have necessary tools • Make to order	• No experience of higher volumes • Might need new equipment
Marketing planning and strategy	• Niche marketing	• No formal strategy • Responsive rather than proactive • No planning system • No control systems
MR/MkIS	• Initiative	• No formal MR/MkIS • No factual knowledge of market sizes, trends, buying motives etc
Product	• Custom-built • Good design • High quality	• None apparent
Price	• Negotiable • Potentially premium	• No formal costings
Promotion	• Recommendation • Demonstration • Some personal selling • Club PR	• No promotional skills • No promotional budget • No agency
Place	• Some existing space (production) • Direct delivery/collection	• No showroom space? • No distribution channels • No office

(c) *Conclusion*

Although the proposed new company has a number of important strengths, there is an almost equal number of weaknesses. Following Kotler's recommendations the strengths and weaknesses should be *scored* and their degrees of importance assessed so as to facilitate *prioritisation*. For example it seems clear that product design and mechanical quality would have both a high *score* and a high *importance* and should therefore be ranked as a major strength. However, lack of finance, lack of marketing skills and lack of market knowledge would rank as major weaknesses. Worked through in this way, it would seem major weaknesses exceed major strengths. Issues arising are as follows.

(i) It is unlikely that sufficient funding could be attracted without a formal business plan (I would be pleased to assist in producing one).

(ii) Should the new company outsource marketing/sales/distribution so as to exploit better its design/production skills?

(iii) I propose a management team is elected from the group to further the group's interests.

7   **FLEXIBLE MATRIX**

(a) *Introduction*

The logic of product portfolio analysis is the same as that applied to share portfolios. Just as financial investors have different investments with varying risks and rates of return, firms should have a portfolio of products (and possibly strategic business units (SBUs)) characterised by different market growth rates and relative market shares. A number of alternative models of portfolio analysis have been developed which include the BCG growth-share matrix, the General Electric multifactor portfolio model, the Shell directional policy matrix, Abell and Hammond's 3X3 matrix and Arthur D. Little strategic condition model (Wilson and Gilligan, 1998).

(b) *BCG Growth-Share Matrix*

The Boston Consulting Group in the mid 1960s developed the BCG matrix as a strategic planning tool with the rationale that relative market share and market growth rates are important for determining appropriate marketing strategies.

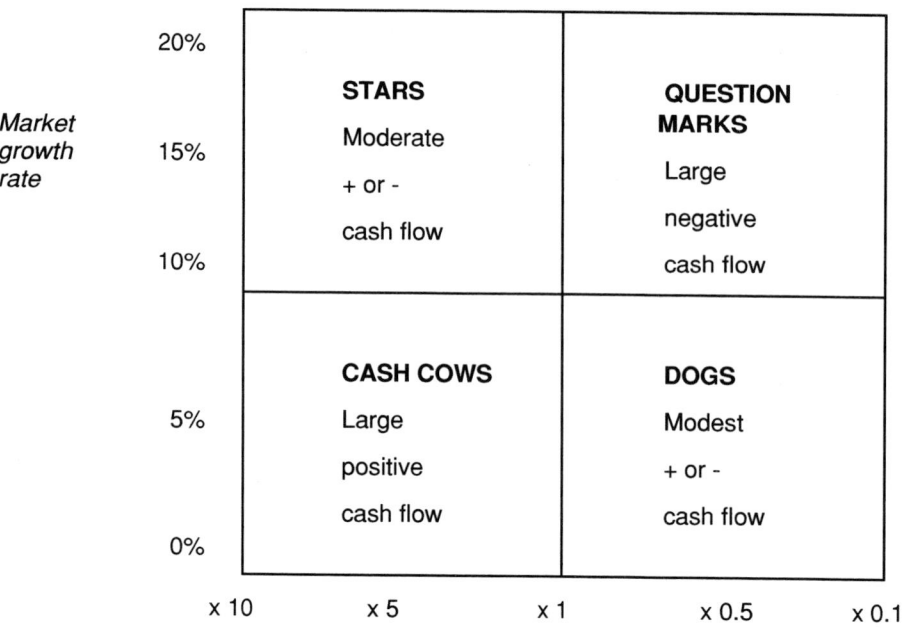

The logic of the matrix is based on four assumptions.

(i)   Margins and funds generated increase with market share as a result of experience and scale effects.

(ii)   Sales growth demands cash to finance working capital and increases in capacity.

(iii) Increases in market share need cash to support share gaining tactics.

(iv) Market growth slows as the product reaches life cycle maturity and at this stage cash surpluses can be generated by high share players to support products still in the growth stages of their life cycle.

BCG stress the need to build a balanced portfolio to ensure sufficient positive net cash flow to ensure long-term success. This means few or no dogs and enough cash cows to turn stars into cash cows as markets mature and to invest in question marks to build market share and hence become stars.

(c) *Weaknesses of the BCG Approach*

(i)   Over simplification. More than two factors that affect cash flow.

(ii)   Cash flow as the performance criteria: some argue return on investment is more important.

(iii) Ambiguity in classifications – it is difficult to separate SBU and product level analysis. In addition, what contributes a high and low share or growth rate? These factors make it difficult to plot positions accurately.

(iv) New products and negative growth situations are not dealt with.

(v)   The *strategies* suggested by the model tend to be highly prescriptive in nature and there are situations where they may be inappropriate. Woo and Cooper point to the success of companies with low market share. Cash flow can be large from a small share player - when scale and experience effects are small, when a firm has a low cost source of raw material or if entry barriers are high. PIMS analysis also indicates that *quality* is a partial substitute for market share.

(vi)   The questionable accuracy of data supplied and/or processing of the data.

(vii)   Derivation of apparently reliable figures for a specific business from a generalist technique or model

(viii) An initial over-optimism of its potential contribution.

(d)   *General Electric's Multifactor Portfolio Model*

In an attempt to overcome some of the weaknesses of the BCG matrix, General Electric's Multifactor portfolio model takes into account more factors to determine market attractiveness and competitive position. Each company needs to determine the factors underlying each dimension in their particular market.

General Electric uses industry attractiveness split into high, medium and low and *business strength* split into strong, medium and weak. The nine cells fall into three distinct strategy and investment recommendations; *invest for growth*, manage selectively for *earnings* and *harvest/withdraw*.

A specific example for the Hydraulic Pumps market (Kotler, 1997) is provided below.

Market attractiveness	Weight	Rating (1-5)	Value
Market size	0.2	4	0.8
Market growth rate	0.2	5	1.0
Profit margin	0.15	4	0.6
Competitive intensity	0.15	2	0.3
Technological requirements	0.15	4	0.6
Inflationary vulnerability	0.05	3	0.15
Energy requirements	0.05	2	0.1
Environmental impact	0.05	3	0.15
			3.70

Business strength	Weight	Rating (1-5)	Value
Market share	0.1	4	0.4
Share growth	0.15	2	0.3
Product quality	0.1	4	0.3
Brand reputation	0.1	5	0.5
Distribution network	0.05	4	0.2
Promotional effectiveness	0.05	3	0.15
Productive capacity	0.05	3	0.15
Productive efficiency	0.05	2	0.1
Unit costs	0.15	3	0.45
Material supplies	0.05	5	0.25
R&D performance	0.1	3	0.3
Managerial personnel	0.05	4	0.2
			3.4

BPP PUBLISHING

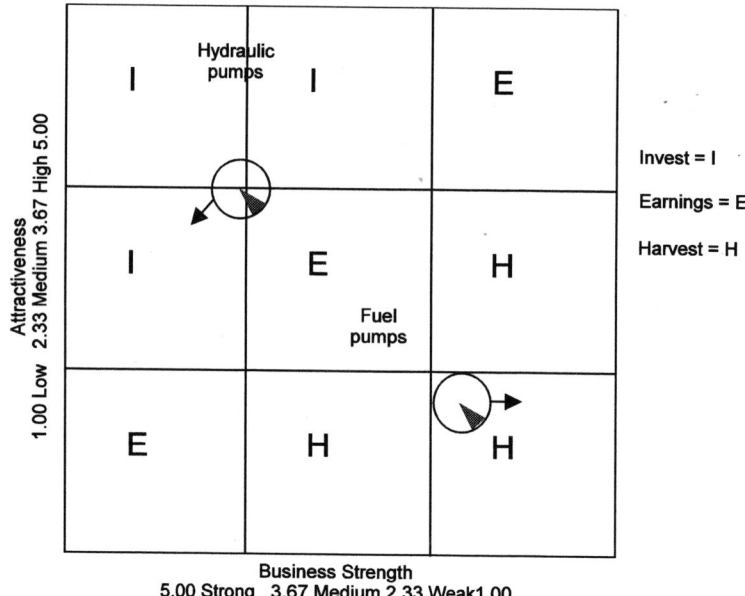

From the portfolio the two BCG factors are subsumed under the two major variables of the GE matrix, and thus the model leads planners to look at more factors in evaluating an actual business or product. In addition, the circle shows the *size* of the overall market and the *company's share* within the market plus the direction the business is likely to move in should no change in strategy occur. The hydraulic pumps business is in a fairly attractive part of the matrix whereas fuel pumps are very unattractive. Overall, this portfolio matrix adds greater information into the decision making process.

Conclusion

Despite their limitations portfolio matrixes do prove useful in the *analysis* and *ideas generation* stage of strategy formulation. As there are a number of matrixes to choose from, the strategic planner should consider using more than one and adapt the model to their own organisational situation.

8   SWOT: NEED FOR RIGOUR

> *Examiner's comment: summary/extracts.* The better responses discussed the nature, source and significance of the weaknesses of SWOT analysis as a prelude to explaining how SWOTs can be conducted far more thoroughly than is typically the case.

SWOT analysis

Strengths **W**eaknesses **O**pportunities **T**hreats analysis is a management tool for organising information and for clarifying the current situation. For a SWOT analysis to be of use to a company it must be considered as part of an overall planning process. We are looking at the 'where are we now?' part of the process, which can be considered as a 'funnel', starting with a lot of information and through techniques such as SWOT we can identify a set of key issues.

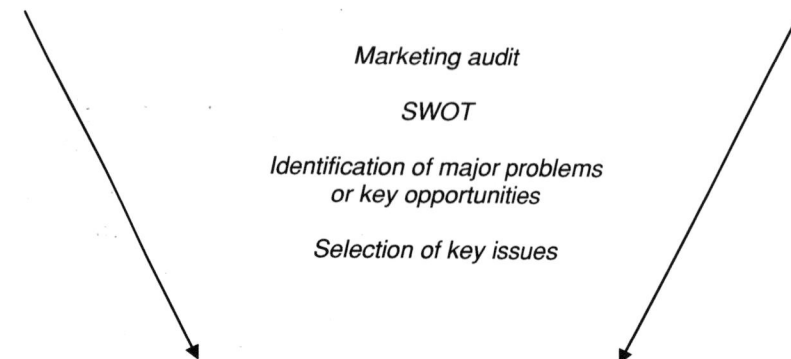

Marketing audit

SWOT

Identification of major problems or key opportunities

Selection of key issues

In order to complete a thorough SWOT analysis, there are four functional areas which need to be covered.

(a)   *Financial*

The organisation's financial position, ratio analysis, gearing, profitability and liquidity.

(b)   *Personnel*

Human resources which are available to the organisation. Time management, skills, training, management, philosophy, turnover and adaptability. Organisational structure and communication channels.

(c)   *Production*

Materials, machines, production capabilities, fixed assets.

(d)   *Marketing*

Marketing environment (both macro and micro). Marketing objectives and strategies. Marketing information systems evaluate and measure marketing effectiveness and the marketing mix.

The results of the SWOT would be displayed as a matrix of strengths, weaknesses, opportunities and threats.

The SWOT analysis tool is attractive due to its apparent simplicity. However if used unrigorously it can turn into descriptive lists of factors of little planning value to the organisation. In a critical review of the tool, Hill and Westbrook (1997) summarise the fundamental concerns about the intrinsic nature of SWOT analysis.

- The length of the lists
- No requirement to prioritise or weight the factors identified
- Unclear and ambiguous words and phrases
- No resolution of conflicts
- No obligation to verify statements and opinions with data or analysis
- Single level of analysis is all that is required
- No logical link with an implementation phase

Therefore to use the tool more rigorously, each of these criticisms should be addressed. An example used by the researchers was of a food company with a dominant customer taking more than 50% of the company's product sales. On their SWOT analysis strengths included, 'the value of our contract with company X', whilst amongst their weaknesses are, 'over-reliance on company X'. This contradiction should have been used as a spur to analytical debate and action. In what circumstances was it a strength? What conditions are needed for over-reliance to do harm? What was a sensible timescale for reduction of this dependence? Raising these questions would move analysis from a single level.

In order to assist decision-making the information should give some indication of the relative importance of the different factors presented. Strengths and weaknesses are internal to the company such as strong cash base, internal conflict etc. and opportunities and threats are external to the company, potential new market segment or development of a substitute product.

Internal to the organisation	**Strengths** in order of priority	**Weaknesses** in order of priority
External to the organisation	**Opportunities** in order of priority	**Threats** in order of priority

This matrix can assist strategy formulation through two options:

- Conversion
- Matching

Conversion strategies

- Convert weaknesses into strengths and be able to take advantage of an existing opportunity.

- Converting threats into opportunities, which can then be taken advantage of through existing strengths.

Matching strategies

- Match company strengths with market opportunities

SWOT analysis can contribute to strategy planning by developing a match between the organisation's environment and its strategic direction. Whilst strong critics such as Mintzberg see the tool as being far too formal and offering false rationality, others such as Wheelen & Hunger (1995) and Weirich (1982) with his TOWS matrix support SWOT as a rigorous analytical tool. It can give initial ideas for strategy and objectives, used in conjunction with other analysis such as PLC, Ansoff and the BCG matrix. If used as the basis for managerial debate, SWOT results in new information and ideas, from which the organisation can go on to make informed decisions on which strategy/ies would be most appropriate to follow.

Although SWOT analysis is a relatively simple model, if applied rigorously in similar manner to the one described it can be an extremely useful tool in organising information for the planning process.

9 FINANCIAL ANALYSIS

> *Tutorial note.* The finance function produces several different kinds of information. Be sure to cover all of them.
>
> *Examiner's comments: summary/extracts.* 'Too many candidates did not use the asked-for format or explain how the results would be used.'

MEMORANDUM

To: Financial Director
From: Marketing Manager
Date: December 1999
Subject: Requirements for financial analysis

Can I take this opportunity to outline my current understanding of how you can aid my marketing decision making. I would welcome your comments on this and recommendations on any other types of financial information you think my be useful to me in my new role.

Having taken my Diploma in Marketing I am aware that there are three important accounting roles which produce different forms of output which are relevant to the marketing department.

(a) Financial accounting which results in the annual report and accounts which includes the key financial statements of the balance sheet, profit and loss and funds flow statement. Whilst important in recording the effects of marketing activities, this information does not aid decision-making.

(b) Corporate finance is concerned with financial management and ensuring that enough funds are made available. Marketing activities are not usually funded separately, but are included in the financial plans produced as part of (c) below.

(c) Management accounting. Management accounts are produced regularly, usually monthly or quarterly, and aid operational decision-making. I would hope that I can receive monthly information which will include a comparison of financial performance to date against my targets as budgeted and assessment of that performance against the budget for the year. In this way financial analysis should aid my marketing analysis, planning and control.

In particular I see financial information being useful in the review and control process related to the areas over which I have some or total control, namely marketing costs, revenue and profits by product, product line, product portfolio, pricing strategy, promotional strategy and distribution channel management. This relationship can be shown diagrammatically.

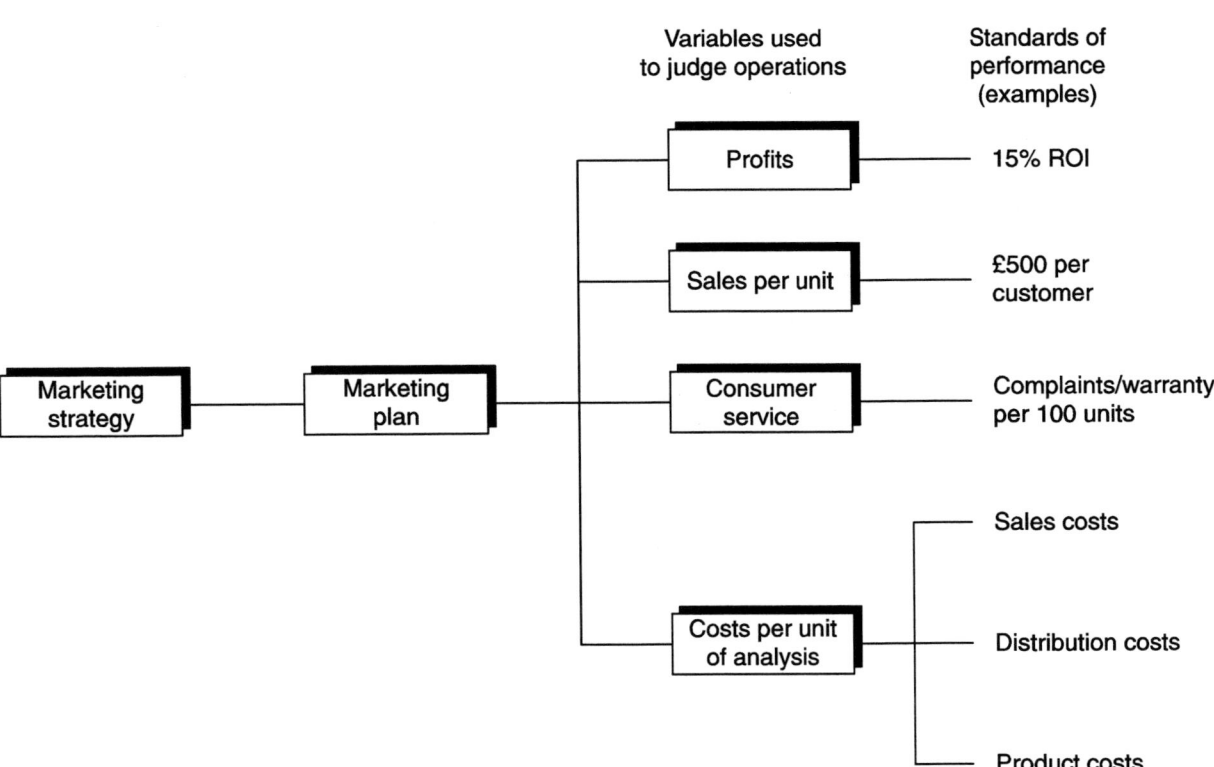

In seeking to control my marketing activities it would be useful for the financial information to conform to the standard characteristics of effective control systems, namely that the information:

- Should be timely
- Should measure the essential nature of the activity being assessed
- Should provide information on trends
- Should facilitate action
- Must be economical and meaningful

With this in mind and from the diagram we can see that as marketing manager I would find financial information relating to the profits, sales and costs of my products useful. More specifically I need this information by product and product line and by the various distribution channels through which we sell our goods. From this variance analysis can be conducted. I should be able to keep close control over my marketing budget each month and be able to assess, longer term, the effectiveness of this expenditure. It would also be useful for the finance department to be able to provide me with comparative performance data on our major competitors. Financial accounting can be used here to help highlight any potential competitive weaknesses which can be exploited.

The results of this financial analysis will be used to make both strategic and tactical decisions. For example, by analysis of sales and profit trends by channel in conjunction with market share analysis I will be able to develop my distribution channel management strategy and thereby allocate trade marketing support accordingly. Looking at financial and market data together, new product development and distribution channel development strategies can be formulated. If specific promotional campaigns can be isolated, their effectiveness can be assessed by analysis of sales trend data. By identification of the most profitable products and channels and in conjunction with the sales manager, sales force targets and compensation programmes can be developed together with sales promotion and advertising support programmes within allocated budgets.

Without this sort of financial information, marketing analysis, planning and control will be less efficient and effective. In view of this fact can we arrange a meeting to discuss the exact detail and form in which the financial information will be provided.

10 FORECASTING OF SALES

MEMO

To: Sales Personnel
From: Mike Jones
Date: 24 November 20XX
Subject: *Sales forecasts and budgetary control information*

(a) *The importance of having accurate forecasts*

Annual forecasts, usually classed as medium-term forecasts, are statements of the estimated volume of sales of an organisation's products and/or services in the next financial year. They are used to assist the organisation's financial planning process since they are expressed in monetary amounts and thereafter feed into the annual budget. It is therefore only by estimating the following year's sales that an organisation can estimate how much money will be available to spend in the future.

It must be remembered, however, that forecasts are only estimates and it is very difficult to produce accurate ones. In being optimistic and overstating the forecasts, several problems can arise.

(i)   High forecasts can lead to high targets for the sales force. This can be demoralising if the sales team do not achieve the target. Moreover they may be relying, to a certain extent, on bonuses that are linked to achieving the forecast sales level.

(ii)   For a company quoted on the Stock Exchange, overstating the forecast could affect the share price if the City loses confidence.

(iii) Sales forecasts feed into production plans. Over-optimistic forecasts can lead to excess stocks in the warehouse. Not only does this tie up capital, it also increases the likelihood of damage and waste.

(iv)   Extra staff may be taken on in sales or production to cope with the expected level of sales. If this does not materialise, there may need to be redundancies which can be very demoralising for the rest of the workforce.

Although there are obvious problems with overstating the expected level of sales, understatement can lead to problems as well. Actual demand will then be greater than supply. This can lead to:

- Competitors benefiting from the organisation's lost sales
- An increase in the amount of overtime required and therefore higher salary costs
- An increase in bonus payments to sales people who exceed their targets

As both overstating and understating forecasts can lead to problems, it is clear that a balance is required. It is therefore important to ensure that forecasts are as accurate as possible. This entails having good, up-to-date internal data and marketing intelligence. Sales statistics should be available in a suitable format and all the factors affecting sales should be understood by the people involved in the forecasting process. In some organisations these people will be accountants, although ideally sales and marketing managers and possibly sales representatives should be involved as they are closer to the market place. Appropriate methods of forecasting should be used, whether quantitative or qualitative or a mixture of the two.

Any assumptions made (such as rate of inflation, exchange rates, rate of adoption of a product, increase in a competitor's promotional activity and so on) should be clearly stated so that if any of these change markedly, adjustments can easily be made. It therefore follows that it is important to review forecasts regularly to take into account any new information and adjust the figures as appropriate. Although totally accurate forecasts cannot be guaranteed, at least the adverse effects of inaccurate forecasts will be minimised.

(b) *The importance of meaningful budgetary control information*

Control is 'the process of ensuring that a firm's activities conform to its plans and that its objectives are achieved' (Drury, *Management & Cost Accounting*).

The budget sets out the company plan in a formal way and really only delivers benefits when it is measured against actual performance. Budgetary control information enables this process to take place. It consists of a report of actual performance set against details of what was expected to be achieved - the budget performance. The result is a formal variance analysis report for management. The variance analysis will contain important indicators as to the reasons for a discrepancy between budgeted and actual results.

Variance analysis information is complex and needs to be fully understood. At first sight it is tempting to dismiss minor variances as unimportant and this *may* be true. However, before dismissing small variances the *cause* as well as the effect has to be appreciated to ensure that the events which gave rise to the variance do not imply serious problems in that particular budget.

In this case, the first step is to find the reason for the shortfall in the sales budget. Ways to produce more accurate information in future must be found.

With errors of such significance further questions also arise. If many of the firm's costs are fixed, the losses in some profit centres might be thought of as inevitable if sales are so far below expectations. However, sensitivity analysis could have been carried out; a thoughtful examination of a 'worst case' scenario could have anticipated the impact of such a large error and contingency plans (increased promotion, cost-cutting) could have been laid. More importantly, as information was being collected the variances should have been seen as so significant that urgent action should have been taken earlier. An important feature of all information is its timeliness and that would appear to have been overlooked. Hence profit centres continued to spend their cost budgets without taking account of the fact that the revenue planned to support the spending was not being achieved.

Budgets are quantitative plans and as such should be based on the nature of a particular organisation as a system with a degree of integration. One figure is likely to be the driver of other figures in the planning process. In this case the errors in the sales forecast inevitably meant that there were related errors in the budgets for purchases, stocks and debtors. These will have further consequences for the company as they drive the payments and receipts pattern which governs the amounts of working capital available.

There appears to be a lack of understanding about the way in which control information is used. For such a large error to exist significant variances of actual to budget must have been evident early in the year (assuming the business is not a particularly seasonal one). It would appear that no action was taken and the reasons for that must be investigated. Finally, effective action should be taken in response to control information and that was clearly lacking. This could have been due to management weakness or more likely to a poor reporting system that simply recorded details without allowing investigation.

11   MISSION AND OBJECTIVES

Wilson, Gilligan and Pearson suggest that to be effective, a strategic planning system must be goal driven. The setting of a mission statement and objectives is therefore a key step in the marketing planning process, since unless it is carried out effectively, everything that follows will lack cohesion and focus.

In the authors' model of the strategic planning process, the development of the mission statement is the second stage after the initial environmental and business analysis.

The *mission statement* comes at the start of both corporate and marketing planning as it represents a *vision* of what the company is or should attempt to become. Brooksbank (in *Marketing Planning: A Seven Stage Process*) also considers it to come at stage two, after establishing a marketing orientation. He outlines three components of the mission statement.

(a)   The firm's basic business in terms of products and/or services to provide and markets to serve.

(b)   The identification of future directions to be pursued by the firm.

(c)   The establishment of business values, attitudes and beliefs (ie how the firm should conduct its affairs).

The basis for deciding on the mission is the firm's response to two fundamental questions:

- 'Where is our business now?'
- 'Where should our business go in the future?'

In reality, formulating a mission is more complicated and difficult than the above two questions make it sound. Most aspects of a company's strategic situation will require analysis first before such long term and strategically significant decisions can be taken.

Once clarified, the business mission should ideally take the form of a concisely written statement, which should then remain the focus of the firm's energies for a considerable time period. In theory at least, the benefit of a well chosen mission statement is that it can provide a powerful source of motivation for all company personnel - based on a shared purpose, opportunity and direction.

BPP
PUBLISHING

As with 'aims', *policy* is somewhere between missions and objectives. Policy can come from legislation, economics or the culture of the organisation. In essence policy comprises the operating decisions which individual managers are not free to make, as they have been made for the organisation as a whole. For example 'It is our policy to prosecute shoplifters', 'It is our policy for staff to spend no more than £55 on one night's hotel accommodation'. Whilst policies and mission are corporate in nature (ie they affect the whole organisation), the key distinction is the *level* at which they operate. The mission has long-term strategic implications whereas policy is operational in nature and unlikely to affect significantly the organisation's long-term direction.

Aims are general statements of intention which focus attention and lead to the need for certain, definitive action. For example, 'Our aim is to be the best employer in town', 'Our aim is to produce the highest quality products'. These are not objectives because they are not performance specific or time related. Very often managers believe they are setting objectives but strictly speaking objectives need to be capable of measurement otherwise they are aims. In this sense, aims are more general statements than objectives. (Sometimes aims are called non-operational goals.)

Objectives are clear statements of what the business or function intends to achieve. Objectives should be hierarchical, measurable, realistic and consistent.

Corporate objectives are concerned with the whole firm and primary objectives relate to key financial factors for business success:

- Profitability - ROCE increase
- Growth - sales, market share
- Risk reduction - increase product, customer, market base
- Cash flow

All functions are deployed strategically towards achieving these objectives. For example, the production function can reduce costs, the finance function can manage funds more efficiently, the personnel function can recruit better people at less cost or increase their productivity and the marketing function can grow sales profitably.

In other words, all functions need to work together to achieve the most common primary corporate objective of profitable growth.

There are often also secondary objectives related to social and ethical obligations (responsibilities or constraints). Most companies seek a good public image and have objectives stating their attempts:

- To be good employers
- To contribute to the local community
- To safeguard the environment

These are often hard to quantify and so strictly speaking should be considered aims for example, 'to become a more environmentally conscious organisation'. Often these 'objectives' can be seen to clearly derive from the core values in the mission statement.

Once corporate objectives have been established and translated into a co-ordinated corporate strategy the various functions can develop their own objectives.

Marketing objectives are usually expressed in sales terms, for example:

- Market share
- Sales revenue
- Sales volume

and are then translated down into tactical objectives for product, pricing, promotion and distribution.

The key feature distinguishing missions, policies, aims and objectives are the time scale and the degree of specificity. Missions are very broad, corporate and long-term in nature whereas objectives are specific, quantifiable and shorter-term in nature.

12 FRANCHISE

Franchising

Compared to a company owned outlet, which is operated by salaried employees, a franchised store is operated by a franchisee who is an independent legal entity. *Franchisees* pay their respective franchisers an initial fee as well as a monthly royalty fee, which is usually specified as a percentage of sales revenue. In addition, franchisees are responsible for investment in the outlet and are expected to closely follow the franchiser's operating norms. Franchising's primary attributes (eg capital formation,

motivated entrepreneurs, standard systems, brand recognition, and procedures to control operations) help to solve key challenges connected with services marketing firms (eg small size, intangibility of services, quality control) and, therefore, represent a 'practical business marriage' (Cross and Walker, 1987).

(a)   *Information required*

As a Taiwan based organisation who has been approached by a UK clothing retailer with a view to franchising their operations in Taiwan certain information will be required before a decision can be made whether to take up this opportunity.

(i)   *Marketing*

(1)   How well recognised is the retail brand in its market and in our home market?

(2)   What marketing support is provided by the franchiser; launch activity, on-going promotions, PR, advertising etc?

(3)   What product range will be available and how much merchandising flexibility will be allowed?

(4)   What happens in terms of stock ownership, returns, old stock etc?

(5)   What pricing policies are involved in the contract?

(6)   How quick and effective are the current logistics?

(ii)   *Finance*

(1)   What are the costs of implementing and maintaining the operation?

(2)   What are the forecasted sales?

(3)   What are the forecasted profit implications?

(4)   What historical sales, cash flow and profit figures are available from current franchisees?

(5)   Are there capital borrowing implications?

(6)   What financial consulting support is offered by franchiser?

(iii)   *Human resources*

(1)   Is there any recruitment, selection, appraisal and disciplinary support offered?

(2)   What training guidelines and workshops are provided?

(3)   Are any HRM software systems available for payroll etc?

(4)   Are there any employment policy principles which will need to be adopted from franchiser's operating philosophy?

(iv)   *Retail operations*

(1)   What systems are required and/or provided (tills, EPOS, procurement etc.)?

(2)   What store location and design support is provided?

(3)   What merchandising support/policies are stipulated?

(4)   What information, monitoring and control procedures are required?

Acquiring this information

As with any research activity, the use of all the elements of a Marketing Information System should be utilised.

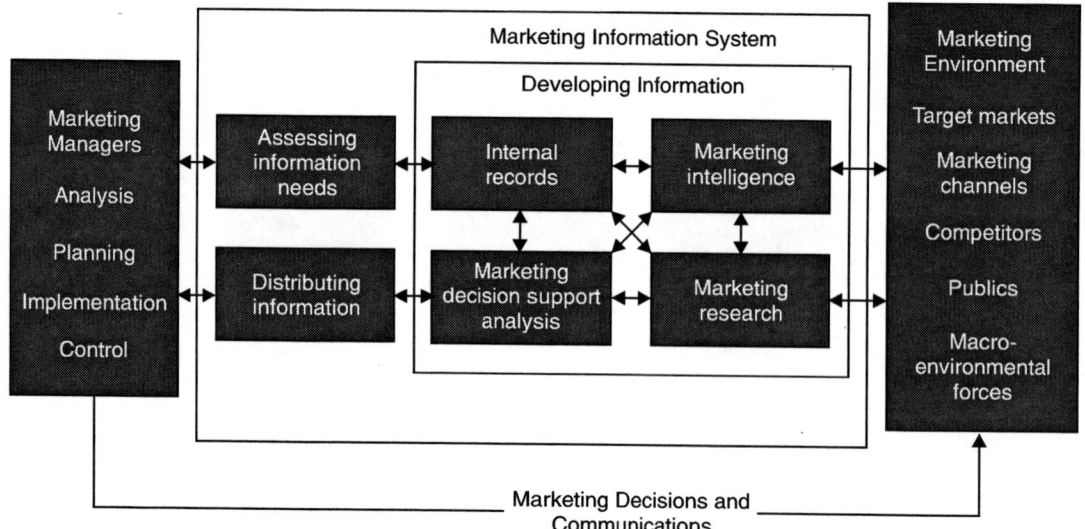

A lot of information can be gathered from *internal records* in the form of franchisee information provided by the UK retailer. Meetings to discuss the questions outlined above should provide a lot of background data. As the UK retailer has approached us, the firm should be receptive to our information requirements and make the relevant personnel in marketing, finance, HR and operations available to us, perhaps via email or a visit to the UK head office. On this visit, it would also be possible to conduct primary research in regard to a retail audit in UK principal town centres to see the retailer in operation in their home country. It would also be important to visit current franchisers in other countries around the world.

In addition, from market *intelligence sources,* reports would be available on retailing trends in both countries, financial performance of the retailer and reports on the retailer's franchising operations.

Meetings with our own *financial advisors* and lawyers would be required to assess the franchise agreement.

Finally, consumer research in Taiwan should be conducted to test the appeal of the new retail concept, store design, merchandise and pricing strategy. This would allow verification of sales forecast data provided by the franchiser.

Once these questions have answers with a reasonable degree of confidence a decision on whether to accept the franchise proposal could be taken.

13   DISCOUNT ORIENTED COMPETITOR

Introduction

Price competition is a factor in many markets ranging from industrial air conditioning to FMCGs such as cat food to the specific case of this question, financial services and motor insurance. In fact the advent of direct insurers such as Direct Line changed the competitive forces in this market by rapidly increasing the direct writers' share of the market at the expense of higher priced insurance brokers.

(a)   *Issues to consider in response to a price-based attack*

   (i)   *Service criteria*

      (1)   Is your service significantly different from the competitor initiating the price attack?

      (2)   Do you have a strong brand?

      (3)   Can you supply a different range of insurance packages?

      (4)   Can you add services to your current range?

   (ii)   *Demand criteria*

      (1)   Is the price cut significant enough to attract consumer attention?

      (2)   Are there a number of market segments with different insurance requirements and price sensitivities?

      (3)   Do you have strong customer loyalty?

(iii) *Competition criteria*

  (1) Why did the competitor change the price?

  - Take market share
  - Utilise excess capacity
  - Meet changing cost conditions
  - Lead an industry-wide price change

  (2) Is it likely to be a permanent price cut?

  (3) What is the likely affect of the price cut on your market share?

  (4) What are other competitors likely to do?

(iv) *Cost criteria*

  (1) What is the likely affect of the price cut on your profitability?
  (2) Will the price cut take your price below your costs?
  (3) Will a price cut increase demand and produce economies of scale effects?

(v) *Strategy criteria*

  (1) How will a change in price affect overall marketing strategy?

(b) *Options available*

If the decision is taken, after considering the answers to the above questions, that the competitor is offering superior value to our customers and taking business away from us, we have several options to consider.

(i) *Maintain price:* if it is decided that by dropping prices the company would lose too much margin, or the insurer would not loose much market share, or it could regain share when necessary, or it would retain the more profitable customers.

  The Radio Times in the TV listings price war maintained its price at 50p when all others dropped theirs in response to price based attacks. At the end of six months a number of the new entrants left the market, unable to sustain an acceptable margin, and the prices stabilised. The Radio Times, whilst losing some market share, came out of the war maintaining higher levels of profitability.

(ii) *Raise perceived quality:* if it is cheaper to maintain price but improve the actual or perceived quality of the insurance package. Improving the product, service and communications could do this.

(iii) *Reduce price:* if the insurer's costs fall with volume, the market is price sensitive, it would be difficult to rebuild share once lost to the new entrant.

However, engaging in price wars can be very costly. When the price wars began in the supermarkets in the early 1990s, Sainsbury's responded to the price cutters such as Kwik Save and Aldi by trying to draw more customers in with their Essentials campaign which cut the price of hundreds of own-label products. This wiped more than £850 million off the stock market value of Sainsburys and sales showed an underlying fall of 1%.

(i) *Increase price and improve quality:* if a target segment can be identified which values quality and is substantial enough to offset the reduction in volumes.

(ii) *Launch lower-price insurance package:* if the company has the resources to have a deeper product line, one higher priced, one the same as the competitors and one lower, this will signal a strong competitive reaction and may dissuade further price erosions or force the competitor to exit the market.

The right decision will be partly dependent on the reactions of the other players in the market. However, by considering the questions outlined above, the chances of making the wrong decision should be greatly reduced.

14 BRAND STRETCHING

Examiner's comments: summary/extracts. Not a popular question, and whilst many candidates identified brand *strategy*, they did not extend this to cover the specific issue of brand stretching.

Introduction

Experts now view *brands* as the *link between a company's* marketing activities and consumers' perceptions of these activities. In the 1990s this brand revolution is particularly relevant to sectors such as financial services. The difficulties consumers have in understanding intangible products and the extent to which the service *becomes* the brand, both present marketing challenges together with the need to exploit brand equity through brand *stretching activities.*

Elements of Brand Strategy

Arnold (1992) in The Handbook of Brand Management, outlines a five stage brand management process.

1. *Market analysis:* Market definition, Market segmentation, Competitor positions, Trends: PEST and Micro factors

2. *Brand situation analysis:* Brand personality, Individual attributes. Internal analysis = is advertising projecting the right image? Is the packaging too aggressive? Does the product need updating? Fundamental evaluation of the brand's character.

3. *Targeting future positions:* Future developments. Brand strategy: any brand strategy should incorporate what has been learnt in steps 1 and 2 into a view of how the market will evolve and what strategic response is most appropriate. Target markets, brand positions and brand scope are the elements of brand strategy.

4. *Testing new offers:* Individual elements of mix and test marketing the total offer.

5. *Planning and evaluating performance:* Level of expenditure. Type of support activity. Measurement against objectives: awareness and availability, attitudes. Information on tracking of performance feeds into step 1 on analysis.

From this we see that brand strategy involves decision on three issues: target market(s), brand positioning and brand stretching.

Brand Stretching

Brand stretching refers specifically to the use of an existing, successful brand being used to launch products in an unrelated market. (Note: a brand extension is the use of an established brand name on a new product within the same broad market.)

The starting point for this activity is to identify the current brand's core values. Brands should only be *stretched* in these cases.

(a) The *core values of the brand have relevance* to the new market into which it is to be launched. Marks & Spencer with its retail operations has established a strong brand image for quality, value and integrity. All these values are also important in the financial services market. This has allowed Marks & Spencer to stretch their brand successfully into the financial services sector.

(b) The *new market area will not effect the value of the brand in its core market.* Virgin's brand name has been successfully stretched into a number of markets including financial services. However the brand may now be affected by the problems it is experiencing operating train services in the UK.

There is a school of thought that states that it may be easier for service companies to stretch umbrella brands across markets. Financial services companies using umbrella brands can also run into database marketing programmes across their whole service range, American Express being a good example. In general though, most financial service brands are currently too weak to support much brand stretching activity.

15 CRITERIA FOR A NEW PROPOSAL

> *Examiner's comments: summary/extracts.* Not a popular question, but it generated some good answers. The better candidates did well by relating their answer to *services* and showing how the criteria could be applied.

Introduction

Whether a good or service, any new product proposal should be professionally evaluated against a number of marketing, financial and internal criteria. It is only by making explicit use of such criteria that more objective and consistent decision-making can be achieved. Ennew (1990) outlines the five stage

new service development process; new service development strategy, idea generation, screening, development and testing and service launch. Criteria are used at the third stage before large investments are made in product development. There is not a definitive list as it will depend on the individual service being evaluated. However the following criteria are likely to be included.

Financial criteria

- Sales volume
- Expected return on investment
- Cost of service operation
- Profit opportunities
- Profit-volume variations and breakeven point
- Pricing issues
- Costs of the marketing support necessary
- Cross subsidy from other operations

Marketing criteria

- Compatibility with current marketing strategy
- Consumer behaviour patterns
- Trends in the industry
- The size of the potential market
- Growth prospects
- Competitive profiles/strategies
- Attractiveness of the market
- Position in the overall product/service offering
- Pricing issues
- Promotional needs/opportunities
- Organisational abilities
- Perceptions of current brand offerings

According to Donelly, screening requires thorough *evaluation* and the application of *weights* to the different criteria according to the key factors for success in the particular service market.

These criteria can then be used in several ways to screen the new service proposal. Specifically they can be used to make the following comparisons.

- This proposed development against other alternative opportunities that the organisation could address.

- The profitability of alternative potential pricing/positioning proposals.

- Our offering against competitors' services.

- Our potential positioning strategies in the market against our competitors.

Conclusions

Should the service proposal score highly enough against the weighted criteria, detailed profit sales and cash flow projections should be developed. More detailed consumer research should follow in the development and test marketing stage of the new service development process.

16 IMPLEMENTATION PROBLEMS

Implementation is not separate from but an integral part of the marketing planning process as illustrated by Wilson, Gilligan and Pearson's cycle of planning.

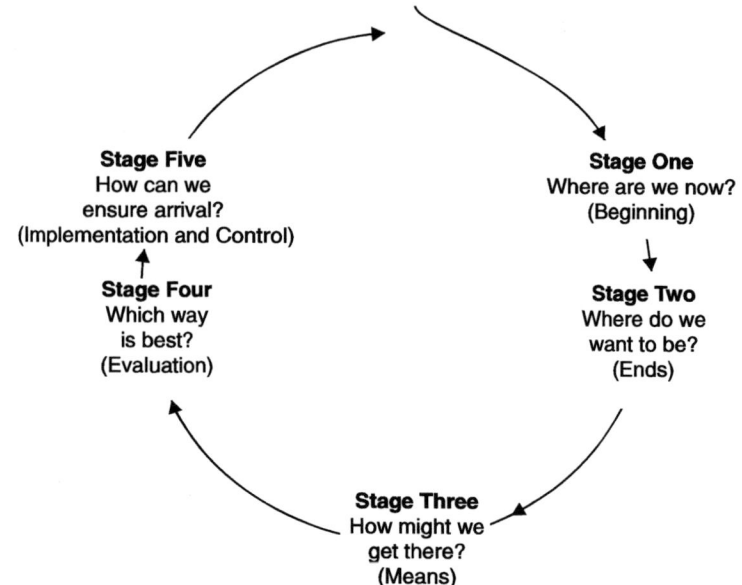

McDonald conducted a four year research project interviewing 200 industrial goods companies regarding their marketing planning process. In reality, it is a far easier job to establish objectives and strategies following the types of prescriptive approaches offered by several authors, than to manage the complex behavioural issues of putting these decisions into action - the implementation dimension of the marketing planner's role.

Frequently encountered implementation problems

(a)   *Weak support from the chief executive and top management.* Without the support, understanding and involvement of the chief executive it is unlikely that other functional managers will take the marketing manager's initiatives very seriously. Marketing planning has to be seen to be important to those in power if 'political' difficulties are to be minimised.

(b)   *Lack of a plan for planning.* It is naive to assume that once a marketing planning system has been designed that it will operate smoothly from day one. The evidence indicates that a period of around three years is required in a large company to overcome resistance to the change that planning inevitably brings. Internal marketing is required which will be discussed later.

(c)   *Lack of line management support.* Operational managers are often unwilling to participate fully because of hostility, lack of skills, lack of information, lack of resources and an inadequate organisational structure without a fully integrated marketing function.

(d)   *Confusion over planning terms.* The initiators of the system are often graduates who have a tendency to use academic planning terminology which line managers see as meaningless jargon. It is unrealistic to expect a process to work if it is not explained clearly and simply and sold in the language of those whose support is required.

(e)   *Numbers in lieu of written objectives and strategies.* Prior to a planning system often all that is used is sales forecasts and financial projections. Making explicit the route to achieving these objectives is a new and difficult skill. It requires managers to express the logic of their objectives and in this sense is a creative process requiring qualitative rather than quantitative information.

(f)   *Too much detail, too far ahead.* Over planning is often associated with too much information and ends with piles of paperwork which confuses and demotivates rather than promoting positive participation. Marketing auditing can result in far too many issues demanding management attention. Key issues need to be identified - the wood needs to be drawn from the trees. However without practice, training and experience it is difficult to extract truly key strategic issues which are buried in piles of detail.

(g)   *Once a year ritual.* This is a common barrier to effective implementation, when the task is seen as just another job to do which gets in the way of the really pressing day-to-day activities. Plans which are written and then filed away until next year do not work. Planning needs to be an integral part of the manager's job with progress towards objectives being reviewed and discussed on a regular basis.

(h)   *Separation of operational planning from strategic planning.* This represented a major problem in McDonald's research. It is the lack of integration between the shorter-term plans of operational

managers and the longer-term plans of senior management. If the activities of the former are not consistent and contributory to the latter then strategic plans are bound to fail. Strategic plans need to be built up from sound analysis at grass-roots level, and all managers need to consider not just continuing in the same direction but what longer-term changes may be required.

(i) *Failure to integrate marketing planning into a total corporate planning system.* This is really a facet of the last point. Unless marketing plans are considered in relation to the plans of finance, production and personnel it becomes impossible to resource accurately the plan's product/market requirements. Many companies require cross-functional planning teams to be able to exploit internal strengths through synergistic efforts.

(j) *Delegation of planning to a planner.* When planning is divorced from the reality of operations, and the people who are expected to put the ideas into action are not involved, it is not surprising that resistance and lack of commitment can exist. In addition, for a planner to be effective it will require him or her to initiate changes in management behaviour and for this to happen top management need to be involved and not simply delegate the task to the 'planner'.

Explicit recognition of these potential barriers is necessary before an internal plan can be developed to try to reduce them, and thereby allow the organisation to reap the benefits of a strategic approach to its business.

The 'flipside' of external marketing is internal marketing which involves 'selling' your marketing plan to your internal customers, ie employees. The following quote from Foreman and Woodruff helps to illustrate the internal culture strived for:

> 'Two stone cutters in the middle ages were asked what they were doing: "I am cutting this damned stone into a square", one of them answered. "I'm working on a cathedral", the other one responded'.

The transformation of emphasis from the stone cutter to the employee building the cathedral is the essence of internal marketing.

17 FEEDBACK AND CONTROL SYSTEM

> *Examiner's comments: summary/extracts.* Too many answers concentrated specifically on the MkIS rather than broader issues of feedback and control, and the use to which this information can be put.

Planning can be defined as 'deciding what to do' whereas control can be defined as 'ensuring that the desired results are achieved'. The feedback and control process can be illustrated by a simple model.

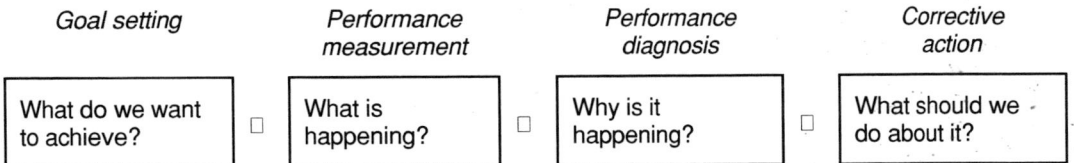

Goal setting		*Performance measurement*		*Performance diagnosis*		*Corrective action*
What do we want to achieve?	□	What is happening?	□	Why is it happening?	□	What should we do about it?

Feedback and control involves goal setting, performance measurement, performance diagnosis and taking corrective action.

Goal setting is the role of the *planning* element of strategic marketing. Ideally, the standards set will have been developed within an understanding of what the organisation is able to deliver. This point is equally true for the development of a marketing feedback and control system. Specifically the factors which should be taken into account include the following.

(a) The type of control information required - financial and non-financial.

(b) The methods used to collect the information - audits, budgets and variance analysis.

(c) Who requires the information?

(d) What form the information should take - weekly, monthly annual reports, presentations, continuous computer based data.

(e) The information systems required.

(f) The resource implications.

(g)   The behavioural implications of controlling peoples' activities.

This final point is less obvious but very important if the control system is to work effectively. The involvement of a range of managers and personnel in the evaluation process is vital, together with the need for good communication, both within the marketing unit and between departments. Effective implementation of the feedback and control system will require internal marketing to employees, motivation of personnel and effective co-ordination of marketing activities.

Fifield and Gilligan (1995) suggest that feedback and control information can be used in five distinct areas of operation.

(a)   Financial analysis
(b)   Market analysis
(c)   Sales and distribution analysis
(d)   Physical resource analysis
(e)   Human resource analysis

Market, sales and distribution analyses are particularly relevant for marketing planning.

Type of analysis	Used to control
Market/sales analysis to consider size and growth of market and market share Demand analysis Sales targets Sales budget	Competitive standing Sales effectiveness Efficiency in use of resources for selling

Information on these areas can be gathered through audits, budgeting or variance analysis. Marketing audits allow for regular monitoring of the successful implementation of marketing plans. For example, a marketing manager might use the information from the mix audit to recognise that communication targets are not being reached. From this point, corrective action would be needed in the form of a campaign review and redevelopment. Budgeting is the most common form of control, it is financial in nature and very useful when applied to marketing implementation. Budgets tend to be short-term and based on the annual plan for achievement of the year's profit and sales forecasts. Monthly deviations from the sales plan tend to require tactical alterations, for example in the form of price increases or decreases to influence demand.

Where budgeting is *longer-term*, this is more appropriate for monitoring strategic decisions such as product portfolio management. For example, in the product plan there will be products identified as question marks or potential stars. The position of each product in the matrix will suggest how much close monitoring and control is needed. Information on high-risk or high-potential new products would be used to manage the risk and to ensure sales forecasts are accurate to avoid back order or production problems. Variance analysis leads on from budgeting, and involves detailed analysis of the difference between actual and expected results. This sort of control information might possibly be used to consider sales-price variances, sales-quantity variances, profit variances and market share variances.

Many marketing activities are not evaluated or controlled but are assumed to be effective. Marketers tend to enjoy planning and tactical implementation but shy away from feedback on the results of their initiatives. This is short-sighted, as it severely limits learning from experience and can, at worst, result in inefficient and ineffective marketing plans.

18   THE LENS SHOP

(a)   Subject: Sources of competitive advantage
       To: The Managing Director
       Prepared by: The Marketing Manager
       Date: December 20XX

Introduction

(i)   *Competitive advantage* is anything which gives an organisation an edge over its competitors - the reason why a customer would select TLS's products or services over other competitive offerings. Once an advantage has been gained, competitors will try to copy or supersede it, so continuous improvements in offerings are needed unless the advantage can be protected.

(ii)   Competitive strategy is the search for a favourable competitive position in an industry. The aim is to establish a profitable and sustainable position. Porter suggests three generic routes to achieving competitive advantage.

(1)   Overall cost leadership
(2)   Overall differentiation
(3)   Focus (segmentation based on costs or differentiation)

Sources of competitive advantage for TLS

(iii)   *Cost leadership*

This strategy seeks to achieve the position of *lowest cost producer* in the industry. This enables the company to compete on price and earn the highest unit profits. Porter (1985) has identified several major factors that affect costs which he terms 'cost drivers'. Not all of these apply.

(1)   *Economies of scale* are not possible. TLS is a *specialist* retail store, as opposed to Dixons with many more locations.

(2)   *Experience and learning effects* can bring efficiencies through repetition of tasks. Experience can be gained through hiring experienced staff and through training. The concept was derived from the manufacturing sector so its application to retail services may be questionable.

(3)   *Capacity utilisation* is important to profits, especially for smaller firms. Our smaller, secondary sites with small stock holdings will be a source of cost advantages.

(4)   *Linkages* between quality control and stock return, for example, can drive costs up or down. External linkages with suppliers can also reduce costs. Our access to discounted products of 'old' product lines will provide a cost advantage.

(5)   *Interrelationships* with other SBUs in a corporate portfolio can help to share costs but this is not possible for our smaller, single business unit organisation.

(6)   *Integration* such as contracting out delivery and/or service can affect costs. As we are not vertically or horizontally integrated this is not an option for competitive advantage.

(7)   *Timing.* Being first to the market can provide access to low cost products, ensure prime locations and gain us technological leadership. As we operate in an established market with a number of general and specialist camera retailers, this is *not* a route to competitive advantage for us.

(8)   *Policy choices* such as product line, service, warranties and so on all affect costs. They also affect the perceived uniqueness of the offer to customers and hence if the competitive strategy is not clear this can create a dilemma. If cost advantage is the strategy then the general rule is to reduce costs on factors which will not significantly affect valued uniqueness.

(9)   *Location* and *institutional factors* can also reduce costs, such as sites near raw material and government regulations. This is not viable for TLS.

From this analysis, discounted 'old' products, small stores in secondary locations and low stock holding all create a cost advantage for TLS. This enables the company to offer lower prices with a price guarantee of being £10 below other local retailers for a similar brand of camera.

(ii)   *Differentiation*

This is a competitive strategy based on raising the quality of the product and thus its costs and sale price. Loyalty is built up and, because customers are not so price sensitive, profits can be increased through higher prices. Organisations following this strategy must continually innovate in order to stay ahead of competitors in quality, thus necessitating larger R&D and promotional budgets. Competitive advantage can be achieved through what Porter calls 'uniqueness drivers'.

(1)   *Product differentiation* seeks to increase the value of the good or service on offer to the customer. Products are made up of four components. The *generic product* which is photography, the *expected product* which is a retail site with a range of products and prices with reasonable customer service, the *augmented product* which constitutes all the extra features and services that go beyond what the normal camera consumer expects and the *potential product* which is anything that could be

BPP
PUBLISHING

offered. TLS offer an augmented product in the form of the buy-back service for upgrades, selection of recent reviews from Camera magazines and sales staff are also knowledgeable and helpful.

(2) *Brand differentiation* is related to the product offer and moves companies from thinking about *tangible product* benefits to *emotional image* benefits. TLS may be able to establish this in the future, through owning the value and service position in the camera market.

(3) *Distribution differentiation* comes from using different outlets, networks or coverage of the market. The less formal, friendly atmosphere of the shops may be a potential source of differentiation from the large, formal multiples.

(4) *Promotional differentiation* involves using different types of promotions at different intensity or content. The TLS colour catalogue is a 'fun' brochure distributed in an innovative way, especially through direct mail to existing customers. This should be a loyalty builder.

(5) *Pricing differentiation* can be successful if TLS enjoys a cost advantage. This is TLS's major point of differentiation with its £10 lower price guarantee, discounted price 'old' stock products, cheap three year extended warranty and buy-back service.

(iii) *Sustainability of current situation*

(1) TLS operate on a *differentiation strategy based on price differentiation* with elements of *product differentiation* based on information and customer service. This is financed through their low cost sources of 'old' product lines from distributors and their location and store size policy. (This is similar to Richer Sounds approach in the hi-fi sector.)

(2) The *risks* of this strategy are the *threat of competition* from lower cost specialist retailers and the vulnerability of a price-based attack by larger competitors such as John Lewis and Dixons, should they go for an aggressive strategy in this product category. Perhaps the greatest risk which needs to be protected is the relationship they have with distributors to clear their shelves of 'old' product lines. If this supply ceased, TLS would lose a significant advantage.

The most useful ways of creating a defensible position lie in exploiting the following.

(1) Unique and valued products
(2) Clear, tight definition of target markets
(3) Enhanced customer linkages
(4) Established brand and company credibility

In the future, creating closer bonds with customers through interactive communications and enhanced service through internal marketing initiatives should strength TLS's position. The buy-back service should help build in switching costs and should be retained together with building the awareness of the brand from specialist camera consumers to the general public. Public relations should help, following the lead of *Richer Sounds* with innovative employee relations policies and incentives together with shouting about their buy-back service.

(b) To: The Managing Director
Prepared by: The Marketing Manager
Date: December 20XX

Report on the development of an *Internal Marketing Programme*

Please find outlined below an overview of an internal marketing programme as requested.

(i) *What is internal marketing?*

'Treating with equal importance the needs of the internal market - the employees - and the external market through proactive programmes and planning to bring about desired organisational objectives by delivering both employee and customer satisfaction.'

Originally, the scope of *internal marketing* was considered to be the motivation, training and development of employees involved at the customer interface, with the aim of delivering a better service to the end customer. This is obviously important in a service industry like camera retailing. However, internal marketing also includes non-contact employees as well. In fact, internal marketing covers any planned effort to overcome any resistance to change in an organisation and to ensure through proper communication, motivation and training that employees effectively implement corporate and functional strategies/plans.

This concept is obviously important in the retail sector where customers' expectations of the service encounter are rising. The head office staff who support the shops are also critical in terms of delivering customer satisfaction.

(ii) *Development and implementation*

People inside the organisation, to whom the plan must be marketed, are considered internal customers. The first stage is to group these internal customers into three segments.

(1) *Supporters*: those likely to gain from improving service levels.

(2) *Neutrals*: those whose gains and losses are in balance.

(3) *Opposers*: those who are likely to lose from the change or are long-term opponents.

An internal marketing mix has to be developed for each of these target groups.

(1) *Product.* This is the plan/strategy itself together with the attitudes, values and actions that are needed to successfully carry it out.

(2) *Price.* The price is what internal customers have to pay as a result of accepting the plan/strategy. This could be changes in work patterns and greater effort to achieve high levels of customer satisfaction.

(3) *Promotion.* This is a critical area in the mix, and involves any communication medium that can be used to effect the attitudes of key groups. The promotional mix includes: presentations, training workshops, discussion groups, written reports etc. This communication has to be a two way process. At times, it may be necessary to adapt the plan in order to gain support.

(4) *Distribution.* This categorises the places where the product and communications are delivered to internal customers, such as in-store, meetings, seminars, informal conversations, away days and so on.

Although an internal marketing programme gives a framework within which to work, successful implementation is reliant on three key skills.

(1) *Persuasion*

- Present a shared vision for the group through a customer service charter.

- Communicate and train.

- Eliminate misconceptions through two-way dialogue.

- Sell the benefits through success stories in the company newsletter, employee of the month awards, incentives for the best store etc.

- Gain acceptance by association, perhaps with Richer Sounds retail success and employee benefits.

- Support words with action, for example the MD rewarding best practice and reviewing the customer feedback comments.

(2) *Negotiation*

- Make the opening proposition high – leave room for negotiation.
- Trade concessions.

(3) *Politics*

- Build coalitions.
- Display support.
- Invite the opposition to contribute.
- Warn opposition.
- Control the agenda.
- Take incremental steps.

Benefits of internal marketing

For TLS, improved *employee satisfaction* and *customer responsiveness* will lead to improved *customer satisfaction*. The higher the relative service quality of any business the higher the return on investment (PIMS research). A clear customer service charter should lead to greater clarity in the purpose and objectives for each store. Customer complaints should reduce thereby saving time dealing with them. Employee turnover should reduce as well. As indicated in the first part of this report, excellence in customer service combined with a competitive pricing strategy should help achieve a sustainable competitive advantage for the business in the highly competitive market in which we operate.

Potential problems to overcome

To achieve the stated benefits, a number of implementation barriers need to be considered. Time is important and potential problems can arise by not taking enough time to allow people to adjust to the changes implied by the plan. Persistence is required in the face of opposition; modifications to the strategy may be necessary on the way. Key detractors and recalcitrant players may exist and if negotiation and persuasion are not successful these people can be removed or if this is not possible, you have to wait till that person leaves or changes job. A final potential problem is lack of resources, both human and financial. Internal marketing programmes require a budget for training, communications and staff time. If this is not available the likely chances of success are greatly reduced.

Bibliography,
List of Key
Concepts and
Index

Further reading is suggested below. It is by no means exhaustive. Note that many exam questions ask you to refer to examples: whilst some case histories do stand the test of time, you should be on the lookout for recent and contemporary examples. Also don't restrict yourself to consumer goods marketing: keep an eye out for industrial marketing, public sector organisations and not for profit organisations.

Magazines, journals and papers

Marketing Business - the CIM's own magazine offers a useful overview of matters of current interest. *Marketing Week, Campaign* and other trade journals offer 'hot' information.

The 'quality' broadsheet newspapers have business sections, which you might find useful for information on current developments. The *Financial Times* has an Inside Track section with articles on matters of business interest. It also covers marketing and advertising at other times. The *Economist* has articles about individual companies and industries and also covers strategic and marketing issues

For a view from the US - a big innovator - the *Harvard Business Review* is often worth a look, if you can find it in your college library. All the main articles are condensed into 'executive summaries' at the back so you can see at a glance what is worth reading further. Note that the context is often the US, and the ideas and recommendations outlined cannot be imported uncritically into other environments.

Your lecturer may well direct you to more specialised articles in journals such as *Long Range Planning*, the *Strategic Management Journal* and others.

Books

Aaker, *Strategic Market Management,* Wiley

Allen D, *Strategic Financial Decisions: A Guide to the Evaluation and Monitoring of Business Strategy,* CIMA

Ames and Hlavecek, *Market Driven Management,* Dow Jones

Ansoff I, *Corporate Strategy,* Penguin

Armstrong M, *A Handbook of Management Techniques,* Kogan Page

Assael, *Marketing Principles and Strategy,* Dryden Press

Buttle F (ed), *Relationship Marketing: Theory and Practice,* Chapman

Cambell A, Devine M, and Young D, *A Sense of Mission,* Hutchinson

Clifton P, Nguyen H, and Nutt S, *Market Research: Using Forecasting in Business,* Butterworth Heinemann

Cowell D, *The Marketing of Services,* Butterworth Heinemann

Cram T, *The Power of Relationship Marketing,* Pitman

Davidson H, *Even More Offensive Marketing,* Penguin

D'Aprix R, *Communicating for Change, Connecting the Workplace to the Marketplace,* Jassey Bass

Dibb S and Simkin L, *Market Segmentation Workbook,* Routledge

Dibb S, Simkin L, Price M, and Ferrell O, *Marketing Concepts and Strategies,* Houghton Mifflin

Doyle P, *Marketing Management and Strategy,* Prentice Hall

Drummond G and Ensor J, *Strategic Marketing Planning and Control,* Butterworth Heinemann (1999)

Fill, C *Marketing Communications: contexts, contents and strategies,* (1999) Prentice Hall

Financial Times (various authors), *Mastering Management* (1996), *Mastering Marketing* (1998)

Goold M and Quinn J, *Strategic Control,* Hutchinson

Halberg G, *All Consumers are not Created Equal,* Wiley

Hamel and Prahalad, *Competing for the Future,* HBS Press

Hammer M, *Re-engineering the Corporation,* NB

Hampden-Turner C, *Corporate Culture,* Piatkus

Bibliography

Handy C, *Gods of Management,* Arrow

      The Empty Raincoat, Century

Hatton A and Oldroyd M, *Economic Theory and Marketing Practice,* Butterworth Heinemann

Holmes K, *Total Quality Management,* Pira

Hooley, Saunders and Piercy, *Marketing Strategy and Competitive Positioning,* Prentice Hall

Johns E, *Perfect Customer Care,* Arrow

Johnson G and Scholes K, *Exploring Corporate Strategy,* Prentice Hall

Kay J, *Foundations of Corporate Success,* OUP

Klein, N, *No Logo,* Harper Collins

Kotler P, *Marketing Management: Analysis, Planning, Control* Prentice Hall

      Principles of Marketing, European Edition, Prentice Hall

Leavy G, *Key Processes in Strategy,* ETP

Lock D, *Project Management,* Gower

MacDonald M, *Marketing Plans,* Butterworth Heinemann

Marsh J, *Managing Financial Services Marketing,* Pitman

Massingham L and Lancaster G, *Marketing Management,* McGraw-Hill

Mercer D, *Marketing Strategy: the Challenge of the External Environment,* Open University/Sage

Mintzberg H and Quin J, *The Strategy Process, Concepts, Context, Cases,* Prentice Hall

Mintzberg H, *The Rise and Fall of Strategic Planning,* Prentice Hall

Moore, J I (ed), *Writers on Strategy and Strategic Management,* Penguin

Palmer A and Worthington E, *The Business and Marketing Environment,* McGraw Hill

Pearson D, *Strategic Marketing Management: Analysis and Decision Tutorial Text,* BPP Publishing

Pedler M, Burgoyne J, and Boydell T, *The Learning Company,* McGraw-Hill

Piercy N, *Market-led Strategic Change,* Butterworth Heinemann

Porter M, *Competitive Advantage,* Free Press

      Competitive Strategy, Free Press

Rice C, *Consumer Behaviour,* Butterworth Heinemann

Rohner K, *Marketing in the Cyber Age,* Wiley

Schiffman and Kanuk, *Consumer Behaviour,* Prentice-Hall

Senge P, *The Fifth Discipline,* Century

Stacey K, *Strategic Management and Organisational Dynamics,* Pitman

Sternberg E, *Just Business,* Fontana

Ward K, *Financial Aspects of Marketing,* Butterworth Heinemann

      Strategic Management Accounting, Butterworth Heinemann

Wilson C, *Customer Base Management*

Wilson R, Gilligan C, and Pearson D, *Strategic Marketing Management,* Butterworth Heinemann

You might also benefit from a look at *Social Trends* (Office of National Statistics, published by The Stationery Office) for aspects of the social and cultural environment of the UK.

BPP
PUBLISHING

List of key concepts

Index

BPP PUBLISHING

Mr/Mrs/Ms (Full name)

Daytime delivery address

Postcode

Daytime Tel   Date of exam (month/year)

	7/01 Texts	9/01 Kit	Success Tapes
CERTIFICATE			
1 Marketing Environment	£18.95 ☐	£9.95 ☐	£12.95 ☐
2 Customer Communications in Marketing	£18.95 ☐	£9.95 ☐	£12.95 ☐
3 Marketing in Practice	£18.95 ☐	£9.95 ☐	£12.95 ☐
4 Marketing Fundamentals	£18.95 ☐	£9.95 ☐	£12.95 ☐
ADVANCED CERTIFICATE			
5 The Marketing Customer Interface	£18.95 ☐	£9.95 ☐	£12.95 ☐
6 Management Information for Marketing Decisions	£18.95 ☐	£9.95 ☐	£12.95 ☐
7 Effective Management for Marketing	£18.95 ☐	£9.95 ☐	£12.95 ☐
8 Marketing Operations	£18.95 ☐	£9.95 ☐	£12.95 ☐
DIPLOMA			
9 Integrated Marketing Communications	£18.95 ☐	£9.95 ☐	£12.95 ☐
10 International Marketing Strategy	£18.95 ☐	£9.95 ☐	£12.95 ☐
11 Strategic Marketing Management: Planning and Control	£18.95 ☐	£9.95 ☐	£12.95 ☐
12 Strategic Marketing Management: Analysis and Decision (9/01)	£25.95 ☐	N/A	£12.95 ☐

SUBTOTAL £ ☐

POSTAGE & PACKING

Study Texts

	First	Each extra	
UK	£3.00	£2.00	£ ☐
Europe*	£5.00	£4.00	£ ☐
Rest of world	£20.00	£10.00	£ ☐

Kits/Success Tapes

	First	Each extra	
UK	£2.00	£1.00	£ ☐
Europe*	£2.50	£1.00	£ ☐
Rest of world	£15.00	£8.00	£ ☐

Grand Total (Cheques to *BPP Publishing*) I enclose
a cheque for (incl. Postage)   £ ☐

Or charge to Access/Visa/Switch

Card Number ☐☐☐☐☐☐☐☐☐☐☐☐

Expiry date _____   Start Date _____

Issue Number (Switch Only) _____

Signature _____

We aim to deliver to all UK addresses inside 5 working days. A signature will be required. Orders to all EU addresses should be delivered within 6 working days.

All other orders to overseas addresses should be delivered within 8 working days.

* Europe includes the Republic of Ireland and the Channel Islands.

REVIEW FORM & FREE PRIZE DRAW

All original review forms from the entire BPP range, completed with genuine comments, will be entered into one of two draws on 31 January 2002 and 30 July 2002. The names on the first four forms picked out on each occasion will be sent a cheque for £50.

Name: _____   **Address**: _____

_____

_____

How have you used this Kit?
(Tick one box only)

☐ Self study (book only)

☐ On a course: college_____

☐ With BPP Home Study package

☐ Other _____

Why did you decide to purchase this Kit?
(Tick one box only)

☐ Have used companion Kit

☐ Have used BPP Texts in the past

☐ Recommendation by friend/colleague

☐ Recommendation by a lecturer at college

☐ Saw advertising in journals

☐ Saw website

☐ Other _____

During the past six months do you recall seeing/receiving any of the following?
(Tick as many boxes as are relevant)

☐ Our advertisement in the *Marketing Success*

☐ Our advertisement in *Marketing Business*

☐ Our brochure with a letter through the post

☐ Our brochure with *Marketing Business*

☐ Saw website

Which (if any) aspects of our advertising do you find useful?
(Tick as many boxes as are relevant)

☐ Prices and publication dates of new editions

☐ Information on product content

☐ Facility to order books off-the-page

☐ None of the above

Have you used the companion Practice & Revision Kit for this subject? ☐ Yes ☐ No

Have you used the companion Success Tapes for this subject? ☐ Yes ☐ No

Your ratings, comments and suggestions would be appreciated on the following areas.

	Very useful	Useful	Not useful
Introductory section (How to use this text, study checklist, etc)	☐	☐	☐
Setting the Scene	☐	☐	☐
Syllabus coverage	☐	☐	☐
Action Programmes and Marketing at Work examples	☐	☐	☐
Chapter roundups	☐	☐	☐
Quick quizzes	☐	☐	☐
Illustrative questions	☐	☐	☐
Content of suggested answers	☐	☐	☐
Index	☐	☐	☐
Structure and presentation			

	Excellent	Good	Adequate	Poor
Overall opinion of this Text	☐	☐	☐	☐

Do you intend to continue using BPP Study Texts/Kits/Success Tapes? ☐ Yes ☐ No

Please note any further comments and suggestions/errors on the reverse of this page.

✂ **Please return to: Kate Machattie, BPP Publishing Ltd, FREEPOST, London, W12 8BR**

REVIEW FORM & FREE PRIZE DRAW (continued)

Please note any further comments and suggestions/errors below.

FREE PRIZE DRAW RULES

1 Closing date for 31 January 2002 draw is 31 December 2001. Closing date for 31 July 2002 draw is 30 June 2002.

2 Restricted to entries with UK and Eire addresses only. BPP employees, their families and business associates are excluded.

3 No purchase necessary. Entry forms are available upon request from BPP Publishing. No more than one entry per title, per person. Draw restricted to persons aged 16 and over.

4 Winners will be notified by post and receive their cheques not later than 6 weeks after the relevant draw date. List of winners will be supplied on request.

5 The decision of the promoter in all matters is final and binding. No correspondence will be entered into.